CHILDREN'S FICTION SOURCEBOOK

DEDICATION

To my father,
with love always

Jennifer Madden

To Philip and Amanda – with love

Margaret Hobson

CHILDREN'S FICTION SOURCEBOOK

A survey of children's books
for 6–13 year olds

Second Edition

Margaret Hobson
Jennifer Madden

© Margaret Hobson and Jennifer Madden, 1995

All rights reserved. No part of this publication may be reproduced, stored in a retrieval system, or transmitted in any form or by any means, electronic, mechanical, photocopying, recording, or otherwise without the prior permission of the publisher.

First edition published by Ashgate Publishing Limited, 1992

Second edition published by
SCOLAR PRESS
Gower House   Ashgate Publishing Company
Croft Road   Old Post Road
Aldershot   Brookfield
Hants GU11 3HR   Vermont 05036
England   USA

British Library Cataloguing in Publication Data

Hobson, Margaret
 Children's Fiction Sourcebook: Survey of Children's
 Books for 6–13 Year Olds. –
 2 Rev.ed
 I. Title
 028.162

Library of Congress Cataloguing-in-Publication Data

Hobson, Margaret
    Children's fiction sourcebook : a survey of children's books for 6–13 year olds / Margaret Hobson, Jennifer Madden —2nd ed.
      p.   cm.
   1. Children—Great Britain—Books and reading.
   2. Children—United States—Books and reading.
   3. Children's stories, English—Bibliography.
   I. Madden, Jennifer.   III. Title.
 Z1037.H647   1995
 016.823008′09282—dc20   94–31292
                              CIP

ISBN 1 85928 083 8

Typeset in Souvenir by Photoprint, Torquay, Devon and printed in Great Britain by Hartnolls Ltd, Bodmin

CONTENTS

◆

Notes on Authors	vi
Preface	vii
Acknowledgements	viii
How to use this book	ix
Main author list	1
Classics	227
Series	237
Television tie-ins	249
List of awards and prize winners	253
Author index	283
Title index	290
Genre index	324

NOTES ON AUTHORS

◆

MARGARET HOBSON

Born in Huddersfield in 1939, she became a library assistant in 1961, eventually specializing in children's work. After qualifying at Liverpool School of Librarianship, she worked first as a children's librarian, then in a College of Education library. With one son and one daughter, she currently works as part of a team in the Books +, the department in Kirklees Cultural Services which deals with schools and junior sections of branch libraries.

JENNIFER MADDEN

Married with one son, Christopher, she is currently the Manager of Books + Kirklees Library Services to Children and Young People. Jennifer is dedicated to making opportunities for as many children as possible to be touched by the magic of the book.

PREFACE

♦

Children's reading is a vital component of education and recreation; parents, teachers and librarians all wish to encourage and foster good reading habits that will provide a sound future base for leisure reading, imaginative skills, and for the everyday requirements of a literate society; all devote much time to the careful collection of a comprehensive stock of children's fiction. The authors urge those choosing titles not to underestimate the young people for whom they are responsible. When presented with fiction that engages their minds and emotions, they are capable of far more than we often anticipate.

The publication of the second edition of this work has justified the authors' conviction that there is a need for a comprehensive source offering thorough guidance on English language fiction for children aged 6 to 13. This selective survey does not include picture books, which are planned to be the subject of a future volume. It covers the best and most popular children's authors, giving a biographical note, address and/or agent, awards and prizes, age-range, and versions of their works with essential bibliographical details.

This edition includes several authors not in the first edition; a few in the first edition have been removed. This ensures that the work reflects current writing for children. To help in the selection of reading material for children, whether by parents, teachers or librarians, each author entry has a brief annotation for a representative number of titles with a list of other children's titles, together with brief bibliographical details, which will help in the selection and contacting of authors for events, promotional meetings, story-times, literary quizzes and readings.

Not every children's author can be represented. We have made a deliberate selection, mainly of those currently writing, and although there is inevitably a UK bias, there is good coverage of Northern American, Australian and other Commonwealth authors.

Appendices offer a number of valuable features. There is a list of recommended available editions of classic tales and anthologies of fairy tales, an updated section on publishers' series and a list of television tie-ins from 1992 to date. The section on prizes and awards from around the world has been brought up to date.

Even with a second edition, some readers will feel there have been errors and omissions. The authors would like to hear from anyone with suggestions for additions and corrections for a future revision.

ACKNOWLEDGEMENTS

◆

The authors wish to express their grateful thanks to Woodfield and Stanley Ltd, children's book suppliers of Moldgreen, Huddersfield, for their support and help.

Their thanks are also due to David Madden for his work in preparing and editing the text.

In compiling this volume we have received help, advice and support from many colleagues, libraries and publishers; we should like to record our thanks to all of them.

HOW TO USE THIS BOOK

◆

The main body of the text is a list, in author order, of those titles selected for review. This is followed by appendices on classics (also in author order with anthologies at the end), series (in series name order, with lists of authors for each series), and television tie-ins (again in author order). The author index lists every author mentioned, whether the name appears in the main text or in the appendices; similarly every title is included in the title index.

Within the entry for each author, the titles are listed in alphabetical order, unless otherwise indicated. However, where the title is part of a series, the first title is listed in its place in the alphabetical order, and subsequent titles follow it immediately. Such titles are indented to indicate that they are part of the series.

For every title listed, at least one bibliographical citation is given. The format for this citation is:

Publisher, year, no. of pages. – notes. – ISBN

The citations for most entries have the full details as shown above. However, while every title has, of course, been read in the course of compiling this work, not every published edition has been examined. The details are as shown in Whitaker's *British Books in Print*, December 1993.

Within notes, the following abbreviations have been used:

Pbk = Paperback edition
L/P = Large print edition
O/P = Out of print. While this means that the title cannot currently be purchased, the titles chosen are all so well known that this version will almost certainly be available from any good public library.

MAIN AUTHOR LIST

◆

ADAMS, Richard

British. Born Newbury, 1920. Educated Bradfield College, Berkshire; Worcester College, Oxford. B.A. Modern History, M.A. British Army WW II. Married Barbara Elizabeth Acland, 1949, two daughters. Civil servant, writer.

Awards: Library Association Carnegie Medal: *Watership Down*, 1972
Guardian Award: *Watership Down*, 1973
Fellow of the Royal Society of Literature, 1975

Address: 26 Church Street, Whitchurch, Hampshire, England

Agent: David Higham Assoc. Ltd, 5–8 Lower John Street, London W1R 4HA, England

WATERSHIP DOWN
A. Lane, 1982, 480p. – 0 7139 1513 7
Ulverscroft, 1981, 683p. – L/P, O/P – 0 7089 8012 0
Penguin, 1974, 480p. – Pbk. – 0 14 003958 9

A book which deserves a place on every bookshelf, in every home and in every library. It tells the story of a group of rabbits forced to flee their home to save their lives. They journey to a better place, facing untold dangers which not all survive. It is funny, sad, exciting and, above all, totally compelling, making unobtrusive but shrewd observations on life as the story progresses. As with all really excellent novels, it is read to and by adults and children of all ages.
Age range: 8–adult

Other publications:
FAIRY TALES
Routledge, 1983. – Pbk. – 0 7100 9997 5

SHIP'S CAT
Cape, 1973. – 0 224 01441 2
TYGER VOYAGE
Hutchinson, 1993. – 0 09 176730 X

AHLBERG, Allan

British. Born Croydon, 1938; grew up in Birmingham. Educated Sunderland College of Education. Married Janet Hall, illustrator, 1969 (died 1994), one daughter. Sometime: postman, soldier, schoolteacher, grave-digger and plumber's mate.

Awards: Children's Rights Workshop Other Award: *Miss Plug the Plumber*, 1980
Emil/Kurt Maschler Award: *The Jolly Postman*, 1986
Children's Book Award: *The Jolly Postman*, 1987
IBBY Honour Award: *Woof!*, 1988
Signal Poetry Award: *Heard it in the Playground*, 1990

Address: 20 Nether Hall Lane, Birstall, Leicestershire LEA 4DT, England

An author with an extraordinary talent. His writing is good, highly original and full of humour. The result is lots of books with enormous appeal to children. His wife has illustrated many of his books, providing complementary illustrations.

THE CLOTHES HORSE AND OTHER STORIES
Penguin, 1989, 32p. – Pbk. – 0 14 032907 2
Viking Kestrel, 1987, 32p. – 0 670 81267 6
illustrated by Janet Ahlberg

AHLBERG

Inventive short stories with superb illustrations. They can be read successfully to younger children, and are equally entertaining for older children to read for themselves. As always, they are fresh and amusing.
Age range: 6–10

HAPPY FAMILIES
Viking Kestrel
Penguin. – Pbk.

A series containing many titles all of the highest quality and versatility. Some are about unusual families, for example a bee-keeper; some are more ordinary, like a plumber or a teacher. They are funny, witty and entertaining. The repetition makes them ideal for children mastering the art of reading, yet all the stories move along at a vigorous pace, making them a real delight to read to younger children. Several different illustrators have been used, which adds to the variety.
Age range: 4–7

IT WAS A DARK AND STORMY NIGHT
Viking, 1993, 32p. – Pbk. – 0 670 84620 1
illustrated by Janet Ahlberg

Antonio is kidnapped by brigands, an act they come to regret. He 'entertains' them and the reader with a new version of the old poem. It is amusing, unusual, and has a safe, happy ending. Excellent for reading aloud with lots to enjoy in the illustrations. The format is large, more of a picture book, but the story is too long and complex to be read at one sitting.
Age range: 6–8

JEREMIAH IN THE DARK WOODS
Penguin, 1989, 32p. – Pbk. – 0 14 032811 4
Viking Kestrel, 1986, 48p. – 0 670 40637 6
illustrated by Janet Ahlberg

An unusual story woven round traditional tales like *Peter Pan* and *The Queen of Hearts*. An excellent read for children becoming confident readers, as it has clear print and plentiful illustrations.
Age range: 7–9

TEN IN A BED
Chivers Press, 1990, 168p. – L/P, O/P –
0 7451 1244 7
Penguin, 1990, 96p. – Pbk. – 0 14 032531 X
Viking, 1989, 112p. – 0 670 82042 3

Witty parodies of well loved stories like *Goldilocks* and *The Sleeping Beauty*. Amusingly told, the full impact can be felt only if the original stories are already familiar.
Age range: 8–10

THE VANISHMENT OF THOMAS TULL
Black, 1988. – 0 7136 2999 1
Penguin, 1985, 64p. – Pbk. – 0 14 031804 6
illustrated by Janet Ahlberg

At the age of seven, Thomas started to shrink. His parents, alarmed, tried many and varied cures, some of which involved Thomas in exciting adventures. The book has a racy tone which encourages young readers, and the illustrations are, as always, perfect.
Age range: 7–9

WOOF
Penguin, 1987, 160p. – Pbk. – 0 14 031996 4
Chivers Press, 1987, 208p. – L/P. –
0 7451 0487 8
Viking Kestrel, 1986, 156p. – 0 670 80832 6
illustrated by Fritz Wegner

Eric – an ordinary name for an ordinary boy who turns into an ordinary dog who loves chocolate buttons and chasing cats. How Eric manages his dual life with the help of his loyal friend Roy makes entertaining reading and became an enjoyable television series.
Age range: 9–11

Other publications:

BABY'S CATALOGUE
Viking, 1985. – O/P – 0 670 80895 4
BAD BEAR
Granada, 1982. – 0 246 11525 4

AHLBERG

BEAR NOBODY WANTED
Viking, 1993. – 0 670 83982 5

BEAR'S BIRTHDAY
Walker Books, 1990. – Pbk. – 0 7445 1606 4

BIG BAD PIG
Walker Books, 1990. – Pbk. – 0 7445 1604 8

BLACK CAT
Little Mammoth, 1992. – Pbk. – 0 7497 1040 3

BLOW ME DOWN!
Walker Books, 1990. – Pbk. – 0 7445 1703 6

BUMPS IN THE NIGHT
Heinemann, 1993. – 0434 96367 4

BURGLAR BILL
Viking, 1992. – 0 14 050301 3

BYE BYE BABY
Little Mammoth, 1991. – Pbk. – 0 7497 0624 4

CINDERELLA SHOW
Viking, 1987. – 0 670 81037 1

CIRCUS
Studio Publications, 1986. – Pbk. – 0 8621 5362 X

CLOWNING ABOUT
Heinemann, 1984. – Pbk. – 0 434 92510 1

COPS AND ROBBERS
Little Mammoth, 1989. – Pbk. – 0 7497 0071 8

CRASH! BANG! WALLOP!
Walker Books, 1990. – Pbk. – 0 7445 1700 1

DINOSAUR DREAMS
Little Mammoth, 1992. – Pbk. – 0 7497 0910 3

DOUBLE DUCKS
Granada, 1982. – 0 246 11524 6

EACH PEACH PEAR PLUM
Viking, 1992. – 0 670 84018 1

FAMILIES
Studio Publications, 1986. – Pbk. – 0 8621 5363 8

FAST FROG
Granada, 1982. – Pbk. 0 583 30467 2

FEE FI FO FUM
Walker Books, 1990. – Pbk. – 0 7445 1499 1

FRED'S DREAM
Collins, 1987 – O/P. – 0 00 138013 3

FUNNYBONES
Heinemann, 1992. – 0 434 92537 3

GHOST TRAIN
Heinemann, 1992. – 0 434 96084 5

GIVE THE DOG A BONE
Heinemann, 1993. – 0 434 96366 6

GOOD OLD DOLLS
Heinemann, 1984. – Pbk. – 0 434 92509 8

GREAT MARATHON FOOTBALL MATCH
Armada Books, 1981. – Pbk. – O/P. – 0 00 661931 2

HA HA BONK BOOK
Kestrel Books, 1982. – 0 7226 5745 5

HAPPY WORM
Walker Books, 1990. – Pbk. – 0 7445 1498 3

HEARD IT IN THE PLAYGROUND
Penguin, 1991. – Pbk. – 0 14 032824 6

HELP!
Walker Books, 1990. – Pbk. – 0 7445 1496 7

HERE ARE THE BRICK STREET BOYS
Picture Lions, 1992. – Pbk. – O/P. – 0 00 664094 X

HIP-HIPPO RAY
Granada, 1983. – Pbk. – 0 583 30549 0

JOLLY CHRISTMAS POSTMAN
Heinemann, 1991. – 0 434 92532 2

JOLLY POSTMAN: OR, OTHER PEOPLE'S LETTERS
Heinemann, 1986. – 0 434 92515 2

JUMPING
Walker Books, 1990. – Pbk. – 0 7445 1497 5

KING KANGAROO
Granada, 1983. – 0 246 11859 8

LOOK OUT FOR THE SEALS!
Walker Books, 1990. – Pbk. – 0 7445 1702 8

MAKE A FACE
Walker Books, 1990. – Pbk. – 0 7445 1605 6

ME AND MY FRIEND
Walker Books, 1990. – Pbk. – 0 7445 1701 X

MIGHTY SLIDE
Penguin, 1989. – Pbk. – 0 14 032335 X

MONSTER MUNCH
Heinemann, 1984. – Pbk. – 0 434 92511 X

MONSTERS
Studio Publications, 1986. – Pbk. – 0 86215 360 3

MR WOLF
Granada, 1983. – 0 246 11860 1

MRS BUTLER SONG BOOK
Viking, 1992. – 0 670 83235 9

MYSTERY TOUR
Little Mammoth, 1992. – Pbk. – 0 7497 0911 1

OLD JOKE BOOK
Viking, 1987. – 0 670 52273 2

ONE AND ONLY TWO HEADS
Collins, 1979. – O/P. – 0 00 138034 6

ONE TRUE SANTA
Heinemann, 1985. – 0 434 92514 4

ONE, TWO, FLEA!
Walker Books, 1987. – Pbk. – 0 7445 1018 X

PAIR OF SINNERS
Granada, 1980. – 0 246 11325 1
PEEK A BOO!
Viking, 1990. – 0 670 83283 9
PEEPO!
Viking, 1990. – 0 670 83282 0
PET SHOP
Little Mammoth, 1992. – Pbk. – 0 7497 1034 9
PLACE TO PLAY
Armada Books, 1976. – Pbk. – 0 00 660871 X
PLAYMATES: SLOT BOOK
Viking, 1984. – 0 670 80071 6
PLEASE MRS BUTLER
Viking, 1985. – 0 670 80617 X
POORLY PIG
Granada, 1982. – Pbk. – 0 583 30471 0
PUSH THE DOG
Walker Books, 1987. – Pbk. – 0 7445 1020 1
READY TEDDY GO!
Heinemann, 1983. – Pbk. – 0 434 92506 3
RENT A ROBOT
Heinemann, 1984. – Pbk. – 0 434 92512 8
RUBBER RABBIT
Granada, 1982. – Pbk. – 0 583 30472 9
SAM THE REFEREE
Collins, 1975. – O/P. – 0 00 138060 5
SHIRLEY'S SHOPS
Walker Books, 1987. – Pbk. – 0 7445 1019 8
SILLY SHEEP
Granada, 1982. – 0 246 11523 8
SKELETON CREW
Heinemann, 1992. – 0 434 96085 3
SO CAN I
Walker Books, 1987. – Pbk. – 0 7445 1016 3
SON OF A GUN
Penguin, 1989. – Pbk. – 0 14032810 6
SPIDER SPY
Granada, 1983. – Pbk. – 0 583 30552 0
STARTING SCHOOL
Penguin, 1990. – Pbk. – 0 14 050737 X
SUMMER SNOWMAN
Heinemann, 1983. – Pbk. – 0 434 92505 5
TELL US A STORY
Walker Books, 1990. – Pbk. – 0 7445 1614 5
TELL-TALE TIGER
Granada, 1983. – Pbk. – 0 583 30553 9
THAT'S MY BABY
Heinemann, 1983. – Pbk. – 0 434 92504 7
TRAVELLING MOOSE
Granada, 1983. – 0 246 11864 4
TWO WHEELS TWO HEADS
Collins, 1979. – O/P. – 0 00 138035 4

WHICH WITCH?
Heinemann, 1983. – Pbk. – 0 434 92507 1
WORM BOOK
Armada Books, 1989. – Pbk. – O/P. – 0 00 663361 7
YUM YUM: SLOT BOOK
Viking, 1984. – O/P. – 0 670 80070 8
ZOO
Studio Publications, 1986. – Pbk. – 0 86215 361 1

AIKEN, Joan (Delano)

British. Born Rye, Sussex, 1924. Daughter of Conrad Aiken, writer; sister of Jane Aiken Hodge, writer. Educated Wychwood School, Oxford. Married: 1) Ronald George Brown, 1945 (died 1955), one son, one daughter; 2) Julius Goldstein, 1976. Information officer, editor, copywriter, writer.

Awards: Guardian Award for Children's Fiction: *The Whispering Mountain*, 1969

Address: The Hermitage,
East Street,
Petworth,
West Sussex SU28 0AB,
England

Agents: A. M. Heath,
40–42 William IV Street,
London WC2N 4DD,
England

Brandt & Brandt,
1501 Broadway,
New York City,
New York 10036,
USA

An author with a special talent – the ability to create magical fantasy stories based firmly on historical reality. She writes for a wide age range, but at all levels readers need to be proficient as she maintains a very high standard of writing. The stories are excellent for reading aloud and serialization; some have become successful television productions.

ARABEL AND MORTIMER
Windrush, 1989, 258p. – L/P. – 1 85089 978 9
Cape, 1980, 144p. – O/P. – 0 224 01765 9

In the same series:

ARABEL AND THE ESCAPED BLACK MAMBA
BBC, 1990. – Pbk. – 0 563 20910 0

MORTIMER AND ARABEL
BBC, 1992. – 0 563 36396 7

MORTIMER AND THE SWORD EXCALIBUR
BBC, 1990. – Pbk. – 0 563 36034 8

MORTIMER SAYS NOTHING AND OTHER STORIES
Cape, 1985, 160p. – 0 224 02335 7

MORTIMER'S CROSS
BBC, 1992, 96p. – Pbk. – 0 563 36385 1
Cape, 1983, 148p. – O/P. – 0 224 02108 7

MORTIMER'S PORTRAIT ON GLASS
BBC, 1990. – Pbk. – 0 563 20915 1

MORTIMER'S TIE
BBC, 1990. – Pbk. – 0 563 20911 9

TALES OF ARABEL'S RAVEN
Cape, 1974, 160p. – 0 224 01059 X
all illustrated by Quentin Blake

These collections of stories describing the adventures of Arabel, her raven and her long-suffering mother were written specially for BBC's *Jackanory*. When published with Quentin Blake's amusing illustrations, they became very popular. Some of the stories have since been published separately in paperback. The large print and plentiful illustrations combine to provide an excellent, easy read for children who need practice in the art of reading.
Age range: 8–10

A CREEPY COMPANY
Gollancz, 1993. 144p. – 0 575 05544 8

Another collection of successful spine-chillers. A worthy successor to her other ghostly collections which have proved so popular.
Age range: 11–13

FAITHLESS LOLLYBIRD AND OTHER STORIES
Cape, 1977, 224p. – O/P. – 0 224 01332 7

In the same series:

HARP OF FISHBONES
Penguin, 1975, 240p. – Pbk. O/P. – 0 14 030729 X
Cape, 1972. 229p. – 0 224 00666 5

MICE AND MENDELSON
Penguin, 1981, 112p. – Pbk. O/P. – 0 14 031253 6
Cape, 1978. 144p. – 0 224 01615 6
illustrated by Babette Cole

SMALL PINCH OF WEATHER
Lutterworth Press, 1988, 192p. – 0 7188 2696 5
Penguin, 1972, 192p. – Pbk. O/P. – 0 14 030544 0

UP THE CHIMNEY DOWN
Cape, 1984, 272p. – 0 224 02198 2

All collections of short stories of endless invention and variety. Some are simply amusing, some scary and some exciting – all are enjoyable and suitable for reading aloud to children who are experienced listeners. They are not for filling in the odd ten minutes, though they are pleasurable enough to do so. They are so well written that they will enrich children's literary experience and provide an introduction to the author's full length novels.
Age range: 8–10

FOG HOUNDS, WIND CAT, SEA MICE
Pan Books, 1987, 75p. – Pbk. – 0 330 29511 X
Macmillan, 1984, 64p. – O/P. – 0 333 36574 7
illustrated by John Lawrence

In the same series:

LAST SLICE OF RAINBOW AND OTHER STORIES
Penguin, 1988, 176p. – Pbk. – 0 14 032301 5
Cape, 1985, 128p. – 0 224 02297 0
illustrated by Margaret Watty

Welcome additions to Joan Aiken's collections of stories, as these are aimed at young readers, while remaining at

AIKEN

the same high level of writing as her books for older readers.
Age range: 7–9

GO SADDLE THE SEA
Penguin, 1980, 288p. – Pbk. – 0 14 031155 6
Cape, 1978, 304p. – 0 224 01546 X

In the same series:
BRIDLE THE WIND
Penguin, 1986, 272p. – Pbk. O/P. –
0 14 031896 8
Cape, 1983, 272p. – 0 224 02137 0

THE TEETH OF THE GALE
Penguin, 1990, 256p. – Pbk. – 0 14 032934 X
Cape, 1988, 256p. – 0 224 02531 7
illustrated by Pat Marriot

A trilogy describing an exciting adventure set in Spain in the early nineteenth century. Felix, the young hero, decides to travel to England, to find his father's relatives when his life is made unbearable for him in his dead mother's ancestral Spanish home. The journey leads him into a variety of dangerous situations which make gripping reading. The unfamiliar Spanish names and the background of political unrest form a barrier for some children which requires a sensitive introduction to overcome, but the initial effort is amply rewarded. Serialized on television.
Age range: 10–12

KINGDOM UNDER THE SEA
Penguin, 1973, 112p. – Pbk. – 0 14 030641 2
Cape, 1971. 112p. – 0 224 61882 2

In the same series:
NECKLACE OF RAINDROPS
Penguin, 1975, 128p. – Pbk, O/P, –
0 14 030754 0
Cape, 1968, 112p. – 0 224 61462 2

PAST EIGHT O'CLOCK: GOODNIGHT STORIES
Penguin, 1990, 128p. – Pbk. – 0 14 032355 4
Cape, 1986, 128p. – 0 224 02856 1

TALE OF A ONE-WAY STREET
Penguin, 1984, 112p. – Pbk. – 0 14 031700 7
Cape, 1978, 128p. – 0 224 01158 8
illustrated by Jan Pienkowski

These books are a special treat. The stories are excellent – unusual, magical, fantastical – and the silhouette illustrations add a dimension of their own. They make splendid leisure reading, but they can also be read at a deeper level and provide an entry into successful discussion. To accommodate the large print which makes these books accessible to children who want to read for themselves, the hardback edition is larger than average. The paperback, though smaller, is equally attractive.
Age range: 8–10

THE KITCHEN WARRIORS
Hodder, 1984, 96p. – Pbk. O/P. –
0 340 33517 3
BBC, 1983, 95p. – O/P. – 0 563 20216 5
illustrated by Jo Worth

Also written for *Jackanory*, this collection of modern fairy tales is woven around such household appliances as the vacuum cleaner. The elves who live in or near them appeal to young children. The usual blend of magic and reality makes this a really satisfying read.
Age range: 7–9

MIDNIGHT IS A PLACE
Red Fox, 1991, 288p. – Pbk. – 0 09 979200 1
Cape, 1974, 304p. – O/P. – 0 224 00968 0

The loneliness suffered by many children is a recurring theme in Joan Aiken's books, and forms the basis for this fantasy. Lucas is driven to confess 'I'm lonely', setting in motion an extraordinary train of events which eventually transforms his life. It is a fast moving story punctuated by flashes of humour.
Age range: 11–13

MOON'S REVENGE
Red Fox, 1990, 32p. – Pbk. – 0 09 975010 4
Cape, 1987, 32p. – 0 224 02477 9
illustrated by Alan Lee

An unusual, evocative and haunting picture book. The story is about a small

child who throws stones at the moon with terrifying consequences. His courage brings the story to a happy conclusion. The illustrations match the mood and atmosphere of the text to perfection.
Age range: 7–11

SHADOW GUESTS
Chivers Press, 1993, 232p. – L/P, – 0 7451 1913 1
Red Fox, 1992, 192p. – Pbk. – 0 09 988820 3
Cape, 1980, 170p. – 0 224 01797 7

A mystery surrounds Cosmo and his family and the way it is resolved makes an unusual story, full of hidden threats. The climax is just as exciting as the build up.
Age range: 11–13

THE WHISPERING MOUNTAIN
Red Fox, 1992, 306p. – Pbk, – 0 09 988830 0
Cape, 1968, 240p. – 0 224 61574 2

Set in Wales and peopled by dwarfs, *The Whispering Mountain* is easy to believe in. Owen, once again a lonely boy, proves himself a worthy opponent of the wicked Marquess. An original plot, told with imagination and humour.
Age range: 10–12

THE WOLVES OF WILLOUGHBY CHASE
Chivers Press, 1986, 272p. – L/P. – 0 7451 0299 9
Hutchinson, 1975, 160p. – O/P. – 0 09 124620 2
Red Fox, 1992, 192p. – Pbk, – 0 09 997250 6

In the same series:

BLACK HEARTS IN BATTERSEA
Red Fox, 1992, 256p. – Pbk. – 0 09 988860 2
Cape, 1965, 192p. – 0 224 60705 7

NIGHT BIRDS ON NANTUCKET
Red Fox, 1993, 202p. – Pbk. – 0 09 988890 4
Cape, 1966, 188p. – 0 224 60687 5

THE STOLEN LAKE
Red Fox, 1993, 318p. – Pbk. – 0 09 988840 8
Cape, 1981, 272p. – 0 224 01924 4

THE CUCKOO TREE
Red Fox, 1992, 304p. – Pbk. – 0 09 988870 X
Cape, 1971, 256p. – O/P. – 0 224 00514 6

DIDO AND PA
Cape, 1986, 252p. – 0 224 02364 0
Red Fox, 1992, 320p. – Pbk. – 0 09 988850 5

Set historically in the first half of eighteenth-century England, but in the wholly imaginary reign of King James III, the first book in this series has a curiously topical appeal as the Channel Tunnel has just been completed. Among the first to use it is a pack of wolves, starving and savage, who add to the dangers facing Bonnie when a sinister new governess arrives. This series illustrates Joan Aiken's unsurpassable ability to blend history, fantasy and reality into an exciting and really funny whole. To read it is to have a true literary and life-enriching experience. *The Wolves of Willoughby Chase* is currently popular owing to the success of the film version recently released.
Age range: 10–12

Other publications:

MYSTERY OF MR JONES'S DISAPPEARING TAXI
BBC, 1990, – Pbk. – 0 563 20917 8
SHOEMAKER'S BOY
Simon and Schuster, 1994, – 0 671 86647 8

ALCOCK, Vivien (Dolores)

British. Born Worthing, Sussex, 1924. Educated at Devizes High School, Wiltshire; Oxford School of Art. Ambulance driver, Auxiliary Territorial Service, WW II. Married Leon Garfield 1948, one adopted daughter. Artist, secretary.

Address: 59 Wood Lane,
           Highgate,
           London N6 5UD,
           England

ALCOCK

Agent: John Johnson Ltd
45–47 Clerkenwell Green,
London EC1R 0HT,
England

Vivien Alcock's writing is characterized by an ability to deal with issues fundamental to children while at the same time creating an original and enjoyable story. Her books are exciting enough to be read aloud and to provide material for fruitful discussion.

CUCKOO SISTER
Heinemann, 1988, 160p. – 0 435 12327 0
Chivers Press, 1987, 256p. – L/P. –
0 7451 0586 6
Armada Books, 1986, 160p. – Pbk. –
0 00 672690 9

Kate finds it difficult to adjust to the startling revelation that she is not an only child. It is impossible to accept that Rosie, with her spiky hair and tight skirt, could possibly be related to the quiet, polite Setons. The tensions brought about by this situation are well portrayed. Serialized on television.
Age range: 10–12

THE HAUNTING OF CASSIE PALMER
Mammoth, 1991, 160p. – Pbk. – 0 7497 0708 9
Methuen, 1980, 155p. – O/P. – 0 416 89250 7

Because Cassie's Mum is a medium, Cassie is used to the idea of spirits, but she does not want to follow in her mother's footsteps. To prove she has no 'powers', she tries to summon a spirit, and, to her horror, succeeds. Worse still, she cannot free herself of him. The reader experiences with Cassie the feeling of growing menace until the climax relieves the tension. Cassie is an outcast at school, and suffers agonizingly as she comes to the realization that parents are only human, fallible and unsuccessful. The greatest worry is being faced with a serious situation that is beyond one's ability to cope.
Age range: 9–11

A KIND OF THIEF
Mammoth, 1992, 160p. – Pbk. – 0 7497 0947 2
Methuen, 1991, 160p. – 0 416 15562 6

There are a very few books which deal with the problems experienced by children whose fathers are in prison. This is one, written from the point of view of Elinor, who, at thirteen, has to shoulder the responsibility for the family without the adult experience to make sound judgments.
Age range: 11–13

MONSTER GARDEN
Chivers Press, 1990, 200p. – L/P. –
0 7451 1063 0
Armada Books, 1989, 128p. – Pbk. –
0 00 673163 5
Methuen, 1988, 144p. – 0 416 09192 X

A moving account of a young girl who 'grows' a monster, and how she comes to accept responsibility for its welfare. The growth of her feelings is well described, but the seriousness of the situation is relieved by the many flashes of humour which combine to make this a well balanced book. It is an exceptionally difficult story to bring to a satisfactory conclusion and there is room for improvement here, but, on the whole, an excellent read.
Age range: 9–11

THE MYSTERIOUS MR ROSS
Chivers Press, 1988, 232p. – L/P. –
0 7451 0759 1
Methuen, 1987, 128p. – 0 416 01312 0

When Felicity saves Mr Ross from drowning, she basks in the acclaim quite naturally afforded to such a heroine. However, there is something mysterious about him, and Felicity's life is transformed by her efforts to unravel the mystery.
Age range: 10–13

OTHERGRAN
Methuen, 1993, 64p. – Pbk. – 0 416 18771 4
illustrated by Elaine Mills

A wonderful story about a child who is instrumental in healing the rift between

her mother and grandmother. Short and easy to read, but a storyline well-handled, and excellent characterization.
Age range: 8–10

SINGER TO THE SEA GOD
Mammoth, 1993, 160p. – Pbk. – 0 7497 1284 8
Methuen, 1992, 160p. – 0 416 18603 3

Basically a novel about the legend of Perseus and Phaidon. It needs careful introduction to children who are likely to be alienated by the Greek names. It is an exciting and often sad adventure story of Phaidon's escape as war begins. A perilous journey to safety is made more arduous as he insists on taking with him his sister who was turned to stone by Medusa. Quite gripping.
Age range: 12+

THE STONE WALKERS
Armada Books, 1982, 144p. – Pbk. –
0 00 671976 7
Methuen, 1981, 180p. – 0 416 20700 6

'Poppy Brown was a liar' – thus the riveting opening of this story. A storm breathes life into a statue, setting in motion a chain of events. Told with humour, the book has a characteristic combination to ensure readers are kept interested to the end. Poppy lies to compensate for her unhappy childhood with many foster mothers. Both Poppy and the adults around her have to face and solve their problems, with the reader a closely involved spectator.
Age range: 9–11

THE SYLVIA GAME
Armada Books, 1984, 160p. – Pbk. –
0 00 672138 9
Methuen, 1982, 154p. – 0 416 21930 6

Emily has many problems. She is convalescing, worried about her over-worked mother, lack of money, and, most of all, her father's strange behaviour. When she meets Oliver and learns about Sylvia and her own resemblance to her, her suspicions about her father increase. The characters are realistically drawn and the story carries the reader swiftly along with a highly satisfactory denouement. Serialized on television.
Age range: 10–12

TRAVELLERS BY NIGHT
Armada Books, 1985, 192p. – Pbk. –
0 00 672383 7
Methuen, 1983, 160p. – 0 416 44830 5

Physical disfigurement is an enormous problem to have to face at any age, but Belle succeeds in coping with it. However, when she learns, first that the circus she works in has to close down, and then that her beloved elephant Tessie has to die, she feels it is all too much. Belle is made of stern stuff and rises to the occasion. In spite of the wealth of unhappiness in this story, there are some light moments of humour. A moving story.
Age range: 9–11

THE TRIAL OF ANNA COTMAN
Mammoth, 1990, 176p. – Pbk. – 0 7497 0444 6
Methuen, 1989, 160p. – 0 416 13952 3

Anna's friendship with Linda involves her with a group of organized bullies at her new school. She tries hard not to be frightened, but when she is put on trial, it proves almost too much for her. Serialized on television.
Age range: 10–12

ALLEN, Judy

British. Born Old Sarum, Wiltshire, 1941. Educated Southsea, Hampshire. Editor, freelance writer. Now lives in South London.

Agent: :   Pat White,
          Rogers, Coleridge & White, Ltd,
          20, Powis Mews,
          London W11 1JN
          England

ALLEN

Awards: Whitbread Literary Award: *Awaiting developments*, 1988
Earthworm Children's Book Award: *Awaiting developments*, 1989

AWAITING DEVELOPMENTS
Walker Books, 1989, 192p. – Pbk. – 0 7445 1321 9
J. MacRae Books, 1988, 176p. – O/P. – 0 86203 356 X

Although published in paperback as part of the 'Teens' series, this book can be appreciated by younger children, especially now it has been televised. It tells the story of a garden about to be redeveloped, and a shy young girl's attempt to save it.
Age range: 11–13

BETWEEN THE MOON AND THE ROCK
J. MacRae, 1992, 156p. – 1 85681 063 1

This novel deals exceptionally well with the idea of a religious sect which controls its members while appearing to offer a solution to life's problems. In spite of the serious topic, Judy Allen's particular brand of humour is very much in evidence. Highly readable.
Age range: 12+

SOMETHING RARE AND SPECIAL
Walker Books, 1989, 144p. – Pbk. – 0 7445 0846 0
J. MacRae Books, 1985, 128p. – O/P. – 0 86203 216 4

Lyn's life is in turmoil – her father has left home, she has to move house, and therefore has to leave her best friend. Describing how Lyn comes to terms with her changed circumstances, Judy Allen shows readers who may be in a similar dilemma that there is always hope.
Age range: 12–14

TRAVELLING HOPEFULLY
Corgi, 1989, 128p. – Pbk. – 0 552 52514 6
J. MacRae Books, 1987, 128p. – O/P. – 0 86203 267 9

An amusingly told story about Clare, who finds herself unexpectedly travelling round Devon with her young aunt, who is a journalist. They are an ill-assorted pair, but gradually they come to accept each other, largely due to a shared sense of humour. A witty book, full of verbal repartee.
Age range: 12–14

Other publications:

CHEAP SHEEP SHOCK
Red Fox, 1992. – Pbk. – 0 09 996810 X
DIM THIN DUCKS
Walker Books, 1991. – Pbk. – 0 7445 2009 6
DREAM THING
Walker Books, 1991. – Pbk. – 0 7445 2058 4
ELEPHANT
Candlewick Press, 1993. – 1 56402069 X
GREAT PIG SPRINT
Walker Books, 1991. – Pbk. – 0 7445 2010 X
LONG-LOAN LLAMA
Red Fox, 1992. – Pbk. – 0 09 996800 2
LORD OF THE DANCE
H. Hamilton, 1976. – 0 241 89476 X
PANDA
Candlewick Press, 1993. – 1 564 02142 4
SEAL
Candlewick Press, 1994. – 1 564 02145 9
SONG FOR SOLO AND PERSISTENT CHORUS
H. Hamilton, 1977. – 0 241 89698 3
SPRING ON THE MOUNTAIN
Penguin, 1977. – Pbk, – O/P, – 0 14 030906 3
STONES OF THE MOON
Cape, 1975. – 0 224 01104 9
TIGER
Candlewick Press, 1992. – 1 564 02083 5
WHALE
Candlewick Press, 1993. – 1 564 02160 2
WHAT IS A WALL, AFTER ALL?
Walker Books, 1993. – 0 7445 2251 X

ALLEN, Linda

British. Born Huddersfield, West Yorkshire. Educated Huddersfield. Married, three children. Secretary, writer.

Address: 51, Churchfields Road,
Cubert,
Newquay,
Cornwall,
England

LIONEL AND THE SPY NEXT DOOR
Pan Books, 1986, 56p. – Pbk. O/P. –
0 330 29528 4
Hamish Hamilton, 1985, 96p. – O/P. –
0 241 11553 1

In the same series:

LIONEL AND THE LONE WOLF
Penguin, 1990, 128p. – Pbk. –
0 14 034183 8
Hamish Hamilton, 1988, 112p. –
0 241 12511 1

LIONEL'S FINEST HOUR
Pan Books, 1986, 90p. – Pbk. –
0 330 29097 5
Hamish Hamilton, 1984, 128p. – O/P. –
0 241 11329 6

Lionel is a boy who knows his own mind, and this leads him into a series of really funny adventures. They are well told, easy to read and well illustrated – books full of appeal for young readers.
Age range: 9–11

Other publications:

CRASH, BANG AND WALLOP
Hodder, 1988. – 0 340 43062 1
DEAD MAN'S SECRET
Hippo Books, 1991. – Pbk. – 0 590 76282 6
MEEKO AND MIRABEL
H. Hamilton, 1985. – 0 241 11599 X
MOUSE BRIDE
Putnam, 1992. – 0 399 22136 0
MRS SIMKIN AND THE GROOVY OLD GRAMOPHONE
H. Hamilton, 1992. – 0 241 13124 3
MRS SIMKIN AND THE MAGIC WHEELBARROW
H. Hamilton, 1987. – 0 241 11992 8
MRS SIMKIN AND THE VERY BIG MUSHROOM
H. Hamilton, 1986. – 0 241 11730 5
MRS SIMKIN AND THE WISHING WELL
H. Hamilton, 1993. – 0 241 13126 X
PARROT IN THE HOUSE
Hodder, 1988. – 0 340 42584 9
RUNAWAY NEST
Abelard-Schuman, 1980. – 0 200 72679 X
WHEN GRANDFATHER'S PARROT INHERITED KENNINGTON COURT
Hodder, 1992. – Pbk. – 0 340 56857 7

ANDERSON, Rachel

British. Pseudonym for Rachel Bradbury. Born Hampton Court, 1943. Married to David Bradbury, University Lecturer. 4 children. Lives in Norfolk and Canterbury. Journalist, reviewer, writer.

Awards: Guardian Children's Fiction Award (joint-winner): *Paper Faces*, 1992

Address: Lower Damsels,
Northrepps,
Norfolk,
England

c/o Lion's Publishing,
Peter's Way,
Sandy Lane West,
Littlemore,
Oxford OX4 5HG
England

Although she has been writing for children for a number of years, she is not as prolific as some, but every book is a gem. She writes about diverse subject matters, each one capable of extending the experience of readers to an important degree.

THE BUS PEOPLE
Red Fox, 1992, 112p. – Pbk. – 0 09 987420 2
OUP, 1989, 95p. – 0 19 271602 6

Undoubtedly one of the best books ever which deals with the problems experienced by children and young people with various handicaps who face a daily battle to live. Honest and unsentimental, it provides the rest of us with valuable insight, not just into their difficulties which are there to be seen, but more importantly into the existence of the essential being trapped inside a damaged body.
Age range: 12+

ANDERSON

LITTLE ANGEL COMES TO STAY
OUP, 1984. – O/P. – 0 19 271472 4

In the same series:

LITTLE ANGEL, BONJOUR!
OUP, 1988. – 0 19 271591 7
both illustrated by Linda Birch

Gabrielle is a naughty, spoilt little girl who spends her time trying, by any means at her disposal, to get her own way, but fate intervenes in an amusing way. The two stories have lots of appeal for younger children who can read with a certain fluency. The print is large and clear; the plentiful line drawings make them very attractive.
Age range: 7–9

PAPER FACES
OUP, 1991, 116p. – 0 19 271654 9

Although there are lots of stories depicting various aspects of war, very few show that declaring peace does not automatically make everything right. Dot was used to having her mother to herself and accepted the rationing and the hardships as normal, but having to cope with the return of her unknown father is frightening.
Age range: 10–12

THE POACHER'S SON
Fontana, 1984, 144p. – Pbk. – 0 00 672251 2
OUP, 1982, 144p. – O/P. – 0 19 271468 6

To read this book is to be transported back in time to rural England in early 1900. The vivid description of the daily grind for the poor allows the reader to suffer with the Betts family in their terrible struggle to survive. Atmospheric, and utterly absorbing, but not an easy read.
Age range: 10–12

WHEN MUM WENT TO WORK
OUP, 1992, 118p. – 0 19 271683 2

When Mrs Garland, hitherto the 'perfect' mother, always available, decides to go to work, her children are passed from one childminder to another, the last one being the most eccentric of all. The most improbable incidents occur and are described in a most amusing style, but still requiring a high degree of fluency. Useful to give to a child who feels resentful at being left while Mum works. Published in paperback with the title *Treasures for Cousin Crystal* (Lions, 1993, 128p. – Pbk. – 0 00 674642 X).
Age range: 9–11

Other publications:
BEST FRIENDS
Young Lions, 1992. – Pbk. – 0 00 674138 X
FOR THE LOVE OF SANG
Lion Publishing, 1990. – Pbk. – 0 7459 1914 6
HAPPY CHRISTMAS, LITTLE ANGEL
OUP, 1991. – 0 19 271514 3
JESSY RUNS AWAY
Armada Books, 1989. – Pbk. – 0 00 673293 3
MOFFATT'S ROAD
Cape, 1978. – O/P. – 0 224 01381 5
RENARD THE FOX
OUP, 1986. – 0 19 274129 2
TIM WALKS
CIO Publishing, 1985. – Pbk. – 0 7151 0422 5
WAR ORPHAN
R. Drew Publishing, 1987. – Pbk. – 0 86267 185 X
WILD GOOSE CHASE
OUP, 1989. – 0 19 279850 2

ANTROBUS, John

British. Born Woolwich, 1933. Educated Bishop Wordsworth Grammar School, Salisbury; Selhurst Grammar School; King Edward Nautical College; Sandhurst Military Academy. East Surrey Regiment, 1952–55. Married Margaret McCormick 1958, three children. Writer.

Agent: Blanche Martin,
21a St John's Wood High Street,
London NW8 7NG,
England

THE BOY WITH ILLUMINATED MEASLES
Hodder, 1980, 64p. – Pbk. – 0 340 25360 6
Robson Books, 1978, 64p. – 0 86051 028 X

In the same series:

HELP! I AM A PRISONER IN A TOOTHPASTE FACTORY
Hodder, 1980, 64p. – Pbk. O/P. – 0 340 25359 2
Robson Books, 1978, 64p. – 0 86051 029 8

RONNIE AND THE FLYING FITTED CARPET
Hodder, 1993, 64p. – 0 86051 822 1

RONNIE AND THE GREAT KNITTED ROBBERY
Hodder, 1984, 64p. – Pbk. O/P. – 0 340 35019 9
Robson Books, 1982, 64p. – 0 86051 180 4

RONNIE AND THE HAUNTED ROLLS ROYCE
Hodder, 1984, 48p. – Pbk. O/P. – 0 340 33988 8
Robson Books, 1982, 48p. – 0 86051 179 0

RONNIE AND THE HIGH RISE
Robson Books, 1992, 64p. – 0 8605 1621 0
illustrated by Rowan Barnes-Murphy

A series of highly original and very amusing stories designed to encourage young readers. Short chapters, plenty of illustrations, and lots of action make these an undemanding but satisfying read.
Age range: 8–10

Other publications:

PICNIC
Carnival, 1989. – 0 00 193324 8
PIRATES
Carnival, 1989. – 0 00 193325 6
POLO TIME
Carnival, 1989. – 0 00 193326 4
SPOOKY TIME
Carnival, 1989. – 0 00 193327 2
TRIXIE AND BABA
Riverrun Press, 1988. – Pbk. – 0 7145 0058 5

APPIAH, Peggy

British. Born Filkins, Gloucestershire, 1921. Daughter of Sir Stafford Cripps (the politician). Educated Norland Place; Queen's College, London; Maltman's Green, Buckinghamshire; Whitehall Secretarial College. Married Joe E. Appiah, 1953, one son, three daughters. Research assistant, secretary.

Address: PO Box 829,
Kumasi,
Ashanti,
Ghana
Agent: David Higham Assoc. Ltd,
5–8 Lower John Street,
London W1R 4HA,
England

THE PINEAPPLE CHILD, AND OTHER TALES FROM ASHANTI
Deutsch, 1989, 176p. – Pbk. – 0 233 98371 6
Deutsch, 1969, 172p. – O/P. – 0 233 95927 0

In the same series:

TALES OF AN ASHANTI FATHER
Beacon Press, 1989, 160p. – 0 8070 8312 7
Deutsch, 1987, 158p. – Pbk. – 0 233 98126 8
both illustrated by Mora Dickinson

Excellent collections of good traditional folk tales from Ghana, with universal appeal. The paperback edition of *The Pineapple Child* is exceptionally well produced, making it a pleasure to handle. Good quality paper, clear print and effective lino cuts combine to give these stories a perfect setting.
Age range: 7–10

Other publications:

RING OF GOLD
Deutsch, 1976. – 0 233 96786 9
WHY THE HYENA DOESN'T CARE FOR FISH
Deutsch, 1977. – 0 233 96903 9

ARKLE, Phyllis

British. Born Chester, 1910. Convent school educated; University of

Liverpool. Married. Lives near Reading, Berkshire. Secretary, Director of the family firm, writer.

MAGIC AT MIDNIGHT
Penguin, 1974, 112p. – Pbk. – 0 14 030693 5
Hodder, 1972, 96p. – O/P. – 0 340 04068 8

In the same series:

MAGIC IN THE AIR
Penguin, 1980, 88p. – Pbk. – 0 14 031179 3
Hodder, 1978, 88p. – O/P. – 0 340 22195 X
both illustrated by Mike Cole

Two stories, involving exciting magical happenings, which have great appeal to younger children who are just beginning to read with a certain fluency.
Age range: 7–9

THE RAILWAY CAT
Penguin, 1985, 96p. – Pbk. – 0 14 031660 4
Hodder, 1983, 88p. – O/P. – 0 340 32593 3

In the same series:

THE RAILWAY CAT AND DIGBY
Penguin, 1986, 80p. – Pbk. – 0 14 031836 4
Hodder, 1984, 80p. – O/P. – 0 340 35077 6

THE RAILWAY CAT AND THE HORSE
Penguin, 1988, 96p. – Pbk. – 0 14 032488 7
Hodder, 1987, 89p. – 0 340 38844 7

THE RAILWAY CAT'S SECRET
Penguin, 1987, 96p. – Pbk. – 0 14 032110 1
Hodder, 1985, 88p. – O/P. – 0 340 36743 1
all illustrated by Lynne Byrnes

An excellent series of books about Alfie, the cat who lives at the railway station, in spite of the porter's attempts to get rid of him. The stories are basic, but well constructed, and full of humour. They are not too long, so young readers are not deterred, yet they are substantial enough to provide a satisfying read. Recently published in one volume by Puffin as *The Adventures of the Railway Cat*.
(Penguin, 1990, 309p. – Pbk. – 0 14 034515 9)
Age range: 8–10

Other publications:
ADVENTURES OF BLUNTER BUTTON
Hodder, 1980. – 0 340 25208 1
DINOSAUR FIELD
Hodder, 1989. – 0 340 49712 2
GRANDMA'S OWN ZOO
Hodder, 1979. – 0 340 24196 9
RODDY AND THE MINIATURE RAILWAY
Hodder, 1980. – O/P. – 0 340 23903 4
RODDY AND THE PUMA
Hodder, 1979. – 0 340 22682 X
RODDY AND THE RUSTLERS
Hodder, 1972. – 0 340 13471 2
RODDY ON THE CANAL
Hodder, 1975. – 0 340 19787 0
RODDY ON THE MOTORWAY
Hodder, 1974. – 0 340 18350 0
RODDY THE ROADMAN
Hodder, 1970. – 0 340 10418 X
TWO VILLAGE DINOSAURS
Penguin, 1981. – Pbk. – 0 14 031304 4
VILLAGE DINOSAUR
Penguin, 1979. – Pbk. – 0 14 031126 2

ASHLEY, Bernard

British. Born Woolwich, South London, 1935. Educated Roan School, Blackheath, London; Sir Joseph Williamson's School, Rochester, Kent; Trent Park College of Education, Certificate of Education; Cambridge Institute of Education, Diploma in Primary Education. Royal Air Force, 1953–55. Married Iris Holbrook, 1958, three sons. Teacher.

Awards: Children's Rights Workshop Other Award: *The Trouble with Donovan Croft*, 1976
Address: 128, Heathwood Gardens, London SE7 8ER, England

Having worked with young people, Bernard Ashley is well placed to know the issues that currently concern them. He takes one or more of these issues and weaves gripping stories around them. He uses words sparingly and to great effect, so his books are not an easy read, but they have great appeal to young readers. They are tough, set firmly in a harsh reality that many children are very familiar with. Many of them concern runaway children who can no longer face a person or situation. All are concerned with growing up and learning to cope, and all of them offer the reader more than just a couple of hours' entertainment.

ALL MY MEN
Penguin, 1979, 160p. – Pbk. – 0 14 031131 9
OUP, 1977, 160p. – 0 19 271390 6

The problem of trying to settle into a new school is not exactly an original theme, but Paul's method of handling this situation, by trying to get picked for the football team, seems a good solution. Learning to deal with the bully who 'controls' the team is a different matter. A book offering hope to every child who suffers at the hands of older children.
Age range: 10–12

BAD BLOOD
Walker Books, 1989, 160p. – Pbk. –
0 7445 0848 7
J. MacRae Books, 1988, 176p. – O/P. –
0 86203 316 0

Determined to save his father, Ritchie sets out to find the missing brother. Slowly, with the help of Sadie, he unravels the mystery that surrounds his father's family. Intriguing.
Age range: 12–14

A BIT OF GIVE AND TAKE
Corgi, 1986, 96p. – Pbk. – 0 552 52348 8
Hamish Hamilton, 1984, 96p. – O/P. –
0 241 11301 6
illustrated by Trevor Stubley

In the same series:

DINNER LADIES DON'T COUNT
Penguin, 1984, 96p. – Pbk. also including 'Linda's Lie'. – 0 14 031593 4
J. MacRae Books, 1981, 48p. – O/P. –
0 86203 017 X
illustrated by Janet Duchesne

I'M TRYING TO TELL YOU
Penguin, 1982, 80p. – Pbk. – 0 14 031337 0
Kestrel Books, 1981, 80p. – O/P. –
0 7226 5725 0
illustrated by Lyn Jones

YOUR GUESS IS AS GOOD AS MINE
Corgi, 1987, 80p. – Pbk. – 0 552 52450 6
J. MacRae Books, 1983, 56p. – O/P. –
0 86203 134 6
illustrated by David Parkins

High quality stories all written for the young reader just beginning to read full-length books. The plots are simple, but well constructed, with their fair share of humour.
Age range: 7–9

BREAK IN THE SUN
OUP, 1983, 190p. – 0 19 271476 7
Penguin, 1981, 192p. – Pbk. – 0 14 031341 9

Like many children today, Patsy has a terrible life with her new step-father. When an opportunity to escape presents itself, she doesn't hesitate. The story of what happens to her, and the eventual pursuit by her step-father, keep the reader engrossed to a very satisfying end. The book made a very successful television drama.
Age range: 10–12

DODGEM
Collins, 1983, 222p. – 0 00 330004 8
Penguin, 1983, 224p. – Pbk. – O/P. –
0 14 031477 6

Simon has a lot to cope with. He is grieving for his mother; his father suffers from severe depression and cannot be left alone, so Simon stays away from school. This eventually lands him in assessment, where he meets Rose, as tough as they come. Together, they run away and join a travelling fair, where life is harsh indeed. A sensitive novel for young secondary school readers. It will help those children who, like Simon, have more than their fair share of difficulties, and will also give more fortunate children some insight into what life can be like for others.
Age range: 12–14

A KIND OF WILD JUSTICE
OUP, 1989, 192p. – 0 19 271617 4
Penguin, 1988, 192p. – Pbk. – 0 14 032745 2

For four years, Ronnie had lived in fear that, if his father failed to please the

ASHLEY

master criminals he worked for, he himself would be severely punished. When his father is arrested and his mother abandons him, he feels certain that life 'in care' can only get worse, and he is right. In such a situation a happy ending would be unrealistic, but a satisfying ending is acceptable, and that is what Ronnie achieves, while offering the reader a chance to understand themselves and others better.
Age range: 11–13

SEEING OFF UNCLE JACK
Puffin Books, 1993, 80p. – Pbk. – 0 14 034794 1
Viking, 1991, 80p. – 0 670 83942 6
illustrated by Kim Harley

Two short stories – each showing how a young person faces up to a difficult situation and emerges wiser and stronger. Easy to read, with short chapters. The illustrations are adequate and serve to break up the text.
Age range: 10–12

TERRY ON THE FENCE
OUP, 1986, 208p. – 0 19 271537 2
Penguin, 1978, 256p. – Pbk. – 0 14 031092 4
illustrated by Charles Keeping

Self-preservation is a very strong instinct. When faced with a tough gang of hostile boys, fear makes Terry cooperate, however reluctantly. He becomes more and more involved in wrong-doing, until he feels he can no longer cope. Such webs of dishonesty exist in every sphere of life, and ordinary, decent people like Terry are often affected by them. An exciting and compelling read, and an excellent television drama.
Age range: 11–13

THE TROUBLE WITH DONOVAN CROFT
OUP, 1980, 162p. – 0 19 277101 9
Penguin, 1977, 192p. – Pbk. – 0 14 030974 8
illustrated by Fermin Rocker

Donovan's short life has been so traumatic that he has decided that he will not talk any more. This makes life difficult for his new foster family, since no-one can penetrate this defensive barrier. The events in the story move rapidly to the conclusion, with Donovan's silence skillfully woven into the narrative. It is not quite all 'doom and gloom' – the reader's heart is allowed a little lift at the end.
Age range: 10–12

Other publications:

ALL I EVER ASK
Orchard Books, 1989. – 1 85213 078 4
BOAT GIRL
J. MacRae, 1990. – 0 86203 445 0
CALLING FOR SAM
Orchard Books, 1987. – 1 85213 075 X
CARETAKER'S CAT
J. MacRae, 1990. – 0 86203 464 7
CLEVERSTICKS
Picture Lions, 1993. – Pbk. – 0 00 663855 4
COUNTRY BOY
J. MacRae, 1989. – Pbk. – 0 86203 387 X
DOCKSIDE SCHOOL STORIES
Walker Books, 1992. – Pbk. – 0 7445 2305 2
DOWN-AND-OUT
Orchard Books, 1988. – 1 85213 077 6
GETTING IN
J. MacRae, 1990. – 0 86203 463 9
GHOST OF DOCKSIDE SCHOOL
J. MacRae, 1990. – 0 86203 446 9
HIGH PAVEMENT BLUES
Penguin, 1990. – Pbk. – 0 14 032589 1
JANEY
Penguin, 1988. – Pbk. – 0 14 032661 8
LINDA'S LIE
J. MacRae, 1982. – 0 86203 099 4
MORE STORIES FROM DOCKSIDE SCHOOL
Walker Books, 1992. – Pbk. – 0 7445 3014 8
ROYAL VISIT
Orchard Books, 1988. – 1 85213 079 2
RUNNING SCARED
Penguin, 1990. – Pbk. – 0 14 032761 4
SALLY CINDERELLA
Orchard Books, 1989. – 1 85213 080 6
SECRET OF THEODORE BROWN
J. MacRae, 1989. – Pbk. – 0 86203 458 2
TALLER THAN BEFORE
Orchard Books, 1987. – O/P. – 1 85213 076 8

B

BAILLIE, Allan

Scottish. Born Prestwick, Scotland, 1943. Moved to Australia, 1950. Married Agnes Chow, 1972, one son, one daughter. Reporter, writer.

Awards: Kathleen Fidler Award: *Adrift*, 1983
IBBY. Honour Award: *Riverman*, 1988

Address: 49 Prince Alfred Parade, Newport, NSW 2106, Australia

ADRIFT
Mammoth, 1989, 112p. – Pbk. – 0 7497 0016 5
Blackie, 1989, 144p. – 0 216 92717 X
J. Murray, 1988, 112p. – 0 7195 4511 0

A powerful and realistic story about two children playing a harmless game in an old crate by the sea. Suddenly they find themselves in the grip of a strong current rushing out to sea, and fear overwhelms them. Their efforts to maintain a sense of proportion in the face of escalating danger are laudable. The fate of the cat is hard to believe, but another upset would be too much for the hard-pressed children, and for the empathizing reader.
Age range: 9–12

CHINA COIN
Blackie, 1991, 190p. – O/P – 0 216 93095 2

This is writing at its best. An excellent plot – half a coin is taking Leah across the world to China to try to find the matching half, and, with it, the other half of her family. Leah is a strongly drawn character, which makes it easy for young readers to identify with her. She is prickly, independent, and with a deep-seated need to find her roots.
The book is topical, as it deals with the political situation in China, culminating in Tiananmen Square. All the human emotions are exploited to make this story a living experience.
Age range: 12+

EAGLE ISLAND
Penguin, 1989, 144p. – Pbk. – 0 14 034045 9
Blackie, 1987, 144p. – 0 216 92096 5

The plot is based on the difference between two characters – the spoilt Lew, and a petty criminal, Col. Thrown together on a deserted island and unable to resolve their differences, hostilities commence. Exciting and undemanding.
Age range: 10–12

LITTLE BROTHER
Puffin Books, 1994. – 0 14 036862 0
Viking, 1992. – 0 670 84381 4
illustrated by Elizabeth Honey

Set in Kampuchea, this book paints a realistic portrait of war, without glamour and without heroes, but with a powerful message of harsh times. Many children have had to suffer the various hard consequences of war. This is the story of two brothers separated while trying to escape. Their efforts to get together provide a suspense-filled drama, maintained to the very end.
Age range: 10–12

MAGICIAN
Blackie, 1992, 160p. – 0 216 93284 X

A futuristic fantasy, telling the story of a community surviving against all odds, but living in fear of the Darkness, which is a threat used by their leader to control them. Kim alone finds the courage to challenge this, but can he persuade others to believe him. Enthralling to the very last page.
Age range: 10–12

BAILLIE

MEGAN'S STAR
Penguin, 1990, 144p. – Pbk. – 0 14 034046 7
Blackie, 1988, 128p. – 0 216 92390 5

A book of many facets, culminating in a well founded whole. Set in Australia, yet not specifically so, it concerns Megan who is struggling to come to terms with her father's sudden departure. She gradually becomes aware that she is different from 'normal' people – just how different is crystallized when a voice inside her head leads her to rescue the voice's owner, Kel, a boy with similar powers to hers. A well produced book with clear print, ensuring that young readers can cope with this complex, exciting story.
Age range: 10–12

RIVER MAN
Blackie, 1986, 144p. – O/P – 0 216 91861 8

Tim felt he had proved himself when he helped with the rescue down the mine. When he accompanies his uncle up river, however, he begins to wonder just how tough he has to be. Alan Baillie has created an excellent character in Tim.
Age range: 10–12

Other publications:

DRAC AND THE GREMLIN
Puffin Books, 1992. – 0 14 054542 5

HERO
Penguin, 1991. – Pbk. – 0 14 034427 6

BANKS, Lynne Reid

British. Born London, 1929. Educated in Canada where she was evacuated during WW II; Italia Centre Stage School, London; Royal Academy of Dramatic Art, London. Married Chaim Stephenson (the sculptor), 1965, three sons. Actress, teacher, writer. Lived in Israel 1963–71.

Agent: Watson Little Ltd,
26, Charing Cross Road,
London WC2H 0DG,
England

A capable writer of modern fantasy, Lynne Reid Banks can draw readers effortlessly into a make-believe world. The stories are accessible to less able readers, as linguistically they are not too demanding.

FAIRY REBEL
Lions, 1992, 116p. – Pbk. – 0 00 673220 8
Cornerstone Books, 1989, 227p. – O/P – L/P. – 1 55736 124 X
Dent, 1985, 128p. – O/P – 0 460 6178 X
illustrated by William Gaunt

Although slow to start, once launched, this fairy story quickly becomes as exciting as any traditional fairy story. Friendship between the fairy world and adult humans is rare, and the resulting dramatic confrontation puts a child's life at risk. Very easy to read.
Age range: 8–10

THE FARTHEST AWAY MOUNTAIN
Armada Books, 1988, 144p. – Pbk. – 0 00 672998 3
Abelard-Schuman, 1976, 142p. – O/P – 0 200 72461 4
illustrated by Victor Ambrus

Using the well tried recipe of a young girl encountering and bravely defeating evil during a difficult journey is a successful ploy. Girls will find much to identify with in the character of Dakin, who dreams of a prince, but finds happiness elsewhere.
Age range: 9–11

I, HOUDINI: THE AUTOBIOGRAPHY OF A SELF-EDUCATED HAMSTER
Armada Books, 1989, 128p. – Pbk. – 0 00 673363 8
Mayflower, 1981, 128p. – Pbk. – 0 583 30482 6
Dent, 1978, 120p. – 0 460 06873 3
illustrated by Terry Riley

Amusing, anecdotal episodes about a hamster who refuses to be caged. It is told in the first person, occasioning many asides which are irritating.

Despite this, the book will be hugely enjoyed by the many hamster-owning readers.
Age range: 9–11

THE INDIAN IN THE CUPBOARD
Dent, 1991, 160p. – 0 460 88099 3
Lions, 1988, 160p. – Pbk. – 0 00 673051 5
Chivers Press, 1987, 280p. – L/P. – 0 7451 0625 0
illustrated by Robin Jacques

In the same series:

THE RETURN OF THE INDIAN
Chivers Press, 1989, 248p. – L/P. – 0 7451 0960 8
Armada Books, 1988, 160p. – Pbk. – 0 00 673052 3
Dent, 1986, 144p. – 0 460 06239 5
illustrated by William Geldert

THE SECRET OF THE INDIAN
Collins, 1991, 144p. – Pbk. – 0 00 673505 3
Chivers Press, 1990, 224p. – L/P. – 0 7451 1232 3
Collins, 1989, 192p. – 0 00 184746 5

Well-sustained fantasies described with wit and the faultless attention to detail which is necessary to make the fantasy world live for the reader. Omri's old cupboard has the magical property of breathing life into plastic toys. The way he comes to understand his responsibility for another life completely dependent on him makes exciting reading.
Age range: 9–11

MAURA'S ANGEL
Penguin, 1985, 128p. – Pbk. – 0 14 031842 9
Dent 1984, 128p. – O/P. – 0 460 06152 6
illustrated by Robin Jacques

An attempt to simplify the situation in Northern Ireland, to make it accessible to children, but the result is a little too bland. Nevertheless, this is an enjoyable and optimistic story which has much to offer all children who find themselves enduring a harsh life at home, and who would benefit from a little angelic interference.
Age range: 9–11

MELUSINE: A MYSTERY
Penguin, 1990, 192p. – Pbk. – 0 14 032793 2
Hamish Hamilton, 1988, 192p. – 0 241 12548 0

Roger, on holiday in France, feels that he alone can help the strange girl who comes with the chateau. Gradually he becomes involved with the mystery that surrounds her. Good ending.
Age range: 12–14

THE MYSTERY OF THE CUPBOARD
Harper Collins, 1993, 160p. – 0 00 185504 2
Lions, 1993, 160p. – Pbk. – 0 00 674 640 3

A further story centred round Omri's cupboard, but this time concerning a mystery connected with a previous owner. Patrick and Omri gradually piece together the clues, while trying as usual to live a normal family life so that no-one else will become curious. As fascinating as the previous books, with the added appeal of a mystery to solve. Easy to read with large, clear print.
Age range: 9–11

Other publications:

ADVENTURES OF KING MIDAS
Harper Collins, 1993. – 0 00 185506 9
MAGIC HARE
Young Lions, 1993. – Pbk. – 0 00 674221 1

BARRY, Margaret Stuart (née Bell)

British. Born Darlington, Co. Durham, 1927. Educated at schools in Richmond, Yorkshire; Teacher Training College, Liverpool, Diploma in Education. Married Pierce Barry, 1957, two daughters, one son. Teacher.

Address: 5 Belvidere Road, Liverpool L8 3TF, England

Agent: Curtis Brown, 162–168 Regent Street, London W1R 5TB, England

BARRY

SIMON AND THE WITCH
Young Lions, 1992, 77p. – Pbk. –
0 00 672064 1
Collins, 1976, 78p. – 0 00 184749 X

In the same series:

THE RETURN OF THE WITCH
Young Lions, 1992, 80p. – Pbk. –
0 00 672063 3
Collins, 1978, 80p. – O/P. – 0 00 184702 3

THE WITCH AND THE HOLIDAY CLUB
Armada Books, 1988, 96p. – Pbk. –
0 00 673262 3
Collins, 1988, 96p. – O/P. – 0 00 184922 0

THE WITCH OF MONOPOLY MANOR
Armada Books, 1981, 80p. – Pbk. –
0 00 671788 8
Collins, 1980, 80p. – O/P. – 0 00 184931 X

THE WITCH ON HOLIDAY
Armada Books, 1984, 80p. – Pbk. –
0 00 672300 4
Collins, 1983, 80p. – 0 00 184932 8

THE WITCH V. I. P.
Armada Books, 1988, 96p. – Pbk. –
0 00 672987 8
Collins, 1987, 96p. – 0 00 184955 7

SIMON AND THE WITCH IN SCHOOL
Armada Books, 1988, 96p. – Pbk. –
0 00 673238 0
Collins, 1987, 96p. – 0 00 184874 7

THE MILLIONAIRE WITCH
Harper Collins, 1992, 96p. – Pbk. –
0 00 185470 4

The first book in this series introduces the reader to an absurd but likable witch who is befriended by Simon, an eminently sensible little boy. In this and subsequent stories, they come together in a variety of unlikely situations, 'helped' by George, the unfortunate cat. The stories are written in an easy-to-read, flowing style, and contain plenty of humour, both verbal and slapstick. They provide a not too taxing and very satisfactory read. Since their successful adaptation into a television series, they are among the most popular stories with children.
Age range: 8–10

Other publications:

BOFFY AND THE MUMFORD GHOSTS
Harrap, 1974. – 0 245 52279 4

BOFFY AND THE TEACHER EATER
Collins, 1973. – Pbk. – 0 00 670595 2

DIZ AND THE BIG FAT BURGLAR
H. Hamilton, 1987. – O/P. – 0 241 12003 9

MAGGIE GUMPTION FLIES HIGH
Hutchinson, 1981. – 0 09 143450 5

MAGGIE GUMPTION
Armada Books, 1981 – Pbk. – 0 00 671 786 1

MONSTER IN A WOOZY GARDEN
Harrap, 1977 – Pbk. – O/P. – 0 245 52832 6

TOMMY MAC BATTLES ON
Kestrel Books, 1974. – 0 7226 6259 9

TOMMY MAC ON SAFARI
Kestrel Books, 1975. – 0 7226 5078 7

TOMMY MAC
Kestrel Books, 1977. – 0 7226 5053 1

WOOZIES GO TO SCHOOL
Harrap, 1973. – 0 245 51972 6

WOOZIES GO VISITING
Harrap, 1977 – Pbk. – O/P. – 0 245 52833 4

WOOZIES HOLD A FRUBARB WEEK
Harrap, 1977 – Pbk. – O/P. – 0 245 52831 8

WOOZIES ON TELEVISION
Harrap, 1973. – 0 245 51973 4

WOOZY AND THE WEIGHT WATCHERS
Harrap, 1977. – Pbk. – O/P. – 0 245 52830 X

WOOZY
Harrap, 1973. – O/P. – 0 245 51970 X

BAWDEN, Nina (née Mabey)

British. Born London, 1925. Educated Ilford County High School, London; Somerville College, Oxford, B.A., M.A. (Modern Greats); Fellow of the Royal Society of Literature. Married: 1) H. W. Bawden, 1946, two sons (one deceased); 2) A. S. Kark, 1954, one daughter, two step-daughters. Reviewer, writer.

Awards: Guardian Award, Children's Fiction: *Peppermint Pig*, 1976

Address: 22 Noel Road, London N1 8HA, England

Nina Bawden has been writing since the 1950s, and is well established as an author of quality for both adults and children. Her books are not for readers lacking fluency, but the storylines are always excellent, often very exciting, and written with humour and a deep understanding of, and faith in, a child's capabilities.

CARRIE'S WAR
Chivers Press, 1985, 248p. – L/P. – 0 7451 0129 1
Penguin, 1974, 144p. – Pbk. – 0 14 030689 7
Gollancz, 1973, 128p. – 0 575 01631 0

Carrie and her younger brother were evacuated from war-torn London to Wales, where they tried hard to combat their natural home-sickness and fit into their new surroundings. Then Carrie does a terrible thing and has to leave the village. Not until she is an adult and takes her own children back for a visit does she learn the final outcome of her action. Serialized for television.
Age range: 10–12

THE FINDING
Chivers Press, 1989, 216p. – L/P. – 0 7451 0922 5
Penguin, 1987, 144p. – Pbk. – 0 14 032023 7
Gollancz, 1985, 128p. – 0 575 03618 4

The drama of this book lies in the skilful handling of events and feelings that can beset an ordinary family. Alex, abandoned by his young mother just after he was born, celebrates his 'Finding Day' rather than guessing his natural birthday. He feels happy and secure with his adoptive family until an old lady dies, leaving him all her possessions. This changes his life to such an extent that he feels he has no choice but to run away, an action which never solves anything. Serialized on television.
Age range: 10–12

A HANDFUL OF THIEVES
Chivers Press, 1990, 232p. – L/P. – 0 7451 1247 1
Penguin, 1970, 141p. – Pbk. – 0 14 030472 X
Gollancz, 1967, 128p. – 0 575 00152 6

What is a thief? Working on the premise 'if you can't beat 'em, join 'em, then perhaps you can beat 'em!', the five children decide to take the law into their own hands. After all, what could be more important than catching the thief who deprived Gran of her savings? This decision leads to danger of an unexpected degree when the Death Wall threatens to live up to its name. The way the children work together to the exclusion of all adults is reminiscent of Enid Blyton's 'Famous Five'!
Age range: 10–12

HUMBUG
Puffin Books, 1994, 160p. – 0 14 036586 9
Chivers Press, 1992, 208p. – L/P. – 0 7451 1670 1
Gollancz, 1992, 144p. – 0 575 05300 3

'Humbug' is the magic word that Cora learns to say when life gets too much for her to bear, particularly when horrid Angelica is up to her sly tricks. It does not seem to work for her on the day when she is falsely accused of stealing her Aunt's diamond ring, and she is powerless to prove her own innocence or Angelica's guilt.
Age range: 9–11

KEEPING HENRY
Chivers Press, 1990, 152p. – L/P. – 0 7451 1064 9
Penguin, 1989, 128p. – Pbk. – 0 14 032805 X
Gollancz, 1988, 128p. – 0 575 04256 7
illustrated by Ian Newsham

On a superficial level, a touching story about a baby squirrel, brought up as a pet and loved by the whole family, which finally attains freedom in the wild again. However, there are many issues

involved – the shadow cast over the lives of ordinary families by war, coming to terms with bereavement and loss, learning to cope with the inevitable changes that life brings. A good quality, highly satisfying book.
Age range: 10–12

KEPT IN THE DARK
Penguin, 1984, 144p. – Pbk. – 0 14 031550 0
Gollancz, 1982, 160p. – 0 575 03113 1

The combination of an intriguing title and excellent jacket gives a good introduction to an exciting story which holds the reader to the very surprising end. Much of the appeal is provided by the interaction of the characters.
Age range: 10–12

ON THE RUN
Penguin, 1967, 192p. – Pbk. – 0 14 030337 5
Gollancz, 1964, 208p. – 0 575 00634 X

A true adventure story – in order to foil the plan to kidnap Thomas, the son of a Prime Minister, Ben organizes an escape plan. It has to expand to include Lil, a refugee from the 'welfare lady', who wants to put her into care. The three children hide in a cave, and find they need all their resourcefulness in order to survive. A sympathetic view of the way children can manage on their own if they have to.
Age range: 10–12

OUTSIDE CHILD
Puffin Books, 1994. – 0 14 036858 2

Life can deal harsh blows to children in various guises. This is the story of just such a situation, and the courage and fortitude it takes to deal with it. Jane's mother is dead, and, unknown to her, her father remarries and has further children. His second wife does not want to have anything to do with his first child, so she becomes an 'outside' child – a heavy burden to bear. Written with such poignancy and yet with a wry humour.
Age range: 11–13

THE PEPPERMINT PIG
Chivers Press, 1987, 264p. – L/P. – 0 7451 0447 9
Penguin, 1977, 160p. – Pbk. – 0 14 030944 6
Gollancz, 1975, 192p. – 0 575 01927 1

A humorous and delightful story about a pig who lives in a house as part of the family. He is very mischievous and helps to keep the children cheerful even in the midst of all their troubles. A sensitive portrayal of family life.
Age range: 9–12

REBEL ON A ROCK
Penguin, 1980, 128p. – Pbk. – 0 14 031123 8
Gollancz, 1978, 160p. – 0 575 02420 8

Jo feels embarrassed by her odd family. She looks so different with her red hair; since her remarriage, her Mum is now called Mrs Sandwich, and finally Mr Sandwich is no oil painting. When they go on holiday to Ithaca, she feels very disappointed with the place. But when she makes friends with Alexis, she comes face to face with alarmingly real problems. Coping with these makes an exciting story.
Age range: 10–13

THE ROBBERS
Chivers Press, 1986, 216p. – L/P. – 0 7451 0328 6
Penguin, 1981, 144p. – Pbk. – 0 14 031317 6
Gollancz, 1979, 144p. – 0 575 02695 2

The strength of this story, as so often with Nina Bawden, is the interaction between the main characters. Philip lives with his grandmother in a safe, happy, comfortable routine. Darcy is street-wise and daring. However unlikely, the boys form a close friendship, but this brings difficulties for Philip, who has to make decisions which will change his life.
Age range: 10–12

RUNAWAY SUMMER
Penguin, 1972, 160p. – Pbk. – 0 14 030539 4
Gollancz, 1969, 176p. – 0 575 00337 5

Feeling fed-up at home, Mary is ready for anything. Finding Krishna, an illegal

immigrant, seems to be the answer to a prayer. Simon helps him to hide while Mary undertakes to search for his family in London. An enjoyable story – girls will really identify with Mary.
Age range: 10–12

THE SECRET PASSAGE
Penguin, 1979, 160p. – Pbk. – 0 14 031166 1
Gollancz, 1968, 192p. – 0 575 00202 6

The secret passage is an excellent cure for the homesickness and grief which Mary, John and Ben are all suffering from. Trying to unravel the mystery keeps their minds occupied and gives their hearts time to heal and adjust. Told with humour, this story is exciting right to the end.
Age range: 10–12

SQUIB
Collins, 1983, 127p. – 0 00 330011 0
Penguin, 1973, 112p. – Pbk. – 0 14 030581 5
Gollancz, 1971, 128p. – 0 575 00665 X
illustrated by Shirley Hughes

Kate came across Squib in the park, and was moved by his loneliness. She determined to find out who he was and why he seemed so unhappy. When she succeeds, she can scarcely believe his appalling circumstances. A shockingly realistic description of the home life of a cruelly ill-treated child and the bravery of more fortunate children with a will to help.
Age range: 10–12

THE WHITE HORSE GANG
Penguin, 1972, 160p. – Pbk. – 0 14 030508 4
Gollancz, 1966, 160p. – 0 575 00841 5

A highly readable story about a gang of children who need a lot of money for a good cause, and who set about kidnapping a rich boy, hoping for a substantial ransom. The plot backfires and they find themselves in Gibbet Wood, facing a terrible danger which needs all their courage.
Age range: 10–12

THE WITCH'S DAUGHTER
Chivers Press, 1988, 288p. – L/P. – 0 7451 0654 4
Penguin, 1969, 160p. – Pbk. – 0 14 030407 X
Gollancz, 1966, 160p. – 0 575 00177 1

Nina Bawden has a special gift for describing lonely, unhappy children. Perdita is an orphan and, because her mother was regarded as a witch, everyone avoids her until Janey arrives. Being blind, Janey understands the problems of being 'different'. She shows Perdita the joys and sorrows that friendship brings. This relationship is woven around discovering hidden treasure, but the adventure story is secondary to the story of Perdita's blossoming.
Age range: 10–12

Other publications:

PRINCESS ALICE
Magnet Books, 1987. – Pbk. – 0 416 96660 8

BERRY, James

British. Born Prospect, Jamaica, 1925. Educated at night school and public libraries in England. Married 1948. Overseas telegraphist, Post Office, 1951–77. Writer.

Awards: C. Day Lewis Fellowship
          Smarties Prize: *A Thief in the Village*, 1987
          Signal Poetry Award: *When I dance*, 1989
          OBE, 1990
          Boston Globe Horn Book Award: *Ajeemah and his son*, 1993
Address: C/O Hamish Hamilton, 27, Wrights Lane, London W8 5TZ, England

ANANCY – SPIDERMAN
Walker Books, 1989, 128p. – Pbk. – 0 7445 1311 1
Walker Books, 1988, 128p. – O/P. – 0 7445 0793 6
illustrated by Joseph Olubo

Caribbean folk tales about Anancy the wily spiderman who outwits everyone. Very popular with children.
Age range: 7–10

THE FUTURE-TELLING LADY
Harper Collins, 1993, 144p. – 0 06 021434 1
Puffin Books, 1993, 160p. – Pbk. –
0 14 034763 1

Seven stories sparkling with the atmosphere of a Caribbean village and its inhabitants. Each story has a racy tone and a strong human element. Highly recommended.
Age range: 12+

A THIEF IN THE VILLAGE AND OTHER STORIES
Puffin Books, 1990, 156p. – 0 14 034357 1
Windrush, 1989, 124p. – L/P. – 1 85089 971 1
Hamish Hamilton, 1987, 144p. – 0 241 12011 X

An excellent collection of short stories so full of atmosphere that the reader feels the heat, smells the cooking, and experiences the fear. Set in the author's native Jamaica, each story vividly portrays children and their view of the world around them in such a way as to cause the reader to query what is happening, not just in their own lives, but in the world generally. A well deserved prize-winner.
Age range: 11–13

Other publications:

AJEEMAH AND HIS SON
Harper Collins, 1994. – 0 06 440523 0
CHAIN OF DAYS
OUP, 1985. – 0 19 211964 8
SPIDERMAN ANANCY
Henry Holt & Co, 1989. – 0 8050 1207 9
WHEN I DANCE
Penguin, 1990. – Pbk. – 0 14 034200 1

BIEGEL, Paul (Johannes)

Dutch. Born Bussum, the Netherlands, 1925. Married, two children.

Awards: Best Children's Book of the Year, Holland: *King of the Copper Mountains*, 1965
Nienke van Hichhum Prize for Children's Literature, 1973
Starte Prize, 1974
Address: Keizersgracht 227, Amsterdam, The Netherlands

Paul Biegel's interest in, and knowledge of, traditional fairy stories is very evident, and enables him to produce high quality books which are fresh and traditional at the same time.

CROCODILE MAN
Dent, 1982, 96p. – O/P. – 0 460 06091 0
illustrated by Eva Jarnerud
A collection of traditional stories retold in Paul Biegel's inimitable style.
Age range: 8–10

THE DWARFS OF NOSEGAY
Penguin, 1980, 128p. – Pbk. – 0 14 031217 X
Blackie, 1978, 125p. – O/P. – 0 216 90452 8
illustrated by Babs van Wely

In the same series:

THE FATTEST DWARF OF NOSEGAY
Blackie, 1980, 128p. – O/P. – 0 216 90879 5

VIRGIL NOSEGAY AND THE CAKE HUNT
Blackie, 1981, 128p. – O/P. –
0 216 91088 9

VIRGIL NOSEGAY AND THE HUPMOBILE
Blackie, 1983, 128p. – O/P. – 0 216 91372 1

VIRGIL NOSEGAY AND THE WELLINGTON BOOTS
Blackie, 1984, 128p. – O/P. – 0 216 91495 7

A popular series of stories about a group of dwarfs and their adventures in the world of 'giants' – alias humans. Full of wry humour, and attractively produced.
Age range: 8–10

THE ELEPHANT PARTY
Penguin, 1977, 96p. – Pbk. – 0 14 030950 0
Kestrel Books, 1977, 112p. – O/P. –
0 7226 5289 5
illustrated by Babs van Wely

A collection of magical stories which are excellent for reading aloud as well as for children to read alone.
Age range: 8–10

THE KING OF COPPER MOUNTAIN
Dent, 1977, 176p. – Pbk, O/P. – 0 460 02742 5
Collins, 1973, 160p. – Pbk. O/P. –
0 00 670480 8
Dent, 1968, 176p. – O/P. – 0 460 05746 4
illustrated by Babs van Wely

Aimed at younger children, this is an excellent introduction to the fantasy genre. In a race against time, the Wonder Doctor searches for a potion to cure the dying King. Each day, the animals come to tell the King stories to ensure his heart keeps beating. The stories they tell are varied – happy, sad, moving. Reading them will keep children's attention from beginning to end.
Age range: 9–11

Other publications:

CLOCK STRUCK TWELVE
Glover & Blair, 1979. – 0 906681 00 6
CURSE OF THE WEREWOLF
Blackie, 1981. – 0 216 90992 9
FAR BEYOND AND BACK AGAIN
Dent, 1977. – 0 460 06737 0
GARDENS OF DORR
Dent, 1975. – 0 460 05888 6
LETTERS FROM THE GENERAL
Dent, 1979. – 0 460 06870 9
LITTLE CAPTAIN AND THE PIRATE TREASURE
Dent, 1980. – 0 460 06906 3
LITTLE CAPTAIN AND THE SEVEN TOWERS
Dent, 1974. – 0 460 05893 2
LITTLE CAPTAIN
Collins, 1973. – Pbk. – 0 00 670737 8
LOOKING-GLASS CASTLE
Blackie, 1979. – 0 216 90537 0
ROBBER HOPSIKA
Armada Books, 1980. – Pbk. – 0 00 671660 1
SEVEN TIMES SEARCH
Dent, 1971. – 0 460 05794 4
TIN CAN BEAST AND OTHER STORIES
Glover & Blair, 1980. – 0 906681 05 7
TWELVE ROBBERS
Penguin, 1978 – Pbk. – O/P. – 0 14 031006 1

BLISHEN, Edward

British. Born Whetstone, Middlesex, 1920. Educated Queen Elizabeth Grammar School, Barnet. Married Nancy Smith, 1948, two sons. Teacher, writer.

Awards: Library Association Carnegie Medal (with Leon Garfield): *The God beneath the Sea*, 1970

Address: 12, Bartrams Lane, Hadley Wood, Barnet, London EN4 0EH, England

CHILDREN'S CLASSICS TO READ ALOUD
Kingfisher Books, 1993, 256p. – Pbk. –
1 85697 026 4
Kingfisher Books, 1992, 256p. – 1 8569 7825 7

Edward Blishen has chosen twenty extracts specifically for reading aloud. They are designed to show children the pleasure to be had from books. Excellent for the classroom, but the original books should also be made available to satisfy the children whose appetite is whetted by the extract.
Age range: 8–11

A TREASURY OF STORIES FOR FIVE YEAR OLDS
Kingfisher Books, 1992, 160p. – Pbk. –
1 8569 7827 3
Kingfisher Books, 1989, 160p. – 0 86272 427 9

In the same series:

A TREASURY OF STORIES FOR SIX YEAR OLDS
Kingfisher Books, 1992, 160p. – Pbk. –
1 8569 7828 1
Kingfisher Books, 1988, 160p. –
0 86272 330 2

A TREASURY OF STORIES FOR SEVEN YEAR OLDS
Kingfisher Books, 1991, 160p. – Pbk. – 0 8627 2808 8
Kingfisher Books, 1988, 160p. – 0 86272 331 0
all illustrated by Patricia Ludlow

Written in conjunction with his wife, these are really excellent collections of stories, as can be expected from such an experienced couple. They combine traditional and modern stories, and are beautifully illustrated. The clear print on beautiful paper makes them lovely books to be read over and over.
Age range: 5–7

Other publications:
GOD BENEATH THE SEA
Kestrel Books, 1976. – O/P. – 0 7226 5093 0
GOLDEN SHADOW
Kestrel Books, 1978. – O/P. – 0 7226 5162 7
KINGFISHER TREASURY OF STORIES FOR CHILDREN
Kingfisher Books, 1992. – 0 8627 2923 8
PENNY WORLD
Trafalgar Square, 1991. – 1 8561 9003 X
ROBIN HOOD
Hodder, 1987 – Pbk. – 0 340 40278 4
SCIENCE FICTION STORIES
Kingfisher Books, 1993. – 1 8569 7889 3

BLUME, Judy (née SUSSMAN)

American. Born Elizabeth, New Jersey, 1938. Educated New York University, B.S. in Education. Married 1) John M. Blume, 1959 (divorced), one daughter, one son; 2) Thomas A. Kitchens, 1976 (divorced); 3) George Cooper, 1987, one step-daughter.

Agent: C/O Claire Smith,
               Harold Ober Associates,
               40 East 49th Street,
               New York City,
               New York 10017,
               USA

Undoubtedly one of the most popular authors writing today, and thereby meriting a place. Girls feel that she understands their problems without criticizing them. Her books are written in a chatty style which breaks down the barriers normally felt between maturing children and adults. It is a pity that the understanding she displays is not accompanied by a similar level of literary merit. Her characters tend to be bland, and the plots sketchy.

ARE YOU THERE, GOD? IT'S ME, MARGARET
Chivers Press, 1985, 192p. – L/P. – O/P. – 0 7451 0130 5
Pan Books, 1980, 128p. – Pbk. – 0 330 26244 0
Gollancz, 1978, 160p. – 0 575 02433 X

Several common problems are dealt with – moving house and trying to fit in with a new set of people; a mix of religions within the same family; Margaret's overwhelming desire to need a bra.
Age range: 10–12

BLUBBER
Cornerstone Books, 1989, 190p. – O/P. – L/P. – 1 55736 025 1
Macmillan, 1982, 160p. – 0 02 711010 9
Pan Books, 1981, 128p. – Pbk. – 0 330 26329 3

The problems of overweight children and the bullying they often attract is the subject of this novel. Of necessity it contains many unpleasant incidents which are not dealt with very satisfactorily. Coming from the pen of someone who has a receptive audience, suggesting a more positive way of coping with this situation would have been preferable to the wishy-washy 'solutions' actually on offer.
Age range: 10–12

IGGIE'S HOUSE
Chivers Press, 1989, 160p. – L/P. – 0 7451 0887 3
Pan Books, 1982, 112p. – Pbk. – 0 330 26682 9
Heinemann, 1981, 112p. – 0 434 92884 4

This book uses the problems that can arise when a black family moves into

an all-white street as the basis for a rather slight story.
Age range: 9–11

OTHERWISE KNOWN AS SHEILA THE GREAT
Pan Books, 1980, 128p. – Pbk. – 0 330 26051 0
Bodley Head, 1979, 128p. – 0 370 30170 6

Sheila is afraid of many things, including life, and suffers accordingly. Full of trepidation, she goes to Summer Camp where she meets Mouse, who is a yo-yo champion. Life takes a turn for the better.
Age range: 9–11

TALES OF A FOURTH GRADE NOTHING
Pan Books, 1991, 160p. – Pbk. – 0 330 69935 0
Chivers Press, 1988, 160p. – L/P. – 0 7451 0722 2
Bodley Head, 1979, 128p. – 0 370 30171 4

In the same series:

SUPERFUDGE
Pan Books, 1991, 144p. – Pbk. – 0 330 69936 9
Chivers Press, 1987, 216p. – L/P. – 0 7451 0488 6
Bodley Head, 1980, 128p. – 0 370 30358 X

Peter has problems with his little brother, Fudge, and some of them are serious. In the sequel, the arrival of a new baby increases the problems. Run-of-the-mill family stories.
Age range: 9–11

Other publications:

DEENIE
Pan Books, 1983 – Pbk. – 0 330 28003 1
FOREVER . . .
Pan Books, 1984. – Pbk. – 0 330 28533 5
FRECKLE JUICE
Pan Books, 1990. – Pbk. – 0 330 30829 7
FUDGE-A-MANIA
Pan Macmillan, 1992. – Pbk. – 0 330 32051 3
HERE'S TO YOU, RACHEL ROBINSON
Orchard Books, 1993. – 0 531 06801 3
IT'S NOT THE END OF THE WORLD
Macmillan, 1982. – 0 02 711050 8
JUST AS LONG AS WE'RE TOGETHER
Pan Books, 1988. – Pbk. – 0 330 30474 7
ONE IN THE MIDDLE IS THE GREEN KANGAROO
Picture Piper, 1993. – Pbk. – 0 330 32749 6
PAIN AND THE GREAT ONE
Pan Books, 1988. – Pbk. – 0 330 29631 0
STARRING SALLY J. FREEDMAN AS HERSELF
Pan Books, 1984. – Pbk. – 0 330 28279 4
THEN AGAIN, MAYBE I WON'T
Heinemann, 1979. – 0 434 92880 1
TIGER EYES
Pan Books, 1983. – Pbk. – 0 330 26954 2

BOND, (Thomas) Michael

British. Born Newbury, Berkshire, 1926. Educated Presentation College, Reading. Royal Air Force, 1943–44, Middlesex Regiment, British Army, 1944–47. Married 1) Brenda May Johnson, 1950 (divorced 1981), one daughter, one son; 2) Susan Marfrey Rogers, 1981. Cameraman, director of Paddington & Co. (Films) Ltd, writer.

Address: 22, Maida Avenue, London W2 1SR, England
Agent: Harvey Unna & Stephen Durbridge Ltd, 24–32 Pottery Lane, London W11 4LZ, England

This author's name has become almost synonymous with his creation Paddington Bear, who is a firm favourite with children all over the world. There are many versions available, from pop-up books for infants to full-length novels. However, there are other equally enjoyable novels by him. The following list gives some of the best available for the age range covered by this book.

THE PADDINGTON LIBRARY
Collins, selected titles by Hutchinson and Crocodile Books.
Selected titles by Windrush Large Print Children's Books.

BOND

A new version of the original stories, with an attractive cover and clear print. It retains the original Peggy Fortnum illustrations, which are an integral part of the Paddington tradition.
Age range: 8–10

FONTANA YOUNG LIONS
Collins, selected titles by Armada Books and Pan Books, Pbk.

A paperback version of the same collections of stories, also attractively produced.
Age range: 8–10

OLGA DA POLGA
Longmans
Penguin, Pbk.

A series of stories about a larger-than-life hamster, whose adventures are recounted with the same dry humour as the Paddington stories. They are enjoyable and amusing, and provide an excellent read, but have not achieved quite the same popularity as Paddington.
Age range: 8–10

PARSLEY THE LION
BBC
Collins or Penguin, Pbk.

Parsley first became popular when he appeared on television, after which demand for the books increased.
Age range: 5–7

Other publications:

CARAVAN PUPPETS
Armada Books, 1985. – Pbk. – 0 00 672462 0
DAY BY THE SEA
Young Lions, 1992. – Pbk. – 0 00 674310 2
DAY THE ANIMALS WENT ON STRIKE
Studio Vista, 1972. – 0 289 70187 2
HERE COMES THURSDAY
Penguin, 1970. – Pbk. – O/P – 0 14 030383 9
JAR OF JOKES
Carnival, 1992. – Pbk. – 0 00 674309 9
JD POLSON AND THE DILLOGATE AFFAIR
Hodder, 1981. – 0 340 27068 3
JD POLSON AND THE LIBERTY HEAD DIME
Octopus Books, 1980. – 0 7064 1381 4
MOUSE CALLED THURSDAY
Chancellor Press, 1989. – 1 8515 2085 6
MR CRAM'S MAGIC BUBBLES
Penguin, 1975. – Pbk. – O/P – 0 14 050072 3
OLIVER THE GREEDY ELEPHANT
Methuen, 1985. – 0 416 53020 6
PICNIC ON THE RIVER
Young Lions, 1993. – Pbk. – 0 00 674 673 X
SOMETHING NASTY IN THE KITCHEN
Young Lions, 1992. – Pbk. – 0 00 674 311 0
THURSDAY AHOY!
Penguin, 1973. – Pbk. – O/P – 0 14 030590 4
THURSDAY IN PARIS
Penguin, 1974. – Pbk. – O/P – 0 14 030730 3
THURSDAY RIDES AGAIN
Penguin, 1970. – Pbk. – O/P – 0 14 030454 1
WINDMILL
Studio Vista, 1975. – 0 289 70452 9

BOSTON, Lucy (Marie, née Wood)

British. Born Southport, Lancashire, 1892. Educated Downs School, Seaford, Sussex; Somerville College, Oxford. Nurse in France in WW I. Married 1917 (dissolved 1935), one son.

Awards: Library Association Carnegie Medal: *A Stranger at Green Knowe*, 1961

Address: The Manor, Hemingford Grey, Huntingdon PE18 9BN, England

THE CHILDREN OF GREEN KNOWE
Chivers Press, 1987, 232p. – L/P. – 0 7451 0626 9
Penguin, 1975, 160p. – Pbk. – 0 14 030789 3
Faber, 1954, 157p. – 0 571 06460 4

In the same series:

THE CHIMNEYS OF GREEN KNOWE
Chivers Press, 1990, 272p. – L/P. – 0 7451 1175 0
Penguin, 1976, 176p. – Pbk. – 0 14 030840 7
Faber, 1958, 186p. – O/P. – 0 571 07030 2

THE RIVER AT GREEN KNOWE
*Chivers Press, 1992, 200p. – O/P. – L/P. –
0 7451 1467 9
Penguin, 1976, 128p. – Pbk. – 0 14 030861 X
Faber, 1959, 144p. – O/P. – 0 571 06660 7*

A STRANGER AT GREEN KNOWE
*Penguin, 1977, 176p. – Pbk. – 0 14 030871 7
Faber, 1961, 160p. – O/P. – 0 571 05903 1*

AN ENEMY AT GREEN KNOWE
*Penguin, 1977, 144p. – Pbk. – 0 14 030910 1
Faber, 1964, 150p. – O/P. – 0 571 05971 6*

GUARDIANS OF THE HOUSE
*Bodley Head, 1974, 56p. – O/P. –
0 370 10934 1*

THE STONES OF GREEN KNOWE
*Penguin, 1979, 128p. – Pbk. – 0 14 031061 4
Bodley Head, 1976, 128p. – O/P. –
0 370 11017 X
all illustrated by Peter Boston*

Green Knowe is a very old house with happy memories of children who have loved it over the years. The magical atmosphere and the characters form a common thread, but each story is different and enjoyable. In particular, *A Stranger at Green Knowe* will be enjoyed by those who feel compassion for wild creatures caged in zoos. *Guardians of the House* is unusual in that it is set in the future, when the house is empty. The stories have lost nothing over the years, and the first title made an excellent television serial.
Age range: 9–12

BRIGGS, Raymond (Redvers)

British. Born Wimbledon, London, 1934. Educated Rutlish School, Merton, Surrey; Wimbledon School of Art; Slade School of Fine Art, National Diploma in Design; University of London, Diploma in Fine Art. British Army, 1953–55. Married Jean Taprel Clark, 1963 (died 1973). Freelance illustrator and writer, part-time lecturer in illustration.

Awards: Library Association Kate Greenaway Medal: *Mother Goose Treasury*, 1966
Library Association Kate Greenaway Medal: *Father Christmas*, 1973
Boston Globe-Horn Book Award: *The Snowman*, 1979 (for the illustrations)
Children's Rights Workshop Other Award: *When the Wind Blows*, 1982
Emil/Kurt Maschler Award: *The Man*, 1992

Address: Weston,
Underhill Lane,
Westmeston,
Hassocks,
Sussex BN6 8XG,
England

Because so many of his books are lavishly illustrated, Raymond Briggs is generally supposed to create books for the very young. In reality, his picture books have much to offer the older child, as the illustrations are very detailed.

FAIRY TALE TREASURY
*Penguin, 1974, 192p. – Pbk. O/P. –
0 14 050103 7
selected by Virginia Haviland*

An excellent compilation of traditional fairy stories brought wonderfully to life by Raymond Briggs's illustrations, both black and white and colour. A worthwhile addition to any child's bookshelf.
Age range: 5–8

FATHER CHRISTMAS
*Hamish Hamilton, 1990, 32p. – 0 241 13011 5
Penguin, 1975, 32p. – Pbk. – 0 14 050125 8*

A story in comic-strip form, without words, about Father Christmas's life with his cat and dog. It is quite long and detailed, requiring a good deal of concentration and several readings to appreciate all it has to offer. It can, of course, be used with younger children, but the humour is best suited to older readers.
Age range: 6–10

FATHER CHRISTMAS GOES ON HOLIDAY
Penguin, 1977, 32p. – Pbk. – 0 14 050187 8
Hamish Hamilton, 1975, 32p. – O/P. – 0 241 89220 1

In comic-strip form again, but more words are used, albeit in the form of conversational 'balloons', and much of it in French. Even an older child may need adult assistance to fully appreciate the humour, although the idea of Father Christmas taking time off has instant appeal.
Age range: 6–10

FUNGUS THE BOGEYMAN
Penguin, 1990, 48p. – Pbk. – 0 14 054235 3
Hamish Hamilton, 1977, 42p. – 0 241 89553 7

A controversial picture book for older children and younger adults, with a certain sense of humour. Fungus awakes as night closes in, and thus begins the story of his 'day', a collection of horrible facts told in Briggs's unique style. Not easy to read.
Age range: 11–adult

GENTLEMAN JIM
Hamish Hamilton, 1981, 30p. – Pbk. – 0 241 10698 2
Hamish Hamilton, 1980, 32p. – 0 241 10281 2

Jim, a cleaner in the public toilets, wants to improve himself, and imagines trying a variety of other jobs. In spite of the usual comic-strip format, some complex issues are dealt with in an unusually (for Raymond Briggs) verbose style. Definitely not a picture book for the young.
Age range: 10–adult

SNOWMAN
Penguin, 1992, 24p. – Pbk. – 0 14 054321 X
Hamish Hamilton, 1991, 16p. – 0 241 13112 X

A book with enormous appeal to children of all ages. It tells of the adventures of a snowman and a little boy, with a realistic, sad ending. It has been produced in a variety of ways in book form, made into a film, and released on video. The illustrations in the original picture-book are pale compared to the vivid colours of the Father Christmas books, making the wordless story a little more difficult to follow.
Age range: 5–10

WHEN THE WIND BLOWS
Penguin, 1983, 40p. – Pbk, O/P. – 0 14 006603 3
Hamish Hamilton, 1982, 40p. – 0 241 10721 0

The terrible story of Jim and his wife trying to understand what is happening and what they should do in the face of nuclear war. They follow the official instructions as best they can, but to no avail. The comic-strip format and occasional spots of humour somehow emphasize the poignancy of this story of faith betrayed.
Age range: 10–adult

Other publications:

FEE FI FO FUM
Penguin, 1969. – Pbk. – 0 14 050012 X
JIM AND THE BEANSTALK
H. Hamilton, 1985. – 0 241 01786 6
THE MAN
J. MacRae, 1992. – 1 8568 1191 3
MIDNIGHT ADVENTURE
Beaver Books, 1985. – Pbk. – 0 09 941870 3
MOTHER GOOSE TREASURY
Penguin, 1973. – Pbk. – 0 14 050088 X
STRANGE HOUSE
Beaver Books, 1985. – Pbk. – 0 09 941860 6

BRINSMEAD, Hesba (Fay, née Hungerford)

Australian. Born Blue Mountains, New South Wales, 1922. Educated Correspondence School; High School, Wahroonga; Avondale College. Married Reginald Brinsmead, 1943, two sons. Teacher, writer.

Awards: Australian Children's Book Council Book of the Year Award: *Pastures of the Blue Crane*, 1965

Australian Children's Book Council Book of the Year Award: *Longtime passing*, 1972

Address: Weathertop,
Shamara Road,
Terranora,
New South Wales 2485,
Australia

One of Australia's most distinguished story tellers for young readers, she brings humour, understanding and the ability to convey, realistically, differing cultures to her audience. Mainly a writer for teenage girls, but the following are intended for younger children:

THE HONEY FOREST
*Hodder, 1980, 60p. – O/P. – 0 340 23048 7
illustrated by Louise Hogan*

A simple story, lovingly told, about Mickey and his father, who spend summer together in the rain forest in the Blue Mountains, and about the lessons Mickey learns there.
Age range: 7–9

ONCE THERE WAS A SWAGMAN
*OUP, 1979, 62p. – O/P. – 0 19 550549 2
illustrated by Noela Young*

This book was written to teach young Australians what a swagman was. Set in the days of the Depression, Teddy has cause to be grateful to Mr Mungo Brodie when she becomes lost in the wild-lands. The sepia illustrations perfectly complement an excellent, deliberately low-key tale.
Age range: 9–12

SOMEPLACE BEAUTIFUL
*Hodder, 1986, 152p. – O/P. – 0 340 35776 2
illustrated by Betina Ogden*

Miss Dove's Flying Trunk Bookshop is to be demolished, as the Council wants to put a betting shop in its place. For the children of Chapple Road, however, the bookshop is 'someplace beautiful' to go, and so they take action. Humorous and simply told; a joy to read.
Age range: 7–9

BROWN, Jeff

No biographical has been received, from either the author or publisher.

FLAT STANLEY
*Mammoth, 1989, 67p. – Pbk. – 0 7497 0137 4
Methuen, 1974, 75p. – 0 416 80360 1
illustrated by Tomi Ungerer*

Although first published in 1968, this extremely funny story is still widely enjoyed. Stanley is flattened when a notice board falls on top of him and life is suddenly completely different.
Age range: 7–9

LAMP FOR THE LAMBCHOPS
*Mammoth, 1989, 96p. – Pbk. O/P. – 0 7497 0138 2
Magnet Books, 1986, 96p. – Pbk. O/P. – 0 416 61870 7
illustrated by Quentin Blake*

Reprinted as:

STANLEY AND THE MAGIC LAMP
*Methuen, 1990, 96p. – 0 416 16852 3
Mammoth, 1990, 96p. – Pbk. – 0 7497 0748 8
illustrated by Quentin Blake*

FLAT STANLEY'S FANTASTIC ADVENTURES
Dean, 1992, 224p. – 0 603 55047 9

STANLEY IN SPACE
*Mammoth, 1991, 80p. – Pbk. – 0 7497 0633 3
Methuen, 1990, 64p. – 0 416 15862 5*

STANLEY'S CHRISTMAS ADVENTURE
*Methuen, 1993, 64p. – 0 416 18896 6
illustrated by Philippe Dupasquier*

As sequels to *Flat Stanley*, they are also enjoyable and amusing, but they do not have the same freshness or rollicking sense of humour as the earlier book.
Age range: 7–9

BURGESS, Melvin

British. Born London, 1954. Partner Avis von Herder, 1 son, 1 daughter. Journalist, craftsman, writer.

Address: 4 Hartley Street,
          Earby,
          Colne,
          Lancashire BB8 6NL,
          England

An author with a growing reputation for his ability to produce powerfully written, impressive stories. Each book contains a strong message for children of today, but the message is wrapped in such a strong storyline that there is no hint of preaching.

AN ANGEL FOR MAY
Chivers Press, 1994, 224p. – 0 7451 2086 5
Andersen Press, 1992, 160p. – 0 8626 4398 8

An adroitly handled time-slip in which an old beggar-woman is the means of transporting Tam back to the time of World War II, where he is befriended and trusted by May, whose experiences have rendered her unable to speak. This teaches him (and the reader) the true horrors of war and the value of individuals, irrespective of outward trappings. It is an imaginative and compelling read.
Age range: 10–12

THE BABY AND FLY PIE
Andersen Press, 1993, 189p. – 0 8626 4461 5

The author's rather depressing view on society today is portrayed by his pessimistic but gripping description of life in the not too distant future for children whose parents cannot or will not take responsibility for them. Hopeful in that it shows how resilient children are, and how well they can cope if they have to. Ultimately, however, the struggles of the three main characters to improve their own circumstances while still trying to do the right thing are very sadly doomed to failure.

A difficult book to read, but useful in awakening social awareness in young readers.
Age range: 12+

BURNING ISSY
Hodder, 1993, 160p. – Pbk. – 0 340 59024 6
Andersen Press, 1992, 128p. – 0 86264 381 3

In the seventeenth century witches were feared and hated. Twelve-year-old Issy is regarded as a witch and suffers accordingly. They were cruel times and Melvin Burgess spares his readers nothing. A book which lingers in the memory.
Age range: 12+

Other publications:

CRY OF THE WOLF
Penguin, 1991. – Pbk. – 0 14 034459 4

BYARS, Betsy (née Cromer)

American. Born Charlotte, North Carolina, 1928. Educated Furman University, Greenville, South Carolina; Queen's College, Charlotte, B.A. English. Married Edward Ford Byars, 1950, three daughters, one son.

Awards: American Library
          Association, Newbery Medal:
          The Summer of the swans,
          1971

          Catholic Library Association,
          Regina Medal, 1987

Address: 4, Riverpoint,
          Clemson,
          South Carolina 29631,
          USA

Betsy Byars is one of the most popular authors currently writing for young people. She is an able, and, at times, powerful storyteller, touching on themes that young people hold dear, as does Judy Blume, but with none of her triviality.

AFTER THE GOAT-MAN
Penguin, 1978, 112p. – Pbk. – 0 14 030992 6
Bodley Head, 1975, 112p. – O/P. –
0 370 10951 1

Figgy is a modern child with a liking for all mod cons, but when he realizes that the newsworthy 'goat-man' is none other than his grandfather, who prefers the simple life in his log-cabin, he has to take some action.
Age range: 10–12

THE ANIMAL, THE VEGETABLE AND JOHN D. JONES
Chivers Press, 1992, 160p. – O/P. – L/P. –
0 7451 1609 4
Penguin, 1984, 144p. – Pbk. – 0 14 031563 2
Bodley Head, 1982, 128p. – 0 370 30914 6

An excellent portrayal of family relationships and the problems encountered by the attempts at uniting two families. The many humorous passages make this a lively, thoroughly enjoyable read.
Age range: 10–12

BEANS ON THE ROOF
Pan Books, 1991, 64p. – Pbk. – 0 330 31029 1
Bodley Head, 1988, 80p. – 0 370 31257 0
illustrated by Melodye Rosales

The Bean family all end up on the roof trying to help Anna write a poem for school. Although short because written for younger children, it still carries the hallmark of Betsy Byars and is therefore a book of quality which can be read again and again.
Age range: 6–8

THE BURNING QUESTIONS OF BINGO BROWN
Penguin, 1990, 160p. – Pbk. – 0 14 034319 9
Chivers Press, 1989, 232p. – L/P. –
0 7451 0961 6
Bodley Head, 1988, 144p. – 0 370 31186 8

Bingo's questions are all concerned with the problems life brings to everyone at one time or another. During the course of the book, he finds some of the answers. Organizing the school rebellion against the ban on T-shirts with words helps him to realize some fundamental facts, but it is the horrific events concerning his teacher which finally teach him to see someone else's point of view.
Age range: 11–14

In the same series:

BINGO BROWN AND THE LANGUAGE OF LOVE
Bodley Head, 1990, 136p. – 0 370 31470 0
Penguin, 1991, 144p. – Pbk. – 0 14 034702 X
Chivers Press, 1990, 176p. – 0 7451 1245 5

BINGO BROWN, GYPSY LOVER
Chivers Press, 1992, 152p. – L/P. –
0 7451 1499 7
Penguin, 1992, 112p. – Pbk. – 0 14 034765 8
Bodley Head, 1991, 108p. – 0 370 31553 7

BINGO BROWN'S GUIDE TO ROMANCE
Chivers Press, 1994, 128p. – L/P. –
0 7451 2037 7
Bodley Head, 1992, 87p. – 0 370 31800 5

The character of Bingo Brown, so wittily drawn by Betsy Byars, has found empathy with young readers, who will enjoy reading these further books.
Age range: 11–14

THE CARTOONIST
Chivers Press, 1991, 152p. – L/P. –
0 7451 1317 6
Penguin, 1981, 112p. – Pbk. – 0 14 031182 3
Bodley Head, 1978, 112p. – O/P. –
0 370 30104 8

Alfie, unhappy at home and at school, takes refuge in the attic, where he spends his time drawing cartoons. He is unable to face losing this refuge when his brother, having some trouble himself, needs to come and stay for a while. In spite of the serious plot, this is an extremely readable story, full of appeal for young readers.
Age range: 11–14

THE COMPUTER NUT
Chivers Press, 1992, 184p. – L/P. –
0 7451 1680 9
Penguin, 1986, 144p. – Pbk. – 0 14 031876 3
Bodley Head, 1984, 128p. – 0 370 30835 2

Kate can't decide whether the message on the computer screen is really from outer space, or just an elaborate joke. Gradually she comes to believe in BB9, and his mission to find the missing element of laughter which has led him to Kate.
Age range: 10–12

CRACKER JACKSON
Chivers Press, 1987, 176p. – L/P. –
0 7451 0493 2
Penguin, 1986, 178p. – Pbk. – 0 14 031881 X
Bodley Head, 1985, 140p. – 0 370 30859 X

A grim story, told with immense perception, yet with a glorious sense of humour. Jackson and his friend Goat are convinced that Alma is in serious trouble at the hands of her violent husband. The 'trouble' is graphically described, just as the attempts to help, which do not always work out, are humorously portrayed. An excellent read.
Age range: 11–14

THE CYBIL WAR
Chivers Press, 1991, 136p. – O/P. – L/P. –
0 7451 1403 2
Collins, 1987, 112p. – Pbk. – 0 00 330043 9
Penguin, 1983, 112p. – Pbk. – 0 14 031458 X
Bodley Head, 1981, 112p. – 0 370 30426 8

A realistic look at growing up and first dates. Simon really likes Cybil, but so does his friend Tony. Their struggles have a humorous side, but nevertheless there is a poignancy about the situation which would be lost on younger, inexperienced readers.
Age range: 12–14

THE EIGHTEENTH EMERGENCY
Chivers Press, 1988, 136p. – L/P. – O/P. –
0 7451 0691 9
Penguin, 1976, 104p. – Pbk. – 0 14 030863 6
Bodley Head, 1974, 128p. – 0 370 10924 4

Fear of being singled out for a 'beating-up' by fellow pupils is something most children experience at school. Mouse and Ezzie have active imaginations, and work out a detailed plan of action in case of an attack by crocodiles.

However, the threat posed by the Hammerman, the biggest bully in the school, is less easy to cope with.
Age range: 10–12

THE GLORY GIRL
Penguin, 1985, 112p. – Pbk. – 0 14 031726 0
Bodley Head, 1983, 128p. – O/P. –
0 370 30997 9

Being left out is one of the worst feelings children have to cope with. They often turn to fellow outcasts for consolation or support. Anna is no exception – unable to join in with her gospel-singing family, she can readily feel sympathy for the rejected ex-con uncle. An exciting story in a rather unlikely setting, and the ending is highly satisfactory.
Age range: 11–14

GOODBYE, CHICKEN LITTLE
Penguin, 1982, 96p. – Pbk. – 0 14 031329 X
Bodley Head, 1979, 96p. – O/P. –
0 370 30212 5

Jimmie's nickname 'Chicken' stems from his fear and embarrassment at the reckless exploits of his family. When his Uncle Pete oversteps the mark, with tragic consequences, Jimmie is overwhelmed by guilt at his own inaction.
Age range: 11–14

THE HOUSE OF WINGS
Penguin, 1977, 112p. – Pbk, O/P. –
0 14 030887 3
Bodley Head, 1973, 136p. – O/P. –
0 370 01247 X

Sammy was fed up with sharing his grandfather's house with all his rare birds, and the resulting mess. He decides to run away, but finds an injured crane which he cannot ignore.
Age range: 9–12

THE MIDNIGHT FOX
Chivers Press, 1989, 184p. – L/P. –
0 7451 0828 8
Penguin, 1976, 128p. – Pbk. – 0 14 030844 X
Faber, 1970, 136p. – O/P. – 0 571 09320 5

A black fox is a rare creature, but it will still cause havoc among livestock. Tom, nevertheless, is determined to prevent his uncle hunting her when she has a cub to care for. A realistic and powerful story, in which Tom learns to rely on himself as his feelings of responsibility for another life develop. It is not a particularly easy book to read, requiring fluency from the child, but it can successfully be read aloud, as there is sufficient plot, tension and humour to keep the interest of a class of children.
Age range: 9–12

THE NIGHT SWIMMERS
Windrush, 1991, 175p. – L/P. – 1 85089 850 2
Penguin, 1982, 144p. – Pbk. – 0 14 031409 1
Bodley Head, 1980, 112p. – O/P. –
0 370 30317 2

At the age of twelve, Retta is faced with bringing up her two brothers. Her mother is dead, and her father gets on with his own life as if the children did not exist. It takes a real emergency and a terrible fright to make him realize his responsibility to his family. Not lacking in humour, this is, nevertheless, a realistic portrayal of a young girl struggling with a situation that is beyond her ability to deal with, yet coping magnificently.
Age range: 10–14

THE NOT-JUST-ANYBODY FAMILY
Chivers Press, 1988, 200p. – L/P. –
0 7451 0756 7
Collins, 1988, 128p. – Pbk. – 0 00 330038 2
Pan Books, 1988, 144p. – Pbk. – 0 330 29974 3
Bodley Head, 1986, 148p. – O/P. –
0 370 30724 0

In the same series:

THE BLOSSOMS MEET THE VULTURE LADY
Chivers Press, 1988, 168p. – L/P. –
0 7451 0824 5
Pan Books, 1988, 128p. – Pbk. –
0 330 29975 1
Bodley Head, 1986, 126p. – 0 370 30760 7

THE BLOSSOMS AND THE GREEN PHANTOM
Chivers Press, 1989, 184p. – L/P. –
0 7451 0924 1
Pan Books, 1988, 136p. – Pbk. –
0 330 30085 7
Bodley Head, 1987, 140p. – 0 370 31041 1

THE BLOSSOM PROMISE
Chivers Press, 1990, 200p. – L/P. –
0 7451 1065 7
Pan Books, 1989, 144p. – Pbk. –
0 330 30730 4
Bodley Head, 1987, 144p. – 0 370 30783 6

WANTED: MUD BLOSSOM
Piper, 1993, 144p. – Pbk. – 0 330 32776 3
Bodley Head, 1991, 140p. – 0 370 31714 9

A series of stories about the Blossom family, written with humour and a sympathetic view of children. They consist of short episodic chapters (a bit like a television 'soap') which appeal to readers who have not developed the ability to concentrate for long. They describe exciting events such as bull-riding at the Rodeo, and making a raft to sail on the flooded creek. Peopled by determined characters, the reader feels compelled to sympathize with them, even when they are engaged in silly activities.
Age range: 9–12

THE PINBALLS
Cornerstone Books, 1988, 186p. – L/P. –
0 55736 028 6
Penguin, 1980, 96p. – Pbk. – 0 14 031121 1
Bodley Head, 1977, 120p. – O/P. –
0 370 30040 8

'The Pinballs' is Carlie's name for herself and the other children in her latest foster home, because she feels they are being tossed about at random by life. It takes a long time and a lot of loving patience from Mrs Mason to show Carlie how to trust and care for people. This sensitive portrayal of what is a common situation today is characterized by a strong sense of humour, provides an excellent read, entertaining and instructive, and has been televised.
Age range: 10–14

BYARS

THE SEVEN TREASURE HUNTS
Red Fox, 1993, 80p. – Pbk. – 0 09 913491 8
Bodley Head, 1992, 56p. – 0 370 31777 7
illustrated by Jennifer Barrett

A light-hearted and amusing story of sibling rivalry, resolved by the last treasure hunt of all.
Age range: 7–9

THE SUMMER OF THE SWANS
Windrush, 1989, 142p. – L/P. – 1 85089 963 0
Penguin, 1984, 144p. – Pbk. – 0 14 031420 2
Kestrel Books, 1984, 144p. – O/P. – 0 7226 5935 0
illustrated by Ted Coconis

Sara finds being a teenager very difficult. She feels out of step with herself and her family, indeed, sometimes, with the whole world. Then her brother goes missing, and suddenly she has to put everything into perspective, and decide just who and what is really important. A compelling read and justifiable prize winner.
Age range: 11–14

THE TV KID
Chivers Press, 1990, 144p. – L/P. – 0 7451 1179 3
Penguin, 1979, 112p. – Pbk. – 0 14 031065 7
Bodley Head, 1976, 128p. – O/P. – 0 370 11018 8

Lennie is a TV addict. The television allows him to escape from his difficult home life and the poor marks he gets at school. Real life, however, forces itself upon Lennie in a horrifying manner, leaving him to ponder about it from a hospital bed. As always, a contemporary problem dealt with sensitively and with humour.
Age range: 10–12

THE TWO-THOUSAND POUND GOLDFISH
Cornerstone Books, 1989, 160p. – L/P. – 1 55736 131 2
Collins, 1987, 128p. – 0 00 330042 0
Penguin, 1984, 112p. – Pbk. – 0 14 031607 8

A funny yet sensitive novel about Warren who lives with his grandmother, but in the constant hope of his mother's return. He consoles himself, meanwhile, by inventing plots for films, one of which has a giant goldfish as the main character. Fun to read, but a story with a sadness that will find an echo in the heart of the many children who feel, or have felt, abandoned.
Age range: 10–12

Other publications:

COAST TO COAST
Bodley Head, 1993. – 0 370 31820 X
GO AND HUSH THE BABY
Bodley Head, 1980. – 0 370 30306 7
GOLLY SISTERS GO WEST
Gollancz, 1993. – Pbk. – 0 575 05593 6
MOON AND ME
Bodley Head, 1993. – 0 370 31827 7
WINGED COLT OF CASA MIA
Penguin, 1979. – Pbk. – 0 14 031067 3

C

CAMERON, Ann

American. Born Rice Lake, Wisconsin, 1943. Educated Radcliffe College, B.A. (Hons); University of Iowa Writers' Workshop. Lives in New York and Guatemala.

JULIAN, SECRET AGENT
Yearling, 1991, 96p. – Pbk. – 0 440 86274 4
Gollancz, 1989, 64p. – 0 575 04602 3
illustrated by Lis Toft

In the same series:

THE JULIAN STORIES
Armada Books, 1984, 80p. – Pbk. –
0 00 672227 X
Gollancz, 1982, 72p. – 0 575 03143 3

JULIAN'S GLORIOUS SUMMER
Collins, 1990, 64p. – Pbk. – 0 00 673539 8
Gollancz, 1988, 64p. – 0 575 04117 X

MORE STORIES JULIAN TELLS
Armada Books, 1987, 80p. – Pbk. –
0 00 672738 7
Gollancz, 1986, 72p. – 0 575 03676 1

JULIAN, DREAM DOCTOR
Gollancz, 1992, 64p. – 0 575 05303 8
all illustrated by Ann Strugnell

Four books of amusing short stories which are a true delight, either for a child to read, or for reading aloud. Julian is the storyteller (in both senses) and young children may have difficulty in making the connection between the first-person and Julian. Linguistically rich, fresh, and full of a warm family atmosphere.
Age range: 7–10

THE MOST BEAUTIFUL PLACE IN THE WORLD
Corgi, 1992, 64p. – Pbk. – 0 552 52601 0
Doubleday, 1989, 64p. – 0 385 26971 4
illustrated by Thomas B. Allen

A simple story told in Ann Cameron's distinctive style, which appeals directly to young readers. Juan is seven and wants to go to school, but he is earning good money as a shoe-shine boy. It is a difficult choice.
Age range: 7–9

CATE, Dick

British. Born Ferryhill, Co. Durham. Educated Spennymore Grammar School, County Durham; Goldsmith's College, London; Bretton Hall, West Yorkshire. Married, four children, three grandchildren. Teacher (retired), full-time writer.

Awards: Children's Rights Other Award: *Old dog, new tricks*, 1978

Address: 2 Bank Lane,
Denby Dale,
Huddersfield,
England

An experienced teacher, married to a teacher, Dick Cate has the ability to speak to children in his books in a way that they can understand. He has written many titles, some for particular series listed elsewhere in this book.

DOOMSDAY DIARY OF ERMENGARDE HULKE
Walker Books, 1993, 112p. – Pbk. –
0 7445 3086 5

Lots of children make a wish in the heat of the moment that their parents would disappear. Ermengarde feels her only hope of peace is if her family were no longer there – and, lo and behold, they disappear, one by one.

A good story, very amusing, with an appealing jacket. The chapters are short

and the pace never lets up, making this a good choice for reluctant readers.
Age range: 9–11

GHOST DOG
Yearling, 1989, 128p. – Pbk. – 0 440 86211 6
Gollancz, 1987, 128p. – 0 575 03926 4

In the same series:

TWISTERS
Yearling, 1989, 176p. – Pbk. – 0 440 86213 2
Gollancz, 1987, 160p. – 0 575 04099 8

FOXCOVER
Yearling, 1989, 179p. – Pbk. – 0 440 86214 0
Gollancz, 1988, 160p. – 0 575 04292 3

FLAMES
Gollancz, 1989, 160p. – 0 575 04501 9

FIBS
Gollancz, 1990, 160p. – 0 575 04901 4
all illustrated by Caroline Binch

Set in a mining village outside Durham, these stories are brought to life by the strongly drawn characters. They are centred around everyday events in the boys' lives, the football team, playing for the school, belonging to the gang. Told with authenticity and humour, they have immense appeal for boys, although Emma is able to fly the flag for the equality of girls.
Age range: 10–12

INCREDIBLE WILLIE SCRIMSHAW
Lions, 1993, 128p. – Pbk. – 0 00 674378 1
Black, 1991, 120p. – 0 7136 3316 6
illustrated by Caroline Holden

In the same series:

WILLIE SCRIMSHAW AND THE HOUNDS OF GOBBOLOT
Lions, 1993, 128p. – Pbk. – 0 00 674651 9
illustrated by John Eastwood

Willie feels unequal to the task of coping with the bullies. A bit of help from the messenger from outer space turns him into a courageous hero, admired by everyone. A very satisfying story. The second volume, in similar vein, sees our unlikely hero tackle the terrible hounds who are organizing everything so well that there is nothing left to grumble about.
Age range: 9–11

RODNEY PENFOLD, GENIUS!
Walker Books, 1993. – Pbk. – 0 7445 3025 3

When a dog is stolen, Rodney feels sure he can solve the mystery, and sets about it with more enthusiasm than knowledge. The other children watch with glee as he conspicuously and hilariously fails.
Age range: 9–11

Other publications:

ALEXANDER AND STAR PART
Pan Books, 1991. – Pbk. – 0 330 31462 9
ALEXANDER AND THE TOOTH OF ZAZA
Piper, 1992. – Pbk. – 0 330 32746 1
BEN'S BIG DAY
Simon & Schuster, 1990. – 0 7500 0261 1
FUNNY SORT OF CHRISTMAS
Penguin, 1979. – Pbk. – O/P. – 0 14 031048 7
OLD DOG, NEW TRICKS
Penguin, 1980. – Pbk. – 0 14 031270 6
SCARED
MacDonald, 1989. – O/P. – 0 356 16781 X

CHAMBERS, Aidan

Also writes as Malcolm Blacklin. British. Born Chester-le-Street, Co. Durham, 1934. Educated Queen Elizabeth I Grammar School, Darlington; Borough Road College, London. Royal Navy, 1953–55. Married Nancy Harris Lockwood, 1968. Teacher, radio presenter, editor, proprietor and publisher, Thimble Press and Signal: approaches to children's books.

Awards: Eleanor Farjeon Award, 1982

Address: Lockwood,
Station Road,
South Woodchester,
Stroud,
Gloucestershire GL5 5EQ,
England

Agent: Pat White,
Deborah Rogers Ltd,
20 Powis Mews,
London W11 1JN,
England

Aidan Chambers is a well known name in the field of children's literature. There are several excellent collections of stories edited by him, as well as the following two books written by him.

THE PRESENT TAKERS
Mammoth, 1991, 126p. – Pbk. – 0 7497 0700 3
Bodley Head, 1983, 128p. – 0 370 30967 7

Bullying in schools is currently an issue much discussed by the media, but for many years adults have refused to acknowledge the seriousness of the problem. This book was one of the first attempts to fictionalize the problem. There is a horrible realism in the description of Melanie and the tortures she inflicts. The solution offered here gives the reader an important lesson in the power of peer cooperation. The book, unfortunately, appears to condone the childhood ethic 'don't tell or it will get worse' by allowing the children to succeed in putting a stop to the bullying where the adults had failed miserably to have any effect.
Age range: 10–12

SEAL SECRET
Red Fox, 1993, 115p. – Pbk. – 0 09 999150 0
Bodley Head, 1980, 128p. – 0 370 30296 6

An unwilling holiday friendship is forced upon William and Gwyn, but the outcome changes William forever. Gwyn has a baby seal, but his plans for it sicken William, who is determined to rescue it. The seal, however, is not at all cooperative. A powerful book.
Age range: 11–13

Other publications:

ANIMAL FAIR
Heinemann, 1979. – O/P. – 0 434 92520 9
BREAKTIME
Bodley Head, 1978. – O/P. – 0 370 30122 6
DANCE ON MY GRAVE
Pan Books, 1986. – Pbk. – O/P. – 0 330 29581 0
FOX TRICKS
Heinemann, 1981. – O/P. – 0 434 93163 2
LOVING YOU LOVING ME
Macmillan, 1980. – O/P. – 0 333 27780 5
NOW I KNOW
Bodley Head, 1987. – Pbk. – 0 370 307739
ON THE EDGE
Pan Books, 1991. – Pbk. – 0 330 31983 3
TOLL BRIDGE
Bodley Head, 1992. – Pbk. – 0 370 31526 X

CHRISTOPHER, John

Pseudonym for Christopher Samuel Youd; has also written as Hilary Ford, William Godfrey, Peter Graaf, Peter Nichols and Anthony Rye.

British. Born Knowsley, Lancashire, 1922. Educated Peter Symonds School, Winchester. Royal Corps of Signals, WW II. Twice married, four daughters and a son from the first marriage.

Awards: Guardian Children's Fiction Award: *The Guardians*, 1971

Address: La Rochelle,
Rye,
East Sussex,
England

Over the years, John Christopher has produced some excellent science fiction for older children. He is able to create imaginative yet believable worlds, peopled by memorable characters. Reading stamina is required to enjoy his novels.

DUSK OF DEMONS
H. Hamilton, 1993. – 0 241 13378 5

An intriguing title which fulfils its promise. Set in a time and place so unlike today's society – machines are evil – it tells the story of Ben, whose life is turned upside down as the

CHRISTOPHER

demons of his dreams become real, and he feels unable to combat them.
Age range: 11–13

FIREBALL
Penguin, 1983, 144p. – Pbk. O/P. – 0 14 031498 9
Gollancz, 1981, 192p. – O/P. – 0 575 02974 9

In the same series:

NEW FOUND LAND
Penguin, 1984, 128p. – Pbk. O/P. – 0 14 031683 3
Gollancz, 1983, 160p. – O/P. – 0 575 03222 7

Brad and Susan learn the hard way that to survive, they must forget their differences and work together. The dangers they face in both books are overwhelming, and keep the reader engrossed to the end.
Age range: 12–14

THE GUARDIANS
Penguin, 1973, 176p. – Pbk. – 0 14 030579 3
Hamish Hamilton, 1970, 160p. – O/P. – 0 241 01795 5

When Rob's father dies, Rob has to live in a state boarding school, where the regime is harsh and bullying is rife. When he cannot stand any more, he runs away to safety, but he is not as safe as he hoped. A tense, exciting story.
Age range: 12–14

THE LOTUS CAVES
Penguin, 1971, 176p. – Pbk. – 0 14 030503 3
Hamish Hamilton, 1969, 160p. – O/P. – 0 241 01729 7

Overwhelmed by the boredom of life on the moon, Marty and Steve break the rules and take a moon vehicle beyond the legal limits. They fall through the crust into a strange land of caves where their troubles really begin.
Age range: 12–14

THE PRINCE IN WAITING
Collins, 1983, 160p. – 0 00 330010 2
Penguin, 1973, 155p. – Pbk. O/P. – 0 14 030617 X

In the same series:

BEYOND THE BURNING LANDS
Penguin, 1973, 160p. – Pbk. O/P. – 0 14 030625 0
Hamish Hamilton, 1971, 160p. – O/P. – 0 241 02033 6

THE SWORD OF THE SPIRITS
Penguin, 1973, 144p. – Pbk. O/P. – 0 14 030630 7
Hamish Hamilton, 1972, 160p. – O/P. – 0 241 02137 5

An excellent trilogy, available both separately and in one volume (Penguin, 1983, 464p. – Pbk. – 0 14 031654 X). Set in a fragmented England in the future, where violence is the norm, someone is urgently needed to unite the country. Luke is heir to one of the settlements, but it would appear that such a task is beyond him. A frightening vision of the future.
Age range: 12–14

THE WHITE MOUNTAINS
Chivers Press, 1989, 256p. – L/P. – 0 7451 1043 6
Kestrel Books, 1984, 160p. – O/P. – 0 7226 5909 1
Penguin, 1984, 160p. – Pbk. O/P. – 0 14 031684 1

In the same series:

THE CITY OF GOLD AND LEAD
Chivers Press, 1990, 280p. – L/P. – 0 7451 1100 9
Kestrel Books, 1984, 160p. – 0 7226 5910 5
Penguin, 1984, 160p. – Pbk. O/P. – 0 14 031685 X

THE POOL OF FIRE
Chivers Press, 1990, 280p. – L/P. – 0 7451 1176 9
Kestrel Books, 1984, 160p. – O/P. – 0 7226 5915 6
Penguin, 1984, 160p. – Pbk. O/P. – 0 14 031686 8

The Tripods trilogy, published separately and in one volume (Penguin, 1984, 448p. – Pbk. – 0 14 031722 8) was a thoroughly enjoyable television serial, and is probably the best of John

Christopher's work. Earth is ruled by the Tripods, until Will, an unlikely hero, is sent to the rescue. It is dangerous, but Will and his companions fight on through the three novels to win in an exciting climax.
Age range: 12–14

WILD JACK
Hamlyn, 1978, 160p. – Pbk. O/P. – 0 600 39405 0
Longmans, 1975, 80p. – Pbk. O/P. – 0 582 53791 6
Hamish Hamilton, 1974, 160p. – O/P. – 0 241 89070 5

A future ruled by an energy crisis seems a real possibility to current readers. Clive is taken prisoner by Wild Jack, a savage who has to live outside the protected city in the Outlands. Here Clive learns a different viewpoint, and finally makes his own decision.
Age range: 12–14

Other publications:

DOM AND VA
H. Hamilton, 1973. – O/P. – 0 241 02329 7
DRAGON DANCE
Viking, 1986. – O/P. – 0 670 81030 4
EMPTY WORLD
Penguin, 1990. – Pbk. – 0 14 032750 9
WHEN THE TRIPODS CAME
Penguin, 1990. – Pbk. – 0 14 0326022

CLEARY, Beverly (Bunn)

Born McMinnville, Oregon, 1916. Educated University of California, Berkeley, B.A.; University of Washington, Seattle, B.A. (Librarianship). Married Clarence Cleary, 1940, twin daughter and son. Librarian, writer.

Awards: American Library Association Laura Ingalls Wilder Award, 1975

Catholic Library Association Regina Medal, 1980

IBBY Honour Diploma: *Ramona and her father*, 1980

American Library Association Newbery Medal: *Dear Mr Henshaw*, 1984

Address: C/o William Morrow Inc, 105, Madison Avenue, New York City, New York 10016, USA

Beverly Cleary has the ability to view young children clearly and shrewdly, and yet lovingly. She also has the fortunate ability to re-create what she sees in the characters in her books, resulting in funny, readable and thoroughly enjoyable stories with lots of appeal to the young reader. The book jackets do not have instant appeal, and therefore, some children will need a personal introduction to these excellent books.

BEEZUS AND RAMONA
Penguin, 1981, 160p. – Pbk. – 0 14 031249 8
Hamish Hamilton, 1978, 192p. – O/P. – 0 241 10014 3
illustrated by Thelma Lambert

In the same series:

RAMONA AND HER FATHER
Cornerstone Books, 1988, 168p. – L/P. – 1 55736 076 6
Penguin, 1981, 144p. – Pbk. – 0 14 031303 6
Hamish Hamilton, 1978, 192p. – O/P. – 0 241 89752 1
illustrated by Alan Tiegreen

RAMONA AND HER MOTHER
Penguin, 1982, 176p. – Pbk. – 0 14 031328 1
Hamish Hamilton, 1979, 192p. – O/P. – 0 241 10280 4
illustrated by Alan Tiegreen

RAMONA FOREVER
Cornerstone Books, 1990, 192p. – L/P. – 1 55736 139 8
Penguin, 1986, 160p. – Pbk. – 0 14 031916 6
J. MacRae Books, 1984, 144p. – O/P. – 0 86203 167 2
illustrated by Alan Tiegreen

CLEARY

RAMONA QUIMBY, AGE EIGHT
Cornerstone Books, 1989, 142p. – O/P. – L/P. – 1 55736 000 6
Penguin, 1984, 160p. – Pbk. – 0 14 031560 8
Hamish Hamilton, 1981, 192p. – O/P. –
0 241 10665 6
illustrated by Alan Tiegreen

RAMONA THE BRAVE
Windrush, 1990, 184p. – L/P. –
1 85089 830 8
Penguin, 1978, 112p. – Pbk. – 0 14 031059 2
Hamish Hamilton, 1975, 190p. –
0 241 89257 0
illustrated by Alan Tiegreen

RAMONA THE PEST
Windrush, 1990, 152p. – L/P. –
1 85089 825 1
Penguin, 1976, 160p. – Pbk. – 0 14 030774 5
Hamish Hamilton, 1974, 192p. –
0 241 02412 9
illustrated by Louis Darling

Ramona is a wonderful, memorable character who, being accident prone, leads a life full of hilarious escapades which cause children to laugh out loud. New editions are being brought out with more attractive jackets, using photographs from the television series.
Age range: 7–9

DEAR MR HENSHAW
Cornerstone Books, 1987, 150p. – L/P. –
1 55736 001 4
Penguin, 1985, 144p. – Pbk. – 0 14 031797 X
J. MacRae Books, 1983, 144p. – O/P. –
0 86203 147 8

As part of a class exercise, Leigh writes a letter to the author of his favourite book. Thus begins a correspondence between them in which Leigh confides the exploits of his family and his highly unusual dog. Completely in letter form, some children may be put off, but others will find the easy, chatty style a welcome change from the formal arrangement of most books.
Age range: 9–11

HENRY AND BEEZUS
Penguin, 1990, 208p. – Pbk. – 0 14 032821 1
Hamish Hamilton, 1980, 192p. – O/P. –
0 241 10431 9

In the same series:

HENRY AND RIBSY
Penguin, 1989, 128p. – Pbk. – 0 14 032820 3
Hamish Hamilton, 1979, 192p. – O/P. –
0 241 10020 8

HENRY AND THE CLUBHOUSE
Penguin, 1989, 128p. – Pbk. – 0 14 032819 X
Hamish Hamilton, 1981, 192p. – O/P. –
0 241 10618 4

all illustrated by Thelma Lambert

A highly entertaining set of stories about a small boy's exploits told in a marvellously funny style. The humorous illustrations perfectly complement the text.
Age range: 7–9

MOUSE AND THE MOTORCYCLE
Windrush, 1990, 160p. – L/P. – 1 85089 960 6
Penguin, 1977, 144p. – Pbk. – 0 14 030970 5
Hamish Hamilton, 1974, 160p. – O/P. –
0 241 89020 9
illustrated by Louis Darling

In the same series:

RALPH S. MOUSE
Windrush, 1990, 134p. – L/P. –
1 85089 800 6
Penguin, 1984, 128p. – Pbk. – 0 14 031669 8
Hamish Hamilton, 1982, 139p. – O/P. –
0 241 10883 7
illustrated by Paul O. Zelinsky

RUNAWAY RALPH
Penguin, 1978, 144p. – Pbk. – 0 14 031020 7
Hamish Hamilton, 1974, 176p. – O/P. –
0 241 89112 4
illustrated by Louis Darling

Through watching television, Ralph has learned to talk. His happiness is complete when he meets a boy with a toy motorbike – just the right size for a mouse. He has many adventures, making this a series of delightful and amusing stories.
Age range: 7–9

MUGGIE MAGGIE
Penguin, 1993, 80p. – Pbk. – 0 14 034816 6
H. Hamilton, 1992, 129p. – 0 241 13135 9
illustrated by Anthony Lewis

Maggie is having difficulty transferring from printing to joined-up writing. She cannot be bothered to make the effort to overcome her problem, until her teacher comes up with a novel and successful idea. Both useful and entertaining.
Age range: 7–8

Other publications:

FIFTEEN
Penguin, 1988. – Pbk. – 0 14 032559 X
HERE COME THE TWINS
Penguin, 1990. – Pbk. – 0 14 032884 X
LUCKY CHUCK
J. MacRae, 1985. – O/P. – 0 8620 31915
STRIDER
Puffin Books, 1993. – Pbk. – 0 14 0348174
TWINS AGAIN
H. Hamilton, 1989. – 0 241 126010

COLWELL, Eileen

Educated University College, London. Pioneer children's librarian. Began children's library service in Hendon, 1926; helped found the Association of Children's Librarians, 1937. Chairman for five years of the International Federation of Library Associations' committee on library work with children. Member of the Carnegie Medal Committee since its inception until her retirement. Librarian, lecturer.

Awards: M.B.E., 1965

Honorary Fellow of Manchester Polytechnic, 1974

Loughborough University Honorary Degree of Doctor of Letters, 1975

BAD BOYS
Kestrel Books, 1975, 172p. – O/P. – 0 7226 5027 2
Penguin, 1972, 176p. – Pbk. – 0 14 030530 0
illustrated by John Riley

In the same series:

CATS IN A BASKET
Viking, 1993, 128p. – 0 670 83710 5
illustrated by Vanessa Julian-Ottie

HIGH DAYS AND HOLIDAYS
Penguin, 1989, 144p. – Pbk. – 0 14 032300 7
Viking Kestrel, 1988, 144p. – O/P. – 0 670 81928 X
illustrated by Maureen Bradley

MORE STORIES TO TELL
Penguin, 1979, 160p. – Pbk. – 0 14 031062 2
illustrated by Caroline Sharpe

TELL ME A STORY
Penguin, 1970, 176p. – Pbk. – 0 14 030159 3
illustrated by Judith Bledsoe

TELL ME ANOTHER STORY
Penguin, 1969, 256p. – Pbk. – 0 14 030210 7

A pioneer and champion of children's librarians, Eileen Colwell was also a master storyteller, able to captivate large or small audiences from the youngest child to adults. Who better, then, to put together collections of stories suitable for telling or reading aloud? Contained in these five volumes is a wide variety of authors, styles and themes, ranging from Joan Aiken and Margaret Mahy to Edward Lear.
Age range: 5–14

COOPER, Susan (Mary)

British. Born Burnham, Buckinghamshire, 1935. Educated Slough High School, Bucks, Somerville College, Oxford, 1953–56, M.A. Married Nicholas J. Grant, 1963 (divorced 1982), one son, one daughter. Moved to USA 1963. Reporter, feature writer, columnist and writer.

Awards: Boston Globe/Horn Book Award: *The Dark is rising*, 1973

American Library Association Newbery Medal: *The Grey King*, 1976

Welsh Arts Council Tir na o'Og Award: *The Grey King*, 1976

Welsh Arts Council Tir na o'Og Award: *Silver on the tree*, 1978

B'nai B'rith Janusz Award, 1984

Address: C/o Athenaeum Publishers,
115 Fifth Avenue,
New York
NY 10003
USA

A writer of extra-ordinary talent, with great appeal for lovers of the fantasy genre.

THE DARK IS RISING
Windrush, 1988, 338p. – L/P. – O/P. – 1 8508 9933 9
Penguin, 1979, 272p. – O/P, – 0 14 095082 6
Bodley Head, 1984, 224p. – 0 370 30815 8

In the same series:

OVER SEA, UNDER STONE
Windrush, 1988, 321p. – L/P. – O/P. – 1 8508 9932 0
Bodley Head, 1984, 238p. – 0 370 30590 6
Penguin, 1968, 224p. – Pbk. – 0 14 030362 6

GREENWITCH
Windrush, 1988, 185p. – L/P. – O/P. – 1 8508 9934 7
Bodley Head, 1984, 168p. – 0 370 30826 3
Penguin, 1977, 160p. – Pbk. – 0 14 030901 2

THE GREY KING
Windrush, 1988, 237p. – L/P. – O/P. – 1 8508 9935 5
Bodley Head, 1984, 210p. – 0 370 30828 X
Penguin, 1977, 192p. – Pbk. – 0 14 030952 7

SILVER ON THE TREE
Windrush, 1988, 394p. – L/P. – O/P. – 1 8508 9936 3
Bodley Head, 1984, 288p. – 0 370 30837 9
Penguin, 1979, 288p. – Pbk. – 0 14 031118 1

This quintet of books, inspired by the myths and legends of Cornwall and Wales, tells the powerful story of the struggle between dark and light, good and evil. The role of the children in defeating evil is a stirring example of what can be achieved while providing an exciting and compelling read.

The covers are exceptionally striking, giving an excellent impression of the fearful content.
Age range: 11–13

THE BOGGART
Penguin, 1994, 192p. – Pbk. 0 14 036488 9
Bodley Head, 1993, 196p. – 0 370 31829 3

A Scottish boggart on the loose in Toronto makes an amusing read, full of surprises, and so enjoyable it requires little effort from the reader.
Age range: 9–11

Other publications:
DAWN OF FEAR
Penguin, 1974. – Pbk. – 0 14 030719 2
SEAWARD
Penguin, 1985. – Pbk. – 0 14 031711 2

CORBETT, W(illiam) J(esse)

British. Born, Birmingham, 1938. Educated Billesley Secondary School, Birmingham. Physical training instructor in the British Army, Merchant Seaman, baker's assistant, furniture removal man, slaughterman, builder and writer.

Awards: Whitbread Literary Award, Children's Novel: *The Song of Pentecost*, 1982

Address: 6, Selborne Grove,
Billesley,
Birmingham,
England

Agent: Murray Pollinger,
4 Garrick Street,
London,
England

Roald Dahl had a very high opinion of this author, whose works, in particular the 'Pentecost' series, he thoroughly enjoyed. The books are funny, witty rather than slapstick, but his descriptions of the countryside are quite poetic.

DUCK SOUP FARM
Little Mammoth, 1993, 160p. – Pbk. –
0 7497 1289 9
Methuen, 1992, 128p. – 0 416 18587 8
illustrated by Tony Ross

Daisy comes up with the idea of putting the patch of waste ground by the cottage to good use – creating a holiday home for pets. The children work hard, but the 'pets' that arrive prove to be rather out-of-the-ordinary. Witty and enjoyable.
Age range: 8–10

LITTLE ELEPHANT
Mammoth, 1993, 128p. – Pbk. – 0 7497 1008 X
Methuen, 1991, 128p. – 0 416 17092 7
illustrated by Tony Ross

A moving beginning when the little elephant returns home to find the whole family killed for their ivory tusks. He is persuaded by Veagle not to give in to his grief, but to travel across Africa in search of another herd. An enjoyable book with a clear but understated message.
Age range: 7–9

SONG OF PENTECOST
Mammoth, 1992, 224p. – Pbk. – 0 7497 0926 X
Chivers Press, 1988, 424p. – O/P. –
0 7451 0794 X
Methuen, 1982, 192p. – 0 416 24730 X

In the same series:

PENTECOST AND THE CHOSEN ONE
Penguin, 1986, 256p. – Pbk. – O/P. –
0 14 031878 X
Methuen, 1984, 160p. – 0 416 50190 7

PENTECOST OF LICKEY TOP
Penguin, 1989, 192p. – Pbk. – O/P. –
0 14 032729 0
Methuen, 1987. – O/P. – 0 416 02372 X
illustrated by Martin Ursell

Pentecost is an intrepid mouse who leads his tribe away from their polluted homes to find a better place to live.

The story of their very eventful journey is told with humour and great style. The character of Pentecost proved to be so popular that two other books followed.
Age range: 9–11

TOBY'S ICEBERG
Mammoth, 1992, 128p. – Pbk. – 0 7497 0452 7
Methuen, 1990, 128p. – O/P. – 0 416 15622 3
illustrated by Tony Ross

An amusing easy-to-read story about Toby the whale who undertakes to push an iceberg to the equator to help his cousins.
Age range: 7–9

Other publications:

BEAR WHO STOOD ON HIS HEAD
Mammoth, 1989. – Pbk. – 0 7497 00327
DEAR GRUMBLE
Mammoth, 1991. – Pbk. – 0 7497 01145
END OF THE TALE AND OTHER STORIES
Penguin, 1987. – Pbk. – O/P. – 0 14 0321373
GRANDSON BOY
Methuen, 1993. – 0 416 187951

CORRIN, Sara and Stephen

British. Stephen born Tedagar, Gwent, Wales, 1916. Educated University of South Wales and University of Lille. Sara born London. Educated Hertfordshire College of Education; Institute of Education, London University, Adv. Diploma in Child Development. Two daughters. Sara Corrin teacher, lecturer in child development, storyteller and editor. Stephen reviewer, writer, translator and editor.

THE FABER BOOK OF FAVOURITE FAIRY TALES
Faber, 1988, 256p. – 0 571 14854 9
illustrated by J. Wijngaard

In the same series:

FABER BOOK OF GOLDEN FAIRY TALES
Faber, 1993, 192p. – 0 571 16348 3
illustrated by Peter Melnyczuk

IMAGINE THAT! FIFTEEN FANTASTIC TALES
Penguin, 1988, 176p. – Pbk. – 0 14 032393 7
Faber, 1986, 175p. – 0 571 13843 8

MODERN FAIRY TALES
Penguin, 1983, 224p. – Pbk. – 0 14 031546 2
Faber, 1981, 312p. – 0 571 11768 6
illustrated by Ann Strugnell

THE PUFFIN BOOK OF CHRISTMAS STORIES
Penguin, 1986, 192p. – Pbk. O/P. – 0 14 031967 0

THE PUFFIN BOOK OF PET STORIES
Penguin, 1987, 208p. – Pbk. – 0 14 032117 9

ROUND THE CHRISTMAS TREE
Penguin, 1985, 144p. – Pbk. – 0 14 031777 5
Faber, 1983, 134p. – O/P. – 0 571 13151 4

STORIES FOR UNDER-FIVES
Penguin, 1979, 160p. – Pbk. – 0 14 031100 9
Faber, 1974, 157p. – 0 571 10371 5

MORE STORIES FOR UNDER-FIVES
Penguin, 1988, 112p. – Pbk. – 0 14 032529 8
Faber, 1988, 96p. – 0 571 15058 6

STORIES FOR FIVE YEAR OLDS AND OTHER YOUNG READERS
Penguin, 1976, 160p. – Pbk. – 0 14 030839 3
Faber, 1973, 167p. – 0 571 10162 3

STORIES FOR SIX YEAR OLDS AND OTHER YOUNG READERS
Penguin, 1976, 176p. – Pbk. – 0 14 030785 0
Faber, 1967, 198p. – 0 571 08114 2

STORIES FOR SEVEN YEAR OLDS
Penguin, 1976, 192p. – Pbk. – 0 14 030882 2
Faber, 1964, 188p. – 0 571 05823 X

MORE STORIES FOR SEVEN YEAR OLDS
Penguin, 1982, 192p. – Pbk. – 0 14 031347 8
Faber, 1978, 183p. – O/P. – 0 571 11196 3

STORIES FOR EIGHT YEAR OLDS AND OTHER READERS
Penguin, 1977, 224p. – Pbk. – 0 14 030975 6
Faber, 1971, 192p. – 0 571 09332 9

STORIES FOR NINE YEAR OLDS AND OTHER YOUNG READERS
Penguin, 1981, 224p. – Pbk. – 0 14 031342 7
Faber, 1979, 159p. – 0 571 11409 1

STORIES FOR TENS AND OVER
Penguin, 1982, 208p. – Pbk. – 0 14 031364 8
Faber, 1976, 240p. – 0 571 10873 3

TIME TO LAUGH: FIFTEEN FUNNY STORIES
Faber, 1989, 116p. – Pbk. – 0 571 15499 9
illustrated by Gerald Rose

LAUGH OUT LOUD: MORE FUNNY STORIES FOR CHILDREN
Faber, 1989, – Pbk, – 0 571 141773

Specialists in collecting folk and fairy tales, both traditional and modern, the Corrins have put together various collections loosely round a theme, for example, heroes and heroines for the eight year olds, humour for the nines. Although they have tried to match the theme to the age group most likely to appreciate it, the stories can, in fact, be used with a variety of age groups. Occasionally extracts are included, for example *The Iron Man* in *Modern Fairy Tales*. These volumes are reprinted time after time as they have proved their value. The Faber Book of Favourite Fairy Tales is a particularly attractive volume.
Age range: 5–12

CRESSWELL, Helen

British. Born Nottinghamshire, 1934. Educated Nottingham Girls' High School; King's College, London University. B.A. (Hons) English. Married Brian Rowe, 1962. Two daughters. Worked as a literary assistant, fashion buyer, teacher.

CRESSWELL

Address: Old Church Farm,
Eakring,
Newark,
Nottinghamshire NG22 0DA,
England

Agent: A. M. Heath,
79 St. Martin's Lane,
London WC2N 4AA,
England

The secret of Helen Cresswell's popularity is the originality of her plots, combined with an odd sense of humour which corresponds with a child's. She writes for a wide age range, but all to the same high standard.

THE BAGTHORPE SAGA comprising:

ABSOLUTE ZERO
Penguin, 1979, 168p. – Pbk. – 0 14 031177 7
Faber, 1978, 168p. – 0 571 11155 6

BAGTHORPES ABROAD
Penguin, 1986, 192p. – Pbk – 0 14 031972 7
Faber, 1984, 186p. – 0 571 13350 9

BAGTHORPES HAUNTED
Penguin, 1987, 208p. – Pbk. – 0 14 032172 1
Faber, 1985, 208p. – 0 571 13585 4

BAGTHORPES LIBERATED
Penguin, 1990, 208p. – Pbk. – 0 14 034428 4
Faber, 1989, 176p. – 0 571 15402 6

BAGTHORPE TRIANGLE
Faber, 1992, 208p. – 0 571 16686 5
illustrated by Jill Bennett

BAGTHORPES UNLIMITED
Penguin, 1980, 192p. – Pbk. – 0 14 031178 5
Faber, 1978, 176p. – 0 571 11245 5

BAGTHORPES VERSUS THE WORLD
Penguin, 1982, 192p. – Pbk. O/P. –
0 14 031324 9
Faber, 1979, 192p. – 0 571 11446 6

ORDINARY JACK
Windrush, 1987, 252p. – L/P. –
1 85089 929 3
Penguin, 1979, 192p. – Pbk. – 0 14 031176 9
Faber, 1977, 192p. – O/P. – 0 571 11114 9
all illustrated by Jill Bennett

The Bagthorpe family are definitely eccentric. Pandemonium reigns, helped on many occasions by Zero, the dog. They stagger from crisis to crisis, providing both hilarious reading and viewing, as the saga became a popular television serial.
Age range: 10–12

THE BARGE CHILDREN
White Lion, 1976, 88p. – O/P. – 0 85686 270 3

Billy and Betsy Moon live on a barge. As the story unfolds, the reader is given a clear picture of what life was like for the bargees in the heyday of Britain's waterways. It is not a long story, but very entertaining.
Age range: 7–9

THE BEACHCOMBERS
Chivers Press, 1987, 192p. – L/P. –
0 7451 0546 7
Penguin, 1978, 144p. – Pbk. O/P. –
0 14 031026 6
Faber, 1972, 128p. – O/P. – 0 571 09932 7
illustrated by Errol le Cain

An unusual story about a boy whose only hope of a holiday is to agree to accompany an only child, when he becomes involved in the rivalry of the beachcombers. In spite of the rising tension, there is no shortage of humour, and the final denouement brings the book to a highly satisfactory close. An excellent book for reading aloud.
Age range: 10–12

THE BONGLEWEED
Penguin, 1981, 176p. – Pbk. – 0 14 031272 2
Faber, 1973, 157p. – O/P. – 0 571 10374 X
illustrated by Ann Strugnell

Owing to the perfect blend of fantasy and realism personified by Becky's pragmatic parents, this book is a first-rate example of the comic fantasy genre. The fantasy element is provided by a new species of plant which, besides threatening to overrun everything, displays more sinister powers. Even if the reader fails to draw the parallels between the blossoming of

CRESSWELL

Becky and the Bongleweed, the sheer vitality of the story pulls them along to the immensely satisfactory ending.
Age range: 10–12

DEAR SHRINK
Penguin, 1988, 160p. – Pbk. – 0 14 032636 7
Windrush, 1987, 236p. – L/P. – O/P. –
1 85089 903 7
Faber, 1982, 221p. – O/P. – 0 571 11912 3

A graphic portrayal of the difference between a loving, sheltered home and the bleakness of being fostered by uncaring people. The reader experiences this with the Saxon family whose parents are working abroad, leaving the children in the care of an elderly baby-sitter, who unfortunately dies. There are many problems, both practical and emotional, to cope with before the moving climax releases the children and the reader.
Age range: 10–12

ELLIE AND THE HAGWITCH
Yearling, 1990, 128p. – Pbk. – 0 440 86263 9
Lutterworth Press, 1987, 80p. – 0 7188 2672 8
illustrated by Jonathon Heap

A strange, chilling fantasy about a little girl struggling alone to combat the witch. Quite easy to read.
Age range: 8–10

GAME OF CATCH
Red Fox, 1990, 80p. – Pbk. – 0 09 975260 3
Chatto, 1969, 64p. – O/P. – 0 7011 0303 5
illustrated by Gareth Floyd

Although not very long because it is intended for young children, this excellently crafted story captures the carefree games of childhood and weaves into them a ghostly echo from a painting. The result is a compelling read.
Age range: 8–10

A GIFT FROM WINKLESEA
Penguin, 1971, 80p. – Pbk. – 0 14 030493 2
Hodder, 1969, 88p. – O/P. – 0 340 10472 4
illustrated by Janina Ede

A seaside souvenir which hatches into something else altogether is the unlikely hero of this unusual and delightful fantasy.
Age range: 7–9

In the same series:

WHATEVER HAPPENED IN WINKLESEA?
Penguin, 1991. – Pbk. – 0 14 034270 2
illustrated by Shoo Rayner

A sequel, telling how the children are re-united with their Winkelsea 'gift'. They are filled with consternation when it is captured, but it does end happily, if a little contrived. Rather slight, but enjoyable – easy and undemanding.
Age range: 7–9

GREEDY ALICE
Corgi, 1989, 64p. – Pbk. – 0 552 52524 3
Deutsch, 1986, 44p. – 0 233 97951 4
illustrated by Kate Simpson

Written for children newly experiencing the delights of reading alone, this is a delightful story. Greedy and curious, Alice decides to eat the cake in the box, and, like her famous namesake, she grows and grows, with equally disastrous results.
Age range: 6–8

LIZZIE DRIPPING
Windrush, 1990, 104p. – L/P. – 1 85089 991 6
Penguin, 1985, 96p. – Pbk. – 0 14 031751 1
BBC, 1973, 96p. – O/P. – 0 563 12411 3

In the same series:

LIZZIE DRIPPING AGAIN
BBC, 1974, 127p. – O/P. – 0 563 12687 6

LIZZIE DRIPPING AND THE LITTLE ANGEL
BBC, 1990, 31p. – Pbk. – 0 563 20908 9

LIZZIE DRIPPING BY THE SEA
BBC, 1990, 64p. – Pbk. – 0 563 20907 0

LIZZIE DRIPPING AND THE WITCH
Chivers Press, 1992, 136p. – 0 7451 1681 7
BBC, 1991, 96p. – 0 563 36210 3
all illustrated by Faith Jacques

A series of stories about a rather irritating little girl who actively seeks out

CRESSWELL

adventure. Very popular on television.
Age range: 8–10

MEET POSY BATES
Red Fox, 1991. – Pbk. – 0 09 985360 4

In the same series:

POSY BATES, AGAIN!
Bodley Head, 1993, 104p. – 0 370 31592 8
Red Fox, 1992. – Pbk. – 0 09 997810 5

POSY BATES AND THE BAG LADY
Bodley Head, 1993, 88p. – 0 370 31764 5
all illustrated by Kate Aldous

The first two titles are volumes of short stories about a little girl full of mischief and bright ideas which often go wrong. The descriptions of her humorous escapades make easy reading. The third is a very accessible, full-length novel about Posy.
Age range: 7–9

MOONDIAL
Penguin, 1988. – Pbk. – O/P. – 0 14 032523 9
Faber, 1987, 220p. – 0 571 14805 0
illustrated by P. J. Lynch

Specially written for television, the story takes place around Belton House, a National Trust property in Lincolnshire. Minty has supernatural powers which allow her to work out the secret of the moondial. Suspenseful, it is easier to watch than read.
Age range: 9–11

THE NIGHT-WATCHMEN
Chivers Press, 1990, 168p. – L/P. – 0 7451 1102 5
Penguin, 1976, 128p. – Pbk. O/P. – 0 14 030851 2
Faber, 1969, 148p. – O/P. – 0 571 08903 8
illustrated by Gareth Floyd

Not a book for those of a nervous disposition, as it is a story with decidedly frightening overtones. Henry is curious about the so-called night-watchmen, and sets out to find out exactly what they do. As the mystery unfolds, Henry's mounting fear is shared by the reader.
Age range: 10–12

THE PIEMAKERS
Faber, 1988, 160p. – 0 571 14761 5
Penguin, 1976, 128p. – Pbk. – 0 14 030868 7
illustrated by V. H. Drummond

Light-hearted and amusing, the story centres on Gravella, feeling fed-up with her never-ending job – helping with the family business of pie-making. When the pie competition is announced, they have a splendid idea, which gradually loses its splendour!
Age range: 9–11

THE SECRET WORLD OF POLLY FLINT
Penguin, 1984, 178p. – Pbk. O/P. – 0 14 031542 X
Faber, 1982, 176p. – 0 571 11939 5

Polly believes in magic, and knows that anything is possible, even the disappearance of a whole world. This intriguing story made a highly successful television series.
Age range: 9–11

TIME OUT
Lutterworth Press, 1987, 76p. – 0 7188 2658 2
illustrated by Tessa Hamilton

Written specifically for the television programme *Jackanory*, this funny story about a green cat and a butler with magic powers has been granted a new lease of life. It is now available in an attractive new edition.
Age range: 7–9

THE WATCHERS: A MYSTERY AT ALTON TOWERS
Puffin Books, 1993, 192p. – Pbk. – 0 14 036140 5
Viking, 1993, 192p. – 0 670 84584 1

Katy and Josh escape from the children's home and make their way to Alton Towers where they hope to be able to disappear. They quickly discover that evil is lurking in the silent rides, and their hopes of a peaceful existence fade. Rather an unrealistic ending, but an easy read, enjoyable and exciting.
Age range: 10–12

CRESSWELL

WHERE THE WIND BLOWS
Faber, 1990, 96p. – Pbk. – 0 571 14425 X
Faber, 1966, 63p. – O/P. – 0 571 06854 5
illustrated by Peggy Fortnum

A delightful book for younger children. The story is simple but appealing. Kirstine feels a little bored living with her grandfather by the slow river. When, by chance, she is shown the boat, she sets off at once on a fairy tale adventure.
Age range: 7–9

Other publications:

ALMOST GOODBYE GUZZLER
Collins, 1991. – Pbk. – 0 00 673881 8
AWFUL JACK
Hodder, 1977. – O/P. – 0 340 20215 7
DRAGON RIDE
Penguin, 1989. – Pbk. – 0 14 032480 1
MY AUNT POLLY BY THE SEA
Wheaton, 1980. – Pbk. – O/P. – 0 08 025622 8
MY AUNT POLLY
Wheaton, 1979. – O/P. – 0 08 024998 1
THE OUTLANDERS
Faber, 1970. – O/P. – 0 571 09405 8
RETURN OF THE PSAMMEAD
BBC, 1993. – Pbk. – 0 563 36766 0
ROSIE AND THE BOREDOM EATER
Heinemann, 1989. – 0 434 93061 X
THE SIGNPOSTERS
Chivers Press, 1988. – 0 8599 7885 0
STORY OF GRACE DARLING
Penguin, 1988. – Pbk. – O/P. – 0 14 0324348
TROUBLE
Gollancz, 1990. – Pbk. – O/P. – 0 575 04772 0
UP THE PIER
Faber, 1989. – Pbk. – O/P. – 0 571 14187 0
WEATHER CAT
Collins, 1989. – O/P. – 0 00 197787 3
WHODUNIT?
Cape, 1986. – O/P. – 0 224 02290 3
THE WILKSES
BBC, 1970. – Pbk. – O/P. – 0 563 10173 3

CROSS, Gillian (Clare, née Arnold)

British. Born London, 1945. Educated North London Collegiate School; Somerville College, Oxford, B.A., M.A.; University of Sussex, D.Phil (Eng). Married Martin Cross, 1967, two sons, two daughters.

Awards: Junior Education Best Historical Fiction: *A Whisper of Lace*, 1981
Carnegie Medal: *Wolf*, 1990
Smarties' Prize: *The Great Elephant chase*, 1992
Whitbread Children's Novel Award: *The Great Elephant chase*, 1992

Address: 39 Main Street,
Wolston,
Coventry CV8 3HH,
England

Children are fortunate that a novelist of this stature should choose to write for them. She has evolved from a competent writer with exceptionally good ideas for stories into a first-rate author, writing equally well for different age groups.

THE DARK BEHIND THE CURTAIN
Hippo Books, 1985, 208p. – Pbk. –
0 590 70349 8
OUP, 1984, 160p. – 0 19 271500 3
illustrated by David Parkins

An above average thriller. The rehearsals for the school play are not progressing well, and there is a real menace lurking behind the stage curtain. The writing is powerful enough to render the book sometimes very frightening, and is a gripping read at all times.
Age range: 10–12

THE DEMON HEADMASTER
OUP, 1990, 96p. – Pbk. – 0 19 831270 9
Chivers Press, 1990, 208p. – L/P. –
0 7451 1150 5
OUP, 1986, 176p. – 0 19 271553 4
illustrated by Gary Rees

In the same series:

THE PRIME MINISTER'S BRAIN
Chivers Press, 1991, 240p. – L/P. – O/P. –
0 7451 1372 9
OUP, 1990, 196p. – 0 19 271641 7
Penguin, 1987, 160p. – Pbk. – 0 14 032312 0
illustrated by Sally Burgess

HUNKY PARKER IS WATCHING YOU
OUP, 1994, 176p. 0 19 271705 7
illustrated by Maureen Bradley

The Demon Headmaster has proved to be an exceptionally popular book. Linguistically accessible to most children, the story has a remarkable appeal. The headmaster is a thoroughly evil man, controlling pupils and staff by fear. Dinah, an exceptional child in many ways, is the only one immune to his hypnotic ministerings. How she succeeds in defeating him makes an exciting and believable story, told with humour. The sequels are equally funny and exciting, but have lost some of the freshness of the original.
Age range: 9–11

GOBBO THE GREAT
Mammoth, 1991, 128p. – Pbk. – 0 7497 0605 8
Methuen, 1991, 144p. – 0 416 17962 2
illustrated by Philippe Dupasquier

In the same series:

THE MINTYGLO KID
Mammoth, 1991, 128p. – Pbk. –
0 7497 0608 2
Methuen, 1983, 128p. – O/P. –
0 416 25420 9
illustrated by Gareth Floyd

SAVE OUR SCHOOL
Mammoth, 1991, 128p. – Pbk. –
0 7497 0591 4
Methuen, 1981, 112p. – O/P. –
0 416 89800 9

SWIMATHON
Mammoth, 1991, 96p. – Pbk. –
0 7497 0609 0
Methuen, 1986, 128p. – O/P. –
0 416 59700 9

Each book describes one of the hilarious adventures experienced by the gang who are never short of ideas which go wrong so humorously. A lively set of stories.
Age range: 9–11

THE GREAT ELEPHANT CHASE
OUP, 1992, 196p. – 0 19 271672 7

A typically innovative theme – Hannibal is determined to posses the elephant. Tad, overwhelmed by the beast, is equally determined to keep him safe, but it is not the easiest of tasks. Very exciting.
Age range: 10–12

THE IRON WAY
OUP, 1990, 138p. – 0 19 271642 5

The beginning of the railway is the setting for this excellent book, full of period detail and atmosphere. Unfortunately, historical novels are not very popular, and without a knowledgeable adult to bridge the gap, many children will miss a very exciting story. The human drama, culminating in a threat to the lives of the children as resentment against the 'navvies' spoiling the countryside with the railway lines reaches fever pitch, is strongly portrayed.
Age range: 11–14

ON THE EDGE
OUP, 1989, 176p. – 0 19 271606 9
Penguin, 1987, 176p. – Pbk. – 0 14 032053 9

The title is an apt description of the readers of this tense thriller, the tension being maintained until the last page. Tug is kidnapped, and very frightened of his captors. Bravely, he tries to attract attention to his plight. Meanwhile, attempts to rescue him fail, putting him in more danger. The television serialization had children glued to their sets.
Age range: 10–14

RESCUING GLORIA
Mammoth, 1991, 137p. – Pbk. – 0 7497 0106 4
Methuen, 1989, 128p. – O/P. – 0 416 13402 5
illustrated by Gareth Floyd

Leo is appalled to learn that the gentle goat has to be put to sleep, and rescues her. The reality of looking after her proves rather more difficult than he anticipated. Then the ducks arrive, and his problems increase. A lively, funny

CROSS

story, well told and attractively produced.
Age range: 7–9

REVOLT AT RATCLIFFE'S RAGS
OUP, 1983, 146p. – 0 19 271477 5
OUP, 1980, 144p. – O/P. – 0 19 271439 2

Reissued as:

STRIKE AT RATCLIFFE'S RAGS
Methuen, 1987, 144p. – Pbk. O/P. – 0 416 97100 8

The slight alteration in the title indicates the main theme of this story. As a school project, the class was studying the working conditions in Ratcliffe's, a small clothing factory. Eventually the parents become involved, taking sides, and a strike results. The subject indicates that this is not an easy, light-weight book, but it is a thought-provoking introduction to the problems of management and workers, albeit as seen through the simplistic eyes of the children.
Age range: 11–14

ROSCOE'S LEAP
Penguin, 1990, 176p. – Pbk. – 0 14 034013 0
OUP, 1987, 160p. – 0 19 271557 7

As expected of this author, the plot is original and enthralling. The setting is an unusual house, built by Samuel Roscoe, which is rapidly going to rack and ruin in spite of the efforts of Stephen and Hannah. Gradually the reader realizes that there is a reason for the children living in one half, almost cut off from the occupants of the other half, and that the reason is some terrible event in the past. The clues are tantalizingly revealed chapter by chapter. A compelling read.
Age range: 12–14

THE RUNAWAY
Magnet Books, 1986, 176p. – Pbk. – 0 416 52100 2
Methuen, 1979, 176p. – O/P. – 0 416 87230 1
illustrated by Reginald Gray

A subject currently receiving media attention is the increasing number of children running away from home, which is also the subject of this book. Children (and some adults) do not find it easy to empathize without personal experience, but a well written book can be the next best thing. This is such a book, describing how so many things go wrong for Denny that he feels he has no other option. Abandoned by his parents, the one stable adult in his life, Gran, has to go to hospital. Victimized by Bouncer Bradley, the school bully, having to live in the same children's home proves to be the last straw. As, in reality, running away is no solution, so it is in the book, and finding an alternative is a painful process.
Age range: 10–12

THE TREE HOUSE
Methuen, 1993, 64p. – 0 416 18876 1
illustrated by Paul Howard

An easy-to-read everyday story about family life, and how love can unite even when circumstances force people apart. Slightly spoilt by the annoying name by which the children refer to their temporarily absent father – 'Dadda'.
Age range: 7–9

TWIN AND SUPER-TWIN
Penguin, 1992, 176p. – Pbk. – 0 14 034825 5
OUP, 1990, 176p. – 0 19 271594 1
illustrated by Maureen Bradley

Ben and Mitch are twins, and between them they have a strange power – Ben is able to change Mitch's arm into anything he chooses – just by thinking hard. Sometimes it is useful, sometimes a nuisance. An amusing read, but rather slight.
Age range: 8–10

A WHISPER OF LACE
OUP, 1981, 143p. – O/P. – 0 19 271447 3

A story centred around the harm to the local lacemakers when Chantilly lace was smuggled in. Lame and weak, Dan nevertheless triumphs when he

becomes dangerously involved with the smugglers to save his sister. An excellent read.
Age range: 12–14

WOLF
*Penguin, 1992, 144p. – Pbk. – 0 14 034826 3
Chivers Press, 1992, 280p. – O/P. –
0 7451 1496 2
OUP, 1990, 144p. – 0 19 271633 6*

An outstanding book – basically a thriller with all the necessary suspense, but also full of powerful human emotions. Excellent, at whichever of its many levels it is read.
Age range: 12+

Other publications:
BEWARE OLGA!
Walker Books, 1993. – 0 7445 2437 7
BORN OF THE SUN
OUP, 1983. – O/P. – 0 19 271475 9
CHARTBREAK
Penguin, 1988. – Pbk. – 0 14 032458 5
FURRY MACCALOO
Heinemann, 1993. – 0 434 96264 3
MAP OF NOWHERE
OUP, 1988. – 0 19 271583 6
MONSTER FROM THE UNDERGROUND
Heinemann, 1990. – 0 434 93070 9
RENT A GENIUS
Penguin, 1993. – Pbk. – 0 14 036130 8

CROSSLEY-HOLLAND, Kevin (John William)

British. Born Mursley, Buckinghamshire, 1941. Educated Bryston School; St Edmund's Hall, Oxford, B.A. (Hons). Married: 1) Caroline Tendall Thompson, 1963, two sons; 2) Ruth Marris, 1972; 3) Gillian Cook, 1982, two daughters. Worked as editor, radio producer and university lecturer in Britain and America.

Awards: Arts Council Award 1968, 1977 and 1978

Carnegie Medal Winner: *Storm*, 1986

Address: The Old Vicarage,
Walsham-le-Willows,
Bury St. Edmunds,
Suffolk,
England

Agent: Rogers, Coleridge & White,
20 Powis Mews,
London W11 1JN,
England

Well known for his interest in mythology and folklore, this author has produced many volumes of collected folk and fairy tales. Many of them require adult introduction or assistance, but some can be tackled directly and with pleasure.

BOO!
Orchard Books, 1988, 64p. – 1 85213 091 1

In the same series:

DATHERA DAD
Orchard Books, 1988, 64p. – 1 85213 092 X

PIPER AND POOKA
Orchard Books, 1988, 64p. – 1 85213 093 8

SMALL-TOOTH DOG
Orchard Books, 1988, 64p. – 1 85213 094 6
all illustrated by Peter Melynczuk

Small books, published so far in a uniform edition, containing very short fairy tales or short stories. Illustrated on every page, they may well be acceptable to the reluctant reader.
Age range: 9–12

BRITISH AND IRISH FOLK TALES
Orchard Books, 1990, 160p. – 1 85213 265 5

Selected very much with children's enjoyment in mind, this collection contains the more popular stories, which children will certainly not find too difficult.
Age range: 9–11

THE DEAD MOON AND OTHER TALES FROM EAST ANGLIA AND THE FEN COUNTRY
*Deutsch, 1990, 108p. – Pbk. – 0 233 98572 7
Deutsch, 1982, 104p. – O/P. – 0 233 97478 4
illustrated by Shirley Felts*

CROSSLEY-HOLLAND

Eleven folk tales from East Anglia showing an excellent and varied mixture of funny and scary stories.
Age range: 9–12

THE FABER BOOK OF NORTHERN FOLK TALES
Faber, 1983, 157p. – Pbk. O/P. – 0 571 13166 2
Faber, 1980, 157p. – 0 571 11519 5
illustrated by Alan Howard

A splendid collection of traditional stories from Scandinavia, Germany, the British Isles and Iceland. They are carefully arranged to follow on easily from each other.
Age range: 9–12

NORSE MYTHS
Simon & Schuster, 1993. – 0 7500 1257 9
Penguin, 1993, 320p. – Pbk. – 0 14 017993 3
illustrated by Gillian McClure

Excellent re-telling of the Viking tales, well illustrated by a specially commissioned artist. Large, clear print puts the finishing touch to a superbly produced book.
Age range: 10–12

WULF
Faber, 1988, 105p. – O/P. – 0 571 15100 0
illustrated by Gareth Floyd

A revised version of a trilogy published much earlier, it tells the story of an Anglo-Saxon boy, converted to Christianity, whose new faith is tested to the full. An excellent book, but a minority choice, in spite of being translated to the television screen in an engrossing serial.
Age range: 10–12

Other publications:
BRITISH FOLK TALES: A SELECTION
Orchard Books, 1991. – Pbk. – 1 8521 3307 4
LABOURS OF HERAKLES
Orion Children's Books, 1993. – 1 8588 1009 4
LONG TOM AND THE DEAD HAND
Deutsch, 1992. – 0 590 54014 9
SEA TONGUE
BBC, 1992. – Pbk. – 0 563 34785 6

SLEEPING NANNA
Orchard Books, 1991. – Pbk. – 1 8521 3356 2
STORM
Heinemann, 1985. – 0 434 93032 6
TALES FROM EUROPE
BBC, 1991. – 0 563 34795 3
UNDER THE SUN AND OVER THE MOON
Orchard Books, 1992. – Pbk. – O/P. – 1 8521 3325 2

CURTIS, Philip

British. Born Westcliffe-on-Sea, 1920. Married, two children. Teacher, writer.

Address: 224 Station Road,
              Leigh-on-Sea,
              Essex SS9 3BS,
              England

BEWARE OF THE BRAIN SHARPENERS
Beaver Books, 1987, 144p. – Pbk. – 0 09 954080 0
Andersen Press, 1983, 136p. – O/P. – 0 86264 055 5

In the same series:

BEWITCHED BY THE BRAIN SHARPENERS
Beaver Books, 1988, 128p. – Pbk. – 0 09 956780 6
Andersen Press, 1986, 128p. – 0 86264 153 5

BRAIN SHARPENERS ABROAD
Andersen Press, 1987, 128p. – 0 86264 183 7

CHAOS COMES TO CHIVY CHASE
Andersen Press, 1988, 128p. – 0 86264 193 4

MR BROWSER AND THE BRAIN SHARPENERS
Penguin, 1982, 80p. – Pbk. – 0 14 031526 8
Andersen Press, 1979, 96p. – 0 905478 59 2

MR BROWSER AND THE COMET CRISIS
Penguin, 1983, 112p. – Pbk. O/P. – 0 14 031527 6
Andersen Press, 1981, 118p. – O/P. – 0 86264 004 0

MR BROWSER AND THE MINI-METEORITES
Beaver Books, 1986, 128p. – Pbk. O/P. –
0 09 943670 1
Andersen Press, 1983, 127p. – 0 86264 030 X

MR BROWSER AND THE SPACE MAGGOTS
Penguin, 1990, 128p. – Pbk. – 0 14 034394 6
Andersen Press, 1989, 126p. – 0 86264 244 2

MR BROWSER IN THE SPACE MUSEUM
Beaver Books, 1988, 144p. – Pbk. –
0 09 956770 9
Andersen Press, 1985, 144p. – 0 86264 095 4

MR BROWSER MEETS THE BURROWERS
Beaver Books, 1986, 128p. – Pbk. –
0 09 943680 9
Andersen Press, 1980, 128p. – O/P. –
0 905478 88 6

MR BROWSER MEETS THE MIND SHRINKERS
Penguin, 1991, 128p. – Pbk. – 0 14 034556 6
Andersen Press, 1989, 128p. – 0 86264 261 2

REVENGE OF THE BRAIN SHARPENERS
Beaver Books, 1987, 120p. – Pbk. – O/P. –
0 09 954090 8
Andersen Press, 1982, 120p. – 0 86264 013 X
all illustrated by Tony Ross

A series of science fiction stories involving the children of Chivy Chase school and their teacher, Mr Browser. The books are funny, with lots of action, maintaining the reader's interest, not just to the end of the book, but throughout the series. Tony Ross's amusing illustrations add the finishing touch.
Age range: 8–10

HOSTAGES OF THE SPACE MAFIA
Andersen Press, 1993, 128p. – 0 8626 4434 8
illustrated by Ken Brown

An unusual story about aliens who kidnap a class of children. They are rescued by using music as a weapon to defeat the aliens. Not very demanding, but enjoyable.
Age range: 9–11

A PARTY FOR LESTER
Andersen Press, 1984, 146p. – 0 86264 066 0
illustrated by Sarah Parker

Quite different from the 'Mr Browser' series, this story concerns Lester, a retarded child, and his struggle to be accepted at school and in society. He undergoes a fundamental change when told he has to attend a special school. Aided by his friend Billy, they go into hiding in the church until a solution can be found. A tense and moving story.
Age range: 10–12

PENFRIEND FROM ANOTHER PLANET
Andersen Press, 1990, 142p. – 0 8626 4296 5
illustrated by Tony Ross

Chris feels left out when he fails to get a French penfriend. It seems too good to be true when the clouds form a funnel to send him a piece of paper covered in pin-pricks. When decoded, it proves to be a letter from outer space, offering to be his penfriend. Very easy to read.
Age range: 9–11

THE QUEST OF THE QUIDNUNCS
Andersen Press, 1985, 128p. – O/P. –
0 86264 113 6
illustrated by Tony Ross

Along the same lines as 'Mr Browser', this science fiction story is set in Austria, where the holiday of a lifetime is not all it promised. Exciting and funny, this will not disappoint Mr Curtis's many fans.
Age range: 8–10

TOOTHLESS WONDER ABROAD
Andersen Press, 1992, 128p. – 0 8626 4383 X

TOOTHLESS WONDER AND THE DOUBLE AGENT
Andersen Press, 1988, 128p. – O/P. –
0 8626 4217 5

TOOTHLESS WONDER IN THE TOWER
Andersen Press, 1986, 128p. – O/P. –
0 8626 4131 4
illustrated by Amelia Rosato

CURTIS

A series of stories about Traynor and his adventures – amusing, light-hearted and highly entertaining. Full of child appeal.
Age range: 9–11

Other publications:
GIFT FROM ANOTHER GALAXY
Andersen Press, 1987. – 0 8626 41667
WELCOME TO THE GIANTS
Andersen Press, 1991. – 0 8626 43341

D

DAHL, Roald

British. Born Llandaff, Glamorganshire, Wales, 1916, died 23 November 1990. Educated Repton School, Yorkshire. RAF in WW II. Wing Commander, 1943–45. Married: 1) Actress Patricia Neal, 1953, divorced 1983, one son, four daughters (one deceased); 2) Felicity Ann Crosland, 1983.

Awards: Federation of Children's Book Groups award: *The Witches*, 1983
Whitbread Award: *The Witches*, 1983
Federation of Children's Book Groups award: *Matilda*, 1988
Oak Award: *Matilda*, 1989
Smarties' Prize for Children's Books: *Esio Trot*, 1990

Undisputedly the most popular children's author of today. The reason for this is the combination of original and ingenious plots, which appeal to the reluctant reader, and a verbal competence which satisfies the more demanding reader. Roald Dahl allied himself with the child reader in much the same way as Enid Blyton. The books are full of crude, even rude humour, which causes raised adult eyebrows, but guarantees delighted readers.

THE BFG
Windrush, 1988, 288p. – O/P. – L/P. –
1 85089 957 6
Penguin, 1989, 208p. – Pbk. – O/P. –
0 14 050856 2
Cape, 1982, 224p. – 0 224 02040 4
illustrated by Quentin Blake

Sophie befriends the friendly giant and together they plot to put an end to the other bogthumping giants. Excellent on television.
Age range: 9–11

CHARLIE AND THE CHOCOLATE FACTORY
Viking, 1993, 160p. – 0 670 85306 2
Windrush, 1986, 184p. – O/P. – L/P. –
1 85089 902 9
Penguin, 1985, 160p. – Pbk. – 0 14 031824 0
illustrated by Michael Foreman

Charlie's winning ticket enabling him to inspect the chocolate factory leads him into some astonishing situations. Many versions are available, including a play; has been filmed and televised.
Age range: 8–10

CHARLIE AND THE GREAT GLASS ELEVATOR
Viking, 1993, 160p. – 0 670 85305 4
Windrush, 1987, 240p. – O/P. – L/P. –
1 85089 907 X
Penguin, 1986, 160p. – Pbk. – 0 14 032043 1
illustrated by Michael Foreman

The sequel to *Charlie and the Chocolate Factory*. Instead of stopping at the correct place, the elevator goes off into space, where they cope as best they can.
Age range: 8–10

DANNY, THE CHAMPION OF THE WORLD
Windrush, 1989, 276p. – O/P. – L/P. –
1 85089 982 7
Penguin, 1989, 176p. – Pbk. – 0 14 032287 6
Cape, 1975, 208p. – O/P. – 0 224 01201 0
illustrated by Jill Bennett

Danny is unusual, in that, at the age of five, his knowledge of cars is second to none. This knowledge comes in useful when he has to rescue his Dad, who has an accident while out poaching. He earns his title by proving that he is a champion poacher, the equal of his Dad. A film version has been shown on television.
Age range: 9–11

DAHL

ESIO TROT
Penguin, 1991, 64p. – Pbk. – 0 14 034728 3
Chivers Press, 1991, 72p. – O/P. – L/P. –
0 7451 1367 2
Cape, 1990, 64p. – 0 224 02786 7
illustrated by Quentin Blake

Mr Hoppy woos his lady-love by the unlikely means of a tortoise. Amusing as always, with large print and lots of illustrations, this makes an excellent easy reading book.
Age range: 9–10

FANTASTIC MR FOX
Viking, 1993, 96p. – 0 670 85303 8
Windrush, 1989, 96p. – O/P. – L/P. –
1 85089 980 0
Penguin, 1988, 96p. – Pbk. – 0 14 032671 5

Wily Mr Fox manages to outwit the combined brains of three farmers, Boggins, Bunce and Bean, who are determined to put an end to him.
Age range: 7–9

GEORGE'S MARVELLOUS MEDICINE
Windrush, 1989, 152p. – L/P. – 1 85089 985 1
Penguin, 1982, 112p. – Pbk. – 0 14 031492 X
Cape, 1981, 96p. – 0 224 01901 5

George finds his unpleasant Grandma too much to bear, so he concocts a medicine which he hopes will 'cure' her. Also televised.
Age range: 8–11

THE GIRAFFE AND THE PELLY AND ME
Penguin, 1993, 80p. – Pbk. – 0 14 036527 3
Cape, 1992, 80p. – 0 224 03580 0

An unlikely trio set up a window cleaning business, and embark upon some hilarious escapades.
Age range: 6–9

JAMES AND THE GIANT PEACH
Viking, 1993, 144p. – 0 670 85302 X
Penguin, 1990, 144p. – Pbk. – 0 14 034269 9
Windrush, 1988, 144p. – O/P. – L/P. –
1 85089 931 2

James travels the world inside an outsize peach, having fantastic adventures.
Age range: 8–10

MATILDA
Chivers Press, 1989, 320p. – O/P. – L/P. –
0 7451 1044 4
Penguin, 1989, 240p. – Pbk. – O/P. –
0 14 032759 2
Cape, 1988, 192p. – 0 224 02572 4

Matilda is a child prodigy who is not appreciated by her parents. She develops her mental powers to a very high degree, and uses them to defeat her cruel headmistress. Televised, and also a very successful play.
Age range: 8–11

THE TWITS
Windrush, 1990, 112p. – O/P. – L/P. –
1 85089 870 7
Penguin, 1982p, 96p. – Pbk. – 0 14 031406 7
Cape, 1980, 80p. – 0 224 01855 8

An amusing anecdotal story about an unpleasant couple who spend their time playing revolting tricks on each other.
Age range: 7–9

THE VICAR OF NIBBLESWICK
Penguin, 1992, 48p. – Pbk. – 0 14 034891 3
Century Publishing Co., 1991, 24p. –
0 7126 5013 X
illustrated by Quentin Blake

A slight but amusing story written specifically to help the Institute for Dyslexia. Robert Lee overcame his problem as a boy, with help from the Institute, only to find it re-occurring embarrassingly in adulthood, requiring a rather unusual solution.
Age range: 7–10

THE WITCHES
Windrush, 1990, 196p. – L/P. – 1 85089 890 1
Penguin, 1985, 208p. – Pbk. – 0 14 031730 9
Cape, 1983, 192p. – 0 224 02165 6

At last – an explanation for the curious fact that most people have never met a black-cloaked witch accompanied by a broomstick. 'Real' witches look the same as everyone else, at first glance, but once you have learned to recognize them, terrible things can happen. The book has been televised and made into a film.
Age range: 9–11

Other publications:
BOY: TALES OF CHILDHOOD
Penguin, 1986. – Pbk. – 0 14 031890 9
DIRTY BEASTS
Hutchinson, 1993. – 0 09 176541 2
ENORMOUS CROCODILE
Penguin, 1980. – Pbk. – 0 14 050342 0
GOING SOLO
Penguin, 1988. – Pbk. – 0 14 032528 X
MAGIC FINGER
Viking, 1993. – 0 670 85301 1
THE MINPINS
Penguin, 1993. – Pbk. – 0 14 054371 6
MY YEAR
Cape, 1993. – 0 224 03647 5
REVOLTING RHYMES AND DIRTY BEASTS
Hutchinson, 1993. – 0 09 176551 X
RHYME STEW
Penguin, 1990. – Pbk. – 0 14 034365 2
WONDERFUL STORY OF HENRY SUGAR AND SIX MORE
Penguin, 1988. – Pbk. – 0 14 032888 2

DALTON, Annie

British. Born Dorset, educated in Suffolk. Married with three children.

Awards: Lancashire County Library Children's Book of the Year: *Out of the Ordinary*, 1989

Nottingham Library Oak Award: *The Afterdark princess*, 1991

A writer of great talent with a distinctive style. Writing mainly in the fantasy genre, she has the ability to make the reader believe utterly in her characters and settings. Some of her books are written for older teenagers and therefore outside the scope of this book.

THE AFTERDARK PRINCESS
Mammoth, 1992, 99p. – Pbk. – 0 7497 0999 5
Methuen, 1990, 128p. – O/P. – 0 416 15902 8

Using the moon-glasses to reveal the secret 'other' world, Alice persuades the reluctant Joe to embark on an adventure in which he discovers within himself a hitherto unsuspected courage.

Exciting, laced with humour, the plot holds the reader's attention to the very end.
Age range: 10–12

DEMON-SPAWN
Penguin, 1993, 128p. – Pbk. – 0 14 036323 8
Blackie, 1991, 96p. – 0 216 93162 2
illustrated by Jo Worth

Immensely readable and enjoyable, this thriller tells the tense, dramatic story of a quarrel between best friends which turns them into deadly enemies. The demons feed on the ensuing hate-filled climate, threatening to overwhelm everyone with evil. Only the reparation of the quarrel will halt the process – not an easy task.
Age range: 9–11

NIGHT MAZE
Mammoth, 1990, 256p. – Pbk. – 0 7497 0322 9
Methuen, 1989, 175p. – O/P. – 0 416 13532 3

Gerard is rescued from a children's home by relatives whose home is a huge house with a maze. There is an element of fantasy as the secret of the maze is gradually revealed. The characters are easy to identify with and perceptive readers will learn a lot about human nature.
Age range: 12+

THE REAL TILLY BEANY
Chivers Press, 1993, 136p. – 0 7451 1807 0
Mammoth, 1993, 128p. – Pbk. – 0 7497 0983 9
Methuen, 1991, 64p. – 0 416 17252 0

TILLY BEANY AND THE BEST-FRIEND MACHINE
Methuen, 1993, 96p. – 0 416 18799 4
both illustrated by Kate Aldous

Two volumes of stories about a resourceful five-year-old, told in an amusing and accessible manner. Lovely to read aloud, and easy for young readers to tackle.
Age range: 5–7

SWAN SISTER
Methuen, 1992, 128p. – 0 416 17982 7

A story causing readers to hold their breath as it draws to a powerful climax, just in case there is to be no happy ending. Ellen's parents, though loving and caring, are too preoccupied with their own problems to realize what is happening, so Ellen takes it upon herself to save her baby sister from the spell cast by the swans. Discovering whether she is equal to the task provides a moving and compelling read.
Age range: 9–11

THE WITCH ROSE
Mammoth, 1991, 99p. – Pbk. – 0 7497 0454 3
Methuen, 1990, 96p. – O/P. – 0 416 15582 0
illustrated by Kate Aldous

Reality and magic run side by side in this story about family life and the problems of relationships.
Age range: 8–10

Other Publications:

ALPHA BOX
Mammoth, 1992. – Pbk. – 0 7497 1178 7
NAMING THE DARK
Methuen, 1992. – 0 416 18628 9
OUT OF THE ORDINARY
Mammoth, 1989. – Pbk. – 0 7497 0007 6

DANN, Colin (Michael)

British. Born Richmond, Surrey, 1943. Educated Richmond and East Sheen Grammar School. Married Janet Stratton, 1977. Writer.

Awards: Arts Council National Award for Children's Literature: *The Animals of Farthing Wood*, 1980

Address: The Old Forge,
Whatlington,
East Sussex,
England

ANIMALS OF FARTHING WOOD
Heinemann, 1993, 80p. – 0 434 96375 5
Mammoth, 1993. – Pbk. – 0 7497 1355 0
Magna, 1981, 496p. – L/P. – 0 86009 338 7

In the same series:

BATTLE FOR THE PARK
Hutchinson, 1993. – 0 09 176183 2
illustrated by Trevor Newton

FLIGHT FROM FARTHING WOOD
Heinemann, 1988, 32p. – 0 434 93398 8

FOX CUB BOLD
Hutchinson, 1993, 164p. – 0 09 176168 9
Red Fox, 1993, 168p. – Pbk. – 0 09 920531 9
Magna, 1986, 256p. – L/P. – 1 85057 016 7
Magna, 1986, 256p. – Pbk. L/P. – 1 85057 017 5
illustrated by Terry Riley

FOX'S FEUD
Hutchinson, 1993, 164p. – 0 09 176163 8
Red Fox, 1993, 176p. – Pbk. – 0 09 920521 1
Magna, 1985, 271p. – L/P. – 0 86009 690 4

IN THE GRIP OF WINTER
Hutchinson, 1993, 164p. – 0 09 176158 1
Red Fox, 1993, 168p. – Pbk. – 0 09 920511 4
illustrated by Terry Riley

IN THE PATH OF THE STORM
Hutchinson, 1993. – 0 09 176178 6
illustrated by Trevor Newton

SIEGE OF WHITE DEER PARK
Hutchinson, 1993, 156p. – 0 09 176173 5
Red Fox, 1993, 160p. – Pbk. – 0 09 920541 6
Magna, 1987, 252p. – L/P. – 0 86009 983 0
Magna, 1987, 252p. – Pbk. L/P. – 0 86009 984 9

A series of books about the animals living in the threatened Farthing Wood. The first story tells how they decide to find a safer home and describes their perilous journey, depending on each other for help and support. Subsequent books reveal that there is to be no 'happy ever after', for the animals find that they still have to work together to survive. The books reflect Colin Dann's deep concern for conservation issues and his knowledge of wild life. They do require a degree of reading

competence, but any effort is richly rewarded by exciting, tense adventure stories of an unusual kind.
Age range: 10–12

In 1994, Heinemann published a new version of these stories, adapted by Clare Dannatt, and illustrated by Stuart Trotter. This complemented the television series, and made them accessible to younger children unable to cope with the full length novels.
Age range: 7–9

THE BEACH DOGS
Beaver Books, 1989, 144p. – Pbk. – 0 09 961380 8
Hutchinson, 1988, 144p. – O/P. – 0 09 173623 4

Jack belongs to the ferry-man and has to spend each winter marooned on his island home. One year he persuades two friends to take the last ferry with him, but life in hiding is not all fun, and they have some hair-raising adventures. Thoroughly enjoyable, with really attractive covers for both the hardback and paperback editions.
Age range: 9–12

A GREAT ESCAPE
Hutchinson, 1990, 164p. – 0 09 174437 7
Red Fox, 1991, 168p. – Pbk. – 0 09 977150 0

Unable to bear the sight of live animals in the pet shop, Eric opens all the cages and sets them free. Thus the amazing troop of monkeys, rabbits and tortoises, etc., make for their meeting place – the windmill.
Age range: 10–12

JUST NUFFIN
Red Fox, 1990, 248p. – Pbk. – 0 09 966900 5
Hutchinson, 1989, 144p. – 0 09 174092 4

Not a very original plot, but the story is tackled without the usual accompanying sentimentality. Roger is bored on holiday until his father finds an abandoned puppy. He is only allowed to keep it until a home can be found, and so he lives in constant fear of losing his beloved friend. A little overlong, it is nevertheless a good story, well handled.
Age range: 9–12

KING OF THE VAGABONDS
Beaver Books, 1988, 160p. – Pbk. – 0 09 957190 0
Hutchinson, 1987, 128p. – 0 09 171960 7

An unusual story about a curious kitten determined to find out who his father is. Attractively produced.
Age range: 9–12

RAM OF SWEETRIVER
Beaver Books, 1987, 224p. – Pbk. – 0 09 951240 8
Hutchinson, 1986, 160p. – 0 09 165070 4

A graphic description of a devastating flood opens this story, which relates how a flock of sheep, led by a courageous and resourceful ram, struggle to survive.
Age range: 10–12

Other publications:

CITY CATS
Red Fox, 1992. – Pbk. – 0 09 993890 1
LEGACY OF GHOSTS
Red Fox, 1992. – Pbk. – 0 09 986540 8

DANZIGER, Paula

American. Born Washington D.C., 1944. B.A. in English, M.A. in Education for reading with a minor in Urban Education. Lives in New York and London.

Address: C/o Delacorte Press,
1 Dag Hammerskjold Plaza,
245 East 47th Street,
New York,
NY 10017,
USA

Paula Danziger has been one of America's leading writers for many years, so it was good news when she turned her considerable talents to writing for younger children. She has a wonderful sense of humour and an enthusiasm for life which positively shines through her writing.

CAN YOU SUE YOUR PARENTS FOR MALPRACTICE?
Pan Books, 1987, 144p. – Pbk. – 0 330 30019 9
Heinemann, 1986, 134p. – 0 434 96570 7

Being the middle child is traditionally difficult – the youngest is treated as a baby and spoiled, while the oldest is treated as an adult and gets away with murder. Laura feels life is unfair, so she enrols for 'Law for children and young people'. In addition to learning about her rights, she meets Zack, whose sense of humour makes him very appealing.
Age range: 11–13

THE CAT ATE MY GYMSUIT
Pan Books, 1987, 120p. – Pbk. – 0 330 29849 6
Heinemann, 1986, 114p. – 0 434 96577 4

A catchy title for this modern school story about a teacher who is suspended because of her new teaching methods. There are many hilarious asides. Mary, full of ingenious excuses for missing gym, cannot stand the injustice, and takes a stand.
Age range: 11–13

EVERYONE ELSE'S PARENTS SAID YES!
Pan Books, 1990. – Pbk. – 0 330 31476 9

The story centres around the ultimate birthday party which Matthew is planning – junk food and no girls! Extremely funny in parts.
Age range: 11–13

Other publications:

AMBER BROWN IS NOT A CRAYON
Heinemann, 1993. – 0 434 96492 1
DIVORCE EXPRESS
Pan Books, 1987. – Pbk. – 0 330 29657 4
EARTH TO MATTHEW
Piper, 1993. – Pbk. – 0 330 32501 9
IT'S AN AARDVARK-EAT-TURTLE WORLD
Chivers Press, 1989. – 0 7451 0889 X

MAKE LIKE A TREE AND LEAVE
Pan Books, 1992. – Pbk. – 0 330 32225 7
NOT FOR A BILLION GAZILLION DOLLARS
Heinemann, 1992. – 0 434 96216 3
PISTACHIO PRESCRIPTION
Pan Books, 1987. – Pbk. – 0 330 30018 0
REMEMBER ME TO HAROLD SQUARE
Pan Books, 1989. – Pbk. – 0 330 30902 1
THERE'S A BAT IN BUNK FIVE
Pan Books, 1988. – Pbk. – 0 330 30234 5
THIS PLACE HAS NO ATMOSPHERE
Pan Books, 1989. – Pbk. – 0 330 30559 X

DAVIES, Andrew (Wynford)

British. Born Cardiff, Glamorganshire, Wales, 1936. Educated Whitchurch Grammar School, Glamorgan; University College, London. B.A. (Eng). Married Diana Huntley, 1960, one son, one daughter. Teacher and lecturer.

Awards: Guardian Award for Children's Fiction: *Conrad's War*, 1979

Boston Globe-Horn Award: *Conrad's War*, 1980

Address: 21 Station Road, Kenilworth, Warwickshire CV8 1JJ, England

Agent: Harvey Unna and Stephen Durbridge Ltd, 24–32 Pottery Lane, London W11 4LZ, England

CONRAD'S WAR
Blackie, 1989, 128p. – 0 216 92564 9
Chivers Press, 1987, 192p. – L/P. – 0 7451 0489 4
Hippo Books, 1980, 144p. – Pbk. – 0 590 70010 3

War books are not unusual, but there are few for younger readers. Conrad, fascinated by the war, suddenly finds he is taking part, and comes to realize that war at first hand is much less glamorous.
Age range: 9–11

Other publications:

ALFONSO BONZO
Magnet Books, 1987. – Pbk. – O/P. –
0 416 05062 X
DANGER – MARMALADE AT WORK
Thames-Magnet, 1984. – Pbk. – O/P. –
0 423 00840 4
EDUCATING MARMALADE
Blackie, 1988. – O/P. – 0 216 92410 3
FANTASTIC FEATS OF DOCTOR BOOX
Magnet Books, 1987. – Pbk. – O/P. –
0 416 03132 3
MARMALADE ATKINS HITS THE BIG TIME
Thames-Magnet, 1984. – Pbk. – O/P. –
0 423 01200 2
MARMALADE ATKINS IN SPACE
Blackie, 1986. – O/P. – 0 216 91887 1
MARMALADE ATKINS' DREADFUL DEEDS
Blackie, 1988. – O/P. – 0 216 92409 X
MARMALADE HITS THE BIG TIME
Blackie, 1984. – O/P. – 0 216 91697 6
POONAM'S PETS
Little Mammoth, 1992. – Pbk. – 0 7497 0417 9

DAVIES, (Edward) Hunter

British. Born Renfrew, Scotland, 1936. Educated University of Durham. B.A., Dip. Ed. Married the novelist Margaret Forster, two daughters, one son. Columnist and broadcaster.

Address: 11 Boscastle Road,
London NW5,
England

COME ON, OSSIE
Armada Books, 1987, 132p. – Pbk. O/P. –
0 00 672739 5
Bodley Head, 1985, 132p. – O/P. –
0 370 30895 6
illustrated by Malou

In the same series:

OSSIE GOES SUPERSONIC
Armada Books, 1988, 144p. – Pbk. O/P. –
0 00 672894 4
Bodley Head, 1986, 144p. – O/P. –
0 370 31007 1

OSSIE THE MILLIONAIRE
Bodley Head, 1987, 144p. – O/P. –
0 370 31111 6
FLOSSIE TEACAKE AGAIN
Armada Books, 1985, 128p. – Pbk. –
0 00 672384 5
FLOSSIE TEACAKE'S FUR COAT
Red Fox, 1993. – Pbk. – 0 09 996710 3
Bodley Head, 1982, 144p. – O/P. –
0 370 30933 2
FLOSSIE TEACAKE STRIKES BACK
Armada Books, 1986, 128p. – Pbk. –
0 00 672555 4
Bodley Head, 1984, 128p. – O/P. –
0 370 30622 8
illustrated by Lawrence Hutchins

Two series to encourage new readers to tackle full length books. Originality and humour, combined with large clear print, makes them ideal.
Age range: 7–9

SNOTTY BUMSTEAD
Red Fox, 1992, 160p. – Pbk. – 0 09 997710 9
Bodley Head, 1991, 144p. – 0 370 31466 2

SNOTTY BUMSTEAD AND THE RENT-A-MUM
Bodley Head, 1993, 144p. – 0 370 31838 2
both illustrated by Paul Thomas

The 'hero' will be the envy of his young readers because he lives alone – no-one to boss him about. The books are well-written with amusing illustrations and appeal to a wide age-range and ability. They are witty, inventive, and often irreverent.
Age range: 9–12

Other publications:
ICE QUEEN
Penguin, 1989. – Pbk. – O/P. – 0 14 032990 0
LET'S STICK TOGETHER
Penguin, 1990. – Pbk. – O/P. – 0 14 032996 X
PARTY, PARTY
Penguin, 1989. – Pbk. – O/P. – 0 14 032989 7
PLAYING AWAY
Penguin, 1990. – Pbk. – O/P. – 0 14 032995 1
RAPPING WITH RAFFY
Penguin, 1989. – Pbk. – O/P. – 0 14 032987 0

SATURDAY NIGHT
Viking, 1989. – 0 670 82370 8
SHE'S LEAVING HOME
Penguin, 1989. – Pbk. – O/P. – 0 14 032988 9
STARS OF THE SIXTH
Penguin, 1990. – Pbk. – O/P. – 0 14 034564 7
SUMMER DAZE
Penguin, 1990. – Pbk. – O/P. – 0 14 032997 8
WHEN WILL I BE FAMOUS?
Penguin, 1990. – Pbk. – O/P. – 0 14 032991 9
WHO DUNNIT?
Penguin, 1990. – Pbk. – O/P. – 0 14 032992 7

DEJONG, Meindert

American. Born Wierum, Netherlands, 1906; moved to the USA when aged 8. Educated Calvin College, Grand Rapids, Michigan; University of Chicago. US Army Corps, WW II. Married: 1) Hattie Overeinter, 1932; 2) Beatrice de Claire McElwee, 1962 (died 1969). Step-children. Worked as college lecturer and farmer.

Awards: American Library Association Newbery Medal: *The Wheel on the School*, 1955

Hans Christian Andersen International Medal Award, 1962

Catholic library Association Regina Medal, 1972

Address: 351 Grand Street,
Allegan,
Michigan 49010,
USA

A gifted writer whose books are read less than they deserve. The book jackets are plain and unattractive, and do not, therefore, appeal to children, but the stories are excellent.

THE ALMOST ALL-WHITE RABBITY CAT
*Penguin, 1977, 96p. – Pbk. O/P. –
0 14 030674 9
Lutterworth Press, 1972, 136p. – O/P. –
0 7188 1998 5
illustrated by Gioia Fiammenghi*

Barney was heart-broken at leaving his rabbits behind. The new city flat was boring until in walked the cat which changed his life.
Age range: 8–10

ALONG CAME A DOG
*Collins, 1971, 128p. – Pbk. O/P. –
0 00 670478 6
illustrated by Maurice Sendak*

A wonderful story about a black dog who befriends and protects an unpopular hen. When she hatches some chicks, the family is complete.
Age range: 9–11

THE HOUSE OF SIXTY FATHERS
*J. Murray, 1988, 160p. – 0 7195 4510 2
Penguin, 1971. – Pbk. – 0 14 030276 X
illustrated by Maurice Sendak*

Based on a true story, this tense book tells of a small boy, very frightened by the destruction of his village by Japanese soldiers, who becomes separated from his parents. Accompanied by his dog, he begins his search for them, while the dangers surrounding him increase.
Age range: 10–12

HURRY HOME, CANDY
*Armada Books, 1977, 159p. – Pbk. –
0 00 671352 1
Lutterworth Press, 1962. – 0 7188 0452 X
illustrated by Maurice Sendak*

A story in which the first chapter brings a lump to the throat that stays throughout the book. Candy is a stray dog, longing for love which never seems to materialize. It's a relief to reach the end!
Age range: 9–11

JOURNEY FROM PEPPERMINT STREET
*Collins, 1973, 192p. – Pbk. O/P. –
0 00 670748 3
Lutterworth Press, 1969, 242p. – 0 7188 1587 4
illustrated by Emily Arnold McCully*

Set in Holland at the turn of the century, this story has to surmount the

barrier of historical fiction. With the right introduction, many children empathize with the anxious Siebren, who, fed up with looking after his baby brother, is allowed to accompany Grandpa on his visit to his great-aunt. This journey brings many surprises, good and bad. Siebren learns (as does the reader) many lessons about life. The book has a highly satisfying ending.
Age range: 9–11

THE WHEEL ON THE SCHOOL
*Penguin, n.d. – Pbk. – 0 14 030152 6
illustrated by Maurice Sendak*

Although not read very much now, this remains an excellent book in many ways. By puzzling over the absence of storks, a solution is found to the nesting problem. Highly satisfactory for all concerned.
Age range: 10–12

Other publications:

EASTER CAT
Lutterworth Press, 1972. – O/P. – 0 7188 1877 6

GOOD LUCK DUCK
Lutterworth Press, 1974. – O/P. – 0 7188 2140 8

HORSE CAME RUNNING
Lutterworth Press, 1970. – 0 7188 1723 0

PUPPY SUMMER
Hodder, 1980. – Pbk. – O/P. – 0 340 25504 8

SHADRACH
Collins, 1972. – Pbk. – O/P. – 0 00 670556 1

DICKINSON, Peter (Malcolm de Brissac)

British. Born Livingston, Zambia, 1927. Educated Eton College (King's Scholar); King's College, Cambridge, B.A. British Army. Married Mary Rose Barnard 1953 (died 1988), two daughters, two sons. Editor and reviewer.

Awards: Boston Globe/Horn Book Award: *Chance, luck and destiny*, 1977

Guardian Children's Fiction Award: *Blue Hawke*, 1977

Whitbread Award: *Tulku*, 1979

Library Association Carnegie Medals: *Tulku*, 1979

Library Association Carnegie Medals: *City of Gold*, 1980

Whitbread Award: *AK*, 1990

Address: Brendeen Lodge, near Alresford, Hampshire SO24 0JN, England

The books produced for children by this author are quite outstanding. His ability as a story-teller is second to none; add his strong characterization, all constructed by a highly intelligent mind, and the result is some very powerful novels, many for older teenagers. Intelligent children will find them a challenging and absorbing read.

ANNERTON PIT
*Penguin, 1979, 176p. – Pbk. – 0 14 031042 8
Gollancz, 1977, 192p. – 0 575 02239 6*

Twelve-year-old Jake is blind, but compensates for his lack of sight by a highly developed sixth sense. It is this attribute which he and his brother heavily rely on when they set off to find their grandfather whose hobby, ghost-hunting, has landed him in a terrifying dangerous situation. Superbly told through Jake's senses, it is a tense thriller.
Age range: 11–13

BONE FROM A DRY SEA
Gollancz, 1992, 191p. – 0 575 05306 2

The theme of archaeological remains will not have universal appeal, but, given the Peter Dickinson treatment, it becomes an absorbing story. A bone forms a link between two children living many years apart, but each heralds a change of monumental importance.
Age range: 11–13

DICKINSON

A BOX OF NOTHING
Chivers Press, 1987, 208p. – O/P. – L/P. –
0 7451 0547 5
Magnet Books, 1987, 128p. – Pbk. –
0 416 96630 6
Gollancz, 1985, 144p. – 0 575 03530 7
illustrated by Ian Newsham

An unusual adventure story set in motion by the purchase of a box of nothing for the princely sum of nothing from nowhere else but the Nothing Shop. Children too young or too reluctant to be able to tackle the fairly dense text and small print will nevertheless enjoy having it read to them.
Age range: 9–12

THE DEVIL'S CHILDREN
Penguin, 1972, 160p. – Pbk. – 0 14 030546 7

In the same series:

HEARTSEASE
Penguin, 1971, 192p. – Pbk. – 0 14 030498 3
Gollancz, 1969, 192p. – 0 575 00223 9

THE WEATHERMONGER
Gollancz, 1984, 144p. – 0 575 03475 0
Penguin, 1970, 176p. – Pbk. O/P. –
0 14 030433 9

Now published by Penguin in a single volume (1985, 348p. – O/P. – 0 14 031846 1) this trilogy is one of the most memorable works of fiction ever produced for children. Successive generations are captivated by the horrifying portrait of a future England in which people have rejected machines, but whose lives have been reduced to hardship and fear. Nicky is convinced that somewhere a machine has been resurrected. Absorbing, right to the final, optimistic chapter of the third book.
Age range: 12–14

THE GIFT
Penguin, 1975, 176p. – Pbk. – 0 14 030731 1
Gollancz, 1973, 176p. – 0 575 01630 2
illustrated by Gareth Floyd

Davy's life is not exactly wonderful, in spite of his ability to see beyond the face into what people are thinking and feeling. It can be just a nuisance, and sometimes, downright dangerous. His Granny always warned him not to make use of the things he learned this way, but the day comes when he has a terrible choice to make. A nail-biting television serial made this book accessible to lots of children who would not otherwise have felt able to tackle it.
Age range: 11–13

TIME AND THE CLOCK MICE ETCETERA
Delacorte Press, 1994. – 0 385 32038 8
illustrated by Emma Chichester-Clark

Two major figures in children's literature have combined their talents to produce a work of outstanding quality. The story of the Hickorys, Dickorys and Docks, generations of mice who have inhabited Branton's Town Hall Clock is inventive, exciting, often very funny, and has a superb ending. The illustrations are plentiful and colourful, adding a dimension of their own.
Age range: 8–10

Other publications:

AK
Corgi, 1992. – Pbk. – 0 552 52719 X
BLUE HAWK
Gollancz, 1985. – 0 575 03649 4
DANCING BEAR
Gollancz, 1985. – 0 575 03650 8
EMMA TUPPER'S DIARY
Penguin, 1973. – Pbk. – O/P. – 0 14 030591 2
EVA
Corgi, 1991. – Pbk. – 0 552 52609 6
GIANT COLD
Gollancz, 1983. – 0 575 03185 9
HEALER
Penguin, 1986. – Pbk. – O/P. – 0 14 031746 5
MERLIN DREAMS
Gollancz, 1988. – 0 575 03962 0
MOLE HOLE
Blackie, 1987. – O/P. – 0 216 91470 1
SEVENTH RAVEN
Penguin, 1989. – Pbk. – 0 14 032667 7
TULKU
Penguin, 1988. – Pbk. – O/P. – 0 14 032514 X

DICKS, Terrance

British. Born London, 1935. Educated East Ham Grammar School; Downing College, Cambridge. Now lives in Hampstead.

A prolific writer capable of producing imaginative stories with great appeal to children. Full of action and easy to read, they are suitable for reluctant readers.

ASK OLIVER
Hodder
Piccadilly Press, Pbk.
illustrated by Valerie Littlewood

Mystery stories aimed at younger children. Oliver and his gang are good at solving mysteries. The reader is given clues, and can try to solve them first. Enjoyable and fun, they encourage new readers to gain confidence.
Age range: 7–9

BAKER STREET IRREGULARS
Blackie
Magnet Books, Pbk.

A series of modern Sherlock Holmes detective stories in which children solve mysteries using the same methods as their hero. Characterization is weak, but the plots are sound.
Age range: 10–12

A CAT CALLED MAX
Piccadilly Press
Piccadilly Press, Pbk.
illustrated by Toni Goffe

Max is no ordinary cat: although he has no home he is well-mannered and exudes a magical aura. An interesting and amusing story, doubtless with more to follow.
Age range: 6–8

DAVID AND GOLIATH
Hodder
Piccadilly Press, Pbk.
illustrated by Valerie Littlewood

Goliath is a huge, happy dog. Together, he and David embark on a series of adventures providing amusing yet short reads for beginners.
Age range: 6–8

THE MACMAGICS
Piccadilly Press, 1991, 64p. – 1 85340 155 2
Piccadilly Press, 1990, 96p. – 1 85340 080 7

In the same series:

MEET THE MACMAGICS
Piccadilly Press, 1990, 96p. – 1 85340 070 X
illustrated by Celia Canning

Mike, trying hard to be a normal, boring schoolboy, is constantly embarrassed by his family displaying their various magical powers. Funny, easy to read, with plenty of illustrations.
Age range: 7–9

T. R. BEAR
Piccadilly Press
Corgi, Pbk.
illustrated by Susan Hellard

Jimmy and his Teddy have many little adventures, amusingly told in large print. Ideal for first time readers.
Age range: 6–8

Other publications:

ADVENTURES OF BUSTER AND BETSY
Piccadilly Press, 1988. – 1 8534 0013 0
Piccadilly Press, 1988. – 1 8534 0001 7
Piccadilly Press, 1989. – 1 8534 0048 3
BIG MATCH
Piccadilly Press, 1991. – 1 8534 0175 7
CAMDEN STREET KIDS ON TV
Piccadilly Press, 1986. – 0 946826 44 7
CAMDEN STREET KIDS: BY THE SEA
Piccadilly Press, 1987. – O/P. – 0 946826 68 4
CAMDEN STREET KIDS: IN THE MONEY
Piccadilly Press, 1986. – 0 946826 33 1
CAMDEN STREET KIDS: SCHOOL FAIR
Piccadilly Press, 1987. – 0 946826 87 0
CINEMA SWINDLE
Blackie, 1986. – O/P. – 0 216 91889 8
COMIC CROOKS
Blackie, 1986. – O/P. – 0 216 91942 8
CRIMINAL COMPUTER
Blackie, 1987. – O/P. – 0 216 92310 7
CRY VAMPIRE!
Hippo Books, 1985. – Pbk. – 0 590 70405 2

CUB SCOUTS
Piccadilly Press, 1989. – 1 8534 0063 7
DEMON OF THE DARK
Blackie, 1983. – O/P. – 0 216 91360 8
DISAPPEARING DIPLOMAT
Blackie, 1986. – O/P. – 0 216 91895 2
EUROPE UNITED
Piccadilly Press, 1991. – 1 8534 0141 2
GEORGE AND THE DRAGON
Blackie, 1991. – 0 216 93116 9
GHOSTS OF GALLOWS CROSS
Blackie, 1984. – O/P. – 0 216 91643 7
GREAT MARCH WEST
Tandem, 1976. – Pbk. – O/P. – 0 426 11092 7
HAUNTED HOLIDAY
Blackie, 1987. – O/P. – 0 216 92101 5
JONATHAN AND THE SUPERSTAR
Red Fox, 1992. – Pbk. – 0 09 995120 7
JONATHAN'S GHOST
Red Fox, 1990. – Pbk. – 0 09 968730 5
KNIGHTSCHOOL
Hodder, 1992. – Pbk. – 0 340 56243 9
LITTLEST DINOSAUR
H. Hamilton, 1993. – 0 241 13382 3
LOST PROPERTY
Blackie, 1990. – 0 216 92926 1
MARVIN'S MONSTER
Blackie, 1982. – O/P. – 0 216 91179 6
MISSING MASTERPIECE
Blackie, 1986. – O/P. – 0 216 91888 X
SALLY ANN AT THE BALLET
Hippo Books, 1990. – Pbk. – 0 590 76351 2
SALLY ANN GOES TO HOSPITAL
Hippo Books, 1990. – Pbk. – 0 590 76191 9
SALLY ANN'S SCHOOL PLAY
Hippo Books, 1989. – Pbk. – 0 590 76165 X
SALLY ANN – ON HER OWN
Hippo Books, 1989. – 0 590 76062 9
SALLY ANN – THE PICNIC
Hippo Books, 1990. – Pbk. – 0 590 76190 0
SALLY ANN – THE PONY
Hippo Books, 1991. – Pbk. – 0 590 76515 9
SCHOOL SPIRIT
Red Fox, 1991. – Pbk. – 0 09 974620 4
SPITFIRE SUMMER
Red Fox, 1991. – Pbk. – O/P. – 0 09 968850 6
SPORTS DAY
Piccadilly Press, 1989. – 1 8534 0041 6
STEAMING SAM
Blackie, 1992. – 0 216 93299 8
STELLA'S WEDDING
Piccadilly Press, 1990. – 1 8534 0098 X

TEACHER'S PET
Piccadilly Press, 1990. – 1 8534 0099 8
WAR OF THE WITCHES
Blackie, 1983. – O/P. – 0 216 91471 X
WEREBOY!
Blackie, 1982. – O/P. – 0 216 91308 X
WHAT'S GOING ON, WILLIAM?
Piccadilly Press, 1991. – 1 8534 0135 8

DOHERTY, Berlie

British. Born Liverpool, 1943. Educated Durham University, County Durham, B.A. (Hons) English; Liverpool University, Post-Graduate Certificate in Social Sciences; Sheffield University, Post-Graduate Certificate in Education. Married Gerard Adrian Doherty, 1966, two daughters and one son. Social worker and teacher.

Awards: Library Association Carnegie Medal: *Granny was a Buffer Girl*, 1986

Library Association Carnegie Medal: *Dear Nobody*, 1991

A writer with an outstanding ability to create vivid pictures in words, as well as absorbing stories.

CHILDREN OF WINTER
Armada Books, 1986, 128p. – Pbk. –
0 00 672583 X
Methuen, 1985, 128p. – O/P. – 0 416 51130 9

Three children are sent away by their parents to live in safety in a cave when their village is struck by the plague. There is humour, suspense and sensitivity in every page. An excellent television drama.
Age range: 9–12

GRANNY WAS A BUFFER GIRL
Chivers Press, 1988, 232p. – L/P. –
0 7451 0725 7
Armada Books, 1988, 128p. – Pbk. –
0 00 672792 1
Methuen, 1986, 128p. – 0 416 53590 9

An unusual framework illustrates how Jess's life is interwoven with her

Granny. It is a love story, an historical novel describing a life of industrial toil, a story of growing up, and is completely compelling.
Age range: 12–14

HOW GREEN YOU ARE
Mammoth, 1992, 144p. – Pbk. – 0 7497 1047 0
Armada Books, 1983, 144p. – Pbk. – 0 00 672210 5
illustrated by Eunice McGregor Turney

In the same series:

THE MAKING OF FINGERS FINNIGAN
Armada Books, 1985, 144p. – Pbk. – 0 00 672340 3
Methuen, 1983, 128p. – O/P. – 0 416 23610 3
illustrated by John Hayson

Stories about a group of children who live in the same street. Everyday happenings vividly described with laughter, sadness and, sometimes, a serious tone combine to provide highly enjoyable reads.
Age range: 9–11

SPELLHORN
Collins, 1990, 192p. – Pbk. – 0 00 673500 2
Hamish Hamilton, 1989, 160p. – 0 241 12624 X

A fantasy firmly based on experience and reality. Laura is blind, and therefore 'sees' the world through her hands and ears, which is how she finds the lost unicorn. The story of her life with the unicorn and his people is utterly compelling.
Age range: 9–14

STREET CHILD
H. Hamilton, 1993, 128p. – 0 241 13058 1

Jim is just one of many orphans who have to live as best they can on the streets of London. It is lonely and dangerous until the day he meets Dr. Barnardo, who is so moved by Jim's plight that he conceives the idea of setting up a refuge for children.
Age range: 11–13

TILLY MINT TALES
Armada Books, 1986, 96p. – Pbk. – 0 00 672557 0
Methuen, 1984, 96p. – 0 416 48220 1
illustrated by Thelma Lambert

In the same series:

TILLY MINT AND THE DODO
Collins, 1989, 112p. – Pbk. – 0 00 673250 X
Methuen, 1988, 128p. – 0 416 04622 3

When Tilly's babysitter, Mrs Hardcastle, falls asleep, it is a signal for the magic to begin for Tilly. Fantasy stories, excellent for reading aloud.
Age range: 7–9

WHITE PEAK FARM
Armada Books, 1986, 112p. – Pbk. – 0 00 672431 0
Methuen, 1984, 112p. – 0 416 47020 3

Describing life on a remote Derbyshire farm, this can be read as one long story, or as individual stories as they were when treated on television and radio. There is something for everyone from the age of 12 to adults, dealing with life and death issues.
Age range: 12–15

Other publications:

DEAR NOBODY
Lions, 1993. – Pbk. – 0 00 674618 7
PADDIWAK AND COSY
Mammoth, 1990. – Pbk. – 0 7497 0299 0
SNOWY
Picture Lions, 1993. – Pbk. – 0 00 664297 7
TOUGH LUCK
Collins, 1989. – Pbk. – O/P. – 0 00 673219 4
WALKING ON AIR
Lions, 1993. – Pbk. – 0 00 674442 7

E

EDWARDS, Dorothy (née Brown)

British. Born Teddington, Middlesex, 1914 (died 9 August 1982). Educated Teddington and Sunbury. Married Francis P. Edwards, 1942, one daughter, one son. Worked as secretary, freelance editor, radio producer, lecturer and broadcaster.

Awards: Children's Rights Workshop Other Award: *A Strong and Willing Girl*, 1981

The mention of Dorothy Edwards's name immediately brings to mind the My naughty little sister stories, which, after 30 years, still claim a place on nursery bookshelves, in spite of being a little old-fashioned now. She is a competent storyteller, and her books are well worth reading.

KING DICKY BIRD AND THE BOSSY PRINCESS
Magnet Books, 1988, 64p. – Pbk. – 0 416 07502 9
Methuen, 1987, 60p. – 0 416 96100 2

A modern, humorous fairy tale about a princess who marries a most unusual beggar.
Age range: 7–9

THE MAGICIAN WHO KEPT A PUB AND OTHER STORIES
Armada Books, 1981, 160p. – Pbk. – 0 00 671785 3
Kestrel Books, 1975, 128p. – O/P. – 0 7226 5452 9
illustrated by Jill Bennett

In the same series:

MARK THE DRUMMER BOY
Magnet Books, 1986, 96p. – Pbk. O/P. – 0 416 61860 X
Methuen, 1983, 96p. – 0 416 26130 2
illustrated by Thelma Lambert

THE OLD MAN WHO SNEEZED: READ ALOUD STORIES
Mammoth, 1992, 50p. – Pbk. – 0 7497 0929 4
Methuen, 1983, 96p. – O/P. – 0 416 26120 5
illustrated by Thelma Lambert

Books of short stories, excellent for reading aloud, of the sort which Dorothy Edwards excels in writing. They are extremely varied, and appeal to both boys and girls.
Age range: 5–7

MISTS AND MAGIC
Armada Books, 1985, 160p. – Pbk. O/P. – 0 00 672357 8
Lutterworth Press, 1983, 160p. – 0 7188 2537 3
illustrated by Jill Bennett

An excellent and wide-ranging collection of stories and poems chosen and edited by Dorothy Edwards. Equally effective, whether read aloud or silently.
Age range: 9–11

A STRONG AND WILLING GIRL
Mammoth, 1993, 112p. – Pbk. – 0 7497 1230 9
Methuen, 1980, 128p. – 0 416 88630 2

The story of a young girl in service, the Victorian age is revealed on every page. Entertaining to read as well as instructive in period detail.
Age range: 12–14

Other publications:

ALL ABOUT 'MY NAUGHTY LITTLE SISTER'
Dean, 1992. – 0 603 55032 0

CRASH!
Hippo Books, 1980. – Pbk. – O/P. – 0 590 70015 4

DAD'S NEW CAR
Methuen, 1976. – O/P. – 0 416 84310 7

EMMIE AND THE PURPLE PAINT
Magnet Books, 1986. – Pbk. – O/P. – 0 416 52080 4

GHOSTS AND SHADOWS
Armada Books, 1981. – Pbk. – O/P. – 0 00 671950 3

HERE'S SAM
Mammoth, 1992. – Pbk. – 0 7497 1035 7

JOE AND TIMOTHY TOGETHER
Magnet Books, 1984. – Pbk. – O/P. – 0 416 21970 5

MORE NAUGHTY LITTLE SISTER STORIES
Mammoth, 1989. – Pbk. – 0 7497 0053 X

MY NAUGHTY LITTLE SISTER AND BAD HARRY'S RABBIT
Mammoth, 1989. – Pbk. – 0 7497 0122 6

MY NAUGHTY LITTLE SISTER AND BAD HARRY
Mammoth, 1990. – Pbk. – 0 7497 0240 0

MY NAUGHTY LITTLE SISTER AND FATHER CHRISTMAS
Little Mammoth, 1989. – Pbk. – 0 7497 0046 7

MY NAUGHTY LITTLE SISTER AT THE FAIR
Little Mammoth, 1989. – Pbk. – 0 7497 0123 4

MY NAUGHTY LITTLE SISTER BIRTHDAY BOOK
Methuen, 1982. – O/P. – 0 416 25450 0

MY NAUGHTY LITTLE SISTER OMNIBUS
Mammoth, 1990. – Pbk. – 0 7497 0701 1

MY NAUGHTY LITTLE SISTER STORYBOOK
Little Mammoth, 1992. – Pbk. – 0 7497 1304 6

MY NAUGHTY LITTLE SISTER'S FRIENDS
Mammoth, 1990. – Pbk. – 0 7497 0237 0

MY NAUGHTY LITTLE SISTER
Mammoth, 1989. – Pbk. – 0 7497 0054 8

ROBERT GOES TO FETCH A SISTER
Methuen, 1986. – O/P. – 0 416 95770 6

TALES OF JOE AND TIMOTHY
Mammoth, 1991. – Pbk. – 0 7497 0577 9

WALK YOUR FINGERS STORY
Methuen, 1976. – O/P. – 0 416 79260 X

WET MONDAY
Methuen, 1975. – O/P. – 0 416 83470 1

WHEN MY NAUGHTY LITTLE SISTER WAS GOOD
Little Mammoth, 1989. – Pbk. – 0 7497 0055 6

WITCHES AND THE GRINNYGOG
Faber, 1981. – O/P. – 0 571 11720 1

F

FARJEON, Eleanor

Also wrote as 'Tomfool'. British. Born London, 1881 (died 5 June 1965). Daughter of novelist Benjamin Leopold Farjeon; sister of the writers Herbert and Joseph Jefferson Farjeon and the composer Harry Farjeon. Educated privately. Columnist, poet, writer.

Awards: Library Association Carnegie Medal: *The Little Bookroom*, 1955

Hans Andersen International Medal, 1956

Catholic Library Association Regina Medal, 1959

Eleanor Farjeon wrote many books for children, for which she received an award. They are now generally considered to be out of date, but it is good that these books, aptly illustrated by Edward Ardizzone, still find a place on the bookshelves.

JIM AT THE CORNER
Magnet Books, 1986, 128p. – Pbk. – O/P. – 0 416 63710 8
J. Goodchild, 1986, 104p. – 0 86391 077 7
illustrated by Edward Ardizzone

Jim was a retired sailor who had lots of stories to tell. Excellent for reading aloud, and, though first published in 1958, they are enjoyed by succeeding generations.
Age range: 6–8

THE LITTLE BOOKROOM
Penguin, 1992, 288p. – Pbk. – 0 14 035136 1
OUP, 1979, 314p. – O/P. – 0 19 277099 3
illustrated by Edward Ardizzone

A collection of stories for older children. They are varied in length and subject, with something for everyone. Magic, fairies, tales of bygone childhood – quite spellbinding.
Age range: 7–9

THE OLD NURSE'S STOCKING BASKET
Penguin, 1981, 80p. – Pbk. O/P. – 0 14 031220 X
OUP, 1980, 108p. – O/P. – 0 19 277093 4
illustrated by Edward Ardizzone

Although first published in 1931, this book is still re-issued because it has a timeless quality that ensures it can be passed from one generation to another. There are 13 short stories for reading aloud, varied in content, but uniformly rich in the poetic use of language, making them a delight to listen to. *Age range:* 3–7

Other publications:

CATS SLEEP ANYWHERE
Orchard Books, 1992. – 1 8521 3372 4

GLASS SLIPPER
J. Goodchild, 1983. – 0 903445 82 4

KALEIDOSCOPE
J. Goodchild, 1986. – 0 86391 078 5

LITTLE DRESSMAKER
Walker Books, 1990. – Pbk. – 0 7445 1443 6

SILVER CURLEW
J. Goodchild, 1984. – 0 86391 012 2

SOMETHING I REMEMBER
Penguin, 1989. – Pbk. – 0 14 032638 3

FARMER, Penelope

British. Born Westerham, Kent, 1939. Educated privately, 1945–1956; St. Anne's College, Oxford, 1957–1960, B.A. (Hons) in History; Bedford College, University of London, Diploma in Social Studies, 1962. Married Michael John Mockridge, 1962 (divorced 1977), one daughter, one son. Teacher and writer.

Address: 39 Mount Ararat Road,
Richmond,
Surrey,
England
Agent: Deborah Owen,
78 Narrow Street,
London E14 8BP,
England

An author whose books have stood the test of time, being enjoyed by and relevant to children today. Belonging to the fantasy genre, she writes with an originality which skilfully combines elements of mythology with modern real-life children with whom the readers can easily identify.

A CASTLE OF BONE
Penguin, 1992, 176p. – Pbk. – 0 14 036064 6
Bodley Head, 1992, 156p. – 0 370 31742 4

Hugh's fierce desire to own the cupboard in the junk shop surprises everyone, including himself. It proves to be the catalyst which changes his life, affects his friends, and leaves the reader with the ability to see the world with a fresh perception, having enjoyed a good laugh en route.
Age range: 10–12

CHARLOTTE SOMETIMES
Penguin, 1993. – Pbk. – 0 14 036084 0

Charlotte is herself only some of the time; the rest of the time, she is Clare, living 40 years earlier, and Clare moves forward in time into Charlotte's place. They communicate by letter until they each become stuck in the other's time, causing untold problems for both. Clever interweaving of period detail.
Age range: 10–12

STONE CROC
Walker Books, 1992, 96p. – Pbk. –
0 7445 2070 3
Walker Books, 1991. – 0 7445 2108 4
illustrated by Robert Bartlett

An imaginative and amusing story about a stone crocodile which comes to life and decides to live with Alice, Meera and Mac. The story is told in such a matter-of-fact way that the impossible becomes readily acceptable. Very easy to read.
Age range: 7–9

Other publications:
RUNAWAY TRAIN
Heinemann, 1980. – O/P. – 0 434 94938 8
SATURDAY BY SEVEN
Walker Books, 1991. – Pbk. – 0 7445 2075 4
THE SEAGULL
Pan Books, 1980. – Pbk. – O/P. –
0 330 26003 0
SUMMER BIRDS
Chivers Press, 1990. – O/P. – 0 7451 1066 5
THICKER THAN WATER
Walker Books, 1991. – Pbk. – 0 7445 1366 9
YEAR KING
Bodley Head, 1984. – Pbk. – O/P. –
0 370 30818 2

FAVILLE, Barry

New Zealander. Born Hamilton, 1939. Educated Waihi College, Auckland University. Married, three children. Teacher, scriptwriter, producer, writer.

Address: c/o OUP (New Zealand),
PO Box 11–149,
Ellerslie,
Auckland 5,
New Zealand
Awards: New Zealand Children's Story Book of the Year Award: *The Keeper*, 1987

A writer who has produced some quite outstanding and original novels. Writing in a deceptively simple, easy style, he makes some profound observations on human nature, while telling an excellent story.

THE KEEPER
OUP, 1988, 160p. – O/P. – 0 19 558146 6

A dramatic story of life in post-nuclear New Zealand. Michael finds a book belonging to the time before the

bombs, and appoints himself its keeper. In it, he records his own and crippled Jean's story, which is explained for the benefit of the reader by secret notes from his teacher. Outside influences, such as the live volcano and the man-eating tiger, pale into insignificance beside the threat of destruction from the hidden cache of guns. Thought-provoking.
Age range: 12+

THE RETURN
Penguin, 1989, 168p. – Pbk. – O/P. – 0 14 032830 0
OUP, 1989, 163p. – O/P. – 0 19 558166 0

The atmosphere and mounting tension of the story ensures it will be read avidly from cover to cover. When Karl Smith moves into a rented house in Wilkes Beach with his mother, the other residents are mildly curious, with the exception of Jonathan. He gradually realises the significance of Karl's white-blond hair, his intense scrutiny, and the strangeness of his speech. The story builds to an exciting climax.
Age range: 11–13

STANLEY'S AQUARIUM
OUP, 1990, 152p. – 0 19 558197 0

A chilling story which begins innocently when Robbie lands a weekend job gardening for Stanley, who does seem a bit odd. As Robbie gradually discovers more about him and his past, she begins to feel distinctly out of her depth.
Age range: 12+

FINE, Anne

British. Born Leicester, 1947. Educated Northampton High School for Girls; University of Warwick, B.A. (Hons) history and politics. Married Kit Fine, 1968, two daughters. Teacher and information officer.

Awards: Scottish Arts Council Award, 1986
Guardian Children's Fiction Award: *Bill's New Frock*, 1989
Smarties Award: *Bill's New Frock*, 1989
Library Association Carnegie Medal: *Goggle-Eyes*, 1989
Guardian Children's Fiction Award: *Goggle-Eyes*, 1990
Oak Award: *Bill's New Frock*, 1990
Library Association Carnegie Medal: *Flour Babies*, 1992
Whitbread Literary Award: *Flour Babies*, 1993

Address: 7 Gray Lane,
Barnard Castle,
Co. Durham DL12 8PD,
England

Agent: Murray Pollinger,
4 Garrick Street,
London WC2E 9BH,
England

A writer of great originality, Anne Fine's books are a true delight to read. She has an extraordinary ability to pitch them at just the right level and she can put across a serious point while at the same time making a joke of it. Every story skilfully combines humour with a deep understanding of the situation portrayed in a straightforward manner.

ANNELI THE ART-HATER
Mammoth, 1991, 112p. – Pbk. – 0 7497 0597 3
Methuen, 1986, 128p. – O/P. – 0 416 61550 3
illustrated by Vanessa Julian-Ottie

Art is Anneli's most hated subject at school, but one day she finds an old oil painting which makes her see things very differently. A good read.
Age range: 8–10

BILL'S NEW FROCK
Mammoth, 1990, 96p. – Pbk. – 0 7497 0305 9
Methuen, 1989, 96p. – 0 416 12152 7
illustrated by Philippe Dupasquier

Bill wakes up one morning to find he is a girl, but only he seems to notice that there has been a change. Everyone acts as if he has always been a girl. This dilemma is skilfully maintained to the very end, causing many hilarious situations.
Age range: 8–10

THE CHICKEN GAVE IT TO ME
*Methuen, 1992, 96p. – 0 416 18627 0
illustrated by Philippe Dupasquier*

This book is best described as 'a little gem'. Original, and extremely funny, it tells the moving story of an intrepid chicken (reminiscent of Dick King-Smith's fox-busting hens) rescuing the human race from an invasion by little green men.
Age range: 7–9

THE COUNTRY PANCAKE
*Mammoth, 1991, 96p. – Pbk. – 0 7497 0567 1
Methuen, 1989, 96p. – 0 416 14982 0
illustrated by Philippe Dupasquier*

Intended for younger readers, this delightful story will amuse and interest children to the last page. Easy to read.
Age range: 7–9

CRUMMY MUMMY AND ME
*Penguin, 1989, 112p. – Pbk. – 0 14 032876 9
Deutsch, 1988, 96p. – 0 233 98059 8
illustrated by David Higham*

Poor Minna has a difficult time trying to behave sensibly when her 'punk' Mum behaves so outrageously. All she wants is a 'normal' Mum like her friends. Excellent light entertainment.
Age range: 9–11

FLOUR BABIES
*H. Hamilton, 1993, 160p. – Pbk. –
0 241 00224 9
H. Hamilton, 1992, 144p. – O/P. –
0 241 13252 5*

Simon is horrified and exasperated when Mr Cartwright explains the project he has chosen for the class. Each pupil has a bag of white flour which they must look after as though it were their child, keeping it safe. Worst of all, they have to keep a diary recording all occurrences. Not only does Simon learn about responsibility, the project also gives him a measure of understanding as to why his own father had felt unable to stay and look after him and his mother. Entertaining and educational.
Age range: 11–13

GOGGLE-EYES
*Penguin, 1993, 144p. – Pbk. – 0 14 036512 5
Chivers Press, 1991, 232p. – O/P. –
0 7451 1369 9*

Divorce is the subject of many books designed to help children come to terms with events in their own life, but good books which deal specifically with a prospective re-marriage and the problems it can cause are less easy to find. Here is one of the best. The story is told by Kitty, the elder daughter, and it realistically portrays the emotional and practical problems that arise when an unwelcome 'outsider' becomes part of the family. The conclusion and the warmth and humour of the telling make this a delightful and useful book to read.
Age range: 11–14

THE GRANNY PROJECT
*Mammoth, 1990, 128p. – Pbk. – 0 7497 0186 2
Collins, 1986, 80p. – Pbk. – 0 00 330234 2
Methuen, 1983, 160p. – O/P. – 0 416 44400 8*

A moving but unsentimental look at a problem facing many families today – what to do for old people who can no longer care for themselves. The children want to keep Granny at home; the parents want to put her in a home. The ensuing battle makes highly entertaining reading.
Age range: 10–12

MADAME DOUBTFIRE
*Chivers Press, 1990, 272p. – L/P. –
0 7451 1228 5
Penguin, 1989, 192p. – Pbk. – 0 14 032633 2
Hamish Hamilton, 1987, 176p. – 0 241 12001 2*

A gem among children's books, this novel shows how the troubles of divorce can be overcome, given the will and a sense of humour. The children's father, out of work, appears incognito for the job of cleaning lady to his ex-wife. It works well at first, but then the inevitable complications set in. This sensitive yet funny story will appeal to everyone, but speaks particularly meaningfully to young people who have experienced divorce.
Age range: 10–12

A PACK OF LIARS
Penguin, 1990, 128p. – 0 14 032954 4
Hamish Hamilton, 1988, 128p. – 0 241 12229 5

A common dilemma – telling lies is wrong, but sometimes expediency makes them necessary. Oliver is unable to resolve this dilemma which eventually leads him into an exciting adventure, related with much humour.
Age range: 10–12

ROUND BEHIND THE ICE-HOUSE
Penguin, 1990, 112p. – Pbk. – 0 14 034067 X
Methuen, 1981, 112p. – O/P. – 0 416 20820 7

This book can be read on two levels. There is the storyline, with the twins pitting themselves against Jamieson and his cruelty. Underlying this is the story of the twins, once so close, now approaching adolescence and painfully growing apart. An exceptionally well written, sensitive story.
Age range: 12–14

THE STONE MENAGERIE
Mammoth, 1991, 128p. – Pbk. – 0 7497 0343 1
Methuen, 1980, 128p. – O/P. – 0 416 88640 X

Unusually set in a mental hospital, this moving story tells how Ally comes to understand the acrimonious relationship he has with his parents. Characteristically full of humour and sadness, this book lives in the memory.
Age range: 12–14

A SUDDEN GLOW OF GOLD
Mammoth, 1992, 64p. – Pbk. – 0 7497 0256 7
Piccadilly Press, 1991, 64p. – 1 8534 0088 2

In the same series:

A SUDDEN PUFF OF GLITTERING SMOKE
Mammoth, 1991, 64p. – Pbk. – 0 7497 0254 0
Piccadilly Press, 1989, 64p. – 1 8534 0046 7

A SUDDEN SWIRL OF ICY WIND
Mammoth, 1991, 64p. – Pbk. – 0 7497 0255 9
Piccadilly Press, 1990, 96p. – 1 8534 0079 3
all illustrated by David Higham

A trilogy of short novels about an unusual genie with a gift for telling stories. Entertaining, easy reads.
Age range: 7–9

Other publications:
ANGEL OF NITSHILL ROAD
Mammoth, 1993. – Pbk. – 0 7497 0974 X
BOOK OF THE BANSHEE
Penguin, 1993. – Pbk. – 0 14 034704 6
DESIGN A PRAM
Heinemann, 1991. – 0 434 97672 5
HAUNTING OF PIP PARKER
Walker Books, 1992. – 0 7445 2436 9
OTHER DARKER NED
Mammoth, 1992. – Pbk. – 0 7497 0185 4
POOR MONTY
Methuen, 1992. – 0 416 17332 2
SCAREDY CAT
Mammoth, 1993. – Pbk. – 0 7497 1632 0
STRANGER DANGER
Penguin, 1991. – Pbk. – 0 14 034302 4
SUMMER HOUSE LOON
Mammoth, 1990. – Pbk. – 0 7497 0184 6

FISK, Nicholas

Pseudonym for David Higginbottom. British. Born London, 1923. Educated Ardingly College, Sussex. RAF WW II. Married Dorothy Antoinette Richold, 1949, twin daughters, two sons. Actor, journalist, musician, editor and publisher, former advertising creative director and consultant.

Awards: Smarties' Prize: *Midnight Blue*, 1990
Address: 59 Elstree Road, Bushey Heath, Hertfordshire WD2 3QX, England
Agent: Laura Cecil, 17 Alwyne Villas, London N1 2HG, England

Often underestimated, perhaps because he is such a prolific writer, Nicholas Fisk has written some really excellent novels. He writes in a chatty style which makes his books readily accessible to all children. The plots are both exciting and thought-provoking, and can make a real contribution to the maturing process which so many children find difficult.

ANTIGRAV
Penguin, 1982, 128p. – Pbk. O/P. – 0 14 031416 4
Kestrel Books, 1978, 128p. – O/P. – 0 7226 5322 0

The classic dilemma of good versus bad, with the outcome dependent on the integrity of three children, who find an apparently harmless red pebble on the beach. It quickly becomes obvious that it is an extra-special pebble which, in the wrong hands, would have evil consequences. Exciting and easy to read.
Age range: 8–11

BACKLASH
Walker Books, 1991, 144p. – Pbk. – 0 7445 1331 6
Walker Books, 1988, 144p. – 0 7445 0808 8

Three children, marooned on an alien planet, are captured by an unpleasant robot. Their escape makes absorbing reading for science fiction enthusiasts.
Age range: 10–12

BROOPS! DOWN THE CHIMNEY
Walker Books, 1992, 96p. – Pbk. – 0 7445 2370 2
Walker Books, 1991. – 0 7445 2121 1
illustrated by Russell Ayto

A slight but amusing story about a child who falls from a spaceship and lands in James' chimney. Is it to be friend or foe?
Age range: 7–9

DARK SUN, BRIGHT SUN
Blackie, 1986, 128p. – O/P. – 0 216 92024 8

An unusual science fiction story set on the distant planet of Merci. The festival of Dany's Day is approaching, and evil forces are about to be unleashed against the unsuspecting children.
Age range: 7–11

GRINNY
Chivers Press, 1989, 168p. – L/P. – 0 7451 0827 X
Collins, 1984, 162p. – 0 00 330020 X
Penguin, 1975, 96p. – Pbk. – 0 14 030745 1

Tim and Beth are shocked when they realize that Great-aunt Emma is, in fact, an alien and highly dangerous. The ensuing battle provides a gripping story, while helping children to come to terms with the realization that adults, even one's parents, are not infallible.
Age range: 10–13

LEADFOOT
Hodder, 1982, 128p. – Pbk. O/P. – 0 340 26809 3
Pelham Books, 1980, 128p. – O/P. – 0 7207 1199 1

An intriguing title for an action-packed thriller, in which a classy Alvis is pitted against a loud Pontiac. It has a special appeal for boys with some knowledge of cars.
Age range: 10–13

LIVING FIRE, AND OTHER SCIENCE FICTION STORIES
Chivers Press, 1990, 192p. – O/P. – 0 86220 860 2
Corgi, 1987, 179p. – Pbk. – O/P. – 0 552 52453 0
illustrated by David Parkins

A good collection of short stories with a twist. They are not very demanding, making this useful for less able readers

FISK

who can choose the stories which particularly appeal to them.
Age range: 10–12

MINDBENDERS
Penguin, 1988, 112p. – Pbk. – 0 14 032164 0
Viking Kestrel, 1987, 114p. – 0 670 81244 7

A nest of ants is an unusual and a rather disappointing present. Gradually Vinny and Toby become fascinated, then virtually hypnotized. Mindbending becomes a habit, but there is danger in store, as there must be when people can be controlled. An excellent read.
Age range: 10–13

MONSTER MAKER
Mammoth, 1989, 144p. – Pbk. – 0 7497 0049 1
Chivers Press, 1986, 200p. – L/P. – O/P. – 0 7451 0301 4
Pelham Books, 1979, 142p. – O/P. – 0 7207 1111 8

Matt is fascinated by the mechanics of constructing monsters for films, and is delighted when Chauncey lets him help. He identifies with the creations to such an extent that he is convinced they are real and he cannot leave them. Local hooligans breaking into the studio, as a result of Matt's actions, bring him back to a frightening reality. A gripping read, for the plot is exciting; a little more difficult to understand are the underlying complexities of Matt's character which shape the story. The book made a strange, compelling television drama.
Age range: 10–13

ON THE FLIP SIDE
Chivers Press, 1987, 200p. – L/P. – 0 7451 0587 4
Penguin, 1985, 128p. – Pbk. O/P. – 0 14 031556 X
Kestrel Books, 1983, 160p. – O/P. – 0 7226 5825 7

A world catastrophe is threatening and can be averted only by Letty, who has an extraordinary affinity with animals. A topical theme with an unusual slant.
Age range: 10–12

A RAG, A BONE AND A HANK OF HAIR
Penguin, 1982, 128p. – Pbk. – 0 14 031417 2
Kestrel Books, 1980, 126p. – O/P. – 0 7226 5550 9

The title is a list of 'ingredients' from which 'reborns' are made. Reborns are necessary since the nuclear accident wiped out so many people. Brin has the job of controlling these newly created children, but his plans go wrong. A chilling portrayal of human engineering at its worst. An exceptional book.
Age range: 10–13

ROBOT REVOLT
Penguin, 1983, 128p. – Pbk. O/P. – 0 14 031551 9
Pelham Books, 1981, 128p. – O/P. – 00 7207 1332 3

Max the robot helps the children in a plot against their father, but when it suits him he stops obeying and makes his own dangerous plans. Not the most original story, but, well written, it makes a good, exciting read.
Age range: 10–12

SNATCHED
Hodder, 1984, 128p. – Pbk. O/P. – 0 340 35847 5
Hodder, 1983, 117p. – O/P. – 0 340 28455 2

Two children are kidnapped because their father is an important ambassador. They are exceptionally brave, and refuse to give way to the fear that their situation naturally inspires. Realistically described in Nicholas Fisk's characteristic colloquial style.
Age range: 10–12

SPACE HOSTAGES
Kestrel Books, 1984, 144p. – 0 7226 5917 2
Penguin, 1970, 144p. – Pbk. – 0 14 030439 8

A top-secret spacecraft with nine children on board is adrift in space. Their struggle to get home, and all the dangers they have to face without adult

help provide the ingredients for an exciting read.
Age range: 10–12

STARSTORMER SAGA:

STARSTORMERS
Blackie, 1984, 112p. – O/P. – 0 216 91691 7
Hodder, 1980, 109p. – Pbk. O/P. – 0 340 24878 5

SUNBURST
Blackie, 1985, 128p. – O/P. – 0 216 91692 5
Hodder, 1980, 125p. – Pbk. O/P. – 0 340 24879 3

CATFANG
Blackie, 1985, 112p. – O/P. – 0 216 91693 3
Hodder, 1981, 96p. – Pbk. O/P. – 0 340 26529 9

EVIL EYE
Blackie, 1986, 112p. – O/P. – 0 216 91694 1
Hodder, 1982, 112p. – Pbk. O/P. – 0 340 27076 4

This is a lengthy and complicated science fiction series. Committed readers of this genre will enjoy it immensely, and will read it strictly in order. However, each volume gives a summary of 'the story so far', so it is possible to read individual books.
Age range: 10–14

TRILLIONS
Kestrel Books, 1984, 128p. – O/P. – 0 7226 5918 0
Penguin, 1973, 128p. – Pbk. – 0 14 030633 1

First published over 20 years ago, this is still a firm favourite with science fiction fans, and is hugely enjoyed by many who would not normally read science fiction. The army wants to destroy the hordes of brittle, hard bright 'things' which have invaded. The children are horrified, and try to rescue them. An excellent television drama.
Age range: 9–12

WHEELIE IN THE STARS
Penguin, 1979, 96p. – Pbk. – 0 14 031066 5

Brave space cadets succeed, against overwhelming odds, in saving the population of a doomed planet. The basic story is derivative, but it is handled with ingenuity.
Age range: 10–12

THE WORM CHARMERS
Walker Books, 1990, 192p. – Pbk. – 0 7445 1448 7
Walker Books, 1989, 192p. – 0 7445 0837 1

An adventure story, full of action, realistic children, and an exciting plot about kidnapping. With clear print, this is an excellent read.
Age range: 10–12

Other publications:

BACK YARD WAR
Pan Books, 1991. – Pbk. – 0 330 31824 1
BONKER'S CLOCKS
Viking, 1985. – O/P. – 0 670 80694 3
HOLE IN THE HEAD
Walker Books, 1992. – Pbk. – 0 7445 2359 1
PIG IGNORANT
Walker Books, 1993. – Pbk. – 0 7445 2351 6
SWEETS FROM A STRANGER AND OTHER SCIENCE FICTION STORIES
Penguin, 1984. – Pbk. – 0 14 031439 3
TALKING CAR
Mammoth, 1990. – Pbk. – 0 7497 0288 5
VOLCANO
Blackie, 1986. – O/P. – 0 216 91695 X
YOU REMEMBER ME!
Penguin, 1986. – Pbk. – 0 14 031656 6

FOX, Paula

American. Born New York City, 1923, the daughter of the writer Paul Hervey Fox. Educated Columbia University, New York. Married: 1) Richard Sigerson 1948 (divorced 1954), two sons; 2) Martin Greenberg, 1962. Now lives in Brooklyn. News Service correspondent, teacher of writing workshops.

Awards: Guggenheim Fellowship 1972
American Academy Award, 1972

FOX

American Library Association Newbery Medal: *The Slave dancer*, 1974

National Endowment of the Arts Award, 1974

Hans Christian Andersen International Medal, 1978

Christopher Award: *One-eyed cat*, 1985

IBBY Honour Award: *One-eyed Cat*, 1986

Boston-Globe Horn Award: *Village by the Sea*, 1989

Agent: Robert Lescher,
Lescher and Lescher,
67 Irving Place,
New York City,
New York 10009,
USA

An exceptionally perceptive writer whose books seem to have limited appeal to children, yet they have much to offer any child willing to make the effort to meet the author half-way. They are not light-hearted, easy reads, but the stories are original and give the reader an insight into aspects of life which would otherwise pass them by.

HOW MANY MILES TO BABYLON
Penguin, 1972, 112p. – Pbk. O/P. – 0 14 030561 0
Macmillan, 1968, 128p. – O/P. – 0 333 08968 5

James, an innocent in the city, is no match for the gang who recognize his potential. They make him help them with stealing, and his life becomes a nightmare. A sad story with an optimistic ending.
Age range: 11–13

IN A PLACE OF DANGER
Lions, 1991, 144p. – Pbk. – 0 00 673493 6
Orchard Books, 1989, 144p. – 1 85213 176 4

The two weeks that Emma has to stay with her strange Aunt Bea while Emma's father is in hospital seem to her to stretch out forever. Luckily she makes friends with Bertie, which helps a lot until the night of the big row.
Age range: 10–12

THE LOST BOY
Pan Books, 1989, 160p. – Pbk. – 0 330 30775 4
Chivers Press, 1989, 240p. – L/P. – 0 7451 0890 3
Dent, 1987, 156p. – 0 460 06271 9

A sensitive book of feelings and emotions rather than actions. Lily and Paul become friends, but Lily is hurt when Jack, newly arrived, steals Paul away from her.
Age range: 11–13

THE ONE-EYED CAT
Cornerstone Books, 1988, 172p. – L/P. – 1 55736 071 5
Collins, 1988, 128p. – Pbk. – 0 00 330037 4
Pan Books, 1988, 144p. – Pbk. – 0 330 29646 9
Dent, 1985, 176p. – 0 460 06186 0

One moment of mischief leads Ned into a nightmare situation. Coming to terms with his feelings of guilt about the injured cat makes a moving story. Light relief is there in the person of the horrible housekeeper who gets her come-uppance.
Age range: 10–12

SLAVE DANCER
Windrush, 1989, 223p. – L/P. – O/P. – 1 8508 9962 2
Pan Books, 1977, 142p. – Pbk. – O/P. – 0 330 25018 3
illustrated by Eras Keith

First published in 1973, this was one of the first books to deal with slavery. It is well written, and just as powerful today, telling how Jessie, press-ganged onto a slave-ship, has to play his flute so the slaves can dance as exercise. It is a nightmare voyage which he recounts in graphic detail.
Age range: 10–13

Other publications:

BLOWFISH LIVE IN THE SEA
Penguin, 1974. – Pbk. – O/P. – 0 14 030701 X

LIKELY PLACE
*Pan Books, 1977. – Pbk. – O/P. –
0 330 25098 1*

LITTLE SWINEHERD AND OTHER TALES
Dent, 1979. – O/P. – 0 460 06904 7

MONKEY ISLAND
Orchard Books, 1992. – 1 8521 3392 9

MOONLIGHT MAN
Dent, 1986. – O/P. – 0 460 06243 3

PLACE APART
Dent, 1981. – O/P. – 0 460 06082 1

PORTRAIT OF IVAN
Macmillan, 1970. – O/P. – 0 333 11803 0

FURLONG, Monica

British. Born 1930. Educated Harrow County Girls' School; University College, London. Married John William Knights (dissolved 1977), one son, one daughter. Journalist, writer.

Address: C/o Anthony Sheil Assoc.,
43 Doughty Street,
London WC1,
England

How privileged children are that this talented author should use her attributes to produce such excellent novels. She combines atmosphere, memorable settings and characters, and believable stories into whole books of outstanding stature, from which every reader emerges wiser.

JUNIPER
Corgi, 1992. – Pbk. – 0 552 52703 3

This goes back in time to when Juniper was a child and felt 'called' to become a wise woman. To achieve this she had to spend time with Evry, her Godmother. It was a time of hardship and learning, but of joy, too. An engrossing read.
Age range: 9–12

WISE CHILD
*Corgi, 1990, 208p. – Pbk. – 0 552 52597 9
Gollancz, 1987, 192p. – 0 575 04046 7*

There is so much packed into this novel that it needs another one to do it justice. The story tells of the childhood of Wise Child on the Isle of Mull, in the seventh century, when superstition is rife, and times are hard. She is 'adopted' by Juniper, a kind, wise woman, suspected to be a witch, with whom she learns how to live. Told with vitality, sympathy, warmth and understanding, the book comes close to sharing the essence of life with discerning readers.
Age range: 12–15

A YEAR AND A DAY
Gollancz, 1990, 224p. – 0 575 04591 4

This is the prequel to *Wise Child*, telling Juniper's story, which proves to be just as absorbing and moving.
Age range: 12–15

G

GARDAM, Jane (née Pearson)

British. Born Coatham, Yorkshire, 1928. Educated Saltburn High School for Girls; Bedford College, London, B.A. (Hons), Graduate Study. Married David Gardam, 1952, two sons and one daughter. Sub-editor and literary editor.

Awards: Fellow, Royal Society of Literature, 1976

Whitbread Award: *The Hollow land*, 1981

Address: Haven House, Sandwich, Kent, England

Agent: Bruce Hunter David Higham Assoc., 5–8 Lower John Street, London W1R 4HA, England

Here is another author whose skill is of the highest quality, and who is able to bring that skill to books for a wide age range, although many are for teenagers. Her character portrayal of both adults and children is superb. The books are interlaced with verbal humour requiring a degree of competence in the reader, even at the youngest level. Reading Jane Gardam's novels is an enriching experience that concerned adults should endeavour to give to every child.

BILGEWATER
Sphere, 1985, 208p. – Pbk. – 0 349 11402 1
Penguin, 1979, 208p. – Pbk. O/P. –
0 14 005368 9
Hamish Hamilton, 1976, 200p. – O/P. –
0 241 89398 4

Marigold Daisy Green, a name to conjure with, feels she is truly ugly, a feeling confirmed by the horrible boys at the school where her father is headmaster. As she and the boys grow older, things change, but with painful slowness. A witty, introspective book for avid girl readers.
Age range: 12–15

BRIDGET AND WILLIAM
Penguin, 1984, 96p. – Pbk. – 0 14 031592 6
J. MacRae Books, 1981, 48p. – O/P. –
0 86203 012 9
illustrated by Janet Rawlins

An easy-to-read story in large print. Bridget's father has no time for the fat pony until his courage in the snowstorm earns him the respect he deserves.
Age range: 6–8

A FEW FAIR DAYS
Walker Books, 1989, 128p. – Pbk. –
0 7445 1337 5
J. MacRae Books, 1987, 120p. – O/P. –
0 86203 302 0

Amusing little anecdotes of Lucy's childhood, told with such humour that children laugh out loud. Easier to listen to than read.
Age range: 8–10

THE HOLLOW LAND
Walker Books, 1992, 160p. – Pbk. –
0 7445 2372 9
Chivers Press, 1987, 272p. – L/P. –
0 7451 0495 9
J. MacRae Books, 1981, 160p. – O/P. –
0 86203 023 4
illustrated by Janet Rawlins

Heart-warming stories about two families, one born and bred in Cumbria, the other moved there from London. It is the superb characterization that gives these stories their appeal. Jane Gardam's love of the Cumbrian fells and the farming communities is much in evidence.
Age range: 12–14

HORSE
*J. MacRae Books, 1982, 48p. – O/P. –
0 86203 066 8*
illustrated by Janet Rawlins

Another easy-to-read novel with large print, but very interesting. The villagers put up a fight to save the 'White Horse' cut into the hillside.
Age range: 6–8

KIT
*J. MacRae Books, 1983, 56p. – O/P. –
0 86203 132 X*
illustrated by William Geldart

In the same series:

KIT IN BOOTS
*J. MacRae Books, 1986, 64p. – O/P. –
0 86203 258 X*
illustrated by William Geldart

KIT IN BOOTS: 'KIT' AND 'KIT IN BOOTS'
Penguin, 1988, 112p. – Pbk. – 0 14 032394 5

Aimed at younger readers, these novels are not very long, but they are, nevertheless, superbly written. Kit is a memorable seven-year-old who lives on a farm. Her escapades, first with the farm bull, and second with a visiting artist, are told in a lively, colloquial style.
Age range: 7–9

THE SWAN
*J. MacRae Books, 1987, 64p. – O/P. –
0 86203 263 6*
illustrated by John Dillow

Henry Wu refuses to speak and appears not to listen. Pratt is given the task of trying to draw him out, but in vain, and the swans in the park have more success. A moving, forthright story.
Age range: 9–11

THROUGH THE DOLL'S HOUSE DOOR
*Walker Books, 1989, 128p. – Pbk. –
0 7445 0849 5
Chivers Press, 1989, 184p. – O/P. –
0 7451 1045 2
J. MacRae, 1987, 121p. – 0 86203 278 4*

The inhabitants of the doll's house suffer terribly when the children grow too old to play, but they pass the time by each telling an extraordinary story from their past. These stories are fascinating reading, and the climax when a new generation of children are born, is superb.
Age range: 9–11

Other publications:

BLACK WOOLLY PONY, WHITE CHALK HORSE
Walker Books, 1993. – Pbk. – 0 7445 2226 9
LONG WAY FROM VERONA
Penguin, 1973. – Pbk. – O/P. – 0 14 030611 0
SUMMER AFTER THE FUNERAL
H. Hamilton, 1986. – O/P. – 0 241 11945 6

GARFIELD, Leon

British. Born Brighton, Sussex, 1921. Educated Brighton Grammar School. Royal Army Medical Corps, WW II. Married Vivien Alcock, children's author, 1948, one daughter. Biochemical technician, 1946–69, writer.

Awards: Guardian Children's Fiction Award: *Devil-in-the-fog*, 1966

Library Association Carnegie Medal: *The God beneath the Sea*, 1970

Whitbread Award: *John Diamond*, 1980

The Children's Book Award: *Fair's Fair*, 1981

Prix de la Foundation de France, 1984

Fellow of the Royal Society of Literature, 1985

Golden Cat Award, Sweden, 1985

Children's Literature Association Phoenix Award, 1987

GARFIELD

Address: 59 Wood Lane,
London N6,
England

Agents: John Johnson Ltd,
45–47 Clerkenwell Green,
London EC1R 0HT,
England

International Creative
   Management,
40 West 57th Street,
New York,
New York 10019,
USA

An author whose command of words is absolute. He is able to create an atmosphere of mystery and suspense, which lingers long after the book is finished, yet there are lots of witty jokes. He weaves several different threads together to make one completely gripping story, peopled by memorable characters.

APPRENTICES
Penguin, 1984, 316p. – Pbk. – 0 14 031595 0
Heinemann, 1982, 316p. – O/P. –
0 434 94044 5

Life for apprentices in eighteenth century London is hard. This book tells the story of twelve of them, one for each month, with their hopes, disappointments, and, above all, the realities of their respective situations.
Age range: 12–14

BLACK JACK
Kestrel Books, 1975, 192p. – O/P. –
0 7226 5092 2
Penguin, 1971, 192p. – Pbk. – 0 14 030489 4
illustrated by Antony Maitland

This book caused quite a stir when it was runner-up for the Carnegie Medal – unusual for a first novel. It is exciting, unusual, and quite compelling, and bestowed respectability on historical novels. It has an effective beginning, with a coffin containing a live person, and goes on to weave a tale of adventure and evil together with love and understanding.
Age range: 12–14

THE CONFIDENCE MAN
Kestrel Books, 1978, 320p. – O/P. –
0 7226 5407 3

An incident in eighteenth century Germany in which Protestants were persecuted provides Leon Garfield with a basis for this superb adventure story. A young boy, journeying to a better future in America, has to face many obstacles.
Age range: 12–14

THE DECEMBER ROSE
Chivers Press, 1987, 344p. – L/P. –
0 7451 0588 2
Viking Kestrel, 1986, 208p. – O/P. –
0 670 81054 1
Penguin, 1986, 208p. – Pbk. – 0 14 032070 9

Originally written for television, this story is set in Victorian London, and is a typical mystery. Barnacle is a likable lad, and the reader follows his fortune and misfortune with avid interest.
Age range: 12–14

DEVIL-IN-THE-FOG
Kestrel Books, 1975, 188p. – O/P. –
0 7226 5089 2
Penguin, 1970. 173p. – Pbk. O/P. –
0 14 030353 7

It is difficult for George to learn at fourteen that he is not a humble Treet, but the son of Sir John Dexter, and must now take his rightful place. This obviously cannot be achieved without some difficulties, but when it leads to attempted murder, George finds out just what he is made of.
Age range: 12–14

THE EMPTY SLEEVE
Penguin, 1989, 176p. – Pbk. – 0 14 032686 3
Viking Kestrel, 1988, 192p. – O/P. –
0 670 80118 6

As the title suggests, this is a ghost story concerning twin boys and their different fortunes. It is full of atmosphere, and has an intriguing plot climaxing with murder most foul.
Age range: 12–14

GARFIELD

THE GHOST DOWNSTAIRS
Kestrel Books, 1975, 96p. – O/P. –
0 7226 5094 9
Penguin, 1975, 96p. – Pbk. – 0 14 030788 5
illustrated by Antony Maitland

Rather more than 'just a ghost story', this book has the capacity to enable readers to experience real horror. Mr Frost and Mr Fishbone, so aptly and wittily named, are characters not easily forgotten.
Age range: 12–14

JACK HOLBORN
Kestrel Books, 1984, 200p. – O/P. –
0 7226 5088 4
Penguin, 1970, 200p. – Pbk. – 0 14 030318 9
illustrated by Antony Maitland

Jack is an orphan who falls into the hands of a pirate crew. The captain is a mysterious character who influences Jack's life to the very exciting end.
Age range: 12–14

JOHN DIAMOND
Chivers Press, 1988, 304p. – L/P. –
0 7451 0757 5
Penguin, 1981, 192p. – Pbk. – 0 14 031366 4
Kestrel Books, 1980, 180p. – O/P. –
0 7226 5619 X

Set in the familiar territory of the back streets of Victorian London, this is the tale of an honest young man trying to put right the wrongs committed by his father, actions easier to plan than to execute. Amusing, yet shocking.
Age range: 12–14

MR CORBETT'S GHOST, AND OTHER STORIES
Kestrel Books, 1982, 88p. – O/P. –
0 7226 5806 0
Penguin, 1971, 144p. – Pbk. – O/P. –
0 14 030510 6
illustrated by Antony Maitland

Three shorter stories, very much in the same vein as his full-length novels, but not so daunting. The first story was made into an excellent film.
Age range: 12–14

THE PRISONERS OF SEPTEMBER
Kestrel Books, 1975, 256p. – O/P. –
0 7226 5097 3

The French Revolution is not the easiest period in which to set a popular story, but it gives an opportunity for an adventure story which Leon Garfield exploits to the full, combining excitement with comedy and romanticism. As always, the characters are vividly portrayed and the conclusion gives an opportunity for discussion about ideals and how they should dictate one's actions. Not an easy book to read.
Age range: 12–14

SMITH
Chivers Press, 1987, 320p. – L/P. –
0 7451 0448 7
Kestrel Books, 1977, 192p. – O/P. –
0 7226 5090 6
Penguin, 1970, 176p. – Pbk. – 0 14 030349 9
illustrated by Antony Maitland

Smith is a pick-pocket in eighteenth century London, where murder is commonplace. Uncharacteristically, he feels sorry for a blind man and helps him – an act of charity which changes his whole life.
Age range: 12–14

THE STRANGE AFFAIR OF ADELAIDE HARRIS
Kestrel Books, 1977, 176p. – O/P. –
0 7226 5095 7
Penguin, 1974, 176p. – Pbk. O/P. –
0 14 030671 4
illustrated by Fritz Wegner

In the same series:

BOSTOCK AND HARRIS
Kestrel Books, 1979, 176p. – O/P. –
0 7226 5529 0
illustrated by Martin Cottam

Entertainment at its best, these amusing and original novels show Leon Garfield at his most inventive. Harris puts his history lesson to the test by taking his baby sister to use in an experiment which goes wrong, with horrifying

GARFIELD

consequences. The sequel is equally gripping.
Age range: 12–14

Other publications:

BLEWCOAT BOY
Gollancz, 1988. – O/P. – 0 575 04394 6
FAIR'S FAIR
Simon & Schuster, 1990. – 0 7500 0333 2
GOD BENEATH THE SEA
Gollancz, 1992. – Pbk. – 0 575 05256 2
GOLDEN SHADOW
Gollancz, 1992. – Pbk. – 0 575 05255 4
GUILT AND GINGERBREAD
Penguin, 1987. – Pbk. – O/P. – 0 14 032195 0
LABOUR IN VAIN
Heinemann, 1977. – O/P. – 0 434 94036 4
LAMPLIGHTER'S FUNERAL
Heinemann, 1976. – O/P. – 0 434 94032 1
LUCIFER WILKINS
Heinemann, 1973. – O/P. – 0 434 94911 6
MIRROR, MIRROR
Heinemann, 1976. – O/P. – 0 434 94031 3
PLEASURE GARDEN
Harper Collins, 1991. – Pbk. – O/P. – 0 00 673678 5
WEDDING GHOST
OUP, 1992. – Pbk. – 0 19 272246 8

GARNER, Alan

British. Born Congleton, Cheshire, 1934. Educated Alderly Edge Primary School, Cheshire; Manchester Grammar School; Magdalene College, Oxford. Second Lieutenant, Royal Artillery. Married: 1) Ann Cook, 1956 (marriage dissolved), one son, two daughters; 2) Griselda Greaves, 1972, one son, one daughter.

Awards: Guardian Children's Fiction Award: *Owl Service*, 1968

Library Association Carnegie Medal: *Owl Service*, 1967

Address: Blackden,
Holmes Chapel,
Crewe,
Cheshire CW4 8BY,
England

Alan Garner has a unique gift for storytelling, coupled with an erudite grasp of language. His books all have a compelling story to tell, but are sometimes inaccessible to readers because of the very high literary standard. This can be overcome by being read out loud by a sympathetic reader.

BAG OF MOONSHINE
Lions, 1992, 104p. – Pbk. – 0 00 674290 4
Collins, 1986, 160p. – 0 00 184403 2
illustrated by Patrick James Lynch

A book of folk tales re-told to make them accessible to his young audience. Large print and lots of varied illustrations give hours of pleasure.
Age range: 8–10

ELIDOR
Windrush, 1989, 244p. – L/P. – 1 85089 945 2
Collins, 1980, 160p. – Pbk. – 0 00 671674 1
Collins, 1965, 160p. – 0 00 184202 1
illustrated by Charles Keeping

Fantasy at its best. Roland finds himself separated from his friends in the old church and in a different world, where evil holds sway. Even when safely back in Manchester, Elidor's power affects him and his friends, until the dramatic climax.
Age range: 10–12

THE STONE BOOK QUARTET
Collins, 1983, 224p. – Pbk. O/P. – 0 00 184289 7
Collins, 1983, 224p. – 0 00 184282 X
illustrated by Michael Foreman

Experienced and confident readers will enjoy these demanding stories about craftsmen and their children. Although short, they are beautifully written.
Age range: 10–12

THE WEIRDSTONE OF BRISINGAMEN
Collins, 1983, 224p. – Pbk. – 0 00 671672 5
Collins, 1965, 224p. – 0 00 183104 6

In the same series:

THE MOON OF GOMRATH
*Harper Collins, 1983, 156p. – Pbk. –
0 00 671673 3
Collins, 1963, 160p. – 0 00 184503 9*

Both books are a wonderful mixture of legend and fact, culled from the Cheshire countryside. They each tell a classic story of the struggle between good and evil, as the wizard's last magic-store turns up in a bracelet. As with Tolkien, there is initial difficulty in getting used to the strange names, but the stories are powerful and compelling.
Age range: 10–12

Other publications:

BREADHORSE
Collins, 1975. – O/P. – 0 00 195069 X
FAIRY TALES OF GOLD
Collins, 1980. – 0 00 183773 7
JACK AND THE BEANSTALK
Picture Lions, 1993. – Pbk. – 0 00 664294 2
OWL SERVICE
Collins, 1981. – Pbk. – 0 00 671675 X
RED SHIFT
Collins, 1975. – Pbk. – 0 00 671000 X

GATES, Susan

British. Born Grimsby, 1950. Educated Warwick University, B.A. English and American Lit.; Coventry College of Education, Dip. Ed. Married, three children. Now lives in Crook, Co. Durham. Teacher and writer.

Address: C/o Oxford University Press,
Walton Street,
Oxford OX2 6DP,
England.

A comparatively new writer for older children, Susan Gates has quickly established herself as a powerful and original storyteller. She has an extraordinary ability to portray life in the raw, telling a remarkably human story in a readable style, while often featuring a particular aspect relevant to the North of England.

AFRICAN DREAMS
OUP, 1993, 136p. – 0 19 271684 0

An unlikely friendship develops between a young tearaway needing a hiding place and a teenage girl who finds her present life with her Mum not to her liking. For a while they share a dream of a new life in Africa, before reality re-asserts itself and separates them.
Age range: 11–13

THE BURNHOPE WHEEL
OUP, 1989, 83p. – 0 19 271620 4

From the first chapter, the reader feels completely involved with Ellen, whether quarrelling with her mother or doing totally foolish things such as getting on a bus that should not be there, has no other passengers, and takes her to Burnhope. The wheel seems to affect her, as does meeting Dave – the past and the present getting all mixed up. A dramatic climax.
Age range: 12+

DEADLINE FOR DANNY'S BEACH
OUP, 1993, 157p. – 0 19 271696 4

Highly topical, the issue in this story is contamination of the coastline by a local chemical plant. The human interest is provided by Danny, brain-damaged at birth, whose hobby is collecting odd items from the beach. Thirteen-years old Martha puts all the weight of her teenage passion into trying to stop the pollution, and is relieved when Alex offers his help. The various strands of the story, including the visiting foxes who are also at risk, are cleverly woven together. An essential read for modern children.
Age range: 12+

DRAGLINE
OUP, 1991, 156p. – 0 19 271663 8

As always with this author, there are several strands to the book. It depicts

with awful realism how open-cast mining spoils the countryside and pollutes the lives of people with unbearable noise levels. There is also the human story of Gideon and his mother, unable to paint because of the divorce, the move and the mine. Then Colin and his enmity which is so strong that it is a layer of menace. All the ingredients for a gripping read.
Age range: 12+

THE LOCK
OUP, 1990, 144p. – 0 19 271635 2

Not a book for the faint-hearted as it is a very realistic portrayal of teenage violence, which is currently an everyday occurrence. 'The Lock' has a dual meaning – a stretch of beach, and the barrier which prevents sixteen-years old Marie from communicating effectively with the rest of the world. Kindly people refer to her as 'slow', her peers as 'thick', or worse. It takes the death of Mr Bishop to provide her with the key. A bleak story, but not without hope.
Age range: 12+

GAVIN, Jamila

Born in India of an Indian father and English mother. Studied music in London, Paris and Berlin. Married, two children. Works in TV and radio.

Address: The Laurels,
All Saints Road,
Uplands,
Stroud,
Gloucestershire GL5 1II,
England

Agent: Jacqueline Korn,
David Higham Assoc. Ltd,
5–8 Lower John Street,
Golden Square,
London W1R 4HA,
England

Being born of mixed parentage has given Jamila Gavin a deeper understanding of the two cultures. She is able, therefore, to convey the differences naturally in her stories. There is nothing artificial to spoil the flow of the plots.

DIGITAL DAN
Methuen, 1984, 128p. – O/P. – 0 416 46050 X
illustrated by Patrice Aitken

Dan daydreams that he has a motor-bike with all the gadgets, so that he can have fantastic adventures. Easy to read.
Age range: 7–9

DOUBLE DARE
Mammoth, 1992, 144p. – Pbk. – 0 7497 0959 6
Methuen, 1982, 144p. – O/P. – 0 416 21540 8
illustrated by Simon Willby

Four stories verging on the supernatural, without being very frightening.
Age range: 8–10

GRANDPA CHATTERJI
Methuen, 1993, 64p. – 0 416 19021 9

A striking method of showing how the cultures of England and India can interact. Two children with one English and one Indian grandfather observe how each learns from the other. There is much for the reader to learn from these warm-hearted stories. Highly recommended.
Age range: 8–10

HIDEAWAY
Methuen, 1987, 128p. – O/P. – 0 416 02382 7

Effie, the unhappy victim of a bitter divorce, is delighted when his Dad gives him a bike, but his mother uses it as a weapon, finally taking it away. For Pete, this is the final straw, so he runs away to the only place where he has been able to find any peace, the hideaway he shares with Jack.
Age range: 9–11

THE HINDU WORLD
MacDonald, 1986, 48p. – Religions of the world series – 0 356 11509 7

A collection of traditional Hindu stories, retold with attention to detail and meaning, yet with imagination. Beautifully illustrated, the stories are made accessible to all children, with or without previous knowledge of Hindu religion.
Age range: 9–11

KAMLA AND KATE
Mammoth, 1991, 112p. – Pbk. – 0 7497 0581 7
Methuen, 1983, 96p. – O/P. – 0 416 22780 5
illustrated by Thelma Lambert

In the same series:

KAMLA AND KATE AGAIN
Mammoth, 1992. – Pbk. – 0 7497 1050 0

The two friends are mischievous, yet at the same time they explore the differences in each other's lives. Very popular books with girls.
Age range: 7–9

THE MAGIC ORANGE TREE AND OTHER STORIES
Magnet Books, 1987, 96p. – Pbk. – 0 416 07322 0
Methuen, 1979, 96p. – O/P. – 0 416 86240 3
illustrated by Ossie Murray

A book of short stories about a group of children living in a city. They have diverse cultural backgrounds, and different experiences to share.
Age range: 9–11

THREE INDIAN PRINCESSES: THE STORIES OF SAVITRI, DAMAYANTI AND SITA
Methuen, 1987, 128p. – 0 416 97030 3

Indian folk tales re-told to make them accessible and enjoyable for children. The story of Rama and Sita is particularly moving.
Age range: 9–11

WHEEL OF SURYA
Methuen, 1992, 160p. – 0 416 18572 X

An extraordinary novel in that it is moving and exciting in equal parts. It tells the story of two children who are forced to flee their home when war breaks out. They make their way with great difficulty to England, where they have many adjustments to make before they find a measure of peace. An excellent story.
Age range: 12+

Other publications:

ALI AND THE ROBOTS
Methuen, 1986. – O/P. – 0 416 53960 2
ANGELS ARE WHITE, AREN'T THEY?
Methuen, 1990. – O/P. – 0 416 15592 8
I WANT TO BE AN ANGEL
Mammoth, 1991. – Pbk. – 0 7497 0987 1
SINGING BOWLS
Mammoth, 1991. – Pbk. – 0 7497 0332 6

GEE, Maurice (Gough)

New Zealander. Born Whakatare, 1931. Educated Avondale College, Auckland; University of Auckland, M.A. (Hons) English; Victoria University, Wellington, D. Litt. Married Margaretha Garden, 1970, one son (previous marriage) and two daughters. Teacher, librarian, writer.

Awards:	Esther Glen Award: *The Motherstone*, 1986
Address:	125, Cleveland Terrace, Nelson, New Zealand
Agent:	Richards Literary Agency, P.O. Box 31240, Milford, Auckland 9, New Zealand

It is always a pleasure to see an author, successful in his own country, being accepted and enjoyed by children in different parts of the world. Maurice Gee's books have become immensely popular, perhaps because some of them have been shown on television, revealing what exciting and dramatic plots they contain.

THE CHAMPION
Penguin, 1990, 176p. – Pbk. – 0 14 034160 9

Jackson Coop, an American soldier in New Zealand during WW II, is wounded and comes to stay with Rex's family to recuperate. There are people who do not welcome black soldiers into their community, and events that take place during Jackson's fortnight in Kettle Week change it forever.
Age range: 11–13

THE HALFMEN OF O
Penguin, 1984, 192p. – Pbk. – 0 14 031712 0
OUP, 1982, 208p. – O/P. – 0 19 558081 8

In the same series:

THE PRIESTS OF FERRIS
Penguin, 1987, 192p. – Pbk. O/P. – 0 14 032061 X
OUP, 1985, 180p. – O/P. – 0 19 558112 1

MOTHERSTONE
Penguin, 1988, 184p. – Pbk. O/P. – 0 14 032361 9
OUP, 1986, 184p. – O/P. – 0 19 558130 X

The planet O is in danger of being destroyed by the evil Halfmen, who have lost all trace of any human virtues. They send a sign to Susan, who bears a special mark on her wrist, asking for help. Together with her cousin, Nick, she sets about the task of restoring the balance of good and evil. Having faced unknown terrors in defeating the Halfmen of O, Susan and Nick are dismayed to learn that a new tyranny, in the form of cruel priests, is threatening to overrun the planet. They are determined to set O free. Just as they are convinced they have succeeded, a new leader with an entirely new weapon arrives, and the hard-won peace is threatened yet again. In the final part of this trilogy, Susan and Nick face one last task, from which they do not flinch.
Age range: 12–14

UNDER THE MOUNTAIN
Penguin, 1982, 160p. – Pbk. O/P. – 0 14 031389 3
OUP, 1979, 164p. – O/P. – 0 19 558040 0

A similar idea of a world being taken over, in this case by evil giants living under extinct volcanoes. Less complicated than his trilogy, the book became an engrossing television serial.
Age range: 10–12

THE WORLD AROUND THE CORNER
Penguin, 1983, 96p. – Pbk. – 0 14 031580 2
OUP, 1981, 80p. – O/P. – 0 19 558061 3
illustrated by Garry Webley

Caroline finds a pair of special spectacles, and is determined to return them. Equally determined to stop her are the evil Grimbles, who have their own plans for the spectacles.
Age range: 8–10

GERAS, Adele (Daphne, née Weston)

British. Born Jerusalem, Israel, 1944. Educated St Hilda's College, Oxford, B.A. (Hons), modern languages. Married Norman Geras, 1967, two daughters. Teacher, writer.

Address: 10 Danesmoor Road, Manchester M20 9JS, England

Agent: Laura Cecil, 17 Alwyne Villas, London N1 2HG, England

Undoubtedly at her best writing for teenagers, Adele Geras can nevertheless write stories which appeal to younger children, and keep their interest.

APRICOTS AT MIDNIGHT
Armada Books, 1989, 192p. – Pbk. – 0 00 673225 9
Hamish Hamilton, 1977, 144p. – O/P. – 0 241 89479 4
illustrated by Doreen Caldwell

A collection of stories reflecting Edwardian England. They are connected by the various materials which make up Aunt Pinny's patchwork quilt. An enjoyable way of learning about everyday life in a bygone age.
Age range: 9–11

THE FANTORA FAMILY FILES
Collins, 1990, 128p. – Pbk. – 0 00 673348 4
Hamish Hamilton, 1988, 128p. – 0 241 12467 0
illustrated by Tony Ross

This book contains sparks of true originality. The story is related by the Fantora cat, who has a nice turn of phrase. Other members of the family have different claims to fame: Aunt Varrora is a vegetarian vampire, others possess strange powers. The short, anecdotal chapters are verbally funny.
Age range: 9–11

THE GIRLS IN THE VELVET FRAME
Armada Books, 1988, 160p. – Pbk. –
0 00 672879 0
Hamish Hamilton, 1978, 160p. – O/P. –
0 241 10011 9

Naomi and her sisters are anxious to hear from Isaac, who is living in America, but has not contacted them. Their aunt arranges for them to be photographed as a birthday present for their mother, hoping it will cheer her up. It proves to be far more significant in helping to reunite Isaac and the family. The romances of the eldest girls will be enjoyed by older girls.
Age range: 13–15

LETTERS OF FIRE AND OTHER UNSETTLING STORIES
Armada Books, 1986, 160p. – Pbk. –
0 00 672556 2
Hamish Hamilton, 1984, 154p. – O/P. –
0 241 11268 0

A masterly collection of mysteries and macabre stories that send shivers down the spine, and cause readers to glance fearfully over their shoulders.
Age range: 12–14

Other publications:

CHRISTMAS CAT
Corgi, 1989. – Pbk. – 0 552 52562 6
CORONATION PICNIC
H. Hamilton, 1989. – 0 241 12554 5
FINDING ANNABEL
H. Hamilton, 1987. – 0 241 12302 X
FISH PIE FOR FLAMINGOES
H. Hamilton, 1987. – O/P. – 0 241 11969 3
GLITTERING RIVER
H. Hamilton, 1990. – 0 241 12925 7
GREEN BEHIND THE GLASS
Armada Books, 1984. – Pbk. – O/P. –
0 00 672397 7
HAPPY ENDINGS
Armada Books, 1988. – Pbk. – O/P. –
0 00 672791 3
LITTLE ELEPHANT'S MOON
H. Hamilton, 1986. – 0 241 11729 1
MAGIC BIRTHDAY
Simon & Schuster, 1992. – 0 7500 1177 7
RICHIE'S RABBIT
H. Hamilton, 1986. – O/P. – 0 241 11801 8
STRANGE BIRD
H. Hamilton, 1988. – 0 241 12261 9
TOWER ROOM
Lions, 1993. – Pbk. – 0 00 673910 5
WATCHING THE ROSES
Lions, 1993. – Pbk. – 0 00 674383 8
YESTERDAY
Walker Books, 1993. – Pbk. – 0 7445 2352 4

GIRLING, Brough

British. Born 1946. Educated Oxford University, B.Ed. Editor, writer.

Address: Flat 4,
55 Cathcart Road,
London SW10 9DH,
England

This author has decided views on children and reading, views which are reflected in the stories he writes, the main ingredient being enjoyment. There is humour in abundance, characters and situations that ordinary children can readily identify with, and an easy style which makes them accessible to reluctant readers.

GIRLING

BANGERS AND CHIPS EXPLOSION
Penguin, 1989, 112p. – Pbk. – 0 14 032695 2

SCHOOL SECRETARY ON THE WARPATH
Puffin Books, 1993, 160p. – Pbk. –
0 14 036095 6
illustrated by Tony Blundell

Exploding school dinners and exploding school secretaries are the main drift of these truly hilarious stories set in St Gertrude's Junior School. With equally amusing and plentiful illustrations, these books can introduce young readers to the delights of reading.
Age range: 7–9

CLEVER TREVOR
Young Lions, 1992, 64p. – Pbk. –
0 00 674402 8
Black, 1991, 64p. – 0 7136 3302 6
illustrated by Tony Blundell

Trevor is a parrot who is unable to keep quiet, bringing him into conflict with everyone, and making Samantha's life at school extremely difficult. The illustrations as always add a dimension of their own. Thoroughly enjoyable.
Age range: 7–9

DUMBELLINA
Penguin, 1990, 96p. – Pbk. – 0 14 032401 1
illustrated by Caroline Sharpe

Rebecca cannot bear the thought of moving house, leaving her friends behind and having to start a new school. Meeting a dumpy little fairy with lots of energy helps to take her mind off her problems, giving her time to adjust. Very easy to read, it is an entertaining story for all, but could be especially helpful to children in the same situation as Rebecca.
Age range: 7–9

Other publications:

AMAZING INVISIBLE INK PUZZLE BOOKS
Pan Books, 1988. – Pbk. – O/P. –
0 330 30380 5

DR DRIVEL'S SERIOUS JOKE BOOK
Red Fox, 1991. – Pbk. – O/P. – 0 09 979190 0
GREAT PUFFIN JOKE DIRECTORY
Penguin, 1990. – Pbk. – 0 14 034177 3
GREEN AND SCALY BOOK
Penguin, 1992. – Pbk. – 0 14 034703 8
I KNOW AN OLD LADY
Walker Books, 1992. – 0 7445 2167 X
MAKE YOUR OWN MERRY CHRISTMAS
Magnet Books, 1987. – Pbk. – O/P. –
0 416 06482 5
NORA BONE
Young Lions, 1993. – Pbk. – 0 00 674512 1
VERA PRATT AND THE BALD HEAD
Penguin, 1990. – Pbk. – O/P. – 0 14 034111 0
VERA PRATT AND THE BISHOP'S FALSE TEETH
Penguin, 1987. – Pbk. – 0 14 032379 1
VERA PRATT AND THE FALSE MOUSTACHES
Penguin, 1987. – Pbk. – 0 14 032248 5

GLEITZMAN, Morris

British. Born Sleaford, Lincolnshire, 1953. Educated Chislehurst and Sidcup Grammar School, Kent; Canberra College, Canberra, B.A. Professional Writing. Resident in Australia since 1969. Married Christine McCaul, 1978 (separated); one daughter, one son. Columnist, author.

Awards: Children's Book Council of Australia Book of the Year for Younger Readers: *Misery Guts*, 1982.

Agent: Sappho Clissitt,
William Morris Agency,
31–32 Soho Square,
London W1V 5DG
England

Already very popular in Australia, Morris Gleitzman is finally achieving recognition here as more children become aware of and approve his books. He has the rare gift of total empathy with children while being able to make them laugh and feel good. He chooses to write about modern issues in urban settings, and hit the headlines when his courageous *Jenny lives with Eric and Martin* was published in 1983, exploring the world of homosexuals.

BLABBER MOUTH
Piper, 1994, 128p. – Pbk. – 0 330 33283 X

Rowena, starting at a new school, needs to make friends. She finds it difficult as she cannot speak, and feels hurt when she discovers she is being used as 'the disadvantaged child' in a classmate's project. Finding a solution takes courage. Easy to read, and full of humour.
Age range: 9–11

MISERY GUTS
Piper, 1992, 128p. – Pbk. – 0 330 932440 3 illustrated by John Levers

Ken's parents refuse to be cheered up, no matter what he does. He finally comes up with a drastic solution – they can move to Australia – but doesn't realize that it will take a disastrous fire to get them to agree. Full of the humour associated with Morris Gleitzman.

TWO WEEKS WITH THE QUEEN
Pan Books, 1990, 128p. – Pbk. – 0 330 31376 2
Blackie, 1989, 128p. – O/P. – 0 216 92761 7

Colin copes with the devastating news of his brother's terminal illness by deciding to act positively. He needs help, and decides the Queen of England is just the person, so he sets off to ask her. Very amusing, quite heart-rending, and deals openly and directly with a difficult subject.
Age range: 10–12

WORRY WARTS
Piper, 1993, 122p. – 0 330 32845 X

Keith's parents are considering divorce. He is appalled, and tries various strategies to put a stop to it, but in vain. Then he hears about the opal fields, and decides this has got to be the answer. Instead, it almost proves fatal.

A wonderful combination of humour and sadness.
Age range: 9–11

Other publications:

OTHER FACTS OF LIFE
Puffin, 1988. – Pbk. – 0 14 036877 9
STICKY BEAK
Pan, 1994. – Pbk. – 0 333 60185 8

GORDON, John (William)

British. Born Jarrow, Co. Durham, 1925. Educated Wisbech Grammar School, Cambridgeshire. Royal Navy, 1943–47. Married Sylvia Ellen Young, 1954, one son and one daughter. Worked as newspaper reporter and sub-editor.

Address: 99 George Barrow Road, Norwich, Norfolk NR4 7HU, England

John Gordon is a writer able to create a compelling story, full of atmosphere and chilling menace, yet maintaining the action at a pace guaranteed to draw the reader to the end.

CATCH YOUR DEATH AND OTHER GHOST STORIES
Magnet Books, 1985, 128p. – Pbk. O/P. – 0 416 54540 8
P. Hardy Books, 1984, 128p. – 0 7444 0029 5

Sinister and scary ghost stories for older readers with good nerves. Very enjoyable.
Age range: 12–14

THE EDGE OF THE WORLD
Armada Books, 1985, 192p. – Pbk. O/P. – 0 00 672249 0
P. Hardy Books, 1983, 192p. – 0 7444 0005 8

Ghost stories are always popular, but this book is above average. Completely believable, the children draw the reader

into the web of mystery. Together, reader and characters are led on a chillingly frightening journey to the edge of the world.
Age range: 12–14

THE GIANT UNDER THE SNOW
Penguin, 1971, 192p. – Pbk. – 0 14 030507 6
Hutchinson, 1968, 192p. – O/P. – 0 09 088370 5

John Gordon's first story proved an instant success. Atmospheric, the hidden menace threatens to erupt at any minute. Jonquil, in possession of the brooch, is constantly aware of it. An exciting and inventive story, but not for those of 'a nervous disposition'.
Age range: 11–13

THE HOUSE ON THE BRINK
Penguin, 1989, 192p. – Pbk. – 0 14 032629 4
P. Hardy Books, 1983, 192p. – 0 7444 0004 X

A most unusual story, as always, filled with a feeling of foreboding. A stump of wood, washed up by the tide, moves about, leaving a silvery trail, just like a giant slug. Full of evil and menace, it affects all within its radius. A really superb climax.
Age range: 11–13

THE QUELLING EYE
Armada Books, 1988, 160p. – Pbk. O/P. – 0 00 672841 3
Bodley Head, 1986, 140p. – 0 370 31011 X

A compelling, tense story with many threads. Chuck's mother feels that Tessa is an unsuitable friend for her son, and tries to separate them. Chuck and Tessa share a secret, a knowledge of magic, that makes them inseparable. Percy Falconer poses a great threat to all, and the young people feel ill-equipped to deal with this.
Age range: 12–14

RIDE THE WIND
Bodley Head, 1989, 140p. – 0 370 31279 1

The sequel to *The Giant Under the Snow*, when the menace of the warlord is resurrected even more strongly than before, and the counter-magic is less effective. Good to read if you enjoyed the first story, but it does not have the same impact.
Age range: 11–13

Other publications:

BURNING BABY AND OTHER GHOSTS
Walker Books, 1993. – Pbk. – 0 7445 3080 6
GHOST ON THE HILL
Penguin, 1989. – Pbk. – O/P. – 0 14 032833 5
GRASSHOPPER
Bodley Head, 1987. – Pbk. – O/P. – 0 370 31159 0
ORDINARY SEAMAN
Walker Books, 1993. – Pbk. – 0 7445 2378 8
SECRET CORRIDOR
Blackie, 1990. – O/P. – 0 216 92986 5
WATERFALL BOX
Kestrel Books, 1978. – O/P. – 0 7226 5490 1

GRANT, Gwen(doline Ellen)

British. Born Worksop, Nottinghamshire, 1940. Educated Open University, B.A.; Diploma in Adult Education. Married Ian Grant, 1964, two sons. Having left school at 15, has had a variety of jobs; now a full-time writer.

Address: 95 Watson Road, Worksop, Nottinghamshire, England

Gwen Grant's books are light-hearted easy-to-read romps which do not demand too much from the reader.

GYPSY RACER
Mammoth, 1992, 160p. – Pbk. – 0 7497 1052 7
Heinemann, 1991, 144p. – 0 434 94132 8

Ruth's longing for a dog is graphically described. It is not surprising, therefore, that when she finds an injured dog with pups, she resolves to rescue them. Against all odds, and with help from a

gypsy family, she succeeds. Good clear print puts this book within reach of all children.
Age range: 8–10

THE LILY PICKLE BAND BOOK
Armada Books, 1983, 160p. – Pbk. - O/P. –
0 00 672081 1
Heinemann, 1982, 160p. – O/P. –
0 434 94137 9
illustrated by Margaret Chamberlain

In the same series:

LILY PICKLE ELEVEN
Collins, 1990, 114p. – Pbk. – O/P. –
0 00 672892 8
Heinemann, 1987, 112p. – O/P. –
0 434 94134 4

Lily is made leader of the band, and is told she must write down everything that happens – which is how the book came to be written. The large print, coupled with the colloquial style, makes this a jolly read, full of fun and enjoyment.
Age range: 8–10

PRIVATE – KEEP OUT!
Armada Books, 1980, 144p. – Pbk. –
0 00 671652 0
Heinemann, 1978, 144p. – O/P. –
0 434 94170 0
illustrated by Faith Jacques

In the same series:

KNOCK AND WAIT
Armada Books, 1981, 144p. – Pbk. O/P. –
0 00 671762 4
Heinemann, 1979, 112p. – O/P. –
0 434 94138 7
illustrated by Gareth Floyd

ONE WAY ONLY
Armada Books, 1985, 128p. – Pbk. –
0 00 672290 3
Heinemann, 1983, 144p. – O/P. –
0 434 94136 0
illustrated by Faith Jacques

A series of anecdotal stories set in Nottinghamshire in the 1950s. Large families, no money, hiding from the rent man – it's all part of everyday life.

In spite of being so realistic, they are amusing to read. Excellent 'period' books.
Age range: 12–14

Other publications:

ENEMIES ARE DANGEROUS
Lions, 1993. – Pbk. – 0 00 673785 4
LAST CHANCE
Heinemann, 1992. – 0 434 96110 8
LITTLE BLUE CAR
Orchard Books, 1991. – 1 8521 3303 1
MATTHEW AND HIS MAGIC KITE
Andersen Press, 1977. – O/P. – 0 905478 14 2
REVOLUTIONARY'S DAUGHTER
Mammoth, 1991. – Pbk. – 0 7497 0422 5
WALLOPING STICK WAR
Heinemann, 1989. – 0 434 93055 5

GREEN, Roger J.

British. Born Buxton, Derbyshire, 1944. Educated Bakewell; University of London, B.A. (History); Teacher Training College, Sheffield. Married, two children. Teacher.

Address: 268 Abbeydale Road South, Dore,
Sheffield S17 3LN,
England

THE FEAR OF SAMUEL WALTON
OUP, 1984, 252p. – 0 19 271474 0

In the same series:

LENGTHENING SHADOW
OUP, 1986, 220p. – 0 19 271509 7

DEVIL FINDS WORK
OUP, 1987, 180p. – 0 19 271556 9

THEY WATCHED HIM DIE
OUP, 1988, 208p. – 0 19 271573 9
all illustrated by David Parkins

An intriguing quartet of quite extraordinary dramatic tension, which, at times, becomes quite unbearable. Set

in Derbyshire at the turn of the century, the central 'character' is the Stone, which in each book is the catalyst for many unpleasant happenings, and which inspires great fear. Excellent for reading to a class.
Age range: 11–13

SHE WAS A WITCH
OUP, 1992, 192p. – 0 19 271660 3

Roger Green's strength lies in his ability to transport his readers into the very centre of his story, such is the atmosphere he can create. In the 1850's, anyone with a knowledge of medicine is suspect, so Betsy and her mother suffer accordingly. The feeling of menace is very strong – a true spine-tingling read.
Age range: 12+

H

HALAM, Ann

Pseudonym for Gwyneth A. Jones. British. Born Manchester, 1952. Educated Sussex University, B.A. (Hons). Married Peter Gwilliam, 1976, one son. Civil servant.

Agent: Herta Ryder,
C/o Toby Eady Assoc.,
7 Gledhow Gardens,
London SW5 0BL,
England

Another writer with an exceptional talent for creating fantasy worlds which can seem as real as our own. Her books are not purely entertainment, but require some thought on the part of intelligent readers, who may glean some insight into the meaning of life itself.

ALLY, ALLY, ASTER
Penguin, 1990, 160p. – Pbk. – 0 14 032924 2
Allen & Unwin, 1981, 144p. – O/P. –
0 04 823192 4

A mixture of reality and fantasy, so well blended that it becomes impossible to separate them. Powerful descriptions of Ally and her element make it seem as if the cold is actually emanating from the page. Richard and Laura try hard to combat the encroachment of a distant past, but the witchcraft is very strong. A thoroughly enjoyable read.
Age range: 11–13

THE DAYMAKER
Penguin, 1989, 176p. – Pbk. O/P. –
0 14 032779 7
Orchard Books, 1987, 174p. – 1 85213 019 9

In the same series:

TRANSFORMATIONS
Penguin, 1990, 224p. – Pbk. – 0 14 034186 2
Orchard Books, 1988, 208p. – 1 8521 3119 5

THE SKYBREAKER
Penguin, 1992, 144p. – Pbk. – 0 14 034857 3
Orchard Books, 1990, 192p. – 1 85213 183 7
Orchard Books, 1990, 192p. – Pbk. –
1 85213 201 9

A trilogy of extraordinary depth set in the future. Zanne possesses powers she is unable to control, and must be trained so that she can destroy the Daymaker before it destroys the peace of Inland. Four years later, she undertakes a new task, to discover the secret hidden by the people of Minith. The conclusion to this book is both surprising and frightening. Both Zanne and the reader embark on the last voyage, to Magia, with some trepidation. A monster, buried for years, is beginning to stir, threatening once again the fabric of their society. Each book is totally compelling, involving the reader deeply.
Age range: 13–15

KING DEATH'S GARDEN
Chivers Press, 1988, 232p. – L/P. –
0 7451 0657 9
Penguin, 1988, 128p. – Pbk. O/P. –
0 14 032292 2
Orchard Books, 1986, 160p. – 1 85213 003 2

Maurice finds himself moving between two worlds. There is the 'real' world of school, where he is a loner, and the supernatural world of the cemetery, which begins to encroach more and more on his life. Where does Moth belong? As his fear increases, tension rises and the book draws to a dramatic conclusion. Very satisfying and enjoyable.
Age range: 11–13

Other publications:
ALDER TREE
Allen & Unwin, 1982. – O/P – 0 04 823205 X
DINOSAUR JUNCTION
Orchard Books, 1992. – 1 8521 3368 6

HALL

HALL, Willis

British. Born 1929. Educated Cockburn High school, Leeds. Married Valerie Shute, 1973, four sons, (three by previous marriage). Writer, playwright.

Address: C/o London Management, 235–241 Regent Street, London W1A 2JT, England

THE 'ANTELOPE' COMPANY ASHORE
Bodley Head, 1986, 156p. – 0 370 30775 5
Armada Books, 1986, 160p. – Pbk. – 0 00 672765 4

In the same series:

THE 'ANTELOPE' COMPANY AT LARGE
Armada Books, 1988, 160p. – Pbk. O/P. – 0 00 672926 6
Bodley Head, 1987, 160p. – 0 370 31151 5

THE RETURN OF THE 'ANTELOPE'
Chivers Press, 1990, 256p. – L/P. – O/P. – 0 7451 1103 3
J. Murray, 1988, 176p. – 0 7195 4508 0
Armada Books, 1985, 176p. – Pbk. – 0 00 672550 3
Bodley Head, 1985, 180p. – 0 370 30693 7
illustrated by Rowan Barnes-Murphy

Originally written as a serial for television, it proved so popular that the plot was turned into a series of novels. Willis Hall is able to maintain the suspense very well as the little people battle against overwhelming odds, helped by two children trying to protect them from the evil Harwell. Period detail adds an extra dimension.
Age range: 9–12

DR JEKYLL AND MR HOLLINS
Young Lions, 1991, 176p. – Pbk. – O/P – 0 00 674060 X
Bodley Head, 1988, 144p. – 0 370 31040 3

In the same series:

DRAGON DAYS
Chivers Press, 1991, 200p. – L/P. – 0 7451 1294 3
Armada Books, 1987, 142p. – Pbk. – 0 00 672614 3
Bodley Head, 1985, 132p. – O/P. – 0 370 30626 0

HENRY HOLLINS AND THE DINOSAUR
Red Fox, 1993, 192p. – Pbk. – 0 09 911611 1
Bodley Head, 1988, 192p. – 0 370 31255 4
Target Books, 1979, 192p. – Pbk. O/P. – 0 426 20043 8

THE INFLATABLE SHOP
Armada Books, 1986, 128p. – Pbk. – 0 00 672436 1
Bodley Head, 1984, 128p. – 0 370 30807 7

THE LAST VAMPIRE
Red Fox, 1993, 160p. – Pbk. – 0 09 911541 7
Chivers Press, 1987, 232p. – L/P. – 0 7451 0589 0
Bodley Head, 1982, 160p. – O/P. – 0 370 30503 5

SUMMER OF THE DINOSAUR
Bodley Head, 1977, 216p. – O/P. – 0 370 30003 3

VAMPIRE'S HOLIDAY
Bodley Head, 1992, 174p. – 0 370 31775 0

VAMPIRE'S REVENGE
Bodley Head, 1993, 144p. – 0 370 31772 6
all illustrated by Maggie Ling

Henry is a lovable and appealing small boy, to whom the most extraordinary and original things happen. Each book has its own individual adventure, always told with great humour. Readers need a certain linguistic competence, but the stories are sufficiently enjoyable to encourage children to tackle these full-length novels.
Age range: 9–11

Other publications:

BACK IN TIME WITH MEGABOT
Kingfisher Books, 1986. – O/P. – 0 86272 117 2
INCREDIBLE KIDNAPPING
Heinemann, 1975. – O/P. – 0 434 94200 6
IRISH ADVENTURES OF WORZEL GUMMIDGE
Sparrow Books, 1984. – Pbk. – 0 09 932970 0
MAKING OF MEGABOT
Kingfisher Books, 1986. – O/P. – 0 86272 116 4
TRIALS OF WORZEL GUMMIDGE
Penguin, 1980. – Pbk. – O/P. – 0 14 031390 7
WORZEL GUMMIDGE AND AUNT SALLY
Severn Ho. Publishers, 1982. – O/P. – 0 7278 0827 3

WORZEL GUMMIDGE AT THE FAIR
Penguin, 1980. – Pbk. – O/P. – 0 14 031381 8
WORZEL GUMMIDGE DOWN UNDER
Grafton Books, 1987. – Pbk. – O/P. – 0 583 31106 7
WORZEL GUMMDIGE GOES TO THE SEASIDE
Penguin, 1980. – Pbk. – O/P. – 0 14 050364 1
WORZEL'S BIRTHDAY
Penguin, 1981. – Pbk. – O/P. – 0 14 031487 3

HALLWORTH, Grace

West Indian. Born Trinidad. Schools and children's librarian, now full-time storyteller and writer.

LISTEN TO THIS STORY: TALES FROM THE WEST INDIES
Mammoth, 1992, 80p. – Pbk. – 0 7497 1058 6
Methuen, 1977, 80p. – 0 416 83220 2
illustrated by Dennis Ranston

In the same series:

MOUTH OPEN, STORY JUMP OUT
Mammoth, 1992, 96p. – Pbk. – 0 7497 1038 1
Methuen, 1984, 128p. – 0 416 23550 6
illustrated by Art Derry

A WEB OF STORIES
Methuen, 1990, 109p. – 0 416 09432 5
illustrated by Avril Turner

Three books of short stories, including an Anansi story, from the Caribbean. They are all traditional, and imbued with a special magic which only a master storyteller can contribute. Better read aloud, but older children will still enjoy reading them for themselves. *Age range: 7–10*

Other publications:

CARNIVAL KITE
Methuen, 1980. – O/P. – 0 416 87880 6

HAMILTON, Virginia (Esther)

American. Born Yellow Springs, Ohio, 1936. Educated Antioch College, Yellow Springs; Ohio State University, Columbia; New School for Social Research, New York. Married Arnold Adolff (poet), 1960, one daughter, one son. Lecturer and Visiting Professor.

Awards: Boston Globe Horn Book Award: *M. C. Higgins the Great*, 1974

American Library Association Newbery Award: *M. C. Higgins the Great*, 1975

Boston Globe Horn Book Award: *Sweet Whispers, Brother Rush*, 1983

Children's Rights Workshop Other Award: *The People could Fly*, 1986

Hans Christian Andersen Award, 1992

Address: Box 293,
Yellow Springs,
Ohio 45387,
USA

Agent: Dorothy Markinko,
McIntosh & Otis Inc,
310 Madison Avenue,
New York City,
New York 10017,
USA

Virginia Hamilton's background enables her to tackle the issue of racial problems. Superb use of language and an honest attitude to the problems of youth ensure each book offers readers a life-enriching experience.

ARILLA SUN DOWN
Heinemann, 1977, 252p. – O/P. – 0 241 89548 0

Arilla, the narrator, is 12 years old, and struggling to come to terms with approaching adulthood. She is the product of a mixed marriage which causes anguish to her older brother, who feels himself to be a full Indian, and dresses accordingly. A book of emotions rather than actions, but compelling reading just the same. There are no easy or glib answers, but at least

there is the promise of future happiness at the end of the book.
Age range: 12–14

COUSINS
Gollancz, 1991, 112p. – O/P. – 0 575 05084 5

A wonderful, moving story, exploring relationships and their importance. Cammy's feelings for her talented cousin fluctuate between loathing and envy, feelings which reach a disturbing climax when she tries to come between Cammy and her best friend. Her death leaves Cammy with an almost unbearable guilt complex which she struggles in vain to come to terms with.
Age range: 10–12

IN THE BEGINNING
*Pavilion Books, 1992, 164p. – 1 85145 865 4
illustrated by Barry Moser*

A lot of research by Virginia Hamilton has resulted in an intriguing collection of Creation stories from many different cultures. She provides notes about the origin of the stories, and the unusual illustrations add an extra dimension to make this an outstanding book.
Age range: 10+

JUSTICE AND HER BROTHERS
Hamish Hamilton, 1979, 256p. – O/P. – 0 241 10152 2

In the same series:

DUSTLAND
J. MacRae Books, 1980, 192p. – O/P. – 0 86203 080 3

THE GATHERING
J. MacRae books, 1981, 192p. – O/P. – 0 86203 037 4

A truly unusual trilogy about a little girl, her twin brothers and a friend. Together they form *The Unit* using super-sensory powers. In each book, they embark on a weird journey which draws the reader into its very heart. Each book is totally original and compelling, each with an outstanding conclusion. Not for the faint-hearted reader.
Age range: 13–15

M.C. HIGGINS THE GREAT
*Cornerstone Books, 1989, 304p. – L/P. – 1 55736 075 8
Armada Books, 1976, 220p. – Pbk. O/P. – 0 00 671172 3
Hamish Hamilton, 1975, 278p. – O/P. – 0 241 89214 7*

Although first published in 1974, this book still has a valid message for young people today. The Higgins family live in the shadow of a huge slag heap which threatens to engulf their home. M.C. daydreams about a better home until Lurhetta wanders into his life, causing him to start actively thinking about the situation. As always, there is a highly dramatic conclusion.
Age range: 12–15

THE PEOPLE COULD FLY: AMERICAN BLACK FOLK TALES
*Walker Books, 1986, 180p. – O/P. – 0 7445 0524 0
illustrated by Leo and Diane Dillon*

A collection of folk tales from American black history, which Virginia Hamilton has studied for many years. These re-tellings reflect her own love of folklore and are highly readable. The language is rhythmic and the stories flow easily. The print is large and clear, while the illustrations provide the perfect complement. A highly attractive book.
Age range: 9–12

PLANET OF JUNIOR BROWN
*Pan Books, 1989, 224p. – Pbk. – O/P. – 0 330 30778 9
Chivers Press, 1988, 312p. – 0 7451 0790 7*

A disturbing picture of what can happen to children who dare to buck the system. Junior plays truant, and finds an empty basement where he can feel private and practice his music. When this haven is deliberately destroyed, he is distraught, and retreats from reality. Only his friend

understands, and fights to stop him being institutionalized.
Age range: 12+

Other publications:
LITTLE LOVE
Pan Books, 1987. – Pbk. – O/P. – 0 330 29684 1
SWEET WHISPERS, BROTHER RUSH
Walker Books, 1990. – Pbk. – 0 7445 1435 5
WHITE ROMANCE
Gollancz, 1988. – O/P. – 0 575 04274 5

HAMLEY, Dennis

British. Born Kent, 1935. Educated Cambridge University, B.A. English. Married, two children. Lives in Hertfordshire. Education Advisor in English and drama. Dennis Hamley has written several books for children over the years, but none has stood the test of time. Recent books, however, deserve mention.

BADGER'S FATE
Deutsch, 1992, 112p. – 0 590 54019 X illustrated by Meg Rutherford

Attempting, perhaps, to capitalize on the success of *Hare's choice*, Dennis Hamley turned it into a trilogy concerning death. Hare's death was accidental, but Badger's was cruelly meant and proved too much for the children to cope with. Two endings to the class story, therefore, were provided, so that each child could choose their preferred ending.
Age range: 10–12

DANGLEBOOTS
*Collins, 1989, 140p. – Pbk. – 0 00 673246 1
Deutsch, 1987, 160p. – 0 233 98075 X
illustrated by Tony Ross*

Andy is so useless at football that he is nicknamed 'Dangleboots'. One day he buys a little pair of football boots as a mascot and his life is changed. The plot positively races along, with lots of humorous happenings, perfectly illustrated by Tony Ross.
Age range: 8–10

HARE'S CHOICE
*Collins, 1990, 112p. – Pbk. – 0 00 673503 7
Deutsch, 1988, 96p. – 0 233 98298 1
illustrated by Meg Rutherford*

A most unusual and memorable book. It begins with a poetic and powerful description of a hare running to her death. The rest of the book concerns two children who find the body and take it to show at school. The class decides to write a story about her, and thus she is immortalized, while the whole school benefits from the original sad event.
Age range: 10–12

HAWK'S VISION
*Deutsch, 1993, 112p. – 0 590 54129 3
illustrated by Meg Rutherford*

A neat drawing together of the first two stories, plus the interest of a new one. The children in Mr. Bray's class are upset because their school is dying in a way – it is designated too small, and must close. They want to do one last story together, and choose a hawk as their subject, appointing her guardian of the animals. She alone can defend them against the threatened invasion.
Age range: 10–12

Other publications:
BLOOD LINE
Deutsch, 1989. – Pbk. – 0 233 98445 3
CODED SIGNALS AND OTHER STORIES
Deutsch, 1990. – Pbk. – 0 233 98541 7
FOURTH PLANE AT THE FLYPAST
Armada Books, 1987. – Pbk. – 0 00 672766 2
HAUNTED UNITED
Armada Books, 1988. – Pbk. – O/P. – 0 00 672889 8
LANDINGS
Mayflower, 1981. – Pbk. – O/P. – 0 583 30422 2
SHIRT OFF A HANGED MAN'S BACK
Armada Books, 1986. – Pbk. – O/P. – 0 00 672530 9

HAMLEY

TIGGER AND FRIENDS
Collins, 1990. – Pbk. – O/P. – 0 00 663507 5
VERY FAR FROM HERE
Mayflower, 1979. – Pbk. – O/P. – 0 583 30286 6
WAR AND FREDDY
Deutsch, 1991. – 0 233 98662 6

QUAKE
Faber, 1990, 160p. – Pbk. – 0 571 14281 8
Faber, 1988, 176p. – 0 571 14698 8

Absorbed in her thoughts of what it would be like to meet her new family, Tarrian had no idea why the train was swaying so alarmingly, until it fell into the hole created by an earthquake. A graphic description of a terrible disaster, and the bravery of those who survived.
Age range: 10–12

HARDCASTLE, Michael

Also writes as David Clark. British, born Huddersfield, Yorkshire, 1933. Educated, Huddersfield. Royal Army Educational Corps. Newspaper reporter, literary editor, feature writer. M.B.E.

Awards: M.B.E.

Address: 17 Molescroft Park,
Beverley,
North Humberside
HU17 7EB,
England

A very experienced and prolific writer for children. He specializes in fictional sports books, including football, cricket, motorbike racing, snooker and horse-riding. They are packed with action, not too demanding, and fill a definite need. A selection of his non-sporting novels is given below.

JAMES AND THE TV STAR
Penguin, 1990, 96p. – Pbk. – 0 14 032736 3
Blackie, 1986, 48p. – 0 216 91894 4
illustrated by Pat McCarthy

A simple and easy to read story in which James contrives to meet his television hero.
Age range: 10–12

MAGIC PARTY
Blackie, 1988, 48p. – 0 216 92108 2
illustrated by Vanessa Julian-Ottie

Katie is dismayed to find her party is on the same day as her friend's. The problem requires an imaginative solution.
Age range: 10–12

Other publications:

ADVANTAGE MISS JACKSON
Mammoth, 1993. – Pbk. – 0 7497 1022 5
AWAY FROM HOME
Mammoth, 1989. – Pbk. – 0 7497 0479 9
AWAY TEAM
Mammoth, 1993. – Pbk. – 0 7497 0962 6
BEHIND THE GOAL
Pelham Books, 1980. – O/P. – 0 7207 1252 1
BLOOD MONEY
Benn, 1971. – O/P. – 0 510 07725 0
CAUGHT OUT
Magnet Books, 1985. – Pbk. – O/P. – 0 416 51930 X
CHASING GAME
M. Hardcastle, 1976. – 0 905519 00 0
COME AND GET ME
Benn, 1970. – O/P. – 0 510 07765 X
CRASH CAR
Benn, 1977. – Pbk. – O/P. – 0 510 07721 8
DEMON BOWLER
Heinemann, 1974. – O/P. – 0 434 95863 8
DOG BITES GOALIE AND OTHER STORIES
Methuen, 1993. – 0 416 18723 4
DON'T TELL ME WHAT TO DO
Heinemann, 1970. – O/P. – 0 434 94234 0
DOUBLE HOLIDAY
Blackie, 1985. – O/P. – 0 216 91701 8
FAST FROM THE GATE
Mammoth, 1990. – Pbk. – 0 7497 0443 8
FREE KICK
Mammoth, 1989. – Pbk. – 0 7497 0127 7
GIGANTIC HIT
Pelham Books, 1982. – O/P. – 0 7207 1305 6
GOAL!
Pan Books, 1979. – Pbk. – O/P. – 0 330 25811 7
GOALS IN THE AIR
Pan Books, 1976. – Pbk. – O/P. – 0 330 24529 5

GREEN MACHINE
Mammoth, 1990. – Pbk. – 0 7497 0289 3
HALF A TEAM
Mammoth, 1989. – Pbk. – 0 7497 0126 9
HIDDEN ENEMY
Methuen, 1986. – O/P. – 0 416 61560 0
IN THE NET
Mammoth, 1988. – Pbk. – 0 7497 0426 8
ISLAND MAGIC
Heinemann, 1973. – O/P. – 0 434 94152 2
JAMES AND THE HOUSE OF FUN
Blackie, 1991. – 0 216 93115 0
JOANNA'S GOAL
Blackie, 1990. – 0 216 92923 7
KICKBACK
Faber, 1992. – Pbk. – 0 571 16505 2
LIFE UNDERGROUND
Heinemann, 1975. – O/P. – 0 434 94141 7
LUCKY BREAK
Blackie, 1990. – O/P. – 0 216 92927 X
MARK ENGLAND'S CAP
Heinemann, 1990. – 0 434 93065 2
MASCOT
Mammoth, 1991. – Pbk. – 0 7497 0901 4
MASCOT; TEAM THAT WOULDN'T GIVE IN; SOCCER SPECIAL
Mammoth, 1992. – Pbk. – 0 7497 1317 8
MONEY FOR SALE
Heinemann, 1975. – Pbk. – O/P. – 0 435 27020 6
NO DEFENCE
Deutsch, 1986. – Pbk. – O/P. – 0 233 97912 3
ONE GOOD HORSE
Dent, 1993. – 0 460 88183 3
ONE KICK
Faber, 1989. – Pbk. – 0 571 15337 2
OWN GOAL
Faber, 1992. – 0 571 16411 0
PENALTY
Dent, 1991. – Pbk. – 0 460 88087 X
PLAYING BALL
Heinemann, 1972. – O/P. – 0 434 94143 3
RIVAL GAMES
Methuen, 1988. – O/P. – 0 416 00382 6
ROAR TO VICTORY
Dean, 1992. – 0 603 55079 7
SATURDAY HORSE
Mammoth, 1990. – Pbk. – 0 7497 0441 1
SECOND CHANCE
Faber, 1991. – O/P. – 0 571 16109 X

SHOOT ON SIGHT
Pan Books, 1979. – Pbk. – O/P. – 0 330 25809 5
THE SHOOTERS
Methuen, 1988. – Pbk. – O/P. – 0 416 07512 6
SNOOKERED!
Hippo Books, 1988. – Pbk. – 0 590 70906 2
SOCCER COMES FIRST
Pan Books, 1979. – Pbk. – O/P. – 0 330 25810 9
SOCCER SPECIAL
Mammoth, 1990. – Pbk. – 0 7497 0705 4
SOCCER SPECIAL; AWAY FROM HOME; IN THE NET
Dean, 1992. – 0 603 55080 0
SOCCER STAR
Heinemann, 1993. – 0 434 97688 1
SWIMMING CLUB: JUMP IN
Hippo Books, 1989. – Pbk. – 0 590 76033 5
SWIMMING CLUB: SPLASHDOWN
Hippo Books, 1989. – Pbk. – 0 590 76032 7
SWITCH HORSE
Mammoth, 1990. – Pbk. – 0 7497 0442 X
TEAM THAT WOULDN'T GIVE IN
Mammoth, 1990. – Pbk. – 0 7497 0556 6
TIGER OF THE TRACK
Mammoth, 1991. – Pbk. – 0 7497 0852 2
TOP OF THE LEAGUE
Heinemann, 1979. – O/P. – 0 434 95833 6
UNITED!
Methuen, 1973. – O/P. – 0 416 76390 1
WALKING THE GOLDFISH
Heinemann, 1990. – 0 434 97542 7
WINNING RIDER
Magnet Books, 1987. – Pbk. – O/P. – 0 416 04532 4

HILL, Douglas (Arthur)

Also writes as Martin Hillman. Canadian. Born Brandon, Manitoba, 1935. Educated in Prince Albert, Saskatchewan; University of Saskatchewan, B.A. (Hons); English University of Toronto. Married Gail Robinson, 1958 (divorced 1978), one son. Editor, science fiction advisor.

Address: 3 Hillfield Avenue,
London N8 7DU,
England

HILL

Agent: Sheila Watson,
Watson Little Ltd,
Suite 8,
Charing Cross Road,
London WC2H 0DG,
England

A highly acclaimed writer of science fiction, with a great ability to make the reader believe in his alien worlds, while telling exciting stories.

BLADE OF THE POISONER
Pan Books, 1989, 192p. – Pbk. – O/P. – 0 330 30692 8
Gollancz, 1987, 160p. – 0 575 03954 X

In the same series:

MASTER OF FIENDS
Pan Books, 1989, 192p. – Pbk. – 0 330 30691 X
Gollancz, 1987, 160p. – 0 575 04095 5

A world full of monsters and demons is the setting for these two novels. Powerful descriptions and excellent characterization bring this story of good versus evil vividly to life.
Age range: 12–14

EXILES OF COLSEC
Penguin, 1985, 128p. – Pbk. O/P. – 0 14 031767 8
Gollancz, 1984, 128p. – 0 575 03348 7

In the same series:

THE CAVES OF KLYDOR
Penguin, 1986, 128p. – Pbk. – 0 14 031768 6
Gollancz, 1984, 128p. – 0 575 03413 0

The first novel describes the harsh life on Earth ruled by the tyrannical ColSec, which causes a group of young people to face untold dangers in search of a better life. They hope that the planet Klydor is the answer. In the sequel, they are dismayed to learn that the dreaded ColSec has followed them. Finding out why proves to be dangerous and frightening.
Age range: 12–14

GALACTIC WARLORD
Pan Books, 1980, 128p. – Pbk. – 0 330 26186 X
Gollancz, 1979, 160p. – 0 575 02663 4

In the same series:

DEATHWING OVER VEYNAA
Pan Books, 1981, 128p. – Pbk. – 0 330 26446 X
Gollancz, 1980, 128p. – 0 575 02779 7

DAY OF THE STARWIND
Pan Books, 1982, 128p. – Pbk. – 0 330 26652 7
Gollancz, 1980, 128p. – 0 575 02917 X

PLANET OF THE WARLORD
Pan Books, 1982, 128p. – Pbk. – 0 330 26713 2
Gollancz, 1981, 128p. – 0 575 03009 7

YOUNG LEGIONARY
Pan Books, 1983, 128p. – Pbk. – 0 330 28104 6
Gollancz, 1982, 128p. – 0 575 03201 4

LAST LEGIONARY QUARTET: 'GALACTIC WARLORD', 'DEATHWING OVER VEYNAA', 'DAY OF THE STARWIND' AND 'PLANET OF THE WARLORD'
Pan Books, 1985, 460p. – Pbk. – 0 330 28954 3

The customary recipe involving a young man of noble character who vows revenge on those who wrecked his home. A space adventure story.
Age range: 12–14

THE HUNTSMAN
Pan Books, 1984, 144p. – Pbk. – 0 330 26956 9
Heinemann, 1982, 128p. – O/P. – 0 434 33601 7

In the same series:

WARRIORS OF THE WASTELAND
Pan Books, 1984, 128p. – Pbk. – 0 330 28452 5

Finn Ferral is the hero in these stories. His task is to rescue the family who adopted him as an abandoned baby. They have been kidnapped by huge

metal beings, and the task is fraught with terrible dangers.
Age range: 12–14

Other publications:

ALIEN CITADEL
Pan Books, 1985. – Pbk. – O/P. – 0 330 28563 7
ALIEN WORLDS
Pan Books, 1982. – Pbk. – O/P. – 0 330 26817 1
COLSEC REBELLION
Penguin, 1986. – Pbk. – O/P. – 0 14 031769 4
COYOTE THE TRICKSTER: LEGENDS OF THE NORTH AMERICAN INDIANS
Pan Books, 1981. – Pbk. – O/P. – 0 330 26263 7
EXPLOITS OF HERCULES
Severn Ho. Publishers, 1979. – O/P. – 0 7278 0423 5
GOBLIN PARTY
Gollancz, 1988. – 0 575 04338 5
HOW JENNIFER AND SPECKLE SAVED THE EARTH
Heinemann, 1986. – 0 434 93036 9
MOON MONSTERS
Mammoth, 1993. – Pbk. – 0 7497 1636 3
PENELOPE'S PENDANT
Pan Books, 1991. – Pbk. – 0 330 31772 5
PLANETFALL
OUP, 1986. – O/P. – 0 19 278113 8
TALE OF TRELLIE THE TROOG
BBC, 1992. – Pbk. – 0 563 34781 3
UNICORN DREAM
Heinemann, 1992. – 0 434 97674 1
VOYAGE OF MUDJACK
Methuen, 1993. – 0 416 18819 2

HOBAN, Russell (Conwell)

American. Born Lansdale, Pennsylvania, 1925. Educated Lansdale High school; Philadelphia Museum School of Industrial Art. US Army Infantry, WW II. Married: 1) Lillian Aberman (i.e. Lillian Hoban, illustrator), 1944 (divorced 1975), one son, three daughters; 2) Gundula Ahl, 1975, three sons. Artist, illustrator, copywriter, full-time writer since 1967.

Awards: Whitbread Award: *How Tom beat Captain Najark and his Hired Sportsmen*, 1974
Agent: David Higham Assoc. Ltd, 5–8 Lower John Street, London W1R 4HA, England

THE MOUSE AND HIS CHILD
Chivers Press, 1990, 312p. – L/P. – 0 7451 1104 1
Penguin, 1976, 192p. – Pbk. – 0 14 030841 5
Faber, 1969, 200p. – 0 571 08844 9
illustrated by Lillian Hoban

Now considered a modern children's classic, this story has much to offer at a variety of levels. The plot is an exciting adventure story as the clockwork mice journey through life searching for their lost home. They suffer many hardships and are always pursued by their arch-enemy, the rat. There are jokes which lighten the sadness of their plight, and man's eternal pursuit of happiness will never be better described.
Age range: 10–12

Other publications:

ACE DRAGON LIMITED
Red Fox, 1992. – Pbk. – 0 09 984200 9
ARTHUR'S NEW POWER
Gollancz, 1980. – O/P. – 0 575 02835 1
BABY SISTER FOR FRANCES
Hippo Books, 1983. – Pbk. – O/P. – 0 590 70276 9
BARGAIN FOR FRANCES
Mammoth, 1992. – Pbk. – 0 7497 1231 7
BATTLE OF ZORMLA
Walker Books, 1990. – Pbk. – 0 7445 1728 1
BEDTIME FOR FRANCES
Hippo Books, 1983. – Pbk. – O/P. – 0 590 70278 5
BEST FRIENDS FOR FRANCES
Hippo Books, 1983. – Pbk. – O/P. – 0 590 70277 7
BIG JOHN TURKLE
Walker Books, 1983. – O/P. – 0 7445 0075 3
BIRTHDAY FOR FRANCES
Hippo Books, 1983. – Pbk. – O/P. – 0 590 70279 3
BREAD AND JAM FOR FRANCES
Penguin, 1977. – Pbk. – 0 14 050176 2

HOBAN

CHARLIE MEADOWS
Walker Books, 1984. – O/P. – 0 7445 0076 1

CHARLIE THE TRAMP
Scholastic Book Services, US, 1979. – Pbk. – O/P. – 0 590 72035 X

CORONA AND THE TIN FROG AND OTHER STORIES
Cape, 1979. – O/P. – 0 224 01397 1

CROCODILE AND PIERROT
Cape, 1975. – O/P. – 0 224 01172 3

DANCING TIGERS
Red Fox, 1990. – Pbk. – 0 09 975020 1

DINNER AT ALBERTA'S
Red Fox, 1992. – Pbk. – 0 09 997690 0

EGG THOUGHTS AND OTHER FRANCES SONGS
Faber, 1973. – O/P. – 0 571 10203 4

EMMET OTTER'S JUG-BAND CHRISTMAS
World's Work, 1973. – O/P. – 0 437 46707 4

FLAT CAT
Methuen/Walker, 1980. – O/P. – 0 416 89960 9

FLIGHT OF BEMBEL RUDZUK
Walker Books, 1990. – Pbk. – 0 7445 1729 X

GREAT FRUIT GUM ROBBERY
Walker Books, 1989. – Pbk. – O/P. – 0 7445 1210 7

HARVEY'S HIDEOUT
Red Fox, 1992. – Pbk. – 0 09 997330 8

HERMAN THE LOSER
World's Work, 1972. – O/P. – 0 437 46706 6

HOW TOM BEAT CAPTAIN NAJORK AND HIS HIRED SPORTSMEN
Red Fox, 1993. – Pbk. – 0 09 922171 3

JIM FROG
Walker Books, 1983. – O/P. – 0 7445 0074 5

JIM HEDGEHOG AND THE LONESOME TOWER
Penguin, 1992. – Pbk. – 0 14 034479 9

JIM HEDGEHOG'S SUPERNATURAL CHRISTMAS
Penguin, 1991. – Pbk. – 0 14 034217 6

LAVINIA BAT
Walker Books, 1984. – O/P. – 0 7445 0077 X

LITTLE BRUTE FAMILY
Pan Books, – Pbk. – O/P. – 0 330 23542 7

MARZIPAN PIG
Penguin, 1988. – Pbk. – 0 14 032683 9

MOLE FAMILY'S CHRISTMAS
Red Fox, 1992. – Pbk. – 0 09 918201 7

MONSTERS
Gollancz, 1993. – Pbk. – 0 575 05578 2

NEAR THING FOR CAPTAIN NAJORK
Red Fox, 1993. – Pbk. – 0 09 922161 6

PEDALLING MAN
Mammoth, 1992. – Pbk. – 0 7497 0913 8

PONDERS
Walker Books, 1989. – Pbk. – 0 7445 0828 2

RAIN DOOR
Macmillan, 1987. – Pbk. – O/P. – 0 333 44648 8

SEA-THING CHILD
Gollancz, 1972. – O/P. – 0 575 01438 5

THE SERPENT TOWER
Methuen, 1981. – O/P. – 0 416 05600 8

STONE DOLL OF SISTER BUTE
Pan Books, 1973. – Pbk. – O/P. – 0 330 23745 4

THEY CAME FROM AARGH!
Walker Books, 1989. – Pbk. – 0 7445 1211 5

TOM AND THE TWO HANDLES
World's Work, 1977. – Pbk. – O/P. – 0 437 96010 2

TWENTY ELEPHANT RESTAURANT
Penguin, 1987. – Pbk. – O/P. – 0 14 033112 3

HOLM, Anne

Born Denmark, 1922. Widow, one son, two grandchildren. Journalist and writer.

Address: C/o Gyldendal Publishers,
3 Klareboderne,
DK – 1001 Copenhagen,
Denmark

THE HOSTAGE
Mammoth, 1990, 192p. – Pbk. – 0 7497 0370 9
Magnet Books, 1982, 180p. – Pbk. – O/P. – 0 416 24580 3

A political thriller set in Denmark, now of historical interest rather than topical. It centres round a plot to force Denmark to withdraw from NATO which fails, placing a boy's life in danger unless he can help himself. Fast paced and exciting, the politics do not intrude.
Age range: 11–13

SKY GREW RED
Mammoth, 1992, 160p. – Pbk. – 0 7497 1041 1
Methuen, 1991, 160p. – O/P. – 0 416 16272 X

A moving story illustrating the difference between the way adults and

children see things. It is set at the time of the Napoleonic wars. Louise is Danish and Tim is English – but instead of regarding each other as enemies, they are firm friends, and vow to do their utmost to prevent Denmark becoming caught up in the war. It is an exciting adventure story, but also serves as an excellent scene setter for children studying this historical period.
Age range: 10–12

Other publications:

I AM DAVID
Mammoth, 1989. – Pbk. – 0 7497 0136 6

HOOVER, Helen Mary

American. Born Stark County, Ohio, 1935. Educated Louisville High School; Mount Union College, Alliance, Ohio; Los Angeles School of Nursing.

Address: 9405 Ulysses Court,
Burke,
Virginia 22015,
USA

Agent: Russell and Volkening,
50 West 29th Street,
New York,
New York 100001,
USA

A prolific writer of imaginative and thought-provoking science fiction. Truths about present society are highlighted by comparison with other worlds, other sets of values.

ANOTHER HEAVEN, ANOTHER EARTH
Methuen, 1983, 174p. – O/P – 0 416 23040 7

A choice has to be made between a simple life on the doomed planet Xilan, and a new technological life on Earth. This is not, by any means, a straightforward choice, as it involves a completely different set of values.
Age range: 12–14

CHILDREN OF MORROW
Penguin, 1987, 240p. – Pbk. – 0 14 031873 9
Methuen, 1975, 240p. – O/P – 0 416 81540 5

Tra's life is unbearably hard; because she is different and can 'see' things, she is an outcast. Gradually she comes to realize she has full telepathic powers, which she uses to try to escape, but time is against her. Undemanding, but totally absorbing.
Age range: 11–13

THE DELIKON
Methuen, 1978, 240p. – 0 416 86220 9

Varina, about to leave Earth and return to her own people, the Delikon, is kidnapped along with her pupils. They succeed in escaping, but time is running out for her if she is to be able to return to the Delikon. A powerful story, and excellent characterization.
Age range: 12–14

THE LOST STAR
Penguin, 1987, 160p. – Pbk. O/P –
0 14 032166 7

A moral tale of choices, movingly told. Lian, investigating the planet Balthor, discovers the gentle 'Lumpies'. (What an evocative name!) She must decide whether to reveal their existence, or to try to protect them.
Age range: 12–14

THE RAINS OF ERIDAN
Methuen, 1979, 292p. – O/P – 0 416 87100 3

Eridan is a beautiful planet, which strongly contrasts with the stark horror of the drama played out in this novel. The whole population is overwhelmed by a fear for which there appears to be no cause. Only when it is almost too late and the rains have begun does it become obvious what the strange, huge, mummified mounds are.
Age range: 11–13

THE SHEPHERD MOON
Methuen, 1984, 144p. – O/P – 0 416 45630 8

Set in the distant future on Earth, Merry

watches the arrival of a young man who has come from an artificial moon, generally believed to be uninhabited. This sparks off an investigation which reveals as much about Earth as it does about the Shepherd Moon. An exciting plot with an underlying serious message.
Age range: 12–14

THIS TIME OF DARKNESS
Penguin, 1987, 176p. – Pbk. O/P. –
0 14 031872 0
Methuen, 1982, 160p. – O/P. – 0 416 21770 2

Amy's whole life has been spent in the underground city until she befriends Axel, who tells her the truth about Outside. They plan to escape, but survival is hazardous, even in the devastated landscape Outside. Pointing the finger at social structures based on class invites comparison with our own culture. The climax is cautiously optimistic.
Age range: 12–14

HOROWITZ, Anthony

British. Born London, 1955. Educated Rugby School; University of York. Married, one son.

Awards: Lancashire County Library Children's Book of the Year Award: *Groosham Grange*, 1989

Address: 32 Wandsworth Bridge Road, London SW6 2TH, England

DAY OF THE DRAGON
Methuen, 1989, 160p. – 0 416 11392 3

In the same series:

THE DEVIL'S DOORBELL
Magnet Books, 1985, 160p. – Pbk. –
0 416 45700 2
P. Hardy Books, 1983, 160p. –
0 7444 0007 4

THE NIGHT OF THE SCORPION
Magnet Books, 1986, 160p. – Pbk. –
0 416 54550 5
P. Hardy Books, 1985, 160p. –
0 7444 0053 8

THE SILVER CITADEL
Methuen, 1987, 160p. – Pbk. –
0 416 02572 2
Methuen, 1987, 150p. – O/P. –
0 416 97000 1

A series of thrillers about a group of children whose task is to defeat the Old Ones in order to break their power. Each one has a different setting, but all are full of action and excitement.
Age range: 12–14

THE FALCON'S MALTESER
Lions, 1991, 160p. – Pbk. – O/P. –
0 00 674210 6
Grafton Books, 1986, 160p. – 0 246 12863 1

A humorous thriller with an unusual beginning when a dwarf walks into a private detective's office and leaves a mysterious parcel. Eventually it is discovered that it contains Maltesers, not sufficient reason for murder. Tim tries to solve the mystery. It is fun to read, especially if readers are already familiar with Raymond Chandler's *The Maltese Falcon*.
Age range: 10–13

Other publications:

ADVENTURER
Corgi, 1987. – Pbk. – O/P. – 0 552 52449 2

CROSSBOW: THE ADVENTURES OF WILLIAM TELL
Penguin, 1987. – Pbk. – O/P. – 0 14 032353 8

ENTER FREDERICK K. BOWER
Granada, 1985. – Pbk. – O/P. – 0 583 30856 2

GROOSHAM GRANGE
Methuen, 1988. – O/P. – 0 416 02462 9

JUST ASK FOR DIAMOND
Armada Books, 1989. – Pbk. – O/P. –
0 00 673396 4

MISHA, THE MAGICIAN AND THE MYSTERIOUS AMULET
Arlington Books, 1981. – O/P. – 0 85140 507 X

MYTHS AND LEGENDS
Kingfisher Books, 1991. – Pbk. – 0 86272 786 3

PUBLIC ENEMY NO. TWO
Lions, 1991. – Pbk. – O/P. – 0 00 674211 4
ROBIN OF SHERWOOD: HOODED MAN
Penguin, 1986. – Pbk. – O/P. – 0 14 032058 X
SINISTER SECRET OF FREDERICK K. BOWER
Arlington Books, 1979. – O/P. – 0 85140 332 8
SOUTH BY SOUTH EAST
Lions, 1991. – Pbk. – 0 00 673821 4

HUGHES, Shirley

British. Born Hoylake, Lancashire, 1929. Educated West Kirby High School for Girls; Liverpool Art School; Ruskin College of Art, Oxford. Married John Vulliamy, 1952, two sons, one daughter. Freelance illustrator and writer.

Awards: Children's Rights Workshop Other Award: *Helpers*, 1976

Eleanor Farjeon Award, 1984

Address: 63 Lansdowne Road, London W11 2LG, England

One of the best known and most talented names in the field of children's literature, equally capable in writing and illustrating. Most of her work is for pre-school children, but some of her books are suitable for older children.

ANOTHER HELPING OF CHIPS
Armada Books, 1988, 64p. – Pbk. –
0 00 672745 X
Bodley Head, 1986, 64p. – 0 370 30751 8

In the same series:

CHARLIE MOON AND THE BIG BONANZA BUST-UP
Red Fox, 1992, 128p. – Pbk. – 0 09 992670 9
Chivers Press, 1990, 184p. – L/P. –
0 7451 1151 3
Bodley Head, 1982, 128p. – 0 370 30918 9

CHIPS AND JESSIE
Armada Books, 1987, 64p. – Pbk. –
0 00 672532 5
Bodley Head, 1985, 64p. – 0 370 30666 X

HERE COMES CHARLIE MOON
Red Fox, 1991, 32p. – Pbk. – 0 09 992230 4
Chivers Press, 1990, 184p. – L/P. –
0 7451 1067 3
Bodley Head, 1980, 144p. – 0 370 30335 0

A wonderful combination of cartoons, pictures and continuous text. Different stories about two friends and their dog and cat entice the reader on to the end.
Age range: 7–9

IT'S TOO FRIGHTENING FOR ME
Viking, 1993, 80p. – 0 670 84904 9
Penguin, 1986, 64p. – Pbk. – 0 14 032008 3

An amusing ghost story with lots of illustrations. Together, they form an irresistible combination for young readers.
Age range: 7–9

Other publications:

ALFIE COLLECTION
Bodley Head, 1992. – 0 370 31753 X
ALFIE GETS IN FIRST
Hutchinson, 1993. – 0 09 176581 1
ALFIE GIVES A HAND
Hutchinson, 1993. – 0 09 176571 4
ALFIE OUT OF DOORS
Bodley Head, 1992. – 0 370 31516 2
ALFIE'S FEET
Hutchinson, 1993. – 0 09 176591 9
ALL SHAPES AND SIZES
Walker Books, 1988. – Pbk. – 0 7445 0926 2
ANGEL MAE
Walker Books, 1991. – Pbk. – 0 7445 2032 0
BATHWATER'S HOT
Walker Books, 1988. – Pbk. – 0 7445 0921 1
BIG ALFIE AND ANNIE ROSE STORYBOOK
Red Fox, 1990. – Pbk. – 0 09 975030 9
BIG CONCRETE LORRY
Walker Books, 1991. – Pbk. – 0 7445 2033 9
BOUNCING
Walker Books, 1993. – 0 7445 2513 6
CLOTHES
Bodley Head, 1974. – O/P. – 0 370 02039 1
COLOURS
Walker Books, 1988. – Pbk. – 0 7445 0924 6
DOGGER
J. MacRae, 1991. – 1 8568 1152 2
EVENING AT ALFIE'S
Hutchinson, 1993. – 0 09 176561 7

GIVING
Walker Books, 1993. – 0 7445 2512 8
HELPERS
Red Fox, 1992. – Pbk. – 0 09 992650 4
HOLLYWELL FAMILY
Bodley Head, 1973. – O/P. – 0 370 01147 3
MOVING MOLLY
J. MacRae, 1992. – 1 8568 1044 5
NOISY
Walker Books, 1988. – Pbk. – 0 7445 0923 8
OUT AND ABOUT
Walker Books, 1990. – Pbk. – 0 7445 1422 3
SALLY'S SECRET
Red Fox, 1992. – Pbk. – 0 09 992660 1
SNOW LADY
Walker Books, 1992. – Pbk. – 0 7445 2357 5
STORIES BY FIRELIGHT
Bodley Head, 1993. – 0 370 31794 7
TROUBLE WITH JACK
Corgi, 1986. – Pbk. – 0 552 52306 2
TWO SHOES, NEW SHOES
Walker Books, 1988. – Pbk. – 0 7445 0925 4
UP AND UP
Red Fox, 1991. – Pbk. – 0 09 992250 9
WHEELS
Walker Books, 1992. – Pbk. – 0 7445 2012 6
WHEN WE WENT TO THE PARK
Walker Books, 1988. – Pbk. – 0 7445 0922 X

HUGHES, Ted (i.e. Edward James)

British. Born Mytholmroyd, Yorkshire, 1930. Educated Mexborough Grammar School, Yorkshire; Pembroke College, Cambridge, B.A. Archaeology and Anthropology, M.A. RAF, 1948–50. Married: 1) Sylvia Plath, poet, 1956 (died 1963), one daughter, one son; 2) Carol Orchard, 1970. Lived in the USA 1957–59. Now lives in North Tawton, Devon. Gardener, night-watchman, zoo attendant, teacher, reader and editor.

Awards: Signal Poetry Award 1979, 1983, 1985.

Guardian Children's Fiction award: *What is the Truth?*, 1985

Kurt Maschler Award: *The Iron Man*, 1985

Hon. Fellow, Pembroke College, Cambridge, 1986
O.B.E., 1977
Poet Laureate, 1984

Address: C/o Faber & Faber Ltd, 3 Queen's Square, London WC1N 3AU, England

Better known for his poetry, it is, therefore, logical that any book for children by Ted Hughes will be a powerful linguistic experience. At the same time, he creates stories so well that his linguistic excellence is no barrier to sheer enjoyment.

HOW THE WHALE BECAME, AND OTHER STORIES
Faber, 1989, 72p. – Pbk. – 0 571 14184 6
Faber, n.d., 72p. – O/P. – 0 571 05615 6
illustrated by George Adamson

Imaginative stories recounting how each of the animals became the way we know them.
Age range: 8–10

THE IRON MAN: A STORY IN FIVE NIGHTS
Faber, 1989, 64p. – Pbk. – 0 571 14149 8
Faber, 1985, 53p. – 0 571 13675 3
illustrated by Andrew Davidson

A modern fairy story or fable with an important message. It has a gripping beginning, and holds the reader, (or listener, as it is superb for reading aloud), spellbound to the very end.
Age range: 8–10

THE IRON WOMAN
Faber, 1993, 128p. – 0 571 17003 X
illustrated by Andrew Davidson

A sequel to The Iron man, making an impassioned plea to humankind to stop and think before the world is polluted out of existence by industrial waste.
Age range: 9–11

TALES OF THE EARLY WORLD
Faber, 1990, 128p. – Pbk. – 0 571 14478 0
Faber, 1988, 128p. – 0 571 15126 4
illustrated by Andrew Davidson

Superbly written, the stories relate how the creatures came to be invented. Lots of humour within this natural, almost chatty, style.
Age range: 9–11

Other publications:

EARTH OWL AND OTHER MOON PEOPLE
Faber, 1963. – O/P. – 0 571 05627 X
FFANGS THE VAMPIRE BAT AND THE KISS OF TRUTH
Faber, 1990. – Pbk. – 0 571 15461 1
MEET MY FOLKS!
Faber, 1987. – Pbk. – 0 571 13644 3
MOON-BELLS AND OTHER POEMS
Bodley Head, 1986. – 0 370 30762 3
MOON-WHALES
Faber, 1991. – Pbk. – 0 571 16320 3
NESSIE THE MANNERLESS MONSTER
Faber, 1992. – Pbk. – 0 571 16213 4
SEASON SONGS
Faber, 1985. – 0 571 13703 2
UNDER THE NORTH STAR
Faber, 1981. – O/P. – 0 571 11721 X
WHAT IS THE TRUTH? : A FARMYARD FABLE FOR THE YOUNG
Faber, 1986. – Pbk. – 0 571 14510 8

HUTCHINS, Pat (née Goundry)

British. Born Catterick Camp, Yorkshire, 1942. Educated Darlington School of Art; Leeds College of Art. Married Laurence Hutchins, 1966, two children. Art Director, illustrator, writer.

Awards: Library Association Kate Greenaway Medal: *The Wind Blew*, 1974

Address: 75 Flask Walk, London NW3 1ET, England

Well known for her admirable picture books, Pat Hutchins shows that her talents easily stretch to writing humorous mystery stories with enormous appeal to young readers who need encouragement.

THE CURSE OF THE EGYPTIAN MUMMY
Armada Books, 1985, 160p. – Pbk. – 0 00 672463 9
Bodley Head, 1983, 160p. – O/P. – 0 370 30983 9

In the same series:

FOLLOW THAT BUS!
Red Fox, 1992, 102p. – Pbk. – 0 09 993220 2
Bodley Head, 1977, 112p. – O/P. – 0 370 30055 6

THE MONA LISA MYSTERY
Armada Books, 1987, 192p. – Pbk. – 0 00 672589 9
Bodley Head, 1981, 192p. – 0 370 30310 5
all illustrated by Laurence Hutchins

Amusing plots, packed with action and told in large, clear print: these books are excellent for readers gaining confidence.
Age range: 7–9

RATS!
Red Fox, 1991, 96p. – Pbk. – 0 09 993190 7
Bodley Head, 1989, 96p. – 0 370 31305 4
illustrated by Laurence Hutchins

Sam loves rats and would like one for a pet. Not surprisingly, Mum says no, but he buys one to prove to her that they are lovable. That is when the fun begins.
Age range: 7–9

Other publications:

BEST TRAIN SET EVER
Red Fox, 1991. – Pbk. – 0 09 993210 5
CHANGES, CHANGES
Penguin, 1973. – Pbk. – O/P. – 0 14 050066 9
CLOCKS AND MORE CLOCKS
Penguin, 1974. – Pbk. – 0 14 050091 X
DON'T FORGET THE BACON
Penguin, 1978. – Pbk. – 0 14 050315 3
DOORBELL RANG
Penguin, 1988. – Pbk. – 0 14 050709 4
GOOD-NIGHT, OWL!
J. MacRae, 1993. – 1 8568 1088 7
HAPPY BIRTHDAY, SAM
Penguin, 1981. – Pbk. – 0 14 050339 0
HOUSE THAT SAILED AWAY
Red Fox, 1992. – Pbk. – 0 09 993200 8

HUTCHINS

KING HENRY'S PALACE
Pan Books, 1988. – Pbk. – 0 330 30389 9

MY BEST FRIEND
J. MacRae, 1993. – 1 8568 1157 3

ONE HUNTER
Penguin, 1984. – Pbk. – 0 14 050399 4

ONE-EYED JAKE
Penguin, 1988. – Pbk. – 0 14 050724 8

ROSIE'S WALK
J. MacRae, 1992. – 1 8568 1074 7

SILLY BILLY
J. MacRae, 1992. – 1 8568 1173 5

SILVER CHRISTMAS TREE
Penguin, 1989. – Pbk. – 0 14 050952 6

SURPRISE PARTY
Red Fox, 1993. – Pbk. – 0 09 920721 4

TALE OF THOMAS MEAD
Bodley Head, 1981. – O/P. – 0 370 30357 1

TIDY TITCH
J. MacRae, 1991. – 1 8568 1151 4

TITCH
J. MacRae, 1991. – 1 8568 1142 5

TOM AND SAM
Red Fox, 1993. – Pbk. – 0 09 920731 1

VERY WORST MONSTER
Penguin, 1986. – Pbk. – 0 14 050565 2

WHAT GAME SHALL WE PLAY?
J. MacRae, 1990. – 0 86203 462 0

WHERE'S THE BABY?
Red Fox, 1992. – Pbk. – 0 09 919621 2

WHICH WITCH IS WHICH?
Penguin, 1991. – Pbk. – O/P. – 0 14 054359 7

WIND BLEW
Penguin, 1978. – Pbk. – 0 14 050236 X

YOU'LL SOON GROW INTO THEM, TITCH
Penguin, 1985. – Pbk. – 0 14 050434 6

I

IMPEY, Rose

British. Born Northwich, Cheshire. Two daughters. Teacher, writer.

Address: 38 Wanlip Road,
Syston,
Leicester LE7 8PA,
England

A champion of equality for women, and a writer of great ability and diversity, Rose Impey speaks loudly and clearly to children of today. She tackles situations which they have to face, and shows that solutions can be found.

THE GIRLS' GANG
*Armada Books, 1989, 192p. – Pbk. –
0 00 672878 2
Heinemann, 1986, 158p. – O/P. –
0 434 94390 8
illustrated by Glenys Ambrus*

Flying the flag for equality of the sexes, this book points out in a most amusing and light-hearted way the various areas in which, for no good reason, it is taken for granted that boys are better or stronger. Mr Mills is at a loss as to how to handle eleven-year-olds who set about disproving his beliefs of a lifetime.
Age range: 9–11

INSTANT SISTERS
*Collins, 1990, 192p. – Pbk. – 0 00 673708 0
Orchard Books, 1989, 192p. – O/P. –
1 8521 3170 5*

A highly realistic portrayal of how difficult it can be when children have to live together through re-marriage, irrespective of their own personal wishes. Tina and Joanne have nothing in common, very little space in which to function, and a great resentment of each other's presence. No easy solution is offered, but it is suggested that with time, patience and tolerance, the situation can improve. A comforting book for those who find themselves in a similar situation – a good story for others.
Age range: 9–11

WHO'S A CLEVER GIRL, THEN?
*Heinemann, 1985, 48p. – 0 434 93029 6
illustrated by Andre Amstutz*

An omnibus edition of various stories published separately. Amusing, easy to read, and well-illustrated, it will appeal to all young readers struggling to gain confidence.
Age range: 7–9

Other publications:

ANKLE GRABBER
Ragged Bears, 1989. – 1 8708 1707 9
THE BADDIES
Dean, 1992. – Pbk. – 0 603 55115 7
BAKED BEAN QUEEN
Penguin, 1988. – Pbk. – 0 14 050701 9
BEDTIME BEAST
Penguin, 1989. – Pbk. – O/P. – 0 14 050703 5
BIRTHDAY FOR BLUEBELL: THE OLDEST COW IN THE WORLD
Orchard Books, 1993. – 1 8521 3455 0
BOOK OF FAIRY TALES
*Ladybird Books, 1980. – Pbk. – O/P. –
0 7214 7512 4*
DEMON KEVIN
Penguin, 1988. – Pbk. – O/P. – 0 14 050700 0
DESPERATE FOR A DOG
Armada Books, 1988. – Pbk. – 0 00 673007 8
FIRST CLASS
Orchard Books, 1993. – Pbk. – 1 8521 3505 0
FLAT MAN
Ragged Bears, 1988. – 1 8708 1705 2
HOT DOG HARRIS: THE SMALLEST DOG IN THE WORLD
Orchard Books, 1993. – 1 8521 3457 7
HOUDINI DOG
Armada Books, 1989. – Pbk. – 0 00 673366 2
JOE'S CAFE
Orchard Books, 1991. – Pbk. – 1 8521 3357 0

IMPEY

JUMBLE JOAN
Ragged Bears, 1989. – 1 8708 1708 7
LETTER TO FATHER CHRISTMAS
Orchard Books, 1992. – Pbk. – 1 8521 3326 0
LITTLE SMASHER
Penguin, 1989. – Pbk. – O/P. – 0 14 050705 1
MY MUM AND OUR DAD
Penguin, 1992. – Pbk. – 0 14 050953 4
NOT-SO-CLEVER GENIE
Heinemann, 1987. – 0 434 93041 5
ORCHARD BOOK OF FAIRY TALES
Orchard Books, 1992. – 1 8521 3382 1
PIED PIPER
Ladybird Books, 1984. – Pbk. – O/P. – 0 7214 7530 2
RABBIT AND TEDDY TALES
Dean, 1993. – 0 603 55124 6
RABBIT'S STORY
Mammoth, 1990. – Pbk. – 0 7497 0245 1
REVENGE OF THE RABBIT
Orchard Books, 1993. – Pbk. – 1 8521 3501 8
SCARE YOURSELF TO SLEEP
Ragged Bears, 1988. – 1 8708 1706 0
TEDDY'S STORY
Mammoth, 1990. – Pbk. – 0 7497 0239 7
TINY TIM: THE LONGEST JUMPING FROG
Orchard Books, 1993. – 1 8521 3453 4
TOO MANY BABIES: THE LARGEST LITTER IN THE WORLD
Orchard Books, 1993. – 1 8521 3451 8
TOOTHBRUSH MONSTER
Penguin, 1989. – Pbk. – 0 14 050702 7
TOUGH TEDDY
Penguin, 1989. – O/P. – 0 14 050704 3
TROUBLE WITH THE TUCKER TWINS
Puffin Books, 1993. – Pbk. – 0 14 054089 X
WHO'S AFRAID NOW?
BBC, 1991. – Pbk. – 0 563 34758 9
YOU HERMAN, ME MARY
Heinemann, 1989. – 0 434 93066 0

IRESON, Barbara

Married. Lives in France. Teacher, writer. Barbara Ireson is an experienced and knowledgeable contributor to the field of children's books and reading. She can always be relied on to provide excellent material (not necessarily written by her), for a variety of age groups. The various collections of poems and stories serve the dual purpose of being suitable for reading aloud and for giving to children to enjoy reading for themselves.

CREEPY-CRAWLY STORIES
Beaver Books, 1987, 96p. – Pbk. – 0 09 951230 0
Hutchinson, 1986, 112p. – 0 09 165080 1
illustrated by Lesley Smith

Delightful, amusing stories by different authors about a variety of insects and mini-beasts.
Age range: 8–10

FANTASY TALES
Hamlyn, 1981, 192p. – Pbk. O/P. – 0 600 20056 6
Faber, 1977, 218p. – 0 571 10922 5

An excellent collection of weird and wonderful stories by first-class authors. Some are chilling, some are exciting – all are gripping.
Age range: 12–14

FIGHTING IN BREAK, AND OTHER STORIES
Penguin, 1989, 128p. – Pbk. – 0 14 032741 X
Faber, 1987, 124p. – 0 571 14623 6
illustrated by Susan Hellard

In the same series:

IN A CLASS OF THEIR OWN: SCHOOL STORIES
Penguin, 1987, 160p. – Pbk. – 0 14 032024 5
Faber, 1985, 149p. – O/P. – 0 571 13474 2

School stories are always popular, being within the experience of every child, and a wide range of themes and styles is included in these collections. Some stories are complete, some are excerpts; undoubtedly something for everyone.
Age range: 9–12

GHOSTLY LAUGHTER
Hamlyn, 1981, 160p. – Pbk. O/P. – 0 600 20322 0

Although some of the ghosts in these stories are frightening, most provoke

laughter. A thoroughly enjoyable collection of stories.
Age range: 10–12

NAUGHTY STORIES: TALES OF TERRIBLE CHILDREN
Red Fox, 1990, 96p. – Pbk. – 0 09 969920 6
Hutchinson, 1989, 96p. – 0 09 173893 8

In the same series:

EVEN NAUGHTIER STORIES
Red Fox, 1991, 96p. – Pbk. – 0 09 980890 0
Hutchinson, 1990, 96p. – 0 09 174388 5

NAUGHTIEST STORIES
Hutchinson, 1993, 88p. – 0 09 176229 4
all illustrated by Tony Ross

An irresistible combination with Barbara Ireson choosing stories about naughty children who won't brush their teeth, or tidy their room, or eat their meals, and Tony Ross providing the perfect illustrations. Large clear print makes this a really attractive book.
Age range: 7–9

NEVER MEDDLE WITH MAGIC
Penguin, 1988, 288p. – Pbk. – 0 14 032269 8

In the same series:

THE RUNAWAY SHOES: PUFFIN BEDTIME STORY CHEST
Penguin, 1989, 304p. – Pbk. – 0 14 032270 1
both illustrated by Glenys Ambrus and Caroline Shaw

Two collections of varied stories, chosen by Barbara Ireson as being particularly suitable for bedtime.
Age range: 5–7

Other publications:

COMPLETE RHYME TIME
Red Fox, 1992. – Pbk. – 0 09 926441 2
GINGERBREAD MAN
Faber, 1968. – O/P. – 0 571 08615 2
MOVING ALONG : POEMS OF TRAVEL AND TRANSPORT
Evans Brothers, 1977. – O/P. – 0 237 44853 X
STORY OF THE PIED PIPER
Faber, 1970. – O/P. – 0 571 09408 2

J

JACQUES, Brian

British. Born Liverpool, 1939. Docker, long distance lorry driver, writer.

Awards: Lancashire County Library Children's Book of the Year Award: *Redwall*, 1988

Lancashire County Library Children's Book of the Year Award: *Mattimeo*, 1991

Lancashire County Library Children's Book of the Year Award: *Salamandastron*, 1993 (Shared)

Once in a while, a new children's author of such stature appears that it is immediately apparent his books will ultimately become classics. Brian Jacques is just such an author. He writes fantasies from a basis of a powerful imagination, creating the magical kingdom of Redwall, which has captivated so many children. The narrative moves along at a spanking pace, exciting, and full of humorous touches, while the descriptive passages are positively poetical. The books are quite thick, making them appear rather demanding to less able readers, but reading them aloud to a class will enable children unwilling to tackle them to experience the thrill of the battle between good and evil. Reminiscent of Tolkien.

The first trilogy:

REDWALL
Beaver Books, 1987, 416p. – Pbk. – 0 09 951200 9
Hutchinson, 1986, 311p. – 0 09 165090 9

MOSSFLOWER
Beaver Books, 1989, 432p. – Pbk. – 0 09 955400 3
Hutchinson, 1988, 360p. – Pbk. – O/P. – 0 09 172160 1

MATTIMEO
Red Fox, 1990, 446p. – Pbk. – 0 09 967540 4
Hutchinson, 1989, 312p. – 0 09 173898 9

The second trilogy:

MARIEL OF REDWALL
Red Fox, 1992, 390p. – Pbk. – 0 09 992960 0
Hutchinson, 1991, 390p. – 0 09 176405 X

SALAMANDASTRON
Hutchinson, 1992, 336p. – 0 09 176433 5

MARTIN THE WARRIOR
Hutchinson, 1993, 375p. – 0 09 176150 6

It is impossible to do more than give a flavour of these books, peopled by small, brave animals, tireless in their quest to defeat evil forces. Each chapter is enlivened by a little humorous drawing. Each book is special and produced by a man who remembers what struggles children face.
Age range: 10–12

Other publications:

SEVEN STRANGE AND GHOSTLY TALES
Red Fox, 1992. – Pbk. – 0 09 987970 0

JARMAN, Julia

British. Born Deeping St. James, 1946. Educated Walton Infant & Junior School, Peterborough and Peterborough County Grammar School for Girls; University of Manchester, B.A. Hons. (English), B.A. Hons (Drama). Married Peter Jarman, Engineer, 1969. One son, two daughters. Teacher of English and drama, Tutor for W.E.A., Journalist, Reviewer, Lecturer in Children's Literature, Writer.

Address: Oakwood,
High Street,
Riseley,
Bedford MK44 1DJ,
England

Now well established as a popular author, she succeeds admirably in writing about real children in a way that appeals to today's young readers. She also manages to convey her concern for the countryside without being overly sentimental. Readable and pertinent.

THE GHOST OF TANTONY PIG
Penguin, 1992, 144p. – Pbk. – 0 14 034523 X
Andersen Press, 1990, 134p. – 0 86264 295 7
illustrated by Laszlo Als

At first glance, this could be just another ghost story, read for pleasure and then forgotten. As the character of Laurie is brought skilfully to life, and the importance of the issue of land development being carried out to the detriment of the locality is brought home to the reader, the book takes on an altogether different aspect. There is an important message here, but it is immensely enjoyable.
Age range: 10–12

THE JESSAME STORIES
Heinemann, 1994, 94p. 0 0 434 96392 5
illustrated by Duncan Smith

Six stories about a small girl with a lively imagination. They describe warm funny or sad events in her life, making this a delightful book for young readers either to share with a parent or to read by themselves.
Age range: 6–9

OLLIE AND THE BOGLE
Penguin, 1989, 128p. – Pbk. – O/P. –
0 14 032879 3
Andersen Press, 1987, 136p. – 0 86264 163 2
illustrated by Katarina Lempinen

When Olwen fails in her attempt to prevent her father chopping down the elder tree, she little realises what trouble lies in store. The bogle holds her responsible, and continually makes things go wrong until she manages to find an acceptable new home for him.
  Skilfully interwoven with this story is the sub-plot of the attempt to steal the eggs of the peregrine falcon. Both stories reach a satisfactory conclusion.
Age range: 10–12

POPPY AND THE VICARAGE GHOST
Andersen Press, 1988, 144p. – 0 86264 192 6

In the same series:

WHEN POPPY RAN AWAY
Andersen Press, 1985, 126p. – 0 86264 114 4
illustrated by Laszlo Als

Poppy is a likable character, full of ideas and the energy to carry them out. Each book is an ingenious story told with humour that makes readers eager for the next one.
Age range: 9–11

TOPHER AND THE TIME-TRAVELLING CAT
Andersen Press, 1992, 144p. – 0 86264 409 7
illustrated by David Atack

This unusual story has many strands interwoven to provide an excellent read. Topher (short for Christopher, to distinguish him from his dad, Chris) is struggling to come to terms with the death of his mother. When the stray cat arrives, he tries to make her stay, but through her he makes the journey back in time to Ancient Egypt, which was his mother's subject, and the cause of her death. Helping him throughout is Ellie, his deaf friend, who has problems of her own. It is interesting to see that her T-shirt is labelled 'Save the Whale', reflecting Julia Jarman's interest in conservation. The new edition was called *The Time-travelling cat* (Lions, 1993, 144p. – Pbk. – 0 00 674634 9).
Age range: 10–12

Other publications:

GEORGIE AND THE DRAGON
Young Lions, 1993. – 0 00 100488 3
GEORGIE AND THE PLANET RAIDER
Black, 1993. – 0 7136 3702 1
NANCY POCKET AND THE KIDNAPPERS
Heinemann, 1991. – 0 434 97678 4
SQUONK
Heinemann, 1989. – 0 434 93062 8

JARVIS, Robin

No information has been received from either the author or publisher.

Awards: Lancashire County Library Children's Book of the Year Award: *The Whitby Witches*, 1992

It would be difficult to say which element of Robin Jarvis' books is the strongest – fantasy or suspense, but his popularity increases with every publication. The strong thread of humour saves them from becoming sinister, although there is a certain amount of violence. The titles and jackets are very eye-catching.

THE DEPTFORD MICE TRILOGY

DARK PORTAL
Simon & Schuster, 1989, 256p. – Pbk. – 0 7500 0628 5

CRYSTAL PRISON
Simon & Schuster, 1990, 272p. – Pbk. – 0 7500 0574 2
Macdonald Purnell, 1989, 272p. – 0 361 08574 5

FINAL RECKONING
Simon & Schuster, 1990, 240p. – 0 7500 0271 9
Simon & Schuster, 1990, 240p. – Pbk. – 0 7500 0272 7

Set in the unlikely place of Deptford sewers, the chain of events is set off by the sad death of a little terrified mouse, and it positively races to a tense and unexpected conclusion.
Age range: 10+

THE WHITBY SERIES

WHITBY WITCHES
Simon & Schuster, 1991, 204p. – Pbk. – 0 7500 0581 5
Simon & Schuster, 1991, 204p. – O/P. – 0 7500 0582 3

WARLOCK IN WHITBY
Simon & Schuster, 1992, 304p. – 0 7500 1202 1
Simon & Schuster, 1992, 304p. – Pbk. – 0 7500 1203 X

Ben, visiting Alice with his sister, discovers he has the gift of second sight, which helps him in his fight against evil, no matter what form it takes. Strong stuff, but thrilling to the last page.
Age range: 10+

THE DEPTFORD HISTORIES

ALCHYMIST'S CAT
Simon & Schuster, 1991, 292p. – 0 7500 0889 X
Simon & Schuster, 1991, 292p. – Pbk. – 0 7500 0890 3

OAKEN THRONE
Simon & Schuster, 1993, 336p. – 0 7500 1392 3
Simon & Schuster, 1993, 336p. – Pbk. – 0 7500 1393 1

Prequels to the Deptford Mice trilogy, beginning in mid-seventeenth century as Dr Spittle's laboratory sets in motion the story of sorcery which culminates in murder. The battle between the bats and squirrels is escalating, threatening to destroy both sides unless a saviour can be found.
Age range: 10+

JONES, Diana Wynne

British. Born London, 1934. Educated Friends' School, Saffron Walden; St Anne's College, Oxford, B.A. Married J. A. Burrow, 1956, three sons. Writer.

Awards: Guardian Children's Fiction Award: *A Charmed Life*, 1978

Address: 9 The Polygon,
Clifton,
Bristol BS8 4PW,
England

Agent: Laura Cecil,
17 Alwyne Villas,
London N1 2HG,
England

An unusually gifted fantasy writer who is able to inject humour even into really grim stories. She makes magic acceptable to sceptics and provides reading that is powerful, moving and thought-provoking. Her stories are products of the imagination, and therefore do not lend themselves easily to illustration. This makes attractive book-jackets hard to provide, thus lessening the immediate appeal to children, and the lack of illustration also makes them less accessible to the many children who require visual appeal in order to be persuaded to read. Children who can overcome this barrier are rewarded with enjoyable and unusual stories.

ARCHER'S GOON
Mammoth, 1992, 192p. – Pbk. – 0 7497 0909 X
Methuen, 1984, 144p. – 0 416 49260 6

Read at face value, this story is a superb mystery, full of surprises which keep the reader's attention. There is, however, much more to it. It is a masterly fantasy told with such literary expertise that reading it provides an enriching experience.
Age range: 12–14

BLACK MARIA
Mammoth, 1992, 208p. – Pbk. – 0 7497 1043 8
Methuen, 1991, 224p. – O/P. – 0 416 17212 1

A good combination of thriller, as the reader together with Chris puzzles out Aunt Maria's secret, and magical fantasy, in which time travel and thought projection are made to seem entirely credible. An excellent read with a satisfactory ending.
Age range: 11–13

CART AND CWIDDER
Mammoth, 1993, 220p. – Pbk. – 0 7497 1252 X
Macmillan, 1975, 208p. – O/P. – 0 333 17939 0

Set in the imaginary kingdom of Dalemark, the story concerns a family of wandering singers. The political climate is unsteady, with the North now free while the South is still oppressed. The situation affects the members of the family in different ways. Intrigues develop as terror mounts when the magic begins its work.
Age range: 12–14

CHARMED LIFE
Chivers Press, 1987, 360p. – L/P. –
0 7451 0490 8
Penguin, 1979, 208p. – Pbk. – 0 14 031075 4
Macmillan, 1977, 216p. – O/P. – 0 333 21426 9

Gwendolen shows such promise that she is being tutored in witchcraft free of charge. Cat, her brother, is worried about the whole situation and becomes more so when they are transported to a castle splendidly named Chrestomanci. It has been prophesied that Gwendolen will rule the world – discovering the truth of this provides a fantasy read of the highest quality, imbued with characteristic humour.
Age range: 12–14

DROWNED AMMET
Mammoth, 1993, 314p. – Pbk. – 0 7497 1253 8
Macmillan, 1977, 262p. – O/P. – 0 333 22620 8

Also set in Dalemark at the time of the Sea Festival, which focuses attention on the wicked Earl and his cruel band of secret police. The Freedom Fighters continue with their struggle, but are in dire need of help which only magic can provide.
Age range: 12–14

EIGHT DAYS OF LUKE
Mammoth, 1992, 176p. – Pbk. – 0 7497 1225 2
Chivers Press, 1988, 176p. – L/P. –
0 8599 7893 1
Macmillan, 1975, 176p. – O/P. – 0 333 17141 1

David's homecoming after school is a dismal affair. No-one wants him or feels pleased to see him. In his misery he curses the family, resulting in an earthquake, followed by a fire, a snake attack, and, finally, the appearance of Luke. David's loneliness and misery disappear until sinister events make him wonder who Luke really is and just where he came from. An excellent

mixture of realism and magic told with warmth and humour.
Age range: 10–13

THE HOMEWARD BOUNDERS
Mammoth, 1990, 224p. – Pbk. – 0 7497 0281 8
Magnet Books, 1984, 224p. – Pbk. O/P. – 0 416 22940 9
Macmillan, 1981, 192p. – O/P. – 0 333 30979 0

Curiosity causes Jamie's downfall. He is banished to another world from which he must try to find his way home. Eventually he finds himself in the company of fellow wanderers all trying to get home. Together they try to defy the mysterious and powerful 'They'. An unusual and absorbing story.
Age range: 10–13

HOWL'S MOVING CASTLE
Mammoth, 1991, 224p. – Pbk. – 0 7497 0903 0
Methuen, 1988, 212p. – O/P. – 0 416 07442 1

In the same series:

CASTLE IN THE AIR
Mammoth, 1991, 192p. – Pbk. – 0 7497 0475 6
Methuen, 1990, 192p. – O/P. – 0 416 15782 3

A modern Arabian Nights story in which the long lost son of a prince falls in love with the daughter of a ferocious Sultan. The genie, however, has other ideas, and it is left to the old but still effective magic carpet to rescue them. Bewitching for fans of the fantasy genre.
Age range: 10–12

THE LIVES OF CHRISTOPHER CHANT
Mammoth, 1989, 256p. – Pbk. – 0 7497 0033 5
Methuen, 1988, 240p. – 0 416 10742 7

Christopher has magic powers, and therefore has nine lives, like a cat. Nevertheless, his enemies seem remarkably successful in using up his lives, so he journeys to Chrestomanci Castle to study magic in the hope of defeating the forces of evil. Characteristic flashes of humour enliven this story of good versus evil, which requires a certain level of fluency to be appreciated.
Age range: 10–13

THE MAGICIANS OF CAPRONA
Mammoth, 1992, 224p. – Pbk. – 0 7497 1224 4
Macmillan, 1980, 224p. – O/P. – 0 333 27891 7

Spells are an essential part of this story. Although Tonino cannot manage them, he can understand cats, who are good with spells. Once again the forces of evil are at work. An unusual and amusing story.
Age range: 10–13

THE OGRE DOWNSTAIRS
Penguin, 1977, 192p. – Pbk. – 0 14 030898 9
Macmillan, 1974, 191p. – O/P. – 0 333 15917 9

The Ogre is the step-father of Johnny and Caspar, and not much loved! However, one day he presents them with a chemistry set, which sets them off on an exciting adventure from which they would never fully recover. Magic can seem very real.
Age range: 10–13

POWER OF THREE
Beaver Books, 1989, 272p. – Pbk. – 0 09 963620 4
Macmillan, 1976, 256p. – O/P. – 0 333 18643 5

To read this story is to enter a fantasy world that all too quickly becomes as real as the reader's own. It is peopled by giants and the sinister, shadowy Dorig. The curse that binds the place is exceptionally strong, and Gair feels he is not equal to the task of freeing them. An intriguing plot told, as always, with warmth and humour.
Age range: 10–13

THE SPELLCOATS
Mammoth, 1993, 282p. – Pbk. – 0 7497 1254 6
Macmillan, 1979, 256p. – O/P. – 0 333 25351 5

Tanaqui has the task of weaving coats that will tell the story and the meaning of the journey the children have to undertake when their father dies. It is a

grim journey, beset by dangers, but courage wins through and finally the weaving is complete.
Age range: 10–13

A TALE OF TIME CITY
Mammoth, 1990, 288p. – Pbk. – 0 7497 0440 3
Methuen, 1989, 288p. – O/P. – 0 416 10192 5
Methuen, 1987, 160p. – 0 416 02362 2

Trying to escape from her kidnappers, Vivian becomes involved in the fate of Time City, which is disintegrating. She must find the architect before the unknown evil destroys it. A detective story in an unusual setting.
Age range: 11–13

THE TIME OF THE GHOST
Beaver Books, 1984, 192p. – Pbk. – 0 09 935950 2
Macmillan, 1981, 160p. – O/P. – 0 333 32012 3

An unusual ghost story in which the ghost is the central character trying to communicate. At first, it only succeeds with the dog, and no-one takes any notice of his alarms. The tension builds as a life is put at risk, but in the midst of high drama there is a welcome thread of humour.
Age range: 10–13

WARLOCK AT THE WHEEL AND OTHER STORIES
Arrow Books, 1989, 192p. – Pbk. – 0 09 965090 8
Macmillan, 1984, 156p. – O/P. – 0 333 37613 7

A volume of excellent short stories of a type similar to her full length novels. It is very welcome, as it means that readers who are reluctant to tackle her long novels may be able to partake of Diana Wynne Jones's enjoyable writing.
Age range: 10–12

WILD ROBERT
Mammoth, 1991, 96p. – Pbk. – 0 7497 0590 6
Chivers Press, 1991, 120p. – L/P. – O/P. – 0 7451 1471 7
Methuen, 1989, 96p. – 0 416 15192 2
illustrated by Emma Chichester Clark

Less substantial than most of her novels, this story is still of a high literary and imaginative standard. Heather leads a lonely life in the Stately Home where her parents are curators. She is pleased to find a companion, until she realizes who it is.
Age range: 10–12

WILKIN'S TOOTH
Penguin, 1975, 176p. – Pbk. – 0 14 030765 6
Macmillan, 1973, 176p. – O/P. – 0 333 14548 8

Desperate to make some extra money when a misdeed causes their father to stop their pocket money, Jess and Frank found their own company, designed to help people who desire revenge. How it all gets out of hand is described in an amusing, lively style.
Age range: 10–13

WITCH WEEK
Mammoth, 1989, 224p. – Pbk. – 0 7497 0174 9
Macmillan, 1982, 192p. – O/P. – 0 333 33189 3

Another story woven around Chrestomanci Castle. Witchcraft is an offence punished by burning. One of the pupils in Mr Crossley's class is a witch. Trying to discover who it is in a race against time provides a dramatic story.
Age range: 10–13

Other publications:

CHAIR PERSON
Penguin, 1991. – Pbk. – O/P. – 0 14 032865 3
CROWN OF DALEMARK
Mammoth, 1993. – Pbk. – 0 7497 1255 4
DOGSBODY
Penguin, 1978. – Pbk. – 0 14 031002 9
FIRE AND HEMLOCK
Mammoth, 1990. – Pbk. – 0 7497 0283 4
FOUR GRANNIES
Beaver Books, 1989. – O/P. – 0 09 963890 8
SKIVER'S GUIDE
Hodder, 1984. – Pbk. – O/P. – 0 340 33985 3
WHO GOT RID OF ANGUS FLINT?
Mammoth, 1990. – Pbk. – 0 7497 0282 6
YES DEAR
Harper Collins, 1992. – 0 00 184643 4

K

KAYE, Geraldine (née Hughesdon)

British. Born Watford, Hertfordshire, 1925. Educated Felixstowe College, Suffolk; Watford Grammar School; London School of Economics, B.Sc. (Hons). WRNS WW II. Married Barrington Kaye, 1948 (divorced 1975), two daughters, one son. Scriptwriter, teacher.

Awards: Children's Rights Workshop Other Award: *Comfort Herself*, 1985

Address: 39 High Kingsdown, Bristol BS2 8EW, England

Agent: A. M. Heath & Co. Ltd, 40–42 William IV Street, London WC2N 4DD, England

A perceptive and versatile author who can sympathize with the problems facing children who have to live in a different country from the one they were born in, or where their relatives are. Sometimes she writes lightweight, amusing and easy-to-read stories. Often she shows she is capable of writing at a greater depth, introducing substantial characters in meaningful situations.

THE BEAUTIFUL TAKE-AWAY PALACE
Magnet Books, 1988, 96p. – Pbk. – 0 416 06462 0
Heinemann, 1987, 68p. – O/P. – 0 434 94571 4
illustrated by Glenys Ambrus

Adjusting to the difference between Hong Kong and his new home in England is hard for a young boy. Finding a sympathetic friend is the first step towards improving his new life.
Age range: 9–11

COMFORT HERSELF
Mammoth, 1990, 160p. – Pbk. – 0 7497 0196 X
Deutsch, 1984, 192p. – 0 233 97614 0
illustrated by Jennifer Northway

In the same series:

GREAT COMFORT
Mammoth, 1990, 192p. – Pbk. – 0 7497 0193 5
Deutsch, 1988, 192p. – Pbk. – 0 233 98300 7

Comfort is devastated by her Mum's death, but quickly realizes that she must now learn to make her own decisions. The first one is whether to stay with her grandparents in England, or to go and live with her father in Ghana. Having decided to share her time, she is devastated for a second time when she arrives in Ghana to find her step-family gone. Moving but enjoyable stories which give an insight into the structure of society in both Africa and England.
Age range: 12–14

SUMMER IN SMALL STREET
Mammoth, 1990, 64p. – Pbk. – 0 7497 0246 X

WINTER IN SMALL STREET
Mammoth, 1991, 80p. – Pbk. – 0 7497 0858 1
Methuen, 1990, 64p. – O/P. – 0 416 15652 5
illustrated by Joanna Carey

Two volumes of humorous stories about the various children and their exploits in Small Street. Thoroughly enjoyable.
Age range: 7–9

Other publications:

BABYSITTING GANG
Hodder, 1990. – 0 340 51421 3
BIGGEST BONFIRE IN THE WORLD
Hodder, 1985. – Pbk. – O/P. – 0 340 36741 5
BILLY BOY
Hodder, 1975. – Pbk. – O/P. – 0 340 18510 4

THE BLUE RABBIT
Hodder, 1975. – Pbk. – O/P. – 0 340 04041 6

BREATH OF FRESH AIR
Mammoth, 1990. – O/P. – 0 7497 0082 3

CALL OF THE WILD WOOD
Hodder, 1986. – Pbk. – O/P. – 0 340 36676 1

CHILDREN OF THE TURNPIKE
Hodder, 1976. – Pbk. – O/P. – 0 340 19544 4

DAY AFTER YESTERDAY
Deutsch, 1981. – O/P. – 0 233 97344 3

DIFFERENT SORT OF CHRISTMAS
Kaye & W, 1976. – Pbk. – O/P. –
0 7182 1026 3

DOG CALLED DOG
Hodder, 1990. – 0 340 51366 7

DONKEY CHRISTMAS
Hodder, 1988. – 0 340 42318 8

DONKEY STRIKE
Hodder, 1984. – Pbk. – O/P. – 0 340 33536 X

EIGHT DAYS TO CHRISTMAS
Macmillan, 1978. – Pbk. – O/P. –
0 333 23531 2

GOODBYE RUBY RED
Hodder, 1974. – Pbk. – O/P. – 0 340 18574 0

HANDS OFF MY SISTER
Hippo Books, 1993. – Pbk. – 0 590 55355 0

KASSIM GOES FISHING
Magnet Books, 1980. – Pbk. – O/P. –
0 416 89260 4

KING OF THE KNOCKDOWN GINGERS
Hodder, 1979. – Pbk. – O/P. – 0 340 24347 3

KOFI AND THE EAGLE
Magnet Books, 1980. – Pbk. – O/P. –
0 416 89270 1

MARIE ALONE
Heinemann, 1973. – Pbk. – O/P. –
0 434 95798 4

NAIL, A STICK AND A LID
Hodder, 1975. – Pbk. – O/P. – 0 340 19642 4

NOWHERE TO STOP
Penguin, 1974. – O/P. – 0 14 030732 X

PENNY BLACK
Heinemann, 1976. – Pbk. – O/P. –
0 434 95809 3

PIECE OF CAKE
Deutsch, 1991. – Pbk. – 0 233 98712 6

PLUM TREE PARTY
Hodder, 1982. – Pbk. – O/P. – 0 340 26574 4

PONY RAFFLE
Hodder, 1974. – Pbk. – O/P. – 0 340 18429 9

RABBIT MINDERS
Hodder, 1987. – Pbk. – O/P. – 0 340 40958 4

ROTTEN OLD CAR
Hodder, 1973. – Pbk. – O/P. – 0 340 17787 X

RUNAWAY BOY
Heinemann, 1971. – Pbk. – O/P. –
0 434 94570 6

SCHOOL POOL GANG
Penguin, 1989. – Pbk. – 0 14 032487 9

SKY-BLUE DRAGON
Hodder, 1983. – Pbk. – O/P. – 0 340 28215 0

SNOW GIRL
Heinemann, 1991. – 0 434 97659 8

SOMEONE ELSE'S BABY
Deutsch, 1990. – Pbk. – 0 233 98575 1

TIM AND THE RED INDIAN HEAD-DRESS
Hodder, 1973. – Pbk. – O/P. – 0 340 17788 8

WHERE IS FRED?
Hodder, 1976. – Pbk. – O/P. – 0 340 19641 6

YELLOW POM-POM HAT
Hodder, 1974. – Pbk. – O/P. – 0 340 18966 5

KEMP, Gene (née Rushton)

British. Born Wigginton, Staffordshire, 1926. Educated Wigginton Church Primary School; Tamworth Girls' High School; University of Exeter, B.A. (Hons), English, M.A. Married: 1) Norman Pattison, 1949 (divorced 1958), one daughter; 2) Allan Kemp, 1958, one daughter, one son. Teacher, now freelance writer.

Awards: Children's Rights Workshop Other Award: *The Turbulent Term of Tyke Tiler*, 1977

Library Association Carnegie Medal: *The Turbulent Term of Tyke Tiler*, 1977

Address: 6 West Avenue,
Exeter,
Devon EX4 4SD,
England

Agent: Gerald Pollinger,
Laurence Pollinger Ltd,
18 Maddox Street,
London W1R 0EU,
England

As an ex-teacher, Gene Kemp is particularly able to portray school life realistically. Cricklepit Primary is the setting for her books, but the stories are varied. She understands children and can give convincing portrayals which allow the reader to empathize fully while enjoying the humour of the situation.

CHARLIE LEWIS PLAYS FOR TIME
Chivers Press, 1987, 168p. – L/P. – 0 7451 0548 3
Collins, 1986, 128p. – 0 00 330025 0
Penguin, 1986, 128p. – Pbk. – 0 14 031864 X
illustrated by Vanessa Julian-Ottie

Charlie is musical, but lives in the shadow of his mother, a famous concert pianist. When his favourite teacher is absent, old 'Garters' takes over, both at school and at home. Charlie finds his own solution to these problems. The characters are amusing, and the various episodes described with a liberal sprinkling of jokes, making the book an easy read.
Age range: 9–11

CHRISTMAS WITH TAMWORTH PIG
Faber, 1990, 96p. – Pbk. – 0 571 14445 4
Faber, 1977, 93p. – O/P. – 0 571 11117 3

In the same series:

THE PRIME OF TAMWORTH PIG
Faber, 1989, 112p. – Pbk. – 0 571 15345 3
Faber, 1972, 112p. – O/P. – 0 571 09780 4

TAMWORTH PIG AND THE LITTER
Faber, 1990, 128p. – Pbk. – 0 571 14290 7
Faber, 1975, 94p. – O/P. – 0 571 10743 5

TAMWORTH PIG RIDES AGAIN!
Faber, 1992, 128p. – 0 571 16611 3

TAMWORTH PIG SAVES THE TREES
Faber, 1989, 104p. – Pbk. – 0 571 14186 2
Faber, 1973, 104p. – O/P. – 0 571 10115 1

TAMWORTH PIG STORIES
Faber, 1987, 212p. – 0 571 14931 6
all illustrated by Carolyn Dinan

Just as much a delight to read today as when first published; these books never lose their appeal. Tamworth is a pig with extraordinary talents, whose encounters with life are described with such humour and fun that the reader is really sorry to reach the end.
Age range: 9–11

THE CLOCK TOWER GHOST
Penguin, 1984, 96p. – Pbk. – 0 14 031554 3
Faber, 1981, 89p. – O/P. – 0 571 11767 8
illustrated by Carolyn Dinan

An unusual story about a mean ghost who meets his match when an equally mean child comes to live in the tower. The resulting clash of personalities provides many amusing situations as they battle for supremacy.
Age range: 9–11

DOG DAYS AND CAT NAPS
Penguin, 1983, 112p. – Pbk. – 0 14 031419 9
Faber, 1980, 110p. – 0 571 11595 0
illustrated by Carolyn Dinan

A collection of ten short stories about a variety of pets and their equally varied owners. Fun to read.
Age range: 9–11

GOWIE CORBY PLAYS CHICKEN
Penguin, 1981, 144p. – Pbk. – 0 14 031322 2
Faber, 1979, 136p. – 0 571 11405 9

An unusual choice for a 'hero', as Gowie is mean, friendless and tough. This is the story of how such a boy becomes integrated into the life of the school he hates so much. It is a realistic yet optimistic portrayal of school life.
Age range: 11–14

JASON BODGER AND THE PRIORY GHOST
Chivers Press, 1988, 192p. – L/P. – 0 7451 0656 0
Penguin, 1987, 144p. – Pbk. – 0 14 032088 1
Faber, 1985, 144p. – O/P. – 0 571 13645 1
illustrated by Elaine McGregor Turney

A particular speciality of Gene Kemp is the unpleasant child who is changed by a supernatural experience, hence Jason Bodger. He is the despair of his teacher and classmates, and looks certain to disrupt the class outing to a priory. Mathilda, prowling the priory for seven

hundred years, decides he is just the person she has been waiting for. Fast-paced and hilarious, this book is a thoroughly enjoyable read.
Age range: 10–12

JUNIPER
Penguin, 1988, 112p. – Pbk. – 0 14 032410 0
Faber, 1986, 112p. – 0 571 13902 7

A serious and haunting tale of a girl who has more than her fair share of problems. She has a physical disability, a criminal father, and a mother who cannot cope. There is a dramatic climax to a situation which is skilfully built up as the story progresses.
Age range: 10–12

JUST FERRET
Penguin, 1991, 126p. – Pbk. – 0 14 034589 2

Set at Cricklepit School, the scene of many enjoyable books, this is undoubtedly one of the very best. Ferret has more than his fair share of problems – he has no mother, his father tends to be a bully, he has to try to fit into yet another new school where he comes up against bullying, and he is dyslexic. Becoming the hero of the hour surprises him as much as everyone else, but victory is sweet!
Age range: 10–12

MR MAGUS IS WAITING FOR YOU
Faber, 1986, 170p. – O/P. – 0 571 14686 4
Faber, 1986, 92p. – Pbk. – 0 571 14687 2
illustrated by Alan Baker

Four children, disgruntled and bored, find themselves in an enchanted garden. Each child reacts differently, but the appearance of the sinister Mr Magus signals the beginning of a frightening adventure. The book became a thrilling television serial.
Age range: 9–12

ROUNDABOUT
Faber, 1993, 128p. – 0 571 16732 2

A fine and varied collection of stories to appeal to older children – some scary, some amusing, all entertaining and well written.
Age range: 11–13

THE TURBULENT TERM OF TYKE TILER
Chivers Press, 1986, 160p. – L/P. – O/P. – 0 7451 0330 8
Penguin, 1979, 128p. – Pbk. – 0 14 031135 1
Faber, 1977, 118p. – 0 571 10966 7
illustrated by Carolyn Dinan

The last term at junior school is often difficult for both teachers and pupils. When the class concerned tends to be difficult anyway, the result is a recipe for disaster. An excellent book.
Age range: 9–11

Other publications:

CROCODILE DOG
Heinemann, 1987. – 0 434 93043 1
I CAN'T STAND LOSING
Penguin, 1989. – Pbk. – 0 14 032677 4
MATTY'S MIDNIGHT MONSTER
Penguin, 1992. – Pbk. – 0 14 054429 1
MINK WAR
Faber, 1992. – 0 571 16312 2
NO PLACE LIKE
Penguin, 1988. – Pbk. – O/P. – 0 14 032543 3
ROOM WITH NO WINDOWS
Faber, 1991. – Pbk. – 0 571 16117 0
WANTING A LITTLE BLACK GERBIL
Heinemann, 1992. – 0 434 97690 3
THE WELL
Penguin, 1988. – Pbk. – O/P. – 0 14 032678 2

KILWORTH, Garry

British. Born 1941. Educated at over twenty schools due to being the son of a Royal Air Force Sergeant; R.A.F. Training School, 1956–1959; South West London Polytechnic, H.N.D. Business Studies, 1974; Kings College, London University, English Hons degree, 1955. Married, one son, one daughter, two grandchildren. Aircraftsman, Telegraphist, Sergeant Cryptographer, Executive with Cable & Wireless (retired 1982), Writer.

Address: Wychwater,
           The Chase,
           Ashingdon,
           Rochford,
           Essex, SS4 3JE,
           England

Garry Kilworth has slowly acquired a well-deserved reputation as a first-rate storyteller, producing books in which readers can lose themselves, and escape for a while from reality.

BILLY PINK'S PRIVATE DETECTIVE AGENCY
Methuen, 1993, 160p. – 0 416 18754 4

Set at the turn of the century, this is the story of Billy, who makes a success out of tracking down criminals, and helps to raise his family out of poverty. When he receives a visit from the celebrated author Arthur Conan Doyle, his life is changed yet again. A lovely period story, but the cover, which reflects the time, may cause children to reject the book.
Age range: 9–11

DARK HILLS, HOLLOW CLOCKS
Mammoth, 1992, 128p. – Pbk. – 0 7497 1048 9
Methuen, 1990, 192p. – O/P. – 0 416 15632 0

A collection of stories based on folklore. Each one is different in style and content. They are chilling, sad or funny, but always compelling.
Age range: 10–12

THE DROWNERS
Mammoth, 1992, 160p. – Pbk. – 0 7497 1049 7
Methuen, 1991, 144p. – 0 416 17682 8

Begins strikingly with the death of a child, followed shortly by his father. With them also dies the knowledge about the drowning of the fields. The mysterious appearance of a young boy gives the farmers hope. An excellent story, well told.
Age range: 10–12

THE WIZARD OF WOODWORLD
Grafton Books, 1987, 128p. – Pbk. – O/P. – 0 583 31137 7

An above average science fiction adventure story. A young space cadet finds himself stranded when his spaceship is forced out of the sky. Life is not too bad, until they learn to make and use weapons.
Age range: 9–11

Other publications:

RAIN GHOST
Chivers Press, 1992. – O/P. – 0 86220 893 9
THIRD DRAGON
Hippo Books, 1991. – Pbk. – O/P. – 0 590 76416 0
VOYAGE OF THE VIGILANCE
Armada Books, 1988. – Pbk. – O/P. – 0 00 693320 3

KING, (David) Clive

British. Born Richmond, Surrey, 1924. Educated King's School, Rochester, Kent; Downing College, Cambridge, B.A. English; School of Oriental and African Studies, London. Sub-Lieutenant, RNVR, WW II. Married: 1) Jane Tuke, 1949 (divorced 1974); 2) Penelope Timmins, 1974, one daughter, one son. British Council Officer 1948–71, acting as lecturer and education advisor.

Address: 65A St. Augustine's Road,
           London NW1,
           England
Agent: Murray Pollinger,
           4 Garrick Street,
           London WC2B 9BH,
           England

Here is an author with extra-special talents. He sees the world rather differently to the average adult, and is, therefore, able to communicate with children on their terms. His use of language is unparalleled, and his descriptions are vigorous and meaningful. The result of this combination is lively stories which capture the imagination of children and at the same time enhance their linguistic ability.

ME AND MY MILLION
Penguin, 1979, 144p. – Pbk. – 0 14 031128 9
Kestrel Books, 1976, 144p. – O/P. –
0 7226 5185 6

Realism and fantasy are combined in this remarkable story. Ringo is an illiterate, street-wise youth who is entrusted with the delivery of a laundry bag, a simple task which goes dramatically wrong. The ensuing chaos becomes increasingly amusing, and yet exciting, as he struggles in vain to put things right.
Age range: 10–13

NINNY'S BOAT
Penguin, 1983, 272p. – Pbk. O/P. –
0 14 031424 5
Kestrel Books, 1980, 256p. – 0 7226 5617 3
illustrated by Ian Newsham

Abandoned to his fate during a flood, Ninny has no-one to rely on but himself. In order to keep his spirits up during his search for his home, he makes jokes about, and enjoys, his situation to the best of his ability. The verbal wit makes the reader laugh out loud, and Clive King makes the reader view the world through the fresh and wondering eyes of his Dark Age hero. A special book.
Age range: 9–12

THE SOUND OF PROPELLERS
Penguin, 1988, 208p. – Pbk. O/P. –
0 14 032106 3
Viking Kestrel, 1986, 208p. – 0 670 81106 8
illustrated by David Parkins

The complex, rewarding story of Morugan, sent from his home in India to boarding school in England. His feelings of bewilderment take second place to the exciting discovery that the sound of propellers heralds a spying raid on the aircraft factory next to the school. The boys cannot ignore the situation, and must decide what action to take.
Age range: 10–13

STIG OF THE DUMP
Chivers Press, 1986, 216p. – L/P. – O/P. –
0 7451 0302 2
Viking Kestrel, 1985, 160p. – 0 670 80027 9
Penguin, 1970. 156p. – Pbk. – 0 14 030196 8
illustrated by Edward Ardizzone

A modern classic, this book has continued to capture the imagination of children for many years. Barney, unable to convince anyone that he has found a Stone Age boy living on the dump, just enjoys being friends with him, and learning about his way of life. It has also been translated to the stage.
Age range: 9–12

THE TOWN THAT WENT SOUTH
Penguin, 1970, 112p. – Pbk. – 0 14 030442 8
Hamish Hamilton, 1969, 124p. – O/P. –
0 241 01717 3
illustrated by Maurice Bartlett

The inhabitants of Ramsly wake up one morning to find their town has broken away from the English coast and drifted across to France – what a splendid idea! Fun to read, it gives an entirely new slant to the concept of twin towns.
Age range: 9–12

Other publications:

NIGHT THE WATER CAME
Penguin, 1976. – Pbk. – O/P. – 0 14 030769 9
SEASHORE PEOPLE
Viking, 1987. – O/P. – 0 670 81723 6
SNAKES AND SNAKES
Kestrel Books, 1975. – Pbk. – O/P. –
0 7226 5012 4

KING-SMITH, Dick

British. Born Bitton, Gloucestershire, 1922. Educated Marlborough College, Wiltshire; University of Bristol, B.Ed. 2nd Lieutenant, Grenadier Guards, WW II. Married Myrle England, 1943, two daughters, one son. Farmer, teacher, freelance writer.

Awards: Guardian Children's Fiction Award: *Sheep-pig*, 1984

KING-SMITH

Address: Diamond's Cottage,
Queen Charlton,
near Keynsham,
Avon BS18 2SJ,
England

Agent: A. P. Watt Ltd,
20 John Street,
London WC1N 2DR,
England

An endlessly inventive author whose intentions are plainly to entertain and amuse. His farming experience has given him detailed knowledge of animal characteristics which he uses, with a certain poetic licence, to good effect to produce original, unsentimental and amusing stories.

ACE
Penguin, 1991, 128p. – Pbk. – 0 14 034481 0
Chivers Press, 1991, 152p. – 0 7451 1405 9
Gollancz, 1990, 128p. – 0 575 04725 9
illustrated by Liz Graham-Yooll

Descended from Sheep-pig (see below), Ace is bound to be above average. He catches the eye of Farmer Tubbs, who saves him from the market. Helped by his friends, he manages to oust the hitherto favourite Corgi, and take his place.
Age range: 8–10

DAGGIE DOGFOOT
Chivers Press, 1990, 192p. – L/P. –
0 7451 1229 3
Penguin, 1982, 160p. – Pbk. – 0 14 031391 5
Gollancz, 1980, 112p. – 0 575 02767 3
illustrated by Mary Rayner

A satisfying story in which the underdog (or 'underpig') triumphs over many difficulties to become a hero. Daggie is the runt of the litter and, with typical farming lack of sentimentality, would have been quickly disposed of in a manner likely to bring a lump to the throat of little pink pig lovers. However, the pigman's attention is diverted and Daggie is rescued, going from strength to strength.
Age range: 8–12

DODOS ARE FOREVER
Chivers Press, 1992, 104p. – L/P. –
0 7451 1682 5
Penguin, 1990, 80p. – Pbk. – 0 14 034044 0
Viking, 1989, 224p. – 0 670 82681 2
illustrated by David Parkins

Here is a book for everyone who regrets the demise of the dodo, as it convincingly puts forward the theory that a few may have survived, but their continued existence is threatened by a colony of rats. There is much to both laugh and cry at.
Age range: 8–12

EMILY'S LEGS
MacDonald, 1988, 48p. – O/P. – 0 356 13685 X
MacDonald, 1988, 48p. – Pbk. – 0 356 13686 8
illustrated by Katinka Kew

Ideal for children who can read but need stimulating yet simple reading material, with lots of illustrations. Emily is easily the fastest spider, but there is a reason for this.
Age range: 6–8

FIND THE WHITE HORSE
Penguin, 1993, 128p. – Pbk. – 0 14 034415 2
Chivers Press, 1993, 144p. – L/P –
0 7451 1804 6
Viking, 1991, 128p. – 0 670 83296 0
illustrated by Larry Wilkes

When Lubber goes to sleep in a removal van, he does not realise how far from home he is when he wakes up. Finding his way back to his owners is not easy – the only clue is a chalk horse he remembers on the hill near his home. Funny, but quite moving.
Age range: 9–11

THE FINGER-EATER
Walker Books, 1992, 64p. – 0 7445 2435 0
illustrated by Arthur Robins

A rather sinister tale about a Troll who has a nasty habit of biting off a finger from anyone he is introduced to. Only Gudrun feels brave enough to tackle the problem. Comic horror – successfully makes readers shudder.
Age range: 7–9

THE FOX-BUSTERS
Chivers Press, 1987, 160p. – L/P. –
0 7451 0492 4
Penguin, 1980, 120p. – Pbk. – 0 14 031175 0
Gollancz, 1978, 128p. – 0 575 02444 5
illustrated by Jon Miller

A band of chickens find a way to defeat the foxes who are determined to eat them. As always, it is highly original, exceptionally funny, and yet some readers will also shed a few tears.
Age range: 8–12

FRIENDS AND BROTHERS
Mammoth, 1989, 96p. – Pbk. – 0 7497 0048 3
Heinemann, 1987, 96p. – O/P. – 0 434 94581 1
illustrated by Susan Hellard

William often feels he would like Charlie, his little nuisance of a brother, to disappear. When Charlie is in trouble, however, William finds himself rushing to his rescue.
Age range: 7–9

GEORGE SPEAKS
Penguin, 1989, 96p. – Pbk. – 0 14 032397 X
Viking Kestrel, 1988, 96p. – 0 670 81798 8
illustrated by Judy Brown

George is a miracle baby. At four weeks he can speak in whole sentences, and this leads to many hilarious situations.
Age range: 7–9

HARRY'S MAD
Chivers Press, 1990, 136p. – L/P. –
0 7451 1101 7
Penguin, 1986, 128p. – Pbk. – 0 14 031897 6
Gollancz, 1984, 120p. – 0 575 03497 1
illustrated by Jill Bennett

Harry inherits a parrot called Madison when his great-uncle dies. The parrot has many exceptional talents which make him a welcome addition to the household. When he is lost, the family realize they cannot manage without him, and so begins a great hunt which ends in a most unusual way.
Age range: 8–12

THE HODGEHEG
Windrush, 1990, 96p. – L/P. – 1 85089 860 X
Penguin, 1989, 96p. – Pbk. – 0 14 032503 4
Hamish Hamilton, 1987, 88p. – 0 241 11980 4

Easy to read and completely absorbing, it tells how Max sets out to solve the problem of how hedgehogs can cross the road in safety.
Age range: 6–9

MAGNUS POWERMOUSE
Chivers Press, 1991, 168p. – L/P. –
0 7451 1296 X
Penguin, 1984, 128p. – Pbk. – 0 14 031602 7
Gollancz, 1982, 128p. – 0 575 03116 6

Magnus is a giant among mice, and causes his mother endless problems. The bigger he grows, the worse the problems, and the more entertaining the child finds it. A wonderfully happy ending.
Age range: 8–10

MARTIN'S MICE
Penguin, 1989, 128p. – Pbk. – 0 14 034026 2
Chivers Press, 1989, 152p. – L/P. –
0 7451 0956 X
Gollancz, 1988, 128p. – 0 575 04264 8
illustrated by Jez Alborough

Martin is an embarrassment. As a farm cat, he is supposed to catch mice, but he prefers tinned food and keeps a mouse as a pet! Extremely funny and quite believable.
Age range: 8–12

THE MERRYTHOUGHT
Viking, 1993, 112p. – 0 670 83688 5
illustrated by Mike Reid

A merrythought (a wishbone) is supposed to make wishes come true, but Nick is taken by surprise at the way his works. Not a dull page in this intriguing story.
Age range: 9–11

THE MOUSE BUTCHER
Chivers Press, 1992, 144p. – L/P. –
0 7451 1498 9
Penguin, 1983, 128p. – Pbk. – 0 14 031457 1
Gollancz, 1981, 128p. – 0 575 02899 8
illustrated by Wendy Smith

Definitely not a book for the faint-hearted. The description of Great Mog, the cat whose experiences caused him to hate everyone and everything, is detailed and gruesome, leaving nothing to the imagination. Tom Plug, the butcher's cat, volunteers to rid them of this fearful menace, an arrangement culminating in a battle to the death. Hard-hitting and realistic, but with a lighter side too, it will appeal to readers already acquainted with books by this author, but is not a good one to start with. Cat lovers will find it hard to decide whose side they are on.
Age range: 10–12

NOAH'S BROTHER
Windrush, 1989, 76p. – L/P. – 1 85089 947 9
Penguin, 1988, 80p. – Pbk. – 0 14 032354 6
Gollancz, 1986, 72p. – 0 575 03876 4
illustrated by Ian Newsham

A short story with lots of illustrations and a highly entertaining plot concerning the truth about the building of the Ark.
Age range: 8–10

PADDY'S POT OF GOLD
Windrush, 1991, 122p. – L/P. – 1 85089 811 1
Penguin, 1991, 96p. – Pbk. – 0 14 034215 X
Viking, 1990, 96p. – 0 670 82903 X
illustrated by David Parkins

Brigid is pleased when the little leprechaun chooses her to show himself to. She and Paddy have many amusing adventures together before the pot of gold is found.
Age range: 8–10

PRETTY POLLY
Viking, 1992, 160p. – 0 670 83687 7
illustrated by David Parkins

Polly the hen is the latest animal creation to capture the hearts of this author's large number of fans. She is endearing, even when talking her head off – it would be terrible if she was stolen because her unique gift made her so valuable.
Age range: 9–11

THE QUEEN'S NOSE
Penguin, 1985, 128p. – Pbk. – 0 14 031838 0
Gollancz, 1983, 128p. – 0 575 03228 6
illustrated by Jill Bennett

An immensely exciting story containing all the ingredients of a first-rate book. It has an unusual plot, a hint of mystery, lots of humour, and a wonderful ending. Harmony has to solve a set of cryptic clues in order to reach her uncle's present. When she finds it, she is a little disappointed, until she realizes its potential.
Age range: 9–12

SADDLEBOTTOM
Chivers Press, 1987, 112p. – L/P. – 0 7451 0629 3
Penguin, 1987, 128p. – Pbk. – 0 14 032177 2
Gollancz, 1985, 128p. – 0 575 03715 6
illustrated by Alice Englander

The hero is a saddleback pig whose 'saddle' has slipped, and who is, therefore, an outcast. Needless to say, he makes good, winning fame and fortune in the end. An entertaining story.
Age range: 8–12

SCHOOL MOUSE
Viking, 1994, 144p. – 0 670 85061 6

Flora lives in a school, unknown to the pupils. She joins in the lessons each day, and learns a great deal. She tries to warn the other mice about the dangers of the blue pellets. They ignore her to their cost. Entertaining, as always.
Age range: 9–11

THE SHEEP-PIG
Chivers Press, 1986, 128p. – L/P – O/P. – 0 7451 0333 2
Penguin, 1985, 128p. – Pbk. – 0 14 031839 9
Gollancz, 1983, 128p. – 0 575 03375 4
illustrated by Mary Rayner

Babe, the piglet, is fostered by Fly, the sheepdog. It is not surprising, therefore, that he grows up wanting to learn how to herd sheep. Excellent animal

characterization, as always, makes this a memorable book.
Age range: 8–12

SOPHIE'S SNAIL
Walker Books, 1989, 96p. – Pbk. – 0 7445 0829 0
Walker Books, 1988, 96p. – O/P. – 0 7445 0820 7
illustrated by Claire Minter-Kemp

In the same series:

SOPHIE HITS SIX
Walker Books, 1992, 128p. – Pbk. – 0 7445 2366 4
Walker Books, 1991, 128p. – 0 7445 2163 7

SOPHIE IN THE SADDLE
Walker Books, 1994, 96p. – 0 7445 3191 8

SOPHIE STORIES
Walker Books, 1993, 3 vols. – 0 7445 3127 6

SOPHIE'S TOM
Walker Books, 1991, 80p. – 0 7445 1932 2
Walker Books, 1991, 80p. – Pbk. – 0 7445 2096 7
illustrated by David Parkins

Stories about a four-year-old girl called Sophie. She has a mind of her own, and everyone knows it. Lovely to read aloud.
Age range: 4–6

THE TOBY MAN
Windrush, 1990, 120p. – L/P. – 1 85089 880 4
Penguin, 1990, 112p. – Pbk. – 0 14 034285 0
Gollancz, 1989, 128p. – 0 575 04485 3
illustrated by Ian Newsham

Dick King-Smith's wonderful but zany sense of humour produces a book to enjoy. Tod sets off with a donkey, a mastiff, a ferret and a magpie to make his fortune as a highwayman.
Age range: 8–10

THE TOPSY-TURVY STORYBOOK
Gollancz, 1992, 64p. – 0 575 05429 8
illustrated by John Eastwood

Wonderful retellings of traditional stories with a slight difference as the contents page reveals – for example, 'Huge Red Riding Hood'. Fantastic – a laugh on every line.
Age range: 7–9

TUMBLEWEED
Penguin, 1988, 144p. – Pbk. – 0 14 032547 6
Windrush, 1988, 149p. – L/P. – 1 85089 939 8
Gollancz, 1987, 96p. – 0 575 03975 2
illustrated by Ian Newsham

It is surprising what a little magic can achieve for a shy knight always in trouble. An unusual theme for this author, but just as enjoyable.
Age range: 8–10

THE WATER HORSE
Penguin, 1992, 96p. – Pbk. – 0 14 034284 2
Chivers Press, 1992, 128p. – L/P – O/P. – 0 7451 1610 8
Viking, 1990, 80p. – 0 670 83044 5
illustrated by David Parkins

Facing up to responsibility is really the lesson taught in this hugely enjoyable story. Kirstie and Angus find a sort of egg on the beach. Back home it hatches into a water horse. Taking care of him becomes harder as he grows, but the problem won't go away. In spite of the difficulties, they find a satisfactory solution.
Age range: 9–11

Other publications:

ALICE AND FLOWER AND FOXIANNA
Heinemann, 1989. – Pbk. – O/P. – 0 434 94578 1
ALL PIGS ARE BEAUTIFUL
Walker Books, 1993. – 0 7445 2517 9
ALPHABEASTS
Gollancz, 1990. – 0 575 04723 2
BEWARE OF THE BILL
Heinemann, 1989. – Pbk. – O/P. – 0 434 94626 5
BLESSU
Penguin, 1992. – Pbk. – 0 14 034698 8
CARUSO'S COOL CATS
BBC, 1991. – Pbk. – 0 563 34779 1
CUCKOO BUSH FARM
Collins, 1990. – O/P. – 0 00 663452 4
CUCKOO CHILD
Penguin, 1992. – Pbk. – 0 14 034414 4

KING-SMITH

DICK KING-SMITH'S ALPHABEASTS
Gollancz, 1992. – Pbk. – 0 575 05327 5
DICK KING-SMITH'S TRIFFIC PIG BOOK
Gollancz, 1991. – Pbk. – O/P. – 0 575 05164 7
DODO COMES TO TUMBLEDOWN FARM
*Heinemann, 1988. – Pbk. – O/P. –
0 434 94627 3*
DRAGON BOY
Viking, 1993. – 0 670 83689 3
DUMPLING
H. Hamilton, 1986. – 0 241 11892 1
ESP: ERIC STANLEY PIGEON
Corgi, 1989. – Pbk. – 0 552 52523 5
FARM TALES
Little Mammoth, 1992. – Pbk. – 0 7497 1193 0
FARMER BUNGLE FORGETS
Walker Books, 1990. – Pbk. – 0 7445 1777 X
GHOST AT CODLIN CASTLE
Viking, 1992. – 0 670 84252 4
GUARD DOG
Corgi, 1992. – Pbk. – 0 552 52731 9
H. PRINCE
Walker Books, 1989. – Pbk. – 0 7445 1357 X
HENRY POND THE POET
Hodder, 1991. – Pbk. – O/P. – 0 340 54595 X
HORACE AND MAURICE
Doubleday, 1991. – 0 385 40050 0
HORSE PIE
Doubleday, 1993. – 0 385 40414 X
THE JENIUS
Gollancz, 1990. – Pbk. – 0 575 04852 2
JOLLY WITCH
Simon & Schuster, 1990. – 0 7500 0202 6
JUNGLE JINGLES AND OTHER ANIMAL POEMS
Corgi, 1992. – Pbk. – 0 552 52657 6
LADY DAISY
Penguin, 1993. – Pbk. – 0 14 034416 0
LIGHTNING STRIKES TWICE
Mammoth, 1991. – Pbk. – 0 7497 0733 X
NARROW AND SQUEAK AND OTHER ANIMAL STORIES
Viking, 1993. – 0 670 84253 2
PETS FOR KEEPS
Penguin, 1986. – Pbk. – O/P. – 0 14 031979 4
SUPER TERRIFIC PIGS
Gollancz, 1992. – Pbk. – 0 575 05457 3
THE SWOOSE
Viking, 1993. – 0 670 84255 9
TOWN WATCH
Penguin, 1987. – O/P. – 0 14 032340 6
TROUBLE WITH EDWARD
Hodder, 1991. – Pbk. – O/P. – 0 340 54616 6
TUMBLEDOWN FARM – THE GREATEST
*Heinemann, 1988. – Pbk. – O/P. –
0 434 94572 2*

UNCLE BUMPO
Deutsch, 1993. – 0 590 54087 4
WATER WATCH
Penguin, 1988. – Pbk. – 0 14 032341 4
WHISTLING PIGLET
Walker Books, 1992. – Pbk. – 0 7445 2051 7
YOB
Heinemann, 1986. – 0 434 93035 0
YOUR FAVOURITE FARM STORIES COLLECTION
Dean, 1993. – 0 603 55095 9

KLEIN, Robin (née McMAUGH)

Australian. Born New South Wales, 1936. Educated Kempsey Primary School, Newcastle Girls High School. Married Karl Klein, 1956, divorced 1979. Two sons, two daughters. Tea lady, Bookshop Assistant, Nurse, Copper Enamelist, Writer.

Awards: Australian Children's Book Council Award Junior Book of the Year: *Thing*, 1983

Australian Council Fellowship, 1985

Agent: Tim Curnow,
Curtis Brown Australia Ltd,
PO Box 19,
Paddington,
New South Wales 2021,
Australia

Robin Klein has an ability to write very varied stories which have enormous appeal to children. Her books are not difficult to read, but the impact lingers on, making the reader more aware.

AGAINST THE ODDS
*Penguin, 1990, 104p. – Pbk. – 0 14 032705 3
illustrated by Bill Wood*

Five strange stories suitable for reading aloud. All different, but equally absorbing, they will be enjoyed by a wide range of reading abilities.
Age range: 9–11

ALL IN THE BLUE, UNCLOUDED WEATHER
Viking, 1992, 208p. – 0 670 83909 4

Nostalgia is the word that springs to mind while reading this book, as it is set in the 1940s when summers were warm and sunny and children enjoyed an innocence which somehow seems absent today. The book captures the atmosphere of these years to perfection, and can be useful for showing how different life today is. The descriptions of the escapades of the four sisters alternates between sadness and humour.
Age range: 10–12

BOSS OF THE POOL
Penguin, 1989, 80p. – Pbk. – 0 14 032246 9
Viking, 1987, 80p. – O/P. – 0 670 81669 8
illustrated by Paul Geraghty

This is quite a short novel, but there is a huge amount of human understanding and compassion packed into it. It tells the story of Shelley, a grumpy, unsympathetic character in the beginning, who is horrified by the overtures of friendship she receives from mentally handicapped Ben. Her gradual development through acceptance to understanding and determination to help Ben is told without sentimentality, and has a stronger effect because of it.
Age range: 10–12

GAMES...
Penguin, 1988, 160p. – Pbk. – O/P. – 0 14 032777 0
Viking, 1987, 164p. – O/P. – 0 670 81403 2

An excellent mixture of suspense and the everyday reality of schoolgirls and their friendships and enmities. Patricia reluctantly goes along with the idea of a seance, but has reason to regret her decision. It maintains the reader's interest to the last.
Age range: 10–12

HALFWAY ALONG THE GALAXY AND TURN LEFT
Penguin, 1987, 160p. – Pbk. – 0 14 031843 7
Viking, 1986, 144p. – O/P. – 0 670 80636 6

An extremely amusing account of the encounters experienced by a family punished by being sent to earth from their home planet Zygon. Never a dull moment.
Age range: 10–12

HATING ALISON ASHLEY
Viking, 1987, 192p. – O/P. – 0 670 80864 4
Penguin, 1984, 192p. – Pbk. – 0 14 031672 8

Demonstrating her understanding of school children as she describes the situation between Alison, newly arrived, and the resident children. Although written in a humorous style, it nevertheless deals with a common and serious problem, showing the futility of bad behaviour.
Age range: 10–12

SEEING THINGS
Viking, 1994, 200p. – 0 670 85282 1

A remarkable piece of writing, in which Robin Klein demonstrates her ability to show both sides of a coin simultaneously. Miranda has a difficult life – living with Grandpa in poor, cramped conditions after the death of her parents, she has to look out for her brother, help to look after the baby, and endure nagging from Uncle Bernie. Consequently, in her unhappiness, she takes revenge by spoiling other children's pleasure. We soon understand why, but the bewilderment of her classmates is plain to see.

When her E.S.P. powers manifest themselves, she cannot see their full potential or the need for secrecy, but the reader can see everyone else is very aware, including her sister's violent boyfriend. This creates the tension as the climax of the story approaches. Brilliantly executed.
Age range: 11–13

Other publications:

BORIS AND BORSCH
Allen & Unwin, 1993. – 0 04 442266 0
BROCK AND THE DRAGON
Hodder, 1984. – O/P – 0 340 35490 9

KLEIN

BROOMSTICK ACADEMY
Hippo Books, 1986. – Pbk. – O/P. –
0 590 70575 X

CAME BACK TO SHOW YOU I COULD FLY
Penguin, 1991. – Pbk. – 0 14 034254 0

DRESSES OF RED AND GOLD
Viking, 1993. – 0 670 84733 X

THE ENEMIES
Angus & R, 1986. – O/P. – 0 207 15117 2

GIRAFFE IN PEPPERELL STREET
Hodder, 1978. – O/P. – 0 340 22731 1

JUNK CASTLE
OUP, 1984. – O/P. – 0 19 271487 2

LAURIE LOVED ME BEST
Penguin, 1990. – Pbk. – 0 14 032708 8

LONELY HEARTS CLUB
OUP, 1988. – 0 19 554648 2

PENNY POLLARD IN PRINT
OUP, 1987. – O/P. – 0 19 554638 5

PENNY POLLARD'S DIARY
OUP, 1986. – Pbk. – 0 19 554649 0

PENNY POLLARD'S LETTERS
OUP, 1985. – O/P. – 0 19 554575 3

PENNY POLLARD'S PASSPORT
OUP, 1990. – 0 19 554868 X

PEOPLE MIGHT HEAR YOU
Viking, 1987. – O/P. – 0 670 80303 0

RATBAGS AND RASCALS
Gollancz, 1991. – Pbk. – O/P. – 0 575 05051 9

SEPARATE PLACES
Kangaroo Press, 1985. – Pbk. – 0 86417 022 X

SNAKES AND LADDERS
OUP, 1986. – O/P. – 0 19 276062 9

TEARAWAYS
Penguin, 1992. – Pbk. – 0 14 034599 X

THING
OUP, 1984. – Pbk. – O/P. – 0 19 554549 4

THINGNAPPED
OUP, 1987. – Pbk. – O/P. – 0 19 554784 5

L

LAIRD, Elizabeth

Also writes under the name Elizabeth Risk. Born New Zealand, 1943. Moved to London 1945. Educated Bristol University, B.A. (Hons) French; Post Graduate Certificate in Education, specializing in teaching English as a foreign language, London; M.Litt, Applied Linguistics, Edinburgh. Married David McDowell, writer, two children. Teacher and writer.

Awards: Children's Book Award: *Kiss the Dust*, 1992.

Address: 31 Cambrian Road, Richmond, Surrey TW10 6JQ, England

A welcome addition to the army of quality writers of fiction for young people, not least because she has the ability to write equally well for both younger and older children.

Her younger books are light-hearted, easy-to-read romps, with lots of appeal, particularly for children experiencing difficulty in learning to read. Her books for older readers reflect, in some measure, her interest in people moving, caused by her somewhat nomadic existence.

Well deserving of acclaim and her award-winning status.

CRACKERS
*Mammoth, 1990, 128p. – Pbk. – 0 7497 0309 1
illustrated by Angus McDowall and James Lightfoot*

A group of enterprising children team up to produce their own comic which is a success until a rival publication appears, offering free gifts.
Age range: 7–9

HIDING OUT
Heinemann, 1993, 128p. – 0 434 96376 3

It is every child's worst nightmare – Peter is accidentally left behind at the picnic site when his family set off for home. The tension is enormous as he realizes with horror that rescue is not going to come as quickly as he first assumed, and may just not come at all. The way he copes makes a superb story, parallelled by the description of the agony of the adults as they realise the part their selfishness has played in the drama – a magnificent contrast. Absolutely gripping from beginning to end.
Age range: 10–13

KISS THE DUST
*Heinemann, 1991, 284p. – 0 434 94703 2
Mammoth, 1991, 176p. – Pbk. – 0 7497 0857 3*

A novel made extra-ordinary by the almost matter-of-fact way Elizabeth Laird describes the terrible, heart-rending events which cause the Kurds to flee Iraq and become refugees with no home, no hope. Understatement makes it all the more powerful.
Age range: 10+

PINK GHOST OF LAMONT
*Mammoth, 1992, 128p. – Pbk. – 0 7497 1051 9
Heinemann, 1991, 128p. – 0 434 94701 6*

On one level, an amusing story about a group of children putting on a play, and the difficulties they encounter before triumphing. It also deals with the problem of moving house, trying to settle in, and making friends with the neighbours. Very enjoyable.
Age range: 7–8

RED SKY IN THE MORNING
*Pan Books, 1989, 192p. – Pbk. – 0 330 30890 4
Heinemann, 1988, 144p. – 0 434 94714 8*

This is really the story of Anna and how she suddenly had to grow up and cope with life. Her new baby brother takes a

LAIRD

lot of looking after as he was born mentally handicapped. She also has to cope with finding her first job, and has problems with her best friends. The reader laughs, cries and worries with Anna, and learns to adjust to life, just as she does. An excellent book.
Age range: 10+

Other publications:
ARCTIC BLUES
Little Mammoth, 1991. – Pbk. – 0 7497 0300 8
BIG DRIP
Buzz Books, 1991. – O/P. – 1 8559 1124 8
BIG GREEN STAR
Collins, 1982. – O/P. – 0 00 123704 7
BLANKET HOUSE
Collins, 1982. – O/P. – 0 00 123702 0
CHUNKY BEARS GO CAMPING
Collins, 1989. – O/P. – 0 00 194849 0
CHUNKY BEARS GO ON THE RIVER
Collins, 1989. – O/P. – 0 00 194850 4
CHUNKY BEARS GO SHOPPING
Collins, 1989. – O/P. – 0 00 194779 6
CHUNKY BEARS' BIRTHDAY PARTY
Collins, 1989. – O/P. – 0 00 194780 X
CHUNKY BEARS' BUSY DAY
Collins, 1988. – O/P. – 0 00 184125 4
CUBBY BEARS GO CAMPING
Collins, 1986. – O/P. – 0 00 123854 X
CUBBY BEARS GO ON THE RIVER
Collins, 1986. – O/P. – 0 00 123856 6
CUBBY BEARS GO SHOPPING
Collins, 1986. – O/P. – 0 00 123855 8
CUBBY BEARS' BIRTHDAY PARTY
Collins, 1986. – O/P. – 0 00 123857 4
DARK FOREST
Collins, 1986. – O/P. – 0 00 171194 6
DAY PATCH STOOD GUARD
Collins, 1992. – 0 00 664190 3
DAY SIDNEY WAS LOST
Harper Collins, 1992. – 0 00 664130 X
DAY THE DUCKS WENT SKATING
Picture Lions, 1992. – 0 00 100458 1
DAY VERONICA WAS NOSY
Picture Lions, 1992. – 0 00 100457 3
DESERT ISLAND DUCKS
Buzz Books, 1991. – O/P. – 1 8559 1126 4
DOCTOR'S BAG
Collins, 1982. – Pbk. – 0 00 123703 9

DOLLY ROCKERS
Little Mammoth, 1992. – Pbk. – 0 7497 1302 X
FIREMAN SAM AND THE MISSING KEY
Heinemann, 1990. – Pbk. – O/P. – 0 434 97335 1
GOPHER GOLD
Little Mammoth, 1991. – Pbk. – 0 7497 0303 2
GRAND OSTRICH BALL
Heinemann, 1989. – 0 434 94741 5
HAPPY BIRTHDAY
Collins, 1987. – O/P. – 0 00 184860 7
HEAVY AND LIGHT
Pan Books, 1987. – O/P. – 0 330 29691 4
HIGH FLYERS
Little Mammoth, 1991. – Pbk. – 0 7497 0302 4
HIGHLAND FLING
Buzz Books, 1991. – O/P. – 1 8559 1125 6
HOT AND COLD
Pan Books, 1987. – O/P. – 0 330 29692 2
INSIDE OUTING
Collins, 1990. – O/P. – 0 00 663609 8
JUMPER
Collins, 1982. – O/P. – 0 00 123701 2
KOOKABURRA CACKLES
Heinemann, 1990. – 0 434 94710 5
LIGHT AND DARK
Pan Books, 1987. – O/P. – 0 330 29690 6
LONG HOUSE IN DANGER
Collins, 1986. – O/P. – 0 00 171192 X
PANDEMONIUM
Little Mammoth, 1992. – Pbk. – 0 7497 1301 1
PEACOCK PALACE SCOOP
Heinemann, 1990. – 0 434 94708 3
ROAD TO BETHLEHEM
Collins, 1987. – O/P. – 0 00 184612 4
SID AND SADIE
Collins, 1988. – O/P. – 0 00 191119 8
SNAIL'S TALE
Buzz Books, 1991. – O/P. – 1 8559 1127 2
WET AND DRY
Pan Books, 1987. – O/P. – 0 330 29671 X
ZIPPI AND ZAC AND THE GRAND OSTRICH BALL
Little Mammoth, 1991. – Pbk. – 0 7497 0301 6

LAVELLE, Sheila

British. Born Gateshead, Co. Durham. Married, two sons. Lives at Bourne End, Buckinghamshire. Writer. A writer of lively, popular books which are not too demanding, and fun to read.

DISASTER WITH THE FIEND
Harper Collins, 1991, 144p. – Pbk. –
0 00 673669 6
Hamish Hamilton, 1988, 128p. – 0 241 12528 6
illustrated by Margaret Chamberlain

In the same series:

CALAMITY WITH THE FIEND
Hamish Hamilton, 1993, 160p. –
0 241 13365 3

FIEND NEXT DOOR
Armada Books, 1983, 112p. – Pbk. –
0 00 672082 X
Hamish Hamilton, 1982, 180p. – O/P. –
0 241 10774 1

HOLIDAY WITH THE FIEND
Armada Books, 1988, 128p. – Pbk. –
0 00 672787 5
Hamish Hamilton, 1986, 128p. –
0 241 11857 3
illustrated by Margaret Chamberlain

MY BEST FIEND
Armada Books, 1980, 128p. – Pbk. –
0 00 671661 X
illustrated by Linda Birch

TROUBLE WITH THE FIEND
Armada Books, 1985, 128p. – Pbk. –
0 00 672433 7
Hamish Hamilton, 1984. – 0 241 11305 9

A series of books about Charlie Ellis and Angela Mitchell who live next door to each other. Life is never dull, for Angela is always full of bright ideas and tricks. Sometimes Charlie gets fed up of being the victim, and plans revenges. Each book is similar – only the tricks are different.
Age range: 7–9

Other publications:

APPLE PIE ALIEN
Orchard Books, 1993. – Pbk. – 1 8521 3502 6
BIG STINK
Mammoth, 1993. – Pbk. – 0 7497 1638 X
BOGGY BAY MARATHON
Orchard Books, 1993. – Pbk. – 1 8521 3556 5
CHOCOLATE CANDY KID
Deutsch, 1986. – O/P. – 0 233 97948 4
COPYCAT
Hodder, 1989. – 0 340 49577 4
DISAPPEARING GRANNY
Heinemann, 1985. – 0 434 93026 1
THE DOGNAPPER
Heinemann, 1993. – 0 434 97681 4
EVERYBODY SAID NO!
Black, 1978. – 0 7136 1805 1
FETCH THE SLIPPER
H. Hamilton, 1989. – 0 241 12660 6
FISH STEW
Paperbird, 1991. – Pbk. – 1 8554 3018 5
HARRY'S AUNT
Pan Books, 1988. – Pbk. – 0 330 30388 0
HARRY'S CAT
H. Hamilton, 1992. – 0 241 13090 5
HARRY'S DOG
H. Hamilton, 1988. – 0 241 12222 8
HARRY'S HAMSTER
H. Hamilton, 1990. – 0 241 12661 4
HARRY'S HORSE
H. Hamilton, 1987. – O/P. – 0 241 11989 8
MAISY IN THE MUD AND MAISY'S MASTERPIECE
Pan Macmillan, 1993. – Pbk. – 0 333 58377 9
MAZY
Macmillan, 1990. – Pbk. – O/P. –
0 333 52950 2
MESSY MAISY AND MAISY'S MEASLES
Pan Books, 1991. – Pbk. – 0 330 31869 1
MONICA'S MONSTER
Hodder, 1990. – Pbk. – 0 340 51620 8
MORE ADVENTURES OF URSULA BEAR
Hamlyn, 1983. – Pbk. – O/P. – 0 600 20540 1
MR GINGER'S POTATO
Black, 1981. – 0 7136 2092 7
MYRTLE TURTLE
Black, 1981. – O/P. – 0 7136 2093 5
SNOWY
OUP, 1993. – 0 19 279909 6
SPOTS IN SPACE
Orchard Books, 1988. – 1 8521 3084 9
STRAWBERRY JAM PONY
Penguin, 1989. – Pbk. – O/P. – 0 14 032977 3
TOO MANY HUSBANDS
H. Hamilton, 1978. – Pbk. – O/P. –
0 241 89835 8
TOPSY-TURVY TEACHER
Orchard Books, 1988. – 1 8521 3083 0

URSULA AT THE ZOO
H. Hamilton, 1986. – 0 241 11728 3

URSULA BALLOONING
H. Hamilton, 1992. – Pbk. – 0 241 13202 9

URSULA BEAR
Hamlyn, 1981. – Pbk. – O/P. – 0 600 20072 8

URSULA BY THE SEA
H. Hamilton, 1986. – 0 241 11914 6

URSULA CAMPING
Corgi, 1987. – Pbk. – 0 552 52447 6

URSULA CLIMBING
Corgi, 1988. – Pbk. – 0 552 52516 2

URSULA DANCING
H. Hamilton, 1979. – Pbk. – O/P. – 0 241 10122 0

URSULA EXPLORING
Corgi, 1989. – Pbk. – 0 552 52542 1

URSULA FLYING
Corgi, 1989. – Pbk. – 0 552 52543 X

URSULA IN THE SNOW
H. Hamilton, 1989. – 0 241 12596 0

URSULA ON SAFARI
H. Hamilton, 1992. – 0 241 13062 X

URSULA ON THE FARM
Pan Books, 1988. – Pbk. – 0 330 30711 8

URSULA RIDING
H. Hamilton, 1985. – O/P. – 0 241 11426 8

URSULA SAILING
Corgi, 1987. – Pbk. – 0 552 52448 4

URSULA SKIING
H. Hamilton, 1989. – 0 241 12529 4

URSULA SWIMMING
H. Hamilton, 1990. – 0 241 12962 1

WINCEY'S WORM
Hodder, 1991. – 0 340 52571 1

LEE, Tanith

British. Born London, 1947. Educated Prendergaste Grammar School; Calford Grammar School; Art College.

Address: C/o Macmillan Ltd,
           4 Little Essex Street,
           London WC2R 3LF,
           England

To be successful at writing fantasy, it is essential to be able to create other worlds that readers can whole-heartedly believe in. To this ability, Tanith Lee adds a wonderful sense of humour and an originality of plot that makes her books both intriguing and thought-provoking, and able to stand the test of time.

THE DRAGON HOARD
Beaver Books, 1989. 176p. – Pbk. – 0 09 957160 9
Macmillan, 1971, 176p. – O/P. – 0 333 12850 8
illustrated by Graham Oakley

Prince Jasleth must seek his fortune in the traditional way of princes. The trouble is, he is cursed, and he turns into a raven when it is most inconvenient. Very amusing.
Age range: 10–12

PRINCE ON A WHITE HORSE
Beaver Books, 1989, 160p. – Pbk. O/P. – 0 09 957150 1
Macmillan, 1982, 160p. – O/P. – 0 333 32929 5

The prince riding along talks to himself, as people on their own do. He is surprised when the horse answers him, and puzzled when the horse stoutly denies being able to talk. How he discovers his identity makes an amusing and enjoyable read.
Age range: 10–12

SHON THE TAKEN
Beaver Books, 1989, 144p. – Pbk. – 0 09 963130 X
Macmillan, 1979, 160p. – O/P. – 0 333 27036 3

In Shon's world, if you were touched by one of Crow's people, you had to die. Shon convinces himself he has not been touched, and dismisses the tiny sense of foreboding. Intent on settling a score with his brother, it is too late when the full realization of events is made plain.
Age range: 10–12

THE WINTER PLAYERS
Beaver Books, 1988, 112p. – Pbk. – 0 09 957140 4
Macmillan, 1976, 112p. – O/P. – 0 333 19840 9

The exciting first chapter plunges the reader directly into a scene of powerful conflict, between Oaive, the young

priestess guarding the shrine, and the young man intent on stealing. Which of them is the ultimate victor makes a superb story.
Age range: 10–12

LEESON, Robert (Arthur)

British. Born Barnton, Cheshire, 1928. Educated Sir John Deane's Grammar School; University of London, external B.A. (Hons). British Army, Middle East, 1946–48. Married Gunvor Hagen, 1954, one son, one daughter. Journalist, Parliamentary correspondent, editor.

Awards: Eleanor Farjeon Award, 1985
IBBY Honour Award: *Slambash Wangs of a Compo Gormer*, 1990

Address: 18 McKenzie Road, Broxbourne, Hertfordshire, England

Although associated by many children with the popular television series *Grange Hill*, Robert Leeson has written several books on various themes for different age groups, some with a specific appeal to boys.

BEYOND THE DRAGON PROW
Collins, 1973, 160p. – O/P. – 0 00 184061 4 illustrated by Ian Robbins

Set in Viking times, this stirring adventure story is a useful book to read to a class studying the Vikings. Once the reader has mastered the strange names, it is an easy and exciting story to read, whilst also conveying a realistic impression of everyday life of the period.
Age range: 10–12

CHALLENGE IN THE DARK
Armada Books, 1979, 98p. – Pbk. – 0 00 671648 2
Collins, 1978, 112p. – O/P – 0 00 184065 7 illustrated by Jim Russell

Young readers will appreciate the skilful combination of realism and humour in this story about Steven, the class bully, and Mike, his victim. When the two of them are challenged to see who can stay in the old air-raid shelter without light, Mike rises to the occasion. Easy, entertaining and exciting.
Age range: 9–11

THE DEMON BIKE RIDER
Armada Books, 1977, 94p. – Pbk. – 0 00 671320 3
Collins, 1976, 96p. – O/P. – 0 00 184163 7 illustrated by Jim Russell

A mixture of mystery and ghosts, this has proved one of Robert Leeson's most popular books. The idea of a ghost on a motorbike appeals to boys. Not very long or demanding, but lots of action.
Age range: 9–11

GENIE ON THE LOOSE
Armada Books, 1984, 128p. – Pbk. – 0 00 672294 6
Hamish Hamilton, 1984, 128p. – O/P. – 0 241 11177 3

In the same series:

THIRD CLASS GENIE
Lions, 1993, 160p. – Pbk. – 0 00 671633 4
Hamish Hamilton, 1981, 128p. – 0 241 10623 0

If you have ever wondered how a genie manages to work miracles, these books have the answer. Alec is lucky enough to own a beer can which houses a genie who is learning the job, and does not yet merit a lamp. His 'miracles' often go wrong, sometimes quite disastrously, leading to many hilarious situations. The stories are full of action, but quite dense in appearance, although competent readers will have no problems.
Age range: 10–12

HAROLD AND BELLA, JAMMY AND ME
Hamish Hamilton, 1982, 128p. – O/P. – 0 241 10722 9
Armada Books, 1980, 128p. – Pbk. – 0 00 671606 7

LEESON

An uninspiring title for a collection of comical stories about four children and their adventures in an unspecified town in the north. There is enough dialect for authenticity, but not too much to spoil the sense of the story. The flavour of bygone days pervades throughout.
Age range: 8–10

SILVER'S REVENGE
Armada Books, 1985, 208p. – Pbk. –
0 00 672466 3
Collins, 1978, 196p. – O/P. – 0 00 184783 X

Cleverly contrived, this sequel to 'Treasure Island' is written in a similar style with the same sense of humour. This book will not have universal appeal, but is rewarding for those who do persevere.
Age range: 10–12

SMART GIRLS
Walker Books, 1993, 80p. – 0 7445 2441 5
illustrated by Axel Scheffler

Five international folk-tales featuring a young girl able to outwit everything and everyone. The tales are short and the print is very clear, making it an easy read, even for struggling readers.
Age range: 8–10

WHEEL OF DANGER
Armada Books, 1987, 96p. – Pbk. –
0 00 672803 0
Collins, 1986, 96p. – 0 00 184790 2
Collins, 1986, 96p. – Pbk. – 0 00 184791 0
illustrated by Anthony Kervins

Mike and his friends are pleased with themselves when they succeed in turning the huge water wheel. Their pleasure is, unfortunately, short-lived, as it floods the mill with the children trapped inside. Tense to read, but with amusing moments, it is an excellent story for children who require coaxing.
Age range: 9–11

Other publications:

ADVENTURES OF BAXTER AND CO
Collins, 1984. – O/P. – 0 00 184124 6

APRIL FOOL AT HOB LANE SCHOOL
Puffin Books, 1993. – Pbk. – 0 14 034744 5

AT WAR WITH TOMORROW
Corgi, 1988. – Pbk. – 0 552 52346 1

BESS
Armada Books, 1983. – O/P. – 0 00 672218 0

BURPER
Heinemann, 1989. – 0 434 93072 5

CANDY FOR KING
Armada Books, 1984. – O/P. – 0 00 672467 1

THE CIMAROONS
Journeyman Press, 1990. – Pbk. –
0 904526 43 7

COMING HOME
Lions, 1992. – Pbk. – 0 00 674305 6

FIRE ON THE CLOUD
Mammoth, 1991. – Pbk. – 0 7497 0841 7

FORTY DAYS OF TUCKER
Armada Books, 1983. – O/P. – 0 00 672176 1

GHOSTS AT HOB LANE
H. Hamilton, 1993. – 0 241 13181 2

GRANGE HILL FOR SALE
Fontana, 1981. – Pbk. – O/P. – 0 00 671813 2

GRANGE HILL GOES WILD
Armada Books, 1980. – O/P. – 0 00 671812 4

GRANGE HILL HOME AND AWAY
BBC, 1982. – O/P. – 0 563 20130 4

GRANGE HILL RULES – OK?
BBC, 1980. – O/P. – 0 563 17794 2

HEY, ROBIN!
Collins, 1991. – Pbk. – 0 00 673724 2

HOME AND AWAY
Armada Books, 1982. – O/P. – 0 00 672091 9

HOW ALICE SAVED CAPTAIN MIRACLE
Heinemann, 1989. – 0 434 93063 6

IT'S MY LIFE
Armada Books, 1981. – Pbk. – 0 00 671783 7

JAN ALONE
Tracks, 1991. – Pbk. – 0 00 673180 5

KARLO'S TALE
Young Lions, 1993. – Pbk. – 0 00 674320 X

LANDING IN CLOUD VALLEY
Mammoth, 1991. – Pbk. – 0 7497 0840 9

LAST GENIE
Lions, 1993. – Pbk. – 0 00 674694 2

MAROON BOY
Armada Books, 1982. – O/P. – 0 00 672097 8

METRO GANGS ATTACK
Corgi, 1988. – Pbk. – 0 552 52347 X

NEVER KISS FROGS
Penguin, 1993. – Pbk. – 0 14 034740 2

NO SLEEP FOR HOB LANE SCHOOL
H. Hamilton, 1992. – 0 241 13180 4

ONE FROG TOO MANY
H. Hamilton, 1991. – 0 241 13106 5

PANCAKE PICKLE AT HOB LANE
Penguin, 1993. – Pbk. – 0 14 034743 7

REVERSIBLE GIANT
Armada Books, 1988. – Pbk. – 0 00 672893 6

RIGHT ROYAL KIDNAP
Young Lions, 1992. – Pbk. – 0 00 674375 7

SLAMBASH WANGS OF A COMPO GORMER
Armada Books, 1988. – O/P. – 0 00 672793 X

THREE AGAINST THE WORLD
Corgi, 1988. – Pbk. – 0 552 52345 3

TIME ROPE
Corgi, 1987. – Pbk. – 0 552 52344 5

WHITE HORSE
Fontana, 1984. – Pbk. – O/P. – 0 00 672252 0

ZARNIA EXPERIMENT: PHASE 3
Mammoth, 1993. – Pbk. – 0 7497 0842 5

ZARNIA EXPERIMENT: PHASE 4
Mammoth, 1993. – Pbk. – 0 7497 0843 3

LINDGREN, Astrid

Swedish. Born Vimmerby, 1907. Married Sture Lindgren, 1931, one son, one daughter. Children's book editor.

Awards: Hans Christian Andersen International Medal, 1958

Welsh Arts Council International Writers' Prize

German Booksellers' Peace Prize for the International Year of the Child

Hon. Doctorate of Letters, Leicester University

Leo Tolstoy Gold Medal

An author with the rare quality of having both international appeal and a popularity that survives the passage of time. Her books portray a strong feeling for the security and happiness to be found in a family circle, something many children are deprived of.

CHERRY TIME AT BULLERBY
Mammoth, 1991, 96p. – Pbk. – 0 7497 0663 5
Methuen, 1965. 93p. – O/P. – 0 416 23100 4

In the same series:

CHRISTMAS AT BULLERBY
Methuen, 1970, 96p. – 0 416 22250 1

DAY AT BULLERBY
Methuen, 1967, 24p. – 0 416 94500 7

HAPPY DAYS AT BULLERBY
Mammoth, 1991, 96p. – Pbk. –
0 7497 0662 7
Methuen, 1965, 96p. – O/P. – 0 416 23100 4

THE SIX BULLERBY CHILDREN
Mammoth, 1991, 91p. – Pbk. –
0 7497 0661 9
Methuen, n.d., 92p. – O/P. – 0 416 26180 9

SPRINGTIME AT BULLERBY
Methuen, 1981, 32p. – O/P. – 0 416 88710 4
all illustrated by Ilon Wikland

Warm, humorous stories about the families living on farms in the Swedish village of Bullerby. Far from being sentimental, they take an honest look at the difficulties as well as the joys of relationships.
Age range: 7–9

ALL ABOUT THE BULLERBY CHILDREN
Penguin, 1974, 192p. – Pbk. O/P. –
0 14 030705 2
Methuen, 1970, 224p. – 0 416 15280 5
illustrated by Ilon Wikland

Combines the stories of the above books; the hardback edition is published with exceptionally clear print, making it accessible to younger children.
Age range: 7–9

EMIL AND HIS CLEVER PIG
Beaver Books, 1984, 144p. – Pbk. O/P. –
0 09 937600 8
Hodder, 1975, 160p. – O/P. – 0 340 18971 1
illustrated by Bjorn Berg

In the same series:

EMIL AND THE BAD TOOTH
Hodder, 1976, 32p. – O/P. – 0 340 20923 2

LINDGREN

EMIL GETS INTO MISCHIEF
Beaver Books, 1985, 126p. – Pbk. O/P. –
0 09 942222 0
Hamlyn, 1979, 126p. – Pbk. O/P. –
0 600 33164 4

EMIL IN THE SOUP TUREEN
Beaver Books, 1985, 96p. – Pbk. O/P. –
0 09 942210 7
Hodder, 1970, 90p. – O/P. – 0 340 10404 X

EMIL'S LITTLE SISTER
Hodder, 1985, 64p. – O/P. – 0 340 38114 0
illustrated by Bjorn Berg

EMIL'S PRANKS
Hodder, 1973, 128p. – O/P. – 0 340 16944 3

EMIL'S STICKY PROBLEM
Hodder, 1986, 60p. – O/P. – 0 340 39842 6
illustrated by Bjorn Berg

THAT EMIL
Hodder, 1973, 32p. – O/P. – 0 340 17213 4

Emil is a naughty child, but his antics delight young readers. Enjoyable when read aloud.
Age range: 6–8

KARLSON FLIES AGAIN
Mammoth, 1992, 114p. – Pbk. – 0 7497 1036 5
Methuen, 1977, 144p. – 0 416 58390 3

In the same series:

KARLSON ON THE ROOF
Mammoth, 1992, 128p. – Pbk. –
0 7497 1037 3
Methuen, 1975, 128p. – 0 416 80240 0

THE WORLD'S BEST KARLSON
Methuen, 1980, 160p. – 0 416 88020 7
all illustrated by Ilon Wikland

Karlson is amazing. He is very small and lives on a roof with a propeller fastened to his back. He cheers Midge up when he flies into his life with his mischievous ideas. Escapism at its amusing best.
Age range: 7–9

LOTTA
Methuen, 1982, 160p. – 0 416 26840 4
Methuen, 1979, 160p. – Pbk. O/P. –
0 416 86510 0

In the same series:

LOTTA LEAVES HOME
Mammoth, 1991, 64p. – Pbk. –
0 7497 0665 1
Methuen, 1969, 64p. – O/P. – 0 416 48170 1

LOTTA'S BIKE
Methuen, 1973, 32p. – 0 416 76600 5

LOTTA'S CHRISTMAS SURPRISE
Magnet Books, 1980, 36p. – Pbk. –
0 416 88600 0
Methuen, 1978, 32p. – O/P. – 0 416 86690 5

LOTTA'S EASTER SURPRISE
Raben & Sjogren, 1992, 34p. –
9 1296 2018 X

THE MISCHIEVOUS MARTENS
Mammoth, 1991, 96p. – Pbk. –
0 7497 0664 3
Methuen, 1969, 96p. – O/P. – 0 416 48160 4
illustrated by Ilon Wikland

Ordinary family stories, told with love and humour. Very easy to read.
Age range: 7–9

MARDIE
Magnet Books, 1979, 156p. – Pbk. O/P. –
0 416 87610 2
Methuen, 1979, 160p. – O/P. – 0 416 57640 0

In the same series:

MARDIE TO THE RESCUE
Methuen, 1981, 196p. – 0 416 20650 6
both illustrated by Ilon Wikland

Endearing stories about a Swedish family in the 1920s. They are poor, but Mardie's rascally adventures take place against the secure family background that Astrid Lindgren portrays so well. The usual mixture of warmth, humour and mischief.
Age range: 7–9

PIPPI LONGSTOCKING
Windrush, 1987, 133p. – L/P. – O/P. –
1 8508 9906 1
Penguin, 1976, 176p. – Pbk. – 0 14 030894 6
OUP, 1954, 128p. – 0 19 271097 4
illustrated by Richard Kennedy

The exception to warm family stories. Pippi has to live alone as her mother is

dead and her father marooned. However, she is very strong, both physically and emotionally, and, instead of feeling sorry for herself, she gets on with life, defying all conventions. It is this successful defiance and energetic, imaginative ideas which children find so easy to identify with. It has to be said that, because her father is a Cannibal King on the island, and tongue-in-cheek references are made to cannibal language and customs, the book is considered by some to be racist. It is, however, all part of the unreal life Pippi leads, a fact children will accept purely at face value, without delving beneath for hidden and unintended meanings.
Age range: 9–11

Other Publications:

CHRISTMAS IN THE STABLE
Hodder, 1990. – Pbk. – 0 340 54176 8
DRAGON WITH RED EYES
Methuen, 1986. – O/P. – 0 416 64180 6
FOX AND THE TOMTEN
Kestrel Books, 1977. – Pbk. – O/P. – 0 7226 5189 9
GHOST OF SKINNY JACK
Methuen, 1988. – O/P. – 0 416 07842 7
I DON'T WANT TO GO TO BED
Raben & Sjogren, 1988, – 9 1295 9066 3
I WANT A BROTHER OR SISTER
Raben & Sjogren, 1988, – 9 1295 8778 6
I WANT TO GO TO SCHOOL TOO
Methuen, 1980. – O/P. – 0 416 88990 5
MY NIGHTINGALE IS SINGING
Methuen, 1985. – O/P. – 0 416 52060 X
ROBBER'S DAUGHTER
Methuen, 1983. – O/P. – 0 416 26220 1
RONIA THE ROBBER'S DAUGHTER
Penguin, 1985. – Pbk. – 0 14 031720 1
RUNAWAY SLEIGH RIDE
Methuen, 1984. – O/P. – 0 416 48200 7
TOMTEN AND THE FOX
Floris Books, 1992. – 0 86315 154 X
THE TOMTEN
Floris Books, 1992. – 0 86315 153 1

LITTLE, (Flora) Jean

Canadian. Born Tainon, Formosa, now Taiwan, 1932. Educated in Guelph, Ontario; Victoria College, University of Toronto, B.A. English; Institute of Special Education. Teacher.

Awards: Canadian Children's Book Award: *Mine for Keeps*, 1961

Canadian Library Association Book of the Year Award: *Mama's Going to Buy you a Mocking Bird*, 1985

Ruth Schwartz Award: *Mama's Going to Buy you a Mocking Bird*, 1985

Address: 198 Glasgow Street North,
Guelph,
Ontario,
Canada

Jean Little has an understanding of children and their problems which enables her to write simply and directly for them. As a result, her books deal honestly with different emotional problems and are meaningful in every way.

DIFFERENT DRAGONS

Penguin, 1988, 144p. – Pbk. – 0 14 031998 0
Viking Kestrel, 1987, 124p. – O/P. – 0 670 80836 9
illustrated by Laura Fernandez

Ben is timid, and feels he will not manage to cope with staying with Aunt Rose, whom he does not know very well. He is sure he cannot cope when she presents him with a big dog, for he is terrified. How this problem is resolved makes a warm, satisfying story.
Age range: 7–9

LOST AND FOUND

Penguin, 1987, 96p. – Pbk. – 0 14 031997 2
Viking Kestrel, 1986, 82p. – 0 670 80835 0
illustrated by Leoung O'Young

A moving story about a little girl, feeling strange in a new town, who finds a stray dog. She is allowed to keep him while a search is made for his owner. Eventually she has to make a difficult decision.
Age range: 9–11

LITTLE

MAMA'S GOING TO BUY YOU A MOCKING BIRD
Penguin, 1986, 224p. – Pbk. – 0 14 031737 6
Viking Kestrel, 1985, 212p. – O/P. –
0 670 80346 4

A brave and successful attempt to face a problem which is real, and which many children have to come to terms with. Jeremy's father has cancer and will die. Dealing with grief is personal, but sometimes books can provide a stimulus which allows both children and adults to express their feelings.
Age range: 10–14

Other publications:

HEY WORLD, HERE I AM!
OUP, 1989. – 0 19 276082 3
JESS WAS THE BRAVE ONE
Viking, 1992. – 0 670 83495 5
MINE FOR KEEPS
Dent, 1970. – O/P. – 0 460 05626 3
ONCE UPON A GOLDEN APPLE
Viking, 1991. – 0 670 82963 3
REVENGE OF THE SMALL SMALL
Viking, 1993. – 0 670 84471 3

LIVELY, Penelope (Margaret, née Low)

British. Born Cairo, Egypt, 1933, came to England 1945. Educated boarding school, Sussex; St Anne's College, Oxford, B.A. (Hons), Modern History. Married Jack Lively, 1957, one daughter, one son. Radio presenter, reviewer.

Awards: Fellow of the Royal Society of Literature

Library Association Carnegie Medal: *The Ghost of Thomas Kempe*, 1973

Whitbread Award: *A Stitch in time*, 1976

Address: Duck End,
Great Rollright,
Chipping Norton,
Oxfordshire OX7 5SB,
England

Agent: Murray Pollinger,
4 Garrick Street,
London WC2E 9BH,
England

A distinguished writer with a fascination for time-slips and a sense of history and the way it can affect the present. Children need to be fluent readers as her style is rather adult and makes no compromise. The originality of the plots and the ever-present air of expectation tempered by verbal humour, however, engage the reader's interest to the end.

ASTERCOTE
Penguin, 1987, 160p. – Pbk. – 0 14 031973 5
Heinemann, 1970, 160p. – 0 434 94890 X
illustrated by Antony Maitland

Peter and Mair discover the ruins of an old village called Astercote. They become fascinated, and delve deeper into the history of the village, gradually bringing it back to life.
Age range: 11–14

THE DRIFTWAY
Mammoth, 1993, 144p. – Pbk. – 0 7497 0792 5
Heinemann, 1972, 144p. – 0 434 94893 4

The Driftway is an old road with a long memory. While hitching a lift to go and visit Gran, Paul and his sister see the ghosts of long dead travellers. A slow-moving but atmospheric story which is strangely compelling.
Age range: 12–14

FANNY AND THE MONSTERS
Mammoth, 1991, 128p. – Pbk. – 0 7497 0600 7
Heinemann, 1983, 128p. – O/P. –
0 434 94888 8
illustrated by John Lawrence

A collection of stories about a Victorian girl who longs to be a boy so that she can have adventures.
Age range: 9–11

THE GHOST OF THOMAS KEMPE
Mammoth, 1992, 160p. – Pbk. – 0 7497 0791 7
Chivers Press, 1986, 256p. – L/P. –
0 7451 0303 0
Heinemann, 1973, 160p. – 0 434 94894 2
illustrated by Antony Maitland

Once James realizes that there is a ghost in the house, he spends all his time trying to ascertain who he is. The humour in this story verges on slapstick at times. Quite riveting, with a highly satisfactory ending.
Age range: 11–14

GOING BACK
Penguin, 1991, 128p. – Pbk. – 0 14 014509 5
Heinemann, 1975, 96p. – 0 434 94896 9

Jane returns to Medleycott where she grew up. She relives her childhood during the Second World War. Excellent period detail and atmosphere, making absorbing reading, but likely to remain a minority choice.
Age range: 11–14

THE HOUSE IN NORHAM GARDENS
Penguin, 1986, 176p. – Pbk. – 0 14 031976 X
Heinemann, 1974, 160p. – 0 434 94895 0

A strange mixture of reality and fantasy. The house is Victorian, and the spirit of the previous owner, an explorer, lives on to disturb the present occupants.
Age range: 11–14

THE REVENGE OF SAMUEL STOKES
Chivers Press, 1991, 216p. – L/P. – O/P. –
0 7451 1406 7
Mammoth, 1991, 144p. – Pbk. – 0 7497 0601 5
Heinemann, 1981, 160p. – 0 434 94889 6
illustrated by Martin J. Cottam

Strange happenings abound on the new housing estate. Washing machines go wrong, televisions won't work, and a greenhouse becomes a Greek Temple. Tim and Jane are convinced a ghost is at work and set out to find out the reason. Amusing and enjoyable.
Age range: 11–14

A STITCH IN TIME
Chivers Press, 1988, 264p. – L/P. –
0 7451 0726 5
Penguin, 1986, 160p. – Pbk. – 0 14 031975 1
Heinemann, 1976, 128p. – 0 434 94897 7

A haunting story about Maria, staying in a cottage while on holiday, who feels the presence of a long dead child. She slowly unravels the mystery of why the child cries. Not very eventful, the book successfully relies on its intriguing atmosphere to hold the reader's interest.
Age range: 11–14

THE VOYAGE OF QV66
Chivers Press, 1992, 280p. – O/P. –
0 7451 1548 9
Mammoth, 1990, 192p. – Pbk. – 0 7497 0360 1
Heinemann, 1978, 192p. – 0 434 94898 5
illustrated by Harold Jones

An unusual book for Penelope Lively in that it is completely light-hearted and funny. A group of animals are travelling to a zoo in a country where there are no people. Their efforts to discover who Stanley is are both amusing and intriguing.
Age range: 11–14

THE WHISPERING KNIGHTS
Chivers Press, 1990, 248p. – L/P. –
0 7451 1153 X
Heinemann, 1989, 160p. – 0 434 94884 5
Penguin, 1987, 160p. – Pbk. – 0 14 031977 8
illustrated by Neil Reed

William and Susie were having fun cooking up a witch's brew and chanting spells in the barn. Martha, knowing about the witch who reputedly lived there many years ago, was worried that things may go wrong – rightly so as it turned out. A malevolent spirit is summoned that is beyond the children to control. An engrossing fantasy in which past and present merge in a realistic way.
Age range: 10–12

THE WILD HUNT OF HAGWORTHY
Mammoth, 1992, 144p. – Pbk. – 0 7497 0786 0
Heinemann, 1989, 144p. – 0 434 94886 1
Chivers Press, 1987, 256p. – L/P. –
0 7451 0491 6
illustrated by Robert Payne

The whole village of Hagworthy is helping in some way to prepare for the fete, but only a few are chosen to take part in the Horn Dance. The happy annual event gradually turns into a

sinister, evil hunt where danger is a reality. Readers are enthralled.
Age range: 11–14

Other publications:
DEBBIE AND THE LITTLE DEVIL
Heinemann, 1987. – 0 434 93047 4
DRAGON TROUBLE
Heinemann, 1984. – 0 434 93022 9
HOUSE INSIDE OUT
Penguin, 1989. – Pbk. – 0 14 032399 6
JUDY AND THE MARTIAN
Simon & Schuster, 1992. – 0 7500 1103 3
STAINED GLASS WINDOW
J. MacRae, 1990. – 0 86203 444 2
UNINVITED GHOSTS, AND OTHER STORIES
Mammoth, 1991. – Pbk. – 0 7497 0788 7

LOWRY, Lois (née Hammersberg)

American. Born Honolulu, 1937. Educated Brown University, Providence, Rhode Island; University of South Maine, Portland, B.A. English. Married Donald Lowry 1956 (divorced 1977), two daughters, two sons.

Awards: IBBY Honour Award: *Autumn Street*, 1982

Boston Globe-Horn Book Award: *Rabble Starkey*, 1987

American Library Association Newbery Medal: *Number the Stars*, 1989

American Library Association Newbery Medal: *The Giver*, 1994

Address: 34 Hancock Street, Boston, Massachusetts 02114, USA

ALL ABOUT SAM
Chivers Press, 1992, 152p. – O/P. – 0 7451 1659 0
Collins, 1990, 128p. – Pbk. – 0 00 673436 5

Sam is the younger brother of Anastasia (see below), and has his own story to tell. Written in the same style, this book is also enjoyable, but if the Anastasia theme has been written to the full, and the author wished to address a different age group, a complete change would have been better.
Age range: 9–11

ANASTASIA AGAIN!
Cornerstone Books, 1989, 200p. – L/P. – O/P. – 1 557 36074 X
Armada Books, 1986, 128p. – Pbk. – 0 00 672636 4

In the same series:

ANASTASIA, ASK YOUR ANALYST
Chivers Press, 1992, 160p. – O/P. – 0 7451 1553 5
Armada Books, 1988, 128p. – Pbk. – 0 00 672870 7

ANASTASIA AT THIS ADDRESS
Lions, 1993, 144p. – Pbk. – 0 00 674380 3

ANASTASIA AT YOUR SERVICE
Cornerstone Books, 1989, 224p. – L/P. – 1 557 36101 0
Armada Books, 1987, 160p. – Pbk. – 0 00 672867 7

ANASTASIA HAS THE ANSWERS
Chivers Press, 1991, 176p. – L/P. – 0 7451 1292 7
Armada Books, 1989, 128p. – Pbk. – 0 00 673011 6

ANASTASIA KRUPNIK
Cornerstone Books, 1988, 176p. – L/P. – 1 557 36073 1
Armada Books, 1986, 128p. – Pbk. – 0 00 672635 6

ANASTASIA ON HER OWN
Cornerstone Books, 1989, 184p. – L/P. – 1 557 36135 5
Armada Books, 1988, 144p. – Pbk. – 0 00 672871 5

ANASTASIA'S CHOSEN CAREER
Chivers Press, 1991, 216p. – L/P. – O/P. – 0 7451 1468 7
Collins, 1989, 160p. – Pbk. – 0 00 673012 4

A series of stories about a young lady with a terrific sense of humour, which she badly needs to see her through the various pitfalls that life seems to save

just for her. There is an obvious American slant, but this is no barrier. For sheer fun reading, they are excellent.
Age range: 11–13

Other publications:

FIND A STRANGER, SAY GOODBYE
Collins, 1988. – O/P. – 0 00 673263 1
NUMBER THE STARS
Lions, 1991. – Pbk. – 0 00 673677 7
ONE HUNDREDTH THING ABOUT CAROLINE
Lions, 1992. – Pbk. – 0 00 674195 9
RABBLE STARKEY
Collins, 1990. – Pbk. – O/P. – 0 00 673764 1
ROAD AHEAD
Chivers Press, 1989. – O/P. – 0 7451 0963 2
SUMMER TO DIE
Collins, 1990. – Pbk. – O/P. – 0 00 673598 3
SWITCHAROUND
Lions, 1992. – Pbk. – 0 00 674194 0
TAKING CARE OF TERRIFIC
Cornerstone Books, US, 1989. – O/P. – 1 5573 6119 3
WOODS AT THE END OF AUTUMN STREET
Armada Books, 1989. – Pbk. – O/P. – 0 00 673054 X
YOUR MOVE JP
Lions, 1992. – Pbk. – O/P. – 0 00 674196 7

M

McBRATNEY, Sam

British. Born Belfast, Northern Ireland. Educated Trinity College, Dublin. Married, three children. Teacher.

Address: 17 Ballynister Road,
          Glenavy,
          Crumlin,
          Co. Antrim,
          N. Ireland

A writer of down-to-earth, enjoyable and accessible stories which boys as well as girls can and do read for pleasure. He has an off-beat sense of humour which ensures a lot of laughs.

ART, YOU'RE MAGIC
Walker Books, 1992, 64p. – 0 7445 2417 2
illustrated by Tony Blundell

When Mervyn comes to school in a new tie, everyone admires it and makes a fuss, so Arthur thinks he will do the same. Unfortunately it all goes wrong. Large print, easy to read, and lots of laughs.
Age range: 6–8

CLAUDIUS BALD EAGLE
Methuen, 1987, 96p. – O/P. – 0 416 96860 0
illustrated by Joanne Carey

Edward Moose is unhappy and his friend, Claudius, is fed up with him. When Harry arrives, determined to get moose antlers for his mantelpiece, Edward has good reason to feel unhappy.
Age range: 8–10

COLVIN AND THE SNAKE BASKET
Magnet Books, 1987, 96p. – Pbk. –
0 416 04492 1
Methuen, 1985, 96p. – O/P. – 0 416 52770 1
illustrated by Carol Holmes

Colvin hates being the middle child and feels nothing ever goes right for him. He finds that hiding himself away in the laundry basket is very helpful. Extremely funny.
Age range: 9–11

THE GHOSTS OF HUNGRYHOUSE LANE
Chivers Press, 1989, 112p. – 0 85997 994 6
Hippo Books, 1988, 112p. – Pbk. –
0 590 70972 0
illustrated by David Farris

An unusual ghost story in which the resident ghosts are terrorized by the children when a family move in.
Age range: 9–11

JIMMY ZEST
Mammoth, 1990, 128p. – Pbk. – O/P. –
0 7497 0290 7
Hamish Hamilton, 1982, 151p. – O/P. –
0 241 10807 1

In the same series:

THE JIMMY ZEST ALL-STARS
Hamish Hamilton, 1985, 128p. – O/P. –
0 241 11699 6
illustrated by Thelma Lambert

ZESTY
Mammoth, 1990, 160p. – Pbk. – O/P. –
0 7497 0291 5
Hamish Hamilton, 1984, 148p. –
0 241 11254 0
illustrated by Susan Hellard

ZESTY GOES COOKING
H. Hamilton, 1989, 96p. – O/P. –
0 241 12614 2

Collections of stories about Jimmy Zest and his cronies. The characters are remarkably true to life and the schemes they dream up are told with humour.
Age range: 9–11

UNCLE CHARLIE WEASEL AND THE CUCKOO BIRD
Magnet Books, 1988, 80p. – Pbk. –
0 416 07492 8
Methuen, 1986, 96p. – O/P. – 0 416 59710 6

In the same series:

UNCLE CHARLIE WEASEL'S WINTER
*Methuen, 1988, 96p. – 0 416 05192 8
illustrated by Mike Daley*

Two stories about a wily weasel whose antics provide amusing reading.
Age range: 8–10

Other publications:

CASE OF BLUE MURDER
Heinemann, 1993. – 0 434 97682 2
CHIEFTAIN'S DAUGHTER
O'Brien Press, 1993. – Pbk. – 0 86278 338 0
FUNNY HOW THE MAGIC STARTS
Mammoth, 1990. – Pbk. – 0 7497 0313 X
GREEN KIDS
Walker Books, 1993. – Pbk. – 0 7445 3111 X
JEALOUS JOOLS AND DOMINIQUE
Penguin, 1991. – Pbk. – O/P. – 0 14 034602 3
MISSING LOLLIPOP
H. Hamilton, 1986. – O/P. – 0 241 11900 6
PUT A SADDLE ON THE PIG
Methuen, 1992. – 0 416 19032 4
SCHOOL TRIP TO THE STARS
*Hippo Books, 1990. – Pbk. – O/P. –
0 590 76356 3*
SECRET OF BONE ISLAND
*Hippo Books, 1989. – Pbk. – O/P. –
0 590 76170 6*
SOMETHING BIG
Heinemann, 1992. – 0 434 97689 X

McCAUGHREAN, Geraldine (née Jones)

British. Born Enfield, Middlesex, 1951. Educated Enfield Grammar School for Girls; Southgate Technical College, Middlesex; Christchurch College of Education, Canterbury, Kent, B.Ed. (Hons). Married John McCaughrean, 1988. Editor, writer.

Awards: Whitbread Award: *A Little lower than the angels*, 1987

Library Association Carnegie Medal: *Pack of Lies*, 1988

Guardian Children's Fiction Award: *Pack of Lies*, 1989

Address: The Bridge House,
Great Shefford,
Berkshire RG16 7DA,
England

Agent: Giles Gordon,
Anthony Shiel Assoc.,
43 Doughty Street,
London WC1N 2LF,
England

A comparative newcomer to the field of children's books, but very welcome. Her two major books to date have been greeted with much praise as being extremely well written and innovative.

A LITTLE LOWER THAN THE ANGELS
*Penguin, 1989, 144p. – Pbk. – 0 14 032818 1
OUP, 1987, 144p. – 0 19 271561 5*

Gabriel is apprenticed to a stonemason who is a hard man. His cruelty forces Gabriel to flee; he escapes by jumping into the middle of a play, and decides to stay. Set in the Middle Ages, and told with compassion and humour, this story is an absorbing read.
Age range: 12–14

A PACK OF LIES
*Penguin, 1990, 176p. – Pbk. – 0 14 034276 1
Chivers Press, 1990, 320p. – L/P. –
0 7451 1154 8
OUP, 1988, 192p. – 0 19 271612 3*

Ailsa's mum is not doing very well at selling antiques, but when MCC arrives (rather like a stray cat), everything changes. He makes up stories to suit the customers' needs, thus persuading them to buy. The stories seem very like lies to Ailsa, who is shocked by them, but the reader is engrossed.
Age range: 12–14

Other publications:

BRAMBLEDOWN TALES: BLACKBERRY BUNNY
*Tiger Books International, 1989. –
1 8704 6180 0*

McCAUGHREAN

BRAMBLEDOWN TALES: HENRY HEDGEHOG'S HAT
Tiger Books International, 1989. –
1 8704 6179 7

BRAMBLEDOWN TALES: HOPPITY HARE'S ADVENTURES
Tiger Books International, 1989. –
1 8704 6181 9

BRAMBLEDOWN TALES: LITTLE BROWN MOUSE
Tiger Books International, 1989. –
1 8704 6176 2

BRAMBLEDOWN TALES: LITTLE CHICK'S TAIL
Tiger Books International, 1989. –
1 8704 6183 5

BRAMBLEDOWN TALES: PIGGY GOES TO MARKET
Tiger Books International, 1989. –
1 8704 6182 7

BRAMBLEDOWN TALES: RABBITS' NEW HOME
Tiger Books International, 1989. –
1 8704 6177 0

BRAMBLEDOWN TALES: YELLOW DUCKLING'S STORY
Tiger Books International, 1989. –
1 8704 6178 9

GOLD DUST
OUP, 1993. – 0 19 271721 9

MY FIRST EARTH BOOK
Crocodile Books, 1989. – O/P. – 1 8513 6018 2

MY FIRST SPACE BOOK
Crocodile Books, 1989. – O/P. – 1 8513 6019 0

ORCHARD BOOK OF GREEK MYTHS
Orchard Books, 1992. – 1 8521 3373 2

STORY OF CHRISTMAS
Price Stern Sloan, 1989. – O/P. – 0 85985 767 0

McGOUGH, Roger

British. Born Liverpool, 1937. Educated Star of the Sea Junior School; St Mary's College, Crosby; Hull University. Married: 1) Thelma Monaghan, 1970 (dissolved 1980), two sons; 2) Hilary Clough, 1986, one son. Teacher, lecturer, poet, performer.

Awards: Signal Award: *Sky in the Pie*, 1984

Agent: A. D. Peters,
5th Floor,
The Chambers,
Chelsea Harbour,
Lots Road,
London SW10 0XF,
England

Better known for his rather zany poetry, he nevertheless has written two highly amusing stories which have special appeal to reluctant readers as they are so obviously funny.

THE GREAT SMILE ROBBERY
Viking Kestrel, 1985, 80p. – 0 670 80021 X
Penguin, 1984, 80p. – Pbk. – 0 14 031437 7
illustrated by Tony Blundell

An original idea to have as a hero a boy who has his smiles stolen. The book describes his adventures as he tries to retrieve them. Rather silly, but very enjoyable; loved by children.
Age range: 8–10

THE STOWAWAYS
Chivers Press, 1992, 80p. – L/P. – O/P. –
0 7451 1702 3
Penguin, 1988, 96p. – Pbk. – 0 14 031649 3
Viking Kestrel, 1986, 96p. – O/P. –
0 670 80135 6
illustrated by Tony Blundell

Four stories about two Liverpool lads who stow away to have an adventure, only to discover the Mersey Ferry doesn't go very far! Lots of laughs.
Age range: 8–10

Other publications:

COUNTING BY NUMBERS
Viking, 1989. – O/P. – 0 670 82671 5

LIGHTHOUSE THAT RAN AWAY
Red Fox, 1993. – Pbk. – 0 09 997960 8

LUCKY: A BOOK OF POEMS
Viking, 1993. – 0 670 84619 8

MY DAD'S A FIRE-EATER
Penguin, 1992. – Pbk. – 0 14 034927 8

NOAH'S ARK
Armada Books, 1988. – Pbk. – 0 00 663068 5

OXFORD 123 BOOK OF NUMBER RHYMES
OUP, 1992. – 0 19 910256 2

YOU TELL ME
Viking, 1989. – O/P. – 0 670 82536 0

MAHY, May Margaret

New Zealander. Born Whakatane, 1936. Educated University of Auckland, B.A., Diploma of Librarianship. Two daughters. Librarian.

Awards: New Zealand Library Association Esther Glen Award: *Lion in the meadow*, 1970

New Zealand Library Association Esther Glen Award: *First Margaret Mahy story book*, 1973

Library Association Carnegie Medal: *The Haunting*, 1982

New Zealand Library Association Esther Glen Award: *The Haunting*, 1983

Library Association Carnegie Medal: *The Changeover*, 1984

New Zealand Library Association Esther Glen Award: *The Changeover*, 1985

IBBY Honour Award: *The Changeover*, 1986

Young Observer Fiction Prize: *Memory*, 1987

New Zealand Library Association Esther Glen Award: *Underrunners*, 1993

Address: R.D.I.,
Lyttelton,
New Zealand

There are many admirable qualities attributable to this extremely gifted author. She has written many books, all of a high standard; she is able to write for all age groups equally successfully. Original and inventive, she successfully marries fantasy, magic and everyday reality, and her use of language is superb. Readers require fluency to be able to reap the full benefit. Simply superb at every level.

ALIENS IN THE FAMILY
Methuen, 1986, 168p. – O/P. – 0 416 97360 4

Being visited by an alien and helping him to return home is not the most original of ideas. However, Margaret Mahy's ability to weave a powerful story sets this above the average. The suspense of the chase builds up an unbearable tension, and the climax does not disappoint.
Age range: 10–12

THE BLOOD AND THUNDER ADVENTURE ON HURRICANE PEAK
Penguin, 1991, 144p. – Pbk. – 0 14 034282 6
Chivers Press, 1990, 192p. – L/P. –
0 7451 1230 7
Dent, 1989, 144p. – 0 460 07031 2
illustrated by Wendy Smith

A school story with a difference, or, rather, several differences, among them a cat as head prefect and a teacher who is a magician. Very funny in a slapstick way; short chapters make it an easy read.
Age range: 8–10

THE BUS UNDER THE LEAVES
Penguin, 1976, 80p. – Pbk. O/P. –
0 14 030721 4
Dent, 1975, 72p. – O/P. – 0 460 05899 1
illustrated by Margery Gill

Adam and David, thrilled at finding an old bus hidden on the dump for years, make it their den in which to escape from the girls. Only Anne is a match for them. Funny and imaginative.
Age range: 7–10

CLANCY'S CABIN
Penguin, 1987, 128p. – Pbk. – 0 14 032175 6
Dent, 1974, 96p. – O/P. – 0 460 05900 9
illustrated by Trevor Stubley

Set in her native New Zealand, this is the story of a camping holiday which turns into a treasure hunt when Skip finds the 'pattern for the finding of the treasure'. An enjoyable, straightforward read with lots of gentle humour.
Age range: 9–11

MAHY

COUSINS QUARTET

GOOD FORTUNES GANG
Doubleday, 1993, 89p. – 0 385 40166 3

FORTUNATE NAME
Doubleday, 1993, 129p. O/P. – 0 385 40349 6

FORTUNE BRANCHES OUT
Doubleday, 1993, 192p. – 0 385 40194 9

TANGLED FORTUNES
Delacarte Press, 1994, – 0 385 32066 3
illustrated by John Farman

Four completely different stories about the Fortune Family, each involving a different cousin, but obviously interwoven. The sense of family and 'belonging' is very strong, whilst preserving the identity of individuals. The illustrations are plentiful and particularly apt.
Age range: 9–11

DANGEROUS SPACES
Penguin, 1992. – Pbk. – 0 14 034571 X
H. Hamilton, 1991, 130p. – 0 241 13066 2

The 'spaces' are the dark areas of Anthea's subconscious, which prove to be powerful when manipulated by the dead child, Henry. The strength of the book lies in the skilful juxtaposition of the supernatural with the normal rough and tumble of family life, which is unacceptable to Anthea. Very readable.
Age range: 10–12

THE DENTIST'S PROMISE
Deutsch, 1993, 64p. – 0 590 54084 X
illustrated by Wendy Smith

A witty short story about a small girl who promises her aunt she will never change her name. She grows up to become a dentist, and when she falls in love, there is only one solution to her dilemma. A perfect match of illustrations and text.
Age range: 9–11

THE PIRATE UNCLE
Penguin, 1987, 125p. – Pbk. – 0 14 032250 7
Dent, 1977, 128p. – O/P. – 0 460 06795 8
illustrated by Mary Dinsdale

Uncle Ludovic is an unusual pirate, for he is trying to stop, but needs help. Caroline is just the person to do so.
Age range: 8–10

THE PIRATES' MIXED-UP VOYAGE: DARK DOINGS IN THE THOUSAND ISLANDS
Penguin, 1993, 176p. – Pbk. – 0 14 036327 0
Dent, 1983, 160p. – 0 460 06132 1
illustrated by Margaret Chamberlain

The crew of the pirate ship 'The Sinful Sausage' are a motley bunch whose escapades on the high seas provide excellent reading.
Age range: 9–11

RAGING ROBOTS AND UNRULY UNCLES
Dent, 1990, 93p. – 0 460 88042 X
Penguin, 1985, 96p. – Pbk. – 0 14 031817 8
illustrated by Peter Stevenson

'A linguistic romp' best describes this tale in which the vocabulary is as imaginative as the plot. Evil Jasper and saintly Julian, both less than pleased with their children, get a nasty shock when the robots arrive.
Age range: 10–12

THE BIRTHDAY BURGLAR AND THE VERY WICKED HEADMISTRESS
Dent, 1990, 144p. – 0 460 88041 1
Mammoth, 1990, 144p. – Pbk. – 0 7497 0249 4
illustrated by Margaret Chamberlain

Age range: 5–7

THE BOY WHO BOUNCED AND OTHER MAGIC TALES
Penguin, 1988, 160p. – Pbk. – 0 14 032468 2
illustrated by Shirley Hughes

Age range: 7–10

THE CHEWING-GUM RESCUE AND OTHER STORIES
Penguin, 1992, 144p. – Pbk, – O/P. – 0 14 036326 2
Dent, 1990, 140p. – 0 460 88043 8
illustrated by Jan Ormerod

Age range: 7–9

CHOCOLATE PORRIDGE AND OTHER STORIES
Penguin, 1989, 176p. – Pbk. – 0 14 032906 4
illustrated by Shirley Hughes

Age range: 8–10

THE DOOR IN THE AIR AND OTHER STORIES
Penguin, 1990, 112p. – Pbk. – 0 14 034283 4
Chivers Press, 1989, 176p. – L/P. –
0 7451 1046 0
Dent, 1988, 128p. – 0 460 06285 9
illustrated by Diana Catchpole

Age range: 10–12

THE DOWNHILL CROCODILE WHIZZ AND OTHER STORIES
Windrush, 1990, 162p. – L/P. – 1 85089 983 5
Penguin, 1987, 112p. – Pbk. – 0 14 032362 7
Dent, 1986, 136p. – Pbk. – 0 460 06237 9
illustrated by Ian Newsham

Age range: 5–7

THE FIRST MARGARET MAHY STORY-BOOK
Dent, 1976, 120p. – Pbk. O/P. – 0 460 02713 1
Dent, 1972, 118p. – O/P. – 0 460 05856 8
illustrated by Shirley Hughes

Age range: 6–10

THE GREAT PIRATICAL RUMBUSTIFICATION, AND THE LIBRARIAN AND THE ROBBERS
Windrush, 1990, 76p. – L/P. – 1 85089 810 3
Penguin, 1981, 80p. – Pbk. – 0 14 031261 7
Dent, 1978, 64p. – 0 460 06871 7
illustrated by Quentin Blake

Age range: 6–8

LEAF MAGIC AND FIVE OTHER FAVOURITES
Magnet Books, 1986, 64p. – Pbk. O/P. –
0 416 63780 9
Dent, 1984, 64p. – 0 460 06151 8
illustrated by Margaret Chamberlain

Age range: 5–7

MAHY MAGIC
Windrush, 1991, 186p. – L/P. – 1 85089 816 2
Dent, 1986, 160p. – 0 460 06184 4
illustrated by Shirley Hughes

Age range: 6–10

NONSTOP NONSENSE
Mammoth, 1990, 128p. – Pbk. – 0 7497 0278 8
Dent, 1977, 128p. – 0 460 06806 7
illustrated by Quentin Blake

Age range: 8–10

THE SECOND MARGARET MAHY STORY-BOOK
Dent, 1977, 124p. – Pbk. O/P. – 0 460 02761 1
Dent, 1973, 124p. – O/P. – 0 460 05887 8
illustrated by Shirley Hughes

Age range: 6–10

THE THIRD MARGARET MAHY STORY-BOOK
Dent, 1975, 116p. – 0 460 06625 0
illustrated by Shirley Hughes

Age range: 6–10

TICK TOCK TALES
Orion Children's Books, 1993, 96p. –
1 8588 1004 3
illustrated by Wendy Smith

Age range: 4–6

Collections of stories and poems published in various anthologies. All are of excellent quality, covering a variety of themes, providing hours of storytelling material.

UNDERRUNNERS
H. Hamilton, 1992, 160p. – O/P. –
0 241 13170 7
Chivers Press, 1992, 248p. – O/P. –
0 7451 1671 X

Tris, finding real life almost unbearable at times, retreats into a world of his imagination. He is pleased when he meets Winola, who can join him in his games. He does not realize until it is too late that there is a real menace. Exciting, but quite frightening.

Age range: 12+

Other publications:

BOY WHO WAS FOLLOWED HOME
Little Mammoth, 1989. – Pbk. – 0 7497 0094 7

BOY WITH TWO SHADOWS
Collins, 1989. – Pbk. – O/P. – 0 00 663070 7

BUBBLE TROUBLE
H. Hamilton, 1991. – 0 241 13086 7
BUSY DAY FOR A GOOD GRANDMOTHER
H. Hamilton, 1993. – 0 241 13409 9
CATALOGUE OF THE UNIVERSE
Mammoth, 1991. – Pbk. – 0 7497 0856 5
THE CHANGEOVER: A SUPERNATURAL ROMANCE
Methuen, 1987. – Pbk. – O/P. – 0 416 08822 8
DAVID'S WITCH DOCTOR
F. Watts, 1976. – O/P. – 0 85166 577 2
DRAGON OF AN ORDINARY FAMILY
Little Mammoth, 1991. – Pbk. – 0 7497 0293 1
GREAT MILLIONAIRE KIDNAP
Dent, 1975. – O/P. – 0 460 06693 5
GREAT WHITE MAN-EATING SHARK
Penguin, 1991. – Pbk. – 0 14 054187 X
THE HAUNTING
Penguin, 1992. – Pbk. – 0 14 036325 4
HORRENDOUS HULLABALOO
H. Hamilton, 1992. – 0 241 13250 9
HORRIBLE STORY AND OTHERS
Chivers Press, 1991. – 0 7451 1293 5
KEEPING HOUSE
Penguin, 1992. – Pbk. – 0 14 054368 6
LION IN THE MEADOW
Dent, 1986. – 0 460 06174 7
LITTLE WITCH
Penguin, 1987. – Pbk. – 0 14 032264 7
MAKING FRIENDS
Penguin, 1991. – Pbk. – 0 14 054205 1
MAN WHOSE MOTHER WAS A PIRATE
Dent, 1985. – 0 460 06171 2
MEMORY
Penguin, 1989. – Pbk. – 0 14 032680 4
PRINCESS AND THE CLOWN
Dobson, 1971. – O/P. – 0 234 77636 6
PUMPKIN MAN AND THE CRAFTY CREEPER
Penguin, 1992. – Pbk. – 0 14 054370 8
QUEEN'S GOAT
Penguin, 1993. – Pbk. – 0 14 054372 4
RAILWAY ENGINE AND THE HAIRY BRIGANDS
Dent, 1973. – O/P. – 0 460 05860 6
RARE SPOTTED BIRTHDAY PARTY
F. Watts, 1974. – O/P. – 0 85166 491 1
ROOMS TO LET
Dent, 1974. – O/P. – 0 460 05845 2
SAILOR JACK AND THE TWENTY ORPHANS
Penguin, 1974. – Pbk. – O/P. – 0 14 050094 4
SEVEN CHINESE BROTHERS
Macmillan, 1992. – Pbk. – 0 333 56609 2
SEVENTEEN KINGS AND FORTY-TWO ELEPHANTS
Armada Books, 1989. – Pbk. – O/P. – 0 00 663071 5
STEPMOTHER
F. Watts, 1974. – O/P. – 0 85166 492 X
TALL STORY AND OTHER TALES
Dent, 1991. – 0 460 88077 2
THREE-LEGGED CAT
H. Hamilton, 1993. – 0 241 13390 4
TIN CAN BAND AND OTHER POEMS
Penguin, 1990. – Pbk. – 0 14 054188 8
THE TRICKSTERS
Windrush, 1989. – L/P. – O/P. – 1 8508 9930 4
ULTRAVIOLET CATASTROPHE
Dent, 1975. – O/P. – 0 460 06626 9
WIND BETWEEN THE STARS
Dent, 1976. – O/P. – 0 460 06661 7
WITCH IN THE CHERRY TREE
Dent, 1974. – 0 460 05884 3

MARK, Jan (Marjorie, née Busland)

British. Born Welwyn, Hertfordshire, 1943. Educated Ashford Grammar School; Canterbury College of Art, National Diploma of Design. Married Neil Mark, 1969, one son, one daughter. Teacher.

Awards: Library Association Carnegie Medal: *Thunder and Lightnings*, 1976

Library Association Carnegie Medal: *Handles*, 1983

Address: 98 Howard Street, Oxford OX4 3BY, England

Agent: Murray Pollinger, 4 Garrick Street, London WC 2E, England

The quality that makes Jan Mark's books so successful is her understanding of children and her ability to portray them sympathetically. The plots are interesting, but often it is the interplay between characters which makes them above average.

DREAM HOUSE
Penguin, 1989, 144p. – Pbk. – 0 14 031589 6
Viking Kestrel, 1987, 128p. – 0 670 80189 5
illustrated by Joan Riley

Hannah loves the manor for its memories, Dina for its glamorous guests. Julia complicates life with her constant plotting, but when Tom enters the drama, the recipe for chaos is complete. An excellent plot with more than a hint of comedy.
Age range: 12–14

FEET, AND OTHER STORIES
Penguin, 1990, 160p. – Pbk. – 0 14 032797 5
Viking, 1983, 160p. – 0 670 82510 7
illustrated by Bert Kitchen

A collection of stories with lots of appeal for older readers. Varied in subject matter, they all have something of value to say.
Age range: 12–14

HANDLES
Chivers Press, 1988, 288p. – L/P. – 0 7451 0760 5
Penguin, 1985, 160p. – Pbk. – 0 14 031587 X
Viking Kestrel, 1985, 160p. – 0 670 80536 X
illustrated by David Parkins

A potentially boring holiday is rescued by providential happenings – not a very original idea. What saves this story from banality is the characters, who are larger than life, including a cat with false teeth. Not especially easy, but very enjoyable to read.
Age range: 12–14

NOTHING TO BE AFRAID OF
Chivers Press, 1985, 176p. – L/P. – 0 7451 0132 1
Viking Kestrel, 1985, 120p. – O/P. – 0 670 80018 X
Penguin, 1982, 128p. – Pbk. – 0 14 031392 3
illustrated by David Parkins

A book of scary yet funny stories. As always, even in short stories, Jan Mark's characterization is excellent.
Age range: 11–13

SCHOOL STORIES
Kingfisher Books, 1989, 256p. – 0 86272 418 X
illustrated by David Parkins

An excellent collection of school stories chosen by Jan Mark. The authors range from Enid Blyton to Charlotte Bronte. A pleasure to read.
Age range: 10–14

THE SHORT VOYAGE OF THE 'ALBERT ROSS'
Mayflower, 1981, 80p. – Pbk. O/P. – 0 583 30373 0
Granada, 1980, 72p. – O/P. – 0 246 11241 7
illustrated by Gavin Rowe

An excellent portrait of a bully and his victim who eventually finds the strength of character to stand up to him. At the same time it is an amusing adventure about Stephen's raft and his accidental journey down river.
Age range: 8–10

THUNDER AND LIGHTNINGS
Chivers Press, 1987, 248p. – L/P. – 0 7451 0496 7
Viking Kestrel, 1985, 176p. – 0 670 80116 X
Penguin, 1978, 176p. – Pbk. – 0 14 031063 0

Superficially the story of aircraft, and the demise of the old jets in particular, this novel is really concerned with the friendship between Victor and Andrew, which grows in spite of their many differences. Sensitive and gently amusing, it is a worthy prize-winner.
Age range: 10–12

TROUBLE HALF-WAY
Chivers Press, 1989, 200p. – L/P. – 0 7451 0958 6
Penguin, 1986, 128p. – Pbk. – 0 14 031588 8
Viking Kestrel, 1985, 128p. – 0 670 80188 7
illustrated by David Parkins

There are now many books about step-parents, but this is a particularly sensitive and perceptive story. Amy is forced, by circumstances, to spend time with her step-father, with whom she does not feel at ease. Among the everyday happenings, their relationship begins to develop – very well handled.
Age range: 11–13

UNDER THE AUTUMN GARDEN
Penguin, 1980, 160p. – Pbk. – 0 14 031248 X
Kestrel Books, 1977, 160p. – O/P. – 0 7226 5347 6

As part of his local history project for school, Matthew decides to dig up his garden in search of relics from the old priory. In reality, it turns out rather differently from the way he planned.
Age range: 10–12

Other publications:
AQUARIUS
Penguin, 1990. – Pbk. – 0 14 034387 3
AT THE SIGN OF THE 'DOG AND ROCKET'
Penguin, 1992. – Pbk. – 0 14 034844 1
CAN OF WORMS
Red Fox, 1992. – Pbk. – 0 09 987160 2
CARROT TOPS AND COTTON TAILS
Andersen Press, 1993. – 0 86264 362 7
DEAD LETTER BOX
H. Hamilton, 1982. – 0 241 10804 7
DIVIDE AND RULE
Penguin, 1990. – Pbk. – 0 14 034385 7
ENOUGH IS TOO MUCH ALREADY AND OTHER STORIES
Red Fox, 1991. – Pbk. – 0 09 985310 8
FINDERS, LOSERS
Lions, 1991. – Pbk. – O/P. – 0 00 673495 2
FRANKIE'S HAT
Viking, 1986. – Pbk. – 0 670 81004 5
FUN WITH MRS THUMB
Walker Books, 1993. – 0 7445 2534 9
FUN
Gollancz, 1993. – Pbk. – 0 575 05680 0
FUR
Walker Books, 1991. – Pbk. – 0 7445 2025 8
HAIRS IN THE PALM OF THE HAND
Penguin, 1983. – Pbk. – 0 14 031441 5
HILLINGDON FOX
Penguin, 1993. – Pbk. – 0 14 036235 5
IN BLACK AND WHITE
Penguin, 1992. – Pbk. – 0 14 034352 0
KINGS AND QUEENS
Heinemann, 1993. – 0 434 97665 2
LONG DISTANCE POET
Dinosaur Publications, 1982. – Pbk. – O/P. – 0 85122 305 2
OUT OF THE OVEN
Viking, 1986. – O/P. – 0 670 80093 7
STRAT AND CHATTO
Walker Books, 1990. – Pbk. – 0 7445 1708 7
THIS BOWL OF EARTH
Walker Books, 1993. – 0 7445 2190 4
TWIG THING
Penguin, 1990. – Pbk. – 0 14 032641 3

MAYNE, William (James Carter)

Also writes as Martin Cobalt, Dynely James, Charles Molin. British. Born Hull, Yorkshire, 1928. Educated Cathedral Choir School, Canterbury. Lives in the Yorkshire Dales. Lecturer, writer.

Awards: Library Association Carnegie Medal: *A Grass Rope*, 1957
Guardian Children's Fiction Award: *Low Tide*, 1993
Agent: David Higham Assoc., 5–8 Lower John Street, London W1R 4HA, England

A brilliant but enigmatic writer with a distinctive style. His books do not have universal popular appeal, but there are children who fall under his spell as the result of a sensitive introduction by a knowledgeable adult. He has been writing for many years and some of his earlier works are out of print, although re-printing is currently under consideration. Some of his books are for older readers.

ALL THE KING'S MEN
Penguin, 1984, 192p. – Pbk. O/P. – 0 14 031682 5
Cape, 1982, 182p. – 0 224 02026 9

Three stories, completely different, but all compelling in their own way.
Age range: 12–14

ANTAR AND THE EAGLES
Walker Books, 1990, 216p. – Pbk. – 0 7445 1464 9
Walker Books, 1989, 224p. – 0 7445 0838 X

A most memorable book, but difficult to classify. Part fairy-tale, part adventure, reminiscent of classical stories where overwhelming tasks are accomplished after much stoical suffering. Antar is far too young to be entrusted with the rescue of the eagle's precious egg, but he manfully faces up to his destiny and tries his best. Powerfully described, it

holds the reader to the very satisfying conclusion.
Age range: 9–12

THE FARM THAT RAN OUT OF NAMES
Red Fox, 1991, 96p. – Pbk. – O/P. – 0 09 985550 X
Cape, 1990, 88p. – 0 224 02757 3

The best fantasy books are those with a firm base in reality, which this one has. Owen is happy on his Welsh farm and becomes extremely upset when he is told that the Birmingham Water Authority want to build a reservoir on it. Not a man to take things lying down, he dreams up a scheme and carries it through. Superb storytelling, funny, touching and a wonderful climax.
Age range: 10–12

HOB AND THE GOBLINS
Dorling Kindersley, 1993, 140p. – 0 7513 7006 1
illustrated by Norman Messenger

Hob, originally a character in a picture book, features in this magic tale in which he must use all his cunning to defeat his enemies. A unique style, an exciting story, a far from disappointing conclusion and a superb book-jacket all combine to make this a winner.
Age range: 9–11

THE LAST BUS
Red Fox, 1990, 64p. – Pbk. – 0 09 975050 3
Hamish Hamilton, 1962, 96p. – O/P. – 0 241 90320 3
illustrated by Helen Parsley

Time has no meaning when you are young and busy, and Peter misses the last bus home. He believes he can catch up with it if he cuts across country. The terrain is difficult, and he needs a variety of help to make it across.
Age range: 7–9

LOW TIDE
Red Fox, 1993, 198p. – Pbk. – 0 09 918311 0
Cape, 1992, 198p. – 0 224 03151 1

Fascinated by what they find in the old wreck, Charlie and Elizabeth, and their Maori friend, are unaware of the approaching tidal wave. They are cast up in the mountains where they have to confront their own fear and the strong influence of legends. Not a lot of action, but a powerful evocation of nature and human nature colliding.
Age range: 10–12

RAVENSGILL
Red Fox, 1990, 171p. – Pbk. – 0 09 975270 0
Hamish Hamilton, 1970, 174p. – O/P. – 0 241 01746 7

Bob and Judith are cousins attending the same school, but they only accidentally discover that they are related. Then they set about finding out what caused the rift. Excellent storytelling, keeping the reader's interest to the last page.
Age range: 12–14

SALT RIVER TIMES
Penguin, 1982, 190p. – Pbk. O/P. – 0 14 031499 7
Hamish Hamilton, 1980, 178p. – O/P. – 0 241 10196 4
illustrated by Elizabeth Honey

Having lived in Australia for a time, William Mayne wrote this collection of stories, which are interwoven, to reveal the solution to a murder mystery in a small Australian community. Evocative and full of atmosphere.
Age range: 11–13

SKIFFY
Penguin, 1980, 96p. – Pbk. O/P. – 0 14 031173 4
Hamish Hamilton, 1977, 120p. – O/P. – 0 241 89670 3

In the same series:

SKIFFY AND THE TWIN PLANETS
Hamish Hamilton, 1982, 144p. – O/P. – 0 241 10835 7

A trip into the realm of science fiction, an unusual theme for this author. Easy to read and very entertaining.
Age range: 8–10

MAYNE

WINTER QUARTERS
*Penguin, 1984, 144p. – Pbk. O/P. –
0 14 031681 7
Cape, 1982, 144p. – 0 224 02035 8*

Most readers will be unfamiliar with the lore of the travelling people, but William Mayne's skilful storytelling makes such a lack unimportant. Issy has been brought up in a house, but his birth made him the best person to seek out the old chief who alone could tell them where to stay for the winter. An absorbing and compelling story which gives some understanding of a group of people who are virtual outcasts from society.
Age range: 11–13

Other publications:

AND NETTA AGAIN
H. Hamilton, 1992. – 0 241 13173 1
BARNABAS WALKS
Walker Books, 1990. – Pbk. – 0 7445 1352 9
THE BATTLEFIELD
Penguin, 1971. – Pbk. – O/P. – 0 14 030469 X
BLEMYAH STORIES
*Walker Books, 1988. – Pbk. – O/P. –
0 7445 0608 5*
CATHEDRAL WEDNESDAY
Hodder, 1972. – O/P. – 0 340 15202 8
CHORISTER'S CAKE
Jade Publishers, 1990. – Pbk. – 0 903461 41 2
COME, COME TO MY CORNER
Walker Books, 1986. – O/P. – 0 7445 0534 8
CORBIE
Walker Books, 1986. – Pbk. – 0 7445 0536 4
DRIFT
Penguin, 1987. – Pbk. – 0 14 032116 0
EARTHFASTS
Red Fox, 1991. – Pbk. – 0 09 977600 6
EGG TIMER
Heinemann, 1993. – 0 434 97676 8
GAME OF DARK
Penguin, 1974. – Pbk. – O/P. – 0 14 030668 4
GIDEON AHOY!
Penguin, 1989. – Pbk. – 0 14 032129 2
GOBBLING BILLY
Hodder, 1969. – Pbk. – O/P. – 0 340 04201 X
GRASS ROPE
OUP, 1972. – Pbk. – O/P. – 0 19 272031 7

HOUSE IN TOWN
Walker Books, 1989. – Pbk. – 0 7445 1394 4
THE INCLINE
Penguin, 1974. – Pbk. – O/P. – 0 14 030714 1
IT
Penguin, 1981. – Pbk. – O/P. – 0 14 031174 2
JERSEY SHORE
Penguin, 1976. – Pbk. – O/P. – 0 14 030823 7
KELPIE
Penguin, 1989. – Pbk. – O/P. – 0 14 032854 8
LAMB SHENKIN
Walker Books, 1987. – O/P. – 0 7445 0728 6
LEAPFROG
Walker Books, 1987. – O/P. – 0 7445 0726 X
MAX'S DREAM
H. Hamilton, 1977. – O/P. – 0 241 89546 4
MEMBER FOR THE MARSH
OUP, 1974. – Pbk. – O/P. – 0 19 272062 7
THE MOULDY
Cape, 1983. – O/P. – 0 224 02092 7
MOUSE AND THE EGG
*Armada Books, 1982. – Pbk. – O/P. –
0 00 661884 7*
MOUSEWING
Walker Books, 1987. – O/P. – 0 7445 0729 4
NETTA NEXT
H. Hamilton, 1990. – 0 241 12991 5
NETTA
H. Hamilton, 1989. – O/P. – 0 241 12708 4
NO MORE SCHOOL
H. Hamilton, 1977. – O/P. – 0 241 89668 1
PARCEL OF TREES
Penguin. – Pbk. – O/P. – 0 14 030195 X
PARTY PANTS
Hodder, 1977. – Pbk. – O/P. – 0 340 21211 X
PATCHWORK CAT
J. MacRae, 1991. – 1 8568 1182 4
PLOT NIGHT
H. Hamilton, 1977. – O/P. – 0 241 89669 X
RINGS ON HER FINGERS
H. Hamilton, 1991. – 0 241 13071 9
ROBIN'S REAL ENGINE
Penguin, 1975. – Pbk. – O/P. – 0 14 030761 3
ROYAL HARRY
Penguin, 1973. – Pbk. – O/P. – 0 14 030644 7
SECOND-HAND HORSE AND OTHER STORIES
Mammoth, 1992. – Pbk. – 0 7497 0948 0
SMALL PUDDING FOR WEE GOWRIE
Macmillan, 1983. – O/P. – 0 333 34080 9
SWARM IN MAY
Jade Publishers, 1990. – Pbk. – 0 903461 40 4
THURSDAY CREATURE
Heinemann, 1990. – 0 434 93089 X
TIBBER
Walker Books, 1986. – O/P. – 0 7445 0535 6

TIGER'S RAILWAY
Walker Books, 1991. – Pbk. – 0 7445 2099 1
WHILE THE BELLS RING
H. Hamilton, 1979. – O/P. – 0 241 89932 X
YEAR AND A DAY
Penguin, 1978. – Pbk. – O/P. – 0 14 031070 3
YELLOW AEROPLANE
Pan Books, 1979. – Pbk. – O/P. – 0 330 25615 7

MORPURGO, Michael

British. Born St Albans, 1943. Educated King's School, Canterbury; King's College, London. Married Clare Allen, 1963 (the daughter of Allen Lane), two sons, one daughter. Teacher, writer, runs a farm for city children.

Address: Langlands,
Iddesleigh,
Winkleigh,
Devon EX19 8SN,
England

Agent: Gina Pollinger,
4 Garrick Street,
London WC2E 9BH,
England

Undoubtedly a leading figure in the field of children's books, Michael Morpurgo has quite a following. He writes for a wide age range, and there is a real sincerity in his writing which gives added weight to what he has to say.

JO-JO, THE MELON DONKEY
Deutsch, 1987, 32p. – 0 233 97945 X
illustrated by Chris Molan

A picture book for older children, as there is a detailed description of the grim life Jo Jo has to endure. He is finally rescued to live a life of ease. A predictable story rescued by the marvellous illustrations.
Age range: 5–7

LITTLE FOXES
Mammoth, 1990, 129p. – Pbk. – 0 7497 0203 6
Kaye & Ward, 1984, 128p. – O/P. – 0 7182 3972 5
illustrated by Gareth Floyd

Billy feels an affinity with the wildlife living on some spare ground by the ruined church. Such things cannot remain private for long, and Billy makes his choice. Some very touching scenes.
Age range: 10–12

MY FRIEND WALTER
Chivers Press, 1991, 224p. – L/P. – O/P. – 0 7451 1408 3
Mammoth, 1989, 160p. – Pbk. – 0 7497 0034 3
Heinemann, 1988, 160p. – 0 434 95203 6

The ghost of Walter Raleigh is really the hero of this light-hearted, amusing story. He and Bess work well together to restore Walter's stolen property to his descendants.
Age range: 10–12

TOM'S SAUSAGE LION
Yearling, 1992, 96p. – Pbk. – 0 440 86290 6
Black, 1986, 56p. – O/P. – 0 7136 2757 3
illustrated by Robina Green

Lacking originality, the story tells how Tom sees a lion but fails to convince anyone he is telling the truth. A slight story, told in a matter-of-fact style, the story proceeds at a brisk pace to the highly satisfactory ending. Useful for reluctant readers.
Age range: 8–10

WAITING FOR ANYA
Mammoth, 1991, 76p. – Pbk. – 0 7497 0634 1
Heinemann, 1990, 176p. – 0 434 95205 2

Jo is unaware that his chance meeting with the stranger will have such far-reaching consequences. Gradually he is drawn into helping with the hazardous task of assisting Jewish children to escape over the French border into Spain. A heart-warming, compelling story which is quite easy to read.
Age range: 11–13

WAR HORSE
Mammoth, 1990, 144p. – Pbk. – 0 7497 0445 4
Windrush, 1989, 151p. – L/P. – 1 85089 943 6
Kaye & Ward, 1982, 128p. – 0 7182 3970 9

A very moving story based on reality, which makes it even more poignant.

Albert is heartbroken when his father sends his beloved horse to war, and believes he will never see him again. The horrors of war which the young horse has to face are graphically described.
Age range: 12–14

WAR OF JENKINS' EAR
Heinemann, 1993, 192p. – 0 434 96219 8

Toby is relieved at first when he strikes up a friendship with the new boy Simon. It helps to overcome his feelings of homesickness. Simon, however, claims to have special healing powers, which makes Toby feel uneasy. When the rivalry between the village boys and the school boarders flares into outright confrontation, Toby finds that divided loyalty is a hard cross to bear.

The issue of healing is not openly resolved – the reader must decide whether to believe it or not. Totally absorbing, with excellent characterization.
Age range: 12+

WHY THE WHALES CAME
Mammoth, 1990, 144p. – Pbk. – 0 7497 0537 X
Chivers Press, 1989, 224p. – L/P. – 0 7451 0925 X
Heinemann, 1985, 160p. – 0 434 95200 1

Set on the Isles of Scilly, this is also a story full of compassion. Gracie and Daniel defy their parents and befriend the deaf Birdman. Life is hard for everyone, including the children, but, undaunted, they force the islanders to reconsider when a stranded whale is about to be butchered. The popularity of this book increased after the release of the film.
Age range: 10–12

Other publications:

ALBERTINE GOOSE QUEEN
Black, 1989. – 0 7136 3113 9
AND PIGS MIGHT FLY
Young Lions, 1992. – Pbk. – 0 00 674135 5

COLLY'S BARN
Heinemann, 1991. – 0 434 97666 0
CONKER
Heinemann, 1987. – 0 434 93044 X
FRIEND OR FOE
Mammoth, 1992. – Pbk. – 0 7497 0130 7
JIGGER'S DAY OFF
Collins, 1990. – Pbk. – 0 00 673883 4
KING IN THE FOREST
Simon & Schuster, 1993. – 0 7500 1363 X
KING OF THE CLOUD FOREST
Pan Books, 1989. – Pbk. – 0 330 30560 3
MARBLE CRUSHER
Heinemann, 1992. – 0 434 97670 9
MARTIANS AT MUDPUDDLE FARM
Black, 1992. – 0 7136 3614 9
MOSSOP'S LAST CHANCE
Young Lions, 1993. – 0 00 100487 5
MR NOBODY'S EYES
Mammoth, 1990. – Pbk. – 0 7497 0104 8
NINE LIVES OF MONTEZUMA
Mammoth, 1993. – Pbk. – 0 7497 1229 5
SANDMAN AND THE TURTLES
Mammoth, 1992. – Pbk. – 0 7497 1045 4
TWIST OF GOLD
Mammoth, 1991. – Pbk. – 0 7497 0621 X
WHITE HORSE OF ZENNOR
Mammoth, 1991. – Pbk. – 0 7497 0620 1

MURPHY, Jill (Francis)

British. Born London, 1949. Educated Ursuline Grammar School, Wimbledon; Chelsea, Croydon and Camberwell Schools of Art. Married, husband Roger, step-children Chloe and Alice. Worked in children's homes, now a freelance writer and illustrator. Lives in Wadebridge, Cornwall.

Agent: A. P. Watt Ltd,
20 John Street,
London WC1N 2DL,
England

A BAD SPELL FOR THE WORST WITCH
Chivers Press, 1993, 96p. – L/P. – 0 7451 1809 7
Viking Kestrel, 1984, 128p. – 0 670 80030 9
Penguin, 1983, 128p. – Pbk. – 0 14 031446 6

In the same series:

THE WORST WITCH
Chivers Press, 1992, 96p. – O/P. –
0 7451 1549 7
Viking, 1988, 112p. – 0 670 82188 8
Penguin, 1978, 112p. – Pbk. – 0 14 031108 4

THE WORST WITCH STRIKES AGAIN
Chivers Press, 1992, 80p. – L/P. – O/P. –
0 7451 1672 8
Viking Kestrel, 1988, 96p. – 0 670 82189 6
Penguin, 1981, 96p. – Pbk. – 0 14 031348 6
all illustrated by the author

This is one of the most popular 'witch' series, becoming even more so after being televised. Mildred, studying at the Academy, seems to do everything wrong, to the delight of the reader.
Age range: 7–9

WORLDS APART
Walker Books, 1990, 112p. – Pbk. –
0 7445 1332 4
Walker Books, 1988, 128p. – O/P. –
0 7445 0803 7
illustrated by Tudor Humphries

Totally different from the 'Worst Witch' stories, this book is more serious. Susan's mother left her father when she was a baby. Not until she is eleven does her mother tell her anything about him. Susan then determines to find him, a quest which leads to an unexpected ending, though one which is unlikely to happen in real life.
Age range: 9–11

Other publications:

ALL IN ONE PIECE
Walker Books, 1991. – 0 7445 2116 5

FIVE MINUTES' PEACE
Walker Books, 1989. – 0 7445 1363 4

GEOFFREY STRANGEWAYS
Walker Books, 1991. – Pbk. – 0 7445 1722 2

ON THE WAY HOME
Macmillan, 1984. – Pbk. – 0 333 37572 6

PEACE AT LAST
Macmillan, 1987. – 0 333 44201 6

WHATEVER NEXT!
Macmillan, 1993. – Pbk. – 0 333 53738 6

N

NAIDOO, Beverley

South African/British. Born Johannesburg, 1943. Educated University of Witwatersrand, B.A; University of York, B.A. (Hons), English & Education; University of Southampton, Ph.D. Married Nandhagopaul Naidoo, 1969, one son, one daughter. Educationalist, writer.

Awards: The Other Award: *Journey to Jo'burg*, 1985.

Child Study Children's Book Committee Award, USA: *Journey to Jo'burg*, 1986.

Best Book for Young Adults, American Library Association: *Chain of Fire*, 1991

Vlag en Wimpel Award, Holland: *Chain of Fire*, 1991

Address: 13 Huntly Road, Bournemouth, Dorset BH3 7HF, England

Agent: Gary Carter, Roger Hancock Ltd, 4 Water Lane, London NW1 8NZ, England

Beverley Naidoo has the rare ability to combine a sense of reality of life in Africa with an accessible reading style. Too often authors who feel strongly they have an important message to impart actually alienate the reader by the very weight of their writing.

Hopefully, she will continue to produce novels through which children can extend their experience.

CHAIN OF FIRE
Collins, 1990, 176p. – Pbk. – 0 00 673059 0
Collins, 1989, 192. – O/P – 0 00 184176 9

It is difficult for those of us so accustomed to freedom and respect for our rights to appreciate what it is like to live under apartheid, but this book makes it startlingly and movingly real. The villagers are told they must leave their homes on the barren land allotted to them by the white government. Although accustomed to subservience and obedience, some try to resist with brutal consequences. A stirring story.
Age range: 11–13

JOURNEY TO JO'BURG
Armada Books, 1987, 80p. – Pbk. – 0 00 672693 3
Longmans, 1985, 80p. – O/P – 0 582 25208 3

When Dineo became ill, Naledi felt she needed her mother, but the trouble was she had been sent 300 miles away to work in Johannesburg. So, unbelievably, she and her younger brother begin the nightmare walk to fetch her. Her mistress, unimpressed by the children's fortitude, will not allow her to leave until a planned party is over. She is then given one week of unpaid leave to visit her sick child. The contrast of this scenario with what happens here when a child is sick is a revelation. Every child should have the opportunity to read and learn from this story.
Age range: 9–12

NEEDLE, Jan

British. Born Holybourne, Hampshire, 1943. Educated Church Street School, Portsmouth; Portsmouth Grammar School; University of Manchester, B.A. (Hons), Drama. Reporter, sub-editor, writer.

Agents: David Higham Assoc.,
5–8 Lower John Street,
London W1R 4HA,
England

Rochelle Stevens Co.,
15–17 Islington High Street,
London N1 1LQ,
England

An author who has original ideas, and who does not fight shy of dealing with serious issues.

ANOTHER FINE MESS
Armada Books, 1982, 192p. – Pbk. O/P. – 0 00 671978 3
Deutsch, 1981, 192p. – O/P – 0 233 97370 2
illustrated by Roy Bentley

When the Professor invents the Cheap Day Return Transferer, Cynthia and George volunteer to test it. Off-beat, funny time-travel adventure.
Age range: 11–13

THE BEE RUSTLERS
Magnet Books, 1983, 80p. – Pbk. O/P. – 0 416 29310 7
Collins, 1980, 80p. – O/P. – 0 00 184043 6
illustrated by Paul Wright

An original storyline, describing Tony and Carol's attempt to save the hives which mean so much to their mother.
Age range: 9–11

BEHIND THE BIKE SHEDS
Methuen, 1985, 128p. – O/P. – 0 416 54990 X
Magnet Books, 1985, 128p. – Pbk. O/P. – 0 416 51840 0

An up-to-date school story in which both the events and the vocabulary reflect life in comprehensive schools today. The chapters are very short and may appeal to young people who believe that books are irrelevant. Successfully televised.
Age range: 11–14

THE BULLY
H. Hamilton, 1993, 133p. – 0 241 13381 5

This is very much in the forefront of life at school at present, and many books tackle the issue. Here is one illustrating an unusual but believable aspect, in that, when teachers begin investigating Simon's behaviour to find out why he has become a bully, they discover, rather surprisingly, that in fact he is the victim. An excellent book.
Age range: 11+

A GAME OF SOLDIERS
Deutsch, 1985, 94p. – 0 233 97744 9
Armada Books, 1985, 96p. – Pbk. – 0 00 672460 4

First written for television, then published as a novel, this is a chilling account of a children's game suddenly turned into a nightmarish reality. It leaves the reader in no doubt about the horror of war.
Age range: 12–14

IN THE DOGHOUSE
Mammoth, 1991, 96p. – O/P. – Pbk. – 0 7497 0669 4
Heinemann, 1988, 96p. – O/P. – 0 434 95329 6
illustrated by Robert Bartelt

In the same series:

SKELETON AT SCHOOL
Mammoth, 1990, 95p. – Pbk. – 0 7497 0074 2
Heinemann, 1988, 96p. – 0 434 95328 8

THE SLEEPING PARTY
Mammoth, 1991, 96p. – O/P. – Pbk. – 0 7497 0670 8
Heinemann, 1988, 96p. – 0 434 95331 8

UNCLE IN THE ATTIC
Heinemann, 1988, 96p. – 0 434 95327 X

A series of books aimed at younger readers. Sam and Springy are twins, and their exploits provide entertaining reading.
Age range: 8–10

LOSERS WEEPERS
Magnet Books, 1983, 128p. – Pbk. O/P. – 0 416 30170 3
Methuen, 1981, 128p. – 0 416 21510 6

Tony is delighted when he finds the ancient sword. He is unaware of the

NEEDLE

strong emotions and totally unsuspected reactions it evokes. The book deals realistically with the problem of treasure trove, but is not without its lighter moments.
Age range: 9–11

MY MATE SHOFIQ
Armada Books, 1979, 164p. – Pbk. – 0 00 671518 4
Deutsch, 1978, 144p. – O/P. – 0 233 96987 X

Because his conscience will not allow him to keep silent, Bernard is forced into defending Shofiq. As a result, they gradually become friends, and Bernard learns the hard way what it means to be 'different'. A refreshing look at racism without dwelling too much on it. Remarkably realistic characterization and dialogue. Made into an enjoyable television drama.
Age range: 11–14

THE THIEF
Penguin, 1989, 108p. – Pbk. – 0 14 032905 6
H. Hamilton, 1989, 96p. – O/P. – 0 241 12607 X

Kevin feels very bitter when he is accused of stealing. Convinced it is because his father is in prison, and because he has often been in trouble before, he takes himself off, but becomes involved with thieves. An exciting read which was later made into a gripping television film.
Age range: 10–12

WAGSTAFF THE WIND-UP BOY
Collins, 1989, 176p. – Pbk. – 0 00 672976 2
Deutsch, 1987, 118p. – 0 233 97715 5
illustrated by Roy Bentley

Black humour, in which a horrible accident is described in detail. Lots of amusing illustrations ensure popularity.
Age range: 10–12

WAR OF THE WORMS
Puffin Books, 1993, 75p. – Pbk. – 0 14 034919 7
illustrated by Kay Widdowson

An unusual venture for Jan Needle, describing the struggle between the would-be despoilers of the countryside, and the farmers, who are aided by the moles. Together, they fight victoriously to preserve the peace of the countryside. With large print, and well illustrated, it is very easy to read.
Age range: 7–9

WILD WOOD
Adlib, 1993, 144p. – Pbk. – 0 590 55356 9
J. Murray, 1989, 192p. – 0 7195 4651 6
illustrated by William Rushton

Although it is not absolutely essential to have read 'The Wind in the Willows', it is cosier to relate to the characters if there is some knowledge of the original story. It is not by any means easy to read, but it is extremely funny.
Age range: 11–14

Other publications:

ALBESON AND THE GERMANS
Armada Books, 1981. – Pbk. – O/P. – 0 00 671900 7

AS SEEN ON TV
Mammoth, 1992. – Pbk. – 0 7497 0924 3

BOGEYMEN
Deutsch, 1992. – 0 590 54015 7

FINE BOY FOR KILLING
Deutsch, 1979. – O/P. – 0 233 97106 8

GOING OUT
Deutsch, 1983. – O/P. – 0 233 97585 3

GREAT DAYS AT GRANGE HILL
Armada Books, 1984. – Pbk. – O/P. – 0 00 672211 3

MAD SCRAMBLE
Mammoth, 1992. – Pbk. – 0 7497 0923 5

PIGGY IN THE MIDDLE
Armada Books, 1983. – Pbk. – O/P. – 0 00 672139 7

PITIFUL PLACE AND OTHER STORIES
Magnet Books, 1985. – Pbk. – O/P. – 0 416 50400 0

ROTTENTEETH
Deutsch, 1980. – O/P. – 0 233 97205 6

SENSE OF SHAME AND OTHER STORIES
Armada Books, 1982. – Pbk. – O/P. – 0 00 671901 5

SIZE SPIES
Armada Books, 1980. – Pbk. – O/P. – 0 00 671701 2

TUCKER IN CONTROL
Deutsch, 1985. – O/P. – 0 233 97897 6
TUCKER'S LUCK
Armada Books, 1984. – Pbk. – O/P. – 0 00 672395 0
WAGSTAFFE AND THE LIFE OF CRIME
Lions, 1992. – 0 00 674344 7

NIMMO, Jenny

British. Born Windsor, Berkshire, 1944. Educated private boarding schools. Married David Wynn Millward, 1974, two daughters, one son. Actress, photographic researcher, floor manager, director, writer of children's television programmes; now a full-time writer.

Awards: Smarties Prize: *The Snow Spider*, 1986

Welsh Arts Council Tir na n'Og Award: *The Snow Spider*, 1987

Address: Henllan Llangynyw, Welshpool, Powys S721 9EN, Wales

A writer of exceptional quality. All her books maintain a high literary standard, yet remain accessible to young readers. Her strong characterization of the children enables the reader to identify easily with them, and her love of Wales and Welsh mythology helps her to weave stories with a fine balance of magic and realism; stories which are both exciting and amusing.

DELILAH AND THE DOGSPELL
Mammoth, 1992, 76p. – Pbk. – 0 7497 0984 7

In the same series:

DELILAH AND THE DISHWASHER DOGS
Methuen, 1993, 96p. – 0 416 18769 2
both illustrated by Ben Cort

A new departure for Jenny Nimmo. Aimed at younger children, they are written in a much lighter style. Delilah is a cat, wise in the ways of magic, which is helpful when dealing with evil. Extremely lively and amusing, with illustrations which exactly match the humour of the story.
Age range: 8–10

THE SNOW SPIDER
Mammoth, 1990. – Pbk. – 0 7497 0831 X
Chivers Press, 1987, 208p. – L/P. – 0 7451 0590 4
Methuen, 1986, 144p. – 0 416 54530 0

In the same series:

EMLYN'S MOON
Chivers Press, 1989, 248p. – L/P. – 0 7451 1047 9
Mammoth, 1989, 144p. – Pbk. O/P. – 0 7497 0140 4
Methuen, 1987, 128p. – 0 416 02392 4

THE CHESTNUT SOLDIER
Mammoth, 1991, 176p. – Pbk. – O/P. – 0 7497 0991 X
Chivers Press, 1990, 312p. – L/P. – 0 7451 1178 5
Methuen, 1989, 192p. – 0 416 11402 4
all illustrated by Joanna Carey

Gwyn gradually realizes that he has magical powers. Reassured by his Gran, he begins to accustom himself to using his gift, aided by the little white spider. Eventually he decides he can try to get in touch with his sister, who went missing when he was small, an event which has cast a shadow over the lives of all the family ever since. In the two sequels, the magical atmosphere is equally strong, which, coupled with intriguing plots, makes the whole trilogy totally compelling. *The Snow Spider* became an excellent television serial.
Age range: 10–12

STONE MOUSE
Walker Books, 1993, 62p. – 0 7445 2430 X
illustrated by Helen Craig

Only Elly realizes at once how special the stone mouse is, but she is unable to stop Ted venting his anger on him by throwing him into the sea. The mouse

feels he has no hope of being rescued, but fate takes a hand. The ending seems contrived to adult eyes, but is eminently satisfactory to young readers. Large print and Jenny Nimmo's ability to make every word count make this an outstanding, short, easy to read novel.
Age range: 7–9

TATTY APPLE
Mammoth, 1990, 96p. – Pbk. – 0 7497 0400 4
Methuen, 1984, 96p. – 0 416 50280 6
illustrated by Priscilla Lamont

Owen-Owen finds a golden rabbit which he takes home. Somehow, life begins to improve for the little family, which has had more than its fair share of problems.
Age range: 7–9

ULTRAMARINE
Chivers Press, 1992, 264p. – L/P. – O/P. – 0 7451 1554 3
Mammoth, 1992, 176p. – Pbk. – 0 7497 0927 8
Methuen, 1990, 160p. – 0 416 15932 X

The legend of the Kelpie, a water sprite which causes people to drown, is the basis for this spell-binding novel. In this version of the legend, the sprite's role is reversed, and it fights to protect the sea. Ned and Nell feel a great affinity with the sea, but at first cannot understand. Only when they discover Ultramarine is the puzzle clarified.
Age range: 10–12

RAINBOW AND MR ZED
Mammoth, 1993, 160p. – Pbk. – 0 7497 1288 0
Methuen, 1992, 160p. – O/P. – 0 416 17222 9

A worthy sequel to Ultramarine. Nell is going away from home for the first time in her life, and is full of trepidation about her ability to cope. Her fear proves to be well-founded when they visit the mysterious Mr Zed on his island. She realises they are somehow connected, and that he will never let her go. In despair, she cries out for help, and her father answers in dramatic fashion.
Age range: 10–12

Other publications:
BEARS WILL GET YOU
Little Mammoth, 1992. – Pbk. – 0 7497 0535 3
THE BREADWITCH
Heinemann, 1993. – 0 434 96355 0
BRONZE TRUMPETER
Angus & R, 1975. – O/P. – 0 207 95595 6
JUPITER BOOTS
Heinemann, 1990. – 0 434 93076 8
RED SECRET
H. Hamilton, 1989. – 0 241 12463 8

NOSTLINGER, Christine

Austrian. Born Vienna, 1936. Married, two daughters. Journalist, writer.

Awards: Hans Christian Andersen Award, 1984

It is a measure of her universal appeal that this author, always a success in her native Austria, has become so popular here. She has an off-beat sense of humour, and her books are varied – some completely light-hearted, some extremely touching.

A DOG'S LIFE
Andersen Press, 1990, 160p. – 0 86264 278 7
illustrated by Jutta Bauer

This book is one great laugh from beginning to end. The juxtaposition of the animal and human situations provides endless scope for humour. The illustrations fit the story to perfection.
Age range: 8–10

ELF IN THE HEAD
Poolbeg Press, 1992, 160p. – Pbk. – 1 8537 1213 2
illustrated by Jutta Bauer

An unusual book which will not find universal approval with parents. Anna's parents are divorced, so she spends half her time with her father, who is portrayed by the illustrator as living in an untidy place full of pictures and statues of naked ladies. Anna herself swears (mildly) from time to time, and falls in love at a very tender age.

Children, however, will totally empathise with her and the problems she copes with (helped all the time by the elf who whispers instructions to her). Good reading ability is needed.
Age range: 8–9

FLY AWAY HOME
Andersen Press, 1985, 134p. – 0 86264 090 3
Tandem, 1978, – Pbk. – O/P. – 0 426 11201 6

Set in Russian occupied Vienna towards the end of the second World War, this book, based on the author's childhood, gives a different perspective to the usual one portrayed in English war novels. Trying to preserve life itself, never mind a semblance of normality, became an almost superhuman feat. Very readable.
Age range: 10+

HELLO FRED
Simon & Schuster, 1992, 64p. – O/P. – 0 7500 1179 3
Simon & Schuster, 1992, 64p. – Pbk. – 0 7500 1180 7

In the same series:

FRED AGAIN
Simon & Schuster, 1992, 64p. – O/P. – 0 7500 1181 5
Simon & Schuster, 1992, 64p. – Pbk. – 0 7500 1182 3
illustrated by Erhard Dietl

Amusing anecdotes about six-year-old Fred, small in body but with a very active mind. Large clear print makes them easily accessible to new readers.
Age range: 6–8

GUARDIAN GHOST
Beaver Books, 1988, 144p. – Pbk. – O/P. – 0 09 955050 4
Andersen Press, 1986, 142p. – 0 86264 152 7

There are times in life when individuals feel they cannot cope without help. Stacey is feeling very much that way when the ghost appears. It is her task to help children in need, and she is able to steer Stacey towards a happy ending.
Age range: 10–12

MARRYING OFF MOTHER
Beaver Books, 1986, 144p. – Pbk. – O/P. – 0 09 942160 7
Andersen Press, 1978, 160p. – O/P. – 0 905478 38 X

Sue and Julia have to go to live with their grandmother when their parents split up. They find their new situation so intolerable that they cast around for ways to change it, and decide the best way is to find their mother a new husband. There is much to laugh at, not least the cat with the unlikely name of Philip, but the realism of this unhappy situation is also captured to perfection.
Age range: 9–11

MR BAT'S GREAT INVENTION
Hippo Books, 1980, 128p. – Pbk. – O/P. – 0 590 70002 2
Andersen Press, 1978, 128p. – 0 905478 29 0
illustrated by F. J. Tripp

Robert has a hard time when he persuades his Granny to try the rejuvenating potion. She takes too much, and the result is a little girl's body with a seventy-year old brain – a recipe for disaster unless he can find an antidote. Very amusing.
Age range: 8–10

Other Publications:

BRAINBOX SORTS IT OUT
Andersen Press, 1985. – 0 86264 096 2
BUT JASPER CAME INSTEAD
Andersen Press, 1983. – O/P. – 0 86264 042 3
CONRAD
Hamlyn, 1978. – Pbk. – O/P. – 0 600 32002 2
CUCUMBER KING
Beaver Books, 1984. – Pbk. – O/P. – 0 09 933940 4
LOLLIPOP
Hamlyn, 1983. – Pbk. – O/P. – 0 600 20707 2
LUKE AND ANGELA
Andersen Press, 1979. – O/P. – 0 905478 64 9

O

O'BRIEN, Robert C.

Pseudonym for Robert Leslie Conly. American. Born Brooklyn, New York, 1918 (died 5 March 1973). Educated Amityville, Long Island, New York; Williams College, Williamstown, Massachusetts; Juilliard School of Music, New York; Columbia University, New York; University of Rochester, New York, B.A. English. Married Sally McCaslin, 1943, one son, three daughters. Advertising agent, researcher, writer, reporter.

Awards: American Library Association Newbery Medal: *Mrs Frisby and the Rats of Nimh*, 1972

MRS FRISBY AND THE RATS OF NIMH

Chivers Press, 1985, 299p. – O/P. – 0 7451 0133 X
Penguin, 1975, 197p. – Pbk. – 0 14 030725 7
Gollancz, 1972, 192p. – 0 575 01552 7

Mrs Frisby enlists the aid of a group of rats when she has to move her young son, who is ill. An excellent story, convincing and enjoyable.
Age range: 9–11

THE SILVER CROWN

Gollancz, 1983, 312p. – 0 7445 0918 1
Collins, 1975, 192p. – Pbk. – 0 00 671005 0

The novel's opening chapter grabs the reader's attention at once by the juxtaposition of the innocence of a little girl out playing at being a queen, and her return to find her house burned to the ground and her family all dead. She bravely sets off to find her aunt, but becomes aware that she is being chased. Full of menacing atmosphere, it promises a gripping read.
Age range: 11–13

Z FOR ZACHARIAH

Windrush, 1989, 234p. – L/P. – 1 85089 955 X
Gollancz, 1984, 192p. – O/P. – 0 575 03378 9
Armada Books, 1976, 192p. – Pbk. – 0 00 671081 6

Compulsive and exciting reading, describing life after a nuclear holocaust. Ann's initial fear when Zachariah turns up is well described. The whole book is full of atmosphere, giving a convincingly frightening vision of a devastated land.
Age range: 12+

O'NEILL, Judith

Australian. Born Melbourne, 1930. Educated Mildura High School, Victoria, 1942–47; University of Melbourne (Derham Prize, 1950; Rotary Foundation Fellowship, 1952) B.A. (Hons), English, M.A. English; University of London (Story-Miller Prize, 1953) Certificate in Education. Married John Cochrane O'Neill, 1954, three daughters. University tutor in English, writer.

Address: 9 Lonsdale Terrace,
Edinburgh EH3 9HN
Scotland

Agent: A. P. Watt,
20 John Street,
London WC1N 2DL
England

Writers of historical fiction for children are unfortunately doomed to be read by a minority of children. When the writer is as talented as Judith O'Neill, it is doubly unfortunate, for she has written several powerful and moving novels which bring historical events vividly to life. She has an innate ability to portray sympathetic characters which in turn make the events surrounding them more meaningful. As an Australian living in England and Scotland, she is well-placed for writing about both sides of the ocean from first-hand experience.

DEEPWATER
Magnet Books, 1989, 160p. – Pbk. – O/P. – 0 416 12642 1
H. Hamilton, 1987, 160p. – O/P. – 0 241 12362 3

Deepwater is a farming community which suffers as men go off to serve in the first World war, leaving the farm work to be done by the women. Although very intelligent, Charlotte has to leave school to work on the farm, which is bad enough, but then drought strikes. Then the white feathers start arriving, and the once close-knit community is split. Ideal for showing how war can affect everyone, not just those involved in the fighting.
Age range: 12+

JESS AND THE RIVER KIDS
Mammoth, 1990, 237p. – Pbk. – 0 7497 0047 5
H. Hamilton, 1984, 128p. – 0 241 11183 8

Although set in Australia during the second World War, this is more an adventure story than an historical one. Jess is a splendid character to identify with, resourceful, able to stick up for herself, yet not rough or cheeky. It is thanks to her quick thinking that old Lizzie was rescued when her boat caught fire. Excellent characterization and atmosphere.
Age range: 11–13

THE MESSAGE
Mammoth, 1991, 144p. – Pbk. – 0 7497 0525 6
H. Hamilton, 1989, 160p. – O/P. – 0 241 12709 2

After a rather weak beginning, when the reason 'compelling' Dan to run away from home seems rather slight, the rest of the book is a powerful message in itself. Wandering about aimlessly, as homeless young people do, he encounters Sal and Gray, who take him 'home'. He is happy to be accepted so readily into their community, but gradually realizes that the message they are expecting could have a sinister meaning, and that they all place too much unquestioning faith in the rival leaders. Dan must find a way to break free.
Age range: 12+

SO FAR FROM SKYE
Penguin, 1993, 224p. – Pbk. – 0 14 034980 4
H. Hamilton, 1992, 256p. – 0 241 13213 4

This is her best book to date. It describes the voyage from their beloved Skye home, where it has become impossible to even scratch a living, to the new life awaiting them on an Australian farm. It is an eventful journey seen through the eyes of Morag and Allan, who cannot always correctly interpret the actions of the adults, whether good or bad. A humanely moving story of despair and hope.
Age range: 10–12

Other publications:

SHARP EYES
Heinemann, 1993. – 0 434 97684 9
STRINGYBARK SUMMER
Mammoth, 1990. – Pbk. – 0 7497 0392 X

P

PARK, (Rosina) Ruth (Lucia)

Australian. Born Auckland, New Zealand. Educated St Benedict's College, University of Auckland. Married D'Arcy Niland, 1942, five children. Proof-reader, editor.

Awards: Australian Children's Book Council Book of the Year Award: *Playing Beatie Bow*, 1982

Boston Globe/Horn Book Award: *Playing Beatie Bow*, 1982

Agent: Curtis Brown,
P.O. Box 19,
Paddington,
New South Wales 2021,
Australia

An experienced writer who has achieved success with both younger and older readers. She has an affinity with children which is reflected in her writing.

MY SISTER SIF
Penguin, 1988, 192p. – Pbk. O/P. – 0 14 032342 2
Viking Kestrel, 1987, 192p. – O/P. – 0 670 815241

A most unusual story about a family whose love for the creatures living in the sea originates with their mother. It is a story full of mystery and romance.
Age range: 13–15

PLAYING BEATIE BOW
Penguin, 1982, 196p. – Pbk. – 0 14 031460 1

A time slip book, extraordinarily well handled, in which Abigail is drawn into Beatie's world. She has to learn to cope with the poverty and hardships of Victorian slum life in Sydney. As she learns, her character changes. Enthralling to such a degree that readers almost hold their breath while trying to guess the outcome which proves highly satisfactory.
Age range: 12–15

THINGS IN CORNERS
Penguin, 1991, 240p. – Pbk. – 0 14 032713 4
Viking, 1989, 184p. – O/P. – 0 670 82225 6

Five superb stories with an unexpected twist to send a shiver down the spine.
Age range: 12–14

Other publications:

ADVENTURES OF THE MUDDLEHEADED WOMBAT
Angus & R, 1980. – O/P. – 0 207 14385 4
BIG BRASS KEY
Hodder, 1984. – O/P. – 0 340 27098 5
CALLIE'S CASTLE
Angus & R, 1974. – O/P. – 0 207 12800 6
COME DANGER, COME DARKNESS
Hodder, 1978. – O/P. – 0 340 22746 X
GIGANTIC BALLOON
Collins, 1976. – O/P. – 0 00 185015 6
HOLE IN THE HILL
Pan Books, 1972. – Pbk. – O/P. – 0 330 02853 7
JAMES
Viking – L/P. 1991. – 0 670 82426 7
MUDDLE-HEADED WOMBAT AND THE INVENTION
Angus & R, 1976. – O/P. – 0 207 13232 1
MUDDLE-HEADED WOMBAT ON A CLEAN-UP DAY
Angus & R, 1976. – O/P. – 0 207 13276 3
MUDDLE-HEADED WOMBAT
Angus & R, 1991. – Pbk. – 0 207 16733 8

PATERSON, Katherine (née Womeldorf)

American. Born Qing Jiang, China, 1932, moved to the USA 1940. Educated King College, Bristol, Tennessee, A.B. (summa cum laude);

Presbyterian School of Christian Education, Richmond, Virginia, M.A.; Kobe School of Japanese Language, Japan; Union Theological Seminary, New York, M.R.E. Married John Barstow Paterson, 1962, two sons and two adopted daughters. Missionary, teacher.

Awards: National Book Award: *Master puppeteer*, 1977

American Library Association Newbery Medal: *Bridge to Terabithia*, 1978

Christopher Award: *The Great Gilly Hopkins*, 1979

National Book Award: *The Great Gilly Hopkins*, 1979

American Library Association Newbery Medal: *Jacob have I loved*, 1981

Catholic Library Association Regina Medal, 1988

Address: C/o E. P. Dutton,
2 Park Avenue,
New York City,
New York 10016,
USA

A widely acclaimed writer whose skill in storytelling and whose sensitivity towards children and their deepest feelings makes her popular with older children.

BRIDGE TO TERABITHIA
Cornerstone Books, 1987, 168p. – L/P. – 1 557 36010 3
Penguin, 1980, 144p. – Pbk. – 0 14 031260 9
Gollancz, 1978, 144p. – 0 575 02550 6

An extremely sad book, but one which gives courage to timid children. Jess's life is very harsh, but with Leslie he learns to create a fantasy world to escape to. The relief from reality together with Leslie's influence gradually build up his courage, so that he is able to cope with the concluding drama.
Age range: 10–12

COME SING, JIMMY JO
J. Murray, 1989, 176p. – 0 7195 4649 4
Penguin, 1987, 208p. – Pbk. – 0 14 032176 4
Gollancz, 1986, 198p. – 0 575 03737 7

Jimmy Jo attains fame as a country singing star, but does not know how to deal with the attendant problems. His grandmother is the only person who can help. Told with understanding and humour.
Age range: 10–12

THE GREAT GILLY HOPKINS
Cornerstone Books, 1987, 184p. – L/P. – 1 557 36011 1
Penguin, 1981, 144p. – Pbk. – 0 14 031302 8
Gollancz, 1979, 160p. – O/P. – 0 575 02587 5

Abandoned as a baby, Gilly has had to learn to be tough, to avoid further hurt. She scornfully rejects her latest foster-parents, only to realize she may have made a mistake. Sad without being sentimental.
Age range: 10–12

PARK'S QUEST
Penguin, 1990, 144p. – Pbk. – 0 14 034076 9
Gollancz, 1989, 160p. – 0 575 04487 X

Not an original story, telling how Park slowly uncovers the skeletons in the cupboard, learning about the father he never knew. As always, Katherine Paterson's skill and understanding have created in Park a memorable and sympathetic character, whose story will be read with interest.
Age range: 10–12

Other publications:

JACOB HAVE I LOVED
Penguin, 1983. – Pbk. – O/P. – 0 14 031471 7
REBELS OF THE HEAVENLY KINGDOM
Penguin, 1985. – Pbk. – O/P. – 0 14 031735 X

PEARCE, (Ann) Philippa

British. Born Great Shelford, Cambridgeshire. Educated Perse Girls' School, Cambridge; Girton College,

PEARCE

Cambridge, B.A. (Hons) English, M.A. History. Married Martin Christie, 1963 (died 1965), one daughter. Scriptwriter, producer, editor, reviewer and lecturer.

Awards: Library Association Carnegie Medal: *Tom's Midnight Garden*, 1959

Whitbread Award: *The Battle of Bubble and Squeak*, 1978

Agent: Laura Cecil,
17 Alwyne Villas,
London N1 2HG,
England

Undoubtedly one of the best writers for children, Philippa Pearce succeeds with all age groups. She is a compelling storyteller, able to create memorable characters, and she allows the reader to escape into a completely satisfying 'created' world, and still be able to leave that world feeling all the better for the brief sojourn. Well written, all the books require a certain degree of fluency.

THE BATTLE OF BUBBLE AND SQUEAK
Chivers Press, 1985, 112p. – L/P. – 0 7451 0134 8
Penguin, 1980, 96p. – Pbk. – 0 14 031183 1
Deutsch, 1978, 112p. – 0 233 96986 1
illustrated by Alan Baker

A drama that has been enacted in countless homes over the years is the setting for this entertaining story. The children want to keep gerbils, Mum says 'No!', loudly, clearly and often. Sensitively written in Philippa Pearce's inimitable style, in which humour is mixed with sadness, this book will be read with pleasure.
Age range: 9–11

A DOG SO SMALL
Chivers Press, 1987, 232p. – L/P. – 0 7451 0497 5
Kestrel Books, 1975, 142p. – O/P. – 0 7226 5261 5
Penguin, 1970, 156p. – Pbk. – 0 14 030206 9
illustrated by Antony Maitland

Many children will sympathize with Ben who longs for a dog. He is bitterly disappointed when his birthday present turns out to be a picture of a dog. The strength of his feelings actually creates a dog in his mind's eye; imagination and reality become blurred. Both heart-rending and heart-warming to the very last page.
Age range: 10–12

LION AT SCHOOL AND OTHER STORIES
Penguin, 1986, 111p. – Pbk. – 0 14 031855 0
illustrated by Caroline Sharpe

A book of really excellent stories which can be read to younger children, or suitable for children to read for themselves if reasonably fluent. They are varied in subject, including one about bullying.
Age range: 6–10

MINNOW ON THE SAY
Penguin, 1978, 256p. – Pbk. – 0 14 031022 3
OUP, 1974, 241p. – 0 19 277064 0
illustrated by Edward Ardizzone

David is delighted when, on holiday, he finds first a canoe, and then the owner who becomes a friend. Together they decide to look for the lost treasure, which, unknown to them, others are also searching for. A classic adventure story for committed readers.
Age range: 10–12

THE SHADOW-CAGE
Penguin, 1978, 160p. – Pbk. – 0 14 031073 8
Kestrel Books, 1977. 142p. – O/P. – 0 7226 5243 7
illustrated by Chris Molan

Stories with a supernatural flavour – mysterious and thoroughly enjoyable.
Age range: 11–14

TOM'S MIDNIGHT GARDEN
Penguin, 1989, 224p. – O/P. – Pbk. – 0 14 034049 1
Windrush, 1987, 261p. – L/P. – 1 85089 914 2
OUP, 1958, 232p. – 0 19 271128 8
illustrated by Susan Einzig

A wonderful, evocative story full of mystery and atmosphere. Tom, feeling bitter at being banished from home, finds solace in the garden which comes to life at midnight. As his friendship with Hetty develops, so does the reader's interest. It has an excellent climax.
Age range: 10–12

THE WAY TO SATTIN SHORE
Chivers Press, 1986, 312p. – L/P. – 0 7451 0332 4
Viking Kestrel, 1985, 176p. – O/P. – 0 670 80616 1
Penguin, 1985, 192p. – Pbk. – 0 14 031644 2
illustrated by Charlotte Voake

Kate gradually comes to realize that there is a mystery involving her family, but no-one will enlighten her. A moving and compelling story, not without its lighter moments, which can be read again and again, with each reading offering something new.
Age range: 11–14

WHAT THE NEIGHBOURS DID AND OTHER STORIES
Chivers Press, 1990, 160p. – L/P. – 0 7451 1246 3
Penguin, 1975, 144p. – Pbk. – 0 14 030710 9
Kestrel Books, 1975, 120p. – O/P. – 0 7226 5262 3
illustrated by Faith Jacques

In the same series:

WHO'S AFRAID?: AND OTHER STRANGE STORIES
Penguin, 1988, 128p. – Pbk. – 0 14 032057 1
Viking Kestrel, 1986, 128p. – 0 670 80907 1
illustrated by Peter Melnyczuk

Two collections of stories, one about every-day happenings, the other ghost stories. Well written and with interesting illustrations.
Age range: 9–11

Other publications:

CHILDREN OF CHARLECOTE
Gollancz, 1991. – Pbk. – 0 575 05082 9

CHILDREN OF THE HOUSE
Kestrel Books, 1977. – 0 7226 5988 1
ELM STREET LOT
Penguin, 1988. – Pbk. – 0 14 031953 0
EMILY'S OWN ELEPHANT
Walker Books, 1989. – Pbk. – 0 7445 1230 1
FREDDY
Deutsch, 1988. – 0 233 98175 6
HERE COMES TOD
Walker Books, 1993. – Pbk. – 0 7445 3089 X
IN THE MIDDLE OF THE NIGHT
BBC, 1991. – Pbk. – 0 563 34765 1
MRS COCKLE'S CAT
Penguin, 1988. – Pbk. – 0 14 032118 7
OLD BELLE'S SUMMER HOLIDAY
Deutsch, 1989. – Pbk. – 0 233 98176 4
SQUIRREL WIFE
Penguin, 1992. – Pbk. – 0 14 034837 9
TOOTH BALL
Penguin, 1989. – Pbk. – 0 14 050823 6

PERRY, Ritchie (John Allen)

Pseudonym for John Allen. British. Born King's Lynn, Norfolk, 1942. Educated King Edward VII Grammar School, King's Lynn; St John's College, Oxford, B.A. Modern History. Wife: Lynne Mary Charlotte Allen, two daughters.

Agent: Michael Sissons,
A. D. Peters & Co.,
10 Buckingham Street,
London WC2N 6BU,
England

Rather lightweight but with the gift of writing thoroughly entertaining stories which encourage the enjoyment of reading.

THE CREEPY TALE
Red Fox, 1990, 111p. – Pbk. – 0 09 966890 4
Hutchinson, 1989, 111p. – 0 09 173943 8

Tom, determined not to be outdone by his sister, agrees to go to the Monson House, looking for conkers. It is against his better judgement, for it is a house to avoid since the violent deaths which occurred there.
Age range: 10–12

PERRY

FENELLA FANG
Beaver Books, 1988. – Pbk. – O/P. –
0 09 951270 X
Hutchinson, 1986, 96p. – O/P. – 0 09 165820 9

In the same series:

FENELLA FANG AND THE GREAT ESCAPE
Beaver Books, 1988, 112p. – Pbk. –
0 09 955460 7
Hutchinson, 1987, 144p. – O/P. –
0 09 171910 0

FENELLA FANG AND THE TIME MACHINE
Hutchinson, 1991, 160p. – 0 09 176367 3

FENELLA FANG AND THE WICKED WITCH
Beaver Books, 1990, 144p. – Pbk. O/P. –
0 09 962260 2
Hutchinson, 1989, 144p. – 0 09 173710 9
illustrated by Jean Baylis

Very popular, these gruesome tales tell how Fenella's friends need rescuing from the hairy situations they find themselves in. Easy reading.
Age range: 9–11

GEORGE H. GHASTLY
Beaver Books, 1987, 80p. – Pbk. –
0 09 952020 6
Hutchinson, 1981, 77p. – O/P. – 0 09 143590 0

In the same series:

GEORGE H. GHASTLY AND THE LITTLE HORROR
Beaver Books, 1987, 144p. – Pbk. –
0 09 952040 0
Hutchinson, 1985, 96p. – O/P. –
0 09 162460 6

GEORGE H. GHASTLY TO THE RESCUE
Beaver Books, 1987, 104p. – Pbk. – O/P. –
0 09 952030 3
Hutchinson, 1983, 103p. – O/P. –
0 09 152100 9
all illustrated by Chris Winn

Excellent combinations of the humorous and the spooky. Failure as a ghost drives George to desperate measures.
Age range: 9–11

PEYTON, K. M.

Pseudonym for Kathleen Wendy Peyton, also writing as Kathleen Herald. British. Born Birmingham, Warwickshire, 1929. Educated Wimbledon High School; Manchester Art School, Art Teacher's Diploma, 1951. Married Michael Peyton, 1950, two daughters. Art teacher.

Awards: Library Association Carnegie Medal: *Edge of the Cloud*, 1969

Guardian Children's Fiction Award: *Flambards*, (the trilogy) 1970

Address: Rookery Cottage, North Fambridge, Chelmsford, Essex CM3 6LP, England

A writer with a deep understanding and sympathy for teenagers and their problems, and the ability to translate this into enjoyable books. Her books for younger readers are also well written and enjoyable. She has remained a popular author over many years.

FLY-BY-NIGHT
Sparrow Books, 1981, 176p. – Pbk. –
0 09 926390 4
OUP, 1979, 172p. – 0 19 277091 8

In the same series:

THE TEAM
Sparrow Books, 1982. 204p. – Pbk. –
0 09 927680 1
OUP, 1975, 177p. – O/P. – 0 19 271372 8
both illustrated by the author

Horse and pony stories continue to be popular with girls. These two are particularly good quality novels. The character of Ruth is well developed over the two books. The problems and expense of keeping a horse are honestly described, but there is still a heart-warming storyline for horse lovers.
Age range: 9–11

FROGGETT'S REVENGE
Penguin, 1987, 96p. – Pbk. – 0 14 032115 2
OUP, 1985, 80p. – 0 19 271513 5
illustrated by Maureen Bradley

A child's delight, in which justice prevails. Wayne, the school bully, finds himself on the receiving end of his own medicine. A very satisfying story.
Age range: 8–10

GOING HOME
Magnet Books, 1985, 96p. – Pbk. –
0 416 50290 3
OUP, 1982, 104p. – 0 19 271459 7
illustrated by Chris Molan

An unusual story about two children on holiday in France. They do not always see eye to eye with the relatives they are staying with, so they decide to make their own way home.
Age range: 8–10

POOR BADGER
Yearling, 1991, 64p. – Pbk. – 0 440 86265 5
Doubleday, 1990, 64p. – 0 385 26998 6
illustrated by Mary Lonsdale

Ros is distressed when she realizes the pony she visits and comes to love is neglected by his owners, but she becomes outraged when she discovers they are actually cruel with him. After many tribulations, the story finally ends happily. A lightweight pony story.
Age range: 8–10

THUNDER IN THE SKY
Red Fox, 1990, 159p. – Pbk. – 0 09 975150 X
Bodley Head, 1985, 168p. – Pbk. –
0 370 30885 9
illustrated by Victor Ambrus

When war breaks out in 1914, Sam cannot understand why Gil refuses to go to fight, yet is willing to work on the barges taking ammunition to France. Sam's gradual understanding of this apparent conflict provides an excellent plot.
Age range: 12–14

WHO, SIR? ME, SIR?
Windrush, 1988. – O/P. – 1 8508 9953 3
Puffin, 1985, 201p. – Pbk. – 0 14 031771 6
OUP, 1983, 171p. – 0 19 271470 8

Deciding his class lacked ambition, Mr Sylvester enters them in a competition against the posh school up the road, hoping it will inspire them. Rising to the occasion, they have to employ some rather ingenious, under-hand methods and hard work to overcome the odds stacked against them, and not to let him down. An excellent school story.
Age range: 11–13

THE WILD BOY AND QUEEN MOON
Doubleday, 1993, 169p. – O/P. – 0 385 40310 0

Sandy lives and breathes horses, and is completely captivated by Queen Moon. She is also drawn to the horse's rider when she finally meets him because of the first of many thefts which the police are investigating. Tracking down the thief makes a good story, while the love of horses is all-pervasive.
Age range: 10–12

Other publications:
APPLE WON'T JUMP
H. Hamilton, 1992. – 0 241 13111 1
BEETHOVEN MEDAL
Magnet Books, 1982. – Pbk. – O/P. –
0 416 24720 2
BOY WHO WASN'T THERE
Doubleday, 1992. – 0 385 40248 1
DARKLING
Corgi, 1991. – Pbk. – 0 552 52594 4
DEAR FRED
Bodley Head, 1981. – O/P. – 0 370 30350 4
DOWNHILL ALL THE WAY
Penguin, 1990. – Pbk. – 0 14 034165 X
EDGE OF THE CLOUD
Penguin, 1989. – Pbk. – 0 14 032621 9
FALLING ANGELS
Magnet Books, 1983. – Pbk. – O/P. –
0 416 27450 1
FLAMBARDS DIVIDED
Penguin, 1988. – Pbk. – O/P. – 0 14 032515 8
FLAMBARDS IN SUMMER
Penguin, 1993. – Pbk. – 0 14 034154 4
FLAMBARDS
Penguin, 1989. – Pbk. – O/P. – 0 14 032620 0
HARD WAY HOME
J. Goodchild, 1986. – 0 86391 087 4
LAST DITCH
OUP, 1984. – O/P. – 0 19 271484 8

MAPLIN BIRD
OUP, 1980. – O/P. – 0 19 277104 3

MIDSUMMER NIGHT'S DEATH
Penguin, 1988. – Pbk. – 0 14 032725 8

NORTH TO ADVENTURE
Collins, 1970. – O/P. – 0 00 164225 1

PATTERN OF ROSES
Sparrow Books, 1982. – Pbk. – 0 09 929410 9

PENNINGTON'S HEIR
Magnet Books, 1982. – Pbk. – O/P. –
0 416 24700 8

PENNINGTON'S SEVENTEENTH SUMMER
Windrush, 1989. – O/P. – 1 8508 9970 3

PLAIN JACK
H. Hamilton, 1988. – 0 241 12146 9

PLAN FOR BIRDSMARSH
OUP, 1980. – O/P. – 0 19 277096 9

PROVE YOURSELF A HERO
Penguin, 1988. – Pbk. – 0 14 032508 5

RIGHT-HAND MAN
Magnet Books, 1983. – Pbk. – O/P. –
0 416 28620 8

SKYLARK
Penguin, 1991. – Pbk. – O/P. – 0 14 034558 2

STORMCOCK MEETS TROUBLE
Collins, 1970. – O/P. – 0 00 164205 7

PILLING, ANN

Also writes as Ann Cheetham. British. Born Warrington, Lancashire, 1944. Educated King's College, University of London, B.A. (Hons), M.Phil., English. Married Joe Pilling, 1968, two sons. English teacher.

Awards: Guardian Children's Fiction Award: *Henry's Leg*, 1986

Address: 57 St. John Street, Oxford OX1 2LQ, England

Agent: Gina Pollinger, 4 Garrick Street, London WC2E 9BH, England

Best known for her originality of plot, Ann Pilling is also able to share her sense of humour in a variety of ways. Sometimes verbal, sometimes slapstick, there is much to laugh at in between the mounting tension which she realistically creates.

THE BIG PINK
Chivers Press, 1989, 328p. – L/P. –
0 7451 0959 4
Penguin, 1988, 160p. – Pbk. – 0 14 032319 8
Viking Kestrel, 1987, 156p. – 0 670 81156 4

Although at times very funny, this book is essentially a moving and painful story. Angela has to struggle to carve out a niche for herself in an alien environment. It will strike a chord with many young readers who also feel out on a limb.
Age range: 11–14

HENRY'S LEG
Chivers Press, 1987, 280p. – L/P. –
0 7451 0550 5
Penguin, 1986, 160p. – Pbk. O/P. –
0 14 032016 4
Viking Kestrel, 1985, 176p. – 0 670 80720 6
illustrated by Rowan Clifford

An original and amusing story. Henry finds a discarded leg from a tailor's dummy. Taking a fancy to it, he lugs it home, where it proves to be a catalyst for some hair-raising events.
Age range: 10–12

ON THE LION'S SIDE
Pan Books, 1990, 192p. – Pbk. – 0 330 31046 1
Heinemann, 1988, 160p. – 0 434 95671 6

The story of a friendship between two boys which begins with open hostility, and cautiously develops throughout the solving of the mystery of the wall. Mutual understanding is achieved at the same time as the final tragedy is unearthed. Simultaneously sensitive and exciting.
Age range: 10–12

OUR KID
Penguin, 1991, 208p. – Pbk. – 0 14 032974 9
Chivers Press, 1991, 368p. – L/P. –
0 7451 1295 1
Viking, 1989, 160p. – 0 670 82584 0

Acquiring a paper round gives Frank an opportunity to get to know the posh part of his home town. The people he gets to know broaden his horizons, and set him on the trail of a mystery. An excellent plot.
Age range: 12–14

REALMS OF GOLD
Kingfisher Books, 1993, 96p. – 0 86272 932 7 illustrated by Nady MacDonald Denton

A lovely collection of myths and legends from all over the world. Some are well-known, such as 'The Willow Pattern Story', some less well-known like the Russian 'Wishing Fish'. Varied and vastly enjoyable, with highly original and suitable illustrations.
Age range: 7–11

STAN
*Penguin, 1989, 192p. – Pbk. – 0 14 032388 0
Viking, 1988. 176p. – O/P. – 0 670 81770 8*

Stan's foster home is intolerable, so he runs away, hoping to find his brother, with whom he can make the real home he has never experienced. His difficult journey becomes a nightmare as he is relentlessly pursued. Totally gripping.
Age range: 12–14

VOTE FOR BAZ
*Penguin, 1993, 192p. – Pbk. – 0 14 034517 5
Viking, 1992, 192p. – 0 670 83486 6*

Winning a scholarship to a posh school means an enormous change for Baz, who refuses to conform. When a mock election is held, he puts himself forward as representative of the Common Man Party. This is an entertaining novel with much to say about present-day society.
Age range: 12+

THE YEAR OF THE WORM
*Chivers Press, 1988, 248p. – L/P. – 0 7451 0825 3
Penguin, 1985, 144p. – Pbk. – 0 14 031821 6
Kestrel Books, 1984, 144p. – 0 7226 5868 0
illustrated by Ian Newsham*

Peter is a timid boy, hence the nickname 'Worm'. He is bullied and made fun of until the holiday proves to him and others that he has more than enough courage.
Age range: 10–12

Other publications:

BAKED BEAN KIDS
Walker Books, 1993. – 0 7445 2420 2
BEAST IN THE BASEMENT
Heinemann, 1988. – 0 434 93046 6
BEFORE I GO TO SLEEP
Kingfisher Books, 1990. – 0 86272 451 1
BIG BISCUIT
Hodder, 1989. – 0 340 49705 X
DONKEY'S DAY OUT
Lion Publishing, 1992. – Pbk. – 0 7459 2348 8
DUSTBIN CHARLIE
Penguin, 1990. – Pbk. – 0 14 032391 0
FRIDAY PARCEL
Blackie, 1986. – 0 216 91892 8
JUNGLE SALE
Blackie, 1989. – 0 216 92607 6
NO GUNS, NO ORANGES
Mammoth, 1993. – Pbk. – 0 7497 1635 5

POWLING, Chris

British. Born London, 1943. Educated Bromley Grammar School; St Catherine's College, Oxford, M.A.; King's College, University of London, Postgraduate Certificate in Education; Royal Academy of Music, Diploma in Speech and Drama; Institute of Education, London, Advanced Diploma in Education, 1970; University of Sussex, M.A. Married Janet Smith, 1966, two daughters. Teacher, lecturer, contributor and presenter, BBC radio.

Address: The Old Chapel,
           Easton,
           near Winchester,
           Hampshire SO21 1EG,
           England

POWLING

A writer whose ideas are firmly based on today's society, making the stories relevant and meaningful. He has particular appeal to boys.

DAREDEVILS OR SCAREDYCATS
Fontana, 1981, 128p. – Pbk. – 0 00 671897 3
Abelard-Schuman, 1979, 128p. – O/P. – 0 200 72623 4
illustrated by Stephen Levis

A collection of stories demonstrating the various ways people can show courage. It includes bullying, coping with an emergency, and other situations children sometimes have to face alone.
Age range: 11–13

FINGERS CROSSED: STORIES FOR NINE-YEAR-OLDS
Hodder, 1988, 128p. – Pbk. – 0 340 48566 3
Blackie, 1987, 112p. – O/P. – 0 216 92113 9
illustrated by Jean Baylis

An excellent collection of stories and poems to suit every mood and taste.
Age range: 8–10

MOG AND THE RECTIFIER
Hodder, 1982, 144p. – Pbk. – 0 340 28046 8
Abelard-Schuman, 1980, 134p. – O/P. – 0 200 72697 8
illustrated by Stephen Levis

The narrator of this story is a nameless child, nameless because he feels too ashamed to 'reveal' his name. He belongs to a gang with Mog as leader. Mog hero-worships the Rectifier, a modern-day Robin Hood. There comes a point when a choice has to be made, Mog or the scholarship and a future.
Age range: 11–13

THE MUSTANG MACHINE
Hodder, 1983, 128p. – Pbk. O/P. – 0 340 32101 6
Abelard-Schuman, 1981, 128p. – O/P. – 0 200 72764 8

A book with an unusual hero – an extraordinary bicycle. Becca and the gang do so want to enter the competition, but without a bike they cannot. Mr Amos introduces them to the Mustang machine and everything changes. An enjoyable adventure story.
Age range: 11–13

STUNTKID
Hodder, 1987, 128p. – Pbk. – 0 340 40437 X
Blackie, 1985, 128p. – O/P. – 0 216 91778 6

An exciting mystery in which Andy has to discover the identity of 'Stuntkid' in order to find out why Vic Hogan's film was never finished.
Age range: 11–13

WHERE THE QUAGGY BENDS
Lions, 1992, 144p. – 0 00 185417 8
Lions, 1992, 128p. – Pbk. – 0 00 674087 1

An atmospheric novel in which Shep and Nimi investigate the secret held by the river in which a boy drowned. Easy to read.
Age range: 10–12

Other publications:

BELLA'S DRAGON
Blackie, 1988. – 0 216 92403 0
BUTTERFINGERS
Blackie, 1991. – 0 216 93127 4
CONKER AS HARD AS A DIAMOND
Viking, 1987. – 0 670 81404 0
DRACULA IN SUNLIGHT
Young Lions, 1992. – Pbk. – 0 00 674297 1
ELF 61
Young Lions, 1992. – Pbk. – 0 00 674272 6
FLY-AWAY FRANKIE
Blackie, 1987. – 0 216 92111 2
HARRY MOVES HOUSE
Black, 1993. – 0 7136 3701 3
HARRY WITH SPOTS ON
Young Lions, 1991. – Pbk. – 0 00 673884 2
HARRY'S PARTY
Armada Books, 1989. – Pbk. – 0 00 673347 6
HICCUP HARRY
Armada Books, 1988. – Pbk. – 0 00 673009 4
HOPPITY-GAP
Collins, 1989. – Pbk. – 0 00 673221 6
PHANTOM CARWASH
Mammoth, 1993. – Pbk. – 0 7497 1633 9
RAZZLE DAZZLE RAINBOW
Viking, 1993. – 0 670 84648 1
SPOOK AT THE SUPERSTORE
Heinemann, 1990. – 0 434 93087 3

UNCLE NEPTUNE
*Abelard-Schuman, 1982. – O/P. –
0 200 72781 8*
WESLEY AT THE WATER PARK
Blackie, 1992. – 0 216 93301 3
ZIGGY AND ICE OGRE
Heinemann, 1988. – 0 434 93051 2

PRATCHETT, Terry

British. Born Beaconsfield, Buckinghamshire, 1948. Married. One daughter. Journalist, press officer, writer.

Address: C/o Colin Smythe,
P.O. Box 6,
Gerrards Cross,
Buckinghamshire SL9 8XA,
England

THE CARPET PEOPLE
*Corgi, 1993, 192p. – Pbk. – 0 552 52752 1
Doubleday, 1992, 208p. – 0 385 40304 6*

Probably Terry Pratchett's first novel, written when he was only 17, but extensively revised. When the carpet was new, nothing lived in it, but as time went by and dust began to accumulate, little creatures appeared, with all the attendant problems facing people in the world. Illuminating, but very funny in parts.
Age range: 9–11

ONLY YOU CAN SAVE MANKIND
*Corgi, 1993, 176p. – Pbk. – 0 552 13926 2
Doubleday, 1992, 144p. – 0 385 40308 9*

In the same series:

JOHNNY AND THE DEAD
*Doubleday, 1993, 199p. – O/P. –
0 385 40301 1*

Johnny, involved in a computer game which becomes reality, suddenly finds he has to do an about-face. Instead of killing enemies, he has to work out conservation methods in order to save the alien race. Lots of appeal for modern, computer-literate children. Having successfully saved mankind, Johnny turns his attention to corpses who felt it was more fun when they were alive. Funny, very unusual, rather macabre, but a certain success.
Age range: 11–13

TRUCKERS
*Chivers Press, 1991, 320p. – O/P. –
0 7451 1469 5
Corgi, 1990, 208p. – Pbk. – 0 552 52595 2
Doubleday, 1989, 169p. – 0 385 26961 7*

In the same series:

DIGGERS
*Chivers Press, 1992, 256p. – O/P. –
0 7451 1637 X
Corgi, 1991, 208p. – Pbk. – 0 552 52586 3
Doubleday, 1990, 152p. – 0 385 26979 X*

WINGS
*Chivers Press, 1993, 232p. – L/P. –
0 7451 1805 4
Corgi, 1991, 160p. – Pbk. – 0 552 52649 5
Doubleday, 1990, 192p. – 0 385 40018 7*

A powerful fantasy about a tribe of gnomes who live under the floorboards of a large department store about to be demolished. They make their plans to escape and face the dangers of Outside. The story of their hazardous journey, so courageously faced, comes to a satisfactory climax.
Age range: 10–12

PRICE, Susan

British. Born Rounds Green, Staffordshire, 1955. Educated Tividale Comprehensive School. Writer.

Awards: Children's Rights Other Award: *Twopence a Tub*, 1975

Library Association Carnegie Medal: *The Ghost Drum*, 1987

PRICE

Address: C/o Faber & Faber Ltd,
3 Queen Square,
London WC1N 3AU,
England

Agent: Michael Thomas,
A. M. Heath,
79 St. Martin's Lane,
London WC2N 4AA,
England

A writer of the highest quality who began writing in her teens and has gone from strength to strength. Her books are often set in the recent past, which she portrays with extraordinary vividness. She is also well known for her imaginative re-tellings of traditional tales.

FORBIDDEN DOORS
Faber, 1993, 112p. – Pbk. – 0 571 16837 X
Faber, 1991, 112p. – O/P. – 0 571 16228 2
illustrated by Patrick Lynch

An unusual collection of stories of mystery and suspense about people who dare to open forbidden doors with a variety of consequences – some good, some bad. A delicious thrill to be had in reading them.
Age range: 11+

THE GHOST DRUM
Faber, 1989, 167p. – Pbk. – 0 571 15340 2
Faber, 1987, 167p. – 0 571 14613 9

A grim tale of a power struggle with a life at stake. Czar Guidon rules by terror, and keeps his son imprisoned in terrible circumstances. Out in the frozen wastes is a witch, who listens to messages from the ghost drum, and hears the cries of the imprisoned son. An excellent story, but the names are difficult and form a barrier which prevents some children tackling the book.
Age range: 12–14

GHOSTS AT LARGE
Penguin, 1986, 96p. – Pbk. – 0 14 032021 0
Faber, 1984, 96p. – O/P. – 0 571 13282 0
illustrated by Allison Price

Lesser known traditional stories re-told by a master storyteller. Weird ghostly happenings in each story ensure the reader will be kept enthralled.
Age range: 11–13

HEADS AND TALES
Faber, 1993, 128p. – 0 571 16914 7

A grisly story about two children who set off on a journey to their grandmother carrying their father's head in obedience to his last request on his death-bed. They have no money and need help – supplied by the head as it tells stories to the fearful and astonished folk they meet on route. Not for the faint-hearted.
Age range: 11–13

HERE LIES PRICE
Faber, 1987, 80p. – O/P. – 0 571 14804 2

A volume of short stories for those readers with nerves of steel. It is impossible to guess the outcome, the stories hold one's interest to the last.
Age range: 12+

HOME FROM HOME
Faber, 1990, 178p. – Pbk. – 0 571 14316 4
Faber, 1977, 123p. – O/P. – 0 571 11022 3

Paul feels completely at odds with everyone at home and at school, and makes no secret of the fact. Mrs Maxwell feels worried and distrustful when she is allotted Paul to visit her as part of the Active Christian scheme, and Paul himself feels appalled. After a shaky start they become friends, and he learns a lot from the clutter around her house. Realistic and down-to-earth, the story can be successfully read to a class, and appeals to children who feel they have a lot in common with Paul.
Age range: 12+

IN A NUTSHELL
Faber, 1983, 120p. – O/P. – 0 571 13075 5
illustrated by Alison Price

A delightful tale of Thumb and

Thumbling banished in nutshells to live with human beings. Being so tiny means that every problem seems so huge as to be insurmountable. Eventually they resolve the problem and achieve happiness.
Age range: 8–10

TWOPENCE A TUB
Faber, 1991, 176p. – Pbk. – 0 571 16125 1
Faber, 1975, 173p. – O/P. – 0 571 10624 2

Many books have been written about coal-mining and the hard life endured by miners in the nineteenth century, but this is one of the best. Readers can experience the anxiety as Jek, committed to striking for the extra pay per tub, struggles to see the point of view of those willing to break the strike. Desperate days, vividly described.
Age range: 11–13

Other publications:

BILLY GOATS GRUFF AND OTHER STORIES
Kingfisher Books, 1992. – Pbk. – 0 86272 893 2
BONE DOG
Hippo Books, 1989. – Pbk. – 0 590 76073 4
THE CARPENTER
Penguin, 1986. – Pbk. – O/P. – 0 14 032049 0
CHRISTOPHER UPTAKE
Faber, 1981. – 0 571 11660 4
CRACK A STORY
Faber, 1990. – 0 571 14136 6
DEVIL'S PIPER
Penguin, 1977. – Pbk. – 0 14 030936 5
FEASTING OF TROLLS
Black, 1990. – 0 7136 3221 6
GHOST SONG
Faber, 1992. – 0 571 16410 2
JACK AND THE BEANSTALK AND OTHER STORIES
Kingfisher Books, 1992. – Pbk. – 0 86272 894 0
KNOCKING JACK
Yearling, 1992. – Pbk. – 0 440 86281 7
MASTER THOMAS KATT
Black, 1988. – 0 7136 3036 1
ODIN'S MONSTER
Black, 1986. – 0 7136 2787 5
PHANTOM FROM THE PAST
Paperbird, 1989. – Pbk. – 1 8554 3005 3
STICKS AND STONES
Faber, 1992. – Pbk. – O/P. – 0 571 16315 7
THREE BEARS AND OTHER STORIES
Kingfisher Books, 1992. – Pbk. – 0 86272 892 4
THUNDERPUMPS
Heinemann, 1990. – 0 434 93093 8

R

RANSOME, Arthur (Michell)

British. Born Leeds, Yorkshire, 1884 (died 3 June 1967). Educated Old College, Windermere; Rugeley College, Warwickshire; Yorkshire College (now Leeds University). Married: 1) Ivy Walker, 1909 (divorced 1924), one daughter; 2) Eugenia Shelepin, 1924. Correspondent, writer.

Awards: Library Association Carnegie Medal: *Pigeon Post*, 1936
University of Leeds: Litt.D.
University of Durham: M.A.
O.B.E.

In a sense, it can be said that Arthur Ransome is the father of children's literature as we know it today. Of course, there were children's books before his, but they were restricted to moralizing and improving. In the midst of this, Arthur Ransome's stirring tales of adventure shine like a beacon. The children in the stories, albeit middle class, are independent, resourceful and imaginative. Their characters are well rounded, and, therefore, memorable, and the books have their share of humorous incidents. They continue to give discerning readers hours of pleasure. Ransome drew all the maps, diagrams and illustrations himself. The new paperback editions have colourful jackets which make them more immediately attractive to today's child, used to seeing everything in colour. The books are listed below in reading order.
Age range for all titles: 10–12

SWALLOWS AND AMAZONS
Red Fox, 1993, 416p. – Pbk. – 0 09 996290 X
Cape, 1930, 352p. – 0 224 60631 X

The first book which introduces readers to the two families, the Walkers and the Blacketts, who are the heroes of most of the other books. Each has a small dinghy, and they spend the summer camping on an island in the lake, playing pirates, sailing, and generally having a wonderful time. The book has been made into a delightful film.

SWALLOWDALE
Red Fox, 1993, 448p. – Pbk. – 0 09 996300 0
Cape, 1931, 454p. – 0 224 60632 8

In a moment of carelessness, Captain John runs Swallow onto a rock, and sinks her. With only one boat for the rest of the holiday, they are forced ashore, and find a secret valley complete with a hidden cave. Their spirits rise as they start to explore, and the climax is the ascent of a local mountain, called Kanchenjunga by the children.

PETER DUCK
Red Fox, 1993, 476p. – Pbk. – 0 09 996310 8
Cape, 1983, 416p. – 0 224 02125 7
Penguin, 1968, 448p. – Pbk. – 0 14 030340 5

Actually a story 'written' by the children themselves during the winter holiday when they are unable to sail. They create a pirate story in which Black Jake pursues Peter Duck, who is sailing with the Swallows and Amazons to find the treasure that Peter Duck once saw being buried.

WINTER HOLIDAY
Red Fox, 1993, 352p. – Pbk. – 0 09 996320 5
Cape, 1933, 360p. – 0 224 60634 4

With their boats laid up for the winter, the children find other roles to adopt. They become Arctic explorers, and a great expedition is planned for the Swallows and Amazons, also joined for the first time by the two Ds. When the lake freezes over, they decide to journey to the 'North Pole'. Fate also takes a hand, in the form of mumps.

COOT CLUB
Red Fox, 1993, 384p. – Pbk. – 0 09 996330 2
Cape, 1934, 352p. – 0 224 60635 2

Tom throws caution to the winds and casts a motor launch adrift so that the noise of the engine cannot disturb a coot nesting nearby. The owners are angry and plot revenge. A different set of children from most of his books.

PIGEON POST
Red Fox, 1993, 336p. – Pbk. – 0 09 996340 X
Cape, 1983, 384p. – 0 224 02124 9

On this holiday, the Swallows and Amazons, always ready to be helpful, decide to go prospecting for gold to help Uncle Jim, whose own expedition to South America has ended in failure. Serious as they are in their quest, there are others who are more so, and they spend much time outwitting a possible 'claim jumper'.

WE DIDN'T MEAN TO GO TO SEA
Red Fox, 1993, 376p. – Pbk. – 0 09 996350 7
Cape, 1983, 344p. – 0 224 02123 0

Perhaps the best of the series, but featuring only the Walker children. When the boat they are spending the night on drags her anchor, they are subjected to a very frightening experience as they drift out to sea, in thick fog. Helpless at first, their confidence and courage increase as the story progresses, and they cross the North Sea successfully.

SECRET WATER
Red Fox, 1993, 432p. – Pbk. – 0 09 996360 4
Cape, 1939, 384p. – 0 224 60638 7

Excited, and a little apprehensive, the children are put ashore on an island, charged with the holiday task of making a map, fending for themselves while they do so. While exploring, they find mysterious tracks which they identify as those of a Mastodon, and also meet up with another group of children whose home ground the island is.

BIG SIX
Red Fox, 1993, 424p. – Pbk. – 0 09 996370 1
Cape, 1940, 400p. – 0 224 60639 5

The children from *Coot Club* are wrongly suspected of setting boats adrift. Proving their innocence is difficult, as evidence is piling up against them. They are joined in this adventure by the two Ds.

MISSEE LEE
Red Fox, 1993, 400p. – Pbk. – 0 09 996380 9
Cape, 1941, 340p. – 0 224 60640 9

A rather more melodramatic plot, dreamed up by the children like *Peter Duck* to while away the winter holiday. Captain Flint (Uncle Jim) accidentally sets his boat on fire, so they abandon ship and sail off in the two boats *Swallow* and *Amazon*, and are subsequently shipwrecked on the coast of China in a storm. They meet Missee Lee, a pirate, who holds them against their will. Their escape makes a lively adventure.

THE PICTS AND THE MARTYRS
Red Fox, 1993, 352p. – Pbk. – 0 09 996390 6
Cape, 1943, 304p. – 0 224 60641 7

The Martyrs are the Amazons, who have to stay indoors and be good, tidy, clean children during the visit of a fearsome Great Aunt. The Picts are the two Ds, who camp out in a hut on the hillside like the Picts of old used to do during raids. When the Great Aunt disappears, their holiday plans take a turn for the better.

GREAT NORTHERN?
Red Fox, 1993, 410p. – Pbk. – 0 09 996400 7
Cape, 1947, 352p. – 0 224 60642 5

Mooring their boat in an isolated cove to get her cleaned up, the children see what turns out to be a pair of rare birds nesting. To their horror, they soon realize that a ruthless egg-collector is about to kill the birds to steal the eggs. They must somehow form a rescue plan.

OLD PETER'S RUSSIAN TALES
Penguin, 1988, 253p. – Pbk. – 0 14 035097 7
Cape, 1984, 256p. – 0 224 02959 2

Arthur Ransome travelled a great deal in Russia when he was a war correspondent. He learnt Russian in order to study the folk-lore, and these stories are his version of the tales Old Peter told his grandchildren during the long winter evenings.

Other publications:

COOTS IN THE NORTH
Red Fox, 1993. – Pbk. – 0 09 996410 4
FOOL OF THE WORLD AND THE FLYING SHIP
H. Hamilton, 1970. – O/P. – 0 241 01788 2
SWALLOWS AND AMAZONS FOR EVER
Red Fox, 1993. – Pbk. – 0 09 996420 1
WAR OF THE BIRDS AND THE BEASTS AND OTHER RUSSIAN TALES
Penguin, 1986. – Pbk. – O/P. – 0 14 031900 X

endorsed this opinion. They find it an easy, fun book to read. The hero, Ruskin Splinter, a name to conjure with, is small, thin, wears glasses, and speaks in a squeaky voice. He has the stuff heroes are made of running through his veins, however. When the Krindlekrax appears, it is just the opportunity he needs to prove himself.
Age range: 9–11

MERCEDES ICE
Armada Books, 1989, 96p. – Pbk. – O/P. – 0 00 673241 0
illustrated by Damon Burnard

An odd little story with a neat ending which is described as a 'fairy-tale for modern children'. Rather than a palace, there is a tower block which casts a huge black shadow, adversely affecting the lives of those who have to live in it.
Age range: 9–11

Other publications:

DAKOTA OF THE WHITE FLATS
Collins, 1991. – Pbk. – O/P. – 0 00 673469 3

RIDLEY, Philip

No biographical has been received, from either the author or publisher.

Awards: Smarties Book Prize, 9–11 category: *Krindlekrax*, 1991

A newcomer to children's fiction, Philip Ridley is proving to be both innovative and very popular with young readers.

KRINDLEKRAX
Red Fox, 1992, 128p. – Pbk. – 0 09 997920 9
Chivers Press, 1992, 192p. – L/P. – O/P. – 0 7451 1638 8
Cape, 1991, 130p. – 0 224 03149 X
illustrated by Mark Robertson

Hailed as 'imaginative' and 'outrageous' by several reviewers, and children have

ROSSELSON, Leon

No biographical has been received, from either the author or publisher. Song writer and performer. An author of outstanding promise. Further books are eagerly awaited.

ROSA'S SINGING GRANDFATHER
Penguin, 1992, 96p. – Pbk. – 0 14 034587 6
Viking, 1991, 96p. – 0 670 83598 6

In the same series:

ROSA'S GRANDFATHER SINGS AGAIN
Penguin, 1993, 96p. – Pbk. – 0 14 034588 4
Viking, 1991, 96p. – 0 670 83599 4
illustrated by Norman Young

Undoubtedly two of the best books ever to be published for children. Delightful stories, full of gentle humour, about Rosa and her beloved grandfather, whose habit of bursting into song is not always convenient. Excellent for reading aloud, they are also published in the 'Reading Aloud' series in extra large print.
Age range: 6–8

Other publications:

BERNIE WORKS A MIRACLE
Young Lions, 1993. – Pbk. – 0 00 674559 8

S

SAMPSON, Fay

British. Born South Devon. Educated University of Exeter, B.A. (Maths). Married, two children. Teacher, author. This author deserves to be more widely read, but as some of her books have a historical flavour, they tend to be overlooked by some children. She creates individual and memorable children in dramatic situations which can sometimes shock the reader, but justifiably so.

FINNGLAS AND THE STONES OF CHOOSING
Lion Publishing, 1986, 128p. – Pbk. – 0 7459 1124 2

In the same series:

FINNGLAS OF THE HORSES
Lion Publishing, 1985, 128p. – Pbk. – 0 8564 8899 2

PANGUR BAN: THE WHITE CAT
Chivers Press, 1991, 128p. – L/P. – O/P. – 0 86220 879 3
Lion Publishing, 1983, 128p. – Pbk. – 0 8564 8580 2

THE SERPENT OF SENARGAD
Lion Publishing, 1989, 128p. – Pbk. – 0 7459 1520 5

SHAPE-SHIFTER: THE NAMING OF PANGUR BAN
Lion Publishing, 1988, 128p. – Pbk. – 0 7459 1347 4

THE WHITE HORSE IS RUNNING
Lion Publishing, 1990, 176p. – Pbk. – 0 7459 1915 4

A series of books set in the kingdom of Senergad where evil triumphs over good. Great battles are waged to try to redress the balance. Exciting fantasy stories.
Age range: 12–15

A FREE MAN ON SUNDAY
Collins, 1990, 160p. – Pbk. – 0 00 673501 0
Gollancz, 1987, 128p. – 0 575 04114 5

Clifford Ramsden is a serious rambler who spends much of his time on and around Kinder Scout. He and his fellow ramblers feel strongly about the right of common people to be able to wander freely. Edie, his daughter, loves to accompany him and desperately wants to show her support for him on the day of the trespass. The outcome of her decision to defy him is unexpected. A very enjoyable fictional account of the Mass Trespass on Kinder Scout in 1932. It echoes the present situation where many public footpaths and rights of way are being eroded and obstructed, and individuals still try to protect the public right.
Age range: 10–12

THE HUNGRY SNOW
Dobson, 1980, 184p. – 0 234 72262 2

A vivid and memorable tale of the days of poverty when baby boys were welcome because they could work and earn money, and baby girls were thought to be too much of a liability. Marie is filled with horror as she comes to realize that babies are deliberately left to die. She finally rebels against her fellow villagers and saves her baby sister.
Age range: 12–14

JOSH'S PANTHER
Penguin, 1988, 96p. – Pbk. – 0 14 032485 2
Gollancz, 1986, 96p. – 0 575 03914 0
illustrated by Jill Bennett

Josh cannot believe that his practical joke has been taken seriously, but all too quickly it becomes impossible for him to confess that his plaster paw print is not really taken from a wild animal.

An amusing, light-hearted story, suitably illustrated.
Age range: 8–10

Other publications:

CHAINS OF SLEEP
Dobson, 1981. – 0 234 72250 9
CHRIS AND THE DRAGON
Penguin, 1985. – Pbk. – 0 14 032121 7
CHRISTMAS BLIZZARD
Lion Publishing, 1991. – Pbk. – 0 7459 2214 7
EMPTY HOUSE
Dobson, 1979. – 0 234 72195 2
HALF A WELCOME
Dobson, 1977. – O/P. – 0 234 72031 X
JENNY AND THE WRECKERS
H. Hamilton, 1984. – O/P. – 0 241 11368 7
LANDFALL ON INNIS MICHAEL
Dobson, 1980. – 0 234 72201 0
PANGUR BAN STORIES
Lion Publishing, 1992. – 0 7459 2616 9
SUS
Dobson, 1982. – 0 234 72299 1
WATCH OF PATTERICK FELL
Dobson, 1978. – 0 234 72077 8

SEFTON, Catherine

For biographical details, see Martin WADDELL.

Martin Waddell claims he writes as Catherine Sefton when he wants to be serious and deeply emotional. There is no doubt that Sefton books are much appreciated by older girls. There is usually an element of mystery or the supernatural, and the plots are intriguing. They do not require much stamina to read, yet they are deeply satisfying. Not too demanding, they can be used to encourage reluctant readers.

ALONG A LONELY ROAD
Penguin, 1993, 160p. – Pbk. – 0 14 034853 0
Chivers Press, 1993, 160p. – L/P. –
0 7451, 1909 3
H. Hamilton, 1991, 160p. – O/P. –
0 241 13136 7

It comes as a shock to Ruth to see her Mum, normally so calm and capable, weeping and subservient to the newly-arrived Dooneys. Gradually she realises they are virtual prisoners, and that it is up to her to act in order to avert a tragedy. A superb build-up to an exciting climax.
Age range: 10–12

BLUE MISTY MONSTERS
Magnet Books, 1986, 112p. – Pbk. –
0 416 61670 4
Faber, 1985, 106p. – O/P. – 0 571 13564 1
illustrated by Elaine McGregor-Turney

A fun science fiction story in which Mo lands her Pod in Spud's garden quite by mistake. Spud is delighted to have a spaceship until it shrinks to the size of a marble, and until Mo takes on human shape, but remains bright blue, which is inconvenient, to say the least
Age range: 8–10

EMER'S GHOST
Mammoth, 1990, 128p. – Pbk. – 0 7497 0690 2
Hamish Hamilton, 1981, 137p. – O/P. –
0 241 10619 2

A timeless ghost story which appeals to succeeding generations of children. A wooden doll which sheds real tears is a portent not to be ignored, as Emer finds out. When she is finally convinced she has seen a ghost, trying to solve the mystery leads her into danger. A dramatic story with an excellent conclusion.
Age range: 9–11

THE EMMA DILEMMA
Magnet Books, 1984, 96p. – Pbk. –
0 416 46800 4
Faber, 1982, 96p. – O/P. – 0 571 11841
illustrated by Jill Bennett

After falling and bumping her head, Emma realizes that a second Emma has appeared, and looks set to stay. Unfortunately, she is full of tricks, which makes life difficult for Emma number one.
Age range: 8–10

SEFTON

THE FINN GANG
*Hippo Books, 1985, 96p. – Pbk, O/P. –
0 590 70353 6
Hamish Hamilton, 1981, 96p. – O/P. –
0 241 10694 X
illustrated by Michael Charlton*

The shed used by the gang as their HQ has been taken over. The children are angry and determined to expose the wrong-doers. An air of mystery is maintained to the end.
Age range: 9–11

THE GHOST AND BERTIE BOGGIN
*Penguin, 1983, 96p. – Pbk. – 0 14 031363 X
Faber, 1980, 94p. – O/P. – 0 571 11524 1
illustrated by Jill Bennett*

Amusing ghost stories are always popular. Bertie Boggin's best friend is a ghost who shows him where the best blackberries are and helps him to build winning sand castles. The ghost's fondness for Florence Nightingale leads to difficulties but there is a highly satisfying ending.

In the same series:

BERTIE BOGGIN AND THE GHOST AGAIN!
Penguin, 1991. – Pbk. – 0 14 034321 0

Age range: 9–11

THE GHOST GIRL
*Mammoth, 1991, 128p. – Pbk. – 0 7497 0889 1
Hamish Hamilton, 1985, 160p. – 0 241 11428 4*

A little bit of everything – ghost story, romance, family story and mystery, set in Ireland. Clare sees a ghost, but perhaps it is her imagination, as she is not enjoying her holiday. Following the clues, she begins to put together Lucie's story. Very light-hearted.
Age range: 11–13

IN A BLUE VELVET DRESS
*Walker Books, 1991, 143p. – Pbk. –
0 7445 2056 8
Chivers Press, 1987, 168p. – O/P. – L/P. –
0 7451 0498 3
H. Hamilton, 1985, 128p. – 0 241 11652 X*

Jane doesn't know a lot about ghosts, but feels sure that one is leaving books for her to read. She wants to try to help, but realizes in the end that the ghost girl only appeared because Jane herself needed help. Lots of humorous passages – a good read which has stood the test of time.
Age range: 9–11

ISLAND OF THE STRANGERS
*Mammoth, 1990, 128p. – Pbk. – 0 7497 0182 X
Hamish Hamilton, 1983, 160p. – O/P. –
0 241 10914 0*

A stirring tale of the residents against the Gobbers – a group of city kids complete with skin-head hair-dos and earrings who 'invade' Inishnagal, the island of strangers. Only Nora goes against the majority and almost pays with her life. Written in her typical racy, undemanding style, there is, however, a more serious lesson to be learned.
Age range: 12–14

SLEEPERS ON THE HILL
*Mammoth, 1990, 128p. – Pbk. – 0 7497 0691 0
Faber, 1973, 126p. – O/P. – 0 571 10305 7*

When Miss Cooney broke her leg, a chain of events began that changed many lives. Tom had to see to her hens, and found the bangle. He could feel its power at once, especially in the vicinity of the graves. Then he discovers the girl hiding in the cottage. An exciting mystery with rather more substance.
Age range: 10–12

Other publications:

BACK HOUSE GHOSTS
Walker Books, 1991. – Pbk. – 0 7445 2057 6
BEAT OF THE DRUM
Mammoth, 1990. – Pbk. – 0 7497 0402 0
BOGGART IN THE BARREL
H. Hamilton, 1991. – 0 241 13032 8
DAY THE SMELLS WENT WRONG
H. Hamilton, 1988. – 0 241 12237 6
FLYING SAM
H. Hamilton, 1986. – 0 241 11915 4

FRANKIE'S STORY
Mammoth, 1990. – Pbk. – 0 7497 0558 2
GHOST SHIP
H. Hamilton, 1985. – 0 241 11596 5
GHOSTS OF COBWEB AND THE CIRCUS STAR
H. Hamilton, 1993. – 0 241 13423 4
GHOSTS OF COBWEB AND THE SKULLY BONES MYSTERY
H. Hamilton, 1993. – 0 241 13346 7
GHOSTS OF COBWEB
H. Hamilton, 1992. – O/P. – 0 241 13130 8
HAUNTED SCHOOLBAG
Penguin, 1993. – Pbk. – 0 14 034838 7
HORACE THE GHOST
H. Hamilton, 1991. – 0 241 13033 6
MY GANG
Corgi, 1987. – Pbk. – 0 552 52415 8
PUFF OF SMOKE
Corgi, 1988. – Pbk. – 0 552 52470 0
SHADOWS ON THE CAKE
H. Hamilton, 1987. – O/P. – 0 241 11997 9
STARRY NIGHT
Mammoth, 1990. – Pbk. – 0 7497 0559 0

SEVERY, Richard

British. Born Nottingham, 1944. Educated Guildford Royal Grammar School; Bristol University, LL.B. (Hons); Bath University, Certificate in Education. Lives with Jann Howarth (illustrator), one son, with three daughters by a marriage dissolved in 1979. (Jann Howarth also has two daughters.) Solicitor, teacher, business man, writer.

Address: Lodge Farm,
Hinton Charterhouse,
Near Bath,
Avon BA3 6BG,
England
Agent: Jon Thurley,
213 Linen Hall,
156–170 Regent Street,
London W1R 5TA,
England

Superb plots laced with humour are Richard Severy's strong point. Some of the stories are written about his own family, which may account for the excellent characterization.

ANGEL
Mammoth, 1989, 144p. – Pbk. – 0 7497 0014 9
Methuen, 1988, 128p. – 0 416 09552 6
illustrated by Jann Haworth

This can best be described as a 'gem'. Angie, a wonderfully drawn character, and her twin brother, travel to school on a steam train because their father is a signalman. Times are changing, and rumours about the projected closure of the railway line are making life at home unhappy. At school, the new headmistress is making life difficult for Angie, who feels she has nowhere to turn. She does, however, fight on to win in a most spectacular way.
Age range: 10–12

BATTLEFIELDS
Methuen, 1987, 144p. – O/P. – 0 416 03882 4

Jerry had looked forward to his new home in the country where he and his dog could explore in safety. It was completely ruined for him by Captain Packham, who, being crippled, takes his frustration with life out on those around him, particularly Jerry and his dog. Each time they meet, the unpleasantness and near-violence escalate until the unexpected climax.
Age range: 11–13

HI JINKS!
J. MacRae, 1986. – O/P. – 0 86203 245 8
illustrated by Karen Haworth

When the children find themselves left in sole charge of the farm due to circumstances beyond their control, they rise magnificently to the occasion. They cope with a variety of situations, some comic, some frightening. An easy and entertaining read.
Age range: 8–10

MYSTERY PIG
J. MacRae Books, 1983, 60p. – O/P. – 0 86203 125 7
illustrated by Karen Haworth

The pig arrived looking tired and damp. Kay and Dee fell in love with him, but he proved to be too much of a handful. Absolutely hilarious.
Age range: 7–9

RAT'S CASTLE
J. MacRae, 1985, 96p. – 0 86203 193 1
illustrated by Karen Haworth

There is so much packed into this short novel. Excellent atmospheric description of the castle in the snow, plus the mysterious footprints and the courage of the children, together combine to make an excellent book.
Age range: 7–9

UNICORN TRAP
J. MacRae, 1984, 82p. – O/P. – 0 86203 156 7
illustrated by Karen Haworth

One rainy day, the children make plasticine models to pass the time. Kay chooses to make a unicorn which she stands on the windowsill in the moonlight. Strange things happen after that, but the children cannot decide if it is proper magic, or man-made magic. A lovely story with a magical ending.
Age range: 7–9

SOUTHALL, Ivan (Francis)

Australian. Born Canterbury, Victoria, 1921. Educated Chatham State School; Mont Albert Central School; Box Hill Grammar School. Australian Army, Royal Australian Air Force, WW II, Distinguished Flying Cross. Married: 1) Joyce Blackburn, 1945, one son, three daughters; 2) Susan Stanton, 1976. Lecturer, writer.

Awards: Australian Children's Book Council Book of the Year Award: *Ash Road*, 1966
Australian Children's Book Council Book of the Year Award: *To the Wild Sky*, 1968
Australian Children's Book Council Picture Book of the Year Award: *Fly Old Wardrobe*, 1969
Australian Children's Book Council Book of the Year Award: *Bread and honey*, 1971
Library Association Carnegie Medal: *Josh*, 1971
I.B.B.Y. Honour Award: *Josh*, 1974
Australian Children's Book Council Book of the Year Award: *Fly West*, 1976
Member: Order of Australia, 1981

Address: PO Box 25,
Healesville,
Victoria 3777,
Australia

A writer of the highest quality who deals with emotions as well as events. He has a firm belief that, when necessary, children can and will rise to the occasion, however disastrous. His books are mostly not easy light reading, but for fluent readers they offer tense, exciting plots and characters they can sympathize with.

ASH ROAD
Penguin, 1970, 192p. – Pbk. – 0 14 030314 6
Angus & Robertson, 1966, 160p. – O/P. – 0 207 94629 9
illustrated by Clem Seale

Fire is very dangerous and destructive, so whenever it starts, everyone sets off to fight it, leaving the children of Ash Road alone. Then the impossible happens, and the children start a fire which gets out of control, threatening them within seconds. A moment's carelessness will affect them forever.
Age range: 12–14

SOUTHALL

CHINAMAN'S REEF IS OURS
Hodder, 1975, 192p. – Pbk. O/P. –
0 340 18744 1
Angus & Robertson, 1970, 160p. – O/P. –
0 207 95365 1

The story, powerfully told, of a group of children who fight to save the town in which they are growing up from the bulldozers.
Age range: 12–14

FLY WEST
Penguin, 1978, 192p. – Pbk. O/P. –
0 14 047118 9
Angus & Robertson, 1975, 176p. – O/P. –
0 207 13002 7

A fictional account of a personal experience, telling of the men who flew Sunderland flying boats during the war.
Age range: 12–14

THE FOX HOLE
Mammoth, 1989, 117p. – Pbk. – 0 7497 0363 6
Methuen, 1967, 126p. – 0 416 11100 9
illustrated by Ian Ribbons

Although this is one of Ivan Southall's easier books, it is nevertheless an excellent combination of an exciting story and a moving description of developing relationships. Ken feels strange with his cousins when he first comes to stay. The tension builds as the children go camping and Ken falls into a hole while chasing a thieving fox. He is genuinely afraid he won't be rescued.
Age range: 10–12

HILL'S END
Penguin, 1970, 224p. – Pbk. – 0 14 030245 X
Angus & Robertson, 1962, 174p. – O/P. –
0 207 94635 3
illustrated by Jim Phillips

A tribute to the sterling courage that children are capable of in times of adversity. While the children are away from home, a cyclonic storm destroys the whole area, so that when they struggle home, there is nothing left. They must somehow survive until help arrives, but the hazards are many, and they are not used to making their own decisions. The suspense is maintained to the very end.
Age range: 12–14

JOSH
Penguin, 1974, 225p. – Pbk. O/P. – 0 14 030598 X
Angus & Robertson, 1978, 179p. – O/P. – 0 207 13656 4

The book spans three days, and, at the same time, a whole lifetime. Josh goes to visit Aunt Clara as a sort of initiation ceremony – if he comes up to scratch there, he can be considered a Plowman. His visit starts badly as he treads in a cowclap and stands on her cat, but worse is to come when he meets the other children, and two worlds collide head-on. It is a different Josh who returns home.
Age range: 12–14

LET THE BALLOON GO
Mammoth, 1990, 128p. – Pbk. – 0 7497 0399 7
Methuen, 1968, 142p. – O/P. – 0 416 29420 0

When first published, this book was innovative as it was one of the few, at that time, to fictionalize the problems of disabled children. Since then, many books have tackled the subject, but this is still among the best. John is spastic, and often feels frustrated by his overprotective mother and the restrictions she puts on his life. One day, he is left alone at home, and, revelling in unaccustomed freedom, he seizes the opportunity to try many of the things he has not previously been allowed to do.
Age range: 10–12

TO THE WILD SKY
Penguin, 1971, 224p. – Pbk. O/P. –
0 14 030483 5
Angus & Robertson, 1967, 192p. – O/P. –
0 207 94634 5

In the same series:

A CITY OUT OF SIGHT
Angus & Robertson, 1985, 143p. – O/P. –
0 207 14943 7

A group of children, involved in an air

crash, find themselves on an uninhabited island. Hoping for rescue, they must nevertheless set about surviving. Tense and absorbing, the story is realistically convincing.
Age range: 12–14

Other publications:

CHRISTMAS IN THE TREE
Hodder, 1986. – O/P. – 0 340 36903 5
GOLDEN GOOSE
Methuen, 1981. – O/P. – 0 416 21360 X
HEAD IN THE CLOUDS
Angus & R, 1972. – O/P. – 0 207 95448 8
KING OF THE STICKS
Penguin, 1981. – Pbk. – O/P. – 0 14 031395 8
LONG NIGHT WATCH
Magnet Books, 1985. – Pbk. – O/P. – 0 416 51900 8
MATT AND JO
Angus & R, 1974. – O/P. – 0 207 95507 7
OVER THE TOP
Mammoth, 1992. – Pbk. – 0 7497 1227 9
SEVENTEEN SECONDS
Hodder, 1977. – Pbk. – O/P. – 0 340 20132 0
SLY OLD WARDROBE
Hodder, 1974. – O/P. – 0 340 18239 3
WHAT ABOUT TOMORROW?
Penguin, 1980. – Pbk. – 0 14 005420 0

STRACHAN, Ian

British. Born Altrincham, Cheshire, 1938. Educated Altrincham County Grammar School; Royal Academy of Dramatic Art. Married Jo Elizabeth Morris, one son, one daughter. Stage director, BBC producer, presenter in Theatre, Radio and Television, writer.

Address: West View,
Fair Oak,
Eccleshall,
Staffordshire ST21 6NT,
England

Agent: Caroline Sheldon Literary Agency,
71 Hillgate Place,
London W8 7SS,
England

A capable author whose successive books are increasingly striking and absorbing. He chooses themes which may not immediately appeal to children, but once started, the books will not be put down until finished.

BANG! BANG! YOU'RE DEAD
Methuen, 1988, 96p. – 0 416 05182 0
illustrated by Paul Wright

Two children are held at gunpoint in their own home by a thief looking for the money he hid there some time ago. Very exciting, but believable at the same time.
Age range: 10–12

THE FLAWED GLASS
Mammoth, 1990, 288p. – Pbk. – 0 7497 0151 X

A remarkable story, told with extreme sensitivity. Shona, an islander, is severely disabled, and because she cannot easily communicate, is often disregarded. The arrival of the American businessman finally results in releasing the Shona who has been imprisoned within her for so many years. A very moving ending.
Age range: 12–14

JOURNEY OF 1000 MILES
Mammoth, 1991, 142p. – Pbk. – 0 7497 0656 2

The very human story that lies behind a news headline for a day or two, and is then mostly forgotten. Lee, together with the rest of his family, flee from Vietnam crammed into a rickety fishing boat, which is itself a hazard. If the patrols or the pirates don't get them, hunger and thirst will. Packed with incidents, exciting and yet sad, it is a book that lingers in the memory.
Age range: 10–12

THE SECOND STEP
Mammoth, 1992, 128p. – Pbk. – 0 7497 0961 8
Methuen, 1991, 160p. – O/P. – 0 416 16152 9

Lee feels that life must have more to offer than the restricted life of the camp. For the second time, he sets off

on a journey which this time ends on a thoroughly happy note. A moving description of life in exile.
Age range: 10–12

THROWAWAYS
Methuen, 1992, 160p. – 0 416 18882 6

Ian Strachan has a great affinity with children who are outcast in society, for whatever reason. This book is dedicated to the hundreds of street children who live appallingly deprived lives. It is harrowing in parts, but also pays tribute to the courage and resilience shown by the young. A powerful story with a lesson for everyone.
Age range: 12+

THE UPSIDE-DOWN WORLD OF GINGER NUTT
Methuen, 1992, 128p. – 0 416 18608 4

Readers will be delighted to make the acquaintance of Ginger – energetic and full of ideas. This is a refreshingly light-hearted novel with lots of humour.
Age range: 9–12

WAYNE LOVES CUSTARD
Mammoth, 1992, 111p. – Pbk. – 0 7497 1039 X
Methuen, 1990, 128p. – O/P. – 0 416 15022 5

Wayne finds he has to stand his ground in his aunt's house if he is to escape the unreasonable limits imposed on him. He is pleased to meet Custard, who does not feel at all bound by rules. As they struggle to make Wayne's raft a reality, they learn a lot about human nature. Excellent characterization.
Age range: 11–13

Other publications:
BOY IN THE BUBBLE
Methuen, 1993. – 0 416 18739 0
FERRYMAN'S SON
Hippo Books, 1990. – Pbk. – 0 590 76279 6
MOSES BEECH
Penguin, 1990. – Pbk. – 0 14 032560 3
PEBBLE ON THE BEACH
Mammoth, 1991. – Pbk. – 0 7497 0764 X

PICKING UP THE THREADS
Hippo Books, 1989. – Pbk. – 0 590 76169 2
SOUTAR RETROSPECTIVE
OUP, 1982. – O/P. – 0 19 271464 3

SUTCLIFF, Rosemary

British. Born West Clandon, Surrey, 1920. Died 1992. Educated Bideford School of Art, Devon. Member of the Royal Society of Miniature Painters. Writer.

Awards: Library Association Carnegie Medal: *The Lantern Bearers*, 1959

Boston Globe-Horn Book Award: *Tristan and Iseult*, 1972

Order of the British Empire, 1975

Children's Rights Workshop Other Award: *Song for a dark queen*, 1978

Fellow of the Royal Society of Literature, 1982

Catholic Library Association Phoenix Award, 1988

Undoubtedly the queen of children's historical fiction, she was renowned for her painstaking research into whatever period she chose to write about. Her novels are by no means easy to read, requiring a good reading ability, but they are exciting and absorbing, if children can only be persuaded to try them. Although not intrusive, each book contains a strong moral sense of right and wrong, a lesson which is to be welcomed.

Rosemary Sutcliff completed about fifty books – only a few of her best are reviewed here. Some are currently out of print, but perhaps her recent death will persuade publishers to re-issue them.

SUTCLIFF

DAWN WIND
Penguin, 1982, 304p. – Pbk. – 0 14 031223 4

The period is the sixth century, and Britain has just been defeated and overrun by the Saxon hordes. Owain, left for dead, begins his journey north with a war-hound for company. Dejected and self-pitying, he is disinclined to accept human company, but Regina is even worse off. Slowly they overcome their mutual mistrust and become close friends, until Regina's illness forces Owain to make the biggest sacrifice of his life.

Unfamiliar Roman and Saxon names can form a barrier to the enjoyment of this stirring tale, but with a small amount of perseverance, they become familiar.
Age range: 11–13

HIGH DEEDS OF FINN MACCOOL
Red Fox, 1992, 206p. – Pbk. – 0 09 997940 3
Penguin, 1968, 192p. – Pbk. – O/P. – 0 14 030380 4

Set in Ireland, the story of Finn MacCool and the grey dog, which has become a legend, is told in a way that makes the old ways live again for the young readers of today.
Age range: 11–13

OUTCAST
Penguin, 1984, 240p. – Pbk. – 0 14 031715 5
OUP, 1980, 240p. – 0 19 277106 X

A story of Roman Britain in which courage is paramount. Beric, adopted into an English clan as a baby, is cast out because of his Roman origins. His agony in exile lasts for so many years that, when he finally finds a home, he feels he cannot shake off the conviction that he is an outcast for ever.
Age range: 11–13

EAGLE OF THE NINTH
Windrush, 1988, 362p. – L/P. – O/P. – 1 8508 9937 1
OUP, 1980, – 264p. O/P. – 0 19 277102 7
Penguin, 1977, 304p. – Pbk. – 0 14 030890 3

In the same series:

SILVER BRANCH
Penguin, 1980, 240p. – Pbk. – 0 14 031221 8
OUP, 1979, 224p. – O/P. – 0 19 277088 8

THE LANTERN BEARERS
Penguin, 1981, 272p. – Pbk. – 0 14 031222 6
OUP, 1979, 254p. – O/P. – 0 19 277082 9
illustrated by Charles Keeping

An excellent trilogy, set in Roman Britain, which tells the story of the doomed Ninth Legion, resurrected when Cullen finds a battered Eagle. Besides being a thrilling adventure story, the books give a real sense of life in Britain as Rome begins to fall.
Age range: 11–13

SWORD AND THE CIRCLE
Red Fox, 1992, 272p. – Pbk. – 0 09 997460 6
Bodley Head, 1981, 256p. – O/P. – 0 370 30387 3

In the same series:

LIGHT BEYOND THE FOREST
Red Fox, 1992, 156p. – Pbk. – 0 09 997450 9
Bodley Head, 1979, 160p. – O/P. – 0 370 30191 9

ROAD TO CAMLANN
Red Fox, 1992, 144p. – Pbk. – 0 09 997930 6
Bodley Head, 1981, 160p. – O/P. – 0 370 30384 9

Three books telling Rosemary Sutcliff's version of King Arthur and his Knights. She faithfully recounts the old legends, but brings a different slant to them. She believed that King Arthur was more than a legend, but also a war leader engaged in battle against the marauding Saxons.
Age range: 12+

TRISTAN AND ISEULT
Red Fox, 1991, 144p. – Pbk. – 0 09 979550 7
Bodley Head, 1971, 136p. – O/P. – 0 370 01257 7

A re-telling of the old Celtic legend in which Tristan falls in love with the lady he is bringing home to marry the king.

Their love is doomed, and ends in tragedy.
Age range: 12+

WITCH'S BRAT
Red Fox, 1990, 144p. – Pbk. – 0 09 975080 5
Bodley Head, 1986, 126p. – Pbk. – O/P. – 0 370 31002 0

The book opens with a vivid description of the anger and hatred people feel towards Lovel simply because he is a hunch-back. The path that takes him from danger to a fulfilling life as a healer in St. Bartholomew's hospital is utterly absorbing.
Age range: 10–12

Other publications:

ARMOURER'S HOUSE
Magnet Books, 1983. – Pbk. – O/P. – 0 416 25160 9
BLACK SHIPS BEFORE TROY
F. Lincoln, 1993. – 0 7112 0778 X
BLOOD FEUD
Penguin, 1978. – Pbk. – O/P. – 0 14 031085 1
BONNIE DUNDEE
Penguin, 1985. – Pbk. – 0 14 031721 X
BROTHER DUSTY-FEET
OUP, 1979. – O/P. – 0 19 271444 9
CAPRICORN BRACELET
Red Fox, 1990. – Pbk. – 0 09 977620 0
CHANGELING
H. Hamilton, 1974. – O/P. – 0 241 89019 5
CHESS-DREAM IN A GARDEN
Walker Books, 1993. – 0 7445 2282 X
CHIEF'S DAUGHTER
Pan Books, 1978. – Pbk. – O/P. – 0 330 25446 4
CIRCLET OF OAK LEAVES
Hamlyn, 1982. – Pbk. – O/P. – 0 600 20470 7
DRAGON SLAYER : STORY OF BEOWULF
Red Fox, 1992. – Pbk. – 0 09 997270 0
EAGLE'S EGG
Hamlyn, 1982. – Pbk. – O/P. – 0 600 20471 5
FLAME COLOURED TAFFETA
Penguin, 1989. – Pbk. – 0 14 034030 0
FRONTIER WOLF
Penguin, 1984. – Pbk. – 0 14 031472 5
HOUND OF ULSTER
Red Fox, 1992. – Pbk. – 0 09 997260 3
KNIGHT'S FEE
Red Fox, 1990. – Pbk. – 0 09 977630 8
LITTLE DOG LIKE YOU
Orchard Books, 1987. – 1 8521 3112 8
LITTLE HOUND FOUND
H. Hamilton, 1989. – 0 241 12505 7
MARK OF THE HORSE LORD
Penguin, 1983. – Pbk. – O/P. – 0 14 031473 3
MINSTREL AND THE DRAGON PUP
Walker Books, 1993. – 0 7445 2174 2
ROUNDABOUT HORSE
H. Hamilton, 1986. – 0 241 11731 3
SHIELD RING
Penguin, 1992. – Pbk. – 0 14 034969 3
SHIFTING SANDS
H. Hamilton, 1977. – O/P. – 0 241 89549 9
SHINING COMPANY
Red Fox, 1991. – Pbk. – 0 09 985580 1
SIMON
OUP, 1979. – O/P. – 0 19 271442 2
SONG FOR A DARK QUEEN
Hodder, 1980. – Pbk. – O/P. – 0 340 24864 5
SUN HORSE, MOON HORSE
Red Fox, 1991. – Pbk. – 0 09 979560 4
TRUCE OF THE GAMES
H. Hamilton, 1971. – O/P. – 0 241 02021 2
WARRIOR SCARLET
OUP, 1980. – O/P. – 0 19 277095 0
WE WENT TO LIVE IN DRUMFYVIE
Blackie, 1975. – O/P. – 0 216 89972 9

SWINDELLS, Robert (Edward)

British. Born Bradford, Yorkshire, 1939. Educated Huddersfield Polytechnic, Teaching Certificate; University of Bradford, M.A., Peace Studies. Royal Air Force, 1957–60. Married Brenda, 1980, 2nd marriage: two daughters from first marriage. Copywriter, advertising clerk, engineer, teacher, writer.

Awards: Children's Rights Workshop Other Award: *Brother in the Land*, 1984

Children's Book Award: *Brother in the Land*, 1984

Children's Book Award: *Room 13*, 1989

SWINDELLS

Address: 3 Upwood Park,
Blackmoor Road,
Oxenhope,
West Yorkshire BD22 9SS,
England

Agent: J. Luithcen,
88 Holmfirth Road,
Leicester,
England

A CANDLE IN THE DARK
*Firecrest Publications, 1987, 136p. –
0 85997 698 X
Hodder, 1983, 144p. – Pbk. O/P. –
0 340 32098 2
illustrated by Gareth Floyd*

Jimmy finds life in the pit hard, but when he discovers that a man is being kept a prisoner, his own life is also put at risk.
Age range: 10–12

DRACULA'S CASTLE
*Yearling, 1991, 80p. – Pbk. – 0 440 86278 7
Doubleday, 1990, 62p. – 0 385 40023 3
illustrated by Jon Riley*

When Marvin walks up the drive of the big, empty old house nicknamed 'Dracula's Castle', and fails to turn up at school, his classmates fear the worst. A slight story, published in extra large print with lots of bold illustrations to encourage children.
Age range: 7–9

THE GHOST MESSENGERS
*Hodder, 1988, 96p. – Pbk. – 0 340 48668 6
Collins, 1988, 128p. – 0 00 330036 6*

Meg finds her school work is suffering as her sleep is disturbed by the ghost of her grandfather who keeps trying to tell her something. Easy to read.
Age range: 10–12

HYDRA
*Yearling, 1993, 208p. – Pbk. – 0 440 86313 9
Doubleday, 1991, 169p. – 0 385 40151 5
illustrated by Mark Robertson*

Easy to read and an interesting subject – this is a highly suitable volume for reluctant reads. Ben and Midge have trouble believing what they discover at Cansfield Farm. How can they convince anyone with influence that these weird creatures exist and how evil they are? A good mixture of horror, fantasy and humour.
Age range: 10–12

THE ICE PALACE
*Penguin, 1992, 96p. – Pbk. – 0 14 034966 9
Hamish Hamilton, 1977, 96p. – O/P. –
0 241 89614 2
illustrated by June Jackson*

Storjik the childtaker steals Ivan's brother, but Ivan is determined to be brave and to rescue him. Easy to read, with very large print, and quite short.
Age range: 7–9

In the same series:

INSIDE THE WORM
*Doubleday, 1993, 160p. – 0 385 40307 0
illustrated by Jon Riley*

ROOM 13
*Chivers Press, 1991, 192p. – O/P. –
0 7451 1371 0
Yearling, 1990, 160p. – Pbk. – 0 440 86227 2
Doubleday, 1989, 160p. – 0 385 26967 6*

Both contain a similar mixture of horror and humour with a satisfactory build-up of tension before the thrilling climax. Easy to read.
Age range: 10–12

THE OUTFIT

THE SECRET OF WEEPING WOOD
*Deutsch, 1993, 128p. – 0 590 54086 6
Hippo Books, 1994, 128p. – Pbk. –
0 590 55658 4*

WE DIDN'T MEAN TO, HONEST!
*Deutsch, 1993, 128p. – 0 590 54100 5
Hippo Books, 1994, 128p. – Pbk. –
0 590 55659 2
both illustrated by Carolyn Dinan*

Written along the lines of Enid Blyton's 'Famous Five', it remains to be seen how popular they will be with children. Not very demanding, with clear print, lots of illustrations, and lots of action.
Age range: 7–9

THE SERPENT'S TOOTH
Penguin, 1990, 144p. – Pbk. – 0 14 034017 3
Hamish Hamilton, 1988, 160p. – 0 241 12207 4

Many issues are touched upon in this highly readable and enjoyable novel. Lucy, just entering her 'teens', is at odds with her parents and their views, but feels at ease with 'daft Alice'. She is pleased when heart-throb Tim Ogden asks her to a party, but is typically disappointed when she gets there. She can't decide just where she stands on the issue of a nuclear waste disposal site.
Age range: 12–14

THE SIEGE OF FRIMLY PRIM
Methuen, 1993, 96p. – 0 416 18671 8
illustrated by Scoular Anderson

A very funny story centred around a serious issue. No-one wants the village school to close, so they organize the usual protests, including sit-ins. Their triumph against all the odds is intended to give hope to all campaigns for right against might.
Age range: 8–10

THE THOUSAND EYES OF NIGHT
Yearling, 1993, 160p. – Pbk. – 0 440 86316 3
Hodder, 1985, 120p. – O/P. – 0 340 35389 9

Little out-of-the-ordinary events are one thing, but a big one, like finding a dead man, is quite a different matter. As the children slowly make the connections the tension builds up to reach a nail-biting climax.
Age range: 10–12

TIM KIPPER
Macmillan, 1992, 32p. – Pbk. – 0 333 56612 2
illustrated by Scoular Anderson

Although produced in picture book format, the aim is to show children the folly of smoking, and it can, therefore, be used with a variety of age groups. It is witty, rhymes, and the illustrations are full of humour.
Age range: 6+

WHEN DARKNESS COMES
Hodder, 1993, 160p. – Pbk. – 0 340 58228 6
Hodder, 1973, 160p. – O/P. – 0 340 17506 0

A primitive tribe is torn apart by jealousy and thwarted ambition. The children are saddened at being separated from their friends, and plot together to re-unite them. Only when an outside danger threatens are they able to forget their differences and work together. A surprising ending.
Age range: 11–13

WORLD-EATER
Hodder, 1983, 112p. – Pbk. O/P. –
0 340 32884 3
Hodder, 1981, 104p. – O/P. – 0 340 26576 0

Orville's overriding interest is his pigeons, but even they take second place as the discovery of a new planet is revealed. Slowly the reader realizes just how badly the planet's existence will affect the world. Quite compelling, yet not too demanding.
Age range: 10–12

Other publications:

BROTHER IN THE LAND
Penguin, 1988. – Pbk. – 0 14 032670 7
DAZ 4 ZOE
Penguin, 1992. – Pbk. – 0 14 034320 2
DRAGONS LIVE FOREVER
Hodder, 1978. – O/P. – 0 340 22769 9
FOLLOW A SHADOW
Penguin, 1991. – Pbk. – 0 14 034016 5
GHOST SHIP TO GANYMEDE
Arnold-Wheaton, 1980. – O/P. – 0 08 025007 6
GO-AHEAD GANG
H. Hamilton, 1992. – 0 241 13141 3
MAVIS DAVIS
OUP, 1988. – 0 19 278213 4
MOONPATH AND OTHER STORIES
Arnold-Wheaton, 1979. – O/P. – 0 08 022903 4
NIGHT SCHOOL
Paperbird, 1989. – Pbk. – 1 8554 3003 7
NORAH AND THE WHALE
Arnold-Wheaton, 1981. – O/P. – 0 08 024980 9
NORAH TO THE RESCUE
Wheaton, 1981. – 0 08 024979 5

SWINDELLS

NORAH'S ARK
Wheaton, 1979. – O/P. – 0 08 024177 8

NORAH'S SHARK
Wheaton, 1979. – O/P. – 0 08 024178 6

POSTBOX MYSTERY
Yearling, 1991. – Pbk. – 0 440 86275 2

ROLF AND ROSIE
Red Fox, 1993. – Pbk. – 0 09 995610 1

SAM AND SUE AND LAVATORY LUE
Simon & Schuster, 1993. – 0 7500 1335 4

STAYING UP
Corgi, 1990. – Pbk. – 0 552 52503 0

VERY SPECIAL BABY
Hodder, 1977. – O/P. – 0 340 21623 9

VOYAGE TO VALHALLA
Hodder, 1976. – O/P. – 0 340 20695 0

THE WEATHER-CLERK
Hodder, 1983. – Pbk. – O/P. – 0 340 34619 1

YOU CAN'T SAY I'M CRAZY
H. Hamilton, 1992. – 0 241 13140 5

T

TAYLOR, Mildred D.

American. Born Jackson, Mississippi, 1943. Educated at schools in Toledo, Ohio; University of Toledo; University of Colorado School of Journalism, M.A. Teacher, study skills coordinator, office worker, writer.

Awards: American Library Association Newbery Medal: *Roll of thunder, hear my cry*, 1977
Coretta Scott King Award: *Let the circle be unbroken*, 1982
Buxtehude Bulle Prize (Germany), 1985
Coretta Scott King Award: *The Friendship*, 1988
Boston Globe-Horn Book Award: *The Friendship*, 1988
Children's Book Council Award: *The Friendship*, 1988

Address: C/o Dial Press,
1 Dag Hammerskjold Place,
New York,
NY 10017,
USA

The power of this author's writing stems in part from the fact that she is recounting her own experiences.

THE FRIENDSHIP, AND OTHER STORIES
Penguin, 1991, 96p, – Pbk. – 0 14 034615 5
Gollancz, 1989, 96p, – 0 575 04495 0

Three extremely powerful stories, demonstrating the difficulties experienced by black children in America around the time of World War II. It vividly shows the harm that prejudice almost automatically causes.
Age range: 11+

Other publications:

LET THE CIRCLE BE UNBROKEN
Penguin, 1988, 320p. – Pbk. – 0 14 032558 1
ROAD TO MEMPHIS
Penguin, 1992, 304p. – Pbk. – 0 14 034806 9
ROLL OF THUNDER, HEAR MY CRY
Cornerstone Books, US, 1990, 304p. – O/P. – 1 55736 140 1

THOMAS, Ruth

British. Born Wellington, Somerset, 1927. Educated Bristol University, BA (Hons) English. Divorced, one son.

Awards: Guardian Children's Fiction Award: *The Runaways*, 1988

Address: 113 Wakeman Road,
Kensal Green,
London NW10 5BH,
England

A comparative newcomer to children's literature, Ruth Thomas appears to have found a recipe for success. Lots of action, realistic children, and events described in a direct way, that readers can relate to.

THE CLASS THAT WENT WILD
Beaver Books, 1989, 224p. – Pbk. –
0 09 963210 1
Hutchinson, 1988, 226p. – 0 09 173618 8

Class 4L are not best pleased when their teacher leaves to have a baby, and they refuse to behave for the constant supply of temporary teachers. Gillian is really worried about her brother, but his disappearance brings matters to a head.
Age range: 11–13

GUILTY!
Hutchinson, 1993, 246p. – 0 09 176426 2

A multi-layered book, set in inner London, with all that implies. Firstly, there is an exciting plot – Desmond's Dad has been accused of stealing, so Kaye helps Desmond to prove his dad's innocence. Secondly, there is an

excellent example of friendship and loyalty. Thirdly, there is stark reality to cope with when they discover who the thief is, and have to come to terms with unwelcome knowledge.
Age range: 10–12

THE NEW BOY
Red Fox, 1990, 264p. – Pbk. – 0 09 973410 9
Hutchinson, 1989, 264p. – 0 09 173799 0

Donovan, newly arrived in class, is a disruptive influence. Fights begin, things are stolen, but Amy defends him and helps him until he needs to be hidden. Then she must make her own decision.
Age range: 11–13

THE RUNAWAYS
Beaver Books, 1988, 256p. – Pbk. –
0 09 959660 1
Hutchinson, 1987, 252p. – 0 09 172633 6

Unpopular children always feel sure that money will buy popularity, so when Julia and Nathan find a substantial amount, they decide to use it for this purpose. But questions are asked, until they become afraid and run away.
Age range: 11–13

THE SECRET
Red Fox, 1991, 250p. – Pbk. – 0 09 984000 6
Hutchinson, 1990, 246p. – 0 09 176341 X

Left at home on their own, and with time passing, Nicky and Roy become anxious when their mother fails to return. Afraid of what will happen if they betray her, they try to cope with the problems. Not very plausible, but young readers will undoubtedly overlook the faults in construction in their enjoyment of the plot.
Age range: 9–12

TOMLINSON, Theresa

British. Born Crawley, 1946. Educated St. Hilda's School, Whitby; Kingston-upon-Hull College of Education. Married Alan Tomlinson, one daughter, two sons. Writer.

Address: 65 Hastings Road,
Sheffield S7 2GT,
England

Theresa Tomlinson possesses a unique gift – an ability to take historical facts and merge them into an exciting fictional story in such a way that the characters and settings come vividly to life. She brings a new dimension to historical fiction by illustrating some of them with photographs. She writes with compassion and obvious feeling for both the real-life and fictional characters.

FLITHER PICKERS
Walker Books, 1992, 96p. – Pbk. –
0 7445 2043 6
J. MacRae Books, 1990, 96p. – 0 86203 450 7

Dedicated to the fishing families of the North east where the author grew up, it tells the story of how fisher-folk had to live in Victorian times. Life was hard, but the women were hardy and brave, and succeeded on one occasion in launching the lifeboat.
Age range: 11–13

FORESTWIFE
J. MacRae, 1993, 166p. – 1 85681 193 X

Basically the story of Maid Marion and the struggle she has in coming to terms with life in the forest where she eventually finds more than the friendship she first sought. A new side of this famous heroine.
Age range: 11–13

RIDING THE WAVES
Walker Books, 1992, 112p. – Pbk. –
0 7445 2312 5
J. MacRae Books, 1990, 112p. – 0 86203 476 0

Matt spends hours longingly watching his heroes, the surfers, just waiting until he is old enough to join them. Meanwhile, he has to interview Florrie for his history project. Through her, he learns how to cope with the difficulties

that come to everyone at some time. Authentic and moving.
Age range: 11–13

THE ROPE CARRIER
Walker Books, 1994, 128p. – Pbk. –
0 7445 3604 9
J. MacRae, 1991, 128p. – 1 85681 241 3

The rope carriers lived underground, and the story concerns Minnie and Netty and their life at the start of the Industrial Revolution. The story is harsh and uncompromising, giving children a flavour of what life could be like. Enjoyable and educational, the illustrations consist of contemporary engravings.
Age range: 11–13

THE SECRET PLACE
Walker Books, 1990, 96p. – Pbk. –
0 7445 1486 X

This was first published under the title *Summer witches*. It tells how two friends make their den in a disused air-raid shelter which was once a secret meeting place for two other girls, now old ladies. Their lives are intertwined, and the old ladies benefit enormously.
Age range: 9–11

THE WATER CAT
Walker Books, 1989, 128p. – Pbk. –
0 7445 1399 5
J. MacRae Books, 1988, 128p. – O/P. –
0 86203 367 5
illustrated by Paul Leith

Newly arrived in the village, Jane and Tom find a strange water cat while exploring. It proves to be a link with the past and the disaster which had threatened the village. Very readable, though not attractively produced.
Age range: 10–12

Other publications:
HERRING GIRLS
J. MacRae, 1994, 160p. – 1 85681 169 7
SUMMER WITCHES
J. MacRae Books, 1989, 96p. – O/P. –
0 86203 373 X

TOWNSEND, John Rowe

British. Born Leeds, West Yorkshire, 1922. Educated Leeds Grammar School; Emmanuel College, Cambridge, B.A., M.A. Royal Air Force, WW II. Married Vera Lancaster, 1948, two daughters, one son. Reporter, editor, lecturer.

Awards: Boston Globe-Horn Award: *The Intruder*, 1970
Address: 72 Water Lane, Cambridge CB4 4LR, England

Almost a household word in the realm of children's literature, John Rowe Townsend has not only written successfully for many years, but he has also made a substantial contribution to the reviewing of children's books. He is particularly successful in writing for teenagers, but his books for younger children are also popular. His male characters are always well drawn, giving them special appeal to boys.

DAN ALONE
Penguin, 1985, 192p. – Pbk. O/P. –
0 14 031626 4
Kestrel Books, 1983, 176p. – O/P. –
0 7226 5812 5

Dan's young life has been a nightmare; deserted by his alcoholic father, then by his mother who cannot cope alone, he has to go to relatives who do not want him. He decides to run away and live rough, which leads him to Leo who is not all he seems. Dan finds he can no longer hold on to his dream of belonging to a family. Realistic, with a finely constructed ending.
Age range: 12–14

GUMBLE'S YARD
Penguin, 1985, 128p. – Pbk. – 0 14 031850 X
Viking Kestrel, 1984, 128p. – 0 670 80081 3

In the same series:

GOOD-BYE TO GUMBLE'S YARD
Penguin, 1987, 158p. – Pbk. – 0 14 031403 2

203

TOWNSEND

When Sandra and Keith are left on their own, they realize the authorities will put them into care, so they move into Gumble's Yard. Unknown to them, it is used by a gang of thieves, who make life uncomfortable for them. Fast-paced and exciting adventure stories.
Age range: 10–12

THE PERSUADING STICK
Penguin, 1988, 96p. – Pbk. O/P. –
0 14 032131 4
Viking Kestrel, 1986, 96p. – O/P. –
0 670 81170 X
illustrated by Pat Fogarty

Sarah realizes she needs help in making Beth and Katherine listen to her. Convinced the special stick she has found has magical powers, she puts it to the test with astonishing success. The way the real magic of the stick is revealed makes an excellent conclusion.
Age range: 9–11

ROB'S PLACE
Penguin, 1988, 176p. – Pbk. O/P. –
0 14 032318 X
Viking Kestrel, 1987, 176p. – 0 670 80998 5

Like Dan in *Dan Alone*, Rob is deserted by everyone he cares about. Finding reality unbearable, he begins to live in a fantasy world which gradually takes over in a frightening way, and he begins to fear he is going insane. A very powerful and sensitive story of a boy under stress.
Age range: 12–14

TOM TIDDLER'S GROUND
Chivers Press, 1987, 168p. – L/P. –
0 7451 0591 2
Penguin, 1987, 112p. – Pbk. O/P. –
0 14 031914 X
Viking Kestrel, 1985, 144p. – 0 670 80689 7
illustrated by Mark Peppe

This book is a straightforward adventure story, with none of the emotional drama that John Rowe Townsend excels at. A group of children find an old barge which they adopt as their den. When they discover an old horse-brass, it sets them off on a mysterious trail.
Age range: 9–11

THE XANADU MANUSCRIPT
Red Fox, 1990, 176p. – Pbk. – 0 09 975180 1
OUP, 1977, 176p. – O/P. – 0 19 271406 6

A fantastic yet convincing story of people coming from the future into the present day. The difficulties they experience are sometimes funny, sometimes sad. A gentle story that is thoroughly enjoyable.
Age range: 12–14

Other publications:

CLEVER DICK: THE DIARY OF A DREADFUL CHILD
OUP, 1982. – O/P. – 0 19 271462 7
CLOUDY-BRIGHT
Penguin, 1985. – Pbk. – O/P. – 0 14 031627 2
DOWNSTREAM
Walker Books, 1989. – Pbk. – 0 7445 0843 6
FOREIGN AFFAIR
Penguin, 1991. – Pbk. – 0 14 032787 8
FOREST OF THE NIGHT
OUP, 1974. – O/P. – 0 19 271368 X
GOLDEN JOURNEY
Penguin, 1990. – Pbk. – 0 14 032891 2
GONE TO THE DOGS
OUP, 1984. – 0 19 271471 6
GOOD-NIGHT, PROF. LOVE
Penguin, 1989. – Pbk. – O/P. – 0 14 032899 8
HALLERSAGE SOUND
Hutchinson, 1971. – O/P. – 0 09 108900 X
HELL'S EDGE
Hutchinson, 1970. – O/P. – 0 09 069851 7
THE INTRUDER
Red Fox, 1993. – Pbk. – 0 09 999260 4
THE INVADERS
OUP, 1992. – O/P. – 0 19 271681 6
THE ISLANDERS
Penguin, 1983. – Pbk. – O/P. – 0 14 031478 4
KING CREATURE, COME
R Drew Pub, 1988. – Pbk. – O/P. –
0 86267 221 X
NOAH'S CASTLE
Penguin, 1988. – Pbk. – 0 14 032513 1
PIRATE'S ISLAND
OUP, 1980. – O/P. – 0 19 277107 8

SAM AND JENNY
Red Fox, 1992. – Pbk. – 0 09 984310 2

SOUNDING OF STORYTELLERS
Kestrel Books, 1979. – 0 7226 5599 1

THE SUMMER PEOPLE
OUP, 1972. – O/P. – 0 19 271346 9

TOP OF THE WORLD
Penguin, 1978. – Pbk. – 0 14 031096 7

WIDDERSHINS CRESCENT
Penguin, 1970. – Pbk. – 0 14 030422 3

WISH FOR WINGS
Heinemann, 1972. – O/P. – 0 434 94907 8

TOWNSON, Hazel

British. Born Nelson, Lancashire, 1928. Educated Accrington High School; Leeds University; Manchester Polytechnic, B.A.; Associate of the Library Association. Married Kenneth Smith (now dead), one son, one daughter. Librarian, writer.

Address: 53 Prestwich Hills,
            Prestwich,
            Manchester M25 9PY,
            England

For a good, light-hearted, entertaining read, Hazel Townson is hard to beat. There are lots of stories, all with original plots, full of humour, with good illustrations – fun to read. Many of her books are illustrated by Tony Ross; they make an excellent combination.

THE BARLEY SUGAR GHOSTS
Red Fox, 1990, 96p. – Pbk. – 0 09 975990 X
Hodder, 1976, 96p. – O/P. – 0 340 20291 2
illustrated by Val Biro

When Nell discovers she has sold her Gran's tin containing her valuables to Black Logan, she sets off to recover it. A recipe for hilarious misadventure.
Age range: 8–10

THE CRIMSON CRESCENT
Beaver Books, 1987, 80p. – Pbk. –
0 09 952110 5
Andersen Press, 1986, 80p. – 0 86264 130 6

In the same series:

FIREWORKS GALORE
Beaver Books, 1989, 88p. – Pbk. –
0 09 965540 3
Andersen Press, 1988, 80p. – 0 86264 214 0

THE GREAT ICE-CREAM CRIME
Red Fox, 1990, 80p. – Pbk. – 0 09 976000 2
Beaver Books, 1986, 80p. – Pbk. –
0 09 948640 7
Andersen Press, 1981, 72p. – 0 86264 005 9

HAUNTED IVY
Beaver Books, 1986, 80p. – Pbk. –
0 09 941320 5
Andersen Press, 1984, 80p. – 0 86264 082 2

THE SIEGE OF COBB STREET SCHOOL
Red Fox, 1990, 80p. – Pbk. – 0 09 975980 2
Andersen Press, 1983, 64p. – 0 86264 041 5

THE STAGGERING SNOWMAN
Beaver Books, 1988, 80p. – Pbk. –
0 09 956820 9
Andersen Press, 1987, 80p. – 0 86264 181 0

THE VANISHING GRAN
Beaver Books, 1985, 80p. – Pbk. –
0 09 935480 2
Andersen Press, 1983, 72p. – 0 86264 058 X
all illustrated by Philippe Dupasquier

WALNUT WHIRL
Red Fox, 1990, 80p. – Pbk. – 0 09 973380 3
Andersen Press, 1989, 80p. – 0 86264 246 9

Adventure stories for younger readers. Racy and humorous, these books feature Lenny and Jake, amateur sleuths who always solve their mysteries.
Age range: 8–10

DANNY – DON'T JUMP
Beaver Books, 1987, 80p. – Pbk. –
0 09 946290 7
Andersen Press, 1985, 80p. – 0 86264 112 8
illustrated by Amelia Rosato

There is a good reason for the accident-prone Danny being on the roof. Discovering what the reason is provides the reader with the usual exciting and funny story.
Age range: 8–10

THE MOVING STATUE
*Beaver Books, 1990, 64p. – Pbk. –
0 09 973370 6
Andersen Press, 1989, 72p. – 0 86264 243 4
illustrated by Shelagh McNicholas*

The issue at stake in this story is whether or not the statue moved. Even those who did not see it swear they did. An easy and entertaining read.
Age range: 7–9

ONE GREEN BOTTLE
*Andersen Press, 1987, 56p. – 0 86264 164 0
illustrated by David McKee*

Tim hopes to make his fortune with his new board-game. He cannot believe it when it disappears. A most engaging story.
Age range: 8–10

PILKIE'S PROGRESS
*Beaver Books, 1988, 64p. – Pbk. – 0 09 956360 6
Andersen Press, 1986, 80p. – 0 86264 149 7
illustrated by Tony Ross*

Benny Pilkington, alias Pilkie, explodes the 'test your heart' machine. He convinces himself he is dying.
Age range: 8–10

THE SHRIEKING FACE
*Beaver Books, 1986, 90p. – Pbk. – 0 09 941310 8
Andersen Press, 1984, 94p. – 0 86264 065 2
illustrated by Tony Ross*

An intriguing title for an unusual story. Angus wins a prize for his picture of a shrieking face, but the attendant publicity is not to his liking.
Age range: 8–10

THE SPECKLED PANIC
*Beaver Books, 1985, 78p. – Pbk. –
0 09 935490 X
Andersen Press, 1982, 76p. – 0 86264 031 8*

In the same series:

THE CHOKING PERIL
*Beaver Books, 1987, 80p. – Pbk. –
0 09 950530 4
Andersen Press, 1985, 72p. – 0 86264 093 8
illustrated by David McKee*

Both books feature Kip and Herbie and are fast and funny. The first involves their headmaster and some toothpaste, while the second addresses the problem of litter.
Age range: 8–10

VICTOR'S PARTY
*Red Fox, 1991, 96p. – Pbk. – 0 09 973390 0
Andersen Press, 1990, 80p. – 0 86264 276 0
illustrated by Tony Ross*

Victor hates parties, especially his own. First, not enough guests, then too many. One escapade swiftly follows another in this extremely funny book.
Age range: 8–10

WHO'S AFRAID OF THE EVIL EYE
*Andersen Press, 1993, 80p. – 0 86264 400 3
illustrated by David McKee*

Adam is superstitious, and when he sleepily puts on his left shoe before his right, he just knows the rest of the day is doomed. The things that go wrong provide endless amusement for the reader. Superbly humorous illustrations.
Age range: 7–9

Other publications:

AMOS SHRIKE, THE SCHOOL GHOST
Red Fox, 1991. – Pbk. – 0 09 979020 3
BLACK-STONE EYE
H. Hamilton, 1979. – O/P. – 0 241 10102 6
BLUE MAGIC
Red Fox, 1993. – Pbk. – 0 09 966870 X
CHARLIE, THE CHAMPION LIAR
Methuen, 1993. – 0 416 18733 1
DEATHWOOD LETTERS
Red Fox, 1991. – Pbk. – 0 09 983500 2
GARY WHO?
Beaver Books, 1989. – Pbk. – 0 09 965530 6
HOPPING MAD
Red Fox, 1992. – Pbk. – 0 09 910291 9
HOT STUFF
Red Fox, 1992. – Pbk. – 0 09 910301 X
JAM SPELL
H. Hamilton, 1977. – O/P. – 0 241 89569 3
KIDNAP REPORT
Red Fox, 1993. – Pbk. – 0 09 920691 9

LENNY AND JAKE ADVENTURES
Red Fox, 1991. – Pbk. – 0 09 991800 5
LOOKING FOR LOSSIE
Hodder, 1975. – O/P. – 0 340 18970 3
PEA-GREEN PIG
H. Hamilton, 1978. – O/P. – 0 241 89812 9
SCHOOL BOOK FAIR : 'SPECKLED PANIC' AND 'CHOKING PERIL'
Red Fox, 1992. – Pbk. – 0 09 922791 6
SECRETS OF CELIA
Red Fox, 1993. – Pbk. – 0 09 913851 4
SNAKES ALIVE
Red Fox, 1992. – Pbk. – 0 09 979030 0
TERRIBLE TUESDAY
Beaver Books, 1987. – Pbk. – O/P. – 0 09 942140 2
THROUGH THE WITCH'S WINDOW
Red Fox, 1990. – Pbk. – 0 09 966860 2
WHAT ON EARTH
Andersen Press, 1990. – 0 86264 282 5

TREASE, (Robert) Geoffrey

British. Born Nottingham, 1909. Educated Nottingham High School, 1920–28; Queen's College, Oxford (Scholar), 1928–29. British Army, 1942–1946. Married Marion Boyer, 1933, one daughter. Social worker, journalist, teacher, writer.

Awards: Fellow of the Royal Society of Literature, 1979

Address: 1 Yomede Park,
Newbridge Road,
Bath, BA1 3LS,
England

Agent: Murray Pollinger,
4 Garrick Street,
London WC2E 9BH,
England

One of the most prolific of writers for children, with over one hundred books to his credit. He is, first and foremost, a genuine, old fashioned story teller, whose ability to interest and excite readers has ensured that new generations of children are captured afresh.

ARPINO ASSIGNMENT
Walker Books, 1989, 224p. – Pbk. – 0 7445 1333 2
Walker Books, 1988, 224p. – 0 7445 0810 X

Geoffrey Trease's fascination with Winston Churchill's Special Operations Executive was the inspiration for this gripping tale of Rick Weston, who is parachuted into Italy to help the Resistance.
Age range: 12+

CALABRIAN QUEST
Walker Books, 1992, 208p. – Pbk. – 0 7445 2304 4
Walker Books, 1990, 208p. – 0 7445 1528 9

An archaeological adventure story which combines the thrill of the chase for lost treasure with sinister elements in the guise of the Mafia, and superstitious locals in the Italian village.
Age range: 12+

FIRE ON THE WIND
Pan Macmillan, 1993, 192p. – O/P. – 0 333 58568 2

The fire is the one that destroyed so much of London in 1666. The friendship between Hugh and Sarah blossoms against the common enemy. Authentic and enthralling.
Age range: 11–13

SHADOW UNDER THE SEA
Walker Books, 1991, 192p. – Pbk. – 0 7445 1450 9
Walker Books, 1990, 192p. – 0 7445 1527 0

An excellent combination of description of a new Russia liberated by 'glasnost' and 'perestroika' with a gripping mystery of smuggling. Also a hint of romance.
Age range: 12+

TOMORROW IS A STRANGER
Pan Books, 1989, 160p. – Pbk. – 0 330 30903 X
Heinemann, 1987, 156p. – O/P. – 0 434 96764 5

TREASE

Set in occupied Guernsey, it describes in vivid detail the lives of the few children who remained behind, and how they managed to cope when danger threatened. So authentic is the story that it makes an excellent introduction for children studying World War II.
Age range: 11–13

Other publications:

AUNT AUGUSTA'S ELEPHANT
Pan Books, 1992. – Pbk. – 0 330 32276 1
BARON'S HOSTAGE
Hodder, 1974. – Pbk. – O/P. – 0 340 17938 4
BOWS AGAINST THE BARONS
Hodder, 1973. – Pbk. – O/P. – 0 340 16380 1
CHOCOLATE BOY
Heinemann, 1975. – O/P. – 0 434 94913 2
CLAWS OF THE EAGLE
Heinemann, 1977. – O/P. – 0 434 94930 2
COMRADES FOR THE CHARTER
Hodder, 1972. – O/P. – 0 340 15836 0
CORMORANT VENTURE
Macmillan, 1984. – O/P. – 0 333 36073 7
CROWN OF VIOLET
Penguin, 1968. – Pbk. – O/P. – 0 14 030330 8
CUE FOR TREASON
J. Goodchild, 1986. – 0 86391 079 3
FLIGHT OF ANGELS
Piper, 1993. – Pbk. – 0 330 32581 7
FOLLOW MY BLACK PLUME
Penguin, 1972. – Pbk. – O/P. – 0 14 030514 9
HIDDEN TREASURE
Evans Brothers, 1992. – 0 237 60278 4
HILLS OF VARNA
Hodder, 1967. – Pbk. – O/P. – 0 340 03994 9
HORSEMAN ON THE HILLS
Macmillan, 1971. – O/P. – 0 333 12973 3
IRON TSAR
Pan Books, 1978. – Pbk. – O/P. – 0 330 25489 8
MANDEVILLE
Macmillan, 1980. – O/P. – 0 333 30574 4
MASQUE FOR THE QUEEN
H. Hamilton, 1970. – O/P. – 0 241 01872 2
POPINJAY MYSTERY
Piper, 1993. – Pbk. – 0 330 32703 8
POPINJAY STAIRS
Penguin, 1977. – Pbk. – O/P. – 0 14 030937 3
RED TOWERS OF GRANADA
Pan Macmillan, 1992. – Pbk. – 0 330 32628 7
RUNAWAY SERF
Pan Books, 1979. – Pbk. – O/P. – 0 330 25815 X
RUNNING OF THE DEER
H. Hamilton, 1982. – O/P. – 0 241 10789 X
SARABAND FOR SHADOWS
Macmillan, 1982. – O/P. – 0 333 32848 5
SEAS OF MORNING
Penguin, 1976. – Pbk. – O/P. – 0 14 030891 1
SHIP TO ROME
Heinemann, 1972. – O/P. – 0 434 94904 3
SONG FOR A TATTERED FLAG
Walker Books, 1993. – Pbk. – 0 7445 3082 2
SPYCATCHERS
H. Hamilton, 1976. – O/P. – 0 241 89420 4
VIOLET FOR BONAPARTE
Pan Books, 1978. – Pbk. – O/P. – 0 330 25490 1
VOICE IN THE NIGHT
Heinemann, 1973. – O/P. – 0 434 95870 0
WHEN THE DRUMS BEAT
Heinemann, 1976. – O/P. – 0 434 94919 1
WHITE NIGHTS OF ST. PETERSBURG
R Drew Pub, 1987. – Pbk. – O/P. – 0 86267, 196 5
WOOD BY MOONLIGHT AND OTHER STORIES
Chatto, 1981. – O/P. – 0 7011 2575 6

U

URE, Jean

Also writes as Sarah McCulloch. British. Born Caterham, Surrey, 1943. Educated Croydon High School, Surrey; Webber-Douglas Academy of Dramatic Art. Married Leonard Gregory, 1967. Full-time writer.

Awards: Lancashire County Library Children's Book of the Year Award: *Plague 99*, 1990

Address: 88 Southbridge Road, Croydon, Surrey CR0 1AF, England

Agent: Maggie Noach Agency, 21 Redan Street, London W14 0AB, England

A talented writer who has the ability in abundance to write compelling, often tense stories peopled by strong, sympathetic characters, and laced with a sense of humour. Her ear for dialogue is remarkable. A new novel by this author is always a cause for celebration. Excellent material for teenagers, but equally successful for younger readers.

A BOTTLED CHERRY ANGEL
Beaver Books, 1987, 151p. – Pbk. – 0 09 951370 6
Hutchinson, 1986, 144p. – 0 09 165280 4

A story for the 'in-betweens'. It concerns three friends of the same age but with different priorities in life. Two of them have begun to go to discos and to shop for clothes. The third, Midge, still enjoys playing with her dolls, and, above all, she hates boys. One day, out sledging by herself, she feels left out and lonely. She meets a boy, who, to her surprise, feels just as she does. Slowly, they both begin to change.
Age range: 11–13

COOL SIMON
Corgi, 1992, 176p. – Pbk. – 0 552 52707 6
Orchard Books, 1990, 192p. – 1 85213 186 1

Simon is deaf, and therefore speaks with an impediment. When he moves to a new school where the children are not used to him, they find they cannot easily understand what he is saying, and will not make any effort. Only Sam tries, and that is because she is full of tricks, and the other children in the class don't want her as a friend. A good read.
Age range: 9–11

DANCING DREAMS
The title of an intended dancing trilogy of which only the first book is published to date.

In the series:

STAR TURN
Hutchinson, 1993, 160p. – 0 09 176219 7

Making use of her own theatrical experience, as well as her inherent story-telling ability, this first book makes an exciting start with a mystery. Karen is very secretive about her ballet lessons, and Jessamy needs to find out why, for Karen's own sake.
Age range: 10–12

FRANKIE'S DAD
Beaver Books, 1989, 144p. – Pbk. – 0 09 959720 9
Hutchinson, 1988, 144p. – 0 09 173491 6

Frankie hates Billie Small, and is horrified to learn that her mother has agreed to marry him. Life becomes intolerable, for he is violent, and Jasper is too pathetic for words, so Frankie is on her own.
Age range: 11–13

URE

THE GHOST THAT LIVED ON THE HILL
Methuen, 1993, 64p. – 0 416 18695 5
illustrated by Ben Cort

A ghost story by such a talented author is certain to be unusual. Joe loves ghost stories, and hopes their new house will be haunted. The humour lies in the fact that it is – but Joe cannot see the ghost, in spite of its utmost efforts to be seen.
Age range: 7–9

HI THERE, SUPERMOUSE
Windrush, 1989, 150p. – L/P. – 1 85089 954 1
Penguin, 1985, 128p. – Pbk. – 0 14 031716 3
Hutchinson, 1983, 124p. – 0 09 152090 8
illustrated by Martin White

Sibling rivalry is the subject of this amusing story of family life. Rose is the talented one, who is expected to go far in the world of show business. Nicola, tall and gangly, has always rather resentfully taken a back seat, until the accident gives her a chance to shine.
Age range: 9–11

NICOLA MIMOSA
Penguin, 1986, 176p. – Pbk. – 0 14 032031 8
Hutchinson, 1985, 166p. – 0 09 160390 0
illustrated by Martin White

The sequel to *Hi there, Supermouse*, in which Nicola has to choose her future career.
Age range: 12+

MEGASTAR
Hippo Books, 1986, 128p. – Pbk. – 0 590 70529 6
Blackie, 1985, 112p. – O/P. – 0 216 91700 X

Jason wants to be an actor, but his command of standard English leaves much to be desired. When the Community Arts Festival decides to make a local video, he seizes the chance to be in it, hoping it will lead to other opportunities.
Age range: 10–12

PETER HIGH SERIES
In the same series:
JO IN THE MIDDLE
Red Fox, 1992, 184p. – Pbk. – 0 09 997730 3
Hutchinson, 1990, 160p. – 0 09 173600 5
FAT LOLLIPOP
Red Fox, 1992, 151p. – Pbk. – 0 09 997740 0
Hutchinson, 1991, 151p. – 0 09 176356 8
BOSSY BOOTS
Red Fox, 1993, 168p. – Pbk. – 0 09 960790 5
Hutchinson, 1991, 172p. – 0 09 176390 8
JAM TODAY
Red Fox, 1993, 192p. – Pbk. – 0 09 960800 6
Hutchinson, 1992, 160p. – 0 09 171950 X
MATCH MAKERS
Red Fox, 1993, 192p. – Pbk. – 0 09 999040 7
Hutchinson, 1992, 154p. – 0 09 176417 3

The setting is a girl's comprehensive school. The stories are varied, while their strength lies in the realistic dialogue and the convincing portrayal of the ebb and flow of school life.
Age range: 11+

SEVEN FOR A SECRET
Blackie, 1993, 128p. – 0 216 93285 8

This book highlights one of Jean Ure's main concerns – animal rights. She puts her point of view very forcefully, while using the kidnapping of Penny by an animal rights group to demonstrate the other side of the argument. The reader is made to think about the rights and wrongs of animal experiments.
Age range: 10–12

TEA-LEAF ON THE ROOF
Windrush, 1989, 158p. – L/P. – 1 85089 965 7
Blackie, 1987, 112p. – 0 216 92112 0
illustrated by Val Sassoon

In the same series:
WILLIAM IN LOVE
Puffin Books, 1993, 112p. – Pbk. – 0 14 036128 6
Blackie, 1991, 96p. – 0 216 93103 7

William is sure he can track down the burglar who is stealing lead from the roofs of houses in his street. It proves

less easy than he expected. In the second volume, William decides it is time he fell in love. The trouble is, Charlotte does not seem to realise it, or reciprocate his feelings. Very much tongue-in-cheek humour.
Age range: 9–11

WAR WITH OLD MOULDY
Mammoth, 1989, 112p. – Pbk. – 0 7497 0015 7
Methuen, 1987, 128p. – 0 416 00262 5
illustrated by Alice Englander

Jody leads the campaign to rid the school of Old Mouldy. The battle commences, with hilarious results.
Age range: 9–11

WIZARD IN THE WOODS
Walker Books, 1991, 176p. – Pbk. –
0 7445 1717 6
Walker Books, 1990, 176p. – 0 7445 1530 0

WIZARD IN WONDERLAND
Walker Books, 1992, 176p. – Pbk. –
0 7445 2341 9
Walker Books, 1991, 176p. – 0 7445, 1934 9
illustrated by David Anstey

Two magical stories full of zany characters. They are fun, and very easy to read.
Age range: 7–9

THE WOODSIDE SCHOOL STORY

In the same series:

THE FRIGHT
Orchard Books, 1987, 64p. – 1 85213 087 3
illustrated by Beverley Lees

KING OF SPUDS
Orchard Books, 1989, 64p. – 1 85213 089 X
illustrated by Lynne Willey

LOUD MOUTH
Orchard Books, 1988, 64p. – 1 85213 086 5
illustrated by Lynne Willey

SOPPY BIRTHDAY
Orchard Books, 1988, 64p. – 1 85213 085 7
illustrated by Beverley Lees

WHO'S FOR THE ZOO?
Orchard Books, 1989, 64p. – 1 85213 090 3
illustrated by Beverley Lees

WHO'S TALKING?
Orchard Books, 1987, 64p. – 1 85213 088 1
illustrated by Beverley Lees

Very short, attractively produced stories, with lots of appeal for younger readers just able to tackle reading a novel.
Age range: 7–9

THE YOU TWO
Beaver Books, 1985, 176p. – Pbk. –
0 09 93810 1
Hutchinson, 1984, 150p. – 0 09 154810 1

Elizabeth cannot face having to attend Gladeside Comprehensive, which is huge, noisy and full of rude children making fun of her posh 'Lady Margaret' accent. Meeting Paddy and becoming inseparable friends (hence the 'You two'), makes life a lot better for a while. Sensitive and realistic character portrayal.
Age range: 10–12

Other publications:

AFTER THURSDAY
Methuen, 1989. – Pbk. – O/P. – 0 416 08282 3

ALWAYS SEBASTIAN
Bodley Head, 1993. – 0 370 31536 7

BRENDA THE BOLD
Mammoth, 1993. – Pbk. – 0 7497 1637 1

COME LUCKY APRIL
Mammoth, 1993. – Pbk. – 0 7497 1015 2

DANCE FOR TWO
J. Goodchild, 1984. – 0 86391 009 2

DREAMING OF LARRY
Doubleday, 1991. – Pbk. – 0 385 40011 X

IF IT WEREN'T FOR SEBASTIAN
Red Fox, 1993. – Pbk. – 0 09 985870 3

MUDDY KIND OF MAGIC
Blackie, 1988. – O/P. – 0 216 92335 2

ONE GREEN LEAF
Corgi, 1990. – Pbk. – 0 552 52506 5

OTHER SIDE OF THE FENCE
Corgi, 1988. – Pbk. – 0 552 52466 2

PHANTOM KNICKER NICKER
Blackie, 1993. – 0 216 94044 3

PLACE TO SCREAM
Doubleday, 1992. – Pbk. – 0 385 40013 6

PLAGUE '99
Mammoth, 1991. – Pbk. – 0 7497 0333 4

URE

PLAY NIMROD FOR HIM
Red Fox, 1992. – Pbk. – 0 09 985300 0

PROPER LITTLE NOORYEFF
Corgi, 1992. – Pbk. – 0 552 52711 4

SAY GOODBYE
Corgi, 1989. – Pbk. – 0 552 52430 1

SEE YOU THURSDAY
Penguin, 1989. – Pbk. – 0 14 032516 6

SPOOKY COTTAGE
Heinemann, 1991. – 0 434 97660 1

SWINGS AND ROUNDABOUTS
Methuen, 1988. – Pbk. – O/P. – 0 416 07372 7

THERE'S ALWAYS DANNIE
Corgi, 1989. – Pbk. – 0 552 52429 8

TOMORROW IS ALSO A DAY
*Mammoth, 1989. – Pbk. – O/P. –
0 7497 0008 4*

TROUBLE WITH VANESSA
Corgi, 1988. – Pbk. – 0 552 52428 X

TWO MEN IN A BOAT
Blackie, 1988. – O/P. – 0 216 92336 0

UNKNOWN PLANET
Walker Books, 1992. – 0 7445 2411 3

YOU WIN SOME, YOU LOSE SOME
Corgi, 1987. – Pbk. – 0 552 52431 X

W

WADDELL, Martin

Also writes as Catherine Sefton. Irish. Born Belfast, Northern Ireland, 1941. Married Rosaleen Canagher, 1969, three sons.

Awards: Arts Council of Northern Ireland Bursaries: 1971, 1974, 1981

Children's Rights Workshop Other Award (as Catherine Sefton): *Starry night*, 1986

Smarties Prize: *Can't you Sleep, Little Bear*, 1988

Emil/Kurt Maschler Award: *The Park in the Dark*, 1989

Address: 139 Central Promenade, Newcastle, County Down, Northern Ireland

Agent: Murray Pollinger, 4 Garrick Street, London WC2E 9BH, England

An able writer who appeals to a wide age range. He has written fictional sports stories for older readers, and many fine picture books for the youngest.

FRED THE ANGEL
Walker Books, 1990, 129p. – Pbk. – 0 7445 0832 0
Walker Books, 1989, 112p. – O/P. – 0 7445 0823 1
illustrated by Patrick Benson

Five stories about an angel who is in the process of learning his job, and who encounters many problems. Amusing and very easy to read.
Age range: 7–9

HARRIET AND THE CROCODILES
Blackie, 1986, 80p. – O/P. – 0 216 91886 3
Abelard-Schuman, 1982, 80p. – O/P. – 0 200 72780 X

In the same series:

HARRIET AND THE FLYING TEACHERS
Hippo Books, 1990, 156p. – Pbk. – 0 590 76345 8
Blackie, 1987, 80p. – O/P. – 0 216 92239 9

HARRIET AND THE HAUNTED SCHOOL
Blackie, 1988, 68p. – 0 216 92408 1
Hippo Books, 1985, 78p. – Pbk. – 0 590 70441 9

HARRIET AND THE ROBOT
Hippo Books, 1988, 96p. – Pbk. – 0 590 70939 9
Blackie, 1985, 80p. – O/P. – 0 216 91806 5
all illustrated by Mark Burgess

A series of amusing easy readers about a little girl with a penchant for disaster.
Age range: 7–9

THE HOUSE UNDER THE STAIRS
Magnet Books, 1984, 96p. – Pbk. – 0 416 46170 0
Methuen, 1983, 96p. – O/P. – 0 416 25040 8
illustrated by Maggie Ling

This is an excellent book. Although fairly short, it has a good story and endearing characters, showing a deep understanding of children and what troubles them. The ending is marvellous.
Age range: 7–9

OWL AND BILLY
Methuen, 1986, 96p. – 0 416 54180 1

In the same series:

OWL AND BILLY AND THE SPACE DAYS
Methuen, 1988, 96p. – O/P. – 0 416 07552 5
illustrated by Carolyn Dinan

Satisfying and amusing, these books are

excellent for reading aloud. They describe incidents as seen through the eyes of Billy and his companion, Owl. Age range: 4–6

Other publications:

ALICE THE ARTIST
Methuen, 1988. – O/P. – 0 416 01652 9

AMY SAID
Walker Books, 1990. – O/P. – 0 7445 1277 8

BIG BAD BERTIE
Methuen, 1984. – O/P. – 0 416 46870 5

BUDGIE SAID GRRR!
Methuen, 1985. – O/P. – 0 416 52150 9

DAISY'S CHRISTMAS
Methuen, 1990. – O/P. – 0 416 12592 1

DAY IT RAINED ELEPHANTS
Methuen, 1986. – O/P. – 0 416 54980 2

GREAT GRAN GORILLA AND THE ROBBERS
Walker Books, 1988. – O/P. – 0 7445 0751 0

GREAT GRAN GORILLA TO THE RESCUE
Walker Books, 1988. – O/P. – 0 7445 0752 9

GREAT GREEN MOUSE DISASTER
Andersen Press, 1981. – O/P. – 0 86264 006 7

JUDY THE BAD FAIRY
Walker Books, 1989. – O/P. – 0 7445 1140 2

LITTLE DRACULA'S CHRISTMAS
Walker Books, 1986. – O/P. – 0 7445 0686 7

LITTLE DRACULA'S FIRST BITE
Walker Books, 1986. – O/P. – 0 7445 0685 9

MAN MOUNTAIN
Viking, 1991. – O/P. – 0 670 82814 9

MY GREAT GRANDPA
Walker Books, 1990. – O/P. – 0 7445 1286 7

MYSTERY SQUAD AND MR MIDNIGHT
Blackie, 1984. – Pbk. – O/P. – 0 216 91420 5

MYSTERY SQUAD AND THE ARTFUL DODGER
Blackie, 1984. – Pbk. – O/P. – 0 216 91418 3

MYSTERY SQUAD AND THE CANDID CAMERA
Blackie, 1985. – Pbk. – O/P. – 0 216 91710 7

MYSTERY SQUAD AND THE CANNONBALL KID
Blackie, 1986. – Pbk. – O/P. – 0 216 91851 0

MYSTERY SQUAD AND THE CREEPING CASTLE
Blackie, 1985. – Pbk. – O/P. – 0 216 91708 5

MYSTERY SQUAD AND THE DEAD MAN'S MESSAGE
Blackie, 1984. – Pbk. – O/P. – 0 216 91416 7

MYSTERY SQUAD AND THE ROBOT'S REVENGE
Blackie, 1986. – Pbk. – O/P. – 0 216 91849 9

MYSTERY SQUAD AND THE WHISTLING TEETH
Blackie, 1984. – Pbk. – O/P. – 0 216 91422 1

NAPPER GOES FOR GOAL
Blackie, 1987. – O/P. – 0 216 92218 6

NAPPER STRIKES AGAIN
Blackie, 1988. – O/P. – 0 216 92377 8

NAPPER'S GOLDEN GOALS
Blackie, 1988. – O/P. – 0 216 92399 9

OUR SLEEPYSAURUS
Walker Books, 1988. – O/P. – 0 7445 0821 5

SCHOOL REPORTER'S NOTEBOOK
Beaver Books, 1985. – Pbk. – O/P. – 0 09 938970 3

TALES FROM THE SHOP THAT NEVER SHUTS
Viking, 1988. – O/P. – 0 670 82066 0

TOUGH PRINCESS
Walker Books, 1986. – O/P. – 0 7445 0540 2

WE LOVE THEM
Walker Books, 1990. – O/P. – 0 7445 1278 6

WALSH, Jill Paton (Gillian Paton Walsh, née Bliss)

British. Born London, 1937. Educated St Michael's Convent, London; St Anne's College, Oxford, Dip.Ed., M.A. (Hons), English. Married Anthony Edmund Paton Walsh, 1961, one son, two daughters. Teacher, co-founder (with John Rowe Townsend) of Green Bay Publishers, 1986.

Awards: Whitbread Award: *The Emperor's Winding Sheet*, 1974

Boston Globe-Horn Book Award: *The Unleaving*, 1976

Arts Council Creative Writing Fellowship, 1976

Smarties Prize: *Gaffer Samson's Luck*, 1985

Address: 72 Water Lane, Histon, Cambridge CB4 4LR, England

A writer of exceptional quality who brings history to life with her stories. Readers undoubtedly require fluency to tackle these stories which are linguistically rich, with complex characters, but the plots are riveting.

BABYLON
Beaver Books, 1988, 32p. – Pbk. –
0 09 938080 3
Deutsch, 1982, 32p. – O/P. – 0 233 97362 1
illustrated by Jennifer Northway

Beautifully illustrated, this story tells of three children playing on an old railway line. Many wise words are spoken in between the poetical reminiscences.
Age range: 6–8

BIRDY AND THE GHOSTIE
Macdonald, 1989, 48p. – 0 356 16779 8
illustrated by Alan Marks

An unusual short story, well illustrated with large print, making it a most attractive book. Birdy learns that second sight is a curse, not a blessing, but it serves her well when the 'ghosties' arrive.
Age range: 7–9

THE BUTTY BOY
Penguin, 1986, 128p. – Pbk. – 0 14 031962 X
Macmillan, 1975, 128p. – O/P. – 0 333 18567 6
illustrated by Juliette Palmer

A wonderfully descriptive novel about life on a narrow boat. Harriet, hating her new home, glimpses a boat and investigates. She is intrigued to discover children managing the narrow boats and helps them through the lock. She decides she is too dirty to return home and stays on the barge. It proves to be the most exciting time of her life.
Age range: 9–11

THE CHANCE CHILD
Chivers Press, 1988, 232p. – L/P. –
0 7451 0659 5
Penguin, 1985, 160p. – Pbk. – 0 14 031816 X
Macmillan, 1978, 160p. – O/P. – 0 333 23833 8

Totally compelling, this book has many facets. The beginning is quite gripping, describing a poor ill-treated scrap of humanity who emerges from a cardboard box. There is a taut air of mystery as Christopher, trying to find Creep, sees his name carved in stone on a bridge, but it is covered by the moss of many years. It focuses on the horror of working conditions in the mills, particularly for children. Not a book for the faint-hearted, but a moving interpretation of a bygone age.
Age range: 12–14

THE DAWNSTONE
Pan Books, 1979, 96p. – Pbk. O/P. –
0 330 25735 8
Hamish Hamilton, 1973, 86p. – O/P. –
0 241 02397 1
illustrated by Mary Dinsdale

Easy to read with an intriguing story. Adam finds a stone which he feels sure belongs to the Stone Age. He sleeps with it under his pillow and has frightening dreams. Eventually it finds its true place when he takes it to the zoo.
Age range: 7–9

THE DOLPHIN CROSSING
Penguin, 1970. 133p. – Pbk. – 0 14 030457 6
Macmillan, 1967, 144p. – O/P. – 0 333 09096 9

In spite of their differences, Pat and John become friends. John is an evacuee from London and finds life difficult. When news of Dunkirk is received, the two boys respond promptly in spite of the danger.
Age range: 11–13

FIREWEED
Penguin, 1972, 128p. – Pbk. – 0 14 030560 2
Macmillan, 1969, 144p. – O/P. – 0 333 10618 0

The setting is London during the blitz. Two young adolescents are hiding from officials because they want to stay in London. At first they enjoy the cat and mouse games, but as the relentless bombing continues they find the effort of surviving too much. Full of

WALSH

atmosphere, it sensitively portrays the youngsters and their friendship.
Age range: 12–15

GAFFER SAMSON'S LUCK
Penguin, 1987, 112p. – Pbk. – 0 14 031765 1
Chivers Press, 1987, 160p. – L/P. – 0 7451 0451 7
Viking Kestrel, 1985, 112p. – 0 670 80122 4

James doesn't like the flatness of the Fens; he is not happy at school, but he does like Gaffer Samson. He sees no harm in helping him find his good luck charm, but the school gang have other ideas. Excellent characterization, and a memorable story.
Age range: 11–13

GOLDENGROVE
Red Fox, 1990, 124p. – Pbk. – 0 09 975210 7
Bodley Head, 1985, 126p. – O/P. – 0 370 30630 9

Madge and Paul meet up every summer in spite of their parents' disapproval. This summer is somehow different. They are not quite at ease together, and Goldengrove also seems different. Growing up can be hard.
Age range: 12–14

THE GREEN BOOK
Macmillan, 1981, 128p. – O/P. – 0 333 31910 9
illustrated by Joanna Stubbs

Leaving doomed Earth forever seems exciting to the children who do not fully understand the implications. The journey is long, and the new planet needs exploring. With so much to do, it takes time to realize how badly they chose which books to take along. Only the children seem to realize the importance of stories.
Age range: 8–10

A PARCEL OF PATTERNS
Chivers Press, 1989, 264p. – L/P. – 0 7451 0926 8
Penguin, 1988, 137p. – Pbk. – O/P. – 0 14 032627 8
Viking Kestrel, 1986, 144p. – 0 670 80861 X

Set in Eyam in Derbyshire at the time of the plague, this novel is quite compelling. The horror of the plague is well described, as is the courage of the villagers who decide they must contain the disease. There is the added dimension of the love between Emmot and Roland and the way the plague affects them.
Age range: 12–15

THE TORCH
Penguin, 1992, 176p. – Pbk. – 0 14 034941 3
Viking, 1987, 176p. – 0 670 81554 3

The story of the Olympic Torch provides a stirring read. When Dio and Cal reluctantly accept the guardianship of the living flame, they must undertake to find where the Games are being held. This leads them into many adventures before their mission is accomplished.
Age range: 10–12

Other publications:

CAN I PLAY FARMER FARMER?
Bodley Head, 1990. – O/P. – 0 370 31448 4
CAN I PLAY JENNY JONES?
Bodley Head, 1990. – O/P. – 0 370 31446 8
CAN I PLAY QUEENIE?
Bodley Head, 1990. – O/P. – 0 370 31449 2
CAN I PLAY WOLF?
Bodley Head, 1990. – O/P. – 0 370 31447 6
CROSSING TO SALAMIS
Heinemann, 1977. – O/P. – 0 434 94925 6
EMPEROR'S WINDING SHEET
Penguin, 1976. – Pbk. – 0 14 030833 4
GRACE
Puffin Books, 1993. – Pbk. – 0 14 034729 1
HENGEST'S TALE
Penguin, 1971. – Pbk. – 0 14 030437 1
ISLAND SUNRISE
Deutsch, 1975. – O/P. – 0 233 96671 4
LOST AND FOUND
Deutsch, 1984. – 0 233 97672 8
MATTHEW AND THE SEA SINGER
Simon & Schuster, 1992. – 0 7500 1175 0
PERSIAN GOLD
Heinemann, 1978. – O/P. – 0 434 94933 7
SHINE
Macdonald, 1988. – O/P. – 0 356 13462 8

TOOLMAKER
Heinemann, 1973. – O/P. – 0 434 94910 8
UNLEAVING
Red Fox, 1990. – Pbk. – 0 09 975320 0
WALLS OF ATHENS
Heinemann, 1977. – O/P. – 0 434 94931 0
WHEN GRANDMA CAME
Viking, 1992. – 0 670 83581 1

WARBURTON, Nick

British. Born Woodford, 1947. Married, one son. Teacher, writer.

Address: 37 Fulbrooke Road,
Newnham,
Cambridge CB3 9EE,
England

Agent: David Higham Associates Ltd.
5–8 Lower John Street,
Golden Square,
London W1R 4HA,
England

A welcome addition to the children's book scene, Nick Warburton brings the full force of his considerable wit and humour to bear on his stories, resulting in thoroughly enjoyable fun reads which will appeal to a wide age range.

APE IN SPACE
Mammoth, 1991, 64p. – Pbk. – 0 7497 0719 4
Black, 1990, 64p. – 0 7136 3223 2
illustrated by Peter Cottrill

Short, amusingly illustrated, it tells how Mr Armpits the ape and Matt the bat solve the puzzle of the disappearing animals.
Age range: 7–9

THE BATTLE OF BAKED BEAN ALLEY
Walker Books, 1993, 176p. – Pbk. – 0 7445 3078 4
Walker Books, 1992, 176p. – 0 7445 2135 1

A thoroughly enjoyable and amusing slant on the serious theme of conservation. Ivor wants to save his oak tree from the threatened baked bean extension. A full length novel, but easy to read.
Age range: 8–10

NORMAL NESBIT
Walker Books, 1993, 192p. – Pbk. – 0 7445 3097 0

Gordon is classified as an average pupil, and he feels doomed to act in an average way for the rest of his life. Fate, however, in the guise of a glamorous new girl takes a hand to change matters. As an ex-teacher, Nick Warburton has lots of experience of playground dialogue which he reproduces (including the occasional swear-word) and which some adults may object to.
Age range: 11–13

SAVING GRACE
Mammoth, 1990, 64p. – Pbk. – 0 7497 0294 X
Black, 1989, 56p. – 0 7136 3122 8
illustrated by Peter Cottrill

A case of mistaken identity leads to a variety of amusing situations, although Sammy finds it increasingly funny. A wonderful play on the words of the title. Very short.
Age range: 7–9

THE THIRTEENTH OWL
Bodley Head, 1993, 124p. – 0 370 31818 8

A new departure with this chilling story of a young girl with a scar where she burnt her face, now the victim of cruel taunts. Through her loneliness, she becomes unwittingly embroiled in Mr Balik's horrific past.
Age range: 10–12

ZARTAN
Black, 1988, 64p. – 0 7136 3067 1
illustrated by Peter Cottrill

An amusing version of the Tarzan story. Short and very easy to read.
Age range: 7–9

Other publications:
FAME AND FORTUNE
Mammoth, 1990. – Pbk. – 0 7497 0201 X
HOODS AND HEROES
Black, 1987. – 0 7136 2882 0
MR PARKER'S AUTUMN TERM
Red Fox, 1991. – Pbk. – 0 09 972220 8
MR TITE'S BELONGINGS
All Books for Children, 1991. – 1 8540 6117 8

WESTALL, Robert (Atkinson)

British. Born Tynemouth, 1929. Died 15 April 1993. Educated Tynemouth High School; Durham University, B.A. (Hons), fine art; Slade School, University of London, D.F.A. Royal Corps of Signals, 1953–55. Married Jean Underhill, 1958, one son (deceased). Art master, antiques dealer, art critic, writer.

Awards: Library Association Carnegie Medal: *The Machine-gunners*, 1975

Library Association Carnegie Medal: *The Scarecrows*, 1981

Smarties' Prize: *Blitz Cat*, 1989

Guardian Children's Fiction Award: *Kingdom by the sea*, 1991

Lancashire County Library Children's Book of the Year Award: *Gulf*, 1993 (shared)

Address: 2 Dyar Terrace,
Winnington,
Northwich,
Cheshire CW8 4DN,
England

A writer of enormously powerful stories which are capable of stirring deep feelings and, at times, a genuine sense of dread. Many of his books are set during the Second World War, bringing alive this important period for a new generation of children. His strength lies in the realism of his characters and settings.

BLITZCAT
Pan Books, 1990, 240p. – Pbk. – 0 330 31040 2
Chivers Press, 1990, 352p. – L/P. – 0 7451 1177 7
Macmillan, 1989, 240p. – O/P. – 0 333 47498 8

A haunting, heart warming story of a cat which survives an air-raid in Coventry, and is determined not to rest until she is united with the man she adores. It is a hazardous journey of pain and fear, so that the reader is almost afraid to reach the end. Robert Westall gives no guarantees of a happy ending.
Age range: 11–14

THE CREATURE IN THE DARK
Methuen, 1990, 176p. – 0 416 15662 2
Blackie, 1989, 112p. – 0 216 92760 9
Blackie, 1988, 144p. – 0 216 92472 8

An easy to read mystery, beginning with a sheep being worried, then lambs missing, then calves! It is impossible for a dog to be responsible, but neither Sammy nor his father can guess what sort of creature it can be. An exciting, well constructed story with a satisfying ending.
Age range: 9–11

THE KINGDOM BY THE SEA
Mammoth, 1992, 160p. – Pbk. – 0 7497 0796 8
Chivers Press, 1991, 288p. – L/P. – O/P. – 0 7451 1429 6
Methuen, 1990, 176p. – 0 416 15662 2

The story of Harry, and how he copes with the loss of his family in an air-raid during the Second World War, makes stirring reading. His journey along the Tyneside coast, accompanied by a stray dog he befriends equates with his journey to independence. It is moving, exciting, and utterly absorbing.
Age range: 11–13

THE MACHINE-GUNNERS
Penguin, 1977, 187p. – Pbk. – 0 14 030973 X

Now a classic war story, *The Machine-*

gunners tells how Charles, hunting for additions to his collection of war souvenirs, cannot believe his luck when he finds a machine gun in working order in the crashed plane. By fair means or foul, he and his mates manage to conceal it from the adults, but when they also capture a German pilot, matters get out of hand.

A worthy medal winner, this story has been read by successive generations of children, with enjoyment laced with sympathy at the decisions facing the children who must then live with the consequences.
Age range: 10–13

OLD MAN ON A HORSE
Blackie, 1989, 112p. – O/P. – 0 216 92760 9
Hippo Books, 1989, 196p. – Pbk. –
0 590 76082 3

Tobias is brought up by peace-loving parents who have opted out of society and joined a hippy following. Life is suddenly turned upside-down when the police arrest his father. Finding a statue of a man on a horse causes a time-slip to the time of Charles II, which helps to resolve the problems faced by Tobias and his family. Rather easier to read than many of Westall's novels, it is an unusual and accessible read for younger children.
Age range: 10–12

THE SCARECROWS
Penguin, 1989, 176p. – Pbk. – 0 14 032731 2
Windrush, 1989, 283p. – L/P. – 1 85089 973 8
Bodley Head, 1984, 160p. – O/P. –
0 370 30844 1

Being able to empathize with young boys and their interests and fears is one of Robert Westall's strong points. In this novel he has created a memorable character in Simon, who feels at odds with his step-father, and therefore with his mother too. Gradually, and chillingly, the emphasis changes from his feelings of self-pity to the fear that grows in him when the scarecrows appear. A gripping story in which many readers may learn something about themselves, as well as enjoying the plot.
Age range: 11–13

A WALK ON THE WILD SIDE
Mammoth, 1991, 143p. – Pbk. – 0 7497 0147 1
Methuen, 1989, 128p. – 0 416 13592 7

Seven completely different stories about a variety of cats. The animal world is often violent and cruel, and there is no attempt to soften the reality in these stories, some of which are quite scary.
Age range: 12–14

Other publications:

BREAK OF DARK
Penguin, 1988. – Pbk. – 0 14 032767 3
CALL, AND OTHER STORIES
Penguin, 1991. – Pbk. – 0 14 032921 8
CATS OF SEROSTER
Pan Books, 1986. – Pbk. – 0 330 29239 0
CHRISTMAS CAT
Methuen, 1991. – 0 416 16822 1
CHRISTMAS GHOST
Methuen, 1992. – 0 416 18691 2
DEVIL ON THE ROAD
Penguin, 1988. – Pbk. – 0 14 032585 9
ECHOES OF WAR
Penguin, 1991. – Pbk. – 0 14 034208 7
FALLING INTO GLORY
Methuen, 1993. – 0 416 18801 X
FATHOM FIVE
Pan Books, 1992. – Pbk. – 0 330 32230 3
FEARFUL LOVERS AND OTHER STORIES
Piper, 1993. – Pbk. – 0 330 32925 1
FUTURETRACK 5
Penguin, 1988. – Pbk. – 0 14 032768 1
GHOST ABBEY
Macmillan, 1988. – O/P. – 0 333 47564 X
GHOSTS AND JOURNEYS
Pan Books, 1989. – Pbk. – O/P. – 0 330 30904 8
GULF
Methuen, 1992. – 0 416 18590 8
HAUNTING OF CHAS MCGILL AND OTHER STORIES
Penguin, 1988. – Pbk. – 0 14 032665 0
IF CATS COULD FLY
Chivers Press, 1992. – O/P. – 0 7451 1639 6
PLACE FOR ME
Macmillan, 1993. – 0 333 59277 8

WESTALL

THE PROMISE
Pan Books, 1991. – Pbk. – 0 330 31741 5
RACHEL AND THE ANGEL AND OTHER STORIES
Pan Books, 1988. – Pbk. – 0 330 30235 3
SIZE TWELVE
Heinemann, 1993. – 0 434 97683 0
STONES OF MUNCASTER CATHEDRAL
Penguin, 1993. – Pbk. – 0 14 034843 3
STORMSEARCH
Penguin, 1992. – Pbk. – 0 14 034468 3
URN BURIAL
Penguin, 1989. – Pbk. – 0 14 032266 3
WATCH HOUSE
Penguin, 1988. – Pbk. – 0 14 032765 7
WHEATSTONE POND
Viking, 1993. – 0 670 84898 0
WIND EYE
Piper, 1992. – Pbk. – 0 330 32234 6
YAXLEY'S CAT
Pan Books, 1992. – Pbk. – O/P. – 0 330 32499 3

WILDE, Nicholas

British. Born Cheltenham. Educated Cheltenham; King's College, Cambridge. Teacher. A relative newcomer to children's fiction writing, this author is proving himself to be a first-rate mystery writer with an extraordinary ability to create a feeling of tension within a good, strong storyline. It is unusual to find an author whose next book is awaited with such anticipation.

DEATH KNELL
Lions, 1991, 224p. – Pbk. – 0 00 674005 7
Collins, 1990, 224p. – 0 00 107217 X

An atmospheric mystery which Tim and Jamie are determined to solve. They cannot decide how much relevance the legend of the crypt has to the body found in the locked crypt. As the sense of danger mounts, they begin to wish they had kept out of it. The final solution is ingenious and plausible.
Age range: 12–14

DOWN CAME A BLACKBIRD
Harper Collins, 1991, 208p. – O/P. – 0 00, 192110 X

Not quite as absorbing as his previous two novels, but highly original nonetheless. It tells the story of James' last chance to make a life for himself when, rejected on all sides, he goes to stay in his ancestral home. History provides the beginning of the healing process, and stops his deep desire to hurt everything and everyone.
Age range: 12+

INTO THE DARK
Collins, 1989, 176p. – Pbk. – 0 00 673517 7
Collins, 1987, 160p. – 0 00 184426 1

Matthew is excited at the prospect of a proper holiday for the first time. Set in Norfolk, the site of many holidays for the author, there is a strong feeling of mystery which is maintained to the end. A superb story which the reader is sorry to finish.
Age range: 11–13

Other publications:

HUFFLE
Hodder, 1984. – O/P. – 0 340 34466 0
SIR BERTIE AND THE WYVERN
Debrett's, 1981. – O/P. – 0 905649 46 X

WILDER, Laura (Elizabeth Ingalls)

American. Born Pepin, Wisconsin, 1867 (died 10 February 1957). Educated Walnut Grove, Minnesota; Burn Oak, Iowa; De Smet, Dakota Territory. Married Almanzo James Wilder, 1885 (died 1949), one daughter. Schoolteacher, columnist, writer.

Awards: American Library Association Laura Ingalls Wilder Award, 1954

Fictional autobiographical books usually have little appeal for children, but this series is an exception. Based on her childhood memories as a member of a pioneering family, the books have such an authentic tone that they are all the more memorable. They are, of course, old-fashioned, but they radiate a gentle family happiness which contrasts with the isolated, vulnerable position of the house.

LITTLE HOUSE IN THE BIG WOODS
Mammoth, 1992, 224p. – Pbk. – 0 7497 0931 6
Windrush, 1987, 167p. – L/P. – 1 85089 913 4
Methuen, 1970, 220p. – 0 416 07130 9

In the same series:

LITTLE HOUSE ON THE PRAIRIE
Mammoth, 1992, 224p. – Pbk. –
0 7497 0930 8
Windrush, 1986, 252p. – L/P. –
1 85089 900 2
Methuen, 1970, 220p. – 0 416 07140 6

ON THE BANKS OF PLUM CREEK
Mammoth, 1992, 224p. – Pbk. –
0 7497 0932 4
Windrush, 1988, 276p. – L/P. –
1 85089 941 X
Methuen, 1970, 220p. – 0 416 07150 3

BY THE SHORES OF SILVER LAKE
Windrush, 1990, 272p. – L/P. –
1 85089 994 0
Penguin, 1969, 224p. – Pbk. – 0 14 030303 0
Lutterworth Press, 1961, 304p. –
0 7188 0128 8

THE LONG WINTER
Penguin, 1968, 256p. – Pbk. – 0 14 030381 2
Lutterworth Press, 1962, 352p. –
0 7188 0520 8

LITTLE TOWN ON THE PRAIRIE
Penguin, 1969, 224p. – Pbk. – 0 14 030417 7
Lutterworth Press, 1963, 320p. –
0 7188 0519 4

THESE HAPPY GOLDEN YEARS
Penguin, 1970, 240p. – Pbk. – 0 14 030461 4
Lutterworth Press, 1964, 304p. –
0 7188 0918 1

Age range: 10–12

Other publications:
FARMER BOY
Penguin, 1972. – Pbk. – 0 14 030568 8

FIRST FOUR YEARS
Penguin, 1978. – Pbk. – 0 14 031028 2

WILSON, David Henry

British. Born London, 1937. Educated Pembroke College, Cambridge, B.A., M.A. (Cantab.). Married Elizabeth Ayo Amaworo, 1965, two sons, one daughter. University lecturer.

Address: 3 Beech Close,
Hope Corner Lane,
Taunton,
Somerset TA2 7NZ,
England

Light, easy books to tempt the reluctant reader to try to tackle full length novels.

BESIDE THE SEA WITH JEREMY JAMES
Pan Books, 1985, 96p. – Pbk. – 0 330 28695 1
Chatto, 1980, 96p. – O/P. – 0 7011 2537 3

In the same series:

DO GOLDFISH PLAY THE VIOLIN?: ADVENTURES WITH JEREMY JAMES
Pan Books, 1987, 128p. – Pbk. –
0 330 29594 2
Dent, 1985, 128p. – O/P. – 0 460 06220 4

ELEPHANTS DON'T SIT ON CARS
Pan Books, 1980, 96p. – Pbk. –
0 330 26005 7
Chatto, 1977, 96p. – O/P. – 0 7011 2273 0

GETTING RICH WITH JEREMY JAMES
Pan Books, 1984, 112p. – Pbk. –
0 330 28383 9
Chatto, 1979, 112p. – O/P. – 0 7011 2441 5

HOW TO STOP A TRAIN WITH ONE FINGER: ADVENTURES WITH JEREMY JAMES
Pan Books, 1985, 112p. – Pbk. –
0 330 28978 0
Dent, 1984, 112p. – 0 460 06150 X
all illustrated by Patricia Drew

PLEASE KEEP OFF THE DINOSAUR
Pan Macmillan, 1993, 96p. – O/P. –
0 333 58766 9
illustrated by Ann Johns

A series of amusing stories about a small boy who seems to attract trouble like a magnet. Good for reading aloud.
Age range: 6–9

SUPERDOG
Hodder, 1992, 96p, – Pbk. – 0 340 58008 9
Hodder, 1984, 88p. – O/P. – 0 340 34905 0

In the same series:

SUPERDOG IN TROUBLE
Hodder, 1992, 96p. – Pbk. – 0 340 58011 9
Hodder, 1988, 80p. – 0 340 43061 3

SUPERDOG THE HERO
Hodder, 1992, 96p. – Pbk. – 0 340 58010 0
Hodder, 1986, 96p. – O/P. – 0 340 38872 2
both illustrated by Linda Birch

Woofer belongs to the Brown family. He believes he is very special and proves it by such escapades as falling into the toilet. Very amusing.
Age range: 8–10

THERE'S A WOLF IN MY PUDDING: TWELVE TWISTED, TORTURED, GRIM AND GRUESOME TALL AND TERRIBLE TALES
Pan Books, 1988, 128p. – Pbk. – 0 330 29900 X
Dent, 1986, 128p. – O/P. – 0 460 06240 9

In the same series:

YUCKY DUCKY
Pan Books, 1990, 128p. – Pbk. –
0 330 31044 5
Dent, 1988, 128p. – 0 460 07025 8
both illustrated by Jonathan Allen

Well known stories related with slight differences. Lots of fun.
Age range: 10–12

Other publications:

COACHMAN RAT
Robinson Pub, 1989, 144p. – Pbk. –
1 85487 002 5

FASTEST GUN ALIVE AND OTHER NIGHT ADVENTURES
Pan Books, 1981, 96p. – Pbk. – O/P. –
0 330 26053 7

GANDER OF THE YARD: FATHER GOOSE'S CRIMES
Pan Books, 1990. 128p. – Pbk. – 0 330 31488 2

GIDEON GANDER SOLVES THE WORLD'S GREATEST MYSTERIES
Piper, 1993, 128p. – Pbk. – 0 330 32550 7

LITTLE BILLY AND THE WUMP
Hodder, 1990. 32p. – 0 340 51830 8

WILSON, Jacqueline

British. Born Bath 1945. Educated Coombe Girls School, Surrey; Carshalton Technical College, Surrey. Married William Mellow Wilson, 1965, one daughter. Journalist, writer.

Awards: Oak Award: *The Story of Tracy Beaker*, 1992

Children's Book Award (overall winner): *The Suitcase Kid*, 1993

Address: 1–B Beaufort Road, Kingston-on-Thames, Surrey KT1 2TH, England

Agent: Gina Pollinger, Murray Pollinger, 4 Garrick Street, London WC2E 9BH, England

A bubbly, enthusiastic personality with a great sense of humour and enormous empathy with children. All this shines through the stories she writes. Her books are inventive, warm and human, with universal appeal to modern children. Some of her books are aimed at teenagers.

THE BED AND BREAKFAST STAR
Doubleday, 1994, 129p. – 0 385 40434 4
illustrated by Nick Sharratt

Elsa has to live in bed and breakfast accommodation provided by the Council when her father loses his job.

She puts a brave face on her problems, jokes when she really wants to cry, and proves herself to be a worthy successor to Tracy Beaker, Sadie and Andrea.
Age range: 9–12

GLUBBSLYME
*OUP, 1987, 112p. – 0, 19 271563 1
illustrated by Jane Cope*

A wonderful combination of realism, as Rebecca falls out with her best friend and suffers acute distress over the quarrel, and fantasy in the shape of the speaking toad able to work magic. Very easy and pleasurable to read.
Age range: 7–9

THE MUM-MINDER
*Doubleday, 1993, 60p. – 0 385 40321 6
illustrated by Nick Sharratt*

Sadie's mum is a child-minder. When she becomes ill, it is up to Sadie to organize the other mums to help her to look after her own mother. Full of humorous escapades and wonderful illustrations.
Age range: 8–10

THE OTHER SIDE
*Armada Books, 1986. – Pbk. – O/P. – 0 00 672596 1
OUP, 1984, 172p. – O/P – 0 19 271501 1*

A moving, yet dramatic account of a particularly difficult period in Alison's life. Her mother suffers a nervous breakdown, so she has to go to live with her father, his new wife, and her obnoxious daughter. She also has to attend a new school – it is all too much for her to cope with, but it has a satisfactory yet realistic ending.
Age range: 11–13

STORY OF TRACY BEAKER
*Yearling, 1992, 160p. – Pbk. – 0 440 86279 5
illustrated by Nick Sharratt*

A really amusing and yet deeply moving story of Tracy, who lives in a children's home, and longs to be fostered. It is an effective if unusual way of giving readers insight into the lives of the many children in care.
Age range: 9–12

THE SUITCASE KID
*Yearling, 1993, 160p. – Pbk. – 0 440 86311 2
Doubleday, 1992, 129p. – 0 385 40175 2
Chivers Press, 1992, 152p. – L/P. – 0 7451 1703 1
illustrated by Nick Sharratt*

Andrea's parents are divorcing and she dislikes her feelings when she has to go from mum to dad. Told with compassion laced with humour. A superb book.
Age range: 8–11

TAKE A GOOD LOOK
*Blackie, 1990, 96p. – 0 216 92878 8
illustrated by Michael Slater
Penguin, 1993, 96p. – Pbk. – 0 14 036108 1
illustrated by Jo Worth*

Such a lot is packed into this short book. An exciting plot – Mary witnesses a hold-up at the post-office and is taken hostage. Excellent characterization and an example of personal courage as she plots her escape.
Age range: 7–9

Other publications:

AMBER
Armada Books, 1988. – Pbk. – O/P. – 0 00 672767 0
DREAM PALACE
OUP, 1991. – 0 19 271677 8
FALLING APART
OUP, 1989. – 0 19 271629 8
HOW TO SURVIVE SUMMER CAMP
OUP, 1985. – 0 19 271504 6
KILLER TADPOLE
Corgi, 1987. – Pbk. – O/P. – 0 552 52414 X
LEFT OUTS
Penguin, 1991. – Pbk. – 0 14 034419 5
LONELY HEARTS
Firecrest Pub, 1988. – 0 85997 990 3
MARK SPARK IN THE DARK
H. Hamilton, 1993. – 0 241 13379 3
MARK SPARK
H. Hamilton, 1992. – 0 241 13203 7

MONSTER IN THE CUPBOARD
Blackie, 1986. – 0 216 91893 6
NOBODY'S PERFECT
OUP, 1987. – O/P. – 0 19 271576 3
POWER OF THE SHADE
Armada Books, 1989. – Pbk. – 0 00 672970 3
RAT RACE
Armada Books, 1988. – Pbk. – O/P. – 0 00 692809 9
SCHOOL TRIP
H. Hamilton, 1984. – O/P. – 0 241 11153 6
SUPERSLEUTH
Firecrest Pub, 1989. – 0 85997 989 X
THIS GIRL
Collins, 1990. – Pbk. – O/P. – 0 00 673497 9
VAMPIRE
Armada Books, 1988. – Pbk. – O/P. – 0 00 692810 2
VIDEO ROSE
Blackie, 1992. – 0 216 93273 4
WAITING FOR THE SKY TO FALL
Armada Books, 1985. – Pbk. – 0 00 672438 8
THE WEREPUPPY
Penguin, 1993. – Pbk. – 0 14 036129 4

WRIGHTSON, (Alice) Patricia (née Furlonger)

Australian. Born Lismore, New South Wales, 1921. Educated Correspondence School; St Catherine's College, Stanthorpe, Queensland. Married 1943 (divorced 1953), one daughter, one son. Secretary, editor, writer.

Awards: Australian Children's Book Council Book of the Year Award: *Crooked Snake*, 1956

I.B.B.Y. Honour Award: *I Own the Racecourse*, 1970

Australian Children's Book Council Book of the Year Award: *Nargun and the Stars*, 1974

I.B.B.Y. Honour Award: *The Nargun and the Stars*, 1976

Australian Children's Book Council Book of the Year Award: *The Ice is Coming*, 1978

Order of the British Empire, 1978

Australian Children's Book Council Book of the Year Award: *A Little Fear*, 1984

Boston Globe/Horn Award: *A Little Fear*, 1984

Dromkeen Children's Literature Foundation Medal, 1986

Hans Christian Andersen Award, 1986

Address: Box 91,
Maclean,
New South Wales 2463,
Australia

An excellent storyteller whose books appeal to the older and more competent reader. A student of Aboriginal mythology, she bases many of her books around its themes.

BALYET
Red Fox, 1990, 144p. – Pbk. – O/P. – 0 09 966040 7
Hutchinson, 1989, 144p. – 0 09 173794 X

The aboriginal legend of Balyet, frozen in time and living in isolation, is very moving. Her longing for friendship puts Jo into danger until she is finally able to set Balyet free.
Age range: 11–13

I OWN THE RACECOURSE
Penguin, 1971, 160p. – Pbk. – O/P. – 0 14 030452 5
illustrated by Margaret Horder

Andy is mentally handicapped, and finds it difficult to understand the games his friends play, so when a tramp offers to sell him the racecourse, he is thrilled. The staff play along, referring to him as 'the owner'. Joe thinks it has gone too far, and tries, unsuccessfully, to tell him the truth. Heartbreak seems certain, but eventually a satisfactory ending is

contrived. Sympathetic handling of the characters makes this relevant, even after 25 years.
Age range: 11+

THE ICE IS COMING
Penguin, 1983, 224p. – Pbk. O/P. – 0 14 031628 0
Hutchinson, 1977, 223p. – 0 09 129150 X

In the same series:

THE DARK BRIGHT WATER
Penguin, 1983, 224p. – Pbk. O/P. – 0 14 031630 2
Hutchinson, 1979, 224p. – O/P. – 0 09 136180 X

BEHIND THE WIND
Penguin, 1983, 168p. – Pbk. O/P. – 0 14 031629 9
Hutchinson, 1981, 158p. – O/P. – 0 09 144620 1

A powerful trilogy centred round Wirrun, an Aboriginal boy, who is struggling to live in modern society, but is unable to turn his back on the ancient knowledge and wisdom. This awareness causes him to interpret events differently. Rather difficult, but rewarding.
Age range: 12–14

A LITTLE FEAR
Penguin, 1985, 112p. – Pbk. O/P. – 0 14 031847 X
Hutchinson, 1983, 110p. – O/P. – 0 09 152710 4

A difficult book to classify, for it can be read and enjoyed by both children and adults. Mrs Tucker escapes from the old peoples' home and takes up residence in a lonely cottage with her dog. She finds, however, there is another resident, an evil one, who is trying to drive her out. She vigorously resists. Highly original, more than a little tense, and thoroughly enjoyable.
Age range: 12–adult

MOONDARK
Hutchinson, 1987, 146p. – 0 09 172559 3
illustrated by Noela Young

A haunting but difficult story about the peaceful existence being shattered and the lives of the animals put in danger as the balance of nature is disturbed. They have to appeal to the spirit of the land, who does not fail them in their hour of need. It has limited appeal, but is enormously rewarding if children are introduced to it personally.
Age range: 12+

NARGUN AND THE STARS
Hutchinson, 1989, 144p. – 0 09 157440 4
Penguin, 1976, 160p. – Pbk. – 0 14 030780 X

A sinister description of the ancient Nargun makes an exciting beginning. As the plot progresses and the bulldozers move in, the spirit is moved to exact revenge.
Age range: 12+

AN OLDER KIND OF MAGIC
Penguin, 1974, 151p. – Pbk. – O/P. – 0 14 030739 7
Hutchinson, 1972, 151p. – O/P. – 0 09 111430 6
illustrated by Noel Young

Waiting for the comet to appear, the children are blissfully unaware of the possible consequences when the spirits appear, wielding their own brand of music.
Age range: 11–13

THE ROCKS OF HONEY
Hutchinson, 1974, 184p. – O/P. – 0 09 119760 0
Penguin, 1966, 176p. – Pbk. – 0 14 030269 7

Barry only half believed in the existence of the stone axe, but agreed to go with Eustace to search the rocks. As the legend begins to reveal itself, the tension mounts. Of limited appeal, but worth trying to convince readers of its value.
Age range: 11–13

Other publications:

BUNYIP HOLE
Hutchinson, 1973. – O/P. – 0 09 116780 9
CROOKED SNAKE
Hutchinson, 1973. – O/P. – 0 09 114570 8
DOWN TO EARTH
Penguin, 1973. – Pbk. – 0 14 030559 9

CLASSICS

◆

This section has been included because of a firm belief that children's classics are an important part of the heritage bequeathed to children, and one which should be preserved. At a time when reading standards have apparently dropped to a record low, and recognizing that such books are by no means easy to read, it is imperative that attractive editions continue to be made available. Too many editions are dull and difficult. Books have so much competition for children's attention, and to stand a chance of winning must be of a high standard. The titles listed here are all very attractive editions which it is a pleasure to handle. Obviously such books are expensive, ranging in price up to £17, but they guarantee lasting pleasure. This is not a comprehensive list as it includes only books which were available on bookshop shelves at the time of going to press. There may well be many other similar titles.

AESOP

AESOP'S FABLES
Pavilion Books, 1990, 95p. – 1 85145 567 1

Compiled by Russell Ash and Bernard Higton, this version includes a variety of illustrations chosen from editions published during the last 150 years. It is a unique collection, including notes on the tales and their illustrators. A delightful book for children, but also a useful and pleasurable book for adult collectors.

AESOP'S FABLES
Walker, 1990, 64p. – 0 7445 1009 0

Retold by Mary Clark and illustrated by Charlotte Voake, this volume provides a thoroughly enjoyable book to use with younger children. The text is simple and the illustrations match perfectly, adding touches of humour.

ANDERSEN, Hans Christian

THUMBELINA
Macmillan, 1990, 32p. – Pbk. – 0 333 54184 7

THE WILD SWANS
Macmillan, 1989, 40p. – Pbk. – 0 333 49223 4
both illustrated by Susan Jeffers

Retold by Amy Ehrlich to make them suitable for reading to young children. Beautifully illustrated, with the illustrations occupying the major part of the books.

FAIRY TALES
New Orchard Editions, 1990, 256p. – 1 85079 144 9
illustrated by Margaret Tarrant

Black-and-white and coloured full-page illustrations by an Edwardian illustrator. Large print.

ARDIZZONE'S HANS ANDERSEN: FOURTEEN CLASSIC TALES
Deutsch, 1989, 196p. – 0 233 98372 4
selected and illustrated by Edward Ardizzone; translated from the original by Stephen Corrin

Small black-and-white plus full-page coloured line-drawings in pastel shades.

FAVOURITE HANS CHRISTIAN ANDERSEN FAIRY TALES
Methuen, 1981, 168p. – 0 416 22080 0
illustrated by Michael Hague

Beautiful large clear print on good paper. Nine stories with full-page paintings. Some are vibrant with colour, others pastel, depending on the tone of the story.

HANS ANDERSEN: HIS CLASSIC FAIRY TALES
Gollancz, 1985, 192p. – 0 575 03558 7
illustrated by Michael Foreman

A book to treasure. Eighteen stories, translated by Eric Haugaard, each introduced by an attractive illustration. Black-and-white illustrations are interspersed throughout, and there are 21 full-page colour plates of differing styles, matched perfectly to the individual story.

STORIES AND FAIRY TALES
Heinemann, 1993. – 0 434 92904 2

Eric Blegvad has chosen, translated and illustrated this collection which is a pleasing mixture of old favourites and lesser known stories. The text is in extra clear print and the illustrations seem particularly apt. They are in a large variety of sizes, all in colour, and are interspersed with the text.

STORIES FROM HANS CHRISTIAN ANDERSEN
Orchard, 1993, 80p. – 1 8521 3450 X
illustrated by Alan Snow

Andrew Matthews has retold many of the best known stories with the aim of making 'the stories immediate and enjoyable for a modern audience'. Alan Snow's illustrations are equally modern, and very humorous, the print is large and clear. The book has lots of appeal.

BARRIE, Sir James M.

THE STORY OF PETER PAN
*Bell & Hyman, 1982, 128p. – O/P. –
0 7135 1351 9
illustrated by Alice B. Woodward; retold from
the play by Daniel O'Connor*

Large print with a small amount of text on each page. Lots of full-page colour illustrations which complement the text perfectly.

PETER PAN AND WENDY
*Hodder, 1993, 128p. – Pbk. – 0 340 59755 0
illustrated by Shirley Hughes*

May Byron produced this rather shorter version which Barrie did not object to. Shirley Hughes's black-and-white illustrations are perfectly attuned to the text.

PETER PAN AND WENDY
*Hodder, 1989, 123p.
illustrated by Mabel Lucie Attwell*

The same retelling by May Byron with the original Attwell illustrations which many adults will remember from their childhood, and which they may prefer to more modern editions. The large print makes it attractive to younger children.

PETER PAN
*Viking Kestrel, 1988, 206p. – 0 670 80862 8
illustrated by Jan Ormerod*

The complete text, beautifully enhanced by black-and-white and coloured illustrations.

PETER PAN
*Methuen, 1988, 144p. – 0 416 09392 2
illustrated by Michael Hague*

Distinctive illustrations in a glorious combination of colours.

PETER PAN AND WENDY
*Pavilion Books, 1989, 160p. – 1 85145 449 7
illustrated by Michael Foreman*

Imaginative, colourful illustrations, with attractive decorations at the beginning and the end of chapters.

PETER PAN
Random House, 1989, 72p. – 0 394 89226 7

A set consisting of a hardback book edited by Josette Frank, illustrated in colour by Diane Goode, and with a cassette by Lyn Redgrave.

PETER PAN
*Brimax, 1993, 112p. – 0 86112 648 3
illustrated by Eric Kincaid*

A full-length adaptation which is exceptionally well illustrated, with a picture on every page. Subtle use of colour has produced atmospheric pictures which will be remembered after the story is finished.

BURNETT, Frances Hodgson

THE SECRET GARDEN
*Michael Joseph, 1986, 224p. – O/P. –
0 7181 2664 5*

A LITTLE PRINCESS
*Michael Joseph, 1989, 129p. – 0 7181 3317 X
both illustrated by Graham Rust*

Both contain a variety of illustrations – coloured, sepia, and little snippets of decoration, all interspersed with the text. The period detail is excellent, with clear print and good page design.

THE SECRET GARDEN
*Gollancz, 1988, 256p. – 0 575 04168 4
illustrated by Shirley Hughes*

Both black-and-white and 16 full-page colour plates in typical Shirley Hughes style make this a very attractive book. The period detail is excellent.

THE SECRET GARDEN
*Heinemann, 1990, 314p. – 0 434 93088 1
illustrated by Charles Robinson*

BURNETT

A facsimile edition of the original, published in 1911. Excellent illustrations.

CARROLL, Lewis

ALICE'S ADVENTURES IN WONDERLAND
J. MacRae Books, 1988, 128p. – O/P. – 0 86203 324 1
illustrated by Anthony Browne

All the illustrations are coloured, with striking combinations. Typically distinctive.

ALICE IN WONDERLAND
New Orchard, 1990, 256p. – 1 85079 148 1
illustrated by Margaret Tarrant

Full-page coloured illustrations by an Edwardian illustrator. Large print.

ALICE'S ADVENTURES IN WONDERLAND
Dragon's World, 1990, 96p. – 1 85028 105 X

ALICE THROUGH THE LOOKING GLASS
Dragon's World, 1989, 124p. – 1 85028 073 8
both illustrated by Malcolm Ashman

Both books have excellent page design and the illustrations are superb, mainly full-page colour with some small insets. A distinctive and personal interpretation.

ALICE'S ADVENTURES IN WONDERLAND
Gollancz, 1988, 160p. – Pbk. – 0 575 04332 6

THROUGH THE LOOKING GLASS
Gollancz, 1986, 176p. – 0 575 03756 3
both illustrated by Justin Todd

Vivid, memorable pictures, verging on the surreal, and a perfect complement to the stories. Clear print, and good spacing and layout.

ALICE'S ADVENTURES IN WONDERLAND
Hutchinson, 1989, 224p. – 0 09 173764 8
illustrated by Peter Weevers

Beautifully drawn illustrations on every page, some full-page, some smaller. Paintings of Alice were done from life, with the illustrator's daughter sitting for him. Excellent quality paper and clear print.

COLLODI, Carlo

PINOCCHIO
OUP, 1988, 96p. – 0 19 279855 3
illustrated by Victor G. Ambrus

A completely new version, retold by James Riordan from the original Italian story. Lots of excellent illustrations in both black-and-white and colour.

ADVENTURES OF PINOCCHIO
Cape, 1988, 144p. – 0 224 02523 6
illustrated by Roberto Innocenti

Illustrations of outstanding originality and forcefulness combined with excellent print and high quality paper make this book a pleasure to own. The design provides many surprises as each page has a different lay-out; some full-page illustrations are also included.

DICKENS, Charles

A CHRISTMAS CAROL
Cape, 1990, 152p. – 0 224 02900 2
illustrated by Roberto Innocenti

Full-page paintings in glorious colour, good period detail, clear print, beautiful paper and excellent page layout. Total excellence.

A CHRISTMAS CAROL
Gollancz, 1989, 128p. – Pbk. – 0 575 04956 5
illustrated by Michael Foreman

Black-and-white drawings interspersed through the text, plus full-colour plates.

A CHRISTMAS CAROL IN PROSE
Guild Publishing, 1990.
illustrated by Liz Summers

Also contains *The Story of the Goblins who Stole a Sexton*. Lots of bright, cheerful illustrations, with some black-and-white. The whole book has child appeal as the illustrations have an immediacy which is absent from the more formal illustrations in other editions.

GRAHAME, Kenneth

THE WIND IN THE WILLOWS
Methuen, 1980, 216p. – 0 416 20629 4
illustrated by Cosgrove Hall

Colourful illustrations on decorated pages.

THE WIND IN THE WILLOWS
Gollancz, 1988, 192p. – 0 575 03892 6
illustrated by Justin Todd

A talented artist brings his personal interpretation of the story to the full-page colour paintings. Good quality paper and clear print.

THE WIND IN THE WILLOWS
Methuen, 1951, 178p. – 0 416 53260 8
illustrated by Arthur Rackham

First published in 1939 in America, it is constantly reprinted so that consecutive generations can enjoy Rackham's illustrations.

THE WIND IN THE WILLOWS
Methuen, 1971, 284p. – 0 416 16980 5
illustrated by E. H. Shephard

THE WIND IN THE WILLOWS
Penguin, 1980, 240p. – Pbk. – 0 14 031544 6
illustrated by John Burningham

Although all the illustrations are black and white, there are over 60 humorous sketches which enhance the charm of the story.

THE WIND IN THE WILLOWS
Pavilion and National Trust, 1991, 176p. – 1 85145 603 1
illustrated by Graham Percy

Unusual use of colour giving the effect of being seen through a glass or through water. Some small black and white sketches are also included.

GRIMM, Jacob and Wilhelm

THE BROTHERS GRIMM: POPULAR FOLK TALES
Gollancz, 1990, 192p. – Pbk. – 0 575 04030 0
illustrated by Margaret Chamberlain

A welcome re-issue of this volume of stories chosen by Brian Alderson. The illustrations are plentiful and excellent, while the prose is particularly good for reading aloud.

FAVOURITE FAIRY TALES FROM GRIMM
Four Winds Press, 1982, 224p. – 0 590 07791 0
illustrated by Mercer Meyer

All the well known stories strikingly and fittingly illustrated in a highly individual style. Good quality paper and clear print with little silhouette decorations interspersed.

POPULAR FOLK TALES
Gollancz, 1990, 192p. – Pbk. – 0 575 04030 0
illustrated by Michael Foreman

Thirty-one stories translated from the German by Brian Alderson, and superbly illustrated with 25 full-colour plates, both humorous and atmospheric, and supported by black-and-white sketches interspersed throughout.

TALES FROM GRIMM
F. Lincoln, 1992, 112p. – 0 7112 0737 2
illustrated by Margaret Chamberlain

Retold by Antonia Barber, who is well known for her interest in folk and fairy tales. Each page is designed and decorated with a view to giving pleasure to the reader. The illustrations add a new dimension to well-known tales, giving them life, and bringing out the humour. Each illustration contains much detail which is rewarding to study and discuss with children. A beautiful book to own.

HARRIS, Joel Chandler

THE TALES OF UNCLE REMUS
Bodley Head, 1987, 176p. – 0 370 31089 6
illustrated by Jerry Pinkney

The adventures of Brer Rabbit as told to Julius Lester, illustrated by an award-winning artist. These 48 American folk tales are made accessible to modern children by updating the language without losing the point.

KINGSLEY, Charles

THE WATER BABIES
New Orchard Editions, 1990, 256p. –
1 85079 146 5
illustrated by Harry G. Theaker

Full-page colour illustrations with some black and white, by an Edwardian illustrator. Large print.

THE WATER BABIES
Dragon's World, 1981, 144p. – 0 905895 50 9
illustrated by Susan Rowe

Both black-and-white and water-colour paintings.

THE WATER BABIES
Gollancz, 1986, 224p. – Pbk. – 0 575 03879 9
illustrated by Harold Jones

Attractively illustrated and designed with a variety of illustrations, some small, some L-shaped, and some full-page. The print is very clear.

KIPLING, Rudyard

THE JUNGLE BOOK
Macmillan, 1993, 192p. – 0 333 59313 8

This collaboration between Maurice and Edward Detmold has produced a most accessible version of the famous stories. The print is clear, each page having a lot of space round the edges, with an unusual page design. The water-colour illustrations evoke the feeling of India.

THE JUNGLE BOOK
Pavilion and National Trust, 1991, 128p. –
1 85145 503 5
illustrated by Gregory Alexander

This version will be appreciated by an older child, as the illustrations have more adult appeal. There are full-colour pages and full-page spreads, with smaller insets interspersed throughout the text. Unusual and effective.

THE JUNGLE BOOK
Viking, 1987. – 0 670 80241 7
illustrated by Michael Foreman

In order to produce the right sort of illustrations, Michael Foreman visited India to see the colours and absorb the atmosphere. The result is full-page illustrations in vibrant colour, together with black and white sketches on half-pages. Very effective indeed.

THE JUST SO STORIES
Michael Joseph, 1989, 96p. – Pbk. –
1 85145 454 3
illustrated by Safaya Salter

Beautiful evocative illustrations.

THE JUST SO STORIES
Little Brown and Company, 1993, 160p. –
0 316 90696 4
illustrated by Isabelle Brent

A book of all-round, outstanding quality. Each full-page illustration has a beautiful, mosaic border which is repeated on the next page of text. The book is a riot of colour and gold-leaf on excellent paper with a clear, attractive print.

TALES OF MOWGLI
Heinemann, 1990, 192p. – 0 434 94641 9
illustrated by Patricia McCarthy

Both black-and-white and coloured illustrations in a very distinctive style which resembles batik.

LEWIS, C. S.

THE CHRONICLES OF NARNIA
in reading order:

THE MAGICIAN'S NEPHEW
Windrush, 1986, 198p. – L/P. – 1 85089 094 3

THE LION, THE WITCH AND THE WARDROBE
Windrush, 1986, 177p. – L/P. – 1 85089 084 6

A HORSE AND HIS BOY
Windrush, 1986, 208p. – L/P. – 1 85089 098 6

PRINCE CASPIAN
Windrush, 1986, 209p. – L/P. – 1 85089 099 4

THE VOYAGE OF THE 'DAWN TREADER'
Windrush, 1986, 237p. – L/P. – 1 85089 103 6

THE SILVER CHAIR
Windrush, 1986, 225p. – L/P. – 1 85089 104 4

THE LAST BATTLE
Windrush, 1986, 197p. – L/P. – 1 85089 108 7
all illustrated by Pauline Baynes

Designated as a 'Handi-read', it has large, very clear print, intended for partially-sighted readers, but equally good for children who are put off by small print. Also available as a boxed set.

MASEFIELD, John

THE BOX OF DELIGHTS
Heinemann, 1984, 168p. – 0 434 095952 1
illustrated by Faith Jacques

Abridged by Patricia Crampton, as this is a particularly difficult book for children to read, but she succeeds in preserving the essence of the book. Black-and-white illustrations interspersed with the text, with several full-page colour plates, beautifully painted.

MILNE, A. A.

THE HOUSE AT POOH CORNER
Methuen, 1928, 178p. – 0 416 34180 2
Mammoth, 1989, 176p. – Pbk. – 0 7497 0116 1

WINNIE THE POOH
Methuen, 1928, 158p. – 0 416 39380 2
Mammoth, 1989, 192p. – Pbk. – 0 7497 0210 9
both illustrated by E. H. Shephard

These books are both available in the same edition as originally published. The illustrations are an integral part of the book.

NESBIT, E.

THE RAILWAY CHILDREN
Heinemann, 1989, 188p. – 0 434 95456 X
illustrated by Pamela Kay

A mixture of black-and-white interspersed with the text, and full-colour plates. The pastel colours are very appealing, and there is good attention to period detail.

FIVE CHILDREN AND IT
BBC, 1990, 197p. – 0 563 36065 8
illustrated by John Holder

Excellent illustrations in pastel colours with good period detail. Ties in with the serialization shown on television.

FIVE CHILDREN AND IT
Heinemann, 1990, 192p. – 0 434 95458 6
illustrated by Larry Wilkes

These illustrations, based on research in Aylesford, Kent, where the story is set, capture all the sense of fun and atmosphere of E. Nesbit's story. A pleasing mixture of black-and-white and colour, small, large and full-page. A refreshing new look at an old favourite.

PERRAULT, Charles

CINDERELLA
Hamish Hamilton, 1986, 32p. – 0 241 11780 1
illustrated by Susan Jeffers

Retold by Amy Ehrlich, this is the story of Cinderella at its most basic, and best known. The pastel illustrations on every page, with some double-page spreads, make this a quality picture book.

LITTLE RED RIDING HOOD AND TEN OTHER CLASSIC STORIES
Pavilion, 1993, – 1 85793 934 4
illustrated by Sally Holmes

An attractive addition to the books of fairy stories. The print is large and clear, making even the pages with no illustration look attractive. The illustrated pages have a variety of layouts, and the colours are pale rather than garish.

POTTER, Beatrix

THE COMPLETE TALES OF BEATRIX POTTER
Warne, 1989, 384p. – 0 7232 3618 6
illustrated by the author

A beautiful book for Potter fanatics, containing 23 stories and poems, set out in chronological order with all the original illustrations, printed on good quality paper. There is a brief introduction linking the stories to places and events in the Lake District. Worth every pound!

SEWELL, Anna

BLACK BEAUTY
Gollancz, 1988, 224p. – 0 575 03924 8
illustrated by Charles Keeping

A mixture of black-and-white, half-colour and full-colour, some interspersed with the text, some full-page. Typical Keeping illustrations are a perfect match for this story.

BLACK BEAUTY
Macmillan, 1989, 72p. – Pbk. – 0 333 49334 6
illustrated by Susan Jeffers

Retold by Robin McKinley – an excellent adaptation, keeping as true as possible to the original. As always with the Papermac series, the illustrations are the major part, and are superb.

BLACK BEAUTY
Pavilion and National Trust, 1993, 192p. – 1 85793 068 1
illustrated by Dinah Dryhurst

The artist obviously feels in tune with the mood of the Victorian period, which is reflected in the excellent water colours and line drawings produced for this edition. The quality of the paper is excellent, but the print is rather small.

SPYRI, Johanna

HEIDI
Heinemann, 1991, 192p. – 0 434 96423 9
illustrated by Kate Aldous

There have been many versions of this popular classic over the years, but this one is particularly outstanding. Although the print is rather small, it is clear, and the text is well-broken with coloured or black and white illustrations of very high quality. Some full-page colour illustrations are included.

STEVENSON, Robert Louis

TREASURE ISLAND
Gollancz, 1990, 288p. – Pbk. – 0 575 04840 9
illustrated by N. C. Wyeth

Originally commissioned in 1911, 14 paintings were included. This edition was first published in hardback in 1982. The print is attractive and clear, but not large, and the paintings are striking. Recommended for older children.

TREASURE ISLAND
Heinemann, 1990, 204p. – 0 434 96508 1
illustrated by John Lawrence

An excellent colourful version with illustrations reminiscent of Edward Ardizzone. Clear print on good paper make it easy to read.

TREASURE ISLAND
Dragons World, 1992, 176p. – 1 85028 202 1
illustrated by Robert Ingpen

This version contains illustrations which are capable of conveying as much as the text to the reader. There are both paintings and drawings on every page, and at times could be taken for photographs. Full of atmosphere, they give a whole new perspective to the story.

TOLKIEN, J. R. R.

THE HOBBIT
Unwin, 1987, 304p. – Pbk. – 0 04 823803
illustrated by Michael Hague

Highly unusual paintings in colours which reflect the atmosphere and mystery of this story.

THE HOBBIT
Windrush, 1990, 384p. – L/P. – 1 85089 805 7
illustrated by the author

This is a large print edition of the original version which will make it more accessible to children who struggle with small print.

WILDE, Oscar

THE FAIRY STORIES OF OSCAR WILDE
Gollancz, 1985, 224p. – Pbk. – 0 575 03614 1
illustrated by Harold Jones

Nine stories, including *The Happy Prince* and *The Selfish Giant*, with lots of black-and-white illustrations, either half or full-page, and very clear print.

THE FAIRY TALES OF OSCAR WILDE
Michael O'Mara, 1993, 192p. – 1 85479 118 4
illustrated by Michael Hague

An artist of exceptional talent has excelled himself producing paintings to illustrate these stories.

ANTHOLOGIES

CARTER, Angela
SLEEPING BEAUTY AND OTHER FAVOURITE FAIRY TALES
Gollancz, 1991, 128p. – Pbk. – 0 575 05086 1
illustrated by Michael Foreman

An unusual selection of stories, edited by Angela Carter, includes some of the less well-known, with Foreman's lavish illustrations in colour and black and white on every page.

CORRIN, Sara and Stephen
THE FABER BOOK OF FAVOURITE FAIRY TALES
Faber, 1988, 256p. – 0 571 14854 9
illustrated by Juan Wijngaard

Chosen by Sara and Stephen Corrin, the 26 wide-ranging fairy tales are published in clear print on good paper. The pages are decorated, and look most attractive. The award-winning artist has painted 15 full-page pictures of excellent quality.

EHRLICH, Amy
THE WALKER BOOK OF FAIRY TALES
Walker Books, 1986, 208p. – O/P. – 0 7445 0339 6
illustrated by Diane Goode

Nineteen of the best known fairy tales, adapted by Amy Ehrlich, and marvellously illustrated on every page, both black-and-white and full-colour. Excellent paper and large, clear print. A superb book.

FOREMAN, Michael
WORLD OF FAIRY TALES
Pavilion Books, 1990, 144p. – 1 85145 466 7
illustrated by the editor

Twenty-two stories from around the world, some well known, others less so. The illustrations use vibrant colour on excellent quality paper. A book to savour, and guaranteed to make children love books for life.

FOSS, Michael
A FIRST TREASURY OF FAIRY TALES
M. O'Mara Books, 1989, 160p. – 0 948397 30 6
Macmillan Children's Books, 1988, 80p. – Pbk. – 0 333 48057 0

A SECOND TREASURY OF FAIRY TALES
Macmillan Children's Books, 1988, 80p. – Pbk. – 0 333 48058 9

Edited by Michael Foss, with illustrations by such classic illustrators as Arthur Rackham and Leslie Brook. Good quality paper, excellent page layout, and lots of very varied illustrations. Some of the stories have been slightly abbreviated for easier accessibility by younger readers.

IMPEY, Rose
ORCHARD BOOK OF FAIRY TALES
Orchard, 1993, 128p. – 1 85213 382 1
illustrated by Ian Beck

Rose Impey retells the favourites, and, combined with Ian Beck, could not fail to produce a top-quality book. There are fourteen stories on good paper, with clear print and complementary illustrations on every page. A winner!

SERIES

◆

Publishing books in a series is one way of producing good quality material at an economical price. It is also helpful for readers who have found a book enjoyable to have a reliable means of recognizing similar material. Most publishers try to obtain highly regarded authors, first because good material is important at all levels, and second because it is hoped that children will recognize and read the same authors later. Not all series maintain a consistently high standard. Every book should be examined critically. The entries in this section show for whom the series is primarily intended, followed by examples of the best titles.

ANTELOPE

Hamish Hamilton.

A long established series aimed at 7–9 year olds, and designed to give young readers practice in order to achieve fluency. Recently given a face-lift with better covers and a new design, the formula remains the same: fairly short chapters, restricted vocabulary, and plenty of illustrations to back up the text, which is in large print. Many of the earlier titles have been re-issued in paperback in the **Young Puffin Story Book Series.**

ALCOCK, V.
  The Wreckers

BALL, B.
  Magic on the tide

CROSS, G.
  Rent-a-genius

DALTON, A.
  Ugly mug

DHAMI, N.
  Cat's eyes

FINE, A.
  Diary of a killer cat

JONES, D. W.
  Chair Person

NICHOLLS, C.
  Good and bad witch

NIMMO, J.
  The Red Secret

OPPEL, K.
  Bad case of robots

SWINDELLS, R.
  Go ahead, gang

WHITEHEAD, A.
  Eric the first flying penguin

BANANA

Heinemann

A very successful series best suited to 7–9 year olds. An attractive small format, with colourful illustrations, covering a wide range of interests. They are fun to read, amusing, and not too difficult or long.

BENJAMIN, F.
  Snotty and the rod of power

CROSS, G.
  Monster from the underground

DARKE, M.
  Imp

FINE, A.
  Design a pram

IMPEY, R.
  You Herman, me Mary

JARMAN, J.
  Nancy Pocket and the kidnappers

KAYE, G.
  Snow girl

KEMP, G.
  Wanting a little black gerbil

LIVELY, P.
  Debbie and the Little Devil

MORPURGO, M.
  Marble crusher

URE, J.
  Spooky cottage

WILSON, G.
  Polly pipes up

BLACKIE BEARS

Blackie

Aimed at 6–8 year olds requiring reading practice. Very attractive and distinctive in bright yellow, but not, however, divided into chapters, which is a pity, for 50 pages is a lengthy read to manage all at once for children just becoming accustomed to a full-length book. Some titles are now available in the *Young Puffin Read Alone Series*.

BERESFORD, E.
Rola Polar Bear and the heatwave

BULL, A.
Yellow wellies

DICKS, T.
Steaming Sam

ESCOTT, J.
Matthew's surprise

HARDCASTLE, M.
Joanne's goal

ENNINGS, L.
Luke's holiday

KRAILING, T.
Marlene the monster

OLDFIELD, P.
Cat with no name

PILLING, A.
The Friday Parcel

POWLING, C.
Wesley at the water park

WADDELL, M.
The Tall Story of Wilbur Small

WILSON, J.
Monster in the cupboard

BLACKIE SNAPPERS

Blackie

Aimed at 'younger readers', but rather vague. The stories are full of humour, and move along at a fast pace. The vocabulary, however, is quite complex, as are some of the concepts, and the books require a certain ability and stamina. They are illustrated in black-and-white, but several pages do not have illustrations. Suitable for age 8–10.

BEVAN, C.
Ask me no questions

HOOPER, M.
Revolting wedding

IRONS, J.
How to swap your parents without really trying

McCALL SMITH, A.
The Cowgirl aunt of Harriet Bean
Harriet Bean and the league of cheats

MASTERS, A.
Playing with fire

PIROTTA, S.
Operation carrot

RYAN, M.
The Saturday Knight

SAMPSON, D.
The Boy who was twins

WILSON, J.
The Were puppy

WISEMAN, D.
Goliath takes the bait

CARTWHEELS

Hamish Hamilton

As children are learning to read, it is important that they find it fun, and feel successful. This series supplies material just right for that purpose, bridging the gap between picture books and full-length story books. Bold type, colourful illustrations and stories of a consistently high standard ensure success.

ALLEN, J.
Percy goes to Spain

BALL, B.
Bella's concert

CARTWHEELS

DINAN, C.
　Goodnight monster

ELLIS, A.
　Out in the woods

GERAS, A.
　The Glittering River

HARKER, L.
Charlie's dragon

LAMBERT, T.
　Benny's best friend

LAVELLE, S.
Harry's cat

MAYNE, W.
　Oh, Grandma

OFFEN, H.
　S.O.S. for Rita

PEYTON, K. M.
　Apple won't jump

POWLING, C.
　That dragon again

PRATER, J.
　Bear's den

BENNETT, L.
　Kat's goblin

EADINGTON, J.
　Jonny Briggs and the Silver Surprise

HACKNEY, J.
　Alec's dragon

JONES, I.
　Battle for Muck Farm

KAYE, G.
　A Dog called Dog

MANGAN, A.
　Nan's Palace

MORSE, B.
　Sauce for the Fox

PEARSON, M.
　Save this tree

ZABEL, Jennifer
　Under the Pudding basin

CHEETAHS

Hodder & Stoughton

Aimed at the age group 6–8 years, there are no fixed rules of vocabulary, but fairly standard length, usually divided into chapters. Any author would be considered on merit, but there is a tendency to rely on known authors who have expertise in writing for this particular age group. The overriding criterion is a good strong story suitable for children of this age.

ALLEN, L.
　Crash, Bang and Wallop

ARKLE, P.
　The Dinosaur Field

COMETS and CRACKERS

Black

Similar to **CHEETAHS**, these two companion series are uniform in length, with attractive covers, lots of illustrations, and clear print, all designed to encourage children aged between 8 and 10 to read. Some are much better than others.

COMETS

DEARY, T.
　The Dream Seller

EYLES, H.
　The Double

FREEMAN, M.
　Spaceball

LEESON, R.
　Right Royal Kidnap

240

LISHAK, A.
Coming round
Ten pound note

PRICE, S.
Master Thomas Katt

SIMISTER, J.
Where dragons breathe

SOUTER, A.
Scrapyard

WILLSON, R. B.
Haunting music

WRIGHT, B. R.
Christina's ghost

CRACKERS

DEARY, T.
Joke factory
Windmill of nowhere

PREGER, J.
The Terrible Trials of Mattie McCrum

STRONG, J.
Fatbag
It's a tough life
Pandemonium at school
Viking in trouble

TALBOT, J.
Big Swig and Fling

UMANSKY, K.
Big Izzy
Fwog Pwince and the twuth

WARBURTON, N. J.
Ape in space
Saving Grace

GANDERS

Hodder & Stoughton

An outwardly attractive series for children who have mastered reading, but who need good quality material that will not overwhelm them. The stories are lively and amusing, and the print is large and clear. Coloured illustrations would have enhanced the attractiveness of the series, as the front covers promise more than the contents can yield. Nevertheless, the black and white drawings have charm and humour. Shortly to be replaced by a new series.

ALLEN, E.
Emily in the News

DEARY, T.
The Skeleton in the Cupboard

HILL, D.
Matthew's mog

LAVELLE, S.
Copycat
Wincey's worm

LINDSAY, F.
Runaway Bim

MAY, K.
Lenny's dinosaur bone

NEWMAN, M.
Green monster magic

PEARSON, M.
Silly Tilly
Strong Tom

THOMPSON, C.
Ethel the chicken
A Giant called Norman Mary

WEBB, D.
Lilly's lollipop wand

GAZELLE

Hamish Hamilton

Aimed at 6–8 year olds and, like **ANTELOPES**, a well established series which has recently been redesigned to make it more up-to-date and appealing. Small and quite short (about 50 pages), bold print and lots of illustrations make it a series which will

GAZELLE

help children gain reading fluency. There are now many titles in the series, some re-issued in paperback, and some are much more worth reading than others.

BROWNE, E.
Caraway and the cup final

DICKS, T.
Littlest dinosaur

FINE, A.
Same old story every year

GERAS, A.
Nina's magic

GOWAR, M.
Sir Pellinore, the Knight who never gave up

HANNAH, S.
Carrot the goldfish

LAMBERT, T.
Jenny and Big L

LEESON, R.
One frog too many

MATTHIAS, B.
Kate's skates

NEWMAN, M.
Skipper at school

SEFTON, C.
Ghosts of cobweb

TOOMEY, P.
Lance and the singing rat

WILSON, J.
Mark Spark in the dark

HEDGEHOG

Hodder & Stoughton

A series designed like **CARTWHEELS** to encourage new readers to practise their new-found skills and achieve fluency. Very enjoyable stories, bold print and lively colourful illustrations all combine to produce excellent reading material.

BALL, B.
Cat up the clock

COCKETT, M.
Bridesmaids

DAVIES, G.
James and the jumble

MANGAN, A.
School cat
Umbrella tree

MORTON, C.
The Pig that bathed

PAUL, B.
Unlucky lucky

STRONG, J.
Little Pig goes to school

TAYLOR, M.
Aunt Lizzie's lion

WEBB, D.
Ben and the amazing pot plant

WILSON, D. H.
Little Billy and the Wump

JETS

Black – hardback
Young Lions – paperback

This series is aimed at children who can read, but who require practice with lots of encouragement. This is provided by illustrations on every page, both conventional and comic-strip, which appeal more to some readers. The stories are humorous, interesting and imaginative. They are not, however, straightforward to read, as the child has to follow two texts, the story and the 'extras' in bubbles. Authors invited to contribute to the series are well established, and write stories with a clear continuity line.

ANDERSON, R.
  Best friends

BURNARD, D.
  Ernest the heroic lion-tamer

GIRLING, B.
  Clevor Trevor
  Nora Bone

HENDRY, D. and HEAP, S.
  The Thing in-a-box

JARMAN, J.
  Georgie and the dragon

MORPURGO, M.
  And pigs might fly
  Jigger's day off

OFFEN, H.
  Grubble trouble

TAYLOR, L.
  Pesters of the west

THOMSON, P.
  Rhyming Russell

WEST, C.
  Monty, the dog who wore glasses

WILSON, B.
  Stone the crows, it's a vacuum cleaner

JUMBO JETS

A new addition aimed at children who can cope easily with **JETS** and need stretching.

BRUMPTON, K.
  Forecast of fear

ROSSELSON, L.
  Bornie works a miracle

RYAN, M.
  Fergus the forgetful

UMANSKY, K.
  Sir Quinton Quest hunts the yeti

ORCHARD STORYBOOKS

KITES

Viking Kestrel

Intended for the age group 7–9, and for children with a certain competence as they are quite long – 100 pages. The print is large, and every page is illustrated with line drawings, but they do look a little dull when compared with new series illustrated in colour. Many of the titles in this series have been re-issued in paperback.

BRANDRETH, G.
  The Hiccups at No. 13

DUFFEY, B.
  Gadget war

FINDLATER, E.
  Ginger Spike

GIRLING, B.
  Dumbellina and the vanishing video

JUNGMAN, A.
  Septimouse, Big-cheese

KIDD, D.
  Onion tears

KING-SMITH, D.
  Mr. Potter's pet

KINGSLAND, R.
  Zoldo the magnificent

RODGERS, F.
  Intergalactic kitten goes prehistoric

UMANSKY, K.
  King Keith and the Jolly Lodger

WADDELL, M.
  Herbie whistle

ORCHARD STORYBOOKS

Orchard

There are several excellent mini-series within this group, each written by the same author to ensure reliability and to

ORCHARD STORYBOOKS

encourage children to further reading through familiarity. Best suited for the 7–9 year-olds, with short chapters and good illustrations.

ASHLEY, B.
  Clipper Street
Six stories set in a South London street, dealing with the problems that face children daily – violence, racism, homelessness.

CROSSLEY-HOLLAND, K.
  Folk Tales
Short adaptations of popular British folk stories in four volumes.

IMPEY, R.
  Animal crackers
A series of very easy and highly amusing animal stories based on record-breaking animals. Shoo Rayner's illustrations carry equal weight.

LAVELLE, S.
  Jupiter Jane
Four science fiction stories that are also very amusing.

LIMB, S.
  Green Books
Two books about environmental problems dealt with in a humorous way.

URE, J.
  Woodside School
Six stories about the children from Woodside Primary School.

READ ALONE

Viking Kestrel

'Designed for all new readers who want to start reading a whole book on their own.' Attractive covers lead to disappointing interiors, as the illustrations are a dull black and white. However, the print is large and clear, the chapters are short, and the stories, on the whole, are fun to read. The series includes some titles published in hardback as **TIGER** series, and some titles are now available in **Young Puffin Read Alone.**

ANDERSON, S.
  Amazing Mark in Creepstone Castle

BERG, L.
  Dear Billy and other stories

BEVAN, B.
  Simon's magic bobble hat

CASTOR, H.
  Fat Puss and Slimpup

FINE, A.
  Only a show

FORD, N.
  Lost wag

HAYES, R.
  Smell that got away

HUNTER, J.
  Hector the spectre

JOY, M.
  Addy the baddy

JUNGMAN, A.
  Leila's magical monster party

McCALL SMITH, A.
  Ice-cream bicycle

PILLING, A.
  Dustbin Charlie cleans up

ROSSELSON, L.
  Grandfather sings again
  Rosa's singing grandfather

TAYLOR, R.
  Kitnapping of Mittens

READ IT YOURSELF

Gollancz

A very attractive series, but not as young as the name implies. Approximately 50 pages, not particularly large print, but very clear, lots of coloured illustrations, but not divided into chapters, which is a disadvantage. Lower juniors will enjoy them.

BYARS, B.
  Golly Sisters go west

HILL, D.
  Goblin Party

HOBAN, J.
  Quick chick

KING-SMITH, D.
  The Jeanius

RYLANT, C.
  Henry and Mudge

READY, STEADY, READ

Puffin

A new series for children who have learned to read and want to practise on 'proper books'. Good clear print, well illustrated, and a good storyline which contrives to be both repetitious and interesting, ensure children will gain enjoyment from reading.

FRENCH, V.
  Hedgehogs don't eat hamburgers

MOSTYN, D.
  Captain Daylight and the big hold-up

OSBAND, G.
  Farmer Jane
  Farmer Jane's birthday treat

RAYNER, S.
  Cyril's cat and the big surprise

ROSSELSON, L.
  Swim, Sam, swim

SAGE, A.
  Little blue book of the Marie Celeste
  Little pink book of the woolly mammoth

WADDELL, M.
  Lucky duck song

ROOSTERS

Hodder & Stoughton

Designed to 'boost children's confidence in their ability to read "a whole book"'. Good stories of real interest to encourage reluctant readers. The very large, clear print and bold black and white illustrations look quite inviting.

ALLEN, E.
  Emily in the news

DEARY, T.
  Skeleton in the Cupboard

HILL, D.
  Matthew's Mog

LINDSAY, F.
  Runaway Bim

LYONS, G.
  Lonely basilisk

NEWMAN, M.
  Green monster magic

PEARSON, M.
  Peter Pepper and the Goblin

RUFFELL, A.
  Grand Bristleton Easter Egg

WEBB, D.
  Lilly's lollipop wand

THE STORY FACTORY

Blackie

A new series 'written especially for younger readers'. They are too difficult for first readers, but children with a

245

THE STORY FACTORY

basic ability who need practice to build on their newly acquired skill will enjoy the challenge. The print is large, the chapters short, and there are lots of illustrations. So far, the story content has proved to be very good.

CAVE, K.
  Jumble

ESCOTT, J.
  Crocodile surprise

KRAILING, T.
  Supersnail

McCALL SMITH, A.
  Marzipan Max

PITCHER, C.
  The Sun Tribe

RYAN, M.
  Griselda F, G, M

WARD, N.
  Gran in space

SUPERCHAMPS

Heinemann

A series for competent readers who need encouraging to read for pleasure. Small so they do not appear daunting, bright and attractive inside and outside, clear print and unusually good quality paper. The stories are interesting and amusing, not too long and divided into manageable chapters.

ANDERSON, R.
  Tough as old boots

GORDON, J.
  Blood brothers

GRANT, G.
  Crash!

HARDCASTLE, M.
  Mark England's Cap

HOFFMAN, M.
  Dog Powder

KAYE, G.
  The Stone boy

MARCH, J.
  All the kings and queens

MAYNE, W.
  Egg timer

O'NEILL, J.
  Sharp eyes

PILLING, A.
  Boy with his leg in the air

PRICE, S.
  Thunderpumps

WESTALL, R.
  Size twelve

TIGERS

A series aimed at 6–9 year olds, which is quite a wide age range. Some are very simple, and restricted to 3000 words with an illustration on every page, others are longer and more difficult, so it is necessary to choose with care. They are divided into chapters, which is useful. Some established authors are commissioned, but a new author with a suitable script would be teamed with a well-known illustrator.

BURNAND, D.
  Revenge of the killer vegetables

CAMP, L.
  Cabbages from outer space

FITZMAURICE, M.
  Morris MacMillipede

HAWKINS, E.
  Henry's most unusual birthday

246

MAY, K.
   Cat's witch and the last birthday

SPELLER, P.
   I want to be on TV

SWINDELLS, R.
   Rolf and Rosie

TALBOT, J.
   Stanley makes it big

TOWNSON, H.
   Blue magic

WILLS, J.
   Lily and Lorna
   Salt and pepper boys

TELEVISION TIE-INS

◆

A list of books which have featured on television since 1992. Much has been said about the detrimental effect of television on the reading habits of children. No doubt there is some truth in this, but there is also a positive side. Many good quality books are dramatized, which allows children who would otherwise miss out completely to experience the author's message, and can often stimulate them to read books which they would otherwise have felt unable to tackle.

AHLBERG, A.
  Master Money and the Millionaire's Son
  Mrs Plug the Plumber
  Mr and Mrs Hay the Horse
  Mr Biff the Boxer
  Mr Tick the Teacher
  Woof!

AIKEN, J.
  Night Birds on Nantucket

APPS, R.
  Marlene Marlowe Investigates...

ASHLEY, B.
  Dodgem
  Seeing off Uncle Jack

ASHLEY, C. and B.
  Three Seven Eleven

AVERY, G.
  A Likely Lad

BENEDICTUS, D.
  Little Sir Nicholas

BRESLIN, T.
  Simon's Challenge

BROWN, J.
  Flat Stanley
  Flat Stanley in Space

COLLODI, C.
  Pinocchio

CRESSWELL, H.
  Lizzy Dripping and the Witch

DAHL, R.
  The BFG
  Charlie and the Chocolate Factory
  Dirty Beasts
  Revolting Rhymes

DANN, C.
  The Animals of Farthing Wood

DESAI, A.
  Village by the Sea

DOHERTY, B.
  Children in Winter

EADINGTON, J.
  Jonny Briggs and the Galloping Wedding
  Jonny Briggs and the Junior Tennis
  Jonny Briggs and the Silver Surprise
  Stand up Jonny Briggs
  Well done, Jonny Briggs

ELDRIDGE, J.
  Bud Boyes
  Time Riders
  Uncle Jack and Operation Green
  Uncle Jack and the Loch Ness Monster

FINE, A.
  Angel of Nitshill Road
  Flour Babies
  Goggle-eyes

GERRARD, R.
  Mik's Mammoth

GETZ, D.
  Thin Air

GLEITZMAN, M.
  Misery Guts
  Two Weeks with the Queen

GRAHAME, K.
  The Wind in the Willows

GREGORY, P.
  Florizella and the Wolves

HANDFORD, M.
  Where's Wally?

HENDRY, D.
  Harvey Angell

HENKES, K.
  Jessica

HICYILMAZ, G.
  Against the Storm

IMPEY, R.
  Who's a Clever Girl, Then?

JENNINGS, P.
  Round the Twist

JONES, D. W.
  Archer's Goon

JONES, T.
  Fantastic Stories

KING-SMITH, D.
  Harry's Mad
  Queen's Nose

KIPLING, R.
  The Cat that Walked by Itself
  The Just So Stories

LAIRD, E.
  Kiss the Dust

LEWIS, C. S.
  The Lion, the Witch and the
    Wardrobe
  Prince Caspian
  The Voyage of the 'Dawn Treader'

LOFTING, H.
  The Story of Dr Dolittle

MONTGOMERY, L. M.
  Anne of Green Gables
  The Road to Avonlea

MORPURGO, M.
  Marble Crusher
  Mr Nobody's Eyes

NABB, M.
  Josie Smith
  Josie Smith and Eileen
  Josie Smith at School
  Josie Smith at the Seaside
  Josie Smith in Hospital

NESBIT, E.
  Five Children and It

NIMMO, J.
  Delilah and the Dogspell

NORTON, M.
  The Borrowers
  The Borrowers Afield
  The Borrowers Afloat

PEARCE, P.
  The Way to Sattin Shore

PEYTON, K. M.
  Who Sir, Me Sir?

PORTER, E. H.
  Pollyanna

PRATCHETT, T.
  Truckers

RUTSLER, W.
  Mr Merlin

RUSHDIE, S.
  Haroun and the Sea of Stories

STEIG, W.
  Real Thief

STRACHAN, I.
  Flawed Glass

SWINDELLS, R.
  Ice Palace

UMANSKY, K.
  Fwog Pwince – the Twuth
  Sir Quinton Quest Hunts the Yeti

VARLEY, S.
  Badger's Parting Gifts

WADDELL, S.
  Sloggers

WALSH, J. P.
  Torch

WHITE, H.
  Children's Ward

LIST OF AWARDS AND PRIZE WINNERS

◆

HANS CHRISTIAN ANDERSEN AWARDS

Made biennially by the International Board on Books for Young People (IBBY), and given to an author in respect of their complete works, judged as a lasting contribution to literature for children. The medal was first awarded in 1956, jointly to Eleanor Farjeon and Jella Lepman – founder of IBBY.

1956	Eleanor Farjeon	(Great Britain)
1958	Astrid Lindgren	(Sweden)
1960	Erich Kästner	(Germany)
1962	Meindert Dejong	(USA)
1964	René Guillot	(France)
1966	Tove Jannson	(Finland)
1968	James Kruss	(Germany)
	Jose Maria Sanchez Silva	(Spain)
1970	Gianni Rodari	(Italy)
1972	Scott O'Dell	(USA)
1974	Maria Gripe	(Sweden)
1976	Cecil Bodker	(Denmark)
1978	Paula Fox	(USA)
1980	Bohumil Riha	(Czechoslovakia)
1982	Lygia Bojunga Nunes	(Brazil)
1984	Christine Nostlinger	(Austria)
1986	Patricia Wrightson	(Australia)
1988	Annie M. G. Schmidt	(Netherlands)
1990	Tormod Haugen	(Norway)
1992	Virginia Hamilton	(USA)

AWARDS AND PRIZE WINNERS

BOSTON GLOBE-HORN BOOK AWARD

Co-sponsored by the *Boston Globe* newspaper and the *Horn Book* magazine, awards were first given in 1967. From 1976 there have been awards for non-fiction and illustration in addition to the fiction awards of which the winners are listed here.

1967	The Little Fishes	Erik Christian Haugaard	Houghton Mifflin
1968	The Spring Rider	John Lawson	Crowell
1969	The Wizard of Earthsea	Ursula K. Le Guin	Parnassus
1970	The Intruder	John Rowe Townsend	Lippincott
1971	A Room made of Windows	Eleanor Cameron	Atlantic Little Brown
1972	Tristan and Iseult	Rosemary Sutcliff	Dutton
1973	The Dark is Rising	Susan Cooper	Atheneum
1974	M. C. Higgins, the Great	Virginia Hamilton	Macmillan
1975	Transport 7–41–R	T. Degens	Viking
1976	Unleaving	Jill Paton Walsh	Farrar Straus & Giroux
1977	Child of the Owl	Laurence Yep	Harper & Row
1978	The Westing Game	Ellen Raskin	Dutton
1979	Humbug Mountain	Sid Fleischman	Atlantic Little Brown
1980	Conrad's War	Andrew Davies	Crown
1981	The Leaving	Lynn Hall	Scribner
1982	Playing Beatie Bow	Ruth Park	Atheneum
1983	Sweet Whispers, Brother Rush	Virginia Hamilton	Philomel
1984	A Little Fear	Patricia Wrightson	Atheneum
1985	The Moves Make the Man	Bruce Brooks	Harper & Row
1986	In Summer Light	Zibby Oneal	Viking
1987	Rabble Starkey	Lois Lowry	Houghton Mifflin
1988	The Friendship	Mildred D. Taylor	Dial
1989	The Village by the Sea	Paula Fox	Orchard
1990	Maniac Magee	Jerry Spinelli	Little, Brown
1991	The True Confessions of Charlotte Doyle	Avi	Orchard
1992	Missing May	Cynthia Rylant	Orchard/A Richard Jackson Book
1993	Ajeemah and his Son	James Berry	Harper Collins

AWARDS AND PRIZE WINNERS

CANADIAN LIBRARY ASSOCIATION – BOOK OF THE YEAR FOR CHILDREN AWARD

Presented annually since 1947 for an English language book by a Canadian or permanent Canadian resident.

1947	Starbuck Valley Winter	Roderick Haig-Brown	Morrow
1948	No award given		
1949	Kristli's Trees	Mabel Dunham	McClelland & Stewart
1950	Franklin of the Arctic: a Life of Adventure	Richard S. Lambert	McClelland & Stewart
1951	No award given		
1952	The Sun Horse	Catherine Anthony Clark	Macmillan
1953	No award given		
1954	No award given		
1955	No award given		
1956	Train for Tiger Lily	Louise Riley	Macmillan
1957	Glooskap's Country and Other Indian Tales	Cyrus Macmillan	OUP
1958	Lost in the Barrens	Farley Mowat	Little Brown
1959	The Dangerous Cove: a Story of Early Days in Newfoundland	John F. Hayes	Copp Clark
1960	The Golden Phoenix and Other French Canadian Fairy Tales	Charles Marius Barbeau	OUP
1961	The St Lawrence	William Toye	OUP
1962	No award given		
1963	The Incredible Journey: a Tale of Three Animals	Sheila Every Burnford	Little Brown
1964	The Whale People	Roderick Haig-Brown	Collins
1965	Tales of Nanabozho	Dorothy Reid	OUP
1966	Tikta' Liktak: an Eskimo Legend	James Houston	Longman
1967	The Raven's Cry	Christie Harris	McClelland & Stewart
1968	The White Archer: an Eskimo Legend	James Houston	Academic
1969	And Tomorrow the Stars: the Story of John Cabot	Kay Hill	Dodd
1970	Sally Go Round the Sun	Edith Fowke	McClelland & Stewart
1971	Carter Discovers the St Lawrence	William Toye	OUP
1972	Mary of Mile 18	Ann Blades	Tundra
1973	The Marrow of the World	Ruth Nichollls	Macmillan
1974	The Miraculous Hind	Elizabeth Cleaver	Holt Rinehart & Winston
1975	Alligator Pie	Dennis Lee	Macmillan
1976	Jacob Two-Two Meets the Hooded Fang	Mordecai Richler	McClelland & Stewart

257

AWARDS AND PRIZE WINNERS

1977	Mouse Woman and the Vanished Princesses	Christie Harris	McClelland & Stewart
1978	Garbage Delight	Dennis Lee	Macmillan
1979	Hold Fast	Kevin Major	Clarke Irwin
1980	River Runners: a Tale of Hardship and Bravery	James Houston	McClelland & Stewart
1981	The Violin Maker's Gift	Donn Kushner	Macmillan
1982	The Root Cellar	Janet Lunn	Lester & Orpen Dennys
1983	Up To Low	Brian Doyle	Groundwood
1984	Sweetgrass	Jan Hudson	Tree Frog Press
1985	Mama's Going to Buy you a Mockingbird	Jean Little	Viking Kestrel
1986	Julie	Cora Taylor	Western Producer
1987	Shadow in Hawthorn Bay	Janet Lunn	Lester & Orpen Dennys
1988	A Handful of Time	Kit Pearson	Penguin
1989	Easy Avenue	Brian Doyle	Groundwood
1990	The Sky is Falling	Kit Pearson	Penguin
1991	Redwork	Michael Bedard	Lester & Orpen Dennys
1992	Eating between the Lines	Kevin Major	Doubleday
1993	Ticket to Curlew	Celia Barker Lettridge	Groundwood/Douglas McIntyre

AWARDS AND PRIZE WINNERS

THE CARNEGIE MEDAL

The Carnegie Medal is given for an outstanding book for children written in English and contenders are appraised for characterization, plot, style, accuracy, imaginative quality and that indefinable element that lifts the book above the others. Presented annually by the Library Association since 1936.

Year	Title	Author	Publisher
1936	Pigeon Post	Arthur Ransome	Cape
1937	The Family from One End Street	Eve Garnett	Muller
1938	The Circus is Coming	Noel Streatfield	Dent
1939	Radium Woman	Eleanor Doorl	Heinemann
1940	Visitors from London	Kitty Barne	Dent
1941	We Couldn't Leave Dinah	Mary Treadgold	Cape
1942	The Little Grey Men	BB	Eyre & Spottiswoode
1943	No award given		
1944	The Wind on the Moon	Eric Linklater	Macmillan
1945	No award given		
1946	The Little White Horse	Elizabeth Goudge	Bockhampton Press
1947	Collected Stories for Children	Walter de la Mare	Faber & Faber
1948	Sea Change	Richard Armstrong	Dent
1949	The Story of Your Home	Agnes Allen	Transatlantic
1950	The Lark on the Wing	Elfrida Vipont	OUP
1951	The Wool-Pack	Cynthia Harnett	Methuen
1952	The Borrowers	Mary Norton	Dent
1953	A Valley Grows Up	Edward Osmond	OUP
1954	Knight Crusader	Ronald Welch	OUP
1955	The Little Bookroom	Eleanor Farjeon	OUP
1956	The Last Battle	C. S. Lewis	Bodley Head
1957	A Grass Rope	William Mayne	OUP
1958	Tom's Midnight Garden	A. Philippa Pearce	OUP
1959	The Lantern Bearers	Rosemary Sutcliff	OUP
1960	The Making Of Man	I. W. Cornwall	Phoenix
1961	A Stranger at Green Knowe	Lucy M. Boston	Faber & Faber
1962	The Twelve and the Genii	Pauline Clarke	Faber & Faber
1963	Time of Trial	Hester Burton	OUP
1964	Nordy Bank	Sheena Porter	OUP
1965	The Grange At High Force	Philip Turner	OUP
1966	No award given		
1967	The Owl Service	Alan Garner	Collins
1968	The Moon in the Cloud	Rosemary Harris	Faber & Faber
1969	The Edge of the Cloud	K. M. Peyton	OUP
1970	The God Beneath the Sea	Leon Garfield and Edward Blishen	Longman
1971	Josh	Ivan Southall	Angus & Robertson
1972	Watership Down	Richard Adams	Collins
1973	The Ghost of Thomas Kempe	Penelope Lively	Heinemann

AWARDS AND PRIZE WINNERS

1974	The Stronghold	Mollie Hunter	Hamish Hamilton
1975	The Machine-gunners	Robert Westall	Macmillan
1976	Thunder and Lightnings	Jan Mark	Kestrel
1977	The Turbulent Term of Tyke Tiler	Gene Kemp	Faber & Faber
1978	The Exeter Blitz	David Rees	Hamish Hamilton
1979	Tulku	Peter Dickinson	Gollancz
1980	City of Gold	Peter Dickinson	Gollancz
1981	The Scarecrows	Robert Westall	Chatto & Windus
1982	The Haunting	Margaret Mahy	Dent
1983	Handles	Jan Mark	Kestrel
1984	The Changeover	Margaret Mahy	Dent
1985	Storm	Kevin Crossley-Holland	Heinemann
1986	Granny Was A Buffer Girl	Berlie Doherty	Methuen
1987	The Ghost Drum	Susan Price	Faber & Faber
1988	A Pack of Lies	Geraldine McCaughrean	OUP
1989	Goggle Eyes	Anne Fine	Hamilton
1990	Wolf	Gillian Cross	Oxford
1991	Dear Nobody	Berlie Doherty	Hamish Hamilton
1992	Flour Babies	Anne Fine	Hamish Hamilton

AWARDS AND PRIZE WINNERS

THE CHILDREN'S BOOK AWARD

The Children's Book Award is organized by the Federation of Children's Book Groups and is sponsored by Save and Prosper Educational Trust. The award is an annual prize for the 'best book of the year', judged by the children themselves and has been awarded since 1980. Thousands of children from all over the country help the Federation to test the books.

Year	Title	Author	Publisher
1980	Mr Magnolia	Quentin Blake	Cape
1981	Fair's Fair	Leon Garfield	Macdonald
1982	The BFG	Roald Dahl	Cape
1983	Saga of Erik the Viking	Terry Jones	Pavilion
1984	Brother in the Land	Robert Swindells	OUP
1985	Arthur	Amanda Graham	Spindlewood
1986	(No award)		
1987	The Jolly Postman	Janet & Allan Ahlberg	Heinemann
1988	Winnie the Witch	Valerie Thomas and Korky Paul	OUP
1989	Matilda	Roald Dahl	Cape
1990	Room 13	Robert Swindells	Doubleday
1991	Threadbear	Mick Inkpen	Hodder & Stoughton
1992	Kiss the Dust	Elizabeth Laird	Heinemann
1993	The Suitcase Kid	Jacqueline Wilson	Heinemann

AWARDS AND PRIZE WINNERS

CHILDREN'S BOOK COUNCIL OF AUSTRALIA – BOOK OF THE YEAR AWARDS

Started in 1946 to encourage new talent and to recognize outstanding achievement in books of lasting merit; in 1983 a Junior Book of the Year Award was added, and in 1987 the Awards were retitled Book of the Year – Older readers, and Book of the Year – Younger readers. (An Award is also made for picture books.)

Year	Title	Author	Publisher
1946	Karrawingi the Emu	Leslie Rees	Sands
1947	No award given		
1948	Shackleton's Argonauts	Frank Hurley	Angus & Robertson
1949	No competition		
1950	Whales of the Midnight Sun	Alan Villiers	Angus & Robertson
1951	Verity of Sydney Town	Ruth Williams	Angus & Robertson
1952	The Australian Book	Eve Pownall	Sands
1953	Good Luck to the Rider	Joan Phipson	Angus & Robertson
	Aircraft Today and Tomorrow	J. H. Martin	Angus & Robertson
1954	Australian Legendary Tales	K. L. Parker	Angus & Robertson
1955	The First Walkabout	Norman Tindale	Longmans Green
1956	The Crooked Snake	Patricia Wrightson	Angus & Robertson
1957	Boomerang Book of Legendary Tales	Enid Heddle	Longmans Green
1958	Tiger in the Bush	Nan Chauncey	OUP
1959	Devil's Hill	Nan Chauncey	OUP
1960	All the Proud Tribesmen	Kylie Tennant	Macmillan
1961	Tangara	Nan Chauncey	OUP
1962	Racketty Street Gang	L. H. Evers	Hodder & Stoughton
1963	Family Conspiracy	Joan Phipson	Constable
1964	Green Laurel	Eleanor Spence	OUP
1965	Pastures of the Blue Crane	Hesba Brinsmead	OUP
1966	Ash Road	Ivan Southall	Angus & Robertson
1967	The Min-min	Mavis Clark	Lansdowne
1968	To the Wild Sky	Ivan Southall	Angus & Robertson
1969	When Jays Fly to Barmbo	Margaret Balderson	OUP
1970	Uhu	Annette Macarthur-Onslow	Ure Smith
1971	Bread and Honey	Ivan Southall	Angus & Robertson
1972	Longtime Passing	Hesba Brinsmead	Angus & Robertson
1973	Family at the Lookout	Noreen Shelley	OUP
1974	The Nargun and the Stars	Patricia Wrightson	Hutchinson
1975	No award given		
1976	Fly West	Ivan Southall	Angus & Robertson
1977	October Child	Eleanor Spence	OUP
1978	The Ice is Coming	Patricia Wrightson	Hutchinson
1979	The Plum-Rain Scroll	Ruth Manley	Hodder & Stoughton
1980	Displaced Person	Lee Harding	Hyland House
1981	Playing Beatie Bow	Ruth Park	Nelson
1982	Valley Between	Colin Thiele	Rigby
1983	Master of the Grove	Victor Kelleher	Kestrel

262

1984	A Little Fear	Patricia Wrightson	Hutchinson
1985	True Story of Lilli Stubeck	James Aldridge	Hyland
1986	The Green Wind	Thurley Fowler	Rigby

JUNIOR BOOK OF THE YEAR AWARD

1983	Thing	Robin Klein	OUP
1984	Bernice Knows Best	Max Dann	OUP
1985	Something Special	Emily Roberts	Angus & Robertson
1986	Arkwright	Mary Steele	Hyland

BOOK OF THE YEAR – OLDER READERS

1987	All we Know	Simon French	Angus & Robertson
1988	So Much to Tell You	John Marsden	Walter McVitty
1989	Beyond the Labyrinth	Gillian Rubinstein	Hyland
1990	Came Back to Show You I Could Fly	Robert Klein	Viking Kestrel/Penguin
1991	Strange Objects	Gary Crew	William Heinemann Australia
1992	The House Guest	Eleanor Nilsson	Viking/Penguin
1993	Looking for Alibrandi	Melina Morchetta	Puffin

BOOK OF THE YEAR – YOUNGER READERS

1987	Pigs Might Fly	Emily Rodda	Angus & Robertson
1988	My Place	Nadia Wheatley	Collin Dove
1989	The Best Kept Secret	Emily Rodda	Angus & Robertson
1990	Pigs and Honey	Jeanis Adams	Omnibus Bks
1991	Finders Keepers	Emily Rodda	Omnibus Bks
1992	The Magnificent Nose and Other Marvels	Anna Fienberg	Allen & Unwin
1993	The Bamboo Flute	Gay Disher	Collins

AWARDS AND PRIZE WINNERS

EARTHWORM CHILDREN'S BOOK AWARD

The Earthworm Award has been set up by Friends of the Earth in order to encourage the writing of children's books which reflect concern about environmental issues. Books eligible are those published during the preceding year, written in English and either published or distributed in the UK.

1987	The Boy and the Swan	Catherine Storr	A. Deutsch
1988	Where the Forest meets the Sea	Jeannie Baker	J. MacRae
1989	Awaiting Developments	Judy Allen	J. MacRae
1990	The Young Green Consumer guide (non-fiction)		Gollancz
1991	The Last Rabbit	Jennifer Curry (editor)	Methuen
1992	Captain Eco and the Fate of the Earth	Jonathon Porritt	Dorling Kindersley
1993	Strange Orbit	Margaret Simpson	Scholastic

AWARDS AND PRIZE WINNERS

THE ELEANOR FARJEON AWARD

The Eleanor Farjeon Award was first presented in 1965. The Award is made for distinguished service to the world of children's books, and is open to anyone whose commitment and contribution is deemed to be outstanding.

1965	Margery Fisher
1966	Jessica Jenkins
1967	Brian Alderson
1968	Anne Wood
1969	Kaye Webb
1970	Margaret Meek
1971	Janet Hill
1972	Eleanor Graham
1973	Leila Berg
1974	Naomi Lewis
1975	Joyce and Court Oldmeadow
1976	Elaine Moss
1977	Peter Kennerley
1978	Joy Whitby
1979	Dorothy Butler
1980	Margaret Marshall
1981	Virginia Allen Jenson
1982	Nancy and Aidan Chambers
1983	Jean Russell
1984	Shirley Hughes
1985	Robert Leeson
1986	Judith Elkin
1987	Valerie Bierman
1988	National Library for the Handicapped Child
1989	Anna Home
1990	Jill Bennett
1991	Patricia Crampton
1992	Stephanie Nettell
1993	Susan Belgrave

AWARDS AND PRIZE WINNERS

THE EMIL/KURT MASCHLER AWARD

The Emil/Kurt Maschler Award was established in 1982 by the late Kurt Maschler for a work of imagination in the children's field in which text and illustration are of excellence and so presented that each enhances yet balances the other. The prize is £1000 and in addition the winner receives an 'Emil' – a bronze figure of Erich Kästner's famous character. It was Kurt Maschler's publishing company, William Verlag, which originally published Emil and the Detectives (1929).

1982	Sleeping Beauty and other Favourite Fairy Tales	Angela Carter	Gollancz
1983	Gorilla	Anthony Browne	J. MacRae
1984	Granpa	John Burningham	Cape
1985	The Iron Man	Ted Hughes	Faber
1986	The Jolly Postman	Allan & Janet Ahlberg	Heinemann
1987	Jack the Treacle Eater	Charles Causley	Macmillan
1988	Alice's Adventures in Wonderland	Anthony Browne	J. MacRae
1989	The Park in the Dark	Martin Waddell	Walker Books
1990	All join in	Quentin Blake	Cape
1991	Have you seen who's just moved in next door?	Colin McNaughton	Walker Books
1992	The Man	Raymond Briggs	Macrae
1993	Think of Eel	Karen Wallace & Mike Bostock	Walker Books

THE KATHLEEN FIDLER AWARD

The Kathleen Fidler Award was set up in 1980 to encourage both new and established authors to submit their work for the 8–12 age group. It is sponsored by Blackie publishers and administered by Book Trust Scotland. The winner is then published by Blackie.

1983	Adrift	Alan Baillie	Blackie
1984	Barty	Janet Collins	Blackie
1985	No Shelter	Elizabeth Lutzeir	Blackie
1986	Diamond	Caroline Pitcher	Blackie
1987	Simon's Challenge	Theresa Breslin	Blackie
1988	Flight of the Solar Duck	Charles Morgan	Blackie
1989	Mightier than the Sword	Clare Bevan	Blackie
1990	Magic with Everything	Roger Burt	Blackie
1991	Greg's Revenge	George Hendry	Blackie
1992	Richard's Castle	Susan Coon	Blackie
1993	48 Hours with Franklin	Mij Kelly	Blackie

AWARDS AND PRIZE WINNERS

ESTHER GLEN AWARD

Established in 1944 by the New Zealand Library Association; awarded to the author considered to have made the most distinguished contribution to literature for children during the year. Esther Glen, born in 1881, was a journalist and pioneer writer of children's books in New Zealand.

1945	Book of Wiremu	Stella Morice	Progressive Publication Society
1946	No award		
1947	Myths and Legends of Maoriland	Alexander Reed	Reed
1948	No award		
1949	No award		
1950	The Adventures of Nimble, Rumble and Tumble	Joan Smith	Paul
1951–58	No awards		
1959	Falter Tom and the Water Boy	Maurice Duggan	Paul
1960–63	No awards		
1964	Turi: the Story of a Little Boy	Lesley Powell	Paul
1965–69	No awards		
1970	A Lion in the Meadow	May Margaret Mahy	Watts
1971	No award		
1972	No award		
1973	The First Margaret Mahy Story Book	May Margaret Mahy	Dent
1974	No award		
1975	My Cat likes to Hide in Boxes	Eve Sutton	Hamilton
1976	No award		
1977	No award		
1978	The Lighthouse Keeper's Lunch	Ronda Armitage	Hutchinson
1979	Take the Long Path	Joan de Hamel	Lutterworth Press
1980	No award		
1981	No award		
1982	The Year of the Yelvertons	Katherine O'Brien	OUP
1983	The Haunting	May Margaret Mahy	Dent
1984	Elephant Rock	Caroline Macdonald	Hodder & Stoughton
1985	The Changeover: a Supernatural Romance	May Margaret Mahy	Waiatarua
1986	Motherstone	Maurice Gee	OUP
1987	No award		
1988	Alex	Tessa Duder	OUP
1989	The Mangrove Summer	Jack Lazenby	OUP

AWARDS AND PRIZE WINNERS

1990	Alex in Winter	Tessa Duder	OUP
1991	Agnes the Sheep	William Taylor	OUP
1992	Alessandra: Alex in Rome	Tessa Duder	OUP
1993	Underrunners	May Margaret Mahy	Hamilton

AWARDS AND PRIZE WINNERS

GUARDIAN CHILDREN'S FICTION AWARD

The Guardian Children's Fiction Award has been given annually since 1967 for an outstanding work of fiction for children by a British or Commonwealth author, which was first published in the UK during the preceding year. The award is chosen by a panel of authors and *The Guardian*'s children's book review editor. Picture books are not included for consideration.

Year	Title	Author	Publisher
1967	Devil-in-the-Fog	Leon Garfield	Longman
1968	The Owl Service	Alan Garner	Collins
1969	The Whispering Mountain	Joan Aiken	Cape
1970	Flambards (The Trilogy)	K. M. Peyton	OUP
1971	The Guardians	John Christopher	Hamish Hamilton
1972	A Likely Lad	Gillian Avery	Collins
1973	Watership Down	Richard Adams	Collins
1974	The Iron Lily	Barbara Willard	Longman Young
1975	Gran at Coalgate	Winifred Cawley	OUP
1976	The Peppermint Pig	Nina Bawden	Gollancz
1977	The Blue Hawk	Peter Dickinson	Gollancz
1978	A Charmed Life	Diana Wynne Jones	Macmillan
1979	Conrad's War	Andrew Davies	Blackie
1980	The Vandal	Ann Schlee	Macmillan
1981	The Sentinels	Peter Carter	OUP
1982	Goodnight Mister Tom	Michelle Magorian	Kestrel
1983	The Village by the Sea: an Indian Family Story	Anita Desai	Heinemann
1984	The Sheep-Pig	Dick King-Smith	Gollancz
1985	What is the Truth? a Farmyard Fable for the Young	Ted Hughes	Faber & Faber
1986	Henry's Leg	Ann Pilling	Viking Kestrel
1987	The True Story of Spit MacPhee	James Aldridge	Viking Kestrel
1988	The Runaways	Ruth Thomas	Hutchinson
1989	A Pack of Lies	Geraldine McCaughrean	OUP
1990	Goggle Eyes	Anne Fine	Hamilton
1991	Kingdom by the Sea	Robert Westall	Methuen
1992	The Exiles	Hilary McKay	Gollancz
	Paper Faces	Rachel Anderson	OUP
1993	Lowtide	William Mayne	Cape
1994	The Mennyms	Sylvia Waugh	Julia MacRae Books

AWARDS AND PRIZE WINNERS

IBBY HONOUR DIPLOMAS

Awarded every two years, to call attention to some of the best books for children and young people on an international level. Awards for writing are given below; there are also awards for illustration and translation.

1980
AUSTRALIA
A Dream of Seas   Lilith Norman   Collins
CANADA
Holdfast   Kevin Najor   Clarke-Irwin
UK
The Gods in Winter   Patricia Miles   H. Hamilton
USA
Ramona and her Father   Beverley Cleary   W. Morrow & Co.

1982
AUSTRALIA
Playing Beatie Bow   Ruth Park   T. Nelson
CANADA
The Keeper of the Isis Light Monica Hughes   H. Hamilton
UK
Tulku   Peter Dickinson   Gollancz
USA
Autumn Street   Lois Lowry   Houghton Mifflin

1984
AUSTRALIA
The Watcher in the Garden   Joan Phipson   Methuen
CANADA
The Root Cellar   Janet Lunn   Lester & Orpen Dennys
UK
All the King's Men   William Mayne   Cape
USA
Sweet Whispers, Brother
Rush   Virginia Hamilton   Philomel

1986
AUSTRALIA
Dancing in the Anzal Deli   Nadia Wheatley   OUP
CANADA
Sweetgrass   Jan Hudson   Tree Frog Press
UK
The Changeover   Margaret Mahy   Dent
USA
One-eyed cat   Paula Fox   Scaisdale

1988
AUSTRALIA
Riverman   Allan Baillie   Nelson

271

AWARDS AND PRIZE WINNERS

CANADA
Shadow in Hawthorne Bay   Janet Lunn   Lester & Orpen Dennys
UK
Woof!   Allan Ahlberg   Viking Kestrel
USA
Sarah, plain and tall   Patricia MacLachlan   Harper & Row

1990
AUSTRALIA
My Place   Nadia Wheatley & Donna
                           Rawlins   Collins Dove
CANADA
Bad Boy   Diana J. Wieler   Groundwood
UK
Slambash Wangs of a
Compo Gormer   Robert Leeson   Collins
USA
Lincoln: a photobiography Russell Freedman   Clarion Books

1992
AUSTRALIA
Dodger   Libby Gleeson   Turton & Chambers Ltd
CANADA
Redwork   Michael Bedard   Lester & Orpen Dennys
GHANA
The Cats and the Mice   Abenaa Karama   Educational Press
UK
No Award
USA
Shabanu – Daughter of   Suzanne Fisher Staples   Alfred A. Knopf Books for
the Wind   Young Readers

LANCASHIRE COUNTY LIBRARY CHILDREN'S BOOK OF THE YEAR AWARD

Awarded to a fiction title suitable for the 11–14 age range, and sponsored by the National Westminster Bank. Judged by 13–14 year-old pupils from Lancashire schools.

1987	Ruby in the Smoke	Philip Pullman	OUP
1988	Redwall	Brian Jacques	Hutchinson
1989	Groosham Grange	Anthony Horowitz	Methuen
1990	Plague 99	Jean Ure	Methuen
1991	Mattimeo	Brian Jacques	Hutchinson
1992	Whitby Witches	Robin Jarvis	Simon & Schuster
1993	Gulf	Robert Westall	Methuen
	Salamandastron	Brian Jacques	Hutchinson

AWARDS AND PRIZE WINNERS

THE NEWBERY MEDAL

The Newbery Medal is given annually for the most distinguished contribution to American literature for children. It is named after John Newbery (1713–67), a London bookseller and the first British publisher of children's books. It is administered by the American Library Association and was first awarded in 1922.

Year	Title	Author	Publisher
1922	The Story of Mankind	Hendrick W. van Loon	Liveright
1923	The Voyages of Doctor Dolittle	Hugh Lofting	Lippincott
1924	The Dark Frigate	Charles Boardman Hawes	Atlantic Little Brown
1925	Tales from Silver Lands	Charles J. Finger	Doubleday
1926	Shen of the Sea	Arthur Bowie Chrisman	Dutton
1927	Smoky, the Cowhorse	Will James	Scribner
1928	Gay-Neck, the Story of a Pigeon	Dhan Gopal Mukerji	Dutton
1929	The Trumpeter of Krakow	Eric P. Kelly	Macmillan
1930	Hitty, her First Hundred Years	Rachel Field	Macmillan
1931	The Cat Who Went to Heaven	Elizabeth Coatsworth	Macmillan
1932	Waterless Mountain	Laura Adams Armer	Longman
1933	Young Fu of the Upper Yangtze	Elizabeth F. Lewis	Winston
1934	Invincible Louisa	Cornelia Meigs	Little Brown
1935	Dobry	Monica Shannon	Viking
1936	Caddie Woodlawn	Carol Ryrie Brink	Macmillan
1937	Roller Skates	Ruth Sawyer	Viking
1938	The White Stag	Kate Seredy	Viking
1939	Thimble Summer	Elizabeth Enright	Holt, Rinehart & Winston
1940	Daniel Boone	James Daugherty	Viking
1941	Call It Courage (UK title: The Boy who was Afraid)	Armstrong Sperry	Macmillan
1942	The Matchlock Gun	Walter D. Edmonds	Dodd Mead
1943	Adam of the Road	Elizabeth Janet Gray	Viking
1944	Johnny Tremain	Esther Forbes	Houghton Mifflin
1945	Rabbit Hill	Robert Lawson	Viking
1946	Strawberry Girl	Lois Lenski	Lippincott
1947	Miss Hickory	Carolyn Sherwin Bailey	Viking
1948	The Twenty-One Balloons	William Pene du Bois	Viking
1949	King of the Wind	Marguerite Henry	Rand McNally
1950	The Door in the Wall	Marguerite de Angeli	Doubleday
1951	Amos Fortune, Free Man	Elizabeth Yates	Aladdin
1952	Ginger Pye	Eleanor Estes	Harcourt Brace
1953	Secret of the Andes	Ann Nolan Clark	Viking
1954	... And Now Miguel	Joseph Krumgold	Crowell
1955	The Wheel on the School	Meindert Dejong	Harper & Row
1956	Carry On, Mr Bowditch	Jean Lee Latham	Houghton Mifflin

AWARDS AND PRIZE WINNERS

1957	Miracles on Maple Hill	Virginia Sorenson	Harcourt Brace
1958	Rifles for Watie	Harold Keith	Crowell
1959	The Witch of Blackbird Pond	Elizabeth G. Speare	Houghton Mifflin
1960	Onion John	Joseph Krumgold	Crowell
1961	Island of the Blue Dolphins	Scott O'Dell	Houghton Mifflin
1962	The Bronze Bow	Elizabeth G. Speare	Houghton Mifflin
1963	A Wrinkle in Time	Madeleine L'Engle	Farrar Straus & Giroux
1964	It's Like This, Cat	Emily Cheney Neville	Harper & Row
1965	Shadow of a Bull	Maia Wojciechowska	Atheneum
1966	I, Juan de Pareja	Elizabeth de Trevino	Farrar Straus & Giroux
1967	Up A Road Slowly	Irene Hunt	Follett
1968	From the Mixed-Up Files of Mrs Basil E. Frankweiler	Elaine L. Konigsburg	Atheneum
1969	The High King	Lloyd Alexander	Holt, Rinehart & Winston
1970	Sounder	William H. Armstrong	Harper & Row
1971	The Summer of the Swans	Betsy Byars	Viking
1972	Mrs Frisby and the Rats of Nimh	Robert C. O'Brien	Atheneum
1973	Julie of the Wolves	Jean Craighead George	Harper & Row
1974	The Slave Dancer	Paula Fox	Bradbury
1975	M. C. Higgins, the Great	Virginia Hamilton	Macmillan
1976	The Grey King	Susan Cooper	Atheneum
1977	Roll of Thunder, Hear My Cry	Mildred D. Taylor	Dial
1978	Bridge to Terabithia	Katherine Paterson	Crowell
1979	The Westing Game	Ellen Raskin	Dutton
1980	A Gathering of Days	Joan W. Blos	Scribner
1981	Jacob Have I Loved	Katherine Paterson	Crowell
1982	A Visit to William Blake's Inn	Nancy Willard	Harcourt Brace
1983	Dicey's-Song	Cynthia Voigt	Atheneum
1984	Dear Mr Henshaw	Beverly Cleary	Morrow
1985	The Hero and the Crown	Robin McKinley	Greenwillow
1986	Sarah, Plain and Tall	Patricia McLachlan	Harper & Row
1987	The Whipping Boy	Sid Fleischman	Greenwillow
1988	Lincoln: A Photobiography	Russell Freedman	Houghton Clarion
1989	Joyful Noise	Paul Fleischman	Harper & Row
1990	Number the Stars	Lois Lowry	Houghton Mifflin
1991	Maniac Magee	Jerry Spinelli	Little, Brown
1992	Shiloh	Phyllis R. Naylor	Atheneum
1993	Missing May	Cynthia Rylant	Orchard/A Richard Jackson Book
1994	The Giver	Lois Lowry	Houghton Mifflin

AWARDS AND PRIZE WINNERS

NOTTINGHAMSHIRE CHILDREN'S BOOK AWARD

Jointly organized and promoted by Nottinghamshire Libraries and Dillons Bookstore. The aim of the award is to encourage reading, to draw attention to the range of exciting new children's books available, and to involve children in enjoying and evaluating new books. The award is presented annually in two categories, the Acorn Award for an outstanding book written and illustrated for the 0–7 age group, and the Oak Tree Award for an outstanding book written and illustrated for the 8–12 age group. The first awards were presented in 1989.

1989
ACORN AWARD
Sidney the monster	David Wood	Walker Books

OAK TREE AWARD
Matilda	Roald Dahl	Viking

1990
ACORN AWARD
Knickerless Nicola	Kara May	Macmillan

OAK TREE AWARD
Bill's New Frock	Anne Fine	Methuen

1991
ACORN AWARD
Threadbear	Mick Inkpen	Hodder & Stoughton

OAK TREE AWARD
The Afterdark Princess	Annie Dalton	Methuen

1992
ACORN AWARD
Kipper	Mick Inkpen	Hodder & Stoughton

OAK TREE AWARD
The Story of Tracy Beaker	Jacqueline Wilson	Doubleday

1993
ACORN AWARD
Jonpanda	Gwen Grant	Heinemann

OAK TREE AWARD
Pongwiffy and the Spell of the Year	Kaye Umansky	Viking

AWARDS AND PRIZE WINNERS

THE OTHER AWARD

The Other Award was established in 1975 as a counter-award to the already existing awards and aimed to draw attention to important new or neglected work of a progressive nature from children's writers and illustrators. It took the form of an annual commendation to a number of children's books published during the preceding year and was not accompanied by a prize or money. The award was discontinued in 1988 after 13 years because the administrators chose not to go down the road of sponsorship and because they no longer considered an award an appropriate way to promote 'other' concerns.

1976	Nobody's Family is Going to Change	Louise Fitzhugh	Gollancz
	Trouble with Donovan Croft	Bernard Ashley	OUP
	Helpers	Shirley Hughes	Bodley Head
1977	East End at your Feet	Farrukh Dhondy	Macmillan
	Turbulent Term of Tyke Tiler	Gene Kemp	Faber
1978	Song for a Dark Queen	Rosemary Sutcliff	Pelham
	Goalkeeper's Revenge	Bill Naughton	Puffin
	Gypsy Family	Mary Waterson and Lance Brown	Black
1979	Old Dog, New Tricks	Dick Cote	Hamilton
	Come to Mecca	Farrukh Dhondy	Collins
	Two Victorian Families	Sue Wagstaff	A. & C. Black
1980	Mr Plug the Plumber	Allan Ahlberg	Kestrel
	Green Bough of Liberty	David Rees	Dobson
1981	A Strong and Willing Girl	Dorothy Edwards	Methuen
	Have You Started Yet?	Ruth Thomson	Heinemann
1982	Welcome Home, Jellybean	Marlene Fanta Shyer	Granada
	When the Wind Blows	Raymond Briggs	Gollancz
1983	Nowhere to Play	Karusa	A. & C. Black
	Will of Iron	Gerard Melia	Longman
	Everybody's Here	Michael Rosen	Bodley Head
	Talking in Whispers	James Watson	Gollancz
1984	Brother in the Land	Robert Swindells	OUP
	Who Lies Inside	Timothy Ireland	Gay Men's Press
	Wheel Around the World	Chris Searle	Macdonald
	A Chair for my Mother	Vera Williams	J. MacRae
1985	Our Kids	Peckham Publishing Project	
	Journey to Jo'burg	Beverley Naidoo	Longman
	Vila	Sarah Baylis	Longman
	Motherland	Elyse Dodgson	Heinemann
	Comfort Herself	Geraldine Kaye	Andre Deutsch
1986	Say It Again, Granny	John Agard	Bodley Head
	Starry Night	Catherine Sefton	Hamish Hamilton
	The People Could Fly	Virginia Hamilton	Walker Books

277

AWARDS AND PRIZE WINNERS

1987	Grandma's Favourite	Peter C. Heaslip	Methuen
	Which Twin Wins?	Peter C. Heaslip	Methuen
	Push Me Pull Me	Sandra Chick	Women's Press
1988	Award discontinued		

AWARDS AND PRIZE WINNERS

SMARTIES PRIZE FOR CHILDREN'S BOOKS

The Smarties Prize for Children's Books has been established to encourage high standards and stimulate interest in books for children. It is sponsored by Rowntree Mackintosh and administered by Book Trust. Eligible books are any published during the preceding year, written in English by a citizen of the UK or an author resident in the UK and the author must be living at the time of publication.

1985	GRAND PRIX AND OVER 7 YEARS CATEGORY WINNER		
	Gaffer Samson's Luck	Jill Paton Walsh	Viking Kestrel
	UNDER 7 YEARS CATEGORY WINNER		
	It's Your Turn Roger!	Susanna Gretz	Bodley Head and Fontana
1986	GRAND PRIX AND 7–11 YEARS CATEGORY WINNER		
	The Snow Spider	Jenny Nimmo	Methuen
	6 YEARS AND UNDER CATEGORY WINNER		
	The Goose that Laid the Golden Egg	Geoffrey Patterson	André Deutsch
1987	GRAND PRIX AND 9–11 YEARS CATEGORY WINNER		
	A Thief in the Village	James Berry	Hamish Hamilton
	6–8 YEARS CATEGORY WINNER		
	Tangle and the Firesticks	Benedict Blathway	J. MacRae
	5 YEARS AND UNDER CATEGORY WINNER		
	The Angel and the Soldier Boy	Peter Collington	Methuen
1988	GRAND PRIX AND UNDER 5 YEARS WINNER		
	Can't You Sleep Little Bear	Martin Waddell	Walker Books
	9–11 YEARS WINNER		
	Rushavenn Time	Theresa Whistler & Brixworth Primary School	
	6–8 YEARS WINNER		
	Can It Be True?	Susan Hill	Hamish Hamilton
1989	GRAND PRIX AND UNDER 5 YEARS WINNER		
	We're Going on a Bear Hunt	Michael Rosen	Walker Books
	9–11 YEARS WINNER		
	Blitz Cat	Robert Westall	Macmillan

AWARDS AND PRIZE WINNERS

	6–8 YEARS WINNER		
	Bill's New Frock	Anne Fine	Methuen
1990	GRAND PRIX AND 9–11 YEARS CATEGORY WINNER		
	Midnight Blue	Pauline Fisk	Lion Publishing
	6–8 YEARS WINNER		
	Esio Trot	Roald Dahl	Jonathan Cape
	0–5 YEARS WINNER		
	Six Dinner Sid	Inga Moore	Simon & Schuster
1991	GRAND PRIX AND UNDER 5 YEARS WINNER		
	Farmer Duck	Martin Waddell & Helen Oxenbury	Walker Books
	9–11 YEARS WINNER		
	Krindlekrax	Philip Ridley	Cape
	6–8 YEARS WINNER		
	Josie Smith and Eileen	Magdalen Nabb	Harper Collins
1992	GRAND PRIX AND 9–11 YEARS CATEGORY WINNER		
	The Great Elephant Chase	Gillian Cross	OUP
	6–8 YEARS WINNER		
	The story of Creation	Jane Ray	Orchard
	UNDER 5 YEARS WINNER		
	Nice Work, Little Wolf!	Hilda Offen	Hamish Hamilton
1993	GRAND PRIX AND 6–8 YEARS CATEGORY WINNER		
	War Game	Michael Foreman	Pavilion
	9–11 YEARS CATEGORY WINNER		
	Listen to the Dark	Maeve Henry	Heinemann
	0–5 YEARS CATEGORY WINNER		
	Hue Boy	Rita Phillips Mitchell & Caroline Binch	Gollancz

WHITBREAD LITERARY AWARD CHILDREN'S NOVEL

The Whitbread Literary Award Children's Novel was first awarded in 1972. The award is for a book for children of seven and up, published in the UK or Republic of Ireland and written by a British or Irish author or one who has been settled in Britain or Ireland. It is sponsored by Whitbread and administered by the Booksellers' Association.

Year	Title	Author	Publisher
1972	The Diddakoi	Rumer Godden	Macmillan
1973	The Butterfly Ball and the Grasshopper's Feast	William Plomer	Cape
1974	How Tom Beat Captain Najork and His Hired Sportsmen	Russell Hoban	Cape
1975	No award		
1976	A Stitch in Time	Penelope Lively	Heinemann
1977	No End to Yesterday	Shelagh Macdonald	André Deutsch
1978	The Battle of Bubble and Squeak	A. Philippa Pearce	André Deutsch
1979	Tulku	Peter Dickinson	Gollancz
1980	John Diamond	Leon Garfield	Kestrel
1981	The Hollow Land	Jane Gardam	J. MacRae
1982	The Song of Pentecost	William Corbett	Methuen
1983	The Witches	Roald Dahl	Cape
1984	The Queen of the Pharisees' Children	Barbara Willard	J. MacRae
1985	The Nature of the Beast	Janni Howker	J. MacRae
1986	The Coal House	Andrew Taylor	Collins
1987	A Little Lower than the Angels	Geraldine McCaughrean	OUP
1988	Awaiting Developments	Judy Allen	J. MacRae
1989	Why Weep the Brogan	Hugh Scott	Walker Books
1990	AK	Peter Dickinson	Gollancz
1991	Harvey Angel	Diana Hendry	J. MacRae
1992	The Great Elephant Chase	Gillian Cross	OUP
1993	Flour Babies	Anne Fine	Hamish Hamilton

AWARDS AND PRIZE WINNERS

LAURA INGALLS WILDER AWARD

Awarded by the Association for Library Services for Children in the American Library Association to an author or illustrator whose books, published in the USA, have made a substantial and lasting contribution to literature for children over a period of years. Now awarded every three years.

1954	Laura Ingalls Wilder
1960	Clara Judson
1965	Ruth Sawyer
1970	E. B. White
1975	Beverly Cleary
1980	Theodor Giesl (Dr Seuss)
1983	Maurice Sendak
1986	Jean Fritz
1989	Elizabeth Speare
1992	Marcia Brown

AUTHOR INDEX

Adams, Jeanis 263
Adams, Richard 2, 259, 270
Aesop 228
Agard, John 277
Ahlberg, Allan 3, 261, 266, 272, 277
Ahlberg, Janet 261
Aiken, Joan 266
Alcock, Vivien 9, 238
Alderson, Brian 265
Aldridge, James 263, 270
Alexander, Lloyd 275
Allen, Agnes 259
Allen, Eleanor 241, 245
Allen, Joy 239
Allen, Judy 11, 264, 281
Allen, Linda 12, 240
Andersen, Hans Christian 228
Anderson, Rachel 13, 243, 246, 270
Anderson, Scoular 244
Angeli, Marguerite De 274
Antrobus, John 14
Appiah, Peggy 15
Apps, Roy 250
Arkle, Phyllis 15, 240
Armer, Laura Adams 274
Armitage, Ronda 268
Armstrong, Richard 259
Armstrong, William H. 275
Ashley, Bernard 16, 244, 250, 277
Ashley, Chris 250
Avery, Gillian 250, 270
Avi 256

Bailey, Carolyn Sherwin 274
Baillie, Allan 19, 267, 271
Baker, Jeannie 264
Balderson, Margaret 262
Ball, Brian 238, 239
Banks, Lynne Reid 20
Barbeau, Charles Marius 257
Barne, Kitty 259
Barrie, Sir James M. 229
Barry, Margaret Stuart 21
Bawden, Nina 22, 270
Baylis, Sarah 277
BB 259

Bedard, Michael 258, 272
Belgrave, Susan 265
Benedictus, David 250
Benjamin, Floella 238
Bennett, Jill 265
Bennett, Leonie 240
Beresford, Elisabeth 239
Berg, Leila 244, 265
Berry, James 25, 256, 279
Bevan, Bill 244
Bevan, Clare 239, 267
Bierman, Valerie 265
Biegel, Paul 26
Binch, Caroline 280
Blades, Ann 257
Blake, Quentin 261, 266
Blathway, Benedict 279
Blishen, Edward 27
Blos, Joan W. 275
Blume, Judy 28
Bodker, Cecil 255
Bois, William Pene du 274
Bond, Michael 29
Bostock, Mike 266
Boston, Lucy M. 30, 259
Brandreth, Giles 243
Breslin, Theresa 250, 267
Briggs, Raymond 31, 266, 277
Brink, Carol Ryrie 274
Brinsmead, Hesba 32, 262
Brixworth Primary School 279
Brooks, Bruce 256
Brown, Jeff 33, 250
Brown, Lance 277
Brown, Marcia 282
Browne, Anthony 266
Browne, Eileen 242
Brumpton, Keith 243
Bull, Angela 239
Burgess, Melvin 34
Burnard, Damon 243, 246
Burnett, Frances Hodgson 229
Burnford, Sheila Every 257
Burningham, John 266
Burt, Roger 267
Burton, Hester 259

283

AUTHOR INDEX

Butler, Dorothy 265
Byars, Betsy 34, 245, 275

Cameron, Ann 39
Cameron, Eleanor 256
Camp, Lindsay 246
Carroll, Lewis 230
Carter, Angela 239, 266
Carter, Peter 270
Castor, Harriet 244
Cate, Dick 39
Causle, Charles 266
Cave, Kathryn 246
Cawley, Winifred 270
Chambers, Aidan 40, 265
Chambers, Nancy 265
Chauncey, Nan 262
Chick, Sandra 278
Chrisman, Arthur Bowie 274
Christopher, John 41, 270
Clark, Ann Nolan 274
Clark, Catherine Anthony 257
Clark, Mavis 262
Clarke, Pauline 259
Cleary, Beverly 43, 271, 275, 282
Cleaver, Elizabeth 257
Coatsworth, Elizabeth 274
Cockett, Mary 242
Collington, Peter 279
Collins, Janet 267
Collodi, Carlo 230, 250
Colwell, Eileen 45
Coon, Susan 267
Cooper, Susan 45, 256, 275
Corbett, William J. 46, 281
Cornwall, I. W. 259
Corrin, Sara 47, 236
Corrin, Stephen 47, 236
Cote, Dick 277
Crampton, Patricia 265
Cresswell, Helen 48, 250
Crew, Gary 263
Cross, Gillian 52, 238, 260, 280, 281
Crossley-Holland, Kevin 55, 244, 260
Curry, Jennifer 264
Curtis, Philip 56

Dahl, Roald 59, 250, 261, 276, 280, 281
Dalton, Annie 61, 238, 276
Dann, Colin 62, 250
Dann, Max 263
Danziger, Paula 63
Darke, Marjorie 238

Daugherty, James 274
Davies, Andrew 64, 256, 270
Davies, Gill 242
Davies, Hunter 65
Deary, Terry 240, 241, 245
Degens, T. 256
De Jong, Meindert 66, 255, 274
De La Mere, Walter 259
Desai, Anita 250, 270
Dhami, Narinder 238
Dhondy, Farrukh 277
Dickens, Charles 230
Dickinson, Peter 67, 260, 270, 271, 281
Dicks, Terrance 69, 239, 242
Dinan, C. 240
Disher, Gay 263
Dodgson, Elyse 277
Doherty, Berlie 70, 250, 260
Doorl, Eleanor 259
Doyle, Brian 258
Duder, Tessa 268, 269
Duffey, B. 243
Duggan, Maurice 268
Dunham, Mabel 257

Eadington, Joan 240, 250
Edmonds, Walter D. 274
Edwards, Dorothy 72, 277
Ehrlich, Amy 236
Eldridge, Jim 250
Elkin, Judith 265
Ellis, A. 240
Enright, Elizabeth 274
Escott, John 239, 246
Estes, Eleanor 274
Evers, L. H. 262
Eyles, Heather 240

Farjeon, Eleanor 74, 255, 259
Farmer, Penelope 74
Faville, Barry 75
Field, Rachel 274
Fienberg, Anna 263
Findlater, Evelyn 243
Fine, Anne 76, 238, 242, 244, 250, 260, 270, 276, 280, 281
Finger, Charles J. 274
Fisher, Margery 265
Fisk, Nicholas 78
Fisk, Pauline 280
Fitzhugh, Louise 277
Fitzmaurice, Mick 246
Fleischman, Paul 275

AUTHOR INDEX

Fleischman, Sid 256, 275
Forbes, Esther 274
Ford, N. 244
Foreman, Michael 236, 280
Foss, Michael 236
Fowke, Edith 257
Fowler, Thurley 263
Fox, Paula 81, 255, 256, 271, 275
Freedman, Russell 272, 275
Freeman, Maggie 240
French, Simon 263
French, Vivien 245
Fritz, Jean 282
Furlong, Monica 83

Gardam, Jane 84
Garfield, Leon 85, 261, 270, 281
Garner, Alan 88, 259, 270
Garnett, Eve 259
Gates, Susan 89
Gavin, Jamila 90
Gee, Maurice 91, 268
George, Jean Craighead 275
Geras, Adele 92, 240, 242
Gerrard, Roy 250
Getz, David 250
Giesl, Theodor 282
Girling, Brough 93, 243
Gleeson, Libby 272
Gleitzman, Morris 94, 250
Godden, Rumer 281
Gordon, John 95, 246
Goudge, Elizabeth 259
Gowar, M. 242
Graham, Amanda 261
Graham, Eleanor 265
Grahame, Kenneth 231, 250
Grant, Gwen 96, 246, 276
Gray, Elizabeth Janet 274
Green, Roger J. 97
Gregory, Philippa 250
Gretz, Susanna 279
Grimm, Jacob 231
Grimm, Wilhelm 231
Gripe, Maria 255
Guillot, René 255

Hackney, Jo 240
Haig-Brown, Roderick 257
Halam, Ann 99
Hall, Lynn 256
Hall, Willis 100
Hallworth, Grace 101
Hamel, Joan De 268

Hamilton, Virginia 101, 255, 256, 271, 275, 277
Hamley, Dennis 103
Handford, Martin 250
Hannah, S. 242
Hardcastle, Michael 104, 239, 246
Harding, Lee 262
Harker, L. 240
Harnett, Cynthia 259
Harris, Christie 257, 258
Harris, Joel Chandler 232
Harris, Rosemary 259
Haugaard, Erik Christian 256
Haugen, Tormod 255
Hawes, Charles Boardman 274
Hawkins, Elizabeth 246
Hayes, John F. 257
Hayes, Rosemary 244
Heap, Sue 243
Heaslip, Peter C. 278
Heddle, Enid 262
Hendry, Diana 243, 250, 281
Hendry, George 267
Henkes, Kevin 250
Henry, Maeve 280
Henry, Marguerite 274
Hicyilmaz, Gaye 250
Hill, Denise 241, 245
Hill, Douglas 105
Hill, Janet 265
Hill, Kay 257
Hill, Susan 279
Hoban, Julia 245
Hoban, Russell 107, 281
Hoffman, Mary 246
Holm, Anne 108
Home, Anna 265
Hooper, Mary 239
Hoover, Helen Mary 109
Horowitz, Anthony 110, 273
Houston, James 257, 258
Howker, Janni 281
Hudson, Jan 258, 271
Hughes, Monica 271
Hughes, Shirley 111, 265, 277
Hughes, Ted 112, 266, 270
Hunt, Irene 275
Hunter, Jana 244
Hunter, Mollie 260
Hurley, Frank 262
Hutchins, Pat 113

Impey, Rose 115, 236, 238, 244, 250
Inkpen, Mick 261, 276

285

AUTHOR INDEX

Ireland, Timothy 277
Ireson, Barbara 116
Irons, Jane 239

Jacques, Brian 118
James, Will 274
Jannson, Tove 255
Jarman, Julia 118, 238, 243
Jarvis, Robin 120, 273
Jenkins, Jessica 265
Jennings, Linda 239
Jennings, Paul 250
Jenson, Virginia Allen 265
Jones, Diana Wynne 120, 238, 250, 270
Jones, Ivan 240
Jones, Terry 251, 261
Joy, Margaret 244
Judson, Clara 282
Jungman, Ann 243, 244

Karama, Abenaa 272
Karusa 277
Kastner, Erich 255
Kaye, Geraldine 124, 238, 240, 246, 277
Keith, Harold 275
Kelleher, Victor 262
Kelly, Eric P. 274
Kelly, Mij 267
Kemp, Gene 125, 238, 260, 277
Kennerley, Peter 265
Kidd, Diana 243
Kilworth, Garry 127
King, Clive 128
King-Smith, Dick 129, 243, 245, 251, 270
Kingsland, R. 243
Kingsley, Charles 232
Kipling, Rudyard 232, 251
Klein, Robin 134, 263
Konigsburg, Elaine L. 275
Krailing, Tessa 239, 246
Krumgold, Joseph 274, 275
Kruss, James 255
Kushner, Donn 258

Laird, Elizabeth 137, 251, 261
Lambert, Richard S. 257
Lambert, Thelma 240, 242
Latham, Jean Lee 274
Lavelle, Sheila 138, 240, 241, 244
Lawson, John 256
Lawson, Robert 274
Lazenby, Jack 268
Lee, Dennis 257, 258

Lee, Tanith 140
Leeson, Robert 141, 240, 242, 265, 272
Le Guin, Ursula K. 256
L'Engle, Madeleine 275
Lenski, Lois 274
Lettridge, Celia Barker 258
Lewis, C. S. 233, 251, 259
Lewis, Elizabeth F. 274
Lewis, Naomi 265
Limb, Su 244
Lindgren, Astrid 143, 255
Lindsay, Frances 241, 245
Linklater, Eric 259
Lishak, Antony 241
Little, Jean 145, 258
Lively, Penelope 146, 238, 259, 281
Lofting, Hugh 251, 274
Loon, Hendrick W. van 274
Lowry, Lois 148, 256, 271, 275
Lunn, Janet 258, 271, 272
Lutzeir, Elizabeth 267
Lyons, Greg 245

Macarthur-Onslow, Annette 262
McAll Smith, Alexander 239, 244, 246
McBratney, Sam 150
McCaughrean, Geraldine 150, 260, 270, 281
Macdonald, Caroline 268
Macdonald, Shelagh 281
McGough, Roger 152
McKay, Hilary 270
McKinley, Robin 275
McLachlan, Patricia 272, 275
Macmillan, Cyrus 257
McNaughton, Colin 266
Magorian, Michelle 270
Mahy, Margaret 153, 260, 268, 269, 271
Major, Kevin 258, 271
Mangan, Anne 240, 242
Manley, Ruth 262
March, Jan 246
Mark, Jan 156, 260
Marsden, John 263
Martin, J. H. 262
Masefield, John 233
Marshall, Margaret 265
Masters, Anthony 239
Matthias, Beverley 242
May, Kara 241, 247, 276
Mayne, William 158, 240, 246, 259, 270, 271
Meek, Margaret 265
Meigs, Cornelia 274

AUTHOR INDEX

Melia, Gerard 277
Miles, Patricia 271
Milne, A. A. 233
Mitchell, R. P. 280
Montgomery, L. M. 251
Moore, Inga 280
Morchetta, Melina 263
Morgan, Charles 267
Morice, Stella 268
Morpurgo, Michael 161, 238, 243, 251
Morse, Brian 240
Morton, Christine 242
Moss, Elaine 265
Mostyn, David 245
Mowat, Farley 257
Mukerji, Dhan Gopal 274
Murphy, Jill 162

Nabb, Magdalen 251, 280
Naidoo, Beverley 264, 277
National Library For the Handicapped Child 265
Naughton, Bill 277
Naylor, Phyllis R. 275
Needle, Jan 164
Nesbit, E. 233, 251
Nettell, Stephanie 265
Neville, Emily Cheney 275
Newman, Marjorie 241, 242, 245
Nicholls, C. 238
Nicholls, Ruth 257
Nilsson, Eleanor 263
Nimmo, Jenny 167, 238, 251, 279
Norman, Lilith 271
Norton, Mary 251, 259
Nostlinger, Christine 168, 255
Nunes, Lygia Bojunga 255

0O'Brien, Katherine 268
O'Brien, Robert C. 170, 275
O'Dell, Scott 255, 275
Offen, Hilda 240, 243, 280
Oldfield, Pamela 239
Oldmeadow, Court 265
Oldmeadow, Joyce 265
O'Neal, Zibby 256
O'Neill, Judith 170, 246
Oppel, Kenneth 238
Osband, Gillian 245
Osmond, Edward 259
Oxenbury, Helen 280

Park, Ruth 172, 256, 262, 271
Parker, K. L. 262
Paterson, Katherine 172, 275

Patterson, Geoffrey 279
Paul, Bette 242
Paul, Korky 261
Pearce, Philippa 173, 251, 259, 281
Pearson, Kit 258
Pearson, Maggie 240, 241, 245
Peckham Publishing Project 277
Perrault, Charles 234
Perry, Ritchie 175
Peyton, K. M. 176, 240, 251, 259, 270
Phipson, Joan 262, 271
Pilling, Ann 178, 239, 244, 246, 270
Pirotta, Saviour 239
Pitcher, Caroline 246, 267
Plomer, William 281
Porritt, Jonathon 264
Porter, Eleanor H. 251
Porter, Sheena 259
Potter, Beatrix 234
Powell, Lesley 268
Powling, Chris 179, 239, 240
Pownall, Eve 262
Pratchett, Tony 181, 251
Prater, John 240
Preger, Jane 241
Price, Susan 181, 241, 246, 260
Pullman, Philip 273

Ransome, Arthur 184, 259
Raskin, Ellen 256, 275
Rawlins, Donna 272
Ray, Jane 280
Rayner, Shoo 245
Reed, Alexander 268
Rees, David 260, 277
Rees, Leslie 262
Reid, Dorothy 257
Richler, Mordecai 257
Ridley, Philip 186, 280
Riha, Bohumil 255
Riley, Louise 257
Roberts, Emily 263
Rodari, Gianni 255
Rodda, Emily 263
Rodgers, Frank 243
Rosen, Michael 277, 279
Rosselson, Leon 186, 243, 244, 245
Rubinstein, Gillian 263
Ruffell, Ann 245
Rushdie, Salman 251
Russell, Jean 265
Rutsler, William 251
Ryan, Margaret 239, 243, 246
Rylant, Cynthia 245, 256, 275

AUTHOR INDEX

Sage, Angie 245
Sampson, Derek 239
Sampson, Fay 188
Sawyer, Ruth 274, 282
Schlee, Ann 270
Schmidt, Annie M. G. 255
Scott, Hugh 281
Searle, Chris 277
Sefton, Catherine 189, 242, 277
Sendak, Maurice 282
Seredy, Kate 274
Seuss, Dr 282
Severy, Richard 191
Sewell, Anna 234
Shannon, Monica 274
Shelley, Noreen 262
Shyer, Marlene Fanta 277
Silva, Jose Maria Sanchez 255
Simister, Jean 241
Simpson, Margaret 264
Smith, Joan 268
Sorenson, Virginia 275
Souter, Andy 241
Southall, Ivan 192, 259, 262
Speare, Elizabeth G. 275, 282
Speller, Penny 247
Spence, Eleanor 262
Sperry, Armstrong 274
Spinelli, Jerry 256, 275
Staples, Suzanne Fisher 272
Spyri, Johanna 234
Steele, Mary 263
Steig, William 251
Stevenson, Robert Louis 235
Storr, Catherine 264
Strachan, Ian 194, 251
Streatfeild, Noel 259
Strong, Jeremy 241, 242
Sutcliff, Rosemary 195, 256, 259, 277
Sutton, Eve 268
Swindells, Robert 197, 238, 247, 251, 261, 277

Talbot, John 241, 247
Taylor, Andrew 281
Taylor, Cora 258
Taylor, Lisa 243
Taylor, Mildred D. 201, 256, 275
Taylor, Minna 242
Taylor, R. 244
Taylor, William 269
Tennant, Kylie 262
Thiele, Colin 262
Thomas, Ruth 201, 270
Thomas, Valerie 261

Thompson, Colin 241
Thomson, Pat 243
Thomson, Ruth 277
Tindale, Norman 262
Tolkien, J. R. R. 235
Tomlinson, Theresa 202
Toomey, P. 242
Townsend, John Rowe 203, 256
Townson, Hazel 205, 247
Toye, William 257
Treadgold, Mary 259
Trease, Geoffrey 207
Trevino, Elizabeth de 275
Turner, Philip 259

Umansky, Kaye 241, 243, 251, 276
Ure, Jean 209, 238, 244, 273

Varley, Susan 251
Villiers, Alan 262
Vipont, Elfrida 259
Voigt, Cynthia 275

Waddell, Martin 213, 239, 243, 245, 266, 279, 280
Waddell, Sid 251
Wagstaff, Sue 277
Wallace, Karen 266
Walsh, Jill Paton 214, 251, 256, 279
Warburton, Nick 217, 241
Ward, Nick 246
Waterson, Mary 277
Watson, James 277
Waugh, Sylvia 270
Webb, Kaye 265
Webb, Diana 241, 242, 245
Welch, Ronald 259
West, Colin 243
Westall, Robert 218, 246, 260, 270, 273, 279
Wheatley, Nadia 263, 271, 272
Whistler, Theresa 279
Whitby, Joy 265
White, E. B. 282
White, Helen 251
Whitehead, A. 238
Wieler, Diana J. 272
Wilde, Nicholas 220
Wilde, Oscar 235
Wilder, Laura Ingalls 220, 282
Willard, Barbara 270, 281
Willard, Nancy 275
Williams, Ruth 262
Williams, Vera 277
Wills, Jean 247

AUTHOR INDEX

Willson, Robina Beckles 241
Wilson, Bob 243
Wilson, David Henry 221, 242
Wilson, Gina 238
Wilson, Jacqueline 222, 239, 242, 261, 276
Wiseman, David 239
Wojciechowska, Maia 275
Wood, Anne 265
Wood, David 276
Wright, Betty Ren 241
Wrightson, Patricia 224, 255, 256, 262, 263

Yates, Elizabeth 274
Yep, Laurence 256

Zabel, Jennifer 240

TITLE INDEX

♦

Absolute Zero   49
Ace   130
Ace Dragon Limited   107
Adam of the Road   274
Addy the Baddy   244
Adrift   19, 267
Advantage Miss Jackson   104
Adventurer   110
Adventures of Baxter and Co   142
Adventures of Blunter Button   16
Adventures of Buster and Betsy   69
Adventures of King Midas   21
Adventures of Nimble Rumble and Tumble   268
Adventures of Pinocchio   230
Adventures of the Muddleheaded Wombat   172
Aesop's Fables   228
African Dreams   89
After the Goat-Man   35
After Thursday   211
Afterdark Princess   61, 276
Against the Odds   134
Against the Storm   250
Agnes the Sheep   269
Aircraft Today and Tomorrow   262
Ajeemah and His Son   26, 256
AK   68, 281
Albertine Goose Queen   162
Albeson and the Germans   166
Alchymist's Cat   120
Alder Tree   99
Alec's Dragon   240
Alessandra   269
Alex   268
Alex in Winter   269
Alexander and Star Part   40
Alexander and the Tooth of Zaza   40
Alfie Collection   111
Alfie Gets in First   111
Alfie Gives a Hand   111
Alfie Out of Doors   111
Alfie's Feet   111
Alfonso Bonzo   65
Ali and the Robots   91
Alice and Flower and Foxianna   133

Alice in Wonderland   230
Alice the Artist   214
Alice Through the Looking Glass   230
Alice's Adventures in Wonderland   230, 266
Alien Citadel   107
Alien Worlds   107
Aliens in the Family   153
All About My Naughty Little Sister   72
All About Sam   148
All About the Bullerby Children   143
All I Ever Ask   18
All in One Piece   163
All in the Blue Unclouded Weather   135
All Join In   266
All My Men   17
All Pigs Are Beautiful   133
All Shapes and Sizes   111
All the King's Men   158, 271
All the Kings and Queens   246
All the Proud Tribesmen   262
All We Know   263
Alligator Pie   257
Ally Ally Aster   99
Almost All-White Rabbity Cat   66
Almost Goodbye Guzzler   52
Along a Lonely Road   189
Along Came a Dog   66
Alpha Box   62
Alphabeasts   133
Always Sebastian   211
Amazing Invisible Ink Puzzle Books   94
Amazing Mark in Creepstone Castle   244
Amber   223
Amber Brown Is Not a Crayon   64
Amos Fortune Free Man   274
Amos Shrike the School Ghost   206
Amy Said   214
Anancy – Spiderman   25
Anastasia Again!   148
Anastasia Ask Your Analyst   148
Anastasia at This Address   148
Anastasia at Your Service   148
Anastasia Has the Answers   148
Anastasia Krupnik   148
Anastasia on Her Own   148

TITLE INDEX

Anastasia's Chosen Career   148
And Netta Again   160
And Now Miguel   274
And Pigs Might Fly   162, 243
And Tomorrow the Stars   257
Angel   191
Angel and the Soldier Boy   279
Angel for May   34
Angel Mae   111
Angel of Nitshill Road   78, 250
Angels Are White Aren't They?   91
Animal Crackers   244
Animal Fair   41
Animal the Vegetable and John D. Jones   35
Animals of Farthing Wood   62, 250
Ankle Grabber   115
Anne of Green Gables   251
Anneli the Art-Hater   76
Annerton Pit   67
Another Fine Mess   165
Another Heaven Another Earth   109
Another Helping of Chips   111
Antar and the Eagles   158
Antelope Company Ashore   100
Antelope Company at Large   100
Antigrav   79
Ape in Space   217, 241
Apple Pie Alien   139
Apple Won't Jump   177, 240
Apprentices   86
Apricots at Midnight   92
April Fool at Hob Lane School   142
Aquarius   158
Arabel and Mortimer   7
Arabel and the Escaped Black Mamba   7
Archer's Goon   121, 250
Arctic Blues   138
Ardizzone's Hans Andersen   228
Are You There God? It's Me Margaret   28
Arilla Sun Down   101
Arkwright   263
Armourer's House   197
Arpino Assignment   207
Art You're Magic   150
Arthur   261
Arthur's New Power   107
As Seen on TV   166
Ash Road   192, 262
Ask Me No Questions   239
Ask Oliver   69
Astercote   146
At the Sign of the Dog and Rocket   158

At War with Tomorrow   142
Aunt Augusta's Elephant   208
Aunt Lizzie's Lion   242
Australian Book   262
Australian Legendary Tales   262
Autumn Street   271
Awaiting Developments   12, 264, 281
Away from Home   104, 105
Away Team   104
Awful Jack   52

Baby and Fly Pie   34
Baby Sister for Frances   107
Baby's Catalogue   4
Babylon   215
Babysitting Gang   124
Back House Ghosts   190
Back in Time with Megabot   100
Back Yard War   81
Backlash   79
Bad Bear   4
Bad Blood   17
Bad Boy   272
Bad Boys   45
Bad Case of Robots   238
Bad Spell for the Worst Witch   162
Baddies   115
Badger's Fate   103
Badger's Parting Gifts   251
Bag of Moonshine   88
Bagthorpe Triangle   49
Bagthorpes Abroad   49
Bagthorpes Haunted   49
Bagthorpes Liberated   49
Bagthorpes Unlimited   49
Bagthorpes Versus The World   49
Baked Bean Kids   179
Baked Bean Queen   115
Baker Street Irregulars   69
Balyet   224
Bamboo Flute   263
Bang! Bang! You're Dead   194
Bangers and Chips Explosion   94
Bargain for Frances   107
Barge Children   49
Barley Sugar Ghosts   205
Barnabas Walks   160
Baron's Hostage   208
Barty   267
Bathwater's Hot   111
Battle for Muck Farm   240
Battle for the Park   62
Battle Of Baked Bean Alley   217
Battle of Bubble and Squeak   174, 281
Battle of Zormla   107

TITLE INDEX

Battlefield   160
Battlefields   191
Beach Dogs   63
Beachcombers   49
Beans on the Roof   35
Bear Nobody Wanted   5
Bear Who Stood on His Head   47
Bear's Birthday   5
Bear's Den   240
Bears Will Get You   168
Beast in the Basement   179
Beat of the Drum   190
Beautiful Take-Away Palace   124
Bed and Breakfast Star   222
Bedtime Beast   115
Bedtime for Frances   107
Bee Rustlers   165
Beethoven Medal   171
Beezus and Ramona   43
Before I Go to Sleep   179
Behind the Bike Sheds   165
Behind the Goal   104
Behind the Wind   225
Bella's Concert   239
Bella's Dragon   180
Ben and the Amazing Pot Plant   242
Ben's Big Day   40
Benny's Best Friend   240
Bernice Knows Best   263
Bernie Works a Miracle   187
Bertie Boggin and the Ghost Again!   190
Beside the Sea with Jeremy James   221
Bess   142
Best Friends   14, 243
Best Friends for Frances   107
Best Kept Secret   263
Best Train Set Ever   113
Between the Moon and the Rock   12
Beware of the Bill   133
Beware of the Brain Sharpeners   56
Beware Olga!   55
Bewitched by the Brain Sharpeners   56
Beyond the Burning Lands   42
Beyond the Dragon Prow   141
Beyond the Labyrinth   263
BFG   59, 250, 261
Big Alfie and Annie Rose Storybook   111
Big Bad Bertie   214
Big Bad Pig   5
Big Biscuit   179
Big Brass Key   172
Big Concrete Lorry   111
Big Drip   138

Big Green Star   138
Big Izzy   241
Big John Turkle   107
Big Match   69
Big Pink   178
Big Six   185
Big Stink   139
Big Swig and Fling   241
Biggest Bonfire in the World   124
Bilgewater   84
Bill's New Frock   76, 276, 280
Billy Boy   124
Billy Goats Gruff...   183
Billy Pink's Private Detective Agency   128
Bingo Brown and the Language of Love   35
Bingo Brown Gypsy Lover   35
Bingo Brown's Guide to Romance   35
Birdy and the Ghostie   215
Birthday Burglar and the Very Wicked Headmistress   154
Birthday for Bluebell   115
Birthday for Frances   107
Bit of Give and Take   17
Blabber Mouth   95
Black Beauty   234
Black Cat   5
Black Hearts in Battersea   9
Black Jack   86
Black Maria   121
Black Ships Before Troy   197
Black Woolly Pony White Chalk Horse   85
Black-Stone Eye   206
Blade of the Poisoner   106
Blanket House   138
Blemyah Stories   160
Blessu   133
Blewcoat Boy   88
Blitz Cat   218, 279
Blood and Thunder Adventure on Hurricane Peak   153
Blood Brothers   246
Blood Feud   197
Blood Line   103
Blood Money   104
Blossom Promise   37
Blossoms and The Green Phantom   37
Blossoms Meet the Vulture Lady   37
Blow Me Down!   5
Blowfish Live in the Sea   82
Blubber   28
Blue Hawk   68, 270

292

TITLE INDEX

Blue Magic   206, 247
Blue Misty Monsters   189
Blue Rabbit   125
Boat Girl   18
Boffy and the Mumford Ghosts   22
Boffy and the Teacher Eater   22
Bogeymen   166
Boggart   46
Boggart in the Barrel   190
Boggy Bay Marathon   139
Bone Dog   183
Bone from a Dry Sea   67
Bongleweed   49
Bonker's Clocks   81
Bonnie Dundee   197
Boo!   55
Book of Fairy Tales   115
Book of the Banshee   78
Book of Wiremu   268
Boomerang Book of Legendary Tales   262
Boris and Borsch   135
Born of the Sun   55
Bornie Works a Miracle   243
Borrowers   251, 259
Borrowers Afield   251
Borrowers Afloat   251
Boss of the Pool   135
Bossy Boots   210
Bostock and Harris   87
Bottled Cherry Angel   209
Bouncing   111
Bows Against the Barons   208
Box of Delights   233
Box of Nothing   68
Boy: Tales of Childhood   61
Boy and the Swan   264
Boy in the Bubble   195
Boy Who Bounced . . .   154
Boy Who Was Afraid   274
Boy Who Was Followed Home   155
Boy Who Was Twins   239
Boy Who Wasn't There   177
Boy with His Leg in the Air   246
Boy with Illuminated Measles   15
Boy with Two Shadows   155
Brain Sharpeners Abroad   56
Brainbox Sorts It Out   169
Brambledown Tales: Blackberry Bunny   151
Brambledown Tales: Henry Hedgehog's Hat   152
Brambledown Tales: Hoppity Hare's Adventures   152

Brambledown Tales: Little Brown Mouse   152
Brambledown Tales: Little Chick's Tail   152
Brambledown Tales: Piggy Goes to Market   152
Brambledown Tales: Rabbits' New Home   152
Brambledown Tales: Yellow Duckling's Story   152
Bread and Honey   262
Bread and Jam for Frances   107
Breadhorse   89
Breadwitch   168
Break in the Sun   17
Break of Dark   219
Breaktime   41
Breath of Fresh Air   125
Brenda the Bold   211
Bridesmaids   242
Bridge to Terabithia   173, 275
Bridget and William   84
Bridle the Wind   8
British and Irish Folk Tales   55
British Folk Tales   56
Brock and the Dragon   135
Bronze Bow   275
Bronze Trumpeter   168
Broomstick Academy   136
Broops! Down the Chimney   79
Brother Dusty-Feet   197
Brother in the Land   199, 261, 277
Brothers Grimm: Popular Folk Tales   231
Bubble Trouble   156
Bud Boyes   250
Budgie Said Grrr!   214
Bully   165
Bumps in the Night   5
Bunyip Hole   225
Burglar Bill   5
Burnhope Wheel   89
Burning Baby. . .   96
Burning Issy   34
Burning Questions of Bingo Brown   35
Burper   142
Bus People   13
Bus Under the Leaves   153
Busy Day for a Good Grandmother   156
But Jasper Came Instead   169
Butterfingers   180
Butterfly Ball and the Grasshopper's Feast   281
Butty Boy   215

293

TITLE INDEX

By the Shores of Silver Lake 221
Bye Bye Baby 5

Cabbages from Outer Space 246
Caddie Woodlawn 274
Calabrian Quest 207
Calamity With the Fiend 139
Call and Other Stories 219
Call it Courage 274
Call of the Wild Wood 125
Callie's Castle 172
Calling for Sam 18
Camden Street Kids on TV 69
Camden Street Kids: by the Sea 69
Camden Street Kids: in the Money 69
Camden Street Kids: School Fair 69
Came Back To Show You I Could Fly 136
Can I Play Farmer Farmer? 216
Can I Play Jenny Jones? 216
Can I Play Queenie? 216
Can I Play Wolf? 216
Can It Be True? 279
Can of Worms 158
Can You Sue Your Parents for Malpractice? 64
Can't You Sleep Little Bear 279
Candle in the Dark 198
Candy for King 142
Capricorn Bracelet 197
Captain Daylight and the Big Hold-Up 245
Captain Eco and the Fate of the Earth 264
Caravan Puppets 30
Caraway and the Cup Final 242
Caretaker's Cat 18
Carnival Kite 101
Carpenter 183
Carpet People 181
Carrie's War 23
Carrot the Goldfish 242
Carrot Tops And Cotton Tails 158
Carry on Mr Bowditch 274
Cart and Cwidder 121
Carter Discovers the St Lawrence 257
Cartoonist 35
Caruso's Cool Cats 133
Case of Blue Murder 151
Castle in the Air 122
Castle of Bone 75
Cat Ate My Gymsuit 64
Cat Called Max 69
Cat That Walked by Itself 251
Cat Up the Clock 242

Cat Who Went to Heaven 274
Cat with No Name 239
Cat's Eyes 238
Cat's Witch and the Last Birthday 247
Catalogue Of the Universe 156
Catch Your Death . . . 95
Catfang 81
Cathedral Wednesday 160
Cats and the Mice 272
Cats in a Basket 45
Cats of Seroster 219
Cats Sleep Anywhere 74
Caught Out 104
Caves of Klydor 106
Chain of Days 26
Chain of Fire 164
Chains of Sleep 189
Chair for My Mother 277
Chair Person 123, 238
Challenge in the Dark 141
Champion 92
Chance Child 215
Changeling 197
Changeover 156, 260, 268, 271
Changes Changes 113
Chaos Comes to Chivy Chase 56
Charlie and the Chocolate Factory 59, 250
Charlie and the Great Glass Elevator 59
Charlie Lewis Plays for Time 126
Charlie Meadows 108
Charlie Moon and the Big Bonanza Bust-Up 111
Charlie the Champion Liar 206
Charlie the Tramp 108
Charlie's Dragon 240
Charlotte Sometimes 75
Charmed Life 121, 270
Chartbreak 55
Chasing Game 104
Cheap Sheep Shock 12
Cherry Time at Bullerby 143
Chess-Dream in a Garden 197
Chestnut Soldier 167
Chewing-Gum Rescue. . . 154
Chicken Gave It to Me 77
Chief's Daughter 197
Chieftain's Daughter 151
Child of the Owl 256
Children in Winter 250
Children Of Charlecote 175
Children of Green Knowe 30
Children of Morrow 109
Children of the House 175

294

TITLE INDEX

Children of the Turnpike   125
Children of Winter   70
Children's Classics to Read Aloud   27
Children's Ward   251
Chimneys of Green Knowe   30
China Coin   19
Chinaman's Reef Is Ours   193
Chips and Jessie   111
Chocolate Boy   208
Chocolate Candy Kid   139
Chocolate Porridge...   155
Choking Peril   206
Chorister's Cake   160
Chris and the Dragon   189
Christina's Ghost   241
Christmas at Bullerby   143
Christmas Blizzard   189
Christmas Carol   230
Christmas Carol in Prose   231
Christmas Cat   93, 219
Christmas Ghost   145
Christmas in the Stable   194
Christmas in the Tree   126
Christmas with Tamworth Pig   183
Christopher Uptake   233
Chronicles of Narnia   138
Chunky Bears Go Camping   138
Chunky Bears Go on the River   138
Chunky Bears Go Shopping   138
Chunky Bears' Birthday Party   138
Chunky Bears' Busy Day   138
Cimaroons   142
Cinderella   234
Cinderella Show   5
Cinema Swindle   69
Circlet of Oak Leaves   197
Circus   5
Circus Is Coming   259
City Cats   63
City of Gold   260
City of Gold and Lead   42
City Out of Sight   193
Clancy's Cabin   153
Class That Went Wild   201
Claudius Bald Eagle   150
Claws of the Eagle   208
Clever Dick   204
Clever Trevor   243
Cleversticks   18
Clevor Trevor   94
Clipper Street   244
Clock Struck Twelve   27
Clock Tower Ghost   126
Clocks and More Clocks   113

Clothes   111
Clothes Horse...   3
Cloudy-Bright   204
Clowning About   5
Coachman Rat   222
Coal House   281
Coast to Coast   38
Coded Signals...   103
Collected Stories for Children   259
Colly's Barn   162
Colours   111
ColSec Rebellion   107
Colvin and the Snake Basket   150
Come and Get Me   104
Come Come to My Corner   160
Come Danger Come Darkness   172
Come Lucky April   211
Come on Ossie   65
Come Sing Jimmy Jo   173
Come to Mecca   277
Comfort Herself   124, 277
Comic Crooks   69
Coming Home   142
Coming Round   241
Complete Rhyme Time   117
Complete Tales of Beatrix Potter   234
Computer Nut   35
Comrades for the Charter   208
Confidence Man   86
Conker   162
Conker As Hard As a Diamond   180
Conrad   169
Conrad's War   64, 256, 270
Cool Simon   209
Coot Club   185
Coots in the North   186
Cops and Robbers   5
Copycat   139, 241
Corbie   160
Cormorant Venture   208
Corona and the Tin Frog...   108
Coronation Picnic   93
Counting by Numbers   152
Country Boy   18
Country Pancake   77
Cousins   102
Cousins Quartet   154
Cowgirl Aunt of Harriet Bean   239
Coyote the Trickster   107
Crack a Story   183
Cracker Jackson   36
Crackers   137
Crash!   72, 246
Crash Bang and Wallop   13

TITLE INDEX

Crash! Bang! Wallop! 5, 240
Crash Car 104
Creature In the Dark 218
Creepy Company 7
Creepy Tale 175
Creepy-Crawly Stories 116
Criminal Computer 69
Crimson Crescent 205
Crocodile and Pierrot 108
Crocodile Dog 127
Crocodile Man 26
Crocodile Surprise 246
Crooked Snake 225, 262
Crossbow 110
Crossing to Salamis 216
Crown of Dalemark 123
Crown of Violet 208
Crummy Mummy and Me 77
Cry of the Wolf 34
Cry Vampire! 69
Crystal Prison 120
Cub Scouts 70
Cubby Bears Go Camping 138
Cubby Bears Go on the River 138
Cubby Bears Go Shopping 138
Cubby Bears' Birthday Party 138
Cuckoo Bush Farm 133
Cuckoo Child 133
Cuckoo Sister 10
Cuckoo Tree 9
Cucumber King 169
Cue for Treason 208
Curse of the Egyptian Mummy 113
Curse of the Werewolf 27
Cybil War 36
Cyril's Cat and the Big Surprise 245

Dad's New Car 72
Daggie Dogfoot 130
Daisy's Christmas 214
Dakota of the White Flats 186
Dan Alone 203
Dance for Two 211
Dance on My Grave 41
Dancing Bear 68
Dancing Dreams 209
Dancing in the Anzac Deli 271
Dancing Tigers 108
Danger – Marmalade at Work 65
Dangerous Cove 257
Dangerous Spaces 154
Dangleboots 103
Daniel Boone 274
Danny – Don't Jump 205
Danny the Champion of the World 59

Daredevils Or Scaredycats 180
Dark Behind the Curtain 52
Dark Bright Water 225
Dark Forest 138
Dark Frigate 274
Dark Hills Hollow Clocks 128
Dark Is Rising 45, 256
Dark Portal 120
Dark Sun Bright Sun 79
Darkling 177
Dathera Dad 55
David and Goliath 69
David's Witch Doctor 150
Dawn of Fear 46
Dawn Wind 196
Dawnstone 215
Day After Yesterday 125
Day at Bullerby 143
Day by the Sea 30
Day It Rained Elephants 214
Day of the Dragon 110
Day of the Starwind 106
Day Patch Stood Guard 138
Day Sidney Was Lost 138
Day the Animals Went on Strike 30
Day the Ducks Went Skating 138
Day the Smells Went Wrong 190
Day Veronica Was Nosy 138
Daymaker 99
Daz 4 Zoe 199
Dead Letter Box 158
Dead Man's Secret 13
Dead Moon . . . 55
Deadline for Danny's Beach 89
Dear Billy . . . 244
Dear Fred 177
Dear Grumble 47
Dear Mr Henshaw 44, 275
Dear Nobody 71, 260
Dear Shrink 50
Death Knell 220
Deathwing Over Veynaa 106
Deathwood Letters 206
Debbie and the Little Devil 148, 238
December Rose 86
Deenie 29
Deepwater 171
Delikon 109
Delilah and the Dishwasher Dogs 167
Delilah and the Dogspell 167, 250
Demon Bike Rider 141
Demon Bowler 104
Demon Headmaster 52
Demon Kevin 115

TITLE INDEX

Demon of the Dark   70
Demon-Spawn   61
Dentist's Promise   154
Deptford Histories   120
Deptford Mice Trilogy   120
Desert Island Ducks   138
Design a Pram   78, 238
Desperate for a Dog   115
Devil Finds Work   97
Devil on the Road   219
Devil's Children   68
Devil's Doorbell   110
Devil's Hill   262
Devil's Piper   183
Devil-In-The-Fog   86, 270
Diamond   267
Diary of a Killer Cat   238
Dicey's-Song   275
Dick King-Smith's Alphabeasts   134
Dick King-Smith's Triffic Pig Book   134
Diddakoi   281
Dido and Pa   9
Different Dragons   145
Different Sort of Christmas   125
Diggers   181
Digital Dan   90
Dim Thin Ducks   12
Dinner At Alberta's   108
Dinner Ladies Don't Count   17
Dinosaur Dreams   5
Dinosaur Field   16, 240
Dinosaur Junction   99
Dirty Beasts   61, 250
Disappearing Diplomat   70
Disappearing Granny   139
Disaster with the Fiend   139
Displaced Person   262
Divide and Rule   158
Divorce Express   64
Diz and the Big Fat Burglar   22
Do Goldfish Play the Violin?   221
Dobry   274
Dockside School Stories   18
Doctor's Bag   138
Dodgem   17, 250, 272
Dodo Comes to Tumbledown Farm   134
Dodos Are Forever   130
Dog Bites Goalie . . .   104
Dog Called Dog   125, 240
Dog Days and Cat Naps   126
Dog Powder   246
Dog So Small   174
Dog's Life   168
Dogger   111

Dognapper   139
Dogsbody   123
Dolly Rockers   138
Dolphin Crossing   215
Dom and Va   43
Don't Forget the Bacon   113
Don't Tell Me What to Do   104
Donkey Christmas   125
Donkey Strike   125
Donkey's Day Out   179
Doomsday Diary of Ermengarde Hulke   39
Door in the Air . . .   155
Door in the Wall   274
Doorbell Rang   113
Double   240
Double Dare   90
Double Ducks   5
Double Holiday   104
Down-And-Out   18
Down Came a Blackbird   220
Down to Earth   225
Downhill All the Way   177
Downhill Crocodile Whizz . . .   155
Downstream   204
Dr Drivel's Serious Joke Book   94
Dr Jekyll and Mr Hollins   100
Drac and the Gremlin   20
Dracula In Sunlight   180
Dracula's Castle   198
Dragline   89
Dragon Boy   134
Dragon Dance   43
Dragon Days   100
Dragon Hoard   140
Dragon of an Ordinary Family   156
Dragon Ride   52
Dragon Slayer   197
Dragon Trouble   148
Dragon with Red Eyes   145
Dragons Live Forever   199
Dream House   157
Dream of Seas   271
Dream Palace   223
Dream Seller   240
Dream Thing   12
Dreaming Of Larry   211
Dresses of Red and Gold   136
Drift   160
Driftway   146
Drowned Ammet   121
Drowners   128
Duck Soup Farm   47
Dumbellina   94

TITLE INDEX

Dumbellina and the Vanishing Video 243
Dumpling 134
Dusk of Demons 41
Dustbin Charlie 179
Dustbin Charlie Cleans Up 244
Dustland 102
Dwarfs of Nosegay 26

Each Peach Pear Plum 5
Eagle Island 19
Eagle of the Ninth 196
Eagle's Egg 197
Earth Owl and Other Moon People 113
Earth to Matthew 64
Earthfasts 160
East End at Your Feet 277
Easter Cat 67
Easy Avenue 258
Eating Between the Lines 258
Echoes of War 219
Edge of the Cloud 177, 259
Edge of the World 95
Educating Marmalade 65
Egg Thoughts... 108
Egg Timer 160, 246
Eight Days of Luke 121
Eight Days to Christmas 125
Eighteenth Emergency 36
Elephant 12
Elephant Party 27
Elephant Rock 268
Elephants Don't Sit on Cars 221
ELF 61 180
Elf in the Head 168
Elidor 88
Ellie and the Hagwitch 50
Elm Street Lot 175
Emer's Ghost 189
Emil and His Clever Pig 143
Emil and the Bad Tooth 143
Emil Gets Into Mischief 144
Emil in the Soup Tureen 144
Emil's Little Sister 144
Emil's Pranks 144
Emil's Sticky Problem 144
Emily in the News 241, 245
Emily's Legs 130
Emily's Own Elephant 175
Emlyn's Moon 167
Emma Dilemma 189
Emma Tupper's Diary 68
Emmet Otter's Jug-Band Christmas 108
Emmie and the Purple Paint 72
Emperor's Winding Sheet 216

Empty House 189
Empty Sleeve 86
Empty World 43
End of the Tale... 47
Enemies 136
Enemies Are Dangerous 97
Enemy at Green Knowe 31
Enormous Crocodile 61
Enough Is Too Much Already... 158
Enter Frederick K Bower 110
Eric the First Flying Penguin 238
Ernest the Heroic Lion-Tamer 243
Esio Trot 60, 280
ESP: Eric Stanley Pigeon 134
Ethel the Chicken 241
Europe United 70
Eva 68
Even Naughtier Stories 117
Evening at Alfie's 111
Everybody Said No! 139
Everybody's Here 277
Everyone Else's Parents Said Yes! 64
Evil Eye 81
Exeter Blitz 260
Exiles 270
Exiles of ColSec 106
Exploits of Hercules 107

Faber Book of Favourite Fairy Tales 47, 236
Faber Book of Golden Fairy Tales 48
Faber Book of Northern Folk Tales 56
Fair's Fair 88, 261
Fairy Rebel 20
Fairy Stories Of Oscar Wilde 235
Fairy Tale Treasury 31
Fairy Tales 3, 228
Fairy Tales of Gold 89
Fairy Tales of Oscar Wilde 235
Faithless Lollybird... 7
Falcon's Malteser 110
Falling Angels 177
Falling Apart 223
Falling Into Glory 219
Falter Tom and the Water Boy 268
Fame and Fortune 218
Families 5
Family at the Lookout 262
Family Conspiracy 262
Family from One End Street 259
Fanny and the Monsters 146
Fantastic Feats of Doctor Boox 65
Fantastic Mr Fox 60
Fantastic Stories 251
Fantasy Tales 116

TITLE INDEX

Fantora Family Files   93
Far Beyond and Back Again   27
Farm Tales   134
Farm That Ran Out of Names   159
Farmer Boy   221
Farmer Bungle Forgets   134
Farmer Duck   280
Farmer Jane   245
Farmer Jane's Birthday Treat   245
Farthest Away Mountain   20
Fast Frog   5
Fast from the Gate   104
Fastest Gun Alive . . .   222
Fat Lollipop   210
Fat Puss and Slimpup   241
Fatbag   243
Father Christmas   31
Father Christmas Goes on Holiday   32
Fathom Five   219
Fattest Dwarf of Nosegay   26
Favourite Fairy Tales from Grimm   231
Favourite Hans Christian Andersen Fairy Tales   228
Fear of Samuel Walton   97
Fearful Lovers . . .   219
Feasting of Trolls   183
Fee Fi Fo Fum   5, 32
Feet . . .   157
Fenella Fang   176
Fenella Fang And the Great Escape   176
Fenella Fang and the Time Machine   176
Fenella Fang and the Wicked Witch   176
Fergus the Forgetful   243
Ferryman's Son   195
Fetch the Slipper   139
Few Fair Days   84
Ffangs the Vampire Bat and the Kiss of Truth   113
Fibs   40
Fiend Next Door   139
Fifteen   45
Fighting In Break   116
Final Reckoning   120
Find a Stranger Say Goodbye   149
Find the White Horse   130
Finders Losers   158
Finding   23
Finding Annabel   93
Fine Boy for Killing   166
Finger-Eater   130
Fingers Crossed   180
Finn Gang   190
Finnglas and the Stones of Choosing   188

Finnglas of the Horses   188
Fire and Hemlock   123
Fire on the Cloud   142
Fire on the Wind   207
Fireball   42
Fireman Sam and the Missing Key   138
Fireweed   215
Fireworks Galore   205
First Class   115
First Four Years   221
First Margaret Mahy Story Book   158, 268
First Treasury of Fairy Tales   236
First Walkabout   262
Fish Pie for Flamingoes   93
Fish Stew   139
Five Children and It   233, 251
Five Minutes' Peace   163
Flambards   270
Flambards Divided   177
Flambards in Summer   177
Flame Coloured Taffeta   193
Flames   40
Flat Cat   108
Flat Man   115
Flat Stanley   33, 250
Flat Stanley's Fantastic Adventures   33, 250
Flawed Glass   194, 251
Flight from Farthing Wood   62
Flight of Angels   208
Flight of Bembel Rudzuk   108
Flight of the Solar Duck   267
Flither Pickers   202
Florizella and the Wolves   250
Flossie Teacake Again   65
Flossie Teacake Strikes Back   65
Flossie Teacake's Fur Coat   65
Flour Babies   77, 250, 260, 281
Fly Away Home   169
Fly West   193, 262
Fly-Away Frankie   180
Fly-By-Night   176
Flying Sam   190
Fog Hounds Wind Cat Sea Mice   7
Folk Tales   244
Follow A Shadow   199
Follow My Black Plume   208
Follow That Bus!   113
Fool of the World and the Flying Ship   186
For the Love of Sang   14
Forbidden Doors   182
Forecast of Fear   243

299

TITLE INDEX

Foreign Affair 204
Forest of the Night 204
Forestwife 202
Forever . . . 29
Fortunate Name 154
Fortune Branches Out 154
Forty Days of Tucker 142
Forty-Eight Hours with Franklin 267
Four Grannies 123
Fourth Plane at the Flypast 103
Fox and the Tomten 145
Fox-Busters 131
Fox Cub Bold 62
Fox Hole 193
Fox Tricks 41
Fox's Feud 62
Foxcover 40
Frankie's Dad 209
Frankie's Hat 158
Frankie's Story 191
Franklin of The Arctic 257
Freckle Juice 29
Fred Again 104
Fred the Angel 203
Fred's Dream 5
Freddy 175
Free Kick 104
Free Man on Sunday 188
Friday Parcel 179, 239
Friend Or Foe 162
Friends and Brothers 131
Friendship 201, 256
Fright 211
Froggett's Revenge 177
From the Mixed-Up Files of Mrs Basil E. Frankweiler 275
Frontier Wolf 197
Fudge-A-Mania 29
Fun 158
Fun with Mrs Thumb 158
Fungus the Bogeyman 32
Funny How the Magic Starts 151
Funny Sort of Christmas 40
Funnybones 5
Fur 158
Furry Maccaloo 55
Future-Telling Lady 26
Futuretrack 5 219
Fwog Pwince – the Twuth 241, 251

Gadget War 243
Gaffer Samson's Luck 216, 279
Galactic Warlord 106
Game of Dark 50, 160
Game of Soldiers 165

Games . . . 135
Gander of the Yard 222
Garbage Delight 258
Gardens of Dorr 27
Gary Who? 206
Gathering 102
Gathering of Days 275
Gay-Neck the Story of a Pigeon 274
Genie on the Loose 141
Gentleman Jim 32
Geoffrey Strangeways 163
George and the Dragon 70
George H. Ghastly 176
George H. Ghastly and the Little Horror 176
George H. Ghastly to the Rescue 176
George Speaks 131
George's Marvellous Medicine 60
Georgie and the Dragon 119, 243
Georgie and the Planet Raider 119
Getting In 18
Getting Rich with Jeremy James 221
Ghost Abbey 219
Ghost and Bertie Boggin 190
Ghost at Codlin Castle 134
Ghost Dog 40
Ghost Downstairs 87
Ghost Drum 182, 260
Ghost Girl 190
Ghost Messengers 198
Ghost of Dockside School 18
Ghost of Skinny Jack 145
Ghost of Tantony Pig 119
Ghost of Thomas Kempe 146, 259
Ghost on the Hill 96
Ghost Ship 191
Ghost Ship to Ganymede 199
Ghost Song 183
Ghost That Lived on the Hill 210
Ghost Train 5
Ghostly Laughter 116
Ghosts and Journeys 219
Ghosts and Shadows 73
Ghosts at Hob Lane 142
Ghosts at Large 182
Ghosts of Cobweb 191, 242
Ghosts of Cobweb and the Circus Star 191
Ghosts of Cobweb and the Skully Bones Mystery 191
Ghosts of Gallows Cross 70
Ghosts of Hungryhouse Lane 150
Giant Called Norman Mary 241
Giant Cold 68

300

TITLE INDEX

Giant Under the Snow 96
Gideon Ahoy! 160
Gideon Gander Solves the World's
  Greatest Mysteries 222
Gift 68
Gift from Another Galaxy 58
Gift from Winklesea 50
Gigantic Balloon 172
Gigantic Hit 104
Ginger Pye 274
Ginger Spike 243
Gingerbread Man 117
Giraffe and the Pelly and Me 60
Giraffe in Pepperell Street 136
Girls in the Velvet Frame 93
Girls' Gang 115
Give the Dog a Bone 5
Giver 275
Giving 112
Glass Slipper 74
Glittering River 93, 240
Glooskap's Country... 257
Glory Girl 36
Glubbslyme 223
Go and Hush the Baby 38
Go Saddle the Sea 8
Go-Ahead Gang 199, 238
Goal! 104
Goalkeeper's Revenge 277
Goals in the Air 104
Gobbling Billy 160
Gobbo the Great 53
Goblin Party 107, 245
God Beneath the Sea 28, 88, 259
Gods in Winter 271
Goggle Eyes 77, 250, 260, 270
Going Back 147
Going Home 177
Going Out 166
Going Solo 61
Gold Dust 152
Golden Goose 194
Golden Journey 204
Golden Phoenix 257
Golden Shadow 28, 88
Goldengrove 216
Goliath Takes the Bait 239
Golly Sisters Go West 38, 245
Gone to the Dogs 204
Good and Bad Witch 238
Goodbye Chicken Little 36
Goodbye Ruby Red 125
Good-Bye to Gumble's Yard 203
Good Fortunes Gang 154

Good Luck Duck 67
Good Luck to the Rider 262
Goodnight Mister Tom 270
Goodnight Monster 240
Good-Night Owl! 113
Good-Night Prof. Love 204
Good Old Dolls 5
Goose That Laid the Golden Egg 279
Gopher Gold 138
Gorilla 266
Gowie Corby Plays Chicken 126
Grace 216
Gran at Coalgate 270
Gran in Space 246
Grand Bristleton Easter Egg 245
Grand Ostrich Ball 138
Grandfather Sings Again 244
Grandma's Favourite 278
Grandma's Own Zoo 16
Grandpa Chatterji 90
Grandson Boy 47
Grange at High Force 259
Grange Hill for Sale 142
Grange Hill Goes Wild 142
Grange Hill Home and Away 142
Grange Hill Rules – OK? 142
Granny Project 77
Granny Was a Buffer Girl 70, 260
Granpa 266
Grass Rope 160, 259
Grasshopper 96
Great Comfort 124
Great Days at Grange Hill 166
Great Elephant Chase 53, 280, 281
Great Escape 63
Great Fruit Gum Robbery 108
Great Gilly Hopkins 173
Great Gran Gorilla and the Robbers 214
Great Gran Gorilla to the Rescue 214
Great Green Mouse Disaster 214
Great Ice-Cream Crime 205
Great Marathon Football Match 5
Great March West 70
Great Millionaire Kidnap 176
Great Northern? 185
Great Pig Sprint 12
Great Piratical Rumbustification 155
Great Puffin Joke Directory 94
Great Smile Robbery 152
Great White Man-Eating Shark 156
Greedy Alice 50
Green and Scaly Book 94
Green Behind the Glass 93
Green Book 216

301

TITLE INDEX

Green Books   244
Green Bough of Liberty   277
Green Kids   151
Green Laurel   262
Green Machine   105
Green Monster Magic   241, 245
Green Wind   263
Greenwitch   46
Greg's Revenge   267
Grey King   46, 275
Grinny   79
Griselda Fgm   246
Groosham Grange   110, 273
Grubble Trouble   243
Guard Dog   134
Guardian Ghost   169
Guardians   42, 270
Guardians of the House   31
Guilt and Gingerbread   88
Guilty!   201
Gulf   219, 273
Gumble's Yard   203
Gypsy Family   277
Gypsy Racer   96

H. Prince   134
Ha Ha Bonk Book   5
Hairs in the Palm of the Hand   158
Half a Team   105
Half a Welcome   105, 189
Halfmen of O   92
Halfway Along the Galaxy and Turn Left   175
Hallersage Sound   204
Handful of Thieves   23
Handful of Time   258
Handles   157, 260
Hands Off My Sister   125
Hans Andersen: His Classic Fairy Tales   228
Happy Birthday   138
Happy Birthday Sam   113
Happy Christmas Little Angel   14
Happy Days at Bullerby   143
Happy Endings   93
Happy Families   4
Happy Worm   5
Hard Way Home   177
Hare's Choice   103
Harold and Bella Jammy and Me   141
Haroun and the Sea of Stories   251
Harp of Fishbones   7
Harriet and the Crocodiles   213
Harriet and the Flying Teachers   213
Harriet and the Haunted School   213

Harriet and the Robot   213
Harriet Bean and the League of Cheats   239
Harry Moves House   180
Harry with Spots On   180
Harry's Aunt   139
Harry's Cat   139, 240
Harry's Dog   139
Harry's Hamster   139
Harry's Horse   139
Harry's Mad   131, 251
Harry's Party   180
Harvey Angel   250, 281
Harvey's Hideout   108
Hating Alison Ashley   135
Haunted Holiday   70
Haunted Ivy   205
Haunted Schoolbag   191
Haunted United   103
Haunting   156, 260, 268
Haunting Music   241
Haunting of Cassie Palmer   10
Haunting of Chas McGill . . .   219
Haunting of Pip Parker   78
Have You Seen Who's Just Moved in Next Door   266
Have You Started Yet?   277
Hawk's Vision   103
Head in the Clouds   194
Heads and Tales   182
Healer   68
Heard It in The Playground   5
Heartsease   68
Heavy and Light   138
Hector the Spectre   244
Hedgehogs Don'T Eat Hamburgers   245
Heidi   234
Hell's Edge   204
Hello Fred   169
Help!   5
Help! I Am a Prisoner in a Toothpaste Factory   15
Helpers   112, 277
Hengest's Tale   216
Henry and Beezus   44
Henry and Mudge   245
Henry and Ribsy   44
Henry and the Clubhouse   44
Henry Hollins and the Dinosaur   100
Henry Pond the Poet   134
Henry's Leg   178, 270
Henry's Most Unusual Birthday   246
Herbie Whistle   243
Here Are the Brick Street Boys   5

TITLE INDEX

Here Come the Twins   45
Here Comes Charlie Moon   111
Here Comes Thursday   30
Here Comes Tod   175
Here Lies Price   182
Here's Sam   73
Here's to You Rachel Robinson   29
Herman the Loser   108
Hero   20
Hero and the Crown   275
Herring Girls   203
Hey Robin!   142
Hey World Here I Am!   146
Hi Jinks!   191
Hi There Supermouse   210
Hiccup Harry   180
Hiccups at No. 13   243
Hidden Enemy   105
Hidden Treasure   208
Hideaway   90
Hiding Out   137
High Days and Holidays   45
High Deeds of Finn MacCool   196
High Flyers   138
High King   275
High Pavement Blues   18
Highland Fling   138
Hill's End   193
Hillingdon Fox   158
Hills of Varna   208
Hindu World   91
Hip-Hippo Ray   5
Hitty Her First Hundred Years   274
Hob and the Goblins   159
Hobbit   235
Hodgeheg   131
Hold Fast   258, 271
Hole in the Head   81
Hole in the Hill   172
Holiday with the Fiend   139
Hollow Land   84, 281
Hollywell Family   112
Home and Away   142
Home from Home   182
Homeward Bounders   122
Honey Forest   33
Hoods and Heroes   218
Hopping Mad   206
Hoppity-Gap   180
Horace and Maurice   134
Horace the Ghost   191
Horrendous Hullabaloo   156
Horrible Story and Others   156
Horse   85

Horse and His Boy   233
Horse Came Running   67
Horse Pie   134
Horseman on the Hills   208
Hostage   108
Hostages Of the Space Mafia   57
Hot and Cold   138
Hot Dog Harris   115
Hot Stuff   206
Houdini Dog   115
Hound of Ulster   197
House at Pooh Corner   233
House in Norham Gardens   147
House in Town   160
House Inside Out   148
House of Sixty Fathers   66
House of Wings   36
House on the Brink   96
House That Sailed Away   113
House Under the Stairs   213
How to Stop a Train with One Finger   221
How Alice Saved Captain Miracle   142
How Green You Are   71
How Jennifer and Speckle Saved the Earth   107
How Many Miles to Babylon   82
How the Whale Became   112
How to Survive Summer Camp   223
How to Swap Your Parents Without Really Trying   239
How Tom Beat Captain Najork and His Hired Sportsmen   108, 281
Howl's Moving Castle   122
Huffle   220
Humbug   23
Humbug Mountain   256
Hungry Snow   188
Hunky Parker Is Watching You   53
Huntsman   106
Hurry Home Candy   66
Hydra   198

I Am David   109
I Can't Stand Losing   127
I Don't Want to Go to Bed   145
I Houdini   20
I Juan De Pareja   275
I Know an Old Lady   94
I Own the Racecourse   224
I Want a Brother Or Sister   145
I Want to Be an Angel   91
I Want to Be on TV   247
I Want to Go to School Too   145
I'm Tying to Tell You   17

TITLE INDEX

Ice-Cream Bicycle 244
Ice Is Coming 225, 262
Ice Palace 198, 251
Ice Queen 65
If Cats Could Fly 219
If It Weren't for Sebastian 211
Iggie's House 28
Imagine That! Fifteen Fantastic Tales 48
Imp 238
In a Blue Velvet Dress 190
In a Class of Their Own 116
In a Nutshell 182
In a Place of Danger 82
In Black and White 158
In Summer Light 256
In the Beginning 102
In the Doghouse 165
In the Grip of Winter 62
In the Middle of the Night 175
In the Net 105
In the Path of the Storm 62
Incline 160
Incredible Journey 257
Incredible Kidnapping 100
Incredible Willie Scrimshaw 40
Indian in the Cupboard 21
Inflatable Shop 100
Inside Outing 138
Inside the Worm 198
Instant Sisters 115
Intergalactic Kitten Goes Prehistoric 243
Into the Dark 220
Intruder 204, 256
Invaders 204
Invincible Louisa 274
Irish Adventures of Worzel Gummidge 100
Iron Lily 270
Iron Man 112, 266
Iron Tsar 208
Iron Way 53
Iron Woman 112
Island Magic 105
Island of the Blue Dolphins 275
Island of the Strangers 190
Island Sunrise 216
Islanders 204
It 160
It Was a Dark and Stormy Night 4
It's a Tough Life 241
It's an Aardvark-Eat-Turtle World 64
It's Like This, Cat 275
It's My Life 142
It's Not the End of the World 29

It's Too Frightening for Me 111
It's Your Turn Roger! 279
Jack and the Beanstalk 89, 183
Jack Holborn 87
Jack the Treacle Eater 266
Jacob Have I Loved 173, 275
Jacob Two-Two Meets the Hooded Fang 257
Jam Spell 206
Jam Today 210
James 172
James and the Giant Peach 60
James and the House Of Fun 105
James and the Jumble 242
James and the TV Star 104
Jan Alone 142
Janey 18
Jar of Jokes 30
Jason Bodger and the Priory Ghost 126
JD Polson and the Dillogate Affair 30
JD Polson and the Liberty Head Dime 30
Jealous Jools And Dominique 151
Jeanius 245
Jenius 134
Jenny and Big L 242
Jenny and the Wreckers 189
Jeremiah in the Dark Woods 4
Jersey Shore 160
Jess and the River Kids 171
Jess Was the Brave One 146
Jessame Stories 119
Jessica 250
Jessy Runs Away 14
Jigger's Day Off 162, 243
Jim and the Beanstalk 32
Jim at the Corner 74
Jim Frog 108
Jim Hedgehog and the Lonesome Tower 108
Jim Hedgehog's Supernatural Christmas 108
Jimmy Zest 150
Jimmy Zest All-Stars 150
Jo in the Middle 210
Jo-Jo the Melon Donkey 161
Joanna's Goal 105, 239
Joe and Timothy Together 73
Joe's Cafe 115
John Diamond 87, 281
Johnny and the Dead 181
Johnny Tremain 274
Joke Factory 241
Jolly Christmas Postman 5

304

TITLE INDEX

Jolly Postman   5, 261, 266
Jolly Witch   134
Jonathan and the Superstar   70
Jonathan's Ghost   70
Jonny Briggs And The Galloping Wedding   250
Jonny Briggs and the Junior Tennis   250
Jonny Briggs and the Silver Surprise   240, 250
Jonpanda   276
Josh   193, 259
Josh's Panther   188
Josie Smith   251
Josie Smith and Eileen   251, 280
Josie Smith at School   251
Josie Smith at the Seaside   251
Josie Smith in Hospital   251
Journey from Peppermint Street   66
Journey of 1000 Miles   194
Journey to Jo'burg   164, 277
Joyful Noise   275
Judy and the Martian   148
Judy the Bad Fairy   214
Julian Dream Doctor   39
Julian Secret Agent   39
Julian Stories   39
Julian's Glorious Summer   39
Julie   258
Julie of The Wolves   275
Jumble   246
Jumble Joan   116
Jumper   138
Jumping   5
Jungle Book   232
Jungle Jingles . . .   134
Jungle Sale   179
Juniper   83, 127
Junk Castle   136
Jupiter Boots   168
Jupiter Jane   244
Just As Long As We're Together   29
Just Ask for Diamond   110
Just Ferret   127
Just Nuffin   63
Just So Stories   232, 251
Justice and Her Brothers   102

Kaleidoscope   74
Kamla and Kate   91
Kamla and Kate Again   91
Karlo's Tale   142
Karlson Flies Again   144
Karlson on the Roof   144
Karrawingi the Emu   262
Kassim Goes Fishing   125

Kat's Goblin   240
Kate's Skates   242
Keeper   75
Keeper of the Isis Light   271
Keeping Henry   23
Keeping House   156
Kelpie   160
Kept in the Dark   24
Kickback   105
Kidnap Report   206
Killer Tadpole   223
Kind of Thief   10
Kind of Wild Justice   17
King Creature Come   204
King Death's Garden   99
King Dicky Bird and the Bossy Princess   72
King Henry's Palace   114
King in the Forest   162
King Kangaroo   5
King Keith and the Jolly Lodger   243
King of Copper Mountain   27
King of Spuds   211
King of the Cloud Forest   162
King of the Knockdown Gingers   125
King of the Sticks   194
King of the Vagabonds   63
King of the Wind   274
Kingdom by the Sea   218, 270
Kingdom Under the Sea   8
Kingfisher Treasury of Stories for Children   28
Kings and Queens   158
Kipper   276
Kiss the Dust   137, 251, 261
Kit   85
Kit in Boots   85
Kitchen Warriors   8
Kitnapping of Mittens   244
Knickerless Nicola   276
Knight Crusader   259
Knight's Fee   197
Knightschool   70
Knock and Wait   97
Knocking Jack   183
Kofi and The Eagle   125
Kookaburra Cackles   138
Krindlekrax   186, 280
Kristli's Trees   257

Labour In Vain   88
Labours of Herakles   56
Lady Daisy   134
Lamb Shenkin   160
Lamp for the Lambchops   33

TITLE INDEX

Lamplighter's Funeral 88
Lance and the Singing Rat 242
Landfall on Innis Michael 189
Landing in Cloud Valley 142
Landings 103
Lantern Bearers 196, 259
Lark on the Wing 259
Last Battle 233, 259
Last Bus 159
Last Chance 97
Last Ditch 177
Last Genie 142
Last Legionary Quartet 106
Last Rabbit 264
Last Slice Of Rainbow... 7
Last Vampire 100
Laugh Out Loud 48
Laurie Loved Me Best 136
Lavinia Bat 108
Leadfoot 79
Leaf Magic and Five Other Favourites 155
Leapfrog 160
Leaving 256
Left Outs 223
Legacy of Ghosts 63
Leila's Magical Monster Party 244
Lengthening Shadow 97
Lenny and Jake Adventures 207
Lenny's Dinosaur Bone 241
Let the Balloon Go 193
Let the Circle Be Unbroken 201
Let's Stick Together 65
Letter to Father Christmas 116
Letters from the General 27
Letters of Fire... 93
Librarian And the Robbers 155
Life Underground 105
Light and Dark 138
Light Beyond the Forest 196
Lighthouse Keeper's Lunch 268
Lighthouse That Ran Away 152
Lightning Strikes Twice 134
Likely Lad 250, 270
Likely Place 83
Lilly's Lollipop Wand 241, 245
Lily and Lorna 247
Lily Pickle Band Book 97
Lily Pickle Eleven 97
Lincoln 272, 275
Linda's Lie 18
Lion at School... 174
Lion in the Meadow 156, 268

Lion, the Witch and the Wardrobe 233, 251
Lionel and the Lone Wolf 13
Lionel and the Spy Next Door 13
Lionel's Finest Hour 13
Listen to This Story 101
Little Angel Bonjour! 14
Little Angel Comes to Stay 14
Little Billy and the Wump 222, 242
Little Blue Book of the Marie Celeste 245
Little Blue Car 97
Little Bookroom 74, 259
Little Brother 19
Little Brute Family 108
Little Captain 27
Little Captain and the Pirate Treasure 27
Little Captain and the Seven Towers 27
Little Dog Like You 197
Little Dracula's Christmas 214
Little Dracula's First Bite 214
Little Dressmaker 74
Little Elephant 47
Little Elephant's Moon 93
Little Fear 225, 256, 263
Little Fishes 256
Little Foxes 161
Little Grey Men 259
Little Hound Found 197
Little House in the Big Woods 221
Little House on the Prairie 221
Little Love 103
Little Lower Than the Angels 151, 281
Little Pig Goes to School 242
Little Pink Book of the Woolly Mammoth 245
Little Princess 229
Little Red Riding Hood... 234
Little Sir Nicholas 250
Little Smasher 116
Little Swineherd... 83
Little Town on the Prairie 221
Little White Horse 259
Little Witch 156
Littlest Dinosaur 70, 242
Lives of Christopher Chant 122
Living Fire... 79
Lizzie Dripping 50
Lizzie Dripping Again 50
Lizzie Dripping and the Little Angel 50
Lizzie Dripping and the Witch 50, 250
Lizzie Dripping by the Sea 50
Lock 90
Lollipop 169

TITLE INDEX

Lonely Basilisk   245
Lonely Hearts   223
Lonely Hearts Club   136
Long Distance Poet   158
Long House in Danger   138
Long-Loan Llama   12
Long Night Watch   194
Long Tom and the Dead Hand   56
Long Way from Verona   85
Long Winter   221
Longtime Passing   262
Look Out For the Seals!   5
Looking for Alibrandi   263
Looking for Lossie   207
Looking-Glass Castle   27
Lord of the Dance   12
Losers Weepers   165
Lost and Found   145, 216
Lost Boy   82
Lost in the Barrens   257
Lost Property   70
Lost Star   109
Lost Wag   244
Lotta   144
Lotta Leaves Home   144
Lotta's Bike   144
Lotta's Christmas Surprise   144
Lotta's Easter Surprise   144
Lotus Caves   42
Loud Mouth   211
Loving You Loving Me   41
Low Tide   159, 270
Lucifer Wilkins   88
Lucky   152
Lucky Break   105
Lucky Chuck   45
Lucky Duck Song   245
Luke and Angela   169
Luke's Holiday   239

M. C. Higgins the Great   102, 256, 275
Machine-Gunners   218, 260
Macmagics   69
Mad Scramble   166
Madame Doubtfire   77
Maggie Gumption   22
Maggie Gumption Flies High   22
Magic at Midnight   16
Magic Birthday   93
Magic Finger   61
Magic Hare   21
Magic in the Air   16
Magic on the Tide   238
Magic Orange Tree . . .   91

Magic Party   104
Magic with Everything   267
Magician   19
Magician Who Kept a Pub . . .   72
Magician's Nephew   233
Magicians of Caprona   122
Magnus Powermouse   131
Mahy Magic   155
Maisy in the Mud   139
Maisy's Masterpiece   139
Make a Face   5
Make Like a Tree and Leave   64
Make Your Own Merry Christmas   94
Making Friends   156
Making of Fingers Finnigan   71
Making of Man   259
Making of Megabot   100
Mama's Going to Buy You a Mocking Bird   146, 258
Man   32, 266
Man Mountain   214
Man Whose Mother Was a Pirate   156
Mandeville   208
Mangrove Summer   268
Maniac Magee   256, 275
Map of Nowhere   55
Maplin Bird   178
Marble Crusher   162, 238, 251
Mardie   144
Mardie to the Rescue   144
Marie Alone   125
Mariel Of Redwall   118
Mark England's Cap   105, 246
Mark of the Horse Lord   197
Mark Spark   223
Mark Spark in the Dark   223, 242
Mark the Drummer Boy   72
Marlene Marlowe Investigates . . .   250
Marlene the Monster   239
Marmalade Atkins Hits the Big Time   65
Marmalade Atkins in Space   65
Marmalade Atkins' Dreadful Deeds   65
Marmalade Hits the Big Time   65
Maroon Boy   142
Marrow of the World   257
Marrying Off Mother   169
Martians At Mudpuddle Farm   162
Martin the Warrior   118
Martin's Mice   131
Marvin's Monster   70
Mary of Mile 18   257
Marzipan Max   246
Marzipan Pig   108
Mascot   105

307

TITLE INDEX

Masque for The Queen 208
Master Money and the Millionaire's Son 250
Master of Fiends 106
Master of the Grove 262
Master Thomas Katt 183, 241
Match Makers 210
Matchlock Gun 274
Matilda 60, 261, 276
Matt and Jo 194
Matthew and His Magic Kite 97
Matthew and the Sea Singer 216
Matthew's Mog 241, 245
Matthew's Surprise 239
Mattimeo 118
Matty's Midnight Monster 127
Maura's Angel 21
Mavis Davis 199
Max's Dream 160
Mazy 139
Me and My Friend 5
Me and My Million 129
Meeko and Mirabel 13
Meet My Folks! 113
Meet Posy Bates 50
Meet the Macmagics 69
Megan's Star 20
Megastar 210
Melusine 21
Member for the Marsh 160
Memory 156
Mercedes Ice 186
Merlin Dreams 68
Merrythought 131
Message 171
Messy Maisy 139
Maisy's Measles 139
Metro Gangs Attack 142
Mice and Mendelson 7
Midnight Adventure 32
Midnight Blue 280
Midnight Fox 36
Midnight Is a Place 8
Midsummer Night's Death 178
Mightier Than the Sword 267
Mighty Slide 5
Mik's Mammoth 250
Millionaire Witch 22
Min-Min 262
Mindbenders 80
Mine for Keeps 146
Mink War 127
Minnow on the Say 174
Minpins 61

Minstrel And the Dragon Pup 197
Mintyglo Kid 53
Miracles on Maple Hill 275
Miraculous Hind 257
Mirror Mirror 88
Mischievous Martens 144
Misery Guts 95, 250
Misha the Magician and the Mysterious Amulet 110
Miss Hickory 274
Missee Lee 185
Missing Lollipop 151
Missing Masterpiece 70
Missing May 256, 275
Mists and Magic 72
Modern Fairy Tales 48
Moffatt's Road 14
Mog and the Rectifier 180
Mole Family's Christmas 108
Mole Hole 68
Mona Lisa Mystery 113
Money for Sale 105
Monica's Monster 139
Monkey Island 83
Monster from the Underground 55, 238
Monster Garden 10
Monster in a Woozy Garden 22
Monster in the Cupboard 224
Monster Maker 80
Monster Munch 5
Monsters 5, 108
Monty the Dog Who Wore Glasses 243
Moon and Me 38
Moon-Bells... 113
Moon in the Cloud 259
Moon Monsters 107
Moon of Gomrath 89
Moon-Whales 113
Moon's Revenge 8
Moondark 225
Moondial 51
Moonlight Man 83
Moonpath... 199
More Adventures of Ursula Bear 139
More Naughty Little Sister Stories 73
More Stories for Seven Year Olds 48
More Stories for Under-Fives 48
More Stories From Dockside School 18
More Stories Julian Tells 39
More Stories to Tell 45
Morris Macmillipede 246
Mortimer And Arabel 7
Mortimer and the Sword Excalibur 7
Mortimer Says Nothing... 7

TITLE INDEX

Mortimer's Cross 7
Mortimer's Portrait on Glass 7
Mortimer's Tie 7
Moses Beech 195
Mossflower 118
Mossop's Last Chance 162
Most Beautiful Place in the World 39
Mother Goose Treasury 32
Motherland 277
Motherstone 92, 268
Mouldy 160
Mouse and His Child 107
Mouse and the Egg 160
Mouse and the Motorcycle 44
Mouse Bride 13
Mouse Butcher 131
Mouse Called Thursday 30
Mouse Woman and the Vanished Princesses 258
Mousewing 160
Mouth Open Story Jump Out 101
Moves Make the Man 256
Moving Along 117
Moving Molly 112
Moving Statue 206
Mr and Mrs Hay The Horse 250
Mr Bat's Great Invention 169
Mr Biff the Boxer 250
Mr Browser and the Brain Sharpeners 56
Mr Browser and the Comet Crisis 56
Mr Browser and the Mini-Meteorites 57
Mr Browser and the Space Maggots 57
Mr Browser in the Space Museum 57
Mr Browser Meets the Burrowers 57
Mr Browser Meets the Mind Shrinkers 57
Mr Corbett's Ghost . . . 87
Mr Cram's Magic Bubbles 30
Mr Ginger's Potato 139
Mr Magnolia 261
Mr Magus Is Waiting for You 127
Mr Merlin 251
Mr Nobody's Eyes 162, 251
Mr Parker's Autumn Term 218
Mr Plug the Plumber 277
Mr Potter's Pet 243
Mr Tick the Teacher 250
Mr Tite's Belongings 218
Mr Wolf 5
Mrs Butler Song Book 5
Mrs Cockle's Cat 175
Mrs Frisby and the Rats of NIMH 170, 275

Mrs Plug the Plumber 250
Mrs Simkin and the Groovy Old Gramophone 13
Mrs Simkin and the Magic Wheelbarrow 13
Mrs Simkin and the Very Big Mushroom 13
Mrs Simkin and the Wishing Well 13
Muddle-Headed Wombat 172
Muddle-Headed Wombat and the Invention 172
Muddle-Headed Wombat on a Clean-Up Day 172
Muddy Kind of Magic 211
Muggie Maggie 44
Mum-Minder 223
Mustang Machine 180
My Aunt Polly 52
My Aunt Polly by the Sea 52
My Best Fiend 139
My Best Friend 114
My Cat Likes to Hide in Boxes 268
My Dad's a Fire-Eater 152
My First Earth Book 152
My First Space Book 152
My Friend Walter 161
My Gang 191
My Great Grandpa 214
My Mate Shofiq 166
My Mum and Our Dad 116
My Naughty Little Sister 73
My Naughty Little Sister and Bad Harry 73
My Naughty Little Sister and Bad Harry's Rabbit 73
My Naughty Little Sister and Father Christmas 73
My Naughty Little Sister at the Fair 73
My Naughty Little Sister Birthday Book 73
My Naughty Little Sister Omnibus 73
My Naughty Little Sister Storybook 73
My Naughty Little Sister's Friends 73
My Nightingale Is Singing 145
My Place 263, 272
My Sister Sif 172
My Year 61
Myrtle Turtle 139
Mysterious Mr Ross 10
Mystery of Mr Jones's Disappearing Taxi 9
Mystery of the Cupboard 21
Mystery Pig 191
Mystery Squad and Mr. Midnight 214

TITLE INDEX

Mystery Squad and the Artful Dodger 214
Mystery Squad and the Candid Camera 214
Mystery Squad and the Cannonball Kid 214
Mystery Squad and the Creeping Castle 214
Mystery Squad and the Dead Man's Message 214
Mystery Squad and the Robot's Revenge 214
Mystery Squad and the Whistling Teeth 214
Mystery Tour 5
Myths and Legends 110
Myths and Legends of Maoriland 268

Nail a Stick and a Lid 125
Naming the Dark 62
Nan's Palace 240
Nancy Pocket and the Kidnappers 119, 238
Napper Goes for Goal 214
Napper Strikes Again 214
Napper's Golden Goals 214
Nargun and the Stars 225, 262
Narrow and Squeak . . . 134
Nature of the Beast 281
Naughtiest Stories 117
Naughty Stories 117
Near Thing for Captain Najork 108
Necklace of Raindrops 8
Nessie the Mannerless Monster 113
Netta 160
Netta Next 160
Never Kiss Frogs 142
Never Meddle with Magic 117
New Boy 202
New Found Land 42
Nice Work Little Wolf 280
Nicola Mimosa 210
Night Birds on Nantucket 9, 250
Night Maze 61
Night of the Scorpion 110
Night School 199
Night Swimmers 37
Night the Water Came 129
Night-Watchmen 51
Nina's Magic 242
Nine Lives of Montezuma 162
Ninny's Boat 129
No Defence 105
No End to Yesterday 281
No Guns No Oranges 179

No More School 160
No Place Like 127
No Shelter 267
No Sleep for Hob Lane School 143
Noah's Ark 152
Noah's Brother 132
Noah's Castle 204
Nobody's Family Is Going to Change 277
Nobody's Perfect 224
Noisy 112
Nonstop Nonsense 155
Nora Bone 94, 243
Norah and The Whale 199
Norah to the Rescue 199
Norah's Ark 200
Norah's Shark 200
Nordy Bank 259
Normal Nesbit 217
Norse Myths 56
North to Adventure 178
Not for a Billion Gazillion Dollars 64
Not-Just-Anybody Family 37
Not-So-Clever Genie 116
Nothing to Be Afraid Of 157
Now I Know 41
Nowhere to Play 277
Nowhere to Stop 125
Number the Stars 149, 275

Oaken Throne 120
October Child 262
Odin's Monster 183
Ogre Downstairs 122
Oh Grandma 240
Old Belle's Summer Holiday 175
Old Dog New Tricks 40, 277
Old Joke Book 5
Old Man on a Horse 219
Old Man Who Sneezed 72
Old Nurse's Stocking Basket 74
Old Peter's Russian Tales 186
Older Kind of Magic 225
Olga Da Polga 30
Oliver the Greedy Elephant 30
Ollie and the Bogle 119
Outfit 198
On the Banks of Plum Creek 221
On the Edge 41, 53
On the Flip Side 80
On the Lion's Side 178
On the Run 24
On the Way Home 163
Once There Was a Swagman 33
Once Upon a Golden Apple 146

TITLE INDEX

One and Only Two Heads   5
One-Eyed Cat   82, 271
One-Eyed Jake   114
One Frog Too Many   143, 242
One Good Horse   105
One Green Bottle   206
One Green Leaf   211
One Hundredth Thing About Caroline   149
One Hunter   114
One in The Middle Is the Green Kangaroo   29
One Kick   105
One True Santa   5
One Two Flea!   5
One Way Only   97
Onion John   275
Onion Tears   243
Only a Show   244
Only You Can Save Mankind   181
Operation Carrot   239
Orchard Book of Fairy Tales   116, 236
Orchard Book of Greek Myths   152
Ordinary Jack   49
Ordinary Seaman   96
Ossie Goes Supersonic   65
Ossie the Millionaire   65
Other Darker Ned   78
Other Facts of Life   95
Other Side   223
Other Side of the Fence   211
Othergran   10
Otherwise Known As Sheila the Great   29
Our Kid   178
Our Kids   277
Our Sleepysaurus   214
Out and About   112
Out in the Woods   240
Out of the Ordinary   62
Out of the Oven   158
Outcast   196
Outlanders   52
Outside Child   24
Over Sea Under Stone   46
Over the Top   194
Owl and Billy   213
Owl and Billy and the Space Days   213
Owl Service   89, 259, 270
Own Goal   105
Oxford 123 Book of Number Rhymes   152

Pack of Liars   78
Pack of Lies   151, 260, 270

Paddington Library   29
Paddiwak and Cosy   71
Paddy's Pot of Gold   132
Pain and the Great One   29
Pair of Sinners   6
Pancake Pickle at Hob Lane   143
Panda   12
Pandemonium   138
Pandemonium at School   241
Pangur Ban   188
Pangur Ban Stories   189
Paper Faces   14, 270
Parcel of Patterns   216
Parcel of Trees   160
Park in the Dark   266
Park's Quest   173
Parrot in the House   13
Parsley the Lion   30
Party for Lester   57
Party Pants   160
Party Party   65
Past Eight O'clock   8
Pastures of The Blue Crane   262
Patchwork Cat   160
Pattern of Roses   178
Pea-Green Pig   207
Peace at Last   163
Peacock Palace Scoop   138
Pebble on the Beach   195
Pedalling Man   108
Peek a Boo!   6
Peepo!   6
Penalty   105
Penelope's Pendant   107
Penfriend from Another Planet   57
Pennington's Heir   178
Pennington's Seventeenth Summer   178
Penny Black   125
Penny Pollard in Print   136
Penny Pollard's Diary   136
Penny Pollard's Letters   136
Penny Pollard's Passport   136
Penny World   28
Pentecost and The Chosen One   47
Pentecost of Lickey Top   47
People Could Fly   102, 277
People Might Hear You   136
Peppermint Pig   24, 270
Percy Goes To Spain   239
Persian Gold   216
Persuading Stick   204
Pesters of the West   243
Pet Shop   6
Peter Duck   184

311

TITLE INDEX

Peter Pan 229
Peter Pan and Wendy 229
Peter Pepper and the Goblin 245
Pets for Keeps 134
Phantom Carwash 180
Phantom from the Past 183
Phantom Knicker Nicker 211
Picking Up the Threads 195
Picnic 15
Picnic on the River 30
Picts and the Martyrs 185
Piece of Cake 125
Pied Piper 116
Piemakers 51
Pig Ignorant 81
Pig That Bathed 242
Pigeon Post 185, 259
Piggy in the Middle 166
Pigs Might Fly 263
Pilkie's Progress 206
Pinballs 37
Pineapple Child 15
Pink Ghost of Lamont 137
Pinocchio 230, 250
Piper and Pooka 55
Pippi Longstocking 144
Pirate Uncle 154
Pirate's Island 204
Pirates 15
Pirates' Mixed-Up Voyage 154
Pistachio Prescription 64
Pitiful Place . . . 166
Place Apart 83
Place for Me 219
Place to Play 6
Place to Scream 211
Plague '99 211, 273
Plain Jack 178
Plan for Birdsmarsh 178
Planet of Junior Brown 102
Planet of the Warlord 106
Planetfall 107
Play Nimrod for Him 212
Playing Away 65
Playing Ball 105
Playing Beatie Bow 172, 256, 262, 271
Playing with Fire 239
Playmates 6
Please Keep Off the Dinosaur 222
Please Mrs Butler 6
Pleasure Garden 88
Plot Night 160
Plum Tree Party 125
Plum-Rain Scroll 262

Poacher's Son 14
Polly Pipes Up 238
Pollyanna 251
Polo Time 15
Ponders 108
Pongwiffy and the Spell of the Year 276
Pony Raffle 125
Pool of Fire 42
Poonam's Pets 65
Poor Badger 177
Poor Monty 78
Poorly Pig 6
Popinjay Mystery 208
Popinjay Stairs 208
Poppy and the Vicarage Ghost 129
Popular Folk Tales 231
Portrait of Ivan 83
Postbox Mystery 200
Posy Bates Again! 50
Posy Bates and the Bag Lady 51
Power of the Shade 224
Power of Three 122
Present Takers 41
Pretty Polly 132
Priests of Ferris 92
Prime Minister's Brain 52
Prime of Tamworth Pig 126
Prince Caspian 233, 251
Prince in Waiting 42
Prince on a White Horse 140
Princess Alice 25
Princess and The Clown 156
Prisoners of September 87
Private – Keep Out! 97
Promise 220
Proper Little Nooryeff 212
Prove Yourself a Hero 178
Public Enemy No Two 111
Puff of Smoke 191
Puffin Book of Christmas Stories 48
Puffin Book of Pet Stories 48
Pumpkin Man and the Crafty Creeper 156
Puppy Summer 67
Push Me Pull Me 278
Push the Dog 6
Put a Saddle on the Pig 151

Quake 104
Queen of the Pharisees' Children 281
Queen's Goat 156
Queen's Nose 132, 251
Quelling Eye 96
Quest of the Quidnuncs 57
Quick Chick 245

TITLE INDEX

Rabbit and Teddy Tales   116
Rabbit Hill   274
Rabbit Minders   125
Rabbit's Story   116
Rabble Starkey   149, 256
Rachel and the Angel . . .   220
Racketty Street Gang   262
Radium Woman   259
Rag a Bone And a hank of Hair   80
Raging Robots and Unruly Uncles   154
Railway Cat   16
Railway Cat and Digby   16
Railway Cat and the Horse   16
Railway Cat's Secret   16
Railway Children   233
Railway Engine and the Hairy Brigands   156
Rain Door   108
Rain Ghost   128
Rainbow and Mr Zed   168
Rains of Eridan   109
Ralph S. Mouse   44
Ram of Sweetriver   63
Ramona and Her Father   43, 271
Ramona and Her Mother   43
Ramona Forever   43
Ramona Quimby Age Eight   44
Ramona the Brave   44
Ramona the Pest   44
Rapping with Raffy   65
Rare Spotted Birthday Party   156
Rat Race   224
Rat's Castle   192
Ratbags and Rascals   136
Rats!   113
Raven's Cry   257
Ravensgill   159
Razzle Dazzle Rainbow   180
Ready Teddy Go!   6
Real Thief   251
Real Tilly Beany   61
Realms Of Gold   179
Rebel on a Rock   24
Rebels of the Heavenly Kingdom   173
Red Secret   168, 238
Red Shift   89
Red Sky in the Morning   137
Red Towers of Granada   208
Redwall   118, 273
Redwork   258, 272
Remember Me to Harold Square   64
Renard the Fox   14
Rent a Genius   55, 238
Rent a Robot   6

Rescuing Gloria   53
Return   76
Return of the 'Antelope'   100
Return of the Indian   21
Return of the Psammead   52
Return of the Witch   22
Revenge of Samuel Stokes   147
Revenge of the Brain Sharpeners   57
Revenge of the Killer Vegetables   246
Revenge of the Rabbit   116
Revenge of the Small Small   146
Reversible Giant   143
Revolt at Ratcliffe's Rags   54
Revolting Rhymes   250
Revolting Rhymes and Dirty Beasts   61
Revolting Wedding   239
Revolutionary's Daughter   97
Rhyme Stew   61
Rhyming Russell   243
Richard's Castle   267
Richie's Rabbit   93
Ride the Wind   96
Riding the Waves   202
Rifles for Watie   275
Right Royal Kidnap   143, 240
Right-Hand Man   178
Ring of Gold   15
Rings on Her Fingers   160
Rival Games   105
River at Green Knowe   31
River Man   20
River Runners   258
Riverman   271
Road Ahead   149
Road to Avonlea   251
Road to Bethlehem   138
Road to Camlann   196
Road to Memphis   201
Roar to Victory   105
Rob's Place   204
Robber Hopsika   27
Robber's Daughter   145
Robbers   24
Robert Goes to Fetch a Sister   73
Robin Hood   28
Robin of Sherwood   111
Robin's Real Engine   160
Robot Revolt   80
Rocks of Honey   225
Roddy and the Miniature Railway   6
Roddy and the Puma   16
Roddy and the Rustlers   16
Roddy on the Canal   16
Roddy on the Motorway   16

313

TITLE INDEX

Roddy the Roadman 16
Rodney Penfold Genius! 40
Rola Polar Bear and the Heatwave 239
Rolf and Rosie 200, 247
Roll of Thunder Hear My Cry 201, 275
Roller Skates 274
Ronia the Robber's Daughter 145
Ronnie and the Flying Fitted Carpet 15
Ronnie and the Great Knitted Robbery 15
Ronnie and the Haunted Rolls Royce 15
Ronnie and the High Rise 15
Room Made of Windows 256
Room 13 198, 261
Room with No Windows 127
Rooms to Let 156
Root Cellar 258, 271
Rope Carrier 203
Rosa's Grandfather Sings Again 186
Rosa's Singing Grandfather 186, 244
Roscoe's Leap 54
Rosie and the Boredom Eater 52
Rosie's Walk 114
Rotten Old Car 125
Rottenteeth 166
Round Behind the Ice-House 78
Round the Christmas Tree 48
Round the Twist 250
Roundabout 127
Roundabout Horse 197
Royal Harry 160
Royal Visit 18
Rubber Rabbit 6
Ruby in the Smoke 273
Runaway 54
Runaway Bim 241, 245
Runaway Boy 125
Runaway Nest 13
Runaway Ralph 44
Runaway Serf 208
Runaway Shoes 117
Runaway Sleigh Ride 145
Runaway Summer 24
Runaway Train 75
Runaways 202, 270
Running of the Deer 208
Running Scared 18
Rushavenn Time 279

S.O.S. for Rita 240
Saddlebottom 132
Saga of Erik the Viking 261
Sailor Jack and the Twenty Orphans 156
Saint Lawrence 257
Salamandastron 118, 273
Sally Ann at the Ballet 70
Sally Ann Goes to Hospital 70
Sally Ann's School Play 70
Sally Ann – On Her Own 70
Sally Ann – The Picnic 70
Sally Ann – The Pony 70
Sally Cinderella 18
Sally Go Round the Sun 257
Sally's Secret 112
Salt and Pepper Boys 247
Salt River Times 159
Sam and Jenny 205
Sam and Sue and Lavatory Lue 200
Sam the Referee 6
Same Old Story Every Year 242
Sandman and the Turtles 162
Saraband for Shadows 208
Sarah Plain And Tall 272, 275
Saturday by Seven 75
Saturday Horse 105
Saturday Knight 239
Saturday Night 66
Sauce for the Fox 240
Save Our School 53
Save This Tree 240
Saving Grace 217, 241
Say Goodbye 212
Say It Again Granny 277
Scare Yourself to Sleep 116
Scarecrows 219, 260
Scared 40
Scaredy Cat 78
School Book Fair 207
School Cat 242
School Mouse 132
School Pool Gang 125
School Reporter's Notebook 214
School Secretary on the Warpath 94
School Spirit 70
School Stories 157
School Trip 224
School Trip to the Stars 151
Science Fiction Stories 28
Scrapyard 241
Sea Change 259
Sea-Thing Child 108
Sea Tongue 56
Seagull 75
Seal 12
Seal Secret 41
Seas of Morning 208
Seashore People 129
Season Songs 113

TITLE INDEX

Seaward 46
Second Chance 105
Second Margaret Mahy Story-Book 155
Second Step 194
Second Treasury of Fairy Tales 236
Second-Hand Horse . . . 160
Secret 202
Secret Corridor 96
Secret Garden 229
Secret of Bone Island 151
Secret of the Andes 274
Secret of the Indian 21
Secret of Theodore Brown 18
Secret of Weeping Wood 198
Secret Passage 25
Secret Place 203
Secret Water 185
Secret World of Polly Flint 51
Secrets of Celia 207
See You Thursday 212
Seeing Off Uncle Jack 18, 250
Seeing Things 135
Sense of Shame . . . 166
Sentinels 270
Separate Places 136
Septimouse Big-Cheese 243
Serpent of Senargad 188
Serpent Tower 108
Serpent's Tooth 199
Seven Chinese Brothers 156
Seven for a Secret 210
Seven Strange and Ghostly Tales 118
Seven Times Search 27
Seven Treasure Hunts 38
Seventeen Kings and Forty-Two Elephants 156
Seventeen Seconds 194
Seventh Raven 68
Shackleton's Argonauts 262
Shabanu – Daughter of the Wind 272
Shadow Guests 9
Shadow in Hawthorn Bay 258, 272
Shadow of a Bull 275
Shadow Under the Sea 207
Shadow-Cage 174
Shadows on the Cake 191
Shadrach 67
Shape-Shifter 188
Sharp Eyes 171, 246
She Was a Witch 98
She's Leaving Home 66
Sheep-Pig 132, 270
Shen of the Sea 274
Shepherd Moon 109

Shield Ring 197
Shifting Sands 197
Shiloh 275
Shine 216
Shining Company 197
Ship to Rome 208
Ship's Cat 3
Shirley's Shops 6
Shirt Off A Hanged Man's Back 103
Shoemaker's Boy 9
Shon the Taken 140
Shoot on Sight 105
Shooters 105
Short Voyage of the 'Albert Ross' 157
Shrieking Face 206
Sid and Sadie 138
Sidney the Monster 276
Siege of Cobb Street School 205
Siege of Frimly Prim 199
Siege of White Deer Park 62
Signposters 52
Silly Billy 114
Silly Sheep 6
Silly Tilly 241
Silver Branch 196
Silver Chair 233
Silver Christmas Tree 114
Silver Citadel 110
Silver Crown 170
Silver Curlew 74
Silver on the Tree 46
Silver's Revenge 142
Simon 197
Simon and the Witch 22
Simon and the Witch in School 22
Simon's Challenge 250, 267
Simon's Magic Bobble Hat 244
Singer to the Sea God 11
Singing Bowls 91
Sinister Secret of Frederick K Bower 111
Sir Bertie and the Wyvern 220
Sir Pellinore the Knight Who Never Gave Up 242
Sir Quinton Quest Hunts the Yeti 243, 251
Six Bullerby Children 143
Six Dinner Sid 280
Size Spies 166
Size Twelve 220, 246
Skeleton at School 165
Skeleton Crew 6
Skeleton in the Cupboard 241, 245
Skiffy 159

315

TITLE INDEX

Skiffy and the Twin Planets   159
Skipper at School   242
Skiver's Guide   123
Sky Grew Red   108
Sky Is Falling   258
Sky-Blue Dragon   125
Skybreaker   99
Skylark   178
Slambash Wangs of a Compo Gormer   143, 272
Slave Dancer   82, 275
Sleepers on the Hill   190
Sleeping Beauty   236, 266
Sleeping Nanna   56
Sleeping Party   165
Sloggers   251
Small Pinch of Weather   194
Small Pudding for Wee Gowrie   7
Small-Tooth Dog   160
Smart Girls   55
Smell That Got Away   142, 244
Smoky the Cowhorse   87, 274
Snail's Tale   138
Snakes Alive   207
Snakes and Ladders   136
Snakes and Snakes   136
Snatched   129
Snookered!   80
Snotty and the Rod of Power   105, 238
Snow Girl   125, 238
Snow Lady   112
Snow Spider   167, 279
Snowman   32
Snowy   71, 139
So Can I   6
So Far from Skye   171
So Much to Tell You   263
Soccer Comes First   105
Soccer Special   105
Soccer Star   105
Someone Else's Baby   125
Someplace Beautiful   33
Something Big   151
Something I Remember   74
Something Nasty in the Kitchen   30
Something Rare and Special   12
Something Special   263
Son of a Gun   6
Song for A Dark Queen   197, 277
Song for a Tattered Flag   208
Song for Solo and Persistent Chorus   12
Song of Pentecost   47, 281
Sophie Hits Six   133
Sophie in the Saddle   133

Sophie Stories   133
Sophie's Snail   133
Sophie's Tom   133
Soppy Birthday   211
Sound of Propellers   129
Sounder   275
Sounding of Storytellers   205
Soutar Retrospective   195
South by South East   111
Space Hostages   80
Spaceball   240
Speckled Panic   206
Spellcoats   122
Spellhorn   71
Spider Spy   6
Spiderman Anancy   26
Spitfire Summer   70
Spook at the Superstore   180
Spooky Cottage   212, 238
Spooky Time   15
Sports Day   70
Spots in Space   139
Spring on the Mountain   12
Spring Rider   256
Springtime at Bullerby   143
Spycatchers   208
Squib   25
Squirrel Wife   175
Squonk   119
Staggering Snowman   205
Stained Glass Window   148
Stand Up Jonny Briggs   250
Stanley and the Magic Lamp   33
Stanley in Space   33
Stanley Makes It Big   247
Stanley's Aquarium   76
Stanley's Christmas Adventure   33
Star Turn   209
Starbuck Valley Winter   257
Starring Sally J Freedman As Herself   29
Starry Night   191, 277
Stars of the Sixth   66
Starstormers   81
Starting School   6
Staying Up   200
Steaming Sam   70, 239
Stella's Wedding   70
Stepmother   156
Sticks and Stones   183
Sticky Beak   95
Stig of the Dump   129
Stitch in Time   147, 281
Stolen Lake   9
Stone Book Quartet   88

TITLE INDEX

Stone Boy   246
Stone Croc   75
Stone Doll of Sister Bute   108
Stone Menagerie   78
Stone Mouse   167
Stone the Crows It's a Vacuum Cleaner   243
Stone Walkers   11
Stones of Green Knowe   31
Stones of Muncaster Cathedral   220
Stones of The Moon   12
Stories and Fairy Tales   228
Stories by Firelight   112
Stories for Eight Year Olds . . .   48
Stories for Five Year Olds . . .   48
Stories for Nine Year Olds . . .   48
Stories for Seven Year Olds   48
Stories for Six Year Olds . . .   48
Stories for Tens and Over   48
Stories for Under-Fives   48
Stories from Hans Christian Andersen   228
Storm   56, 260
Stormcock Meets Trouble   178
Stormsearch   220
Story of Christmas   152
Story of Creation   280
Story of Dr Dolittle   251
Story of Grace Darling   52
Story of Mankind   274
Story of Peter Pan   229
Story of the Goblins Who Stole a Sexton   231
Story of the Pied Piper   117
Story of Tracy Beaker   223, 276
Story of Your Home   259
Stowaways   152
Strange Affair of Adelaide Harris   87
Strange Bird   93
Strange House   32
Strange Orbit   264
Stranger at Green Knowe   31, 259
Stranger Danger   78
Strat and Chatto   158
Strawberry Girl   274
Strawberry Jam Pony   139
Street Child   71
Strider   45
Strike at Ratcliffe's Rags   54
Stringybark Summer   171
Strong and Willing Girl   72, 277
Strong Tom   241
Stronghold   260
Stuntkid   180

Sudden Glow of Gold   78
Sudden Puff of Glittering Smoke   78
Sudden Swirl of Icy Wind   78
Suitcase Kid   223, 261
Summer After The Funeral   85
Summer Birds   75
Summer Daze   66
Summer House Loon   78
Summer in Small Street   124
Summer of the Dinosaur   100
Summer of the Swans   38, 275
Summer People   205
Summer Snowman   6
Summer to Die   149
Summer Witches   203
Sun Horse   257
Sun Horse Moon Horse   197
Sun Tribe   246
Sunburst   81
Super Terrific Pigs   134
Superdog   222
Superdog in Trouble   222
Superdog the Hero   222
Superfudge   29
Supersleuth   224
Supersnail   246
Surprise Party   114
Sus   189
Swallowdale   184
Swallows and Amazons   184
Swallows and Amazons for Ever   186
Swan   85
Swan Sister   62
Swarm in May   160
Sweet Whispers Brother Rush   103, 256, 271
Sweetgrass   258, 271
Sweets from a Stranger . . .   81
Swim Sam Swim   245
Swimathon   53
Swimming Club: Jump In   105
Swimming Club: Splashdown   105
Swings and Roundabouts   212
Switch Horse   105
Switcharound   149
Swoose   134
Sword and the Circle   196
Sword of the Spirits   42
Sylvia Game   11

T.R. Bear   69
Take a Good Look   223
Take the Long Path   268
Taking Care of Terrific   149
Tale of a One-Way Street   8

317

TITLE INDEX

Tale of Thomas Mead   114
Tale of Time City   123
Tale of Trellie the Troog   107
Tales from Europe   56
Tales from Grimm   231
Tales from Silver Lands   274
Tales from the Shop That Never Shuts   214
Tales of a Fourth Grade Nothing   29
Tales of an Ashanti Father   15
Tales of Arabel's Raven   7
Tales of Joe and Timothy   73
Tales of Mowgli   232
Tales of Nanabozho   257
Tales of the Early World   112
Tales of Uncle Remus   232
Talking Car   81
Talking in Whispers   277
Tall Story . . .   156
Tall Story of Wilbur Small   239
Taller Than Before   18
Tamworth Pig and the Litter   126
Tamworth Pig Rides Again!   126
Tamworth Pig Saves the Trees   126
Tamworth Pig Stories   126
Tangara   262
Tangle and the Firesticks   279
Tangled Fortunes   154
Tatty Apple   168
Tea-Leaf on the Roof   210
Teacher's Pet   70
Team   176
Team That Wouldn't Give In   105
Tearaways   136
Teddy's Story   116
Teeth of the Gale   8
Tell Me a Story   45
Tell Me Another Story   45
Tell Us a Story   6
Tell-Tale Tiger   6
Ten in a Bed   4
Ten Pound Note   241
Terrible Trials of Mattie Mccrum   241
Terrible Tuesday   207
Terry on the Fence   18
That Dragon Again   240
That Emil   144
That's My Baby   6
Then Again Maybe I Won't   29
There's a Bat in Bunk Five   64
There's a Wolf in My Pudding   222
There's Always Dannie   212
These Happy Golden Years   221
They Came from Aargh!   108

They Watched Him Die   97
Thicker Than Water   75
Thief   166
Thief in the Village   26, 279
Thimble Summer   274
Thin Air   250
Thing   136, 263
Thing In-a-Box   243
Thingnapped   136
Things in Corners   172
Think of Eel   266
Third Class Genie   141
Third Dragon   128
Third Margaret Mahy Story-Book   155
Thirteenth Owl   217
This Bowl of Earth   158
This Girl   224
This Place Has No Atmosphere   64
This Time of Darkness   110
Thousand Eyes of Night   199
Threadbear   261, 276
Three Against the World   143
Three Bears . . .   183
Three Indian Princesses   91
Three Seven Eleven   250
Three-Legged Cat   156
Through the Doll's House Door   85
Through the Looking Glass   230
Through the Witch's Window   207
Throwaways   195
Thumbelina   228
Thunder and Lightnings   157, 260
Thunder in the Sky   177
Thunderpumps   183, 246
Thursday Ahoy!   30
Thursday Creature   160
Thursday in Paris   30
Thursday Rides Again   30
Tibber   160
Tick Tock Tales   155
Ticket to Curlew   258
Tidy Titch   114
Tiger   12
Tiger Eyes   29
Tiger in the Bush   262
Tiger of the Track   105
Tiger's Railway   161
Tigger and Friends   104
Tikta' Liktak   257
Tilly Beany and the Best-Friend Machine   61
Tilly Mint and the Dodo   71
Tilly Mint Tales   71
Tim and the Red Indian Head-Dress   125

TITLE INDEX

Tim Kipper   199
Tim Walks   14
Time and the Clock Mice Etcetera   68
Time of the Ghost   123
Time of Trial   259
Time Out   51
Time Riders   250
Time Rope   143
Time to Laugh   48
Tin Can Band . . .   156
Tin Can Beast . . .   27
Tiny Tim   116
Titch   114
To the Wild Sky   193, 262
Toby Man   133
Toby's Iceberg   47
Toll Bridge   41
Tom and Sam   114
Tom and the Two Handles   108
Tom's Midnight Garden   174, 259
Tom's Sausage Lion   161
Tom Tiddler's Ground   204
Tommy Mac   22
Tommy Mac Battles On   22
Tommy Mac on Safari   22
Tomorrow Is a Stranger   207
Tomorrow Is Also a Day   212
Tomten   145
Tomten and the Fox   145
Too Many Babies   116
Too Many Husbands   139
Toolmaker   217
Tooth Ball   175
Toothbrush Monster   116
Toothless Wonder Abroad   57
Toothless Wonder and the Double Agent   57
Toothless Wonder in the Tower   57
Top of the League   105
Top of the World   205
Topher and The Time-Travelling Cat   119
Topsy-Turvy Storybook   133
Topsy-Turvy Teacher   139
Torch   216, 251
Tough As Old Boots   246
Tough Luck   71
Tough Princess   214
Tough Teddy   116
Tower Room   93
Town That Went South   129
Town Watch   134
Train for Tiger Lily   257
Transformations   99

Transport 7-41-R   256
Travellers By Night   11
Travelling Hopefully   12
Travelling Moose   6
Treasure Island   235
Treasury of Stories for Five Year Olds   27
Treasury of Stories for Seven Year Olds   28
Treasury of Stories for Six Year Olds   27
Tree House   54
Trial of Anna Cotman   11
Trials of Worzel Gummidge   100
Tricksters   156
Trillions   81
Tristan and Iseult   196, 256
Trixie and Baba   15
Trouble   52
Trouble Half-Way   157
Trouble with Donovan Croft   18, 277
Trouble with Edward   134
Trouble with Jack   112
Trouble with the Fiend   139
Trouble with the Tucker Twins   116
Trouble with Vanessa   212
Truce of the Games   197
Truckers   181, 251
True Confessions of Charlotte Doyle   256
True Story of Lilli Stubeck   263
True Story of Spit MacPhee   270
Trumpeter of Krakow   274
Tucker in Control   167
Tucker's Luck   167
Tulku   68, 260, 271, 281
Tumbledown Farm – the Greatest   134
Tumbleweed   133
Turbulent Term of Tyke Tiler   127, 260, 277
Turi   268
TV Kid   38
Twelve and the Genii   259
Twelve Robbers   27
Twenty Elephant Restaurant   108
Twenty-One Balloons   274
Twig Thing   158
Twin and Super-Twin   54
Twins Again   45
Twist of Gold   162
Twisters   40
Twits   60
Two Men in a Boat   212
Two Shoes New Shoes   112
Two-Thousand Pound Goldfish   38
Two Victorian Families   277

TITLE INDEX

Two Village Dinosaurs 16
Two Weeks with The Queen 95, 250
Two Wheels Two Heads 6
Twopence a Tub 183
Tyger Voyage 3

Ugly Mug 238
Uhu 262
Ultramarine 168
Ultraviolet Catastrophe 156
Umbrella Tree 242
Uncle Bumpo 134
Uncle Charlie Weasel and the Cuckoo Bird 150
Uncle Charlie Weasel's Winter 150
Uncle in the Attic 165
Uncle Jack and Operation Green 250
Uncle Jack and the Loch Ness Monster 250
Uncle Neptune 181
Under the Autumn Garden 157
Under the Mountain 92
Under the North Star 113
Under the Pudding Basin 240
Under the Sun and Over the Moon 56
Underrunners 155, 269
Unicorn Dream 107
Unicorn Trap 192
Uninvited Ghosts . . . 148
United! 105
Unknown Planet 212
Unleaving 217, 256
Unlucky Lucky 242
Up a Road Slowly 275
Up and Up 112
Up the Chimney Down 7
Up the Pier 52
Up to Low 258
Upside-Down World of Ginger Nutt 195
Urn Burial 220
Ursula at the Zoo 140
Ursula Ballooning 140
Ursula Bear 140
Ursula by the Sea 140
Ursula Camping 140
Ursula Climbing 140
Ursula Dancing 140
Ursula Exploring 140
Ursula Flying 140
Ursula in the Snow 140
Ursula on Safari 140
Ursula on the Farm 140
Ursula Riding 140
Ursula Sailing 140

Ursula Skiing 140
Ursula Swimming 140

Valley Between 262
Valley Grows Up 259
Vampire 224
Vampire's Holiday 100
Vampire's Revenge 100
Vandal 270
Vanishing Gran 205
Vanishment of Thomas Tull 4
Vera Pratt and the Bald Head 94
Vera Pratt and the Bishop's False Teeth 94
Vera Pratt and the False Moustaches 94
Verity of Sydney Town 262
Very Far from Here 104
Very Special Baby 200
Very Worst Monster 114
Vicar of Nibbleswick 60
Victor's Party 206
Video Rose 224
Viking in Trouble 241
Vila 277
Village by the Sea 250, 256, 270
Village Dinosaur 16
Violet for Bonaparte 208
Violin Maker's Gift 258
Virgil Nosegay And the Cake Hunt 26
Virgil Nosegay and the Hupmobile 26
Virgil Nosegay and the Wellington Boots 26
Visit To William Blake's Inn 275
Visitors from London 259
Voice in the Night 208
Volcano 81
Vote for Baz 179
Voyage of Mudjack 107
Voyage of QV66 147
Voyage of the 'Dawn Treader' 233, 251
Voyage of the Vigilance 128
Voyage to Valhalla 200
Voyages of Doctor Dolittle 274

Wagstaffe and the Life of Crime 167
Wagstaffe the Wind-Up Boy 166
Waiting for Anya 161
Waiting for the Sky to Fall 224
Walk on the Wild Side 219
Walk Your Fingers Story 73
Walker Book of Fairy Tales 236
Walking On Air 71
Walking the Goldfish 105

TITLE INDEX

Walloping Stick War   97
Walls of Athens   217
Walnut Whirl   205
Wanted   37
Wanting a Little Black Gerbil   127, 238
War and Freddy   104
War Horse   161
War of Jenkins' Ear   162
War of the Birds and the Beasts   186
War of the Witches   70
War of the Worms   166
War Orphan   14
War with Old Mouldy   211
Warlock at The Wheel . . .   123
Warlock in Whitby   120
Warrior Scarlet   197
Warriors of the Wasteland   106
Watch House   220
Watch of Patterick Fell   189
Watcher in the Garden   271
Watchers: A Mystery at Alton Towers   51
Watching the Roses   93
Water Babies   232
Water Cat   203
Water Horse   133
Water Watch   134
Waterfall Box   96
Waterless Mountain   274
Watership Down   3, 259, 270
Way to Sattin Shore   175, 251
Wayne Loves Custard   195
We Couldn't Leave Dinah   259
We Didn't Mean to Go to Sea   185
We Didn't Mean to Honest!   198
We Love Them   214
We Went to Live in Drumfyvie   197
We're Going on a Bear Hunt   279
Weather Cat   52
Weather-Clerk   200
Weathermonger   68
Web of Stories   101
Wedding Ghost   88
Weirdstone of Brisingamen   88
Welcome Home Jellybean   277
Welcome to the Giants   58
Well   127
Well Done Jonny Briggs   250
Were Puppy   239
Wereboy!   70
Werepuppy   224
Wesley at the Water Park   181, 239
Westing Game   256, 275
Wet and Dry   138
Wet Monday   73

Whale   12
Whale People   257
Whales of the Midnight Sun   262
What About Tomorrow?   194
What Game Shall We Play?   114
What Is a Wall After All?   12
What Is the Truth?   113, 270
What on Earth   207
What the Neighbours Did . . .   175
What's Going on William?   70
Whatever Happened in Winklesea?   51
Whatever Next!   163
Wheatstone Pond   220
Wheel Around the World   277
Wheel of Danger   142
Wheel of Surya   91
Wheel on the School   67, 274
Wheelie in the Stars   81
Wheels   112
When Darkness Comes   199
When Grandfather's Parrot Inherited
   Kennington Court   13
When Grandma Came   217
When I Dance   26
When Jays Fly to Barmbo   262
When Mum Went to Work   14
When My Naughty Little Sister Was
   Good   73
When Poppy Ran Away   119
When the Drums Beat   208
When the Tripods Came   43
When the Wind Blows   32
When We Went to the Park   112
When Will I Be Famous?   66
Where Dragons Breathe   241
Where Is Fred?   125
Where the Forest Meets the Sea   264
Where the Quaggy Bends   180
Where the Wind Blows   52
Where's the Baby?   114
Where's Wally   250
Which Twin Wins?   278
Which Witch?   6
Which Witch Is Which?   114
While the Bells Ring   161
Whipping Boy   275
Whisper of Lace   54
Whispering Knights   147
Whispering Mountain   9, 270
Whistling Piglet   134
Whitby Series   120
Whitby Witches   120, 273
White Archer   257
White Horse   142

TITLE INDEX

White Horse Gang 25
White Horse Is Running 188
White Horse of Zennor 162
White Mountains 42
White Nights of St. Petersburg 208
White Peak Farm 71
White Romance 103
White Stag 274
Who Dunnit? 66
Who Got Rid of Angus Flint? 123
Who Lies Inside 277
Who Sir? Me Sir? 251
Who's a Clever Girl Then? 115, 250
Who's Afraid Now? 116
Who's Afraid? . . . 175
Who's Afraid of the Evil Eye 206
Who's for the Zoo? 211
Who's Talking? 211
Whodunnit? 52
Why the Hyena Doesn't Care for Fish 15
Why the Whales Came 162
Why Weep the Brogan 281
Widdershins Crescent 205
Wild Boy and Queen Moon 177
Wild Goose Chase 14
Wild Hunt of Hagworthy 147
Wild Jack 43
Wild Robert 123
Wild Swans 228
Wild Wood 166
Wilkin's Tooth 123
Wilkses 52
Will of Iron 277
William in Love 210
Willie Scrimshaw and the Hounds of Gobbolot 40
Wincey's Worm 140, 241
Wind Between the Stars 156
Wind Blew 114
Wind Eye 220
Wind in the Willows 231, 250
Wind on the Moon 259
Windmill 30
Windmill of Nowhere 241
Winged Colt Of Casa Mia 38
Wings 181
Winnie the Pooh 233
Winnie the Witch 261
Winning Rider 105
Winter Holiday 184
Winter in Small Street 124
Winter Players 140
Winter Quarters 160

Wise Child 83
Wish for Wings 205
Witch and the Holiday Club 22
Witch in the Cherry Tree 156
Witch of Blackbird Pond 275
Witch of Monopoly Manor 22
Witch on Holiday 22
Witch Rose 62
Witch V. I. P. 22
Witch Week 123
Witch's Brat 197
Witch's Daughter 25
Witches 60, 281
Witches and the Grinnygog 73
Wizard in the Woods 211
Wizard in Wonderland 211
Wizard of Earthsea 256
Wizard of Woodworld 128
Wolf 260
Wolves of Willoughby Chase 9
Wonderful Story of Henry Sugar and Six More 61
Wood by Moonlight . . . 208
Woods at the End of Autumn Street 149
Woodside School Story 211, 244
Woof 4, 55, 272
Wool-Pack 259
Woozies Go to School 22
Woozies Go Visiting 22
Woozies Hold a Frubarb Week 22
Woozies on Television 22
Woozy 22
Woozy and the Weight Watchers 22
World Around the Corner 92
World-Eater 199
World of Fairy Tales 236
World's Apart 163
World's Best Karlson 144
Worm Book 6
Worm Charmers 81
Worry Warts 95
Wouf! 250
Worst Witch Strikes Again 163
Worzel Gummidge and Aunt Sally 100
Worzel Gummidge at the Fair 101
Worzel Gummidge Down Under 101
Worzel Gummidge Goes to the Seaside 101
Worzel's Birthday 101
Worst Witch 163
Wreckers 238
Wrinkle in Time 275
Wulf 56

Xanadu Manuscript 204

TITLE INDEX

Yaxley's Cat 220
Year and a Day 83, 161
Year King 75
Year of the Worm 179
Year of the Yelvertons 268
Yellow Aeroplane 161
Yellow Pom-Pom Hat 125
Yellow Wellies 239
Yes Dear 123
Yesterday 93
Yob 134
You Can't Say I'm Crazy 200
You Herman, Me Mary 116, 238
You Remember Me! 81
You Tell Me 152
You Two 211
You Win Some You Lose Some 212
You'll Soon Grow Into Them Titch 114
Young Fu of The Upper Yangtze 274

Young Green Consumer Guide 264
Young Legionary 106
Your Favourite Farm Stories Collection 134
Your Guess Is As Good As Mine 17
Your Move JP 149
Yucky Ducky 222
Yum Yum 6

Z for Zachariah 170
Zarnia Experiment: Phase 3 143
Zarnia Experiment: Phase 4 143
Zartan 217
Zesty 150
Zesty Goes Cooking 150
Ziggy and Ice Ogre 181
Zippi and Zac and the Grand Ostrich Ball 138
Zoldo the Magnificent 243
Zoo 6

GENRE INDEX

◆

ADVENTURE

Adrift   19
Another Fine Mess   165
BFG   59
Big Six   185
Black Jack   86
Box of Nothing   68
Charlie and the Chocolate Factory   59
Charlie and the Great Glass Elevator   59
Clancy's Cabin   153
Confidence Man   86
Coot Club   185
Different Dragons   145
Digital Dan   90
Dr Jekyll and Mr Hollins   100
Dragon Days   100
Finn Gang   190
Fox Hole   193
Going Home   177
Great Northern?   185
Gumble's Yard   203
Handful of Thieves   23
Henry Hollins and the Dinosaur   100
Inflatable Shop   100
Jack Holborn   87
James and the Giant Peach   60
Last Bus   159
Last Vampire   100
Minnow on the Say   174
Missee Lee   185
On the Run   24
Peter Duck   184
Picts and the Martyrs   185
Pigeon Post   185
Pippi Longstocking   144
Pirates' Mixed-Up Voyage   154
Prisoners of September   87
River Man   20
Runaway Summer   24
Secret Water   185
Short Voyage of the 'Albert Ross'   157
Silver's Revenge   142
Summer of the Dinosaur   100
Swallowdale   184
Swallows and Amazons   184
Tom Tiddler's Ground   204

We Didn'T Mean to Go to Sea   185
Wheel of Danger   142
Where the Wind Blows   52
White Horse Gang   25
Winter Holiday   184
Witch's Daughter   25

ANIMAL

Ace   130
Almost All-White Rabbity Cat   66
Along Came a Dog   66
Animals of Farthing Wood   62
Battle of Bubble and Squeak   174
Beach Dogs   63
Blitzcat   218
Cat Called Max   69
Cat That Walked by Itself   251
Christmas with Tamworth Pig   126
Creature in the Dark   218
Daggie Dogfoot   130
Dog Days and Cat Naps   126
Dog so Small   174
Flight from Farthing Wood   62
Fly-By-Night   176
Fox Cub Bold   62
Fox-Busters   131
Fox's Feud   62
Great Escape   63
Harry's Mad   131
Hodgeheg   131
House of Wings   36
Hurry Home, Candy   66
I, Houdini   20
In the Grip of Winter   62
Jo-Jo, the Melon Donkey   161
Just Nuffin   63
Keeping Henry   23
King of the Vagabonds   63
Little Foxes   161
Lost and Found   145
Magnus Powermouse   131
Martin's Mice   131
Midnight Fox   36
Mouse Butcher   131

324

GENRE INDEX

Mystery Pig   191
Olga Da Polga   30
One-Eyed Cat   82
Peppermint Pig   24
Prime of Tamworth Pig   126
Puffin Book of Pet Stories   48
Railway Cat   16
Railway Cat and Digby   16
Railway Cat and the Horse   16
Railway Cat's Secret   16
Ram of Sweetriver   63
Rats!   113
Rescuing Gloria   53
Saddlebottom   132
Seal Secret   41
Sheep-Pig   136
Siege of White Deer Park   62
Superdog   222
Superdog in Trouble   222
Superdog the Hero   222
Tamworth Pig and the Litter   126
Tamworth Pig Saves the Trees   126
Tamworth Pig Stories   126
Team   176
Toby Man   133
Tom's Sausage Lion   161
Travellers by Night   11
Uncle Charlie Weasel and the Cuckoo Bird   150
Uncle Charlie Weasel's Winter   150
Voyage of Qv66   147
Walk on the Wild Side   219
Watership Down   3
Wild Wood   166

CONSERVATION

Animals of Farthing Wood   62
Awaiting Developments   12
Chinaman's Reef Is Ours   193
Flight from Farthing Wood   62
Fox Cub Bold   62
Fox's Feud   62
Green Book   216
In the Grip of Winter   62
M.C. Higgins the Great   102
On the Flip Side   80
Rebel on a Rock   24
Rescuing Gloria   53
Serpent's Tooth   199
Siege of White Deer Park   62
Someplace Beautiful   33
When the Wind Blows   32
Why the Whales Came   162

FAIRY STORIES, FOLK TALES AND TRADITIONAL STORIES

Anancy – Spiderman   25
Bag of Moonshine   88
British and Irish Folk Tales   55
Dead Moon   55
Faber Book of Favourite Fairy Tales   47, 236
Faber Book of Northern Folk Tales   48
Fairy Tale Treasury   31
Ghosts at Large   182
Hindu World   91
How the Whale Became...   112
Listen to This Story   101
Mouth Open, Story Jump out   101
Old Peter's Russian Tales   186
People Could Fly   102
Pineapple Child...   15
Tales of An Ashanti Father   15
Three Indian Princesses   91
Web of Stories   101

FAMILY

All About the Bullerby Children   143
Animal, the Vegetable and John D Jones   35
Bagthorpes Abroad   49
Bagthorpes Haunted   49
Bagthorpes Liberated   49
Bagthorpes Unlimited   49
Bagthorpes Versus the World   49
Blossom Promise   37
Blossoms and the Green Phantom   37
Blossoms Meet the Vulture Lady   37
By the Shores of Silver Lake   221
Cherry Time at Bullerby   143
Christmas at Bullerby   143
Crummy Mummy and me   77
Day at Bullerby   143
Dear Mr Henshaw   44
Friends and Brothers   131
Goodbye, Chicken Little   36
Granny Project   77
Happy Days at Bullerby   143
Little House in the Big Woods   221
Little House on the Prairie   221
Little Town on the Prairie   221
Long Winter   221
Lotta   144
Lotta Leaves Home   144
Lotta's Bike   144

325

GENRE INDEX

Lotta's Christmas Surprise   144
Mardie   144
Mardie to the Rescue   144
Mischievous Martens   144
Not-Just-Anybody Family   37
On the Banks of Plum Creek   221
Peppermint Pig   24
Ravensgill   159
Six Bullerby Children   143
Springtime at Bullerby   143
Tatty Apple   168
These Happy Golden Years   221

FANTASY

Antar and the Eagles   158
'Antelope' Company Ashore   100
'Antelope' Company at Large   100
Archer's Goon   121
Black Hearts in Battersea   9
Bongleweed   49
Cart and Cwidder   121
Charmed Life   121
Cuckoo Tree   9
Daymaker   99
Dido and Pa   9
Diggers   181
Dragon Hoard   140
Drowned Ammet   121
Dwarfs of Nosegay   26
Eight Days of Luke   121
Elidor   88
Fairy Rebel   20
Fantasy Tales   116
Farm that Ran out of Names   159
Fattest Dwarf of Nosegay   26
Finnglas and the Stones of Choosing   188
Finnglas of the Horses   188
Gift from Winklesea   50
Greedy Alice   50
Halfmen of O   92
Homeward Bounders   122
In a Nutshell   182
Indian in the Cupboard   21
Iron Man   112
Karlson Flies Again   144
Karlson on the Roof   144
King of Copper Mountain   27
Lives of Christopher Chant   122
Magicians of Caprona   122
Midnight Is a Place   8
Moon of Gomrath   89

Moon's Revenge   8
Motherstone   92
Mouse and his Child   107
Mr Magus Is Waiting for You   127
Night Birds on Nantucket   9
Ogre Downstairs   122
Paddy's Pot of Gold   132
Pangur Ban   188
Power of Three   122
Priests of Ferris   92
Prince on a White Horse   140
Return of the 'Antelope'   100
Return of the Indian   21
Secret of the Indian   21
Serpent of Senargad   188
Shape-Shifter   188
Shon the Taken   140
Skybreaker   99
Snowman   32
Spellcoats   122
Spellhorn   71
Stig of the Dump   129
Stolen Lake   9
Tom's Midnight Garden   174
Town that Went South   129
Transformations   99
Truckers   181
Under the Mountain   92
Unicorn Trap   192
Virgil Nosegay and the Cake Hunt   26
Virgil Nosegay and the Hupmobile   26
Virgil Nosegay and the Wellington Boots   26
Warlock at the Wheel...   123
Weirdstone of Brisingamen   88
Whispering Mountain   9
White Horse Is Running   188
Wings   181
Winter Players   140
Witch Week   123
Wolves of Willoughby Chase   9
World Around the Corner   92

HISTORICAL

Apprentices   86
Apricots at Midnight   92
Astercote   146
Barge Children   49
Beyond the Dragon Prow   141
Black Jack   86
Bostock and Harris   87
Bridle the Wind   8

GENRE INDEX

Butty Boy 215
Chance Child 215
Children of Winter 70
Confidence Man 86
December Rose 86
Devil-In-The-Fog 86
Empty Sleeve 86
Fanny and the Monsters 146
Free Man on Sunday 188
Go Saddle the Sea 8
Granny Was a Buffer Girl 70
Hungry Snow 188
Iron Way 53
Jack Holborn 87
John Diamond 87
Little Lower Than the Angels 151
My Friend Walter 161
Old Man on a Horse 219
Once There Was a Swagman 33
Parcel of Patterns 216
Playing Beatie Bow 172
Prisoners of September 87
Revolt at Ratcliffe's Rags 54
Stone Book Quartet 88
Strange Affair of Adelaide Harris 87
Strong and Willing Girl 72
Teeth of the Gale 8
When Darkness Comes 199
Whisper of Lace 54
Wulf 56

HUMOUR

Beezus and Ramona 43
Bill's New Frock 76
Blood and Thunder Adventure on Hurricane Peak 153
Boy with Illuminated Measles 15
Country Pancake 77
Emil and his Clever Pig 143
Emil and the Bad Tooth 143
Emil Gets into Mischief 144
Emil in the Soup Tureen 144
Emil's Little Sister 144
Emil's Pranks 144
Emil's Sticky Problem 144
Emily's Legs 130
Esio Trot 60
Fantastic Mr Fox 60
Father Christmas 32
Father Christmas Goes on Holiday 31
Flat Stanley 33
Fred the Angel 213

Fungus the Bogeyman 32
Gentleman Jim 32
George Speaks 131
George's Marvellous Medicine 60
Giraffe and the Pelly and me 60
Great Smile Robbery 152
Harriet and the Crocodiles 213
Harriet and the Flying Teachers 213
Harriet and the Haunted School 213
Harriet and the Robot 213
Help! I Am a Prisoner in a Toothpaste Factory 15
Henry and Beezus 44
Henry and Ribsy 44
Henry and the Clubhouse 44
Lamp for the Lambchops 33
Lionel and the Lone Wolf 13
Lionel and the Spy Next Door 13
Lionel's Finest Hour 13
Paddington Library 29
Pirate Uncle 154
Raging Robots and Unruly Uncles 154
Ramona and Her Father 43
Ramona and Her Mother 43
Ramona Forever 43
Ramona Quimby, Age Eight 44
Ramona the Brave 44
Ramona the Pest 44
Ronnie and the Great Knitted Robbery 15
Ronnie and the Haunted Rolls Royce 15
Stanley and the Magic Lamp 33
Stanley in Space 33
Stowaways 152
Time to Laugh 48
Travelling Hopefully 12
Twits 60
Woof 4, 55

MYSTERY

Annerton Pit 67
Archer's Goon 121
Bad Blood 17
Baker Street Irregulars 69
Creature in the Dark 218
Crimson Crescent 205
Curse of the Egyptian Mummy 113
Dark Behind the Curtain 52
December Rose 86
Fireworks Galore 205
Follow that Bus! 113
Ghost Girl 190

327

GENRE INDEX

Great Ice-Cream Crime 205
Haunted Ivy 205
Into the Dark 220
Melusine 21
Mona Lisa Mystery 113
Mysterious Mr Ross 10
Night-Watchmen 51
Our Kid 178
Queen's Nose 132
Rat's Castle 192
Roscoe's Leap 54
Salt River Times 159
Secret Passage 25
Shadow Guests 9
Siege of Cobb Street School 205
Sleepers on the Hill 190
Staggering Snowman 205
Stitch in Time 147
Stuntkid 180
Sylvia Game 11
Vanishing Gran 205
Way to Sattin Shore 175

SCHOOL

Behind the Bike Sheds 165
Class that Went Wild 201
Demon Headmaster 52
Fibs 40
Fighting in Break... 116
Flames 40
Foxcover 40
Ghost Dog 40
Gowie Corby Plays Chicken 126
In a Class of Their Own 116
Mintyglo Kid 53
New Boy 202
Prime Minister's Brain 52
Runaways 202
Save Our School 53
School Stories 157
Secret 202
Swimathon 53
Turbulent Term of Tyke Tiler 127
Twisters 40
War with Old Mouldy 211

SCIENCE FICTION

Another Heaven, Another Earth 109
Antigrav 79

Beware of the Brain Sharpeners 56
Bewitched by the Brain Sharpeners 56
Beyond the Burning Lands 42
Blade of the Poisoner 106
Blue Misty Monsters 189
Brain Sharpeners Abroad 56
Catfang 81
Caves of Klydor 106
Children of Morrow 109
City of Gold and Lead 42
Computer Nut 35
Dark Sun, Bright Sun 79
Day of the Starwind 106
Deathwing Over Veynaa 106
Delikon 109
Devil's Children 68
Evil Eye 81
Exiles of Colsec 106
Fireball 42
Galactic Warlord 106
Grinny 79
Heartsease 68
Huntsman 106
Last Legionary Quartet 106
Lost Star 109
Lotus Caves 42
Master of Fiends 106
Megan's Star 20
Mindbenders 80
Monster Garden 10
Mr Browser and the Brain Sharpeners 56
Mr Browser and the Comet Crisis 56
Mr Browser and the Mini-Meteorites 57
Mr Browser and the Space Maggots 57
Mr Browser in the Space Museum 57
Mr Browser Meets the Burrowers 57
Mr Browser Meets the Mind Shrinkers 57
New Found Land 42
Planet of the Warlord 106
Pool of Fire 42
Prince in Waiting 42
Quest of the Quidnuncs 57
Rag, a Bone and a Hank of Hair 80
Rains of Eridan 109
Revenge of the Brain Sharpeners 57
Robot Revolt 80
Shepherd Moon 109
Skiffy 159
Skiffy and the Twin Planets 159
Space Hostages 80
Starstormers 81
Sun Burst 81

GENRE INDEX

Sword of the Spirits 42
This Time of Darkness 110
Thousand Eyes of Night 199
Trillions 81
Warriors of the Wasteland 106
Weathermonger 68
Wheelie in the Stars 81
White Mountains 42
Wild Jack 43
World-Eater 199
Xanadu Manuscript 204
Young Legionary 106
Z for Zachariah 170

SHORT STORIES

Arabel and Mortimer 7
Bad Boys 45
Beside the Sea with Jeremy James 221
Birthday Burglar and the Very Wicked Headmistress 154
Boy Who Bounced... 154
Catch Your Death... 95
Chewing-Gum Rescue... 154
Chocolate Porridge... 155
Clothes Horse... 3
Creepy-Crawly Stories 116
Daredevils Or Scaredycats 180
Do Goldfish Play the Violin? 221
Dog Days and Cat Naps 126
Door in the Air... 155
Downhill Crocodile Whizz... 155
Elephant Party 27
Elephants Don'T Sit on Cars 221
Even Naughtier Stories 117
Faithless Lollybird... 7
Fantasy Tales 116
Feet... 157
Fighting in Break... 116
Fingers Crossed 180
First Margaret Mahy Story-Book 158
Fog Hounds, Wind Cat, Sea Mice 7
Fred the Angel 213
Getting Rich with Jeremy James 221
Ghostly Laughter 116
Great Piratical Rumbustification 155
Harp of Fishbones 7
High Days and Holidays 45
How to Stop a Train with One Finger 221
Imagine That! 48
In a Class of Their Own 116
Julian, Secret Agent 39

Julian Stories 39
Julian's Glorious Summer 39
Kingdom Under the Sea 8
Last Slice of Rainbow... 7
Leaf Magic... 155
Letters of Fire... 93
Librarian and the Robbers 155
Listen to This Story 101
Little Bookroom 74
Lizzie Dripping 50
Lizzie Dripping Again 50
Lizzie Dripping and the Little Angel 50
Lizzie Dripping by the Sea 50
Magic Orange Tree... 91
Magician Who Kept a Pub... 72
Mahy Magic 155
Mark the Drummer Boy 72
Mice and Mendelson 7
Mists and Magic 72
Modern Fairy Tales 48
More Stories for Seven Year Olds 48
More Stories for Under-Fives 48
More Stories Julian Tells 39
More Stories to Tell 45
Mortimer Says Nothing... 7
Mortimer's Cross 7
My Naughty Little Sister Stories 73
Naughty Stories 117
Necklace of Raindrops 8
Never Meddle with Magic 117
Nonstop Nonsense 155
Nothing to Be Afraid of 157
Old Man Who Sneezed 72
Old Nurse's Stocking Basket 74
Past Eight O'Clock 8
Puffin Book of Christmas Stories 48
Puffin Book of Pet Stories 48
Round the Christmas Tree 48
Runaway Shoes 117
School Stories 157
Second Margaret Mahy Story-Book 155
Shadow-Cage 174
Small Pinch of Weather 194
Sophie's Snail 133
Stories for Eight Year Olds... 48
Stories for Five Year Olds... 48
Stories for Nine Year Olds... 48
Stories for Seven Year Olds 48
Stories for Six Year Olds... 48
Stories for Tens and Over 48
Stories for Under-Fives 48
Tale of a One-Way Street 8
Tales of Arabel's Raven 7
Tell me a Story 45

GENRE INDEX

Tell me Another Story 45
Ten in a Bed 4
There's a Wolf in My Pudding 222
Thief in the Village... 26
Things in Corners 172
Third Margaret Mahy Story-Book 155
Time to Laugh 48
Topsy Turvy Tales 133
Treasury of Stories for Five Year Olds 27
Treasury of Stories for Seven Year Olds 28
Treasury of Stories for Six Year Olds 27
Up the Chimney Down 7
Warlock at the Wheel... 123
What the Neighbours Did... 175
Who's Afraid? 175
Yucky Ducky 222

SOCIAL SITUATIONS

Are You There, God? It's Me, Margaret 28
Ash Road 192
Beautiful Take-Away Palace 124
Big Pink 178
Bridge to Terabithia 173
Colvin and the Snake Basket 150
Comfort Herself 124
Cracker Jackson 36
Dan Alone 203
Daredevils or Scaredycats 180
Dodgem 17
Great Comfort 124
Hill's End 193
Home from Home 182
Mama's Going to Buy You a Mocking Bird 146
Park's Quest 173
Rob's Place 204
Runaway 54
Squib 25
Stone Walkers 11
To the Wild Sky 193
Travellers by Night 11
Trial of Anna Cotman 11
Two-Thousand Pound Goldfish 38

SOCIAL SITUATIONS: ADOPTION

Finding 23

SOCIAL SITUATIONS: BULLYING

All My Men 17
Blubber 28
Challenge in the Dark 141
Eighteenth Emergency 36
Froggett's Revenge 177
Guardians 42
Present Takers 41
Year of the Worm 179

SOCIAL SITUATIONS: CRIME

How Many Miles to Babylon 82
Kind of Wild Justice 17
Terry on the Fence 18
Thief 166

SOCIAL SITUATIONS: DISABILITY

Cool Simon 209
Flawed Glass 194
Into the Dark 220
Juniper 127
Let the Balloons Go 193
Party for Lester 57

SOCIAL SITUATIONS: DIVORCE

Hideaway 90
Madame Doubtfire 77
Worlds Apart 163

SOCIAL SITUATIONS: FOSTERING

Dear Shrink 50
Great Gilly Hopkins 173
Pinballs 37

SOCIAL SITUATIONS: LYING

Pack of Liars 78

SOCIAL SITUATIONS: RACIAL ISSUES

Arilla Sun Down 101
Champion 92

GENRE INDEX

Iggie's House   28
My Mate Shofiq   166

SOCIAL SITUATIONS: RELATIONSHIPS

Beachcombers   49
Bottled Cherry Angel   209
Cybil War   36
Danny, the Champion of the World   59
Eagle Island   19
Glory Girl   36
Goldengrove   216
Keeping Henry   23
Lost Boy   82
Night Swimmers   37
On the Lion's Side   178
Otherwise Known As Sheila the
   Great   29
Robbers   24
Round Behind the Ice-House   78
Stone Menagerie   78
Summer of the Swans   38
Thunder and Lightnings   157
Witch's Daughter   25
You Two   211

SOCIAL SITUATIONS: SIBLINGS

Cuckoo Sister   10
Hi There, Supermouse   210
Superfudge   29
Tales of a Fourth Grade Nothing   29

SOCIAL SITUATIONS: STEP-FAMILIES

Break in the Sun   17
Frankie's Dad   209
Goggle-Eyes   77
Ogre Downstairs   122
Scarecrows   219
Trouble Half-Way   157

SOCIAL SITUATIONS: WITHDRAWAL

Cartoonist   35
Swan   85
TV Kid   38
Trouble with Donovan Croft   18

SUPERNATURAL

Ally, Ally, Aster   99
Chestnut Soldier   167
Children of Green Knowe   30
Chimneys of Green Knowe   30
Devil Finds Work   97
Double Dare   90
Dustland   102
Emlyn's Moon   167
Emma Dilemma   189
Enemy at Green Knowe   31
Fear of Samuel Walton   97
Gathering   102
Ghost Drum   182
Giant Under the Snow   96
Gift   68
Guardians of the House   31
Haunting of Cassie Palmer   10
House on the Brink   96
Justice and Her Brothers   102
King Death's Garden   99
Lengthening Shadow   97
Letters of Fire . . .   93
Little Fear   225
Moondial   51
Mustang Machine   180
Nothing to Be Afraid of   157
Quelling Eye   96
Ride the Wind   96
River at Green Knowe   31
Scarecrows   219
Snow Spider   167
Stones of Green Knowe   31
They Watched Him Die   97
Twin and Super-Twin   54
Ultramarine   168
Whispering Knights   147
Wild Hunt of Hagworthy   147

SUPERNATURAL: GHOSTS

Barley Sugar Ghosts   205
Catch Your Death and Other Ghost
   Stories   95
Clock Tower Ghost   126
Demon Bike Rider   141
Driftway   146
Edge of the World   95
Emer's Ghost   189
Empty Sleeve   86
George H. Ghastly   176

GENRE INDEX

George H. Ghastly and the Little Horror 176
George H. Ghastly to the Rescue 176
Ghost and Bertie Boggin 190
Ghost Downstairs 87
Ghost Girl 190
Ghost Messengers 198
Ghost of Thomas Kempe 146
Ghostly Laughter 116
Ghosts at Large 182
Ghosts of Hungryhouse Lane 150
House in Norham Gardens 147
Jason Bodger and the Priory Ghost 126
Mr Corbett's Ghost... 87
My Friend Walter 161
Revenge of Samuel Stokes 147
Stitch in Time 147
Time of the Ghost 123
Wild Robert 123

SUPERNATURAL: MAGIC

Genie on the Loose 141
Kitchen Warriors 8
Macmagics 69
Magic at Midnight 16
Magic in the Air 16
Meet the Macmagics 69
Secret World of Polly Flint 51
Tatty Apple 168
Tilly Mint and the Dodo 71
Tilly Mint Tales 71
Time out 51

SUPERNATURAL: WITCHES

Bad Spell for the Worst Witch 162
Ellie and the Hagwitch 50
Return of the Witch 22
Simon and the Witch 22
Simon and the Witch in School 22
Witch and the Holiday Club 22

Witch of Monopoly Manor 22
Witch on Holiday 22
Witch V.I.P. 22
Witches 60
Worst Witch 163

THRILLERS

Baker Street Irregulars 69
Bang! Bang! You're Dead 194
Candle in the Dark 198
Day of the Dragon 110
Death Knell 220
Devil-In-The-Fog 270
Devil's Doorbell 110
Falcon's Malteser 110
Henry's Leg 178
Leadfoot 79
Night of the Scorpion 110
On the Edge 53
Silver Citadel 110
Silver Crown 170
Snatched 129
Sound of Propellers 129
Tea-Leaf on the Roof 210
Worm Charmers 81

WAR

Carrie's War 23
Conrad's War 64
Dolphin Crossing 215
Fireweed 215
Fly West 193
Game of Soldiers 165
House of Sixty Fathers 66
Journey of 1,000 Miles 194
Kingdom by the Sea 218
Little Brother 19
Thunder in the Sky 177
Waiting for Anya 161
War Horse 161